BUSINESS RESEARCH METHODS

SECOND EDITION

Quinlan | Babin | Carr | Griffin | Zikmund

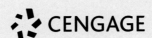 CENGAGE

Australia • Brazil • Mexico • Singapore • United Kingdom • United States

Business Research Methods, Second Edition
Christina Quinlan, Barry Babin, Jon Carr, Mitch Griffin and William Zikmund

Publisher: Annabel Ainscow

List Manager: Abigail Coppin

Content Developer: Hayley Wallbridge

Marketing Manager: Sophie Clarke

Senior Content Project Manager: Phillipa Davidson-Blake

Manufacturing Manager: Eyvett Davis

Typesetter: SPi Global

Cover Design: Simon Levy Associates

Cover Image: © Andrekart Photography/Shutterstock Inc.

For product information and technology assistance, contact us at
emea.info@cengage.com

For permission to use material from this text or product
and for permission queries,
email **emea.permissions@cengage.com**

British Library Cataloguing-in-Publication Data

A catalogue record for this book is available from the British Library.

ISBN: 978-1-4737-6035-6

Cengage Learning, EMEA
Cheriton House, North Way
Andover, Hampshire, SP10 5BE
United Kingdom

Cengage Learning is a leading provider of customized learning solutions with employees residing in nearly 40 different countries and sales in more than 125 countries around the world. Find your local representative at: **www.cengage.co.uk.**

Cengage Learning products are represented in Canada by Nelson Education Ltd.

For your course and learning solutions, visit **www.cengage.co.uk.**

Purchase any of our products at your local college store or at our preferred online store **www.cengagebrain.com.**

Printed in China by RR Donnelley
Print Number: 01   Print Year: 2018

BRIEF CONTENTS

CONTENTS

PREFACE

This textbook aims to provide a balanced introduction to research methods for today's undergraduate business students. It does this by synthesising rigorous coverage of methodologies with an accessible 'real-world' approach. The text follows course learning objectives for undergraduates in business and provides examples drawn from the full range of business subjects from marketing and strategy to human resource management.

The text has unique features: for example, it introduces the four frameworks approach to the research project. The four frameworks approach provides beginner researchers, as well as more advanced researchers, with a simple model that will guide them in the development of their research projects. It facilitates researchers in the task of developing properly focused, fully integrated research projects. The textbook is very sympathetic to the challenges facing a student engaging with the subject for the first time and provides an integrated and balanced approach to quantitative and qualitative research. The writing is simple and direct and the examples and case studies presented were selected particularly with an undergraduate readership in mind. In summary, the text provides a unique and simple yet comprehensive introduction to research methods for business students.

Business Research Methods is a valuable resource for all undergraduate business students, particularly for second- and third-year students on business research methods courses. It provides an excellent introduction to the work of undertaking research in an academic environment. This text is essential reading for all business students required to undertake research projects. Postgraduate students, and indeed students from other non-business disciplines, will also find the text very helpful.

Christina Quinlan,
May 2018

ACKNOWLEDGEMENTS

For our families.

The publisher would like to thank Gideon Els, Desmond Gargan and Eric Shiu
for their valuable reviews of this textbook.

INTRODUCTION

FOR STUDENTS

Business Research Methods sets out to help students design and develop their research projects from inception to completion. The text has been written in an accessible style and will provide useful support for those undertaking investigative projects for the first time. Covering all aspects of the research process in some detail, this is an ideal introductory 'how-to-do' text. The book introduces a model called the four frameworks approach (see below) designed to help researchers with the process of undertaking research. The narrative of the text is enhanced with a number of key features, among them skills activities, end of chapter questions and case studies of real-world research.

This book is designed and written in such a way as to take you, the reader, through the subject of business research methods in a comprehensive but very clear, simple and straightforward manner. If you read the book to the end, you will have a complete understanding of business research methods, and the confidence and the capacity to competently undertake a business research project. Whether you read the book from beginning to end, or choose to read particular chapters, you will find this book an invaluable companion as you undertake your research.

THE FOUR FRAMEWORKS

- Conceptual Framework
- Theoretical Framework
- Methodological Framework
- Analytical Framework

FOR LECTURERS

Business Research Methods is designed to fill a perceived gap in the market in terms of teaching research methods to undergraduate business students. This is a vast market, with all undergraduate and postgraduate students undertaking research projects at some time in their academic career. This text closely follows the learning objectives of business research method programmes and will complement the academic support received during the research process, providing a useful point of reference for students. The text aims to match balanced coverage with accessibility.

This text recognises the institutional pressures on business research courses, including: (a) large class cohorts; (b) increasingly diverse and international student profiles with different learning approaches; (c) the issue of plagiarism; and (d) increasing use of virtual learning environments (VLEs) in teaching. To accommodate these pressures, the book utilises unique skills and real-world relevance emphasis matched with blended content, so that both students and lecturers will be more engaged with the material and many of the current anxieties over course delivery will be overcome.

KEY FEATURES

The following key features are included:

- Balance of coverage and accessibility: the text's structure has evolved from close examination of the standard learning objectives on undergraduate business research methods courses, ensuring all of the key topics are addressed in a balanced and thorough way. Matching this is a strong awareness of the realities of undergraduate courses, in terms of student interest and difficulties with some areas of the curriculum. There is a focus on accessibility and engaging the student throughout.

- Wide-ranging examples: recognising that students on research methods courses come from a wide range of business disciplines, the text uses wide-ranging examples including examples from small and medium enterprises (SMEs), the public sector, as well as not-for-profit business undertakings.
- Clear coverage of research theory: many research methods texts avoid, gloss over or over-integrate into other aspects of research methodology.
- Clear and accessible chapters for undergraduates: lecturers can integrate these easily into the teaching to the level required. 'Real World Research' boxes throughout the text also provide examples of theoretical and methodological issues, which, again, can be used where appropriate based on the direction of the course.
- Outward looking: recognising that undergraduate students should be introduced to as wide a range of research methodologies and methods as possible. One of the key objectives of this textbook is to detail a wide variety of research methodologies and methods, including documentary analysis, content analysis, discourse analysis, archival research, life histories, narratives, semiotics, image-based research, scales and project techniques. The field of social research is very broad. The researcher within the field is concerned with producing methodologically sound research. Within that endeavour there is scope for great creativity and individuality. The methodologies and methods detailed here are some of the ways in which researchers creatively design and conduct sound systematic research.
- Emphasis on research skills: Chapter 1 sets out the practicalities of actually conducting research (formulating arguments, referencing skills, negotiating access, etc.). This chapter provides a clear pathway, at the start of the text, for students to begin moving on their research project. This chapter can be linked into earlier study skills modules provided during the students' course of study and it can be linked with wider institutional emphasis on student skills development.

At the end of this learning exercise, the student should be able to:

- Discuss many ways of engaging in research.
- Design, conduct and complete a research project.
- Use a variety of methodologies and methods.
- Explain the creative scope of scientific research.
- Outline the constraints on creativity within scientific research.
- Design, conduct and complete multi-method research projects.
- Critique the design of research projects.

PEDAGOGICAL FEATURES

Strong pedagogical features are essential for undergraduate students and the text includes the following range of features:

The Value of Good Research – These boxed features appear consistently throughout the text providing 'real-world' examples of research projects. At the beginning of the chapters these boxed features focus primarily on reports of research in the media. They also appear in the middle of chapters, where they focus on demonstrating the link between theory and research. In many of these box features, an article from an academic journal is used to demonstrate this link.

Your Research – These boxed features explore common research issues and problems students encounter while undertaking research, and propose solutions to them or provide a means to deal with them.

Real World Research – This boxed feature appears in every chapter and discusses real-life examples of research in a variety of business examples. This feature is used to discuss the real issues faced by researchers and the methods they use.

Research in Practice – Each of the boxed features focuses on exploring in detail a different research methodology, providing examples of research projects developed using the methodology. Further resources for reading are provided on the methodology in question in these boxed features.

End of Chapter Questions – There is a questions section at the end of each chapter. These questions are designed to encourage students to check their progress and to review the material covered in the chapter.

Case Studies – There is a case study at the end of most chapters. Each case study draws on a student example or on a recently published business research project. These examples are drawn from across all business disciplines.

Glossary – There is a comprehensive glossary of terms.

References – There is a complete and comprehensive bibliography at the end of the textbook, with references and a list of recommended readings at the end of each chapter.

SUPPLEMENTS AND BLENDED LEARNING

Research methods courses typically have large student numbers and consequently require the core textbook to supply a robust set of supplementary materials. Using a companion website, this textbook provides the following supplements:

- PowerPoint slides – A full set of slides matched to each chapter, including all of the main figures from the text.
- Instructor's manual – A detailed manual provides suggested answers to the end of chapter questions and case study questions.
- Extra tutorial questions – Gives lecturers a set of extra discussion questions with answers for use in tutorials and assignments.
- Testbank.
- Online glossary.
- Extensive weblinks.

Students taking business research methods courses often require flexibility in accessing textbook material, calling on chapters when required in an ad hoc and remote fashion (from home, while researching in the library, etc.). This new text recognises this by offering an electronic version via the cengagebrain platform (see www.cengagebrain.com) whereby students can purchase the entire e-textbook; and/or simply subscribe to the e-textbook for a set period of time. The emphasis throughout in the text is on accessibility, on rendering research methodologies and methods more accessible to all students.

ABOUT THE AUTHORS

BARRY BABIN

In addition to co-authoring four textbooks, Barry Babin has published over 70 research publications in prestigious periodicals such as the *Journal of Marketing*, the *Journal of Consumer Research*, the *Journal of Business Research*, the *Journal of Retailing*, *Psychological Reports*, *Psychology and Marketing* and the *Journal of the Academy of Marketing Science*. According to Googlescholar, his publications have been cited 150,000 times. Dr Babin also has won numerous honours for his research, including the University of Southern Mississippi Louis K. Brandt Faculty Research Award (on three occasions), the 1996 Society for Marketing Advances (SMA) Steven J. Shaw Award, and the 1997 Omerre DeSerres Award for Outstanding Contributions to Retail and Service Environment Research. His research focuses on the effect of the service environment on employees and customers, and his expertise lies in building successful outcomes that support long-lasting, mutually beneficial relationships with employees and customers. He also has expertise in encouraging creativity in the workplace and in wine marketing. Dr Babin's primary teaching specialties involve consumers and service quality, marketing research and creative problem solving and he is a popular and frequent international presenter, having lectured in Australia, South Korea, France, Germany, Canada and the United Kingdom. Dr Babin is current Chair of the Board for the Academy of Marketing Sciences, at Louisiana Tech University former president of the Society of Marketing Advances and past marketing editor for the *Journal of Business Research*.

JON CARR

Jon Carr is the Jenkins Distinguished Professor of Entrepreneurship at North Carolina State University where he teaches courses in new venture planning at the undergraduate and graduate level. He previously taught at Texas Christian University and the University of Southern Mississippi. He has published articles in journals such as the *Academy of Management Journal*, *Journal of Applied Psychology*, *Entrepreneurship Theory & Practice*, *Journal of Management* and the *Journal of Business Research*.

MITCH GRIFFIN

Mitch is a Professor of Marketing at Bradley University. Mitch has previous teaching experience at Southern Illinois University and Louisiana State University. His current teaching interests include pricing and product strategies, marketing research and advanced marketing research. In recognition of his teaching and research, Dr Griffin has received numerous teaching, research and service awards. His research has appeared in the *Journal of Consumer Research*, *Journal of Retailing*, *Journal of the Academy of Marketing Science*, *Journal of Business Research*, *Journal of Consumer Affairs*, *Journal of Satisfaction, Dissatisfaction and Complaining Behaviour*, *Journal of Nonprofit and Public Sector Marketing* and *Advances in Consumer Research*.

CHRISTINA QUINLAN

Dr Christina Quinlan is a social scientist. She is currently Director of the Institute for Research in Criminology, Community, Education and Social Justice, in the School of Applied Social Science at De Montfort University in Leicester. Previously, Christina taught research methods to both undergraduate and postgraduate students at Dublin City University. Her PhD research was a study of women's experiences of imprisonment in Ireland. Using critical ethnography, discourse analysis and semiotics, Christina explored the manner in which the identities of imprisoned women are constructed and represented in different discourses, historical discourses, architectural discourses, organisational/managerial discourses and media discourses. Christina also engaged with the imprisoned women themselves and explored with them, using in-depth interviews and photography, the manner in which they constructed and represented their own identities. Christina's book on women's experiences of imprisonment in Ireland was published in 2011 by Irish Academic Press. In postdoctoral research Christina studied the experiences of women in Ireland of social control and criminalisation. She is currently studying women's experiences in criminal justice systems in Britain and Ireland. Her research interests include: qualitative and quantitative research methods, critical research, ethnographic research, action research, image-based research, feminist research, social control, prisons and penality.

WILLIAM G. ZIKMUND

A native of the Chicago area, William G. Zikmund was a Professor of Marketing at Oklahoma State University. Before beginning his academic career, Professor Zikmund worked in marketing research for Conway/Millikin Company (a marketing research supplier) and Remington Arms Company (an extensive user of marketing research). During his academic career, Professor Zikmund published dozens of articles and papers in a diverse group of scholarly journals, ranging from the *Journal of Marketing* and *Accounting Review* to the *Journal of Applied Psychology*. Professor Zikmund was a member of several professional organisations, including the American Marketing Association, the Academy of Marketing Science, the Association for Consumer Research, the Society for Marketing Advances, the Marketing Educators' Association and the Association of Collegiate Marketing Educators. He served on the editorial review boards of the *Journal of Marketing Education*, *Marketing Education Review*, *Journal of the Academy of Marketing Science* and *Journal of Business Research*.

CENGAGE

Teaching & Learning Support Resources

Cengage's peer reviewed content for higher and further education courses is accompanied by a range of digital teaching and learning support resources. The resources are carefully tailored to the specific needs of the instructor, student and the course. Examples of the kind of resources provided include:

- A password protected area for instructors with, for example, a testbank, PowerPoint slides and an instructor's manual.

- An open-access area for students including, for example, useful weblinks and glossary terms.

Lecturers: to discover the dedicated lecturer digital support resources accompanying this textbook please register here for access: login.cengage.com.

Students: to discover the dedicated student digital support resources accompanying this textbook, please search for **Business Research Methods 2e** on: cengagebrain.co.uk.

BE UNSTOPPABLE

Learn more at cengage.co.uk/education

PART ONE
INTRODUCTION

CHAPTER 1

INTRODUCING BUSINESS RESEARCH

LEARNING OBJECTIVES

At the end of this chapter, the student should be able to:

- Outline the model of the research process.

- Outline and briefly explain each of the stages in the research process.

- Outline and apply the model of the four frameworks approach to the research project.

- Understand how research contributes to business success.

- Know how to define business research.

RESEARCH SKILLS

At the end of this chapter, the student should be able to:

- Differentiate between a research idea and a research statement or question.

- Outline the steps in the research process.

- Trace the elements of the research process in a given sample project.

The aim of this chapter is to introduce you, the student, to the process of carrying out research. As you read through this book, you will see that the process is generally the same in every research project. However, the approaches taken to each step in the process vary a great deal and are, in many cases, unique to each research project.

INTRODUCTION

Figure 1.1 is a model of the **research process**. As you can see, the process of undertaking research involves a number of steps. In the first place, you begin with an idea for a research project. You then start to refine that idea, by thinking about it, reflecting on it and by engaging with the literature in the area. You engage with the literature in order to explore and examine how other researchers have engaged with this issue, or this idea, in their own research.

> **research process** The means or process by which research is carried out.

In the context of a research project, literature is research that has already been carried out and published. Such research is published in books, in articles in scientific journals, in theses, conference reports, government reports, the reports of non-governmental organizations (NGOs) and, sometimes, in the media.

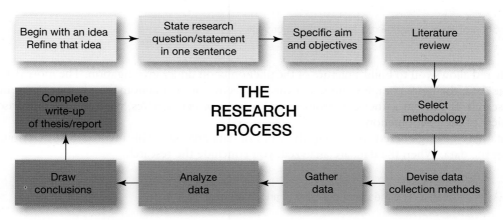

Figure 1.1 The work of research process

The work of the researcher is reflection. As you reflect on your research idea and engage with the literature, you will begin to develop and refine your idea. While you are doing this, it is a good discipline to try to achieve a very clear understanding of your research idea. Try to express your idea in one sentence, it can be a statement or a question. When you are satisfied that it does properly and fully express your research idea, this one sentence becomes the conceptual framework for your research project. This one sentence contains all of the key concepts, all of the keywords and phrases in your research project.

When you have got to the point of being able to state your research idea in one sentence, you will begin the process of developing an aim and a series of objectives for your research. While you are doing all of this work, you will also be engaging with the published literature in your field. When you have a clear understanding of the literature, you will start to write a review of the literature for your research project. This is a review of all of the published literature that you have read for your research. The **literature review** that you develop and write for your research project becomes the theoretical framework on which your research project will be built.

> **literature review** Literature is research already carried out and published, in books, in journal articles, in conference reports, in government reports and in the reports of NGOs. To carry out a literature review, the researcher sources, reads and then writes a review of the literature. A literature review is always undertaken in order to embed the researcher and research project in the body of knowledge.

You then select a research **methodology** for your research project. Examples of research methodologies include case study, survey, attitude research, action research, ethnography grounded theory, image-based research and feminist research. The different research methodologies used in social research and business research are explored in detail in this textbook.

> **methodology** The overall approach to the research project, the way in which the research is carried out. Examples of research methodologies include survey, case study, attitude research and ethnography.

You will then decide on the **data collection methods** to be used in your research. Examples of collection methods include observation, questionnaires, interviews and focus groups. Other data collection methods you might choose from include scales, projective techniques, diaries, images, narratives, life histories, the use of documents, archives, printed material, film and symbols. All of these data sources, and data collection methods, and more, are explained in this textbook.

> **data collection methods** The means by which data are gathered for a research project. Examples of data-gathering methods include observation, interviews, focus groups and questionnaires.

Then you will begin to gather **data**. Data in a research project are information, or evidence, that the researcher gathers in order to be able to explore the phenomenon under investigation, or to prove or disprove the research hypothesis.

data Information or evidence gathered for a research project.

The data gathered allows you to build a picture of the phenomenon under investigation. The more data and the better the quality of the data, the more complex and richer the perspective of the phenomenon you can present in the written report of the research. If you can gather data from several sources or perspectives, you can use comparisons to produce an even richer view of the phenomenon.

When the data have been gathered, you begin the work of data **analysis**. This involves first describing the data and then interpreting the data. When the data are analyzed, you conclude the research.

 analyzing Data are analyzed by means of description and interpretation.

Conclusions are drawn from analyzed data. These conclusions are theorized; this means that you knit them into the body of knowledge and in this way the body of knowledge in this field grows and develops.

 conclusion Essentially a judgement, or a final decision, drawn from evidence and argument.

Finally, you complete the writing of the thesis or the report of the research.

The model of the research process (Figure 1.1) starts with 'Begin with an idea, Refine that idea', and then follows the arrows all the way around to the last element 'Complete write-up of thesis/report'. In practice, researchers do not wait until all of the steps have been taken to begin writing the research report: in an academic setting the report of the research is called a thesis. Instead, they begin writing as they start the research process. As the research process develops and becomes more complex, so too does the written account of the research.

Research projects are very creative endeavours; they might be said to be one part creative and one part **rigorous** and scientific.

 rigorous For a research project to be rigorous, it must adhere to the scientific principles of research. The research must be systematic and valid.

The nature of business research

Business research covers a wide range of phenomena. For managers, the purpose of research is to provide knowledge regarding the organization, the market, the economy or some other area of uncertainty. A financial manager may ask, 'Will the environment for long-term financing be better two years from now?' A personnel manager may ask, 'What kind of training is necessary for production employees?' or 'What is the reason for the company's high employee turnover?' A marketing manager may ask, 'How can I monitor my retail sales and retail trade activities?' Each of these questions requires information about how the environment, employees, customers or the economy will respond to executives' decisions. Research is one of the principal tools for answering these practical questions.

The ultimate goal of business research is to supply accurate information that reduces the uncertainty in managerial decision making. Decisions are often made with little information for various reasons, including cost considerations, insufficient time to conduct research, or management's belief that enough is already known. Relying on seat-of-the-pants decision making – decision making without research – is like betting on a long shot at the racetrack because the horse's name is appealing. Occasionally there are successes, but, in the long run, intuition without research leads to losses. Business research helps decision makers shift from intuitive information gathering to systematic and objective investigation.

Business research defined

Business research is the application of social science research methods in the process of examining business phenomena. The process, as can be seen from the model outlined at the start of this chapter (Figure 1.1), includes idea and theory development, problem definition, searching for and collecting information, analyzing data, and communicating the findings and their implications.

> **business research** The application of the scientific method in searching for the truth about business phenomena. These activities include defining business opportunities and problems, generating and evaluating ideas, monitoring performance and understanding the business process.

This definition suggests that business research information, or data, is not intuitive or haphazardly gathered. Literally, research (re-search) means 'to search again'. The term connotes patient study and scientific investigation as the researcher takes another more careful look at the data to discover all that is known about the subject. Ultimately, all findings are tied back to the underlying theory.

Our definition makes it clear that business research is designed to facilitate the managerial decision-making process for all aspects of the business: finance, marketing, human resources, and so on. Business research is an essential tool for management in virtually all problem-solving and decision-making activities. By providing the necessary information on which to base business decisions, research can decrease the risk of making a wrong decision in each area. However, it is important to note that research is an aid to managerial decision making, never a substitute for it.

This definition of business research is limited by one's definition of business. Certainly, research regarding production, finance, marketing and management in for-profit corporations like DuPont is business research. However, business research also includes efforts that assist not-for-profit organizations such as the American Heart Association, London Zoo, the Berlin Philharmonic Orchestra, or a local school or community organization. Further, governmental agencies such as the French Development Agency (Agence Française de Développement, AFD) and the US Food and Drug Administration (FDA) perform many functions that are similar, if not identical, to those of for-profit business organizations. For instance, the FDA is an important user of research, employing it to address the way people view and use various foods and drugs. Not-for-profit and governmental agencies use research in much the same way as managers at Starbucks or Gap. This book explores business research as it applies to all institutions.

Applied and basic business research

One useful way to describe research is based on the specificity of its purpose. **Applied business research** is conducted to address a specific business decision for a specific firm or organization. **Basic business research** (sometimes referred to as pure research) is conducted without a specific decision in mind and it usually does not address the needs of a specific organization. It attempts to expand the limits of knowledge in general and as such it is not aimed at solving a particular pragmatic problem. Basic research can be used to test the validity of a general business theory (one that applies to all businesses) or to learn more about a particular business phenomenon. For instance, a great deal of basic research is conducted in the area of employee motivation. How can managers best encourage workers to dedicate themselves toward the organization's goals? From such research, we can learn the factors that are most important to workers and how to create an environment where employees are more highly motivated. This basic research does not examine the problem from any single organization's perspective. However, Starbucks' or Gap's management may become aware of such research and use it to design applied research studies examining questions about their own employees. Thus, the two types of research are not completely independent, as basic research often provides the foundation for later applied research.

> **applied business research** Research conducted to address a specific business decision for a specific firm or organization.
>
> **basic business research** Research conducted without a specific decision in mind that usually does not address the needs of a specific organization. It attempts to expand the limits of knowledge in general and is not aimed at solving a particular pragmatic problem.

While the distinction between basic and applied is useful in describing research, there are very few aspects of research that apply only to basic or only to applied research. We will use the term business research more generally to refer to either type of research. The focus of this text is more on applied research – studies that are undertaken to answer questions about specific problems or to make decisions about particular courses of action or policies. Applied research is emphasized in this text because most students will be oriented towards the day-to-day practice of management, and most students and researchers will be exposed to short-term, problem-solving research conducted for businesses or non-profit organizations.

Business research in the twenty-first century

Business research, like all business activity, continues to change. Changes in communication technologies and the trend towards an ever more global marketplace have played a large role in many of these changes.

Communication technologies

Virtually everyone is 'connected' today. Increasingly, many people are 'connected' nearly all the time. Within the lifetime of the typical undergraduate, the way information is exchanged, stored and gathered has been revolutionized completely. Today, the amount of information formally contained in an entire library can rest easily in a single personal computer.

The speed with which information can be exchanged has also increased tremendously. During the 1970s, exchanging information overnight through a courier service from anywhere in the continental United States was heralded as a near miracle of modern technology. Today, we can exchange information from nearly anywhere in the world to nearly anywhere in the world almost instantly. Internet connections are now wireless. Our mobile phones and handheld data devices can be used not only to converse with people, but also as a means of communication that can involve business research.

Changes in computer technology have made for easier data collection and data analysis. In consumer research, for example, many consumer household panels now exist and can be accessed via the internet. Thus, there is less need for the time and expense associated with regular mail survey approaches. Furthermore, the computing power necessary to solve complicated statistical problems is now easily accessible. Again, as recently as the 1970s, such computer applications required expensive mainframe computers found only in very large corporations, major universities and large governmental/military institutions. Researchers could expect to wait hours or even longer to get results from a statistical program involving 200 respondents. Today, even the most basic laptop computers can solve complicated statistical problems involving thousands of data points in practically a nanosecond.

Global business research

Like all business activities, business research has become increasingly global as more and more firms operate with few, if any, geographic boundaries. Some companies have extensive international research operations. The German car manufacturer BMW is part of the 'German big 3' luxury car manufacturers, along with Audi and Mercedes-Benz, and they are the three best-selling luxury car makers in the world. The Nielsen Company, known for its television ratings, is the world's largest research company. Starbucks can now be found in nearly every developed country on the planet.

Companies that conduct business in foreign countries must understand the nature of those particular markets and judge whether they require customized business strategies. For example, although the nations of the European Union (EU) share a single formal market, research shows that Europeans do not share identical tastes for many consumer products. Business researchers have found no such thing as a 'typical' European consumer; culture, language, politics, religion, climate and centuries of tradition divide the nations of Europe. A firm involved in market research, advising companies on colour preferences, found inexplicable differences in Europeans' preferences in medicines. It seems the French prefer to pop purple pills, but the English and Dutch favour white ones. Consumers in all three countries dislike bright red capsules, which are big sellers in the USA. This example shows that companies that do business in Europe must research throughout Europe so that they can adapt to local customs and buying habits.

Even companies that produce brands that are icons in their own country are now doing research internationally. The internationalization of research places greater demands on business researchers and heightens the need for research tools that allow researchers to **cross-validate** research results; in other words, researchers need to be able to establish whether or not the empirical findings from one culture also exist and behave similarly in another culture. The development and application of these international research tools are an important topic in basic business research.

> **cross-validate** To verify that the empirical findings from one culture also exist and behave similarly in another culture.

The Value of Good Research box contains a study of how well-being can be measured. For a long time, many people have argued that simply relying on economic measures, such as measures of gross domestic product (GDP), is an inadequate way of measuring the well-being of people or the state of a nation. There have been calls for the development of measures of happiness by researchers, heads of state and economists. The research highlighted in the box is useful for our purposes here in that it provides an example of some of the ways in which research can be used, and it highlights one of the debates currently being held within the world of social scientific research.

Perhaps you might develop an idea for a research project from your reading of the article. It might be interesting to design a research project to examine the work of economists who have tried to come up with alternative measures of well-being. You could focus on one economist in particular, and examine the relative successes and failures of his/her theories. Through a research project, you could attempt to develop a measure of well-being. This would require a study of the different measures of well-being that have already been developed. You could conduct a survey among your class-mates in order to establish what it is that they think contributes to their overall sense of well-being and the contribution that economic well-being makes to it.

THE VALUE OF GOOD RESEARCH

Research in the media

How can we measure well-being?

A report in *The Guardian* newspaper (Elliott, 30.11.2017), explained that, according to a new thinktank, News Weather Institute, there had already been an estimated 8700 premature deaths in 2017 in London caused by air pollution. According to the article, some of those deaths could have been avoided if more people worked from home or shared cars to the office. Fewer people travelling to work and fewer single person car journeys, the author explained, would be good for the nation's health, but, with fewer people spending money on transport costs, such changes in travel patterns would not be good for GDP.

Perhaps it seems obvious that while GDP as a measure is of central importance, GDP is not necessarily an indicator of the nation's well-being. The USA and China, for example, have the highest GDPs in the world, but this does not mean that they are necessarily the countries with the 'happiest' populations. If someone wanted to move to the USA from Europe, the high GDP would be one important factor, but there are other important factors to take into account too: lifestyles, politics, culture, etc.

So how can well-being be measured? The OECD (Organisation for Economic Cooperation and Development), publishes an annual report entitled 'How's Life?' The 2017 edition of the report outlines the gains for and the threats to people's well-being in 35 OECD countries and six partner countries. Among the 50 indicators of well-being used in this annual study are: life expectancy; the number of people with jobs; income levels; voter turnout in elections; and the number of people who report feeling supported by friends and family.

In the UK, the Office for National Statistics (ONS) uses an annual survey with 41 measures of national well-being, among them: 'satisfaction with family life', 'participation in 30 minutes of moderate intensity sport once per week' and 'five or more GCSEs A* to C including English and Maths'. There are a number of 'domains' in the survey: personal well-being, relationships, health, what people do, where people live, personal finance, the economy, education, skill, governance and the natural environment. The results of the study, conducted every year, are analyzed in comparison to the previous year's results, as well as to those of other countries. For example, in the 2016/17 survey it was found that average ratings of life satisfaction, feeling that the things we do in life are worthwhile, and happiness, had increased slightly in the UK between the years ending June 2016 and 2017.

How would you go about measuring well-being, and what methods would you use to collect data? ONS relies on surveys and subjective responses, but research on health or resource depletion could be gathered in other ways, for example from archives or by using published statistics.

Do you agree that well-being is an important measure alongside GDP?

THE FOUR FRAMEWORKS APPROACH

The **four frameworks approach** was developed by one of the authors of this text, Christina Quinlan, specifically for students, in order to provide them with a simple guide to help them develop their research projects. Using the four frameworks approach to the research project, the researcher uses their (very well-conceptualized) research question or statement (the first of the four frameworks, the conceptual framework) to direct the development of the research. The first framework, the conceptual framework, directs the development of the other three frameworks: the theoretical framework, the methodological framework and the analytical framework.

four frameworks approach An approach to carrying out research whereby the conceptual framework shapes, supports and directs the other three frameworks: the theoretical framework, the methodological framework and the analytical framework.

The four frameworks approach to the research project helps students avoid the confusion, uncertainty, and even fear that can beset them when they are confronted with undertaking independent research. Beginner researchers can perceive independent research to be a mammoth task, an exercise in scholarship and knowledge creation that is seemingly without boundaries. Christina, one of the authors of this textbook, proposed the four frameworks approach as a model that can be used to map the boundaries of a project.

The four frameworks approach provides a guide to the novice researcher. It helps the researcher maintain focus as research is undertaken and as the project is developed. At the same time, the model does not prevent students from taking on board any new shift in direction that may naturally occur as their research develops. Students are able to incorporate any new insights or ideas they might develop through their review of the literature, their experiences while gathering data, and/or through their reflections on their research.

The four frameworks approach to the research project is shown in Figure 1.2. As can be seen, the first framework in the four frameworks approach is the conceptual framework. This, as previously stated, is contained in the one-sentence research question or statement which you, the researcher, develop from your reflection on your research idea and from your reading of the literature published in the area of your research. Each keyword and phrase in that one sentence is a **key concept** in your research.

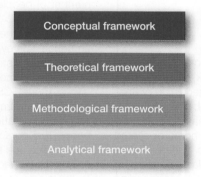

Figure 1.2   The four frameworks

> **key concept**   A key idea expressed in a word or phrase.

The second framework is the theoretical framework. This is contained in the literature review undertaken and written for the research project. The key concepts in the conceptual framework help to guide the researcher towards an appropriate structure and content for the literature review. The key concepts are used as keywords in keyword searches for literature in library resources and online.

The third framework is the methodological framework. It is contained in the research methodology chapter of the thesis, or in the research methodology section of the report of the research. This contains all of the information and detail relating to the research project's research methodology, data-gathering methods, means of data analysis and research ethics. It is a complete and thorough account of how the research was carried out.

The final framework is the analytical framework. This framework is contained in the data analysis chapter of the thesis or in the data analysis section of the report of the research. It contains all of the detail of the analysis carried out for the research that is to be presented in the written account of the research project. The researcher is guided in the work of carrying out and presenting the **data analysis** by the conceptual framework and the theoretical framework constructed for the research project and also by the methodological framework.

> **data analysis**   The process of analyzing data gathered for a research project. The process of data analysis involves describing and interpreting the data. The process also involves drawing conclusions from the data, and in research undertaken in an academic institution (college or university), theorizing those data, i.e. connecting the data gathered with the theory laid out in the literature review.

The four frameworks approach is explained in detail throughout this textbook. It provides a simple framework to guide researchers in the development and completion of thoroughly integrated and sound research projects. As Figure 1.3 shows, the conceptual framework for the research project informs, supports and shapes the three subsequent frameworks: the theoretical framework, the methodological framework and the analytical framework.

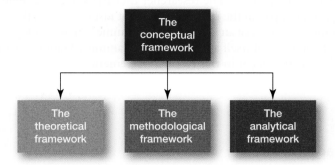

Figure 1.3   The four frameworks approach to the research project

While all of this represents quite a lot of information to take on board, every aspect of the research process is dealt with in this textbook in a relatively simple and straightforward manner. In order to read the material presented in this textbook for understanding, it is best to skim the material quickly to begin with, then read the material through thoroughly for meaning, then finally read it through fluently for understanding and learning. You will find that such an active engagement with the material will help you throughout this book and indeed throughout your studies generally.

THE FOUR FRAMEWORKS AND THE RESEARCH PROCESS

Once you have decided on the topic for your research project it is a good discipline to express this idea in one sentence. This then becomes the conceptual framework, clearly and simply defined, for the research project. The following is an example of a research statement:

> *This research project is a case study designed to facilitate the development of a new induction programme for new employees of Mannings Manufacturing Ltd.*

Defining the research project in one sentence helps exclude all of the concepts that are not relevant to the research and facilitates the researcher in considering and exploring in great detail and depth every concept that is relevant. All of the key concepts in the research project should be included in this sentence (see Table 1.1). Key concepts are something that we will be returning to again and again throughout our study of the research process. You will notice that the research statement just presented also contains a statement of the methodology to be used. It tells us that the research methodology used in (or proposed for use in) the research project is a case study methodology. Through this one sentence we now know exactly what this research project is about and we also know what methodology will be used to develop and carry out the research.

The research statement or question contains the conceptual framework for the research project. This one sentence contains all of the key concepts of the research project. The key concepts are the keywords and/or key phrases in the research statement. Concepts are fundamental to research; they are the building blocks of theory and theory is fundamental to all academic research. It is through building theory that the body of knowledge develops.

Generally, all academic researchers engaging in research undertake a review of the literature in the field of their study. They do this in order to assess the state of knowledge in the field and to identify any gaps in this knowledge. Another reason to conduct a literature review is for the researcher to develop their own expertise in the area or field of their

Table 1.1   Detail of the four frameworks

The conceptual framework	Contained in the research statement, question or hypothesis
The theoretical framework	Contained in the literature review
The methodological framework	Contained in the methodology section
The analytical framework	Contained in the data analysis presented in the thesis

research. In writing a review of the literature, the researcher constructs a theoretical framework for the research they are carrying out. The theoretical framework is contained in the literature review. To put it another way, the literature review is the theoretical framework for the research project. The key concepts in the conceptual framework give the researcher guidance and direction in terms of the reading they need to undertake in order to develop a literature review, or a theoretical framework, for their research project. The researcher uses the key concepts in the conceptual framework in keyword searches for literature. For example, in the research statement just examined, the key concepts (the keywords and phrases) are 'induction programme', 'creation of an induction programme', 'new employees' and 'Mannings Manufacturing'. While 'Mannings Manufacturing' is not itself a key concept, Mannings Manufacturing is a small- to medium-sized enterprise (an SME), and SME is a key concept in this research statement.

YOUR RESEARCH
Keeping a research diary

As you begin to engage with the process of creating, designing and developing your research project, it is important to begin to record your thoughts, ideas, inspirations, references and resources in your research diary. This is a notebook that you have set aside solely for this purpose. It is best to use a hardback notebook as your research diary will be used a lot throughout the project. You do not want it to fall apart and you certainly do not want to lose any pages from it. This written, often scribbled, record of your thoughts and decisions will be invaluable to you when you are writing the formal written account of the research. You will be able to refer back to the research diary for inspiration and ideas and this will save you a lot of time in the writing process, as well as radically improving and enriching the formal written account of the research.

YOUR RESEARCH
The research diary

In the research diary, researchers record their thoughts and ideas about their research project, their observations, understandings and reactions to the phenomena they witness, experience and study in the field. Researchers usually find that, as their research project develops it changes, and, as their acquaintance with the field develops, their perceptions and experiences of it change. These changes occur naturally as the research project deepens and develops. As this happens, records of initial perceptions and experiences are very useful. They provide a point of comparison with more mature experiences, and they provide a challenge to the 'naturalness' of more mature field experiences. In other words, experiences and phenomena that appear extraordinary to researchers fresh to a field can become naturalized as the researcher's field experience deepens and develops. In addition to this, thoughts, impressions and ideas recorded in the research diary often provide researchers with the means to begin the process of writing up different elements, aspects and chapters of the research report/thesis.

Take this opportunity to update your interactive research diary, available on Cengage Brain.

These key concepts are used by the researcher to direct and guide their search for literature for the literature review. In other words, the researcher is searching through the literature for research that has been published on the topics of new employees, induction programmes, induction programmes for new employees and induction programmes for new employees of SMEs. The literature found through these keyword searches represents, in part, the body of knowledge within which this research project is situated. Each research project is situated within a body of knowledge and, in turn, when completed, each research project makes a contribution to that body of knowledge.

When you begin thinking of a research project, you start by identifying an area within which you would like to conduct some research. This might concern, for example, marketing, human resources or perhaps product development. The important thing is to decide on an area that interests you. In writing a thesis or a report on a topic in this area, you are in effect writing a book on that topic and this book may ultimately contain anything from 10 000 to 90 000 words. By the time you have finished, you will be quite expert on your topic. It is therefore very important that you work on a topic that is of particular interest to you. Perhaps this is an area in which you already have some particular expertise, or would like to develop some expertise. You may even be planning a career in this area.

YOUR RESEARCH
Common research problems

It is important to be able to distinguish between an area of interest and a topic for a research project.

Once you have decided on your area, you need an idea for a topic within that area which you can develop into your research project. A common mistake that many beginning researchers make is to define their research project too broadly.

For example, you might be interested in human resources, but the topic for your research project might be, for instance, 'The Development of a New Induction Programme for New Employees of Mannings Manufacturing Ltd'. Mannings Manufacturing Ltd is the company or business within which you will work on your college placement, the company you will work with in your summer job or it is the company you have your part-time job with (or indeed your full-time job, if you are in full-time employment).

So, you see, while your area of interest can be, and probably will be, quite broad, your research project will be very focused, and quite small in relation to the broad area.

It is essential that your research project be very focused and limited in scope because:

- It must be completed within the time allowed for the research.
- It must be completed within the word count allowed for the project.
- It must be 'do-able' or 'researchable' within the scope of the resources available to you, and this includes access to the necessary data.
- It must be to the standard required by your programme of study.
- It must 'fit' with the requirements of your degree programme.

YOUR RESEARCH
Your research diary

Start and maintain a research diary. It is important to do this as you are beginning to think about your research project. Start your research diary by recording your own thoughts in relation to the areas and fields of business and business research that particularly interest you, and the issues and questions that come to mind when you focus on these areas. The purpose of this exercise is to help you move towards selecting an area within which to develop your research project.

The notes that you jot down during your reflections do not need to be very elaborate. They are simply notes you write to yourself in order to maintain a record of your thoughts and ideas with regard to your research. These notes will be very helpful when you begin the process of designing, carrying out and writing up your research project. Take this opportunity to update your interactive research diary, available on Cengage Brain.

The fact that the research process is generally the same for many research projects means that once you have learned the basics of the research process, you can apply your knowledge to every research project that you undertake. Understanding the basic elements of the research process will also allow you to critique the research of others, perhaps research commissioned by your organization, or research carried out by some body or group commenting on your work or on an area of your expertise. Everyone working in a professional capacity should be able to read and understand reports of research and have the ability to critically engage with research relevant to their interests and their work, and indeed research relevant to their family, home and community. They should also possess some skills in carrying out research themselves.

Some problems business students typically encounter when approaching research methods for the first time

Many students new to research methods allow themselves to be put off by the new words, terms and concepts they encounter when they first begin to read into the subject. However, with a little effort, students can become familiar with the terminology and the concepts, and each student can relatively easily begin to develop a valuable new skill. Skilled researchers are highly prized in every organization, in multinational corporations, in small businesses, in the public sector and in not-for-profit organizations. As stated earlier, it is important for every professional to have the skills required to undertake research. It is important too to have the skills required to read and understand other people's research and the research of other organizations. Such research might have important or even critical implications for your own work and organization. Every organization needs people who can make this kind of contribution to the work of the organization.

Research is essentially a creative undertaking. In general, the academy, university or college does not impose a research project on any student, beyond restricting them to researching their own academic field; so students are free to decide for themselves what to research. This means that while all the other subjects that must be studied for a qualification or credential at college or university are created and developed by someone else, this is the one subject that each student designs, creates and develops for themselves. It is very important to be creative in research. The entire research endeavour at university is dedicated to the creation and development of knowledge. In undertaking your research project, you are undertaking to create something new, to create some new knowledge. This might be a new product, a new training programme, a new marketing strategy, a new theory, a new concept or a new idea about an area of business.

Once started on a course of study in research methods, usually undertaken to prepare for the practical exercise of designing and carrying out a research project, many students make the mistake of trying to research something that is too big. It is important that, as you design the research project that you will carry out and complete, you design a project that it will be possible to complete. You yourself will design the mountain that you have to climb; so do not make that mountain too big or too difficult to conquer. As stated earlier, a very common problem is that of students trying to research their idea, which is often too big to research, instead of first turning their idea into a research question or statement, or a research hypothesis, and then researching that question or statement or hypothesis.

Another mistake that is easy to make is to create a research question or statement that has an '*and*' in the middle of it. Take the following research statement, for example:

> *This research project is a survey examining the attitudes of the employees of Swinton Records to the company's new business plan and the proposed relocation of the company to a new greenfield site.*

In effect, this is two research projects. The first project proposed is a survey examining the attitudes of the employees of Swinton Records to the company's new business plan. The second project proposed is a survey of the attitudes of the employees of Swinton Records to the proposed relocation of the company to a new greenfield site. It is neither necessary nor wise to attempt to undertake two research projects. It is sufficient to do one or the other of these. While each alone seems perhaps quite a simple study, each will grow and grow in complexity as they develop. If you find yourself in such a position with your proposed research, with an '*and*' in the middle of the research question or statement, think about how you might eliminate that 'and'. Make a decision and move your project forward. You might decide to pick the project that most appeals to you, the one that makes most sense to you, the one that is perhaps the most useful for the company you are working with or researching. Or you may choose one that works for you in terms of taking you in a direction you wish to go in, with the company or with your career. It could happen that you might decide to keep the '*and*' and do the bigger project because you feel that both aspects to the project are essential. It may be that this is the case. It is important, however, to have an understanding of the size of the project you are undertaking and the implications of that in terms of the amount of work you will have to do and the amount of time you have available for the work required. Whichever decision you make, the important thing is to make a decision. Then once you have made a decision, move on.

Making decisions can in itself be a problem. To be a good researcher you must be able to make decisions. You must be able to decide what to include in your research and what to exclude. You must also be able to move on quickly from a decision and leave behind whatever you have decided to leave behind. As soon as a decision is made to exclude something from the research, your focus must move on from it. If it is excluded, it is no longer relevant. Focus only on what is relevant. It is in this way that your research project becomes more focused and more organized, through all of the decisions, big and small, that you make about it.

As the project develops it is very useful to have these decisions and your reflections on them recorded in the research diary. You can revisit your research diary at any time and read through your thinking and reasoning in relation to any decision made. The record kept in the research diary will provide you with material for writing up your research project. At the very least, this material will give you ideas for your writing.

How to formulate a researchable project

A researchable project is a project that the researcher could possibly undertake and complete. Many students develop ideas for projects that could not possibly be undertaken or completed. The simple test (see Test of Researchability box), can establish very quickly whether or not a research project is researchable.

From time to time you may ponder many issues and questions in relation to the business world. However, while all of these areas interest you, it may perhaps not be possible to conduct research on them. The reason for this may be one of practicality, because research is time-consuming and sometimes expensive. So, while you might think you would like to research the contemporary global experience of the rock music industry, it is unlikely that you will have the necessary resources at your disposal. A research project of this kind would involve a very long set-up period, a lot of privileged access to the world of the global rock music industry, and a great deal of expense in terms of travel, accommodation and subsistence. It might be possible to do some research around this idea on the internet, but this would probably be the only practical option for a researcher working on such a project.

It might be that you feel very strongly that an industry in your locality is causing serious and substantial environmental damage and you might decide that you would like to explore this issue in your research project. This project may also be impossible to conduct. This time the issue is access to data. The industry, if it is causing environmental damage, is unlikely to give you the access you need to gather data required in order to be able to carry out this study. Access to data is a critical issue in all research projects. Researchers are not the police; they do not have any rights of entry or access; they are entirely dependent on the goodwill of the gatekeepers facilitating their research for access to the data they require.

Gatekeepers, in this context, are people who have the capacity to provide or deny access to data. Gatekeepers can have formal roles in an organization or entity. They can be chief executive officers (CEOs) of companies, their personal assistants (PAs) and/or secretaries, human resources (HR) managers, marketing managers, and so on. Gatekeepers can also have informal roles in social settings, such as opinion leaders within groups who can facilitate or deny access to data as easily and quickly as can any formal gatekeeper. The important thing to remember is that a researcher who does not have access to data, who cannot get access to data or who cannot maintain access to data, does not have a research project. The project, because there is no guaranteed access to data, is not researchable.

It is very important to remember that it is often the case that access to data can be withdrawn at any point throughout the lifespan of the research project. Researchers sometimes think that as soon as they actually have the data they require, access can no longer be denied them. This is not the case: even when the researcher has gathered the data, analyzed them and drawn conclusions from them, permission to use the data can be withdrawn. In an academic institution, if there is a dispute over rights to data used in a research project, the project will generally not be accepted by the institution until the differences have been resolved. Your own ethical principles, as a researcher, would probably prohibit you from proceeding with a research project where such a dispute over permission had arisen. The withdrawal of access to data can be a disaster for any researcher, as without that access the research project cannot be completed, or submitted for examination or publication.

So how does a researcher create and develop a researchable project? The researcher does this by ensuring from the start and for the duration of the project that they have the necessary time, money and access to data. Generally, for an undergraduate thesis, students spend six to ten months completing the project, depending on the requirements of the programme. This represents quite a substantial amount of time. Usually, as indicated earlier, there are only relatively minor costs associated with such research, such as the cost of sending out questionnaires, the costs of getting to and from interviews and the costs of printing and binding the final draft of the thesis. However, for a student living off a grant and/or the income from a small part-time job, such relatively minor expenses can represent quite substantial demands on their income. Therefore, it is important when designing the research project to take account of such expenses.

THE TEST OF RESEARCHABILITY

In this simple test, you examine whether or not you have the resources to complete the research project you are thinking of undertaking. The resources you need are:

- The time required to conduct the research: to design the project, carry out the fieldwork, analyze the data, write up your findings, draw conclusions and make recommendations.

- The money required to conduct the research, if any money is needed. In general, even with small-scale research projects, some funds may be required for the fieldwork, for example for posting questionnaires, for travelling to interviews and/or for organizing focus groups.

- Access to data. Many students underestimate the difficulties that researchers can encounter in accessing data, in attempting to access data, in securing access to data and in maintaining access to data over the time required to complete the fieldwork.

Writing up the research: The thesis/report

Like the research process itself, the structure of the thesis or research report follows a conventional pattern, an accepted pattern. The steps of the research project are sequential, as outlined at the start of this chapter; however, there are frequent overlaps in that the researcher moves back and forth through the steps as the project develops. Research projects are very organic, they are living and growing entities and they change all the time. Generally, the changes happen in tiny shifts in emphasis, rather than giant changes or u-turns. All these changes can affect the entire project and the researcher is constantly engaged in a process of editing the thesis or report as it develops, in order to ensure that any changes made are properly incorporated. It is, of course, very useful to record the changes made in the thesis or report, and the reasons and reflections behind them in the research diary.

The thesis or report is the written account of the research project. It is a synopsis of the work that was carried out. As the word count for a thesis is always quite constrained, it is not possible for this written record to be anything more than a synopsis of all of the work that went into the research project

The thesis or report is written following particular social science conventions. The basic layout is shown in Tables 1.2–1.4. The word counts given are simply guides. You can play around with your overall word count, perhaps giving some extra words to the data analysis chapter, and taking those words from some other chapter in the work. It is generally the rule that you must complete the entire thesis/report of the research within the word count; there is usually a 10 per cent margin on either side of the word count. The word counts of the list of references and appendices tend not to be included in the overall word count allowance.

The Gantt chart (see Table 1.5) shows a timeline for a thesis carried out over an eight-month period. It is a good idea to create a model of this kind to plan the progress of your own research. As can be seen from the Gantt chart, and from the model of the research process outlined at the start of this chapter, the research project is developed in phases and the work of developing a research project takes a substantial amount of time. It is helpful therefore to develop a timeline for your research project and to use that timeline to monitor and measure your progress.

You will also find it helpful to look at a number of bound theses in the library. You can use these completed theses as a guide for your own thesis. When you look at these completed and bound theses, study the title pages, abstracts, tables of content, list of references and referencing methods. It is also helpful to examine the appendices of these theses in order to develop an understanding of the kind of material that generally goes into appendices.

Table 1.2 Layout for a 20 000-word thesis

Title pages	Pages with name of project, acknowledgement of research supervisor, dedication and appreciation
Abstract	Three-hundred-word summary of the entire project, generally presented in one paragraph
Table of contents	Entire contents, including lists of tables, figures and photographs
Chapter 1: Introduction, 2000 words	A brief introduction to the entire thesis or report
Chapter 2: Literature review, 5000 words	Contains the theoretical framework for the research project
Chapter 3: Research methodology, 4000 words	Contains the methodological framework for the research project
Chapter 4: Data analysis, 6000 words	Contains the analytical framework for the research project
Chapter 5: Conclusions and recommendations, 3000 words	Contains the fully developed, well-conceptualized conclusions from the research, and usually a bullet point list of the recommendations drawn from the conclusions
List of references	A complete list, using a referencing system, of the books, articles, etc. referred to in the text
Appendices	Each appendix contains a document/table/figure relevant to the research and referenced and discussed in the research. Typically, copies of letters seeking and granting permission for the research are contained in appendices; letters inviting participation in the research; copies of forms designed for the research such as informed consent forms; copies of any data collection methods used in the research, e.g. a copy of the questionnaire, interview/focus group schedule. Long lists and large tables and figures can be placed in appendices

Table 1.3 Layout for a 15 000-word thesis

Title pages	Pages with name of project, acknowledgement of research supervisor, dedication and appreciation
Abstract	Three-hundred-word summary of the entire project, generally presented in one paragraph
Table of contents	Entire contents, including lists of tables, figures and photographs
Chapter 1: Introduction, 1500 words	A brief introduction to the entire thesis or report
Chapter 2: Literature review, 4000 words	Contains the theoretical framework for the research project
Chapter 3: Research methodology, 3500 words	Contains the methodological framework for the research project
Chapter 4: Data analysis, 4000 words	Contains the analytical framework for the research project
Chapter 5: Conclusions and recommendations, 2000 words	Contains the fully developed, well-conceptualized conclusions from the research and usually a bullet point list of the recommendations drawn from the conclusions
List of references	A complete list, using a referencing system, of the books, articles, etc. referred to in the text
Appendices	Each appendix contains a document/table/figure relevant to the research and referenced and discussed in the research. Typically, copies of letters seeking and granting permission for the research are contained in appendices; letters inviting participation in the research; copies of forms designed for the research such as informed consent forms; copies of any data collection methods used in the research, e.g. a copy of the questionnaire, interview/focus group schedule. Long lists and large tables and figures can be placed in appendices

Table 1.4 Layout for a 10 000-word thesis

Title pages	Pages with name of project, acknowledgement of research supervisor, dedication and appreciation
Abstract	Three-hundred-word summary of the entire project, generally presented in one paragraph
Table of contents	Entire contents, including lists of tables, figures and photographs
Chapter 1: Introduction, 1200 words	A brief introduction to the entire thesis or report
Chapter 2: Literature review, 2500 words	Contains the theoretical framework for the research project
Chapter 3: Research methodology, 1800 words	Contains the methodological framework for the research project
Chapter 4: Data analysis, 3000 words	Contains the analytical framework for the research project
Chapter 5: Conclusions and recommendations, 1500 words	Contains the fully developed, well-conceptualized conclusions from the research and usually a bullet point list of the recommendations drawn from the conclusions
List of references	A complete list, using a referencing system, of the books, articles, etc. referred to in the text
Appendices	Each appendix contains a document/table/figure relevant to the research and referenced and discussed in the research. Typically, copies of letters seeking and granting permission for the research are contained in appendices; letters inviting participation in the research; copies of forms designed for the research such as informed consent forms; copies of any data collection methods used in the research, e.g. a copy of the questionnaire, interview/focus group schedule. Long lists and large tables and figures can be placed in appendices

Table 1.5   Gantt chart for a student research project

	Oct.	Nov.	Dec.	Jan.	Feb.	Mar.	April	May
Focus on identifying research area Develop idea in this area for research project Turn idea into a research question/statement	▓							
Commence reading of literature Develop aim and objectives for research project Decide on appropriate methodology for research, and develop the data-gathering methods to be used		▓						
Write research proposal Secure permissions needed to conduct the research Secure ethical approval for the research			▓					
Write Chapter 1, Introduction (this chapter is based on the research proposal) Begin writing literature review for the research (generally Chapter 2 in the thesis)			▓					
Write research methodology chapter (usually Chapter 3 in the thesis)				▓				
Complete writing of literature review Finalize data-gathering techniques (do this with reference to the literature) Gather data					▓			
Analyze data						▓		
Write data analysis chapter/findings chapter (generally Chapter 4 of the thesis)						▓		
Write conclusions and recommendations chapter (generally Chapter 5 of the thesis)						▓		
Complete first draft and submit for feedback							▓	
Complete second draft								▓
Final review of thesis Submit thesis								▓

It is essential that you get some guidance, either from your lecturer in research methodologies or your thesis supervisor, on the word count required, on the format and layout required, and on the referencing method to be used. Your lecturer in research methodologies and/or your thesis supervisor will be able to provide you with guidance on all of the other issues and questions that will arise as you carry out your research. You certainly should avail of all the help and support that they can offer you.

A BRIEF INTRODUCTION TO RESEARCH ETHICS

Social research is the means by which people find out new things about the social world. In order to do this, researchers engage with the theory in the field, by undertaking a review of the literature, and they observe the phenomenon under investigation systematically, by gathering data and by using their imaginations creatively. Researchers must be informed, organized and systematic. They should be sensitive to the people involved in the investigation and they must engage with them, and with the entire research process, in an ethical manner.

The quality of every research project is dependent on the **integrity** of the researcher. When you report your research, you will describe what you set out to do, how you did what you did, what you found, and what that means. Obviously, the written account of the research must be accurate and honest. It should give enough detail to allow the reader to evaluate the work. The literature review must be comprehensive, complete and up-to-date. The data should be properly gathered, properly managed and properly analyzed. The conclusions drawn from the research should be drawn from the findings of the research and these findings must emerge from the data gathered.

integrity The honesty and scholarship of the researcher in carrying out research.

Every researcher has responsibilities to a number of constituencies. These include the institution where the research is being carried out, as well as all of the individuals, groups, institutions and organizations participating in the research. The researcher has a duty of care towards all participants and must, above all, do no harm. The researcher must accurately represent the research to participants, all of whom must participate on an informed, voluntary basis. Covert research can raise particular ethical issues, and consequently it may not be possible to get permission or ethical approval for such a study. If you are thinking of engaging in covert research you should discuss this as soon as possible with your research methods lecturer and/or your thesis supervisor. They will be able to advise and guide you.

It is important in writing your research to reflect broadly on any moral issues and imperatives of the project. This reflection should be detailed in the final report of the research or in the thesis, generally in the methodology chapter. It will enhance the quality of your work. It is important to remember that while there are general ethical principles and issues for all research and all researchers, every individual research project will have ethical issues which are unique to that project and which should be recognized, acknowledged and addressed.

YOUR RESEARCH
A research diary exercise

Think about the possible ethical issues and questions in your research project. Jot down in your research diary some notes in response to these ethical issues and questions.

Consider for a moment any research project in which you have participated. Think about how you felt. Did you feel vulnerable at all? If so, why did you feel vulnerable? What was it about the research, the researcher or the research process that made you feel like this? Think for a moment about yourself as the researcher. How do you want people to perceive your research project? What impression do you want to give people of you yourself as a researcher? How do you want them to feel about participating in your research? How do you want them to feel as they participate in your research?

Write a short research diary entry on these reflections, and on how these reflections will help you when you are designing and carrying out your research. Also write a couple of sentences on how these reflections will help you in writing the 'ethics' section of your thesis. The reflection that you engage in for this exercise may appear, in an edited form, in the ethics section of your research project. The ethics section is usually placed at the end of the research methodology chapter of the thesis (this is often Chapter 3 in the thesis or report of the research).

In your research diary, develop an ethics checklist for your research and for you as a researcher working on that research project.

Try to find in your reading of journal articles particularly good ethical reflections on business research projects. Use these reflections, along with your own reflections, to help you develop your knowledge and skills in terms of research ethics, ethical reflection and writing up research ethics. Take this opportunity to update your interactive research diary, available on Cengage Brain.

REAL WORLD RESEARCH

The article detailed here explores an interesting journal article which outlines the use of a social media strategy in the marketing of a Bollywood film. The journal article is a good example of a research project that has a well-structured and well-written literature review. The research was developed using an interesting research methodology, case study methodology, and the data collection methods used in the research project are clearly detailed, as are the data analysis methods used. The conclusions drawn from the research are clearly and simply outlined and explained.

How theory influences research

In the article examined here (Nanda, Pattnaik and Lu, 2018, 'Innovation in social media strategy for movie success: A study of the Bollywood movie industry', *Management Decision*, 56:1, 233–51), the authors develop an in-depth and

(Continued)

comprehensive case study to examine the promotional strategies adopted through YouTube, Facebook and Twitter throughout the life cycle of a Bollywood movie and its impact on the box office success of the movie. Social media is a key concept in this research. It is interesting to note how the authors use this key concept to facilitate the development of the structure for the entire research project.

As we read the synopsis we will see the different steps in the research process, detailed in Figure 1.1 at the start of this chapter. We suggest that you source the original article and while reading it, you should trace the steps in the research process as they were undertaken for this study.

In the introduction to the article the authors explore, outline and define the concept of social media. They say that in today's world, social media is an essential part of a consumer's everyday life to obtain information, communicate and make purchase decisions. They explain that in this new environment, companies constantly adopt various social media platforms to access new consumers and to engage the existing ones through implementing a variety of promotional strategies involving these platforms. In relation to the movie industry, the authors say that one of the major influencers of a movie's success are the consumers who share their experiences through electronic word of mouth (eWOM) influencing their peers' decisions to watch, or not to watch, a movie. They say that social media also provides rich platforms on which consumers can share their experiences through electronic means and spread the eWOM.

In the study, the authors focus on how movie studios develop an integrated social media strategy in order to engage consumers through promotional strategies so that their movies achieve box office success. They explain that movie studios use a number of social media platforms simultaneously, but they say that a growing body of literature, along with anecdotal evidence, suggests that such promotional strategies are not focused or properly orchestrated. The authors suggest that a more coherent strategy is needed to achieve box office success.

Anecdotal evidence is evidence from anecdotes, it is evidence gathered in informal and/or casual conversation, and consequently it is deemed to have limited value.

The authors engage in an extensive review of the literature through which they explore in great detail the concepts of social media and brand promotion, and social media and movie performance. Social media is a comparatively new field of study, as can be seen from the literature review presented in the article. Throughout the literature review, the authors consider studies of the use of social media platforms such as Twitter, Facebook, YouTube, and Yahoo, in the positioning of a movie in terms of box office success. While there is a substantial and developing body of knowledge, the authors call for further research and they highlight gaps in knowledge in the field.

The authors used a case study methodology in the research. They outline the single, in-depth case study that they developed. In their study they focus on the marketing of one film, and they explain that this narrow focus allows for a very in-depth and comprehensive study of the phenomenon under investigation, the use of social media in the marketing of a Bollywood film. The authors provide a very good overview, a very in-depth discussion, or analysis, of their case, and they present results and a conclusion. They quote Yin (1994) who has written extensively on case study methodology, and, very skilfully, they use Yin and his writings on case study methodology, along with other authors on the topic, to support their justifications for the methodological decisions they made in their study.

In their conclusion, they explain how their case study provides a comprehensive understanding of how an integrative social media strategy led to box office success. They go on to explain the implications of this finding for the development of social media marketing strategies for experiential products generally, and the movie industry in particular. They explain that marketers need to concentrate on generating positive eWOM from consumers, and then on utilizing consumers for further promotion. They conclude the case study with a very clear and simple explanation of how the integrated social media marketing campaign developed for the Bollywood movie they examined in their research, facilitated the box office success of the movie.

The use of social media in marketing and communications is a very interesting area of research. Is it an area that you would consider investigating for your research project? You will find that you get many ideas for your research project as you read published accounts of the research of others.

anecdotal evidence Evidence from anecdotes, evidence gathered in informal and/or casual conversation, and consequently deemed to have limited value.

END OF CHAPTER QUESTIONS

1 Detail the steps in the research process.

2 Outline and explain the use of the four frameworks approach in the research project process.

3 When can a research project be deemed researchable?

4 What is a key concept in research?

5 What is a research diary?

6 Define business research.

7 What is a literature review?

8 What is a theoretical framework?

9 Discuss the value of business research, and use a range of examples of business research projects to support your answer.

10 Write a short reflective piece on research ethics.

REFERENCES

Elliott, L. (2017) 'We're being hurt by the fixation on economic growth at all costs', *The Guardian*, 20.11.2017, www.theguardian.com/commentisfree/2017/nov/30/fixation-economic-growth-gdp-pollution-gambling (Accessed 19.12.2017).

Nanda, M., Pattnaik, C. and Lu, Q. (Steven) (2018) 'Innovation in social media strategy for movie success: A study of the Bollywood movie industry', *Management Decision*, 56(1): 233–251.

OECD (2017) 'How's Life 2017', 'New OECD data expose deep well-being divisions' www.oecd.org/newsroom/new-oecd-data-expose-deep-well-being-divisions.htm (Accessed 19.12.2017).

Yin, R. (1994) *Case Study Research: Design and Methods* (2nd edn), Sage Publications.

RECOMMENDED READING

Bell, J. (2014) *Doing Your Research Project*, Maidenhead: Open University Press.

Collis, J. and Hussey, R. (2013) *Business Research: A Practical Guide for Undergraduate and Postgraduate Students*, Basingstoke: Palgrave Macmillan.

Creswell, J.W. and Creswell, J.D. (2018) *Research Design, Qualitative, Quantitative and Mixed Methods Approaches* (5th edn), London: Sage.

Denscombe, M. (2017) *The Good Research Guide: For Small-scale Social Research Projects* (5th edn), Maidenhead: Open University Press.

Easterby-Smith, M., Thorpe, R. and Jackson, P.R. (2008) *Management Research: Theory and Practice,* (3rd edn), London: Sage.

Jankowicz, A.D. (2005) *Business Research Projects*, London: Cengage.

Kent, R. (2007) *Marketing Research, Approaches, Methods and Applications in Europe*, London: Cengage.

Methodspace: Connecting the Research Community, Sage, www.methodspace.com

Murray, R. (2017) *How to Write a Thesis*, Maidenhead: Open University Press.

Neuman, W.L. (2013) *Social Research Methods: Pearson New International Edition: Qualitative and Quantitative Approaches*, Essex, UK: Pearson Education Limited.

White, B. and Rayner, S. (2014) *Dissertation Skills for Business and Management Students* (2nd edn), London: Cengage.

CHAPTER 2
DEVELOPING RESEARCH SKILLS

LEARNING OBJECTIVES

At the end of this chapter, the student should be able to:

- Recognize their existing level of research skills and identify areas for improvement.

- Create a conceptual framework, the first of the four frameworks.

- Develop a research statement or question for a research project and outline appropriate aims and objectives for the project.

- Identify and source appropriate literature.

- Compile a list of references and properly use appendices.

RESEARCH SKILLS

At the end of this chapter, the student should, using the exercises on Cengage Brain, be able to:

- Generate ideas for research projects.

- Identify, source and use appropriate literature.

The aim of this chapter is to help the reader assess the standard of their basic research skills (using a short review test on the online platform) before setting out these skills in detail throughout the chapter. The chapter covers issues such as how to formulate an argument; how to develop a research statement or question; how to outline a research aim and a series of objectives; how to source literature; how to keep a research diary; how to identify plagiarism; explaining what plagiarism is and why it is strictly outlawed; how to compile a list of references; and the proper use of appendices. There is a focus in the chapter on writing skills and on note keeping. As in all of the chapters in this textbook, keywords and terms are highlighted in the text and explained in a glossary of terms at the end of the book.

INTRODUCTION

The focus of this chapter is on the key skills needed by every researcher. The key skills relate to the different steps in the research process, as outlined at the start of Chapter 1 in Figure 1.1.

It takes time to develop the skills of a good or a competent researcher. The process involves reading textbooks on research methodologies and research methods, reading journal articles that describe research projects and gaining experience in working on research projects. The work of every researcher in academia is both theoretical and applied. Theory is to be found in literature, and literature is found in books and journal articles, in theses, in government reports and papers, in the published work of NGOs and in the reports of conference proceedings. The applied aspect of the research task is in the actual workings of real research projects, carried out in the field.

There are five basic skills required in conducting research. They are detailed in Table 2.1.

Table 2.1 Basic skills required by every researcher

1.	Ability to generate ideas for research projects
2.	Ability to identify, source and use appropriate literature
3.	Ability to develop research projects with a good fit, i.e. where the different parts of the research project fit well together
4.	Ability to gather and analyze data
5.	Ability to write well, to be able to communicate clearly, thoroughly and simply, through writing

RESEARCH IDEAS

The article in the Value of Good Research box focuses on one of Britain's favourite fast foods: fish and chips. Some detail is given in the article on research carried out annually to identify the best fish and chip shop in the UK. Some quantitative data are also presented in the box. Very simply, quantitative data are data in numerical form.

Can you identify some of the issues addressed in the article that could be used to develop ideas for good research projects? Among those ideas, is there an idea that you would consider developing as *your* research project?

One of the most important and fundamental skills every researcher requires is the ability to generate ideas for research projects. There are possibilities for research projects everywhere. For example, the news article from *The Independent* newspaper (see Value of Good Research box) details a competition for the best fish and chip shop. This article could generate several ideas for research projects. Possibilities might include a research project focused on establishing which restaurant is 'the best', an investigation of the factors that make a restaurant 'the best' or perhaps a research project designed to create a campaign to turn a restaurant into 'the best' restaurant.

The key to developing an idea for a research project is to focus on an area of interest and/or of use to you. In general, when students begin to think in this way about ideas for research projects, they find it relatively easy to decide on an idea. An idea for a research project is often simply a statement of the general area within which you wish to situate your research. You might, for example, decide that the area that interests you most is internet sales, or perhaps intercultural workplaces, or training and development, or any one of the very many areas you have covered to a greater or lesser extent in your studies so far for your degree, in your reading for your degree, in your work or place of employment.

Once you have decided on the area in which you wish to situate your research project, you need to begin to develop your idea for the research project from that area. Sometimes research projects come together readily and quickly, and sometimes they do not. It is important that you don't worry if your research project doesn't come to you immediately, because it is worth spending all the time needed in developing a research project. If the idea for the research project is fundamentally sound to begin with, there is a good chance that it will continue to be sound as it develops.

Your research project must be situated within your discipline. If you are taking a degree in business, then your research project must be undertaken on some aspect of business. Similarly, if your degree is in marketing or industrial relations, then your research project must be on some aspect of marketing or industrial relations. The third of the five basic skills required by every researcher, as outlined at the start of this chapter, is the ability to develop research projects with a good fit. One fundamental question is whether or not the research project you are thinking about fits with the requirements of your course of study. Other aspects of the notion of 'fit' relate to:

- whether or not the population you are using in your research is the appropriate population for that research project
- whether or not the research methodology you are using to develop the research project is the appropriate methodology
- whether or not the data collection methods you are using are appropriate to the requirements of the project
- whether or not the data analysis methods and procedures you are using are appropriate in terms of that research project.

The issue of 'fit' in relation to the research project is a very important one, and it is an issue that we will be returning to throughout this textbook.

It is important to be able to distinguish between a broad area for an idea for a research project and a research question or statement. Your idea is the broad area within which you want to conduct your research, for example internet sales, or the intercultural workplace, or perhaps training and development. You might be interested in examining the marketing of computer games or recruitment and selection processes for human resource managers. Other ideas could include business plans for SMEs, the experiences of women in senior management, or possible career paths for new business graduates. These are all ideas for research projects and they are good and useful and interesting ideas, but they are not research questions or statements. Each of these ideas is too broad to be a research project. Your carefully defined research project expressed in your research statement, your research question, or your research hypothesis, would be situated in one of these areas.

THE VALUE OF GOOD RESEARCH

Research in the media: 'UK's Top 10 Fish and Chip Shops Revealed'

In an article in *The Independent*, journalist Kashmira Gander (2017) explains that to make 'the Oscars', the name given to the competition, fish and chip shops all over the UK were judged on their frying skills, menu development and innovation, marketing and staff training, and in addition, the shop managers had to be able to establish that they sourced fish sustainably. According to the Enjoy Fish & Chips website (www.enjoyfishandchips.co.uk/), there are 10 500 independent fish and chip shops operating in the UK; 382 million portions of fish and chips are eaten every year in the UK, and £1.2 billion is spent every year in the UK on fish and chips.

SEAFISH, a non-departmental government body set up in the UK by the Fisheries Act 1981, to raise standards across the seafood industry (www.seafish.org/about-seafish/who-we-are) developed the National Fish and Chip Awards, and the awards are now in their 30th year.

The winner of the competition for the Independent Take-away Fish and Chip Shop of the Year for 2017, the top award, was named as Kingfisher Fish and Chips, Plympton, Devon. Shop owners, Nikki Mutton and Craig Maw, were elated. On their website, (www.kingfisherfishandchips.co.uk/) they said that their shop had the world's most sustainable menu, that they were one of only two fish and chip businesses in the UK to have a three star rating from the Sustainable Restaurant Association, and as well as that award they had another 25 industry and non-industry awards.

According to an article by Saffron Alexander published in *The Telegraph*, (26.01.2017), a member of the judging panel, Ben Bartlett, said that Kingfisher Fish and Chips won the award because of their extensive knowledge and experience, their robust sourcing policies, their forward thinking approach, and their continual business growth.

TURNING RESEARCH IDEAS INTO RESEARCH PROJECTS

Once you have decided on the broad area within which you want to situate your research, the next step is to turn your idea into a precisely defined research project. The key to this process is focus. The questions to ask yourself as you engage in this process of refinement are these: what, precisely, am I interested in researching? What exactly do I want to focus on in my research project?

In addition to focus, you must keep in mind the test of researchability. The **test of researchability** is explained in detail in Chapter 1. Using this simple test, you ask yourself if your project is **researchable**, if you have the time needed, the money needed (if any money is needed), the data required and the level of access to the data required to carry out the study.

> **test of researchability** Deems a research project feasible in relation to the time, money and data needed in order to carry out and complete the research.
>
> **researchable** A project is researchable if you have the time, money, data and the level of access to the data needed to carry out and complete the research.

This simple test can help you decide from the start whether or not it is worthwhile trying to develop your idea into a research project. If you think that you would have difficulty with any one of the items in the test, then the chances are the research project you are proposing to undertake is not researchable. It may be that the project cannot be undertaken because it is too ambitious. It could be that it would not be possible to complete the project in the time allowed. Perhaps the project is too expensive for the budget that you might be in a position to allocate to it. Perhaps the project cannot be undertaken because you could not access the data required for the project, or if you could access the data required, it might be that you could not maintain access to the data for the length of time required to complete the fieldwork. It is important to be very clear about these three issues from the outset: the time allowed for the project, the cost, if there is any cost, of the project, and access to the data required for the project.

Often students have very good and very interesting research projects in mind, but these research projects are, for one reason or another, beyond their capacity or resources. If you find yourself in this situation, the important thing is to accept that the project cannot, for whatever reason, be undertaken and then quickly move on to develop a research project that is possible.

THE FIRST STEP: DEVELOPING A RESEARCH STATEMENT

When you have decided on the broad area within which you wish to situate your research project, the first step is to develop a simple research statement that clearly expresses your idea for your research project. This statement becomes the conceptual framework for your research project. The first framework in the four frameworks approach to the research project, outlined in Chapter 1, is the conceptual framework. The conceptual framework for the research project is contained in the research statement or question, or in the research **hypothesis**. Let us say, for example, that you are interested in examining the marketing of computer games. This is your idea for your research project. The next step is to take this idea and turn it into a research project by creating a research question or statement. This research question or statement will be the **conceptual framework** for the research project, or you might say that it contains the conceptual framework for the research project. The conceptual framework for any research project contains all of the key concepts within that research project.

> **hypothesis** A predicted or expected answer to a research question; a formal statement of an unproven proposition that is empirically testable.
>
> **conceptual framework** The conceptual framework is contained in the one sentence research statement or question. It contains all key concepts (keywords and/or key phrases) in the research project. The entire research project rests on the conceptual framework.

The four frameworks

- *Conceptual Framework*
- Theoretical Framework
- Methodological Framework
- Analytical Framework

If we take the idea of researching the marketing of computer games and we decide to develop this idea into a research statement or question, we have to do two things: we have to ensure that the research statement or question we develop is researchable; and we have to ensure that all of the key concepts that interest you, as the researcher, are contained in the conceptual framework, research statement or question.

For example, if the idea is the marketing of computer games, the research statement might read something like this:

> *This research project is a case study examining the marketing of computer games by three computer games companies: the companies are Zenith Computer Games Ltd, Orbit Computer Games Ltd and Galaxy Computer Games Ltd.*

This research statement is a simple statement of a research project. This is what you, as the researcher, should aim for. While it is clear and simple, the research statement contains all of the key concepts in the research project. The key concepts in this example are 'marketing', 'computer games', 'computer games companies' and 'marketing computer games'. These four key concepts are the essential focus of this research project. We will see in subsequent chapters how the entire research project rests on this conceptual framework and how these four key concepts provide the entire focus of this study.

The proposed research methodology (case study) as indicated in the research statement, would seem to be an appropriate methodology for the research proposed. **Case study methodology** (see Chapter 9), is particularly useful in the in-depth study of bounded entities, such as a company, a team, a class, an organization, a single incident or event, or any entity that is clearly bounded. A bounded entity is an entity with a clear boundary around it. The boundary clearly shows what is in the entity or a part of the entity and what is not in the entity or a part of the entity. The organization, incident or event provides the case (or cases) to be studied. In the case study outlined in the conceptual framework detailed earlier there are three cases: the marketing of computer games by three computer games companies, Zenith Computer Games Ltd, Orbit Computer Games Ltd and Galaxy Computer Games Ltd. Each of the three cases is a bounded entity. Therefore, the proposed case study methodology is a good fit for this research project.

> **case study methodology** Useful in the in-depth study of bounded entities, such as an organization, or a single incident or event. A case study can focus on a single case or on a number of cases.

In this case study, the researcher has clearly outlined the focus of the study (the different marketing campaigns of each company), and has limited the **scope** of the study to three different computer games companies. The decision to use three companies (three cases) was not made arbitrarily; decisions a researcher makes regarding the scope of a research project are dictated by what is possible and what is necessary. It is up to the researcher to decide the scope of the project, with guidance from the research supervisor.

> **scope** The breadth and depth of a project.

There are two dimensions to scope in every research project: breadth and depth. The researcher might decide to undertake a broad study and include three or more companies. Alternatively, the researcher might decide to do a more in-depth study on a single company, or perhaps two companies, and examine their marketing campaigns in greater detail and depth than would be possible if there were more companies included in the study. In a small-scale research project, resource constraints mean that there is always a trade-off between breadth and depth; the broader the study, the less depth is possible. More depth in a study means less breadth.

In terms of this proposed study, which involves the examination of marketing campaigns, access to data may not be an issue. This is because the researcher could decide to use as data only material that is in the public domain, in this case the advertising undertaken by the companies. Such a decision might require a small change to the research statement. The research statement might now read like this:

 This research project is a case study examining the advertising campaigns undertaken for the marketing of computer games by three computer games companies: the companies are Zenith Computer Games Ltd, Orbit Computer Games Ltd and Galaxy Computer Games Ltd.

It is also possible to limit the temporal span (the time span) of the research in the research statement. In the following version of the research statement, the proposed timescale for the study is one year. The reasons for limiting the time span should be detailed in the brief discussion of the research statement or question that usually follows it, as in the following example.

YOUR RESEARCH
The value of a research diary

There is generally a need for a rationale for every decision made in the research project, and that rationale should be logical, reasoned and reasonable. It should be possible to argue the case for every decision made throughout the research process. This is an essential requirement of all research projects because research projects are essentially exercises in reason and logic.

This requirement provides another good reason for keeping a research diary.

The researcher can record, briefly or at length, the decisions made in the process of developing the research project and the reasoning behind those decisions.

These notes are very helpful in the writing of the research. They can provide starting points for the writing and they can become the basis for substantial sections of the thesis or report of the research. The researcher's notes, scribbled in the research diary, can be helpful in tackling writer's block, when the researcher does not know what to write about or how to begin writing.

 This research project is a case study focused on examining the advertising campaigns undertaken in the year 2018, for the marketing of computer games by three computer games companies: the companies are Zenith Computer Games Ltd, Orbit Computer Games Ltd and Galaxy Computer Games Ltd.

The research will focus on the 2018 marketing campaigns of the three companies in order to examine and compare and contrast the most current and up-to-date marketing of the three companies.

In another example, let us consider the student who wishes to examine recruitment and selection processes for HR managers. Once again the student must be able to access data on this topic. If the student works in a company with a HR department, the company may allow the student access to their recruitment and selection processes. If so, then this can be the focus of the student's research. If this is not the case, perhaps the student might develop an ideal recruitment and selection process for a fictitious company, using information on recruitment and selection processes available in books, journal articles and online.

Use your imagination when you are considering the research project you will develop. Do not forget, however, that you are constrained by the requirements of your programme of study. You are also constrained by the standards of **validity** that apply to all research projects.

> **validity**   Relates to how logical, truthful, robust, sound, reasonable, meaningful and useful is the research; the accuracy of a measure or the extent to which a score truthfully represents a concept.

It may be said that the key issue in all research projects is that of validity. This is the issue of how valid the research is; in other words, how logical, truthful, robust, sound, reasonable, meaningful and useful the research is. A related issue is the issue of **reliability**. In social science research, reliability relates to the degree to which the research can be repeated while obtaining consistent results. Validity and reliability are fundamental issues in social science research and we will return to them throughout this textbook.

> **reliability**   An indicator of a measure's internal consistency; dependability of the research, to the degree to which the research can be repeated while obtaining consistent results.

Another fundamental issue in social science research is the issue of **triangulation**. The concept of triangulation and the processes of triangulating research call for more than one approach to answering the research question or responding to the research statement. There are different ways of triangulating research; theoretical triangulation, researcher triangulation, methodological triangulation, and within method and between method (data collection method) triangulation (Denzin, 1970).

> **triangulation**   Studying the phenomenon under investigation from more than one perspective, e.g. researcher, theoretical, methodological and/or method triangulation.

Essentially, using researcher triangulation, more than one researcher is engaged in the work of analyzing and perhaps gathering data. Data analysis is developed by each of the researchers, and each researcher makes their own contribution to the analysis and then to the findings, the conclusions and the recommendations.

With theoretical triangulation, the research is triangulated within different theoretical frameworks, and thus the research is developed, data gathered and analyzed, and conclusions drawn, within different theoretical perspectives.

In methodological triangulation, more than one methodology is used in the research project.

The most popular method of triangulating research at undergraduate, and very often at postgraduate level too, is through the use of within method and between method triangulation. Using between method triangulation, the research question is explored using two different data-gathering methods, for example by using a questionnaire and a series of interviews, or using a series of observations and a focus group. Using within method triangulation, the research issue or phenomenon is explored using the same method, but using the method more than one time. For example, the data might be gathered using two different, and perhaps sequential, questionnaires; or using two different, and perhaps sequential, sets of interviews.

Essentially, triangulation means examining the research issue or phenomenon from more than one perspective.

One of the critiques of triangulation is that it contributes to a naïve realist position by suggesting that social science research can provide an account of what is 'real', thereby implicitly suggesting that there can be a single definitive account of the issue or phenomenon under investigation. Those defending the concept of triangulation would argue that, while there cannot be a single definitive account of the phenomenon under investigation, the process of triangulating research provides a broader view or perspective of the phenomenon under investigation, and consequently a (potentially) more valid view of that phenomenon. The concept of triangulation is explored in detail in later chapters.

A research statement for the project outlined above might read something like this:

 This research project is a case study designed to facilitate the development of a model recruitment and selection process for a fictitious company, 'People for Places Ltd'.

Once again, the research statement contains the conceptual framework for the research project. The conceptual framework is made up of all of the key concepts in the research project. The key concepts in the above research statement are 'recruitment and selection process', 'model recruitment and selection process' and 'development of a model recruitment and selection process'. By outlining the research project in such a disciplined manner, the entire project is stated in one sentence – a question or a statement.

Let us now consider two more research projects. The research statement for the project of the student who is interested in the business plans of SMEs might read as follows:

The research project is a survey of the business plans of 50 SMEs in the Greater Galloway area.

As you can see, this research project is a **survey**, whereas the two previous projects were case studies. The key concepts within the conceptual framework outlined above are 'business plans', 'SMEs' and 'the business plans of SMEs'. These key concepts are the focus of this research; everything else is excluded from the research. The discipline of this focus is important at this stage in the research process because as the research project develops, it will naturally become more complex. Clarity, precision and simplicity at the start of the research process will pay dividends as the research project develops. The scope of this project is 50 SMEs in the particular geographic area indicated. The decisions made around the rationale for how many SMEs to include and the geographic area of the research should be outlined briefly in a short explanation of the research statement, which should appear underneath the research statement.

survey Used to denote survey research methodology. A survey research methodology is particularly useful in facilitating the study of big populations and geographically scattered populations.

The research statement for the student interested in the experiences of women in senior management positions might read something like the following:

This research project is a survey of the experiences of 100 women in senior management positions in multinational corporations in the USA, with a focus on their journeys to those senior positions.

The focus of this study is on women in senior management positions and their journeys to those positions. The key concepts in the project are 'women in senior management', 'the journeys of women to senior management' and 'women in senior management in multinational corporations'. The research statement indicates the scope of the project, 100 women are included. The geographic scope of the project is all of the USA. This broad geographic scope can be readily facilitated through survey research.

Survey research methodology facilitates the study of big populations and samples, and populations and samples that are geographically scattered. Using a survey methodology it is easy, for example, to post or to email a questionnaire to 100 women in different parts of the USA. Using a survey methodology, it would also be feasible to conduct interviews, in particular telephone interviews or Skype interviews, with 100 women located in different parts of the USA. Survey methodology is quite different from case study methodology. While survey methodology readily facilitates very broad studies, case study methodology readily facilitates the in-depth study of clearly defined bounded entities.

We have up to now focused on research statements. Sometimes the conceptual framework for the research project is stated as a statement, and sometimes it is stated as a question. It is easy to restate a research statement as a question. Restated as a question, the above project might read as follows:

What are the experiences of women in senior management positions in multinational corporations in the USA in relation to their journeys to those senior positions? This research project is a survey of the experiences of 100 women in senior management positions in multinational corporations in the USA in relation to their journeys to those senior positions.

Each research project should begin with a statement of the research. Your well-conceptualized research statement or question, the conceptual framework for your research project, should be the first sentence in the first chapter of your thesis, in the report of your research. In this way, the reader/examiner is brought immediately, without preamble, into your research project. On reading the first sentence the reader/examiner knows exactly what your research project is about. They know what methodology you have used, they know the scope of the project, and they have a sense straightaway of the value of your research.

AIMS AND OBJECTIVES

Once the research statement or question has been delineated clearly, the next step is the development, from the research statement/question, of the research **aim and objectives**. The simplest way to do this is to develop one aim and a series of objectives, generally no fewer than two and no more than six objectives. While you can have more than one aim and more than six objectives, it is simpler to stay within these limits, and it is never, in the experience of author Christina Quinlan, necessary to go beyond them. Detailed examples of research aims and objectives follow. The case study at the end of this chapter details a student's experience in developing an idea for a research project into a research statement, and an aim and series of objectives. You should read these examples, you will find them helpful.

> **aim and objectives** The aim is a precise statement of what the researcher intends to accomplish with the research. Objectives specify how the researcher intends to accomplish this aim.

The aim of the research is simply the research statement or question restated as an aim. For example, the research statement reads as follows:

This research project is a case study of the advertising campaigns undertaken in the year 2018 for the marketing of computer games by three computer games companies: the companies are Zenith Computer Games Ltd, Orbit Computer Games Ltd and Galaxy Computer Games Ltd.

The aim of the research is as follows:

The aim of this research is to examine the advertising campaigns undertaken in the year 2018 for the marketing of computer games by three computer games companies: the companies are Zenith Computer Games Ltd, Orbit Computer Games Ltd and Galaxy Computer Games Ltd.

The objectives of the research emerge from the aim of the research. The objectives of the research are the steps the researcher intends to take in order to accomplish the aim of the research. Objectives are generally written in short phrases presented as bullet points. Each phrase uses at least one active verb, examples include the words consider, explore, examine, compare, contrast, develop. The objectives of the above study might read as follows:

- To examine the advertising campaigns of the three companies.
- To compare and contrast the advertising campaigns of the three companies.
- To explore the different advertising appeals used by the three companies.
- To examine the fitness for market of each of the marketing campaigns.

In another example:

This research project is a case study designed to facilitate the development of a model recruitment and selection process for a fictitious company, 'People for Places Ltd'.

The aim of this research is to develop a model recruitment and selection process for a fictitious company 'People for Places Ltd'.

The objectives of the research are as follows:

- To examine the recruitment and selection processes of recruitment companies published on the internet.
- To explore models of recruitment and selection processes published in textbooks.
- To develop a best practice model recruitment and selection process for a fictitious company 'People for Places Ltd'.

In another example:

The research project is a survey of the business plans of 50 SMEs in the Greater Galloway area.

The aim of this research project is to survey the business plans of 50 SMEs in the Greater Galloway area.

The objectives of the study are as follows:

- To examine the business plans of the 50 SMEs.
- To compare and contrast the business plans of the 50 SMEs.

- To establish what the business plans have in common.
- To explore what is unique in each of the business plans.
- To develop and present, based on the findings of this survey, a model business plan for SMEs.

In another example:

What are the experiences of women in senior management positions in multinational corporations in the USA in relation to their journeys to those senior positions? This research project is a survey of the experiences of 100 women in senior management positions in multinational corporations in the USA in relation to their journeys to those senior positions.

The aim of this research project is to examine the experiences of women in senior management positions in multinational corporations (MNCs) in the USA in relation to their journeys to those senior positions.

The objectives of the research are as follows:

- To consider the experiences of women in senior management positions in multinational corporations in the USA.
- To explore the experiences of these senior managers of their journeys to those positions.
- To detail the difficulties, if any, each of the women encountered throughout their journey.
- To examine the women's experiences in order to establish what experiences they had in common.
- To present an account of the critical experiences for women as they rise to senior management positions in MNCs in the USA.

You will notice that the objectives do not contain any statement about reviewing the literature, or any indication of the methodology or data-gathering methods to be used in the research. The objectives are the steps the researcher intends to take in order to accomplish the aim of the research. The objectives of a research project are unique to that project. Every research project involves a review of the literature and every research project needs a methodology and most require data-gathering methods. So the objectives of the research do not contain statements about reviewing literature or about research methodology or methods.

SOURCE APPROPRIATE LITERATURE

Literature, in the context of research projects, is research that has already been carried out and published. The literature that we are interested in is literature that has been published in journal articles, in books, in government papers and reports, in theses, in reports of conference proceedings. In your search for literature, your idea for your research project provides guidance and direction in terms of the literature you need to read. You do have to read some of the literature before you can fully and thoroughly outline a research question or statement for your research project.

Your research project should emerge from the literature of the area or the field within which your research project is situated, and ultimately it should make a contribution to the literature and the theory in that field. It is by reading the literature that you develop an understanding of the kind of research being carried out in your field and the focus of that research, and any gaps in that research, where little or no research has been carried out, or where there are unanswered questions. A gap in the research means that there is a need for research in this area and it would be a very good idea to develop your project as a response to such a gap.

When you have finally decided (following an initial reading of the literature), on the research question or statement for your research project, you will then begin to read the literature in depth in order to develop your literature review. The key concepts, the keywords and phrases in the research statement or question, the conceptual framework for the research project, will indicate the areas within which you should focus your reading for your literature review. The written literature review in your thesis/dissertation or in the report of your research contains the **theoretical framework** for the research project. The theoretical framework is the second framework of the four frameworks approach to the research project. The theoretical framework emerges from the conceptual framework. The example below illustrates this process:

This research project is a case study of the marketing of computer games by three computer games companies: the companies are Zenith Computer Games Ltd, Orbit Computer Games Ltd and Galaxy Computer Games Ltd.

> **theoretical framework** The theoretical framework for the research project is contained in the literature review, or it is the literature review. The literature review contains the theoretical framework for the research project. The key concepts in the conceptual framework guide and direct your reading for the literature review and they provide guidance and direction for the structure for the literature review.

The four frameworks

- Conceptual Framework
- *Theoretical Framework*
- Methodological Framework
- Analytical Framework

As stated earlier in this chapter, the key concepts in this research project are 'marketing', 'computer games', 'computer games companies' and 'marketing computer games'. You use these key concepts to search for appropriate literature, and you use them to help you structure your literature review.

The ability to source appropriate literature is the second of the five basic skills needed in undertaking research. While not all research is theorized, research conducted in an academic setting is always theorized. Theorized research is research that emerges from a body of knowledge and, in turn, makes a contribution to a body of knowledge. Academics are fundamentally engaged in developing theory and adding to the body of knowledge in their field. The researcher reads the literature in order to understand the area within which they are conducting their research to develop some knowledge and expertise in this area, to develop an awareness of what is known in this area and to identify gaps in the knowledge in this area.

In general, published accounts of research projects make recommendations for further research. These recommendations are useful places to explore when attempting to develop an idea for a research project; for an example of a student project developed from the recommendations of another study, see the case study at the end of this chapter.

It is important when conducting a literature search to be able to identify good research. You need to be discerning. Check the date of the publication and try to be as up-to-date as possible in your reading, while including in your research any seminal writers in the field. Seminal writers are writers who have made an original and very substantial contribution to their field. Check the credentials of the authors. What qualifications and experience do they have? Establish whether or not they have a reputation in this field. Check the credentials of the place from where the work originated. Read the account of the research. Try to be critical in your reading, because you need to determine the value of the research. Examine the validity of the research. Is the population of the study appropriate? What sampling **method** has been used, if a sample of a population has been used in the research? What data-gathering methods were used? Were they appropriate? What data were gathered? What data analysis methods and procedures were used? Consider the findings of the research and the conclusions drawn from the research. Do they answer the research question? Do they respond to the research statement? Examine the standard of the writing. Consider the substance of the contribution the work makes to the academic debate in the field. Critique the overall quality of the work.

> **method** Used to denote research methodology such as case study or survey, and data collection method(s) such as observation, interviews, focus groups and questionnaires.

THE DIFFERENT APPROACHES TO RESEARCH

You will find in your reading that there are different approaches to research. It is useful from the start to begin to develop a sense of these different approaches. These different approaches reflect the different philosophical underpinnings of research projects.

In this chapter, we have seen examples of research projects to be developed using survey methodology and case study methodology. Case study and survey research are examples of just two of the many different methodological approaches to social science research.

There are different philosophical frameworks within the world of social research and these frameworks facilitate different kinds of research. There are many different methodologies that can be used in carrying out research and there are also many different data collection methods. These different approaches to research and the ways in which they fit together are summarized in the *methodological pyramid* detailed in Figure 2.1 (see Chapter 4 for a full explanation). The pyramid helps you to see how the fundamental philosophies support research methodologies which in turn support the different data collection methods.

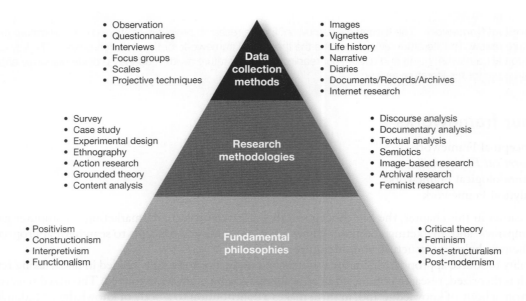

Figure 2.1   The methodological pyramid

RESEARCH IN PRACTICE

Multiple and subjective realities – an example

Imagine that you are reading this paragraph in a seminar or lecture on research methods. Let us say that there are 20 students participating in the seminar or attending the lecture. If this is the case, then there are 20 students attending or participating. That is a fact, an objective fact. It is indisputable. This is the way in which reality can be said to be singular and objective. Then think about how the 20 students are experiencing the seminar or lecture. No two students will experience the seminar or lecture in the same way. Perhaps many of the students spend their time at the lecture thinking about how they can apply all that is being said in the lecture to their own research project. Each student project will be unique, and the ways in which each student applies what is being said in the lecture to their research project will be unique. Perhaps there are students in the seminar or lecture who are really enjoying the experience. This may be, but the reasons why they are enjoying the experience, and ways in which they are enjoying the experience, and the complexity of that enjoyment, will be entirely individual for each student and uniquely their own. Perhaps there are students who spend the time of the seminar or lecture simply wishing that the experience was over. This may be the case, but the reasons for this will be individual and unique for each student. This is an example of the way in which reality can be said to be multiple and subjective.

Now think of the researcher who has to try to document these experiences, explore the patterns and trends in these experiences and to detail all that is unique. The tools that you will learn from this textbook and from undertaking your own research will provide you with real skills in undertaking such research and a real insight into social science research.

AN INTRODUCTION TO RESEARCH METHODOLOGY

The methodological framework, the third framework in the four frameworks approach to the research project, is contained in the methodology section of the thesis or report and it contains all of the detail on how the research was conducted. As explained earlier, there are many different methodologies used in conducting research. Each of these methodologies has a particular application or use. The different research methodologies are dealt with more thoroughly in Chapter 9 of this textbook. Traditionally among business students, the common methodologies tended to be surveys and case studies. The other methodologies mentioned, and others besides, are now being used more and more frequently.

Some research projects can appear to have elements of more than one methodology. You might think that your own project is a survey with case study elements, for example. Or it may be that it is a case study but there is a semiotics element in it. This is frequently the case with social research. As research projects begin and develop, they can often seem to fit quite well with more than one methodology. However, it is essential for the purposes of clarity that the researcher decides which methodology is most appropriate for the project. The decision about the appropriateness of any methodology for any and every research project is a decision around 'fit': how well does the proposed methodology fit the proposed research project?

Along with methodology, the researcher is concerned with data collection methods, the means by which data are gathered. Data are presented as evidence in the research project in order to establish the argument or prove or disprove the hypothesis of the research. Some data collection methods are very familiar to us; we have all filled in questionnaires, and some of us have participated in interviews and focus groups. Every data collection method is designed to focus on, observe and record the observations of some phenomenon. Observation itself is another key data collection method, along with questionnaires, interviews and focus groups. Other data collection methods include scales and projective techniques, visual methods, photographs, pictures, maps, videos, films, the gathering of narratives, the use of field diaries and the use of documentary evidence. The data collection method(s) to be used in any research project is indicated to the researcher by the type of data required, by the population or sample population used, and by the methodology proposed for the project. The data collection methods to be used in the research project are indicated by the data requirements of the project, by the available data, by the location of that data, and by the format or nature of that data.

DATA: WHAT CONSTITUTES EVIDENCE?

Every researcher in undertaking a research project is exploring a phenomenon and/or attempting to establish a case. Conducting research is like going into a court of law and trying to prove a case. In the courtroom, you would present as much evidence as possible. You would be very concerned to ensure that the evidence you presented was valid, trustworthy and correct. In your research project, you are concerned with the amount of evidence you present and with the validity of the evidence you present. So what, in terms of research projects, constitutes evidence? The answer is that it really depends on the phenomenon you are investigating.

In the context of research, evidence is called data. Data can take many forms. They can be the testimony of human participants in a project in, for example, the transcripts of interviews or focus groups. They can be in the responses to a questionnaire. They can also be found in documents, archives, records and reports. Data can be found in maps and charts, field diaries, narratives, photographs or film. They can be in the content of newspapers. In fact, data can take almost any form. The constraint is that the data must be valid. For data to be valid, they must represent that which they are presented as representing. So if, for example, a researcher develops an interview schedule designed specifically to measure, let us say, satisfaction levels among the participants in a training programme, then the interview schedule developed must do precisely that. This issue of validity in the design and development of data collection methods is explored in detail in Chapters 14 and 15 of this textbook.

PLAGIARISM

Plagiarism is the use and/or presentation of somebody else's work or ideas as your own. It is a most serious offence. Students who engage in plagiarism, even unwittingly, can be expelled from their colleges and institutions. This can have seriously detrimental effects on their careers. It can also be devastating for them personally and for their families. You can avoid an accusation of plagiarism by properly referencing everything that you take from any and every source and then use in your own writing or in any work that you present as your own.

> **plagiarism** The use and/or presentation of somebody else's work or ideas as your own. Plagiarism is a serious offence and it is generally avoidable through proper referencing.

It is vitally important that you learn to reference properly. When you get into the habit of referencing, you will no longer find it a chore or at least it will certainly become less onerous. As you practice referencing properly, you will quickly learn to distinguish between somebody else's work and ideas and your own. Where your ideas have developed from somebody else's, you simply reference the ideas that you have built your work on. As stated earlier in this chapter, all research is built on other research and, in turn, all research becomes built upon. This is the way in which knowledge is created and the way in which a body of knowledge develops. You do want to add your own contribution and in doing this, you also want to acknowledge the contribution of others before you. You do this by referencing their work and their ideas.

If you would like to read more about plagiarism, there is a great deal of information about it (and how to avoid it) on the internet. The University of Leeds provides a very useful resource on plagiarism awareness on its website at www .ldu.leeds.ac.uk/plagiarism/. The University of Oxford also provides a lot of information on plagiarism on its website at www.ox.ac.uk/students/academic/guidance/skills/plagiarism. Your own institution will also have guidelines on plagiarism. If you need further information, do discuss this with your research supervisor or research methods lecturer. If you have a particular concern about plagiarism regarding something you have written, you can always submit it to your supervisor or mentor for comment and feedback.

Universities and colleges are now using software such as *Turnitin* (www.turnitin.com) to examine for evidence of plagiarism in assignments and projects submitted by students. There is also free-to-download software now available to check for plagiarism in your own work. A quick internet search will provide you with many options in terms of such software.

Plagiarism really is a serious offence and it does carry very serious penalties. The way to avoid plagiarism and accusations of plagiarism is to submit work that you have written yourself: work that is properly and thoroughly referenced.

COMPILING A LIST OF REFERENCES

The list of references, also known as the **bibliography**, for any research project is one of the most critical elements of the research project. A good list of references is a resource for any scholar interested in the topic of the research. It helps demonstrate the scholarship of the project and the researcher. Readers and examiners tend to read through lists of references before they read any other aspect of the research project. A quick read through the list of references gives the reader a sense of the quality and standard of the work overall.

> **bibliography** A term for a list of all of the published work cited in the research project. All published works cited in the research project must be listed in the bibliography.

The list of references is a list of all of the published work used in the research project: all of the books, chapters in books, journal articles, government reports and papers, theses, conference reports and proceedings, web references, newspaper and magazine articles, radio and television programmes and films, published photographs and other visual material referenced in the thesis/dissertation or report of the research. Every reference detailed in the research project should be listed in the list of references and every reference should be detailed in the text.

The reading that you have done for your research project is evidenced in your referencing throughout the work and in the list of references you present at the end of the work. Try to ensure that your referencing and your list of references adequately evidence the amount of reading that you did and the value and quality of the reading. The list of references demonstrates the breadth and depth of your reading, through the variety and the quality of sources you have used in your research. Ensure that your references are up-to-date, including sources published in the year that you present your thesis. Also ensure that you include any seminal writers on your topic. It may be that a key paper or a key book that influenced and shaped the direction of your topic or field was presented 20 or more years ago, but it is important to reference this work despite its age. It is critically important that your research should reflect the current state of knowledge in the field. You should include all of the seminal works, but focus on the contemporary debate(s).

In compiling the list of references:

- ensure that you are using the style required by your institution
- ensure that you have copied the details of the reference correctly
- be scrupulous about punctuation
- ensure that there are no spelling errors
- place the information for each reference in the list of references in the correct order, according to the convention you are using
- do not use bullet points or any other styling or formatting in the list of references.

Although the work of referencing is painstaking, and it must always be clear, consistent and correct, you will very quickly learn how to reference and get into the routine of referencing. You will learn a great deal about your area of study from the routine work of citing and referencing. You will learn the names of the theorists and become very familiar with their theories. If you apply yourself to this work of referencing properly, you will in no time be readily identifying theorists and their contribution to your field. If you are in doubt as to which referencing method is used in your institution, check with your research or thesis supervisor or your research methods lecturer. They will be able to advise you on the method used in your institution and on the correct way of using it.

There are many books and booklets that can help you in compiling your list of references. It is useful, as always, to visit the library and to examine the list of references in the theses held there and the ways in which the list of references in those theses are presented. De Montfort University, Leicester library has an online guide to referencing every kind of resource using the Harvard Referencing Method. It is available at www.library.dmu.ac.uk/Images/Selfstudy/Harvard .pdf. Another good resource is the very useful online library research skills tutorial provided by Simon Fraser University Library. This can be accessed at www.lib.sfu.ca/help/research-assistance/tutorials#advanced-online-search-techniques.

Finally, there are software packages which can help you in compiling your list of references. Among them are the software packages *EndNote* and *ProCite*. Information on *EndNote* is available from the website www.endnote.com. This website gives free online tutorials as well as access to the software. It is possible that this software package, or a software package like it, is available in your university or college. It is possible too that if the package is available within the university, the university is hosting workshops or tutorials to teach staff and students how to use the software. It is important to develop your computer skills, and other skills, as much as possible and whenever possible. So if the college is offering any training on any software relevant to any area of your study, you should participate in that training.

THE USES OF APPENDICES

Appendices are used to present any information or artefact relevant to the research but not detailed in the body of the research project. Copies of letters written for the research project are placed in appendices. These letters might be letters written to, or received from, formal gatekeepers. These are the people you have sought and received permission from to conduct your research in, for example, their company, or with their employees. Copies of data collection methods and instruments used are also detailed in appendices. For example, copies of questionnaires, interview schedules, observation schedules, focus group schedules, and scales such as Likert scales, would be placed in appendices. It is a good idea to display any long lists that you have used in appendices rather than in the body of the work. Very large tables or figures can also be displayed in appendices. These items tend to interrupt the narrative flow of the written account of your research project and so it is best to place them in appendices.

> **appendices** Used to present any information or artefact relevant to the research but not detailed in the body of the research project.

Appendices are placed after the list of references in the final written report of the research project. Each appendix is numbered at the top and given a title or heading.

It is neither useful nor helpful to place copies of completed data-gathering instruments such as completed questionnaires or scales or transcripts of interviews or focus groups in appendices. In general, you will not be asked to present your raw data and if you are asked to do this, you will not be asked to do so by presenting it in appendices. It is unwise to unnecessarily pad the appendices with any material. Only present in appendices material that is of relevance to the research project. Ensure that all of the material placed in appendices is discussed and explained in the body of the work.

While you should not pad your appendices in any way, and you certainly should not load the appendices with raw data, you should use the facility of appendices as much as you can. As the word count in appendices, as with the word count in the list of references, is not included in the overall word count for the research project, this means that the appendices are a way for you to include elements in your research project without using up the word count. Students generally find it difficult to present research projects within the word count allocated for the project; 10 000 words, 15 000 words or 20 000 words can seem like a lot of words until you actually start to write up the project. It is when you are writing up the research project that you quickly see how few words you really have with which to express the entire research project.

It is a good idea to keep a note in your research diary of the documents and artefacts, the lists and the models and the figures that you wish to place in the appendices of your research project. You should also visit the library and look at the bound copies of theses held there to examine the appendices of those theses and the information and artefacts presented in them. This exercise will give you some ideas for your own appendices.

KEEPING THE RESEARCH DIARY

The research diary is a valuable tool for any researcher. It is a simple notebook within which the researcher records all of their reflections and all of the decisions they make throughout the duration of the research project. Ideally, the researcher starts the diary as soon as they begin to think about their research project and they continue writing notes in the diary until the research project has been completed.

The completed research project represents all of the parts of the research process, as well as the creative, reflective engagement of the researcher. Throughout the process, the researcher is actively engaged with the work of developing the project. This engagement is sustained through the development of the conceptual, theoretical, methodological and analytical frameworks of the research project and throughout the outlining of the conclusions and recommendations from the research.

The reflection that is recorded in the research diary is informal. As ideas arise, through active and reflective engagement with the issues and problems posed in conducting and completing the research project, the researcher records them quickly in the research diary. These ideas can be jotted down in one form and then quickly jotted down again in another form as they develop in the researcher's mind. In this informal way, the researcher develops streams of ideas and inspirations about the research and these can be built upon as the project develops and is completed.

The formal written account of the research is the thesis or report of the research. As the ideas and inspirations recorded in the research diary are moved to the thesis or the research report, they become more polished and are formalized and integrated into the various chapters. In this way, the notes that the researcher makes in the research diary help with the process of writing up the research.

There is no right or wrong way to keep a research diary. You may decide for yourself how much detail you want to record. The notebook you choose as the research diary can be as big or as small as you wish. It is important to use a well-bound notebook, because you do not want pages to fall out of the notebook and get lost.

It is also important to keep a record of the dates and places of all of the entries. These details may be needed in presenting the information in the thesis or report of the research, where they will lend support and credibility, and so validity, to the written account.

You might decide to just use a free-flow method in keeping the diary. Using this method each entry is entered on a new page. If you are recording something that happens during the course of the research, the page is dated and the place is recorded. You might record who was present and write a brief account of what happened. You should also record your impressions. What struck you most about the experience? What did you expect to happen? Why did you expect that to happen? What did happen? What meaning did you make of what happened? Perhaps what happened had different meaning(s) for different people. How? Why?

It is useful to record in the diary the names and roles of the people you encounter throughout the research. You should also record exactly where you encounter each person and the context within which the encounter takes place. You will easily forget details like this and it can be very useful to have it to hand as the research develops. Some of the people you encounter will be gatekeepers in terms of your research and will be in a position, formally or informally, to permit your research to go ahead, or to disrupt, delay or even stop your research. Your encounters with these people will help to shape your research. The record in the research diary will help you to remember the influence each person had on your research.

You use the research diary to record your engagements with the participants in your research. You will have data collection methods, such as questionnaires, interview schedules and focus group schedules to record the engagements with participants formally. There will also in some cases be audio recordings of your engagements with participants, perhaps photographs and maybe even video recordings. The research diary will help supplement these records. Your research diary is for your eyes only. It is your personal record of your own thoughts and ideas, your intuitions and experiences of the people and places you encounter throughout the research process. Use it as you see fit and record as much or as little detail as you wish.

You can use your research diary to help you generate ideas around your research. (see Figure 2.2). You can scribble down any ideas you have and then use your notes to develop these ideas. You can develop ideas for your research statement or question, reflecting on the key concepts you wish to include and how you might do this. You can develop the aim of your research and play around with ideas for objectives. You can think about the issues you want to explore when you engage in data gathering with your participants and you can experiment with questions you might ask them. You can develop lists of questions and issues you would like to explore in the data-gathering phase of your research and you can begin to develop lists of names of potential participants in your research. You can record any thoughts or ideas you have in relation to the ethical issues in your research. You can note your insights into your research project as they come to you. You can begin to create and develop structures for the different chapters of your project. You can jot down insights that you get regarding possible findings that might emerge and conclusions you might draw from the research and recommendations you might make following your research. In short, you can use the research diary to record any aspect of your research project and any thought or idea that you have in relation to it. The research diary is one of the most useful tools in the research process and it is a tool that researchers create by themselves for themselves.

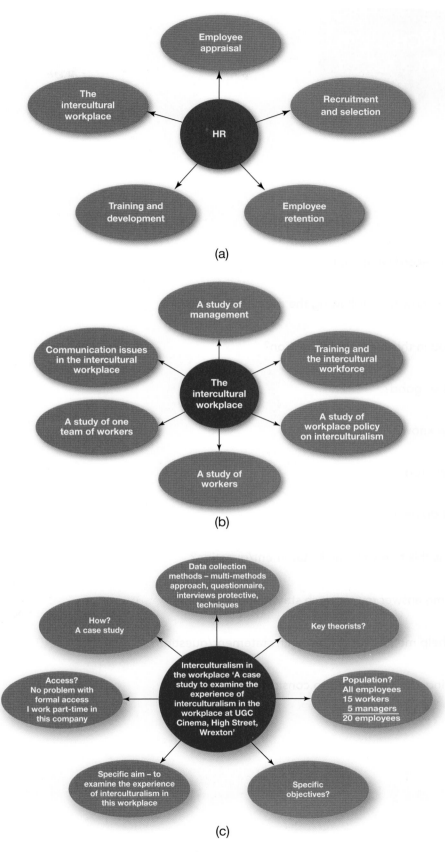

Figure 2.2 Examples of spidergrams included in a research diary

RESEARCH DIARY

Place:

Participants:

Date:

Action: [briefly record what happened]

What ideas do I now have following the meeting/interaction?

What was good in this meeting/interaction?

What was not so good?

What do I now know?

How can I now progress?

What should I do next?

How relevant is this to my research statement/question?

Will this help me answer my research statement/question?

How will this help me answer my research statement/question?

Is there anything else that I need to consider?

Notes:

REAL WORLD RESEARCH

How theory influences research

In the article detailed here (Liang and Xu, 2018, 'Second-hand clothing consumption: A generational cohort analysis of the Chinese market', *International Journal of Consumer Studies*, 42, 120–30), the researchers are concerned with China's rapidly growing economy and the environmental problems caused by high levels of consumption and a throwaway trend attributed to fast fashion changes and short-lived styles.

In their study, they use a survey methodology to gain an insight into Chinese consumption of second-hand clothes and the different values and motivations across four different generations, different age cohorts and in consumer purchase decisions. The authors are concerned that consumers become more aware of the impact of their purchasing decisions on the environment. The article is useful in that it presents some detail on the manner in which this particular survey was carried out. If you are interested in survey research, you should source the original article and trace the steps of the research process, as these steps are detailed in the model of the research process presented at the start of Chapter 1.

In this survey, the authors set out to develop an insight into Chinese consumer behaviours towards purchasing second-hand clothes, in terms of their consumption intentions and the influence of their perceived values and concerns on those behaviours. The authors engaged 350 Chinese consumers in a survey across four generational cohorts. The four cohorts were Post 60s, Post 70s, Post 80s and Post 90s. The study showed significant differences across the cohorts, with younger consumers showing higher values and higher purchase intentions than older consumers.

According to the authors, the review of the literature carried out showed that there has been an enormous growth in the economic power and global scope of the second-hand clothing trade since the early 1990s. They show that the benefits that consumers perceive in relation to the purchase of second-hand clothing include: the economic value of cheaper clothes; the hedonic value of treasure hunting; the uniqueness of purchases; and the environmental value in reducing consumption of new products.

In the article, the authors present a literature review on second-hand clothing consumption in China, and they review the literature on the topic of generational cohort theory. Following the literature review, they detail and explain the research methodology used in the study. The methodology, as explained, is survey methodology. The sampling method used was snowball sampling. The questionnaire was distributed on the internet using WebChat, which, the authors tell us, has over half a billion active users in China. The target participants were those born between 1960 and 1995, covering the four generational cohorts. In all, 350 completed questionnaires were received and from them 334 valid questionnaires were analyzed. It is interesting to note the reasons why the researchers eliminated 16 completed questionnaires from the study. The reasons were as follows: respondents clearly filled in the questionnaire randomly (e.g. straight-lining answers); at least half of the questions were left unanswered; some of the answers given to questions were clearly illogical.

Some key points worth noting with regard to this research:

- The methodology used in the study was survey and the data collection method was a questionnaire. The questionnaire was administered to participants via the internet.
- An extensive review of the literature was undertaken before the questionnaire was designed. The review of the literature informed the development of the questionnaire and the creation and development of the research methodology.
- The authors outline three hypotheses for the study, and they show clearly how each of the three hypotheses were developed.
- The questionnaires were analyzed and many quantitative data from that analysis are presented in the article. (In this textbook, we focus on quantitative data analysis in Chapter 19.)
- The analyzed data are presented, discussed and explored.
- The findings of the research are presented. One of the findings of the research is that younger consumers are more inclined to buy second-hand clothes than older consumers.
- Conclusions are drawn. The authors suggest that the growth in economic value of the second-hand clothes market will continue, and new business models will develop in the market.

In your reading of the article, consider the manner in which theory is used in the article. Consider in particular the way in which the literature review was constructed and presented, and how the literature review was used to develop the study's research methodology.

CASE STUDY

Clara is studying for a degree in Business Management at university in Paris. For her thesis, she wants to research something around vintage clothes. She has a particular interest in vintage clothing and she thinks that she might develop a career in vintage clothing when she graduates from university.

Clara has been reading a journal article that she came across while browsing the e-resources of the university library. The title of the article is as follows 'Identity in old clothes: the socio-cultural dynamics of second-hand clothing in Irbid, Jordan' (Na'amneh and Al Husban, 2012). The journal article explores the socio-cultural dynamics underlying the consumption of second-hand clothing in the city of Irbid in Northern Jordan. The study was an ethnographic study. Data gathering for the study involved in-depth interviews conducted with consumers and shop owners. Clara found the journal article particularly interesting. The study, as presented in the journal article, provides insight into the relationship between consumption and identity, as well as highlighting some of the concerns and reservations people might have about buying second-hand clothes. The study highlighted symbolic rather than economic explanations of consumer practices.

Based on her reading of the journal article, Clara designed the following study.

This research project is an ethnographic study of consumer practices in three vintage clothing stores in Paris.

The aim of this research project is to conduct an ethnographic study of consumer practices in three vintage clothing stores in Paris.

The objectives of the study are as follows:

- To establish why consumers buy vintage clothes.
- To establish precisely what it is that consumers look for in the vintage clothes that they buy.
- To establish any barriers that exist for consumers in the purchase of vintage clothes.
- To explore the market potential of a new venture in vintage clothing.

What do you think of Clara's proposed research? Do you think she will get approval from her research supervisor for the study?

You should read the case study at the end of Chapter 13 which details Dabir's research idea, a study of a nostalgic tourism product, which he based on his reading of a research project he came across in a journal article. As these examples demonstrate, there are ideas for good research projects everywhere.

You may prefer to use a more formal method of recording your thoughts in your research diary. It may help you to devise a series of questions to ask yourself to facilitate a flow of ideas. It is important throughout the research process to stay focused on your research question or statement. Three of the questions outlined in the form that follows relate to checking the relevance of the experiences you are documenting in your diary to your research statement or question. A format such as the Research Diary in this section and the following might be useful.

Here are some useful websites to help you develop skills in creating and generating spidergrams and thought maps:

- www.edrawsoft.com/mind-map-and-spidergram.php
- www.spidergrams.com
- www.mindjet.com/features/spider-diagram
- www.mindmapping.com

END OF CHAPTER QUESTIONS

1 Differentiate between a research idea and a research question.

2 Create a conceptual framework for a research project.

3 Detail a strategy, using the four frameworks approach to research, to source appropriate literature.

4 Detail, describe and explain some of the different approaches to research.

5 Initiate a research diary using a template on the online platform.

6 Evaluate the evidence presented in the research projects presented on the online platform. Critique the list of references outlined.

7 Visit the library and find copies of theses that report research projects which students in your university have carried out using case study and survey methodologies. Be critical in your examination of these projects. Critique the theses in terms of their overall quality. Critically examine the standard of writing in the theses. Critically examine the lists of references in the theses.

8 Read the research statements or questions or hypotheses. As conceptual frameworks for their research projects, how well do you think they work?

9 Read the research methodology chapters. What initial thoughts do you have about them?

10 What research methodology was used?

11 What was the population of the research?

12 Was a sample used and if so what sampling method was used?

13 How is the sampling method described? Is enough detail given to allow the reader to critically evaluate the method used?

14 What data collection methods were used?

15 How are these presented in the thesis? It would be useful to keep a record in your research diary of your critical assessments of the theses. Record briefly in your research diary your reflections on these theses.

REFERENCES

Alexander, S. (2017) 'Britain's Best Fish and Chip Shops Revealed', *The Telegraph*, 25.01.2017, www.telegraph.co.uk/food-and-drink/news/britains-best-fish-chip-shops-revealed (Accessed 15.01.2018).

Denzin, N.K. (1970) *The Research Act in Sociology*, Chicago, IL: Aldine.

De Montfort University, Leicester, (n.d.), 'The Harvard System of Referencing', www.library.dmu.ac.uk/Images/Selfstudy/Harvard.pdf

Gander, K. (2017), 'UK's Ten Best Fish and Chip Shops Revealed', *The Independent*, 15.09.2017, www.independent.co.uk/life-style/food-and-drink/uk-best-fish-chip-shops-top-10-scotland-northern-ireland-england-north-east-west-london-a7947836.html (Accessed 15.01.2018).

Liang, J. and Xu, Y. (2018) 'Second-hand clothing consumption: A generational cohort analysis of the Chinese market', *International Journal of Consumer Studies*, 42: 120–130.

Na'amneh, M.M. and Al Husban, A.K. (2012) 'Identity in old clothes: the socio-cultural dynamics of second-hand clothing in Irbid, Jordan', *Social Identities: Journal for the Study of Race, Nation and Culture*, 18(5): 609–621.

Seafish, 'The authority on seafood from catch to plate', www.seafish.org (Accessed 15.01.2018).

University of Leeds (n.d.) 'Plagiarism awareness', www.ldu.leeds.ac.uk/plagiarism (Accessed 05.02.2018).

University of Oxford (n.d.) 'Plagiarism', www.ox.ac.uk/students/academic/guidance/skills/plagiarism (Accessed 05.02.2018).

RECOMMENDED READING

Bell, J. and Waters, S. (2014) *Doing Your Research Project*, Maidenhead: Open University Press.

Berman Brown, R. (2006) *Doing Your Dissertation in Business and Management*, London: Sage.

Denscombe, M. (2017) *The Good Research Guide: For Small-scale Social Research Projects* (5th edn), Maidenhead: Open University Press.

Easterby-Smith, M., Thorpe, R. and Jackson, P.R. (2008) *Management Research* (3rd edn), London: Sage.

Hart, C. (2018) *Doing a Literature Review: Releasing the Research Imagination*, London: Sage.

May, T. (2011) *Social Research: Issues Methods and Processes*, Maidenhead: Open University Press.

Methodspace: Connecting the Research Community, Sage, www.methodspace.com (Accessed 05.02.2018).

Murray, R. (2017) *How To Write a Thesis*, Maidenhead: Open University Press.

Punch, K.F. (2016) *Developing Effective Research Proposals* (3rd edn), London: Sage.

Quinlan, C. (2011) *Business Research Methods*, Mason, OH: Cengage South-Western.

Trochim, W.M., *The Research Methods Knowledge Base*, www.socialresearchmethods.net (Accessed 05.02.2018).

CHAPTER 3
UNDERSTANDING RESEARCH ETHICS

LEARNING OBJECTIVES

At the end of this chapter, the student should be able to:

- Define ethics and apply ethical principles to business research.

- Explain the importance of research ethics.

- Critique research from an ethical perspective.

- Engage in critical reflection on the ethics of their research.

- Consider, explain and resolve the ethical issues and dilemmas in their own research.

- Seek and secure formal ethical approval, where necessary, for their research project.

RESEARCH SKILLS

At the end of this chapter, the student should, using the exercises on Cengage Brain, be able to:

- Provide an ethical reflection on a given project.

- Critique a given ethical reflection.

The aim of this chapter is to explain ethics, to introduce the student to ethics in business research and to help the student develop an ethical perspective on research in general and business research in particular. The chapter explains the basic precepts of research ethics, explores fundamental ethical issues and details some possible approaches to dealing with the ethical issues and dilemmas of research projects. The chapter will help you, the student, develop a critical reflective ethical approach to research.

INTRODUCTION

Ethics can be defined very simply as a process of reasoning in terms of the right thing to do. In business, as in any other endeavour, ethics is about doing the right thing. In research, it is about doing your work honestly, with integrity, doing it safely and ensuring no harm results to anyone or anything. The model of the research process outlined at the start of Chapter 1 in Figure 1.1 provides a useful tool to aid reflection on the ethical issues that can arise in the different phases of the research process.

Consider each of the stages in the research process, as detailed in Figure 1.1, in relation to your own research. Ask yourself:

- What are the **potential harms** that might arise from your research and from the manner in which you engage with the research and the standard you set for your research throughout every stage of the research process?

- What are the potential risks that might arise from your research and from the manner in which you engage with the research and the standard you set for your research throughout every stage of the research process?

potential harms A potential harm is a harm that might occur.

Think about the ethical issues in your research throughout every step in the research process, and write a reflection in your research diary of how each issue should be addressed. A formal account of this ethical reflection is written into and becomes part of the methodological framework for the research project. Within the four frameworks approach to the research process, the methodological framework is the third framework.

THE VALUE OF GOOD RESEARCH

Research in the media

The ethical practices of organizations and individuals feature frequently in the media. Recently, there has been a great debate in the media about the creation and development of ethical businesses. For example, in *The Guardian* newspaper (07.10.17), Donna Ferguson explained that demand for ethical goods is growing at a great rate. The article featured the founder of the *Big Issue*, John Bird, who launched the magazine in 1991 in order to create, as he explained, a sustainable alternative to begging and crime for very poor people. Currently, according to the article in *The Guardian*, the *Big Issue* is the most widely circulated street newspaper in the world. There is a strong market now, the author of the article explains, for ethical goods. She wrote that the UK market for such goods has quadrupled in size since the year 2000,

and that currently a third of consumers choose to buy goods from firms that they believe are engaged in doing social and/or environmental good.

More recently, in January 2018, in an article in the *South China Post*, journalist Karen Yeung provided detail of the first index to measure the social value competency of Chinese companies, in what she described as a boost for ethical investing. The index, known as China Alliance for Social Value Investment, (CASVIi), Social Value 99 index, evaluates the social value of a company based on whether or not the company has clearly defined targeted social issues in its core business model, and whether it has effectively addressed them through innovative solutions.

In addition, according to an article published in the magazine *Entrepreneur* in January 2018, employees care about the ethical practices of their company, so much so that eight out of ten would be prepared to take lower pay if they believed that the company they worked for operated fairly.

Clearly ethics, ethical practices and ethical businesses are critical issues in business and management. It would be an interesting exercise to try to think of an idea for a research project based on an issue of business ethics.

The four frameworks

- Conceptual Framework
- Theoretical Framework
- *Methodological Framework*
- Analytical Framework

There are many ethical issues in business across the globe. It is worth taking a little time to think about and reflect on the ethical issues in business and in business practices.

Ethics can be defined as the moral principles governing the conduct of an individual, a group or an organization. This definition provides a good point on which to begin a reflection on ethics. In research, as in business, there are fundamental ethical principles. These ethical principles provide guidance for researchers as they design and then carry out research.

ethics Moral principles governing the conduct of an individual, a group or an organization.

ETHICS IN BUSINESS RESEARCH

Ethics in business research is simply the application of ethical principles and standards to business research. Essential in ethics and ethical standards is a capacity to distinguish between right and wrong. YouTube has a number of videos of different people engaging in the Davos Debates on ethics. For five days in January every year, top politicians and business people meet in Davos in Switzerland at the World Economic Forum (www.weforum.org). A good reference for business ethics is the World Economic Forum Code of Ethics, published in 2018 (www.weforum.org/docs/WEF_Code_of_Ethics.pdf). This code of ethics deals with issues such as engaging with the public, engaging with decision makers, supporting diversity and being accountable. You should look up this code of ethics online and read through it. It will provide you with a great deal of information on business ethics, and it might provide you with an idea for your research project.

Politicians from all over the world attend DAVOS, and in 2018 Emmanuel Macron, the French President attended, as did the German Chancellor Angela Merkel, and the American President, Donald Trump. People running global corporations attend the World Economic Forum, people such as Bill and Melinda Gates. Investors such as George Soros attend. Bankers attend, and in 2018, Chetna Sinha, founder and president of Mann Deshi Mahila Sahakari Bank, a bank run for and by women, and Mann Deshi Foundation in India, was one of seven co-chairs of the World Economic Forum Annual Meeting 2018 in Davos.

Davos is attended every year by those running not-for-profit businesses and prominent concerned global citizens such as Bono, Youssou N'Dour, and Malala Yousafzai. The World Economic Forum (WEF) is itself a not-for-profit foundation.

In the Davos YouTube videos on ethics, some of these people can be seen outlining briefly their understanding of ethics and business ethics. In particular, the YouTube video of Rakesh Khurana, Professor of Leadership Development at Harvard Business School and Dean of Harvard College, is of interest. In his video, Professor Khurana considers the question of whether business and management personnel should, like doctors, have an ethical oath and he concludes that they should have one. He says that business is too important to be run by and for self-interest, and he recommends that business people adopt the first maxim of the Hippocratic Oath, first or above all, 'do no harm'.

The American Marketing Association has a highly developed code of ethics. This code covers issues such as the responsibility of the marketer; marketers' professional conduct; and the principles of honesty, fairness and transparency. Reading this code of ethics would be a useful exercise. It would help you develop an understanding of ethical principles in practice. You will find this code online if you search for 'Statement of Ethics – American Marketing Association'.

Another good example of a very highly developed ethical framework for business is that of the Institute of Chartered Accountants Scotland (www.icas.org.uk). The Institute's Code of Ethics is laid out on the website. The current Code of Ethics is the 2017 revised Code of Ethics. The Institute holds that the code applies to all members, including students, in their professional and business activities, whether those activities are paid or voluntary. The Code of Ethics is useful for our purposes in that it provides guidance on five fundamental ethical principles: integrity, professional competence, due care, confidentiality and professional behaviour. These, as you will see as you read on through this chapter, are also fundamental ethical principles in research.

Ethical issues and dilemmas in business research

Ethics in business, and consequently in business research, has in recent years become a critical issue. It has become a critical issue globally because basic ethical standards have not been adhered to in some businesses, even perhaps in some business sectors. Where ethical standards were not adhered to, a culture of greed flourished, within which dishonest and fraudulent activities and behaviours were tolerated and perhaps in some instances even encouraged. Writing in *The Banker* following the recent global economic collapse, Will Hutton (2009) highlighted what he called the 'familiar roll call of villains', among them fabulous bonus systems, poor regulation of financial markets and extraordinary international financial relationships. Globally, we are all now living with the consequences of those unethical practices and the processes put in place to correct those 'mistakes' were costly and painful and their effects are likely to be felt for a long time into the future. The financial readjustments that have taken place, and are taking place, prompted a questioning of ethical standards and practices in business. This questioning has led to more vigorous engagements with ethics in business and in business research. As the processes of adjustment develop, so too will standards and practices in business ethics and in ethics in business research.

Writing in *The Guardian* on this issue of offences against ethical standards and criminal offences, Afua Hirsch (2009) explored the criminal investigations in the USA of banks and businesses and some of the people working in them. She highlighted investigations into Washington Mutual, Freddie Mac and Fannie May, and AIG, as well as the criminal charges that were brought against four executives from Bear Stearns and Crédit Suisse, all of whom were charged with fraud for misleading investors. In the article, Hirsch contrasted the US approach to these cases with the approach taken in the UK to Sir Fred Goodwin, former chairman of the Royal Bank of Scotland. Goodwin retired, according to the article, 'with a knighthood in the bag as well as an £8.4m pension'. He had been forced to step down from his post as chairman of the bank as a non-negotiable condition for the £20 billion bailout of Royal Bank of Scotland and was facing a threat of possible sanctions. Hirsch describes this treatment of Goodwin as mild:

> *In the context of a chairman who oversaw losses of £28billion in investments and purchases in a single year, at a cost to the taxpayer so gargantuan it becomes increasingly impossible to grasp.*

His knighthood was, controversially, cancelled and annulled in 2012 because of the catastrophic impact on the economy of his actions while he was in charge at the Royal Bank of Scotland.

Unethical, and in some cases illegal, behaviour in economics caused the recent global economic downturn. The fact that unfettered markets and unregulated financial systems were responsible for this early twenty-first century economic recession makes this chapter on ethics in business research particularly important.

The importance of ethics in research

When we undertake research, we are representing ourselves and our institution or organization in the wider community and we must consequently adopt in our research endeavour the highest ethical standards. As we mature and become adults every action we take, and are seen to take, contributes to our reputation within our own community and beyond. As this is the case, we should always try to be, and to present ourselves as, ethical practitioners and professionals.

So how do we undertake research ethically? To begin with, we must understand the basic concepts of research and the basic steps in the research process. It is unethical to present yourself as a researcher if you do not know how to conduct research. In order to be able to present yourself as a researcher, you must have the necessary skills and competencies to carry out the research you are proposing to carry out.

Ethics and your research

It is important to begin to think as an ethical practitioner. It is likely that you have been guided all your life by ethical principles. To become an ethical practitioner requires a formal, open and acknowledged critical engagement with ethical standards and behaviours. In research, this critical engagement is formalized through the ethical reflection every researcher engages in and writes about their research project, and through the ethical standards reflected throughout the research project, in the manner in which the research project is carried out and written up.

While the formal ethical reflection appears as a written section in the methodology chapter, the ethical standards of the research project are apparent to the reader of the research project in every element of the written record of a research project. They are evident in the way in which the project was conceptualized, designed and developed, and in the researcher's engagement with the population of the research and the way in which the fieldwork for the research is managed and carried out. The degree of scholarship that the researcher developed in undertaking the research is also reflected in the written account of the research and provides further evidence of the ethical standards of the researcher.

ETHICAL PRINCIPLES

In the following pages, key ethical principles in research are named and explained.

Do no harm

In terms of your own research project, a good place to begin might be to adopt the first maxim of the Hippocratic Oath, above all, 'do no harm', as highlighted by Professor Rakesh Khurana in the YouTube video referred to earlier. In designing and carrying out your research, you must endeavour, above all, to do no harm. In order to accomplish this, you will find it useful to think about the potential harms that *could* arise while you are conducting your research project. Think about the field within which you are situating your research and the institutions, organizations and individuals participating in your study. Try to think of all the different kinds of harm that might possibly befall your participants through their participation in your research. Then try to think of how that harm might be circumvented or avoided. You will find your research diary very useful in recording these thoughts and ideas.

Integrity

A second or allied basic tenet of research ethics is integrity. The value, and indeed the validity, of every aspect of the research project are predicated on the integrity of the researcher. The integrity of the researcher is evident in every aspect of the research and in practically every word written in the research project. The expertise researchers display in the way in which they carry out their research and write about it evidences their integrity.

In the final analysis, the reader of the research must be able to trust that the researcher actually carried out the research as they say they did. The reader will take a critical perspective and search through the research project for evidence of the integrity of the researcher, and also for evidence of any absence of integrity. Examiners in particular are masters at the craft of critical examination of the thesis or report of the research project.

Plagiarism

As we read in Chapter 2, plagiarism is a most serious offence. It is the presentation of somebody else's work as your own. Suspicions of plagiarism can completely undermine perceptions of the integrity of the researcher. It is essential that you clearly understand plagiarism. It is essential that you learn to reference properly. Proper referencing is key to avoiding plagiarism and allegations of plagiarism.

Validity

The most fundamental critique levelled at research projects, as detailed in the earlier chapters, is the critique of the validity of the research project. Above all, the research project must be valid. As defined in Chapter 2, the concept of validity in research is a question of how logical, truthful, robust, sound, reasonable, meaningful and useful is the research. In order to be valid, a research project must make a contribution to knowledge. The issue of validity in terms of the methodology, data-gathering methods and data is dealt with in detail in subsequent chapters.

Power

The next fundamental ethical issue is power. This is an ethical issue in all research. Every researcher, whether they are undergraduates, postgraduates or professional researchers, should critically examine their engagement with their research project in terms of their own power as researchers. The very title of 'researcher' confers a degree of power on the holder because it implies a high degree of expert skill and knowledge. All researchers conducting research within the context of a third-level institution do so under the auspices of that institution and this confers a degree of power on the researcher. The power that accrues to every researcher from these sources is very useful and it is particularly helpful in field research, where the researcher engages with real people and organizations in the process of carrying out their research. However, this power also presents a substantial ethical issue. Researchers must consider the potentially powerful effect in the field of the title of researcher and the affiliation with the university or college. It is likely that both the title and the affiliation will confer on the researcher a degree of power in dealing with gatekeepers and potential research participants. How the researcher uses this power can be a substantial ethical issue.

Transparency

One tried and tested way of avoiding potential harms in the design and development of a research project is through the use of openness and transparency. If you openly, honestly and clearly communicate your research with everyone involved in the project, including your research supervisor, the gatekeepers and the participants in your research, you are likely to uncover potential harms before they become harmful. Once you have uncovered them, you can take steps to ensure that they are neutralized or rendered harmless.

In open discussions around your research, potential issues and pitfalls will arise and they can be dealt with immediately. Any reservations a stakeholder has about your research can be aired and then responded to and dealt with. If this is done, these potential problems can be dealt with properly. If they are not dealt with, they are likely to lead to difficulties that may not become manifest as substantial issues until the research project is very well advanced. As the research project develops, it becomes increasingly difficult to deal with such issues and problems. If the research project is allowed to develop without dealing with the issues and potential problems, these issues and/or problems may even become substantial enough to undermine the research and/or the researcher. They might even cause the research to be stopped.

YOUR RESEARCH
One student's ethical dilemma

I once had a managing director (MD) of a company telephone me to insist that an MSc student who was conducting research under my supervision did not have ethical approval for the research. The student had conducted the fieldwork for the research in this MD's company. Clearly, the student had to have ethical approval from the organization on some level to be able to access the site and conduct the fieldwork in the site. The problem was that, for whatever reason, there was some loss of trust in the project within the organization and this loss of trust manifested itself in the MD's official comment on and complaint about the research. By the time the MD did officially comment and complain about the project, the student had completed the research, finished writing up the project and had just submitted the hardbound thesis.

The response of the university to this situation was to insist that the hardbound thesis be immediately returned to the student. The university would not allow the student to resubmit the thesis until this ethical dilemma was formally resolved. The student could not graduate until the thesis was submitted to the university and accepted by the university. The student had to go back to the MD and renegotiate ethical approval for the research. Ethical approval was eventually given, but, before it was, changes had to be made to some aspects of the text. When these changes were effected to the satisfaction of the MD, the thesis had to be rebound, then resubmitted, and eventually, and finally, examined.

This is not a situation in which any student would want to find themselves.

THE VALUE OF GOOD RESEARCH

Focus on case study research

Case study is a research methodology. It is used a lot in business research. Case study methodology is particularly useful in the in-depth study of bounded entities: for example, a company, or a team, or a class, or any organization, or a single incident or an event: any entity that is clearly bounded. The organization, incident or event provides the case that is to be studied. Case study research can focus on one case or on a number of cases. Decisions about the number of cases to be studied are made in relation to the requirements of the research, the time available for the research and the level and degree of access available to potential cases.

Case study research is holistic. Generally, it involves the study of the case under investigation in great detail or in its entirety.

Case studies tend to involve data from different sources. They can draw on both quantitative and qualitative data. The key to data gathering in case studies is the data requirement in order to, as fully as possible, illustrate or explain the phenomenon under investigation. The researcher using a case study methodology gathers as much data as necessary from as many sources as possible in order to respond to the research question or statement.

For further information on case study research read Yin (2018). See also the guides to case studies provided by the Colorado State University (www.writing.colstate.edu/guides/research/casestudy).

The research article here (Davies, Doherty and Knox, 2010), 'The rise and stall of a fair trade pioneer: The Cafédirect story', *Journal of Business Ethics*, *92*: 127–47, details an interesting research project which was developed using a case study methodology.

In the article, the authors, using a case study methodology, investigate the growth of fair trade pioneer, Cafédirect. The authors state that Cafédirect secured a prominent position in the UK mainstream coffee industry based on its ethical positioning. In their research, the authors explored the marketing, networks and communication channels of Cafédirect that led the brand from a position of niche player to the mainstream. The authors report a slowdown in the brand's meteoric rise, and they ask in the article if the brand can resume its momentum with its current marketing strategy.

The article is interesting on a number of points:

- It presents a useful review of the literature on fair trade.
- It outlines the rise of the brand in question, Cafédirect.
- It presents a lot of detail on the methodology used in the research (in Appendix 1) and on the very wide variety of data used in the study.
- The article provides a teaching appendix (Appendix 2), with interesting questions designed to promote further learning from the case study.
- Finally, the article provides useful references for further reading.

Find the original article online and read it. It is, I think you will agree, an example of a very good case study.

Does the article give you any ideas for your own research project?

RESEARCH IN PRACTICE

Shen's research project – a case study

Shen is studying for a degree in strategic management.

He has decided on the topic for his research project. He read an article in a newspaper about the key issues in taking a venture to market. He was very interested in the article and, as he read the article, he began to think about designing a research project on the topic of bringing new ventures to market.

He decided to read a little more around this topic and to consider how he might develop this idea into a viable research project. He spoke about this to his lecturer in research methodologies who was very encouraging. She advised Shen to develop the idea further and to try to develop the idea into a proposal for a research project.

Shen, after some reading and reflection, came up with the following:

This research project is a case study of the key issues that contribute to success when taking a venture to market.

The research will focus on ten successful startup companies, each of which will have started up in or after 2010. The ten companies will be identified with the help of key informants from the university, and information from media reports.

To be included in the study, each of the new businesses will have to be a 'successful' business. In the first place, 'successful' new businesses will be identified. Then the 'successful' businesses will be contacted. The research will be explained to them and they will be invited to participate in the study. This process will continue until ten successful new companies have agreed to participate in the study.

Data for the research will come from financial reports and marketing plans for each of the ten companies. In addition, in-depth interviews will be conducted with three key informants in each of the ten companies: the CEO, the financial controller and the director of marketing.

The research when complete will make an important contribution to knowledge in relation to the issues that contribute to success when taking a venture to market.

Before he goes any further with this work, Shen intends to discuss his research project with his newly appointed thesis supervisor. He is hoping for some positive and encouraging feedback.

What do you think of Shen's research project?

Do you see any potential problems in the proposed research? We think that Shen needs to define more clearly what is meant by the term 'successful' in relation to this research. Otherwise, we think his research has potential.

Do you think Shen's supervisor will support his idea for his research project?

The ethically reflective practitioner

It is important for standards in ethics in research that each researcher becomes an ethically reflective practitioner. This means that they need to take the time to think critically about the standard of their research, their code of conduct and behaviour as researchers and, in particular, their conduct in relation to their engagement with participants in the field. Researchers should critically reflect on the manner in which they gather, manage and store their data. They should critically reflect on the means and processes through which they analyze their data and they should critically reflect on the way they decide to write up their research. As you can see, research ethics are a part of every aspect of the research process.

Over and over again throughout this textbook, you will find yourself encouraged to critically engage with every aspect of your research. If there are faults in your research in the language, in the words used, in the syntax, the spellings, the punctuation, you would obviously correct them. In the same way, if there are issues with the proposed research, including issues with the research population, the sample of the population, the sampling method, methodology, data-gathering methods, the data, the means and processes of analysis or the findings of the research and the conclusions drawn and/or the recommendations made, you must address them.

As a researcher, you should critically engage with each and every one of these aspects of your research project and you should do the same with every other research project with which you are presented. Remember, one of the most important reasons why anyone would want to develop research skills is in order to be able to critique (to critically engage with) other people's research, particularly if their research has implications for you, for the way that you live or work, for your profession and/or for your career.

Researchers often start out with very simple research projects. Then through the scholarship they bring to these projects, through their engagement with the literature, their work on research methodology and data analysis and through the expert intelligent creative way in which they develop insights into their data and draw conclusions from their data, these simple research projects become extraordinarily complex. The key to developing a good research project is to keep it simple to begin with. This simple research project will, through your scholarly engagement with each and every step of the research process, become quite complex. It is therefore best to begin with a very simple research statement or question. This is particularly important for undergraduate researchers.

Undergraduate researchers are inexperienced researchers. The opportunity to undertake supervised research is offered to students in order to facilitate them in the development of research skills. It is therefore particularly important for undergraduate researchers that they begin with a very simple, very clear, ethically unambiguous and very useful research statement or question or hypothesis. It is important too that they, as students and beginner researchers, make the most of every opportunity available to them for supervision and feedback. The process of **reflexivity** in research will encourage you as a researcher to reflect on your research and to openly discuss your research with all of the participants and stakeholders in the research project. Through this essential reflexive process, the issues, problems and ethical dilemmas, real and potential, in your research project will be acknowledged, discussed and ultimately resolved. If you actively and critically engage in this process you will become a reflective ethical research practitioner.

> **reflexivity** Researcher's active thoughtful engagement with every aspect and development of their research, e.g. self-reflection, self-consciousness, self-awareness.

The ethical issues of anonymity and confidentiality

Two important and basic precepts in research ethics are those of **confidentiality** and **anonymity**. Two aspects of these precepts are those of **informed consent** and data protection. Confidentiality in research generally refers to the guarantee that researchers make to participants, whether they are individuals or organizations, that their contribution to the research project will be confidential. The guarantee is that only the researcher, and perhaps the supervisor of the research project, will have access to the data that participants provide for the research project. Anonymity is a guarantee that researchers make to participants, individuals and/or organizations, that they will not be identified at any time during the research. They will not be identifiable in any way in any written account of the research, the thesis and any other publications based on the research. Often participants consent to participate in research only when these guarantees have been given. It is easy to issue these guarantees, but ensuring that participants remain anonymous and their contributions to research remain confidential is often much more difficult than researchers anticipate.

> **confidentiality** The non-disclosure of certain information.
>
> **anonymity** Free from identification.
>
> **informed consent** Agreement given by a person to participate in some action, after being informed of the possible consequences.

Informed consent

The principle of informed consent is another ethical concern. When a researcher invites a potential participant to participate in their research, they are ethically obliged to inform that potential participant of the nature of the research, the nature and extent of their participation in the research, and any possible consequences for them that might arise from their participation. The potential participant will then consent, or will refuse to consent, to participate in the research. The participant should indicate in an informed consent form as can be seen in this section that they have been advised about the nature and intent of the research and the nature and extent of their engagement with it, and they should then sign the form. The informed consent form is a record of the fact that the participant understands what the research is about and understands what is required of them as a participant. The form also records the fact that the participant is a willing, informed participant, who understands that s/he may withdraw from the research at any time without question or consequence.

A template for an informed consent form is shown in the Your Research feature. The template of the informed consent form provided, as you will see, functions as an information sheet and an informed consent form. Sometimes researchers develop separate information sheets and informed consent forms. This happens usually when the research is very complex, and requires a lot of explaining. It also happens when it is a requirement of a **research ethics committee** (REC), see later. The informed consent form tells the potential participant about the nature of the research and about the kind of participation and the level of participation in the research required of them. The form also provides a structure for the participant to indicate that they have been properly informed (about the research) and that they have freely given their informed consent to participate in the study.

> **research ethics committee** Convened by organizations to monitor and police the ethical standards of research projects in which the parent organization has some gatekeeping role.

YOUR RESEARCH
Common research problems

Let us say, for example, that you decide to conduct your research within your university or college and as part of your research you decide to interview the president of the university or college. You may then, in the written account of the research, wish to highlight a quote or a particular viewpoint given to you by the president. It can be difficult, if not impossible, not to identify the president as the holder of this particular viewpoint. In fact it might be essential to the research and the meaning of the research that the quote or the viewpoint be attributed to the president. The quote or the viewpoint may have meaning only in the context of it being a quote from the president.

This presents an ethical dilemma. For the quote to be meaningful, it must be attributed. If it is attributed, there will a breach of the guarantees of confidentiality and anonymity.

How can this be resolved? The easiest way to resolve such issues is to critically reflect on your research as you design it. Discuss your research with your supervisor. Try, if at all possible, to anticipate dilemmas like this and deal with them.

You might perhaps interview other members of senior management within the college or university, or perhaps you might interview the presidents of other universities and colleges, as well as your own. Both of these approaches would help you maintain your guarantees of anonymity and confidentiality, as you can hide the identity of individual presidents or senior managers in a group of presidents or senior managers. It is worth noting, however, that in such a small group there can be difficulties in maintaining anonymity and confidentiality.

If you discuss your concerns regarding anonymity and confidentiality with the participants or potential participants in the study, you may find that they are happy to go on the record and so will not require that their identities remain anonymous and their contributions confidential. This is another means by which these ethical issues can be overcome.

This brief example illustrates clearly the necessity for openness and dialogue around research and it demonstrates some of the advantages of developing a reflexive (constant process of reflection) critical (questioning) engagement with any proposed research, research strategy or research design.

YOUR RESEARCH
An example informed consent form

(SAMPLE) INFORMED CONSENT FORM
    Research study title: _____
    Researcher's name: _____
    Researcher's status: _____
    (e.g. final year student BSc Management, University of Bellejour)
    Researcher's contact telephone number: _____
    Researcher's email address: _____

Dear Sir/Madam,
You are invited to participate in a research study designed to explore the overall satisfaction of customers of the *Beat Box Music Store* with the store's products and services. If you would like to participate in this research, I would very much appreciate it if you would read this form and sign the bottom of the form. Participation in this study will involve an interview that will last approximately 15 minutes. At the end of the interview, you will be asked to complete a short questionnaire. The questionnaire will comprise ten questions, nine of which require yes or no answers. The final question is an open question, using a sentence completion format.

All information will remain confidential and your identity will remain anonymous. The interview will be audio recorded; the information gathered will be transcribed by the researcher. Only the researcher will have access to the transcripts, and all of the transcripts will be coded. Your name will not appear on any transcript or questionnaire. All of the data gathered for the research will be adequately and properly stored, guarded and disposed of on completion of the study.

Please read the following statements and if you understand the statements and wish to participate in this study, please indicate your agreement to take part by ticking the boxes:

☐ I have read and I understand the description of the study.
☐ I willingly consent to participate in the study.
☐ I understand that I may withdraw from the research at any time without consequence.
☐ I understand that the interviews will be audio recorded and the researcher will take notes.
☐ I understand that my identity will remain anonymous and my contribution will be confidential.

Participant's signature: _____
Name in block capitals: _____
Researcher's signature: _____

As well as informing potential participants about the research and providing a record of their consent to participate in the research, the informed consent form can serve the researcher as a prompt for ethical reflection. The informed consent form also provides an insight for readers and examiners of the ethical standards of the research project.

OTHER ETHICAL ISSUES IN RESEARCH

Other ethical issues in research include the issue of **privileged access**, the issue of **intrusion** and the issue of **vulnerable populations**. Sometimes there can be ethical dilemmas in carrying out research in areas in which you have privileged access. For example, you might in your line of work be in charge of a group of people. You might be a team leader or a manager, and this position places you in a privileged position in relation to that team, and this would become an ethical issue if you decided to conduct your research on or with the team. It might be that the team would welcome any research initiative that you might propose, but if you are in a leadership position, it might be that they would not feel that they could freely refuse to participate in your research. They might feel that to refuse to participate might have consequences for them, either in their work with the team or in their relationship with you. This is an ethical dilemma. While it does not mean that you cannot or should not conduct research in such circumstances, it does mean that you should actively and critically engage with the ethical issues in such research.

> **privileged access** Prior access to an individual or site that provides an advantage in securing access for the purpose of conducting research.
>
> **intrusion** Unwarranted, unnecessary or unwelcome engagement on a person or place.
>
> **vulnerable populations** Populations that have some vulnerability, in terms of their social position or their age or their state of well-being.

Care is needed in asking intrusive questions. These might include questions about how much money a participant earns, about sexual orientation or behaviour, about experiences of imprisonment or experiences in other closed institutions, about criminal activities or potentially criminal activities, or about deviant behaviour. All of these areas, and many others, are potentially sensitive and can be ethically problematic. Great care is needed when undertaking research on topics such as these. The advice, guidance and support of a research supervisor is essential.

The issue of intrusion relates also to the degree of intrusion on the time, goodwill and privacy of participants the research requires. Potential participants have a right to privacy. One question you should ask yourself is whether or not your research is sufficiently important to justify the level of intrusion you are proposing on potential participants. The issue of intrusion has ethical consequences in terms of researchers asking too much of participants. Researchers can trespass too much on the time and goodwill of research participants. You should keep your engagement with participants to the minimum required in order to gather the necessary data. Gathering unnecessary data is another ethical issue. Often researchers gather unnecessary data, too much data, or even the wrong data, when they are unclear about the data they require for their research project. This is one of the reasons why it is important to be properly prepared for the fieldwork, the data-gathering phase of the research.

The issue of vulnerable populations is a substantial ethical issue. Some populations are researched a lot and some are not. Powerful people tend not to be the subjects of research projects. This is often because they feel powerful enough to refuse to participate in research projects, or they are powerful enough to have a **gatekeeper** protecting them and deflecting invitations to participate. Children are considered a vulnerable population in terms of research. People in institutions, hospitals or other care settings are considered vulnerable populations in terms of research. The issue of vulnerable populations can sometimes be a more substantial issue in not-for-profit business research, where researchers may have very laudable intentions, but their research agendas may involve sensitive, ethically problematic research with vulnerable populations. This is of course not to say that such research should not take place, but it warrants substantial critical engagement and ethical reflection on the part of the researcher. Critical reflection on the research project can bring the researcher to the point where they decide, on reflection, to change, perhaps even substantially change, the project in some way or to some degree.

> **gatekeeper** Any person or structure that governs or controls access to people, places, structures and/or to organizations.

One critical question that should be asked of every research project is whether the project warrants all the work, expenditure of resources and trespass on the time and goodwill of potential participants. In order to be worth all of this, the research project must make a substantial contribution to knowledge. Once again, the best way to ensure a good ethical standard for your research project is to be open and honest about the research design as it develops and to engage in dialogue, with your peers and your supervisor and any other advisors you can access, about your research. Remember to keep note of all of these discussions in your research diary; these notes will be invaluable when you are writing up.

This degree of reflexivity will help you to identify and deal with ethical issues and potential pitfalls before they become problems. This reflexivity will also make you a better and more skilled researcher. Remember, the point of the exercise of undertaking a research project for a programme of study is to develop research skills.

Table 3.1 provides a shortlist of the ethical issues and principles we have discussed in this section. It is a useful reminder of the key aspects of a critical ethical reflection on any research project.

Table 3.1 Shortlist of important ethical issues and principles

Do not harm	Power issues	Engaging in a critical reflexive manner with every aspect of the research process
Integrity of the researcher and the research	Maintaining confidentiality	Engaging with vulnerable populations
Scholarship of the researcher	Right to privacy of potential participants	Intrusion – being careful not to intrude too much on the goodwill of participants
Issue of validity	Guaranteeing anonymity to participants	Ethical issues in privileged access
Developing the research in an open and transparent manner	Providing for informed consent	Gaining and maintaining ethical approval for the study

INSTITUTIONAL RESEARCH ETHICS

Many organizations now have a research ethics committee (REC). These committees are made up of people appointed by the organization to oversee the ethical standards of research conducted within it. The people on RECs generally have some degree of expertise in relation to research. Most universities, if not all, have RECs. Many other institutions do too, including hospitals. In general, researchers who wish to conduct research within an institution that has a REC (or under the auspices of such an institution or organization) will be obliged to submit a formal application for ethical approval to this committee.

REC requirements can be substantial and you would be wise to establish from the very beginning whether or not you will be obliged to seek permission for your research from one or more RECs. If it happens that you must secure ethical approval from an REC before you may commence gathering data for your research, then you should, as soon as possible, familiarize yourself with the requirements and the forms (in the plural, as there is usually more than one form to be completed) of those committees. The informed consent form examined earlier is a good, and typical, example of one of the forms that such committees generally require applicants to complete. Other forms frequently required by RECs include letters informing potential participants about the nature of the research and inviting them to participate, and copies of any recruitment material or advertisements used to engage participants in the research. Research ethics committees usually want copies of any data-gathering instrument to be used in the research, such as a copy of the questionnaire or a copy of the interview schedule to be used.

There are two dates that have great significance in relation to any engagement with an REC. The first date is that of the deadline for submission of an application for ethical approval to an REC. The second date is that of the meeting of the REC, which is the date on which a decision will be made as to whether or not ethical approval will be granted to your study. Generally, RECs require changes, and sometimes substantial changes, to research proposals before ethical approval is granted. This has further time implications for the research. Usually, the deadline for submission to the REC is two to four weeks before the actual meeting. RECs tend to meet relatively infrequently, perhaps six or eight times a year. As this is the case, it is important to be aware of the dates that concern you and your application for ethical approval. If you miss the deadline for submission, you have to wait for the next deadline and the delay could have significant implications for your research.

Research ethics checklist of questions/prompts for ethical reflection

The questions that follow are designed to prompt you in terms of your ethical reflection on your research project. The sets of questions relate to different elements of the research process, as outlined in the model of the research process detailed in Figure 1.1 at the start of Chapter 1. You can use these sets of questions to examine your ethical engagement with your own research and also to help you develop the formal ethical reflection you will need to develop in relation to your research.

Questions for the planning phase of the research process

- Is the research useful?
- Will the research make a contribution to knowledge?
- Do I know enough about the topic to conduct this research?
- Do I know enough about research methodology, have I learned enough about research methodology, to conduct this research to a high standard?

Questions for the literature review

- Have I engaged properly and thoroughly with the literature on this topic?
- Does the theoretical framework I have developed for the research project properly and thoroughly support my study?
- Have I scrupulously avoided presenting a skewed perspective on the literature?

Questions for the population and sample

- Is the population chosen for the research the appropriate population?
- Is the sample selected, if using a sample, an appropriate sample?
- Is the sampling method used the appropriate sampling method?

YOUR RESEARCH
Common research problems

Gaining ethical approval for your study

You must of course, to begin with, establish the ethical standards of your own institution. Ensure that in your research you meet the requirements of the ethical standards of your own institution. Ensure too that you have formal acknowledgement, in writing and from the appropriate source, that you have met the requirements of the ethical standards of your own institution.

In presenting research projects to RECs for ethical approval, some research projects require a full ethical review and some research projects require an expedited ethical review.

In general, undergraduate research projects are automatically subject only to a simple expedited review. Postgraduate research projects tend to be subjected to more rigorous ethical review.

It would be a very good idea to establish as early as possible the level of formal ethical review to which your project is likely to be subjected.

As an exercise, visit the websites of some of the university RECs and read and try to understand their requirements. You will find this a very useful exercise in terms of prompting you in ethical reflections on your own research project.

Some examples of university research ethics web pages:

- Cardiff Business School at Cardiff University (www.cardiff.ac.uk/carbs/research/ethics).
- Glasgow School for Business and Society at Glasgow Caledonian University (www.gcu.ac.uk/gsbs/research/researchethicscommittee/researchethics).
- The University of Cambridge, Judge Business School, (www.cbr.cam.ac.uk/research/research-ethics).

Questions for research methodology

- Is the proposed research methodology appropriate?
- Does it fit with the aim of the research, with the nature of the research and with the population of the study?

Questions for data gathering

- Are the data-gathering techniques chosen for and/or designed for the research appropriate?
- Will the data-gathering methods chosen yield the data required for the research?
- Are the data-gathering methods too intrusive or in any other way ethically problematic?

Questions for negotiating access

- Do I have all the permissions needed for the fieldwork?
- Do I have good working relationships with all of the gatekeepers and all of the participants in the research?
- Am I being as open and honest as possible about the research? Are there any ethical issues in the openness and transparency with which the research was conducted?

Questions for an ethical engagement with participants

- Have I, as much as possible, explained to participants and neutralized any potential harms and risks for participants?
- Do I have a clear understanding of the potential risks to participants through their participation in the research?
- Have I thoroughly communicated these potential risks to potential participants?
- Have I, as much as possible, eliminated any and all risks to participants through their participation in the research?
- Have all of the participants read, understood and signed an informed consent form?
- Have I guaranteed the participants' confidentiality and anonymity?
- Can I guarantee confidentiality and anonymity?
- How can I guarantee confidentiality and anonymity?
- Have I provided participants with my contact details should they have any concerns at any stage about the research?
- Do my participants know that they can withdraw from my research at any time without any consequence to them or for them?

Questions for data management

- Do I have a plan for the management of data?
- Where will the data be held?
- Is this a secure place?
- Who will have access to the data?
- Will the data be coded for anonymity and confidentiality?
- Do I have a plan for the appropriate disposal of data?

Questions for data analysis

- Have I the necessary skills to properly analyze the data?
- How will I analyze my data?
- Will I use CADA (Computer Assisted Data Analysis) techniques in analyzing my data? (See Part Four of this textbook for an introduction to CADA.)
- Do I have enough time for data gathering and data analysis?
- Are my conclusions rooted in my data and have they clearly emerged from my data?
- Have I properly and thoroughly theorized my findings? In other words, have I connected my findings with the findings of other researchers/theorists as detailed in the theoretical framework I created for my research project? The theoretical framework, you will remember, is contained in the Literature Review.

Questions for completing the research

- Are my conclusions insightful?
- Do my conclusions add substantially to knowledge in this field?
- Have I theorized my conclusions, i.e. have I knitted my conclusions into the body of knowledge, as detailed in the theoretical framework of the research project?

- Are my recommendations reasonable and achievable?
- Have I properly and thoroughly referenced my work?
- Is my research of a high standard?
- Is my research ethical?

Questions for disseminating the research

- How is my research to be disseminated?
- How will I provide feedback on the findings of my research, if required, to individual and institutional participants?

REAL WORLD RESEARCH

How theory influences research

In the article here (Clegg, Kornberger and Rhodes, 2007, 'Business ethics as practice', *British Journal of Management*, *18*(2): 107–22), the authors explore business ethics as practice.

The authors consider the individual within the business workplace using his/her own conscience as the appropriate standard in ethical and moral judgements. The authors consider the norms and practices of the organization as the arbiter of the appropriate standard in ethical and moral judgements.

They argue that what managers actually do is central to how the individual's sense of the appropriate standard in ethical and moral judgements is formed and challenged within organizations. They examine how the ethics of the individual are shaped by the culture of the organization and how the ethics of individuals shape the ethical culture of organizations.

The article is very useful on a number of levels:

- It is useful in that it is an engaging study of management ethical practices. The focus is on the ethics or the behavioural ethics of individuals situated within business organizations.
- The article is useful in that it presents a highly developed theoretical framework focused on how ethics 'play out in practice'.
- A careful reading of the article gives a good sense of how theory influences research, and vice versa, how research in turn makes a contribution to theory.
- The list of references at the end of the article is a very useful resource for both classical and contemporary references on ethics.

Finally, this article might give you some ideas for your own research project.

The authors present the article as follows:

In this article, we develop a conceptionalization of business ethics as practice. Starting from the view that the ethics that organizations display in practice will have been forged through an ongoing process of debate and contestation over moral choices, we examine ethics in relation to the ambiguous, unpredictable and subjective contexts of managerial action.

The article concludes by discussing how the 'ethics as practice' approach that we expound provides theoretical resources for studying the different ways that ethics manifest themselves in organizations as well as providing a practical application of ethics in organizations that goes beyond moralistic and legalistic approaches.

In recent years, business scandals, ranging from Enron to the Parmalat disasters, have once again redirected the attention of both managers and organization theorists to a consideration of ethics and the moral dilemmas that corporations face in the context of contemporary capitalism (see Donaldson, 2003; Johnson and Smith, 1999; Parker, 2003; Porter and Kramer, 2002; Soule, 2002; Tonge, Greer and Lawton, 2003; Veiga, 2004; Weaver, Treviño and Cochran, 1999; see also Werhane, 2000). Despite such a renewed focus, as Donaldson suggests, the theoretical tools employed to analyze and understand ethics require further development. In the same vein, as Wicks and Freeman argue, 'organization studies need to be fundamentally reshaped . . . to provide room for ethics and to increase the relevance of research' (1998, p. 123). It is an aim that we subscribe to.

The goal of this article is to develop a theoretical framework with which to explore ethics in organization theory that moves beyond being either prescriptive or morally relative. To do so, we argue that ethics is best understood and theorized as a form of practice. Our approach is concerned with theorizing ethics in relation to what managers actually do in their everyday activities.

Finally, this research article concludes with 'a new research agenda' for the practice of ethics for business managers and in business organizations.

When you have read this synopsis, you should source the original article and read it. Does this article give you any ideas for your research project? Does this article give you any ideas for your reflection on the ethical issues in your own research?

CASE STUDY

The Walt Disney Company

Ethics in business is the application of ethical standards throughout every aspect and element of the business. The Walt Disney Company provides a good case study of ethics in business. On its website are details of its ethical framework for business. You can find this on the company's website under the heading Corporate Citizenship. The lead statement from the company reads as follows:

'Acting responsibly is an integral part of our company. At Disney we refer to our broad efforts to conduct our business and create our products in an ethical manner as Disney citizenship.'

The framework covers:

- Disney's international labour standards
- responsible sourcing, designed to create mutually beneficial relationships between the Walt Disney Company and suppliers

- product safety, where the safety of all Disney products is a crucial concern
- product footprint, detailing the efforts to minimize product footprint in order to help protect the environment.

It is worth taking a little time to read through these pages. They give a good overview of a highly structured, carefully developed ethical framework for business. In addition, there is so much data available on the website, that it would be possible to conduct a research project, perhaps a case study, examining the ethical framework of the Walt Disney Company. Is this a research project you would consider undertaking? Perhaps thinking about this gives you some other ideas in terms of potential research projects.

In your research diary, briefly record the key elements of Disney's business ethics framework. If you think any aspect of this framework is of use to you in relation to your own research, write a short paragraph about this.

Question: What are the key ethical issues that the Disney Company focuses on in relation to its hiring practices?

END OF CHAPTER QUESTIONS

1   Define ethics.

2   Name and briefly explain six key ethical issues.

3   What is meant by ethics in business research?

4   What is meant by the term ethical reflection?

5   How does one become a reflexive practitioner?

6   Name and explain two ethical concerns in each step of the research process.

7   Develop two different research questions on ethics in business. Decide whether or not, based on critical ethical reflection, these research questions could or should

be developed into research projects. Explain your ethical reasoning.

8   In your research diary, detail the key ethical concerns in your own research project.

9   In your research diary, write a reflective piece explaining how you intend to overcome these ethical concerns.

10   In your research diary, write a critique of your approach to overcoming the ethical concerns you have about your research project. (The three-part exercise – Questions 8, 9 and 10 – conducted in your research diary, can be used as the basis for the ethical reflection on your research that you present in the methodology section or chapter of your thesis/report of your research.)

REFERENCES

Clegg, S., Kornberger, M. and Rhodes, C. (2007) 'Business ethics as practice', *British Journal of Management, 18*: 107–122.

Colorado State University, 'Writing case studies', writing.colostate.edu/guides/guide.cfm?guideid=60 (Accessed 05.02.2018).

Davies, I.A., Doherty, B. and Knox, S. (2010) 'The rise and stall of a fair trade pioneer: the Cafédirect story', *Journal of Business Ethics, 92*: 127–147.

Donaldson, T. (2003) 'Editor's comments: taking ethics seriously? A mission now more possible', *Academy of Management Review, 28*: 363–366.

Ferguson, D. (2017) 'Start your own ethical business – it could make a world of difference', *The Guardian*, 07.10.17, www.theguardian.com/money/2017/oct/07/start-ethical-business-financially-successful-socially (Accessed 26.01.2018).

Harvard's Rakesh Khurana on Ehics', www.youtube.com/watch?v=gisOW8WOiGQ (Accessed 05.02.2018).

Hirsch, A. (2009) 'Should Sir Fred get away scot-free?', *The Guardian*, www.theguardian.com/commentisfree/2009/jan/20/banking-banks (Accessed 05.02.2018).

Hutton, W. (2009) 'The banking system has shirked its ownership of risk, but governments must be generous if it is to survive', *The Banker*, ec2-54-72-50-240.eu-west-1.compute.amazonaws.com/Banking-Regulation-Risk/Regulation/Will-Hutton?ct=true (Accessed 05.02.2018).

Institute of Chartered Accountants Scotland, 'Code of Ethics', www.icas.com/ethics/icas-code-of-ethics (Accessed 05.02.2018).

Johnson, P. and Smith, K. (1999) 'Contextualizing business ethics: Anomie and social life', *Human Relations, 52*: 1351–1375.

Parker, M. (ed.) (2003) 'Special issue on ethics politics and organization', *Organization, 10*(2): 187–203.

Porter, M. and Kramer, M. (2002) 'The competitive advantage of corporate philanthropy', *Harvard Business Review*, 37–68.

Soule, E. (2002) 'Managerial moral strategies? In search of a few good principles', *Academy of Management Review, 27*: 114–124, www.fsg.org/Portals/0/Uploads/Documents/PDF/Competitive_Advantage.pdf

'Statement of Ethics – American Marketing Association', www.ama.org/AboutAMA/Pages/Statement-of-Ethics.aspx (Accessed 05.02.2018).

The Walt Disney Company, thewaltdisneycompany.com/about (Accessed 05.02.2018).

Tonge, A., Greer, L. and Lawton, A. (2003) 'The Enron story: you can fool some of the people some of the time', *Business Ethics, A European Review, 12*: 4–22.

Veiga, J. (2004) 'Bringing ethics into the mainstream: an introduction to the special topic', *Academy of Management Executive, 18*(2): 37–39.

Weaver, G.R., Treviño, L.K. and Cochran, P.L. (1999) 'Corporate ethics practices in the mid-1990s: an empirical study of the fortune 1000', *Journal of Business Ethics, 18*: 283–294.

Werhane, P.H. (2000) 'Business ethics and the origins of contemporary capitalism: economics and ethics in the work of Adam Smith and Herbert Spence', *Journal of Business Ethics, 24*: 185–198.

Wicks, A.C. and Freeman, R.E. (1998) 'Organization studies and the new pragmatism: positivism, anti-positivism and the search for ethics', *Organization Science, 9*: 123–141.

World Economic Forum, www.weforum.org/en/index.htm

Yeung, K., (2018), 'Chinese index ranking companies by social value commitment aims to help ethical investors', *South China Morning Post*, 19.01.2018, www.scmp.com/business/companies/article/2129721/chinese-index-ranking-companies-social-value-commitment-aims-help (Accessed 26.01.2018).

Yin, R.K. (2018) *Case Study Research and Applications: Design and Methods* (6th edn), London: Sage.

RECOMMENDED READING

Bell, J. and Waters, S. (2014) *Doing Your Research Project*, Maidenhead: Open University Press.

Collis, J. and Hussey, R. (2013) *Business Research, A Practical Guide for Undergraduate and Postgraduate Students* (3rd edn), Basingstoke: Palgrave Macmillan.

Creswell, J. and Creswell, D.J. (2018) *Research Design: Qualitative, Quantitative and Mixed Methods Approaches* (5th edn), London, California, New Delhi, Singapore: Sage.

Davis, D. (2005) *Business Research for Decision Making*, Mason, OH: Cengage South-Western.

Denscombe, M. (2017) *The Good Research Guide: For Small-scale Social Research Projects* (5th edn), Maidenhead: Open University Press.

Denscombe, M. (2010) *Ground Rules for Good Research: Guidelines for Good Practice*, London: Open University Press.

Neuman, W.L. (2013) *Social Research Methods: Pearson New International Edition: Qualitative and Quantitative Approaches*, Essex, UK: Pearson Education Limited.

Webley, S. and Werner, A. (2008) 'Corporate codes of ethics: necessary but not sufficient', *Business Ethics: A European Review, 17*(4): 405–415.

CHAPTER 4

UNDERSTANDING RESEARCH PHILOSOPHY

LEARNING OBJECTIVES

At the end of this chapter, the student should:

● Understand the philosophical underpinnings of research and research methodologies.

● Understand the different world views represented in different philosophical approaches.

● Understand the links between research, theory and knowledge.

RESEARCH SKILLS

At the end of this chapter, the student should, using the exercises on Cengage Brain, be able to:

● **Explain the philosophical underpinnings of sample research projects.**

The aim of this chapter is to explore and explain the philosophical underpinnings of research and research methodologies. The philosophical frameworks explored in this chapter are positivism, constructionism, interpretivism, functionalism, critical inquiry, feminism and postmodernism. Each of these represents a different perspective on the social world, and a fundamental framework within social science research. They have all been written about extensively elsewhere and this chapter contains simply a brief introduction to them. The chapter highlights the importance of theory in research and explains how, through research, knowledge and theory are generated.

INTRODUCTION

In this chapter, the focus is on understanding philosophical frameworks. Every research project is underpinned by a **philosophical framework**, which evidences the world view within which the research is situated, and which can be seen in every step of the research process. This is where the issue of '**fit**' becomes critical. Each step in the research process, as designed by the researcher, should be appropriate to, or should fit with, the purpose and focus of the research. You should by now be quite familiar with the model of the research process, outlined in Figure 1.1 at the start of Chapter 1. Every aspect of the research project, as it is developed by the researcher, should 'fit' with the philosophical framework within which the research project is situated.

> **philosophical framework** The world view within which the research is situated.
>
> **fit** Every step in the research project, should 'fit' with every other step in the research project and 'fit' with the purpose and focus of the project and philosophical framework.

When beginning the process of developing a research proposal, the questions you must ask yourself are:

- What am I going to do? (The research statement/question – the aim of the research.)
- How am I going to do it? (The methodology and methods to be used.)
- Where am I going to do it? (The site of the research.)
- Why am I going to do it? (The rationale for the research.)

The first question 'What am I going to do?' is clearly the most important. The second question, 'How am I going to do it?' relates to (research) methodology and (data collection) methods. In deciding what methodology and methods to use, it is important to bear in mind that you must **justify** these decisions. In answering these questions, you must consider the research question or statement, that is, the purpose of the research. You must consider the methodology and the methods you choose. They must be capable of supporting the research question or statement, capable of providing an appropriate methodological framework and the data necessary for the research project.

> **justify** The researcher is obliged to justify, or explain and defend, the choices they make, especially their methodological choices, in relation to their research.

Our choice and use of particular methodologies and methods, as Crotty (2005: 2) explains, relates to the assumptions about reality that we bring to our work and consequently to our theoretical perspective. Questions about the nature of reality are questions of **ontology**. Questions about the methodology and methods used in the research project relate to our understanding of knowledge and how it is created. In particular, such questions relate to the validity of new knowledge generated by research projects. These are questions of **epistemology**. Table 4.1 outlines three epistemological positions that concern us.

Table 4.1 Three epistemological positions

Positivism	Holds that there is one objective reality; reality is singular and separate from consciousness
Social constructionism	Along with social constructivism, holds that social phenomena develop in social contexts, that reality is socially constructed, and that individuals and groups create, in part, their own realities
Interpretivism	Related to constructivism. It holds that social reality is a subjective construction based on interpretation and interaction

> **ontology** Relates to the study of being, the nature of being and our ways of being in the world.
>
> **epistemology** Relates to knowledge, to what constitutes knowledge and to the processes through which knowledge is created.

As we know, ontology relates to the nature of reality, to the study and nature of being and to our ways of being in the world. There are different understandings of the nature of reality. Positivists see the world as having one reality of which we are all a part. Social constructionists see the world as being co-constituted and socially constructed, and made up of many different realities. For the interpretivist, we each interpret the world in our own way and, through our individual and unique interpretations, we all of us construct our own realities. As there are different understandings about the nature of reality and the nature of being in the world, ontology and ontological issues are important issues in social science research.

The Value of Good Research box 'Research in the media' contains a discussion of feminism. The discussion is interesting in that it highlights the concerns that some feminists have in relation to the roles and representations of women in the film industry. Feminists operate within particular assumptions about the nature of reality and the social world. Feminism, as detailed in Table 4.2, is a philosophical framework. It is also an intellectual and political movement that seeks justice and equality for women. As you read through the discussion in the box feature, highlight the concerns expressed in relation to injustice and inequality. Examine the data presented to support the claims made of injustice and inequality. Do you understand the political argument being made? Politics, in this context, relates to power. In your reading of the box feature, which of the sexes is the more powerful? Very briefly, what do you think are the implications (if any) of that power divide for society and for the way in which society is structured?

THE VALUE OF GOOD RESEARCH

Research in the media

The film industry is a big business internationally. According to the publication *Theatrical Market Statistics*, the 2016 global box office revenue for all films released worldwide was $38.6 billion, and this is up 1 per cent on the previous year. This publication presents a lot of data on the film industry globally, and on the film industry in the USA. If you have an interest in this industry you should access the publication and read through it. This might help you develop some ideas for your research project.

The *Theatrical Markets Statistics* publication (Motion Picture Association of America) shows that in the USA and Canada, slightly more females than males went to the cinema in 2016, while ticket sales were split evenly between them.

These statistics are interesting when considered in relation to the statistics quoted on the Women & Hollywood blog (www.womenandhollywood.com). The blog details that of the top 100 grossing films of 2017, women represented only 8 per cent of directors, 10 per cent of writers, 2 per cent of cinematographers, 24 per cent of producers, and 14 per cent of editors. In addition, of the top 250 grossing films of 2017, women comprised only 3 per cent of the composers, while only five women have ever been nominated for the Oscar for Best Director and Kathryn Bigelow was the only woman ever to have won. She won in 2010.

In an article published in the newspaper *USA Today* (22.02.2018), journalist Maria Puente wrote that things are actually getting worse for women in the film industry. Quoting research undertaken by Dr Martha M. Lauzen at San Diego State University, (Lauzen, 2018), Puente wrote that men continue to dominate the cinema screen; that the number of female protagonists in the top 100 grossing films of 2017 was down 5 per cent from the year before (2016). In the research report, Lauzen noted that black females playing characters in films increased to 16 per cent in 2017, up from 14 per cent; the percentage of Latinas more than doubled to 7 per cent, up from 3 per cent; and the percentage of Asian females increased to 7 per cent from 6 per cent. The research is an annual report entitled 'It's a Man's (Celluloid) World: Portrayals of Female Characters in the 100 Top Films of 2017'. It's published each year, just before the Oscar ceremony in Hollywood. The research carried out for the study is developed using content analysis as the research methodology. In data gathering for the 2018 report, the researcher engaged in a content analysis of 2361 characters appearing in the 100 top films of 2017.

You might think about the film industry when you are trying to develop an idea for your research project. Think about the data highlighted and discussed in the paragraphs above. Think about how you might use data published and available online in your research project.

The term functionalism (see the list of philosophical frameworks in Table 4.2) relates to the way in which society is structured. Using, for example, the concept of gender, think for a moment about some of the ways in which gender impacts on and structures the social world. Critical theory, again one of the philosophical frameworks listed in Table 4.2, calls for a critical engagement with society and the way in which the structures in society privilege some groups over others. Some of the key issues in critical theory are the issues of race, gender and class. You may be able to think of ideas for a business studies research project that you might like to carry out using feminism as your philosophical framework. One example might be a project designed to study the experiences of business women working in a predominantly male environment. Can you think of ideas for a research project that you would like to carry out using critical theory as your philosophical framework? One example might be a study of power, what it is and how it is exercised, from the perspectives of male and female business managers from different ethnic and cultural backgrounds.

THE PHILOSOPHICAL UNDERPINNINGS OF RESEARCH

The epistemological positions we are concerned with are positivism, constructionism and interpretivism. Some of the philosophical frameworks commonly used in social science research are functionalism, symbolic interactionism, feminism, critical inquiry and postmodernism. Each of these represents a particular framework for viewing the social world and each represents particular ontological and epistemological standpoints. The philosophical framework within which each research project is situated evidences the world view within which the research is situated. It tells the reader something of the ontological position of the researcher and their understanding of the nature of reality in relation to the research being undertaken.

It is, of course, possible for a researcher to situate one research project within one epistemological position and another research project within another. For example, one research project might be situated within a framework of positivism, the next within a framework of constructionism. Decisions around the epistemological position used in a research project are dictated by the research being undertaken, its aim, and the kind of data required in order to properly and fully carry out and complete the research.

Table 4.2 Some philosophical frameworks

Positivism	Holds that there is one objective reality; reality is singular and separate from consciousness
Constructivism	Along with social constructivism, holds that social phenomena develop in social contexts and that individuals and groups create in part their own realities
Interpretivism	Holds that all knowledge is a matter of interpretation
Hermeneutics	Theory of interpretation and the study of the processes of interpretation
Symbolic interactionism	Holds that people derive meaning from interaction, that reality comes into being through the shared meaning that develops from human interaction
Functionalism	Within sociology, the study of the structures of society and the manner in which those structures serve societal needs
Structuralism	Holds that human culture can be understood as a system of signs, that meaning is produced and reproduced in society through systems of signs, such as different structures, e.g. economic structures, different practices and ways of doing things
Critical theory	The examination and critique of society, with a view to exposing systems of domination through a focus on values and norms
Feminism	Holds that there should be political, social, sexual and economic equality between women and men
Post-structuralism	Post-structuralism derives from a critique of structuralism
Post-modernism	Post-modernism means after modernity, after the period of modernity. In the period of modernity, which developed from the time of the Enlightenment, scientists attempted to explore, analyze and explain the world in empirical objective rational terms. Post-modernists challenge and reject the simplicity of such approaches

Table 4.2 contains brief definitions of a number of philosophical frameworks or perspectives. It is not possible to simply define complex concepts. Every discipline and every theory is made up of concepts, e.g. key ideas and keywords. However, it is useful to list some of them to give students a sense of the immensity and complexity of this area of science and thought. As you can see, the three epistemological positions of positivism, constructivism (or constructionism) and interpretivism are presented here as philosophical frameworks. Positivism is the framework within which science originally developed, and a great deal of scientific endeavour is carried out today within a framework of positivism. The epistemological positions of constructivism and interpretivism emerged from critiques of positivism which highlighted its limitations in relation to social science research. The other philosophical frameworks listed are embedded in one or other of the three epistemological positions.

It is important to think a little about these frameworks and to develop some sense of their meaning and their contribution to the ways in which we understand the social world. The list provides a starting point for an exploration of the various theoretical and philosophical perspectives on the social world. For further detail and discussion see Crotty (2005); see also the chapter, 'Competing paradigms in qualitative research' (Guba and Lincoln, 1994), in *Handbook of Qualitative Research*, available to download as a pdf document in Google Scholar.

THE PHILOSOPHICAL FRAMEWORKS

In considering the methodology and the data collection methods to be used in the research project, you must consider the kind of knowledge needed to respond to the research question or statement. Research is undertaken in order to make a contribution to knowledge; it is fundamentally concerned with the nature of knowledge and the means of knowledge creation. These are questions of epistemology. Knowledge is created within the research project through the researcher's exploration of the phenomenon under investigation in their review of literature, and by means of the methodology and the methods selected for use in the research. The research methodology and data-gathering methods must be appropriate for, and adequate for, the research project. They must 'fit' with the research project, and they must be capable of generating the knowledge required for the research. In order to answer epistemological questions, the researcher must explain and justify the methodology and methods used in the research project. Such explanations and justifications help to establish the validity of the research. In Figure 4.1 (developed from Crotty, 2005), we can see the five basic elements of research.

In developing the research project, first we state what it is that we are going to do, the research statement or question, the aim of the research. We then explain how we are going to do it and state the methodology to be used. We say, for example, that this research project is a survey, a case study, an action research project, a grounded theory study, or a phenomenological study, and so on. These are statements of methodology. Embedded in each statement of methodology are assumptions about the nature of reality (ontological assumptions) and implicit statements about the kind of knowledge that will be generated by the research (epistemological assumptions). If, for instance, we say we are going to conduct survey research, using that methodology we will produce a particular kind of knowledge (see, for example, Research in Practice box 'Carol's research project'). If we say that we are going to conduct phenomenological research, using that methodology we will produce a different kind of knowledge to the kind of knowledge produced by, for example, a survey methodology (see, for example, Research in Practice box 'Fiona's research project'). In explaining and justifying the methodological decisions made in the design of the research project, we explain and outline the theoretical perspective informing the research, the philosophical underpinnings of the research, and consequently the ontological and epistemological assumptions embedded in the research.

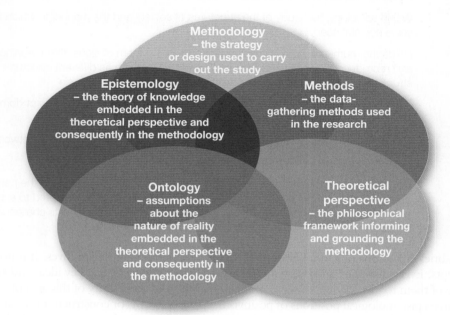

Figure 4.1 The five basic elements of research

In Carol's research project, the methodology proposed is survey and the method (the data-gathering method) is a questionnaire. There is a sample of 100 participants, all of them female managers working in management roles in SMEs. The study is designed to explore and examine their work experiences as managers. The different elements of the project 'fit' well together. The philosophical framework for the study is positivism. This is implicit in the statement of the methodology and methods. Survey research fits within a framework of positivism. Implicit within the statement of the methodology survey are ontological assumptions or assumptions about the nature of reality. As stated at the beginning of this chapter, positivists see the world as having one reality of which we are all a part. Also implicit are epistemological assumptions, about the nature of knowledge and about the kind of knowledge that will be generated by this research project. This research project will generate knowledge about the single reality that each of the participants share, the reality of their work experience as female managers within SMEs. The particular focus of the study is on representing, detailing and explaining the combined patterned experiences of all of these participants, rather than the individual experiences of any or each participant.

In Fiona's research project, detailed below, the same topic is explored using a different methodology.

In Fiona's research project, the methodology proposed is phenomenology and there are two data collection methods: in-depth interviews and a photographic method. There is a sample of 20 participants, all of them female managers and all of them working in management roles in one SME. The study is designed to explore and examine 'the lived experience' of their work experiences as managers. Phenomenological research focuses on lived experience from the perspectives of those living the experience. The elements of the project 'fit' well together. The objectives detailed for the phenomenological study are clear but less explicit than the objectives detailed for the survey (Carol's study). This is because the phenomenological researcher allows the participants in the research to explain and describe their own experiences. The phenomenological researcher does not impose any preconceived ideas that they might have on the experiences of participants. This is the case even when the researcher shares the experience with the participants, as would be the case in this instance if Fiona was, as are all the participants in her study, a female manager in the company within which the study is to be undertaken.

Although Carol and Fiona's studies focus on exploring the same topic, they are designed differently. Each project will produce different data and make its own unique contribution to knowledge. Carol's study is being developed from an epistemological position and theoretical framework of positivism. This is implicit in the statement of methodology in

RESEARCH IN PRACTICE

Carol's research project – a survey

Carol attended a guest lecture recently on the topic of women in management. She was really interested in the area and found the lecture very stimulating. She decided to situate her research project in the area of women in management. She mentioned this to her lecturer in research methods who encouraged her to develop a specific research project in this area. Carol produced the following.

This research project is a survey of the work experiences of 100 women in management in SMEs in Liverpool, UK.

The aim of the research is to examine the work experiences of 100 women in management in SMEs in Liverpool, UK.

The objectives of the study are as follows:

- To explore the work experiences of the women.
- To document the work experiences of the women.

- To highlight any particularly good or bad work experiences the women have had.
- To record what the women learned from those experiences.
- To understand why the women had those good or bad experiences.
- To provide an account of the lessons learned by the women in their work experiences.

The methodology is survey (Fowler, 2014). The data collection method is a questionnaire. The questionnaire will comprise both open and closed questions and there will be two sentence completion exercises. The sentence completion exercises will be used to allow the women who participate in the study to document a particularly good work experience and a particularly bad work experience. The use of survey methodology is justified in this research project because the sample size is relatively big, 100 women will participate in the study and the population of the study is geographically scattered, the participants are located in 100 different companies in the city of Liverpool in the UK. A survey methodology will allow for the participation in the study of such a large and scattered population. A mixture of quantitative and qualitative data is required for the study. The open and closed questions and the sentence completion exercises in the questionnaire will provide the required data.

Carol's research project. The methodology Carol is using is survey research. Survey research engages with participants in order to explore the single 'objective' reality that they all experience. Within a framework of positivism there is one objective reality, and survey research is an appropriate methodology to use in examining and exploring such experiences.

Phenomenological research engages with participants in a different way, exploring the multiple realities of their individual unique lived experiences. Instead of a large sample such as is appropriate in survey research, phenomenology works at a deeper more complex level with smaller samples. The philosophical framework for Fiona's study is symbolic interactionism, from the work of American sociologist George Herbert Mead and the Chicago School. Symbolic interactionism comes from an epistemological position of constructivism and/or interpretivism (see Table 4.2). The epistemological position is implicit in the statement of the methodology. The methodology for Fiona's research project is phenomenology. Phenomenological research fits within a framework of constructivism. Within such a study, no one reality is more valid than any other, and no one person's understanding of 'reality' is more valid than any other person's understanding. Implicit in the statement of the methodology are epistemological assumptions, assumptions about the nature of knowledge and about the kind of knowledge that will be generated by the project. This research project will generate knowledge about multiple realities, the different reality that each participant experiences in her work as a female manager within the SME.

RESEARCH IN PRACTICE

Fiona's research project – a phenomenological study

Fiona also attended the guest lecture on the topic of women in management. She was really interested in the area and found the lecture very stimulating. She too decided to situate

her research project in the area of women in management. She mentioned this to her lecturer in research methods who encouraged her to come up with a specific research project in this area. Fiona produced the following.

This research project is a phenomenological study of the work experiences of 20 women in management in an SME in Liverpool, UK. A sample of 20 is a relatively small sample. Phenomenological studies, according to Smith et al. (2009: 3) are conducted with relatively small samples. This is in order to be able to examine the individual experiences of the small sample of participants in great detail.

(Continued)

The aim of the research is to examine the work experiences of 20 women in management as explained and detailed by the women themselves. All 20 participants work in Hibernia Incorporated, an SME in Liverpool. (The name of the SME has been changed in order to preserve confidentiality.)

The objectives of the study are as follows:

● to explore with the participants their work experiences
● to facilitate the women in reflections on the lessons learned by them in their work experiences.

The methodology is phenomenological. Phenomenology is a research methodology that facilitates the study of lived experience from the perspective of those living the experience. Phenomenology in social science research developed from the work of Edmund Husserl (Moustakas, 1994), who held that although there was 'a real' world that each of us can perceive, there is also an intersubjective world that each of us experiences individually, or in our own unique way.

Three data collection methods will be used in the study. They are as follows:

1. The first data collection method to be used is in-depth interviews. The interviews will allow the researcher to explore in-depth with the women their experiences of work as managers in the SME.
2. The second data collection method will provide a photographic element to the research (Rose, 2016). Each of the participants in the study will be asked to provide a photograph to the study that illustrates for them their work experience within the company.
3. Each photograph will be accompanied by a short narrative written by the participant explaining the meaning for them of the photograph.

Taken together, these data collection methods will facilitate the participants in explaining and detailing their work experiences as women in management.

THE METHODOLOGICAL PYRAMID

In order to help with understanding these key philosophical concepts and how they fit with each other and emerge one from the other, let us now consider the **methodological pyramid** (see Figure 4.2), detailed initially in Chapter 2. In the pyramid, the fundamental philosophies support the (research) methodologies, which, in turn, support the data collection methods. Another way of saying this is that (research) methodologies emerge from the fundamental philosophies, and data collection methods emerge from (research) methodologies. See Crotty (2005) for another account of this complexity. The pyramid helps you to see how the fundamental philosophies fit with the different methodologies, and how the different data collection methods fit with the different methodologies.

methodological pyramid A model showing how the fundamental philosophies fit with the different methodologies and the different data collection methods.

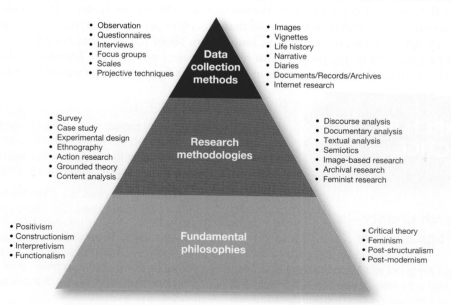

Figure 4.2 The methodological pyramid

The philosophical framework within which the research project is situated emerges during the process of developing the conceptual framework for the research project. The conceptual framework, as we know, is contained in the research statement or question, or it is indicated in the research hypotheses.

When your idea for your research project becomes focused, you can begin to make decisions about the methodology you want to work with for the project. Decisions about which methodology is most appropriate (which is the best fit) for the project are made in light of the aim of the project, what it is that the project is to accomplish, what knowledge the project is designed to provide.

If the aim of the project is to establish the fact(s) of some phenomenon, there is scope for the project to be situated within a framework of positivism. Within a framework of positivism, reality is singular, objective and apart from participants. This is quite a simple understanding of the social world. To illustrate this, let us say that you want to carry out a study of gym/fitness centre memberships among your classmates at college. You ask them whether or not they are members of a gym or fitness centre. They respond that they either are or are not members of a gym/fitness centre. There is one objective reality, there is no ambiguity, they either are or they are not members. This study could be described as positivistic. Let us say that there were 20 students and 5 were members of a gym/fitness centre and 15 were not. The 20, the 5, and the 15, are all numbers. Data in the form of numbers, in numeric format, is quantitative data. Therefore, with this research question, we have generated **quantitative data**. With a research project created and developed within a positivist framework, most of the data generated tends to be quantitative data. Quantitative data are numeric data.

> **quantitative data** Data in the form of numbers, numerical data and/or data that can be coded in numeric format; coding data in a numeric format involves representing phenomena by assigning numbers in an ordered and meaningful way.

The interpretivist and the constructivist hold that reality is unique to each individual and to the manner in which each individual, given his/her own unique set of circumstances and life experiences, constructs, experiences and interprets the world. If it is intended that the research project will explore thoughts and feelings and beliefs about the phenomenon under investigation, then the project may be developed within a framework of interpretivism or constructionism. In this case, each participant will respond to the research or engage with the research in a unique and individual way. Using the gym/fitness centre membership study again, let us suppose that now you know how many of your classmates are members of a gym/fitness centre, you decide that you would like to establish why they are members. In responding to the question of why they are members of a gym/fitness centre, each of the five who are members will give subjective answers. They will each have their own individual and unique reasons for being a member. These unique and individual responses may be quite complex, and as such complexity cannot readily or adequately be represented quantitatively, the data gathered will be qualitative data.

Each of the classmates who is a gym/fitness centre member will have a different reason for joining the centre, a different experience of being a member and a different understanding of the meaning for them of being a member. It is possible that one or two of the respondents will feel guilty about being a member of a gym/fitness centre if they pay for membership but never actually use the centre; however, the nature of, and reasons for, that guilt will be unique to each of them. One or two of the respondents might be very proud of the membership of the gym/fitness centre, and the level of fitness they maintain through their active membership. Their experience of being fit, and the meaning of that in their lives, will be unique to each individual. It may be that others simply enjoy the companionship that comes with being a member of a gym/fitness centre, but again the explanations for and descriptions of enjoying gym/fitness centre membership are likely to be different for each respondent. In any case, the responses you get to the question of why they hold membership will present you with data of a completely different order to the data received in response to the question of how many hold membership. The data are qualitative in nature. They are rich and descriptive. They are not numerical and while it might be possible to code the data numerically, this may not serve the richness, depth and complexity of the data. A simple number cannot convey the complexity of, for example, why a person joins a gym.

Quantitative and qualitative data

There are two types of data that can be collected for any research project, quantitative data and qualitative data (see Table 4.3).

Table 4.3 Quantitative and qualitative data

Quantitative data	Data in the form of numbers or data that can readily be coded numerically
Qualitative data	Data that represent feelings, thoughts, ideas, understandings, non-numeric data

Quantitative data are numerical data. For example, you might ask a participant in a research project to tell you their age and they respond to the question and answer that they are 25 years old. This is a numerical outcome and therefore it is quantitative data.

If you ask the same participant to indicate to you their gender, there are for the most part three possible answers. They will answer that they are male or they are female or they are transgender. Now you have data that are not numerical in form, but data that can readily be coded numerically. As there are, generally, three possible answers to that question on gender, the researcher can assign a code to each of the possible answers. In this case, female might be coded 1, male might be coded 2 and the trans might be coded 3. In this way, the non-numerical data have easily been converted to numerical data, female = 1, male = 2, and trans = 3. We now have numerical values for the data on gender. Positivism holds that there is one objective reality; reality is singular and separate from consciousness. For example, you either are 25 years old or you are not. There is no ambiguity. You either are female or you are not. There is, again, no ambiguity. This is the simplicity of the singular reality. There is a developing perspective that holds that gender is a continuum, rather than a category. Clearly, simple categories or simple categorization will not be useful within such a framework. This illustrates the complexity of the social world, and the complexity of social science research. It also illustrates our evolving understanding of the social world.

Qualitative data are not numerical, although, as we have seen, relatively simple and concise qualitative data can easily be coded numerically. If you have a small number of qualitative responses, it is easy to assign a numerical code to each one as we did above with the data on gender. If you have little variation in the qualitative responses that you receive and they are short and concise, it is a simple procedure to assign a numeric code to each response.

However, often qualitative data are too complex to be coded numerically and sometimes coding qualitative data numerically serves neither the data nor the research project. This is because qualitative data can lose richness, depth and complexity through numerical coding. It may be that the research project actually requires densely descriptive data. If this is the case, reducing the complexity of qualitative data to the level of a numeric code may substantially damage the research project and at the same time raise ethical issues regarding the management of data.

It is important to note that distinctions between qualitative and quantitative occur within data collection methods, at the uppermost point of the methodological pyramid.

In considering your research statement or question, you should ask yourself whether this research project fits within a framework of positivism or a framework of constructionism or interpretivism. You should consider the kind(s) of data that you will need to gather for the research project to be able to answer the research question, or in order to be able to respond to the research statement. Ask yourself whether it is likely that you will need quantitative data or qualitative data. It may be that you will need a mixture of both. If this is the case, ask yourself whether you are likely to need predominantly qualitative or predominantly quantitative data. Ask yourself where the data are to be found and how the data might best be gathered. In answering these questions, you will be able to move towards making a judgement with regard to which research methodology and data-gathering method(s) to use in order to gather the data required to adequately and properly accomplish the aim of the research.

THE USE OF THEORY IN THE GENERATION OF KNOWLEDGE

All research is about the generation of knowledge. All research, certainly all research conducted within an academic setting, is embedded in **theory**. Every academic research project emerges from a particular body of knowledge, a particular body of theory, and it in turn makes a contribution to that body of knowledge. As every research project concludes and makes its own contribution to theory, to the body of knowledge, the body of knowledge grows and this is how a discipline develops.

theory A formal, logical explanation of some events; in the context of a research project, theory is research that has already been carried out, completed and published.

Wherever within theory you decide to situate your research project, you will be entering a theoretical debate that has likely been ongoing for some time. The theoretical debate is conducted by all of the theorists (researchers) working in the field. These researchers conduct research and they publish their findings in theses, in academic journals, in conference papers and proceedings, in government reports and papers, in newspaper reports, in books and online. Through the publication of their research, researchers facilitate other theorists/researchers in an engagement with their research. Other theorists critically examine the research to establish its validity. They critique the philosophical framework within which the research is situated and the methodology used in the research. They critique the data-gathering method(s) and the data gathered. Finally, they critique the findings of the research, the conclusions the researcher drew from the research and the insights into the phenomenon under investigation presented by the researcher as a result of the research. When the validity of the research is established, the research is accepted as making a contribution to knowledge. It is in this way that, through each and every research project, theory is developed and the knowledge base expanded. This is how research is used to expand knowledge. Every research project becomes part of the knowledge base, part of 'what is known' about the particular phenomenon investigated by the research project.

THE IMPORTANCE OF THEORY IN RESEARCH

Theory is of the most fundamental importance in research. However, not all research is embedded in theory. You may even have conducted research for your workplace that did not have a theoretical base. Perhaps you examined sales graphs to establish patterns of sales, peaks and lulls in sales over periods of time. Perhaps you examined employee absentee records to establish patterns of absenteeism among particular employees or particular groups of employees, patterns of absenteeism over particular times, days of the week or days of the month, and so on.

The findings of such research are generally confined to the specific context within which the research was conducted and can make a contribution only in this very limited context. Such research cannot make a contribution to theory. It cannot go towards developing the knowledge base.

As stated earlier, all research conducted in an academic setting is embedded in theory. It emerges from a theoretical framework and, in turn, it makes a contribution to the body of theory in that field.

Concepts, the building blocks of theory

What are concepts? As we have seen in our exploration and use of the conceptual framework, the first of the frameworks in the four frameworks approach to research concepts are key ideas, keywords, key phrases, often the big words in a sentence, a paragraph, in an idea. Every discipline and every theory is made up of concepts. Marketing is a concept. We only have to hear the word marketing, and immediately all the complexity of the concept that is 'marketing' inhabits our minds. We 'know' what marketing is, what is meant by the word (or concept) 'marketing'.

The concept 'marketing' is part of everyday language within business studies. But a concept in business called 'marketing' did not always exist. The concept of 'marketing' was created and developed by theorists working in the field of sales. So the concept of 'marketing' emerged from the body of knowledge that is 'business sales'. It is part of the theory of business sales. As a concept it makes and has made a very substantial contribution to theory in that field. It has facilitated the development of countless more concepts and research projects, all of which have made their own contribution to the marketing body of knowledge. It is in this way that concepts emerge from theory through research and it is in this way that in turn, again through research, they make a contribution to theory.

The same can be said for any and every concept in every discipline that there is or ever has been in existence. Somebody somewhere had to see the pattern or activity, identify the pattern or the activity and then label it with a name. The name, through debate, came to be accepted as representing the concept. It is in this way that concepts come into being.

Concepts, as stated, are keywords or key phrases and they represent key ideas. Each concept contains a great deal of meaning. Each theory is created from different concepts and from the way in which different concepts are grouped together or aligned. This process of developing theory from concepts is not a simple linear process, but a very complex process of creation, organization, development and reflection. It is, as is all creative endeavour, one part inspiration and nine parts perspiration. Each theorist is immersed in the concepts that make up the body of knowledge within which they are working. Through their active engagement with theories and concepts, they try to develop the body of knowledge, to create new concepts, to further develop old concepts and to move the discipline along.

The uses of theory in research

The conceptual framework for every research project is contained in the research question or statement or in the stated hypotheses created and developed for that research project. The conceptual framework contains all of the key concepts in the research project.

There will be many other key concepts that are relevant to the research project and many too of keen interest to the researcher, but the fact that they are excluded from the conceptual framework means that they are not part of the research project, and so they are of no concern to the researcher in their engagement with this particular project. As it develops, the research project will become very complex and it is not possible or desirable to engage with concepts and bodies of knowledge that are not part of the conceptual framework created and developed for the project.

The theoretical framework is the framework created by the researcher from theory relevant to the research project. It is designed by the researcher to support the research and it emerges from the conceptual framework. The theoretical framework for every research project is contained in the literature review. The key concepts in the conceptual framework guide and direct the researcher, through the provision of keywords for keyword searches, in terms of the literature that needs to be sourced for the literature review for the research project. The key concepts in the conceptual framework also provide the researcher with the key concepts to be used in structuring the literature review chapter, providing guidance and direction for the subheadings for the main subsections in the literature review. In this way, the theoretical framework emerges from the conceptual framework, using the four frameworks approach (see Figure 4.3), to the research project.

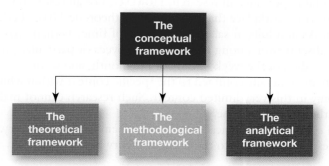

Figure 4.3 The four frameworks approach to the research project

THE VALUE OF GOOD RESEARCH

Focus on image-based research

Image-based research refers to the use of images in research. The images can be photographs or pictures, drawings, cartoons, maps, charts, graphs; they can be images in advertising or other marketing or business material. In fact, any kind of image can be used in image-based research.

In image-based research, the image or images used in the research form the data or part of the data for the research project. Sometimes images are used as data in the research project in conjunction with data from one or more other sources, for example, data from observations, interviews and/or from questionnaires.

The key issue with data from images, as with data from other sources, is the issue of validity. This is the degree to which the data are representative of the phenomenon under investigation.

In the article examined here (Sun, 2017) 'Exploiting femininity in a patriarchal postfeminist way: A visual content analysis of Macau's tourism ads', *International Journal of Communication*, 11, 2624–2646), the author situated her research within a feminist philosophical framework and she conducted the study using image-based research. She used a visual content analysis approach to data analysis. According to the abstract, the study was undertaken:

- To examine gender images in the tourism print ads of Macau.
- To expand understanding of gender roles and relations involved in the Asian tourism industry, especially that of the Greater China Region.

The researcher collected a sample of 439 advertisements published in tourist brochures and leaflets, and distributed in 2015 and 2016. From this sample she selected 320 pictures for analysis which fit with her coding scheme.

Sun tells us her findings indicate that in the advertisements women were closely associated with shopping, decoration and hospitality roles. She notes that the creators of the advertisements relied heavily on stereotypical associations between femininity and glamorous, emotional and caring labour. She concludes that the ads comply with the patriarchal construction of femininity. She states that her findings indicate that patriarchal discourse is still embedded in advertising.

Sun's findings indicate that there is a need for the advertising industry to adjust its communication practices to the changing roles of women in society.

The student project (see Research in Practice box – Ian's research project) proposes a research project using image-based research. Based on your reading of Sun's project and Ian's project, can you think of any ideas for research projects using image-based research?

Several methodologists have published good books on visual methods and image-based research, among them Gillian Rose, Sarah Pink, Marcus Banks and Jon Prosser. You will find copies of their books in your university/college library.

HOW TO CREATE A THEORETICAL FRAMEWORK: THE SECOND OF THE FOUR FRAMEWORKS

In practice, the work of creating a theoretical framework starts the moment the researcher begins to think about creating and developing a research project. Every research project, as has been stated, emerges from a body of knowledge and must make a contribution to knowledge. It is not possible to know what contribution your research project might or could make unless you know what is already known in that body of knowledge.

You must enter the debate within that body of knowledge where that debate is currently. If you do not do this, you may end up conducting research on a topic that has already been well researched, or you may end up conducting research on a topic that is out of date, perhaps a topic which the debate in the field has already dealt with and from which it has already moved on. It is for all of these reasons that you begin reading around a topic as soon as you have an idea for your research project.

You begin reading to develop a sense of what it is that the researchers working in this field know, and what it is that the researchers working in this field would like to know. This will indicate where you can make a useful contribution to research in this field.

We learned in Chapter 2 how to create a conceptual framework for the research project. The conceptual framework contains all of the key concepts in the research project. Each of the key concepts then guides you in terms of your reading for your theoretical framework. For example, if the research question, statement or hypothesis that you have created and developed for your research project contains the key concept 'marketing', then your reading will, obviously, be in the area of marketing.

Conceptual frameworks for research projects contain several key concepts. The researcher decides on the way in which the key concepts are put together in the conceptual framework (the research statement). The researcher aligns the key concepts in such a way as to provide the most apt, the most appropriate, conceptual framework for the research project.

Read the detail given on Kate's research project. Examine the research statement which contains the conceptual framework for the research project. There are several key concepts in this conceptual framework. One of the key concepts is not of relevance to the theoretical framework: this is the key concept 'case study'. The words 'case study' tell the reader what methodology was used in the research. This is relevant to the methodological framework, the third of the frameworks within the four frameworks. We will discuss that framework in later chapters of this book.

RESEARCH IN PRACTICE

Kate's research project

This is an example of a research statement (a conceptual framework). This conceptual framework was developed for Kate for her research project. Kate works in the human resources department of the company, Greene's Biscuits Ltd, which is an SME in the town of Lillington. Kate is interested in examining in detail the training and development provision made in the company for all employees. Kate's research statement is as follows:

This research project is a case study of the training and development provision for the employees of Greene's Biscuits Ltd, Lillington.

The key concepts that are of relevance to the theoretical framework are the concept of training, the concept of development, the concept of training and development, and the concept of training and development for employees. Another key concept of relevance is the concept of an SME. The business within which the research takes place is Greene's Biscuits Ltd, and Greene's Biscuits is an SME. So the theoretical framework that needs to be developed is one around training and development for the employees of SMEs.

The keywords for searches for literature for the theoretical framework for Kate's project are: training and development; training and development for employees; training and development for employees of SMEs. As you can see, each strand of the theoretical framework comes from the conceptual framework. In this way, the conceptual framework provides a guide in the search for literature for the theoretical framework. The literature review is usually Chapter 2 of the thesis or report of the research. Tables 4.4, 4.5 and 4.6 contain a sample structure for the literature review (with different word counts) for the conceptual framework of Kate's research project.

Table 4.4 Example of structure for the literature review (based on 5000-word count)

First section 300 words – in two paragraphs	Introduction (a brief introduction to the chapter and the contents of the chapter)
Second section (first subheading) 1400 words – in three paragraphs	Training and development
Third section (second subheading) 1400 words – in three paragraphs	Training and development for employees
Fourth section (third subheading) 1400 words – in three paragraphs	Training and development for employees of SMEs
Fifth section 500 words – in two paragraphs	Summary (a brief summary of the main points and the main argument developed throughout the chapter)

Table 4.5 Example of structure for the literature review (based on 3000-word count)

First section 200 words – in one paragraph	Introduction (a brief introduction to the chapter and the contents of the chapter)
Second section (first subheading) 800 words – in three paragraphs	Training and development
Third section (second subheading) 800 words – in three paragraphs	Training and development for employees
Fourth section (third subheading) 800 words – in three paragraphs	Training and development for employees of SMEs
Fifth section 400 words – in two paragraphs	Summary (a brief summary of the main points and the main argument developed throughout the chapter)

Table 4.6 Example of structure for the literature review (based on 1000-word count)

First section 100 words – in one paragraph	Introduction (a brief introduction to the chapter and the contents of the chapter)
Second section (first subheading) 250 words – in two paragraphs	Training and development
Third section (second subheading) 250 words – in two paragraphs	Training and development for employees
Fourth section (third subheading) 250 words – in two paragraphs	Training and development for employees of SMEs
Fifth section 150 words – in one paragraph	Summary (a brief summary of the main points and the main argument developed throughout the chapter)

The theoretical framework or literature review contains a discussion, or a review, of the literature in the area of the research project. Each theoretical framework is unique because each is created and designed to support an individual research project. The theoretical framework provides theoretical scaffolding for the research project. The reading that the researcher undertakes for the literature review is focused on the areas indicated by the key concepts in the conceptual framework.

In undertaking the literature review:

1. the researcher first sources the literature
2. then s/he downloads and saves the literature
3. then s/he reads the literature
4. finally, s/he begins to construct from the literature s/he has read the theoretical framework for the research project. The researcher writes the literature review.

As we have stated, the researcher creates the theoretical framework:

- to provide the theoretical framework for the research project
- to establish their expertise in this area
- to detail the current state of knowledge in the area
- to highlight what is known and to highlight any gaps in what is known
- to detail the theory from which the research has emerged
- to outline the theory to which the research will ultimately contribute.

It is important to remember that your conceptual framework is not written in stone. Indeed, practiced researchers often change and rearrange their conceptual frameworks a great deal before finally deciding on the format. It can happen that you, through your reading and reflection, come up with a new key concept that must be included in the theoretical framework. If this is the case then you simply change your conceptual framework so that it encompasses this new concept. Remember that each new or additional concept adds to the complexity of your research project. Unnecessary complexity at the start is inadvisable and undesirable. It is best to keep the conceptual framework simple. As explained earlier, the project will become complex as it develops.

You will see as you read on through this textbook that even the most practiced researchers often begin with very simple ideas for their research projects, and that these initially very simple research ideas become extremely complex research projects, through the scholarship of the researchers and their work on the research project.

The theoretical framework is considered in more detail later in Chapter 6, where more examples are provided.

RESEARCH IN PRACTICE

Ian's research project – an image-based research project

Ian is undertaking an undergraduate degree in business studies. He is spending the summer working in New York, returning to the summer job he held last year working as a business intern in Bloomberg Tower in mid-town Manhattan. He is going to undertake his research for his degree there. He was so impressed by the building housing the headquarters of Bloomberg enterprises in New York City that he decided to focus his research on the building and on how the building itself facilitates Bloomberg's business agenda. He has been given permission to conduct his research in Bloomberg Tower by his manager there and he is now in dialogue with his thesis supervisor in relation to the research project he is proposing.

Ian is particularly keen to focus his research on demonstrating how, through innovative design, the Bloomberg building, Bloomberg Tower, fosters innovation, team building and knowledge spillovers.

He has decided to use image-based research as his methodology. He intends to photograph the structure and organization of the interior of the building. In addition, he has been given access to and permission to copy and use in his research project the architects' designs for the organization and structure of the interior of the building. He intends to use these resources as the data for his project. He is particularly keen to focus on actually demonstrating how, in practice, the interior organization and structure of the building operates as a facilitator of the work of the company.

His research statement is as follows: this research project is a study of the Bloomberg headquarters building, Bloomberg Tower, at 731 Lexington Avenue, New York City, and of the manner in which the interior design of the building facilitates and fosters innovation, team building and knowledge exchange between individuals working within the company.

The literature review for the project will draw on literature in the areas of organizational structure and the impact of organizational structure on innovation, team building and communication.

The methodology will be image-based research.

The data will comprise of photographs of the interior of the building taken by the researcher, and designs for the building drawn up by the architects who designed the building.

The rationale for the study is the unique perspective the study will provide on the manner in which organizational design can impact on and foster innovation, team building and knowledge spillovers in a major company.

Ian's thesis supervisor has provisionally approved the study and has asked Ian to develop a full research proposal for the study.

GENERATING THEORY FROM RESEARCH

The literature that you review gives you material that helps you develop the questions you ask in the data-gathering phase of the research. This is one of the reasons why you read the literature and why you must have a good understanding of the literature before you develop your research question, statement or hypothesis.

The questions you ask in the data-gathering phase of the research emerge from your research question, statement or hypothesis. At all stages through the research, you should be clear as to the relevance of what you are doing to the aim of your research.

When you get to the stage of data analysis, you begin the process of theorizing your data. The process of **theorizing data** is the process of establishing how your data fit with theory laid out in your field. You do this by establishing where and how your data support, and/or contradict, the theory laid out in your literature review. To theorize your research, you knit your findings into the findings of published research. This published research is laid out in the literature review created by the researcher for the research project. We can see this work of theorizing findings in practice in this chapter, when we study the work of Kidwell, Eddleston and Kellerman (2018) in a Real World Research box feature.

theorizing data Explaining and demonstrating how the research findings and conclusions of the research project support or contradict the current research as detailed in the literature review.

Sometimes students worry if their findings contradict the findings of other theorists. However, as long as your research was thorough and valid, your findings stand with the findings of other researchers. There can be many reasons why your research would contradict the research of others. It might be that you are working in a different temporal framework (at a different time), in a different geographic area or in a different cultural setting. It might be that the organization or entity that you are studying is unique in some way and this might account for the differences you are finding in your study. It might simply be that things have changed since the other studies were conducted and those changes account for the differences that you are uncovering in your research. It is important too to be alert to those aspects and elements of your research project, such as the context for the research and the population or sample of the study, which make your research different from that already been carried out. It would be useful to record these insights as they come to you in your research diary. You may be able to include these in the written account of the research, the thesis or research report. If included, they will add depth and complexity to your study. In any case, the important thing is to conduct the research properly and to report your findings honestly and thoroughly.

RESEARCH, THEORY AND KNOWLEDGE

Every research project is designed to make a contribution to knowledge. The researcher creates the conceptual framework for the research project and from that develops the theoretical framework for the research project. The conceptual and theoretical frameworks guide the researcher in the development of the methodological framework for the research project. The conceptual framework, the theoretical framework and the methodological framework guide the researcher in the data-gathering phase of the research in terms of the areas to be explored and/or the questions to be asked. Data are gathered and then analyzed and findings and conclusions are drawn and theorized. Data are theorized by knitting the findings and conclusions drawn from data analysis into the research detailed in the literature review. What results from this process of theorization is a new theory or a new extension of existing theory. This then is presented in the final chapter of the thesis or report of the research (see Figure 4.4, which presents a model of this cycle of research emerging from theory and in turn making a contribution to theory and to knowledge).

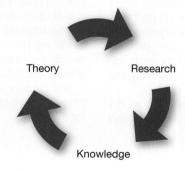

Figure 4.4 The cycle of theory, research and knowledge

REAL WORLD RESEARCH

How theory influences research

This article (Bullough, Moore and Kalafatoglu, 2017, 'Research on women in international business and management: then, now, and next', *Cross Cultural & Strategic Management*, 24:2, 211–230) is a literature review and does not go on to gather and analyze data for the research project. Researchers do this in order to develop their knowledge or

expertise on a topic or on a field of knowledge, and to establish what is known about the topic, and to establish any gaps in knowledge, gaps in what is known about the topic.

This article is worth reading because it is an example of a very good literature review. It is an extensive review of the literature in this field.

The authors explain that this is the first paper to review the body of work on cross-cultural research on women in international business and management. They hope that this literature review will become 'a useful launch pad' for other researchers working on this topic.

You should read this journal article and explore in it the manner in which these authors highlight the need for further research on the topic. Do you think that, on reading this journal article, you might develop an idea for a research

(Continued)

project on this topic? The authors state in the journal article the importance of new cross-cultural scholarship on gender. They provide an overview of four streams of cross-cultural research on gender, and they explain that while these areas of cross-cultural research on gender have been substantially developed, there is still a lot of work to be done. In other words, there are gaps in knowledge in this field.

The article is worth reading too for an exploration of the way in which theory influences research, in this context, in relation to the issue of women in international business and management.

The review also has a very substantial list of references.

As an exercise, critique the list of references. Read the list of references and examine it. How extensive are the references in it? Are the references up-to-date? What period of time do the references cover? Where do the references come from? Are they from books, from journal articles? Are

there any web references? What would you say about the quality overall of the references? What would you say about the quality overall of the literature review? Can you see how a good extensive bibliography like this is very useful for other researchers working on this area of research?

Focus on the writing in the article. Is it clear and to the point? Take note of the structure of the article, the introduction, the body of the work, each subsection and the final conclusions. Take note of the paragraph structure in the article.

The authors used the Harvard referencing method in the article. If you are required to use this referencing method in your research, you might use this article as a guide.

The bibliography is an example of a good and useful, properly compiled bibliography. You could use the list of references as a guide to help you develop an understanding of how you should present your list of references in your own research project.

REAL WORLD RESEARCH

How theory influences research

In the summary of the journal article presented here (Kidwell, Eddleston and Kellermann, 2018, 'Learning bad habits across generations: How negative imprints affect human resource management in the family firm', *Human Resource Management Review*, *28*: 5–17), it can be seen that the authors of the article clearly situate their research within a body of knowledge, a particular area of HRM theory, organizational learning, and they clearly outline the contribution that their research makes to the body of knowledge.

Source the original article online and read it through. Pay close attention to the way in which the authors construct, write and present their theoretical framework. Pay close attention too to the way in which they write and present the final sections of the article, the subsections labelled 'Discussion', 'Implications for Practice', and finally, 'Implications for theory and future research'. Examine the way in which the authors knit their research into the body of knowledge in this area. This is the process of theorizing research, and it is the way in which research makes a contribution to knowledge.

In the Abstract, the authors briefly outline and explain the study.

Abstract

Organizational learning can be a key shared value that perpetuates the family's and the family firm's culture across generations. Imprinting theory helps to explain the impact that lessons learned and transmitted can have on the development of human resources in the family firm. However, the results of imprinting may not necessarily be positive, particularly when imprinting manifests itself in negative processes and expectations. Whereas imprinting and organizational learning are often associated with a "positive halo effect", they have the potential to result in negative behaviours and deleterious firm-level outcomes. Employing imprinting theory as a framework, we highlight the potential dark side of imprinting within the family firm context and how it can damage human resource efforts and threaten company performance and firm survival. Finally, we suggest how bad habits may be broken and replaced with more effective routines so as to ensure the family firm's continuity and success.

The authors detail in the introduction to the article some of the theory on human resource management in the family firm. They explain the imprinting process. They present a model detailing the dark side of imprinting in the family firm. They discuss imprinting and learning culture in the family firm. They talk about re - imprinting, the breaking of bad habits in the family firm.

Throughout the journal article the authors explicitly highlight and explain the contribution to theory that their research makes. You will learn a lot from reading this journal article and examining the way in which it is structured, written and presented. In addition, the journal article may give you ideas for your research project.

CASE STUDY

The research diary

Nadin and Cassell (2006) in their journal article write about the use of a research diary as a tool for reflexive practice, drawing on reflections from management research. This is a useful article in that it demonstrates some of the utility of the research diary in practice. The focus of the article is on the use of the research diary as an aid to reflexivity in management research.

In the article, the authors state that while there have been calls for reflexivity in management research, there has been very little written on how to 'do' reflexivity in practice.

They define reflexivity as involving 'reflecting on the way in which research is carried out and understanding how the process of doing research shapes its outcomes'.

The authors go on to state 'whilst more commonly associated with the disciplines of sociology and ethnography, reflexivity is emerging as a key issue for qualitative researchers within management'.

Drawing on empirical work in the field of small businesses, the authors 'outline a practical example of a research diary in use, and (they) analyze the extent to which it enables reflexivity in practice in the research process'.

The research diary 'was simply an A5 lined notebook'. The entries were made by hand. Each time a firm was visited and data gathered, a new entry was made. This was done as soon as possible after each visit. Reflections on the research, the process and the experience of gathering data were recorded in the diary.

Some of the items recorded were as follows:

- methodological issues
- supplementary thoughts and insights to the interview data gathered
- ideas and thoughts on general themes as they emerged in the data analysis process
- non-verbal aspects of the social encounter (the interview/the site visit)
- thoughts and insights into the management style; anything that the researcher found strange – anomalies or contradictions
- the researcher's reactions to the encounter (how she felt/responded)
- the researcher's engagement with the encounter (researcher's own assumptions, values and beliefs, and how they impact on the research)
- concerns that might, as the authors state, otherwise have been lost or simply not considered.

In addition to all of this, the research diary acted for the researchers as a useful organizational aid to help keep track of the research process as a whole.

In their conclusions, the author's state: 'the use of a research diary was grounded in the epistemological position of social constructionism and the need for reflexivity in research'.

Question: Can you briefly explain the meaning of the concluding statement outlined above?

END OF CHAPTER QUESTIONS

1 What is meant by the term philosophical framework in relation to social research?

2 Name and briefly explain three philosophical frameworks used in social research.

3 What is quantitative data?

4 What is qualitative data?

5 Give an example of how simple and concise qualitative data can be coded numerically.

6 Explain why the numerical coding of qualitative data can be inappropriate.

7 Explain the limits of research developed without a theoretical framework.

8 Explain what is meant by the statement 'concepts are the building blocks of theory'.

9 Briefly explain the process of developing theory, as detailed in this chapter.

10 Explain why it is essential to engage with the literature before making decisions regarding the focus of the research project.

REFERENCES

Bullough, A., Moore, F. and Kalafatoglu, T. (2017) 'Research on women in international business and management: then, now, and next', *Cross Cultural & Strategic Management*, *24*(2): 211–230.

Crotty, M. (2005) *The Foundations of Social Research*, London: Sage.

Fowler, F.J. (2014) *Survey Research Methods*, Thousand Oaks, CA: Sage.

Guba, E.G. and Lincoln, Y.S. (1994) 'Competing paradigms in qualitative research', in Denzin N. and Lincoln Y. (eds), *Handbook of Qualitative Research*, Thousand Oaks, CA: Sage.

Kidwell, R.E., Eddleston, K.A. and Kellermann, F.W. (2018) 'Learning bad habits across generations: How negative imprints affect human resource management in the family firm', *Human Resource Management Review*, *28*: 5–17.

Lauzen, M.M. (2018), 'It's a Man's (Celluloid) World: Portrayals of Female Characters in the 100 Top Films of 2017', womenintvfilm.sdsu.edu/wp-content/uploads/2018/02/2017_Its_a_Mans_Celluloid_World_Report_2.pdf (Accessed 01.03.2018).

Motion Picture Association of America (2017) 'Theatrical Market Statistics 2016', www.mpaa.org/wp-content/uploads/2017/03/MPAA-Theatrical-Market-Statistics-2016_Final.pdf (Accessed 01.03.2018).

Moustakas, C.E. (1994) *Phenomenological Research Methods*, Thousand Oaks, CA: Sage.

Nadin, S. and Cassell, C. (2006) 'The use of a research diary as a tool for reflexive practice: some reflections from management research', *Qualitative Research in Accounting and Management*, *4*(4): 208–217.

Puente, M. (2018) 'Women in film: Bad news all over with bright spots for women of color, annual study shows', *USA Today*, 28.02.2018, www.usatoday.com/story/life/2018/02/22/women-film-bad-news-overall-bright-spots-women-color-annual-study-shows/360242002 (Accessed 01.03.2018).

Rose, G. (2016) *Visual Methodologies: An Introduction to Researching with Visual Materials*, London and Thousand Oaks, CA: Sage.

Smith, J.A., Flowers, P. and Larkin, M. (2009) *Interpretative Phenomenological Analysis*, London: Sage.

Sun, Z. (2017) 'Exploiting femininity in a patriarchal postfeminist way: A visual content analysis of Macau's tourism ads', *International Journal of Communication*, *11*, 2624–46.

Women and Hollywood, blog.womenandhollywood.com (Accessed 02.03.2018).

RECOMMENDED READING

Banks, M. (2007) *Using Visual Data in Qualitative Research*, London: Sage.

Banks, M. and Zeitlyn, D. (2015) *Visual Methods in Social Research*, London, California, New Delhi, Singapore: Sage.

Creswell, J. and Creswell, J.D. (2018) *Research Design: Qualitative, Quantitative and Mixed Methods Approaches*, Thousand Oaks, CA: Sage.

Denscombe, M. (2010) *The Good Research Guide: For Small Scale Social Research Projects*, Maidenhead: Open University Press.

Denscombe, M. (2017) *The Good Research Guide: For Small-scale Social Research Projects* (6th edn), Milton Keynes: Open University Press.

Jankowicz, A.D. (2004) *Business Research Projects* (4th edn), London: Cengage.

Kent, R. (2006) *Marketing Research: Approaches, Methods and Applications in Europe*, London: Cengage.

Lee, N. and Lings, I. (2008) *Doing Business Research: A Guide to Theory and Practice*, London: Sage.

Neuman, W.L. (2014) *Social Research Methods: Qualitative and Quantitative Approaches* (7th edn), Essex, England: Pearson Education Ltd.

Pink, S. (2012) *Advances in Visual Methodology*, London: Sage.

Prosser, J. (ed.) (2003) *Image-based Research: A Sourcebook for Qualitative Researchers*, London: Routledge Falmer.

CHAPTER 5
THE ROLE OF THEORY

LEARNING OBJECTIVES

At the end of this chapter, the student should be able to:

- Define the meaning of theory.
- Understand the role of theory.
- Understand the terms concepts, propositions, variables and hypotheses.
- Discuss how theories are developed.
- Draw on theory and develop theory in a research project.

RESEARCH SKILLS

At the end of this chapter, the student should, using the exercises on Cengage Brain, be able to:

- Explain the key concepts of sample research projects.
- Outline an appropriate theoretical framework for a given project.
- Critique a proposed theoretical framework.
- Outline and explain the contribution to theory of a given research project.

RESEARCH IN PRACTICE

Theory and practice

What if you went home tonight, turned on the light switch and nothing happened? Most of us would immediately start seeking a logical explanation: 'Is the bulb burnt out?', 'Did my housemate forget to pay the electric bill?', 'Is the electricity out?', 'Did a fuse blow?' These are common thoughts that would race through our minds. The order would probably depend on our past experience and we would try to determine the cause through a logical thought sequence. Attribution theory is one framework that helps us explain the world and determine the cause of an event (the light bulb not working) or behaviour (why my housemate is annoyed with me). Simply put, this theory helps us make sense of events by providing a systematic method to assess and evaluate why things occur. Attribution theory is just one of many theoretical models that are useful to business researchers.

INTRODUCTION

All science is concerned with the expansion of knowledge and the search for truth. Theory building is the means by which researchers hope to achieve this purpose.

Students sometimes think their classes or course material are 'too theoretical' or lacking 'practical application'. However, this should certainly not be the case. Theories are simply generalizations that help us better understand reality.

Furthermore, theories allow us to understand the logic behind things we observe. If a theory does not hold true in practice, then that theory holds no value. This chapter will provide a fundamental knowledge of theory, theory development and some terminology regarding theory necessary for business researchers.

What is a theory? A theory consists of a coherent set of general propositions that offer an explanation of some phenomena by describing the way other things correspond to these phenomena. A theory is a formal, testable explanation of some events that includes explanations of how things relate to one another. A simpler way to think of a theory is to consider it a model of reality, a simplification that helps us better understand the logic and relationships among different factors.

THE RESEARCH PROCESS

In this chapter, the focus is on understanding theory and the role of theory in research. Every research project is supported by a theoretical framework. The theoretical framework is the second framework in the four frameworks approach. In the research project, the theoretical framework is contained in the literature review. The literature review is generally the second chapter in the thesis or the report of the research. The material for the literature review comes from theory; that is, research that has already been carried out and published. This published research is to be found in journal articles, in books, in reports of conference proceedings, in government reports and in the reports of NGOs.

The researcher searches for literature relevant to his or her research project. This search is conducted using keywords. The keywords used are the key concepts in the research project. The key concepts for the research project are contained in the conceptual framework for the research project.

It is in this way that the conceptual framework for the research project, which is contained in the research statement or question or in the research hypothesis, guides and directs the search for literature for the literature review or the search for theory for the theoretical framework.

THE VALUE OF GOOD RESEARCH

Research in the media

A 2014 study funded partly by NASA's Goddard Space Flight Center looked into the likelihood of a collapse of the current global industrial civilization. This study argued that advanced empires (such as the Roman, Gupta and Mesopotamian Empires) had fallen, often causing centuries of disruption to civilizations, and that such a collapse of civilization would not be unthinkable in the future.

The research team, led by mathematician Safa Motesharrei, investigated the factors that had caused the historical collapses and they determined that the primary reasons were: population, climate, water, agriculture and energy (all of which are pressing culture and environmental issues today).

The study explored several scenarios to see how our civilization could collapse. The key conclusion was that there must be reductions in economic inequality, resource consumption (or a change to renewable resource consumption) and population growth.

Does this research give you any thoughts and/or ideas in relation to your own research? You might, for instance, consider conducting research on the perceptions of your colleagues to global warming, or perhaps on any steps taken by your colleagues to contribute to reversing the effects of global warming. You might then also think about examining the consequences for businesses of these perceptions and actions.

UNDERSTANDING THEORY

You are probably already familiar with many business theories. For example, one of the most basic theories in the business world is the theory of supply and demand commonly discussed in economics classes. The differing amount of a product or service that a producer is willing to provide at different prices is termed supply. The quantity of the good or service that customers are willing to purchase at differing prices is termed demand. The law of demand states that demand for a product or service will decrease as price increases. While we accept this as common knowledge today, this is actually a theory largely attributed to Alfred Marshall, who recognized that customers played a role in the determination of prices, rather than simply relying on the classical approach of determining prices solely on costs.

A theory can be built through a process of reviewing previous findings of similar studies, through simple logical deduction and/or thorough knowledge of applicable theoretical areas. For example, if a web designer is trying to decide what colour background is most effective in increasing online sales, they may first consult previous studies examining the effects of colour on package design and retail store design. They may also find theories that deal with the wavelength of different colours, affective response to colours, or those that explain retail atmospherics. This may lead to the conclusion that blue is the most effective background colour for a website (Babin *et al.*, 2003).

Research concepts, constructs, propositions, variables and hypotheses

Theory development is essentially a process of describing phenomena at increasingly higher levels of abstraction. In other words, as business researchers, we need to be able to think of things in a very abstract manner, but eventually link these abstract concepts to observable reality. To understand theory and the business research process, it will be useful to know different terminology and how these terms relate to each other.

Research concepts and constructs

A **concept** or **construct** is a generalized idea about a class of objects, attributes, occurrences or processes that has been given a name. If you, as an organizational theorist, were to describe phenomena such as supervisory behaviour or risk aversion, you would categorize empirical events or real things into concepts. Concepts, as explained previously, are the building blocks of theory. In organizational theory, leadership, productivity and morale are concepts. In the theory of finance, gross national product, risk aversion and inflation are frequently used concepts. Accounting concepts include assets, liabilities and depreciation. In marketing, customer satisfaction, market share and loyalty are important concepts.

> **concept (or construct)** A generalized idea about a class of objects that has been given a name; an abstraction of reality that is the basic unit for theory development. Every discipline and theory is made up of concepts, e.g. key ideas, keywords, key phrases.

REAL WORLD RESEARCH

How theory influences research

Let us consider the goals of theory. Suppose a researcher investigating business phenomena wants to know what caused the recent global financial crisis. Another person wants to know if organizational structure influences leadership style. Both of these individuals want to gain a better understanding of the environment and they want to be able to predict behaviour; to be able to say that if we take a particular course of action we can expect a specific outcome to occur. These two issues – understanding and predicting – are the two purposes of theory (Dubin, 1969). Accomplishing the first goal allows the theorist to gain an understanding of the relationship among various phenomena. For example, a financial advisor may believe, or theorize, that older investors tend to be more interested in investment income than younger investors. This theory, once verified, would then allow this advisor to predict the importance of expected dividend yield based on the age of the customer. Thus a theory enables us to predict the behaviour or characteristics of one phenomenon from the knowledge of another phenomenon. The value of understanding and anticipating future conditions in the environment or in an organization is obvious.

Concepts abstract reality. That is, concepts express in one word or in a few words events or objects or experiences. Concepts, however, may vary in degree of abstraction. For example, the concept of an asset is an abstract term that may, in the concrete world of reality, refer to a wide variety of things, from, for example, a bicycle in a cycle courier depot to a major department store in a chain of department stores. The abstraction ladder in Figure 5.1 indicates that it is possible to discuss concepts at various levels of abstraction. Moving up the **ladder of abstraction**, the basic concept becomes more general, wider in scope and less amenable to measurement.

> **ladder of abstraction** Organization of concepts in sequence from the most concrete and individual to the most general.

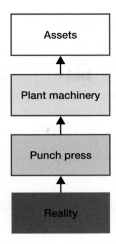

Figure 5.1 A ladder of abstraction for concepts

The basic or scientific business researcher operates at two levels: on the **abstract level** of concepts (and propositions) and on the **empirical level** of data. At the empirical level, we 'experience' reality – that is, we observe, measure, or manipulate objects or events. For example, we commonly use the term 'job performance', but this is an abstract term that can mean different things to different people or in different situations. To move to the empirical level, we must more clearly define this concept and identify actual measures that we can use to assess, measure and represent job performance as shown in Figure 5.2.

> **abstract level** In theory development, the level of knowledge expressing a concept that exists only as an idea, or a quality, apart from an object.
>
> **empirical level** Level of knowledge that is verifiable by experience or observation.

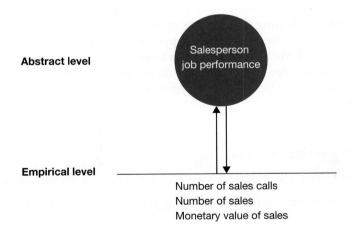

Figure 5.2 Concepts are abstractions of reality

If an organizational researcher says, 'Older workers prefer different rewards than younger workers', two concepts – age of worker and reward preference – are the subjects of this research statement. If the researcher wishes to test this relationship, Jason, age 25, Angela, age 42, and Edward, age 62 – along with other workers – may be questioned about their preferences for salary, retirement plans, intrinsic job satisfaction, and so forth. Recording their ages and assessing their reward preferences are activities that occur at the empirical level.

In the end, researchers are concerned with the observable world, or what we shall loosely term reality. Theorists translate their conceptualization of reality into abstract ideas. Thus, theory deals with abstraction. Things are not the essence of theory; ideas are (Bartels, 1970). Concepts in isolation are not theories. To construct a theory, we must explain how concepts relate to other concepts.

Research propositions and hypotheses

As we just mentioned, concepts are the basic units of theory development. However, theories require an understanding of the relationship among concepts. Thus, once the concepts of interest have been identified, a researcher is interested in the relationship among these concepts. **Propositions** are statements concerned with the relationships among concepts. A proposition explains the logical linkage among certain concepts by asserting a universal connection between concepts. For example, we might propose that treating our employees better will make them more loyal employees. There is certainly a logical link between managerial actions and employee reactions, but it is quite general and not really testable in its current form.

> **propositions** Statements explaining the logical linkage among certain concepts by asserting a universal connection between concepts.

A hypothesis is a formal statement explaining an outcome. In its simplest form, a hypothesis is a guess. A sales manager may hypothesize that the salespeople who are highest in product knowledge will be the most productive. An advertising manager may hypothesize that if consumers' attitudes towards a product change in a positive direction, there will be an increase in consumption of the product. A human resource manager may hypothesize that job candidates with certain degrees will be more successful employees.

A hypothesis is a proposition that is empirically testable. In other words, when one states a hypothesis, it should be written in a manner that can be supported or shown to be wrong through an empirical test. For example, using the colour of the background for a website discussed previously, the researcher may use theoretical reasoning to develop the following hypothesis:

> *H1: A website with a blue background will generate more sales than an otherwise identical website with a red background.*

We often apply statistics to data to empirically test hypotheses. **Empirical testing** means that something has been examined against reality using data. The following abstract proposition, 'Treating our employees better will make them more loyal employees' may be tested empirically with a hypothesis. Figure 5.3 shows that the hypothesis, 'Increasing retirement benefits will reduce intention to leave the organization' is an empirical counterpart of this proposition. Retirement benefits and intention to leave are **variables**, reflecting the concepts of employee treatment and employee loyalty. When the data are consistent with a hypothesis, we say the hypothesis is supported. When the data are inconsistent with a hypothesis, we say the hypothesis is not supported. We are often tempted to say that we prove a hypothesis when the data conforms to the prediction, but this is not really true. Because our result is based on statistics, there is always the possibility that our conclusion is wrong. At times we can be very, very confident in our conclusion, but from an absolute perspective, statistics cannot prove a hypothesis is true.

> **empirical testing** Examining a reality using data.
>
> **variable** A characteristic with more than one value; anything that may assume different values.
>
> **operationalizing** The process of identifying the actual measurement scales to assess the variables of interest.

Because variables are at the empirical level, variables can be measured. In this case, retirement benefits might be measured quite easily and precisely (e.g. the actual percentage change in matching retirement funds), while the construct of intention to leave would be more challenging for the researcher. This step is known as **operationalizing** our variables – the process of identifying the actual measurement scales to assess the variables of interest.

Thus, the scientific inquiry has two basic levels:

- the empirical and the abstract, conceptual – the empirical aspect is primarily concerned with the facts as revealed by observation and experiments
- the abstract or theoretical aspect, which involves a serious attempt to understand the fact, and to integrate them into a coherent logical system, a theory (from Hull, 1952).

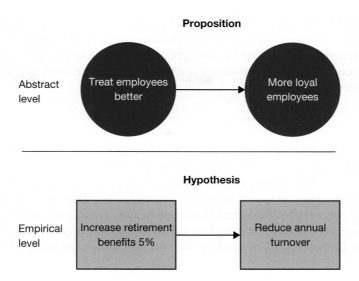

Figure 5.3 Hypotheses are the empirical counterparts of propositions

Understanding theory

Figure 5.4 is a simplified portrayal of a theory to explain voluntary job turnover – the movement of employees to other organizations. Two concepts – (1) the perceived desirability of movement to another organization, and (2) the perceived ease of movement from the present job – are expected to be the primary determinants of intention to quit. This is a proposition. Further, the concept intention to quit is expected to be a necessary condition for the actual voluntary job turnover behaviour to occur. This is a second proposition that links concepts together in this theory. In the more elaborate theory, job performance is another concept considered to be the primary determinant influencing both perceived

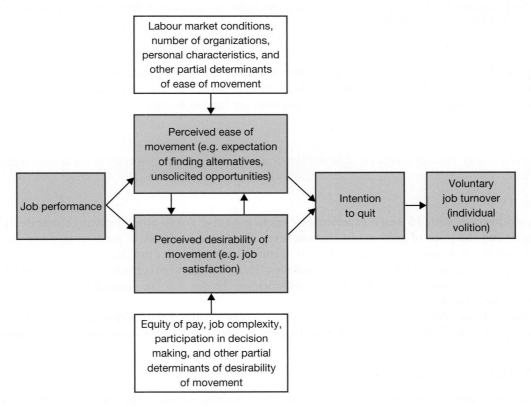

Figure 5.4 A basic theory explaining voluntary job turnover

ease of movement and perceived desirability of movement. Moreover, perceived ease of movement is related to other concepts such as labour market conditions, number of organizations visible to the individual, and personal characteristics. Perceived desirability of movement is influenced by concepts such as equity of pay, job complexity and participation in decision making. A complete explanation of this theory is not possible; however, this example should help you understand the terminology used by theory builders.

Verifying theory

In most situations, there are alternative theories to explain certain phenomena. To determine which is the best theory, researchers make observations or gather empirical data to verify the theories.

Maslow's hierarchical theory of motivation offers one explanation of human behaviour. Maslow theorizes that individuals will attempt to satisfy physiological needs before self-esteem needs. An alternative view of motivation is provided by Freudian (psychoanalytic) theory, which suggests that unconscious, emotional impulses are the basic influences on behaviour. One task of science is to determine if a given theoretical proposition is false or if there are inconsistencies between competing theories. Just as records are made to be broken, theories are made to be tested.

Theory building

You may be wondering, 'Where do theories come from?' Although this is not an easy question to answer in a short chapter on theory in business research, we will explore this topic briefly. In this chapter, theory has been explained at the abstract, conceptual level and at the empirical level. Theory generation may occur at either level.

At the abstract, conceptual level, a theory may be developed with deductive reasoning by going from a general statement to a specific assertion. **Deductive reasoning** is the logical process of deriving a conclusion about a specific instance based on a known general premise or something known to be true. For example, while you might occasionally have doubts, we know that all business professors are human beings. If we also know that Barry Babin is a business professor, then we can deduce that Barry Babin is a human being. You can see the logic in this.

deductive reasoning The logical process of deriving a conclusion about a specific instance based on a known general premise or something known to be true.

At the empirical level, a theory may be developed with inductive reasoning. **Inductive reasoning** is the logical process of establishing a general proposition on the basis of observation of particular facts. All business professors who have ever been seen are human beings; therefore, all business professors are human beings.

inductive reasoning The logical process of establishing a general proposition on the basis of observation of particular facts.

Suppose a stockbroker with 15 years' experience of trading on the Tokyo Stock Exchange repeatedly notices that the price of gold and the price of gold stocks rise whenever there is an outbreak of political hostility. In other words, similar patterns occur whenever a certain type of event occurs. The stockbroker may induce from these empirical observations that the price of gold is related to political stability. Thus, the stockbroker states a proposition based on his or her experience or specific observations: 'Gold prices will increase during times of political instability.' The stockbroker has constructed a basic theory.

Over the course of time, theory construction is often the result of a combination of deductive and inductive reasoning. Our experiences lead us to draw conclusions that we then try to verify empirically, sometimes by testing hypotheses.

Research using hypothesis testing

Research using hypothesis testing is sometimes known as 'the **scientific method**'. The scientific method is a process that moves an idea from hypothesis testing to theory. The scientific method is a set of prescribed procedures for establishing and connecting theoretical statements about events, for analyzing empirical evidence and for predicting events yet unknown. It is useful to look at the analytic process of scientific theory building as a series of stages. While there is not complete consensus concerning exact procedures for the scientific method, we suggest seven operations may be viewed as the steps involved in the application of the scientific method:

1. assessment of relevant existing knowledge of a phenomenon
2. formulation of concepts and propositions
3. statement of hypotheses
4. design of research to test the hypotheses
5. acquisition of meaningful empirical data
6. analysis and evaluation of data
7. proposal of an explanation of the phenomenon and statement of new problems raised by the research (Zaltman *et al.*, 1972).

scientific method A set of prescribed procedures for establishing and connecting theoretical statements about events, for analyzing empirical evidence, and for predicting events yet unknown; techniques or procedures used to analyze empirical evidence in an attempt to confirm or disprove prior conceptions.

THE VALUE OF GOOD RESEARCH

Focus on the scientific method

An excellent overview of the scientific method is presented in Robert Pirsig's book *Zen and the Art of Motorcycle Maintenance*:

> Actually I've never seen a cycle-maintenance problem complex enough really to require full-scale formal scientific method. Repair problems are not that hard. When I think of formal scientific method an image sometimes comes to mind of an enormous juggernaut, a huge bulldozer – slow, tedious, lumbering, laborious, but invincible. It takes twice as long, five times as long, maybe a dozen times as long as informal mechanic's techniques, but you know in the end you're going to get it. There's no fault isolation problem in motorcycle maintenance that can stand up to it. When you've hit a really tough one, tried everything, racked your brain and nothing works, and you know that this time Nature has really decided to be difficult, you say, 'Okay, Nature, that's the end of the nice guy,' and you crank up the formal scientific method.
>
> For this you keep a lab notebook. Everything gets written down, formally, so that you know at all times where you are, where you've been, where you're going and where you want to get. In scientific work and electronics technology this is necessary because otherwise the problems get so complex you get lost in them and confused and forget what you know and what you don't know and have to give up. In cycle maintenance things are not that involved, but when confusion starts it's a good idea to hold it down by making everything formal and exact. Sometimes just the act of writing down the problems straightens out your head as to what they really are.
>
> The logical statements entered into the notebook are broken down into six categories: (1) statement of the problem, (2) hypotheses as to the cause of the problem, (3) experiments designed to test each hypothesis, (4) predicted results of the experiments, (5) observed results of the experiments, and (6) conclusions from the results of the experiments. This is not different from the formal arrangement of many college and high-school lab notebooks but the purpose here is no longer just busywork. The purpose now is precise guidance of thoughts that will fail if they are not accurate.
>
> The real purpose of scientific method is to make sure Nature hasn't misled you into thinking you know something you don't actually know. There's not a mechanic or scientist or technician alive who hasn't suffered from that one so much that he's not instinctively on guard. That's the main reason why so much scientific and mechanical information sounds so dull and so cautious. If you get careless or go romanticizing scientific information, giving it a flourish here and there, Nature will soon make a complete fool out of you. It does it often enough anyway even when you don't give it opportunities. One must be extremely careful and rigidly logical when dealing with Nature: one logical slip and an entire scientific edifice comes tumbling down. One false deduction about the machine and you can get hung up indefinitely.
>
> In Part One of formal scientific method, which is the statement of the problem, the main skill is in stating absolutely no more than you are positive you

(Continued)

know. It is much better to enter a statement 'Solve Problem: Why doesn't cycle work?' which sounds dumb but is correct, than it is to enter a statement 'Solve Problem: What is wrong with the electrical system?' when you don't absolutely know the trouble is in the electrical system. What you should state is 'Solve Problem: What is wrong with cycle?' and then state as the first entry of Part Two: 'Hypothesis Number One: The trouble is in the electrical system.' You think of as many hypotheses as you can, then you design experiments to test them to see which are true and which are false.

This careful approach to the beginning questions keeps you from taking a major wrong turn which might cause you weeks of extra work or can even hang you up completely. Scientific questions often have a surface appearance of dumbness for this reason. They are asked in order to prevent dumb mistakes later on.

Part Three, that part of formal scientific method called experimentation, is sometimes thought of by romantics as all of science itself because that's the only part with much visual surface. They see lots of test tubes and bizarre equipment and people running around making discoveries. They do not see the experiment as part of a larger intellectual process and so they often confuse experiments with demonstrations, which look the same. A man conducting a gee-whiz science show with 50 000 dollars' worth of Frankenstein equipment is not doing anything scientific if he knows beforehand what the results of his efforts are going to be. A motorcycle mechanic, on the other hand, who honks the horn to see if the battery works is informally conducting a true scientific experiment. He is testing a hypothesis by putting the question to nature. The TV scientist who mutters sadly, 'The experiment is a failure; we have failed to achieve what we had hoped for,' is suffering mainly from a bad scriptwriter. An experiment is never a failure solely because it fails to achieve predicted results. An experiment is a failure only when it also fails adequately to test the hypothesis in question, when the data it produces don't prove anything one way or another.

Skill at this point consists of using experiments that test only the hypothesis in question, nothing less, nothing more. If the horn honks, and the mechanic concludes that the whole electrical system is working, he is in deep trouble. He has reached an illogical conclusion. The honking horn only tells him that the battery and horn are working. To design an experiment properly he has to think very rigidly in terms of what

directly causes what. This you know from the hierarchy. The horn doesn't make the cycle go. Neither does the battery, except in a very indirect way. The point at which the electrical system directly causes the engine to fire is at the spark plugs, and if you don't test here, at the output of the electrical system, you will never really know whether the failure is electrical or not.

To test properly the mechanic removes the plug and lays it against the engine so that the base around the plug is electrically grounded, kicks the starter lever and watches the spark-plug gap for a blue spark. If there isn't any he can conclude one of two things: (a) there is an electrical failure or (b) his experiment is sloppy. If he is experienced he will try it a few more times, checking connections, trying every way he can think of to get that plug to fire. Then, if he can't get it to fire, he finally concludes that (a) is correct, there's an electrical failure, and the experiment is over. He has proved that his hypothesis is correct.

In the final category, conclusions, skill comes in stating no more than the experiment has proved. It hasn't proved that when he fixes the electrical system the motorcycle will start. There may be other things wrong. But he does know that the motorcycle isn't going to run until the electrical system is working and he sets up the next formal question: 'Solve problem: What is wrong with the electrical system?'

He then sets up hypotheses for these and tests them. By asking the right questions and choosing the right tests and drawing the right conclusions the mechanic works his way down the echelons of the motorcycle hierarchy until he has found the exact specific cause or causes of the engine failure, and then he changes them so that they no longer cause the failure.

An untrained observer will see only physical labour and often get the idea that physical labour is mainly what the mechanic does. Actually the physical labour is the smallest and easiest part of what the mechanic does. By far the greatest part of his work is careful observation and precise thinking. That is why mechanics sometimes seem so taciturn and withdrawn when performing tests. They don't like it when you talk to them because they are concentrating on mental images, hierarchies, and not really looking at you or the physical motorcycle at all. They are using the experiment as part of a program to expand their hierarchy of knowledge of the faulty motorcycle and compare it to the correct hierarchy in their mind. They are looking at underlying form. (Pirsig, 1974)

The extract just examined from the book *Zen and the Art of Motorcycle Maintenance* is very helpful in explaining the scientific method and hypothesis testing. The extract is particularly useful because it highlights and explains the need for precision in research. When you chose, for example, a concept for your research project, you must be sure that that concept represents what you think it represents and the concept must be necessary to the research project.

Think about the conceptual framework for your research project. Think about all of the key concepts in that conceptual framework. Let us say, for example, that your conceptual framework reads as follows:

'This research project is a case study designed to examine the perceptions of global warming among final-year undergraduate students in Business Studies at the University of Wollongong.'

Each of the keywords and phrases in this conceptual framework is a key concept in your research project. The conceptual framework is very precisely structured in order to include all of the required, and necessary, concepts, and to exclude all of the possible but unnecessary concepts.

In a second example, let us say that you developed the following conceptual framework for your research project:

'This research project is a case study designed to examine the perceptions of global corporations among final-year undergraduate students in Business Studies at the University of Wollongong.'

As you can see, only one word has changed from the first example to the second example, but this one word is a key concept. As a result of this one word change, this change in a key concept in the research project makes the second research project an entirely different research project.

This very simple example demonstrates the need for precision in defining the research project. In fact, precision is required throughout the research process. The researcher is very careful and very precise in the manner in which s/he designs, conducts and completes their research project. The researcher is very precise in the way in which s/he uses language in the research project, in designing different elements of the research project, and in writing up the research. This level of precision is necessary in order to meet the scientific standards of research.

As you know from your reading of this textbook, the conceptual framework for the research project is the first framework in the four frameworks approach to the research project. When the conceptual framework for the research project has been very clearly and very precisely outlined, then all three remaining frameworks, the theoretical framework, the methodological framework, the analytical framework, can be developed. The conceptual framework provides direction and focus for the three remaining frameworks. In this way, the entire research project rests on the conceptual framework.

The four frameworks

- *Conceptual Framework*
- Theoretical Framework
- Methodological Framework
- Analytical Framework

In social science research generally and in business research, a great deal of scientific research is conducted without testing hypotheses. The researcher outlines a research statement, or question, (the conceptual framework for the research project). S/he then develops a theoretical framework for the research project, which is outlined in the literature review. The researcher devises a methodology for the research project, for example, a survey methodology, or a case study methodology, or an action research methodology or an ethnographic methodology. The researcher then devises data-gathering methods for the research project. In the Research in Practice box, you can read Nelson's preliminary thoughts in relation to the research project he plans to develop and carry out for his degree in Business Management.

As explained in the previous chapter, the data-gathering methods must 'fit' with the other elements of the research project. As explained in this chapter, the data-gathering methods must be capable of providing the research project with the data necessary to properly and thoroughly answer the research question or to properly and thoroughly respond to the research statement, or to answer the research hypothesis/hypotheses.

When data are gathered for the research project, they are analyzed. The researcher draws findings and conclusions from the analyzed data. The findings are theorized, by comparing the findings to the findings of other theorists, whose work is laid out in the literature review (which contains the theoretical framework) of the research project. The researcher makes explicit connections, by showing how the findings of the research project agree with, or contradict, the findings of the other theorists. In this way, the researcher devises new theory, and/or contributes to and expands and develops existing theory.

The conclusions the researcher draws from the study must be logical conclusions based on the findings of the study. The conclusions of the study must answer the research question/respond to the research statement. In this way, the research comes full circle (see the model of the research process, Figure 1.1 in Chapter 1) and the research project is completed. Finally, if appropriate, the researcher makes recommendations. The recommendations must be logical and achievable and they must clearly emerge from the conclusions drawn from the study.

Nelson's research project

Nelson is studying for a BSc in Business Management. He is very interested in online networks, and he intends to study an online network in his research project. Following lectures, and his reading of research methodology textbooks, Nelson has decided that a case study methodology is the most appropriate research methodology for his research project. He developed the following research statement.

This research project is a case study documenting the use of online networking in the business management practices of a family run business importing African arts and crafts.

Nelson's family own and run this business, and Nelson works part-time in the business. He believes that the business has developed a good online networking capacity, and he believes that his case study will be a study of best practice in relation to online networking in business management. He hopes to score a very high mark for his dissertation.

Nelson is developing a theoretical framework for his dissertation based on his conceptual framework. We know from our reading of this textbook that the research statement for the research project contains the conceptual framework for the research project. The key concepts in Nelson's conceptual framework are as follows: online networking, online networking in business and online networking in business management practice.

Based on Nelson's careful outline of the key concepts in his research project, can you identity the keywords that Nelson will use in keyword searches for literature for his literature review? Can you also see the structure for his literature review that Nelson has outlined, is based on, and has developed from, his key concepts? Nelson has to write 3000 words for his literature review. He has decided to structure his literature review as follows:

Chapter Two Literature review	
Introduction	200 words
Online networking	800 words
Online networking in business	800 words
Online networking in business management practice	800 words
Summary	400 words

As you can see, the conceptual framework Nelson developed for his research project gave him the guidance and direction he needed in order to be able to develop the theoretical framework for his research project.

In practice, as Nelson reads for his literature review, and as he writes his literature review, the subsections and the subtitles he has conceptualized for them may grow, develop and change. This is appropriate. The important thing for now is that Nelson has a framework for his literature review. This framework will guide him in reading for and writing his literature review. Nelson is happy with the way in which his research project is developing, and so too is his dissertation supervisor.

Practical value of theories

Theories allow us to generalize beyond individual facts or isolated situations. Theories provide a framework that can guide strategy by providing insights into general rules of behaviour. When different incidents may be theoretically comparable in some way, the scientific knowledge gained from theory development may have practical value. A good theory allows us to generalize beyond individual facts so that general patterns may be understood and predicted. For this reason it is often said there is nothing as practical as a good theory.

Social network theory

Researchers have developed theories about the links and structure of social networks, complete with constructs and propositions about how linkages are formed. Each separate entity (individual or organization) is referred to as a node. The relationships among nodes are referred to as ties. When nodes become linked they yield social contacts.

What creates ties? How do the nodes become linked? Many factors have been identified, including family relationships, friendship, professional association, common interest and activities and shared beliefs. When linked together with ties these nodes form a social network.

Network theory is used to examine social networks. The links between and among nodes can be simple or complex.

(Continued)

They can be as simple as a single family or so complex as to operate on a national or international level. The network can play an important role in the success of an individual, how a family functions and how a business makes decisions. The value derived from the social network is termed social capital.

While electronic social networking is a relatively recent development, businesses are already examining ways to utilize social networks to spread information, better serve their customers and grow profits. The next few years will be exciting as the theory of social networks develops and businesses continue to explore how they can gain social capital from engaging in social networking.

It might be interesting to do some reading around social network analysis and to think about how you might use social network analysis in a research project. There are many simple and useful guides to social network analysis provided by different universities on the internet. You could begin by reading one or two of these.

REAL WORLD RESEARCH

How theory influences research

In this journal article by Soboleva *et al*. (2017) the focus is on the factors that encourage retweets on Twitter, in eWOM (electronic Word of Mouth) marketing. The title of the article is 'Retweet for a Chance to . . .': an analysis of what triggers consumers to engage in seeded eWOM on Twitter', *Journal of Marketing Management*, 33:13–14, 1120–48. In the abstract, the authors explain that Twitter provides an important channel for seeded eWOM. Seeded eWOM is a marketing strategy whereby a business enterprise in some way facilitates or encourages consumers to engage in eWOM. What actually happens is that followers on Twitter retweet brand messages.

This journal article is particularly interesting to us, because the authors present and test a theoretical model 'incorporating interactive, textual and visual tweet features to predict eWOM, using tweets by leading brands from three industries'.

You should source the journal article online and read through it. The authors present a very good theoretical framework. We know from our reading of this textbook that the theoretical framework for the research project is the literature review. You should read through the theoretical framework presented in the journal article. You might use this theoretical framework as a model for your own literature review, when you write your literature review for your research project.

The authors present a theoretical model of what predicts retweeting, presented in Figure 1 (Soboleva *et al*., p. 1124). It is interesting to note that among the mechanisms that facilitate retweeting behaviour, as detailed in the model, is the word please. The authors explain that the use of the word please in requests for a retweet, in line, as they explain, with politeness theory, will be associated with a higher retweet rate.

CASE STUDY

Altimeter is a company in the USA that provides advice to businesses on technology and the human side of business (www.prophet.com/altimeter/). One of the leading analysts at Altimeter is Charlene Li who is a leading expert in business and technology. According to her biography on the Altimeter website, she was the founder and CEO of Altimeter before Altimeter joined Prophet. In 2015, she published an article in the *Harvard Business Review* with the intriguing title 'Why No One Uses the Corporate Social Network', (hbr.org/2015/04/ why-no-one-uses-the-corporate-social-network). In the article she makes a number of key points about tech-based enterprise social networks. She writes that:

- In many companies, collaboration platforms and enterprise social networks are presented as the cure for all collaboration and networking needs.
- Most installed enterprise collaboration tools are underutilized.
- It is often the case that leaders in organizations don't see collaboration and engagement as a good use of their time, so the workers that they lead don't either.
- Leaders should engage with workers through digital and social channels, but, generally, they don't.

(Continued)

Li goes on to present three brief case studies of good examples of engaged, networked leadership in three different companies. One of the companies is UPS (United Parcel Service), an American multinational package delivery company. Li writes that Rosemary Turner, the President of UPS in northern California, uses Twitter to keep people connected. She chose to use Twitter because it was the platform with which employees were already comfortable. She uses Twitter for rapid communication, for example of traffic snags in different locations, warning employees of them so that they can avoid them. She also uses Twitter to recognize good employees, posing for photographs with them while applauding their work and their commitment. In addition, Turner says that employees and customers use the platform to engage with the company's leadership. She says that this immediate and effective means of communication promotes trust in the company, in its products and services, in its employees and in its leadership. Turner said, 'I am finding that when I send out a blast on Twitter, I get just as much if not more reaction than if I send out a survey internally.' Li said that Turner's approach to sharing 'enables employees to reach her anytime – thereby achieving her goals as well as the larger corporate mandate for openness'.

Question: Write a reflective paragraph in your research diary on the value to a business enterprise of the online news and social networking site Twitter. Based on your reading of this case study, and your reflection detailed in this paragraph in your research diary, would you be able to develop an idea on the topic of online social networking for a research project?

END OF CHAPTER QUESTIONS

1 Find another definition of theory. How is the definition you found similar to this book's definition? How is it different?

2 What does the statement, 'There is nothing as practical as a good theory' mean? Do you agree with this statement?

3 Name and briefly detail some of the theories offered to explain aspects of your field of business.

4 Compare and contrast deductive logic with inductive logic. Give an example of both.

5 Why is precision so important in scientific research?

6 How does the conceptual framework contribute to the research process?

7 Develop a conceptual framework for a research project.

8 Use the conceptual framework developed in answer to Question 7 to develop an outline for a theoretical framework for that research project.

9 Use the outline of the theoretical framework developed in answer to Question 8 to list the theories and theorists to be drawn on in that research project.

10 Reflect on your own social network. How are the nodes in your social network linked? What social capital do you gain from your social network? Does this reflection give you any ideas for a research project?

REFERENCES

Altimeter, Prophet, Charlene Li, Principal Analyst, www.prophet.com/author/charlene (Accessed 03.03.2018).

Babin, B.J., Hardesty, D.M. and Suter, T.A. (2003) 'Color and shopping intentions: the effect of price, fairness and perceived affect', *Journal of Business Research*, 56: 541–551.

Bartels, R. (1970) *Marketing Theory and Metatheory*, Chicago, IL: American Marketing Association.

Dubin, R. (1969) *Theory Building*, Free Press: New York.

Hull, C.L. (1952) *A Behavioural System*, New York: John Wiley & Sons.

Li, C. (2015) 'Why no one uses the corporate social network', *Harvard Business Review*, 07.04.2015, hbr.org/2015/04/why-no-one-uses-the-corporate-social-network (Accessed 03.03.2018).

Pirsig, R.M. (1974) *Zen and the Art of Motorcycle Maintenance*, New York: Harper Collins.

Soboleva, A., Burton, S., Mallik. G. and Khan. A. (2017) '"Retweet for a chance to . . . ": An analysis of what triggers consumers to engage in seeded eWOM on Twitter', *Journal of Marketing Management*, 33: 13–14, 1120–1148.

Zaltman, G., Pinson, C. and Anglemar, R. (1972) *Metatheory and Consumer Research*, New York: Holt, Rinehart & Winston.

RECOMMENDED READING

Creswell, J. and Creswell, D.J. (2018) *Research Design: Qualitative, Quantitative and Mixed Methods Approaches* (5th edn), London, California, New Delhi, Singapore: Sage.

Denscombe, M. (2017) *The Good Research Guide: For Small-scale Social Research Projects* (6th edn), Milton Keynes: Open University Press.

Fielding, N.G., Lee, R.M. and Blank, G. (2017) *The SAGE Handbook of Online Research Methods* (2nd edn), London, California, New Delhi, Singapore: Sage.

Jankowicz, A.D. (2004) *Business Research Projects* (4th edn), London: Cengage.

Kent, R. (2006) *Marketing Research: Approaches, Methods and Applications in Europe*, London: Cengage.

Lee, N. and Lings, I. (2008) *Doing Business Research: A Guide to Theory and Practice*, London: Sage.

Neuman, W.L. (2014) *Social Research Methods: Qualitative and Quantitative Approaches* (7th edn), Essex, England: Pearson Education Ltd.

Worthington, I. (2013) *Greening Business, Research, Theory and Practice*, Oxford: Oxford University Press.

Yin, R.K. (2018) *Case Study Research and Applications: Design and Methods* (6th edn), Thousand Oaks, CA: Sage.

PART TWO

BEGINNING THE RESEARCH PROCESS

CHAPTER 6
THE LITERATURE REVIEW

LEARNING OBJECTIVES

At the end of this chapter, the student should be able to:

- Identify and source appropriate literature.

- Evaluate the quality of literature sourced.

- Evaluate the utility for the research project of the literature sourced.

- Review literature.

- Create a theoretical framework.

- Write a literature review.

RESEARCH SKILLS

At the end of this chapter, the student should, using the exercises on Cengage Brain, be able to:

- Outline a keyword search strategy for a given research project.

- Create a theoretical framework for a given research project.

- Critique a given literature review.

The aim of this chapter is to consider, explore and explain the literature review. The chapter begins with a definition of 'literature' in the context of research. This is followed by a discussion on where to source literature and a discussion on the importance of exercising discernment, of being discerning, in relation to literature reviewed. There are explanations of how to select appropriate literature and how to use literature. There is a discussion and an explanation of how to construct the theoretical framework, the second framework in the four frameworks approach to the research project. There is a demonstration of how to write a literature review. In the case study at the end of the chapter, two sample literature reviews are presented: the first is an example of a poorly written literature review, the second an example of a better literature review.

INTRODUCTION

Literature, in the context of research, is research that has already been carried out and published. Such research is published in journal articles, books, theses, government reports, the reports of NGOs and in conference reports. The literature in a field or area of research constitutes the body of knowledge in that field or area of research; it contains the theory in that field. The researcher undertakes a review of the literature in order to:

- develop his/her own expertise and scholarship on the topic or phenomenon
- establish what is known and what is not known in the field
- highlight gaps in the knowledge base in the area or on the topic; the researcher may decide to use their research project to try to fill in one or more of those gaps
- create a theoretical framework for the research project.

> **literature** Research that has already been carried out and published.

In Figure 1.1, the model of the research process detailed at the start of Chapter 1, indicates that the literature review is the fourth stage in the research process. In fact, the process of reviewing the literature begins as soon as the researcher has decided to undertake a research project. As soon as s/he decides on an area of research, or on a particular topic within an area of research, the researcher begins to read literature around that topic or that broad area. The reading then continues all the way through the research project.

RESEARCH IN PRACTICE

There are many useful and readily available research resources that you can easily access and use to develop your research skills. We suggest having a quick look at *The Guardian Online Datablog*. Datablog is a very interesting website for any researcher, particularly a beginner. The blog presents all kinds of data in different ways, for example, in table format or visual format. In later chapters of this textbook, we will focus in more depth on the different ways of representing data.

Do you know why data are sometimes presented in tables, and sometimes presented in graphs and figures? If you study the tables and the figures on Datablog, you may be able to answer this question.

There are lots of data on many different topics in *The Guardian's Datablog*. If you spend some time browsing this website, you will learn a great deal about data and about the different ways of presenting data. You might also get some ideas for your own research project.

The table on World Happiness Report 2017 is from *The Guardian Datablog*. Study the data. Think about the data presented, and what that data represents. Remember the Value of Good Research box in Chapter One of this textbook, and the focus in that on the development of measures of happiness. Look at this table (right) and the way the data are presented in the table. Can you see how the table presents a great deal of data in a relatively simple easy-to-read format? Data are sometimes presented in tables, and in graphs, charts and figures, in order to facilitate the simple and clear communication of complex data.

World Happiness Report 2017 — GDP and Happiness Rankings

Top 20 countries by GDP per capita

Country	GDP ranking	Happiness ranking
Qatar	1	35
Luxembourg	2	18
Singapore	3	26
Kuwait	4	39
United Arab Emirates	5	21
Norway	6	1
Switzerland	7	4
Hong Kong S.A.R., China	8	71
United States	9	14
Ireland	10	15
Saudi Arabia	11	37
Netherlands	12	6
Sweden	13	9
Bahrain	14	41
Germany	15	16
Austria	16	13
Australia	17	10
Denmark	18	2
Iceland	19	3
Canada	20	7

LITERATURE IN RESEARCH

The word 'literature' in social science research refers to research that has already been carried out and published. As we have seen earlier, such literature is published in many different places, including in the media. In general, media reports of research projects tend to be very short. Generally, what is reported in the media tends to be a brief synopsis of the research, often without any reference to the theoretical framework within which the research project was situated and developed.

The distinction between research that is presented within a theoretical context and research that is not, is, in scientific terms, substantial.

In previous chapters, we discussed epistemology and epistemological questions. These are:

- questions of knowledge
- questions of what is known

- questions of how what is known is known
- questions of the nature of knowledge, and
- questions of the means of knowledge creation.

Every research project is designed to contribute to knowledge. The rules, processes and procedures of research are rigorous, and they must be adhered to for the research project to be deemed to have contributed to knowledge.

For a research project to be established as valid, it must meet rigorous scientific standards. When a research project does meet these standards, the findings of the research are accepted as a valid contribution to knowledge. In many cases, research is subjected to peer review. Such peer-reviewed research is published primarily in journal articles, in books and in reports. While it can be useful and interesting to source material from other sources, such as the media, it is primarily these **peer-reviewed sources** that are used in compiling a literature review for a research project.

> **peer-reviewed sources** Published accounts of research that have been subjected to rigorous critical review by the peers of the authors of the research.

THE CONCEPTUAL FRAMEWORK AS A GUIDE TO THE REVIEW OF THE LITERATURE

The researcher begins the research process with a research idea and s/he develops this idea into a properly designed, well-conceptualized research project.

The researcher states the research project in the research statement or question, or in the research hypothesis/hypotheses. This becomes the conceptual framework for the research project.

This is the first framework in the four frameworks approach to the research project. The research statement or question is (ideally) a short succinct sentence. It is simple and clear and it is, at the same time, a complete expression of the research project.

The four frameworks

- *Conceptual Framework*
- Theoretical Framework
- Methodological Framework
- Analytical Framework

Each of the key concepts in the research project is articulated in this one sentence. The key concepts are the keywords or phrases in the research project. The keywords are important in the conceptual framework, and they are important also in terms of the literature review. This is because most searches for literature are **keyword searches**, and keyword searches are essentially key concept searches.

> **keyword searches** A search of the literature, in library databases, carried out using the key concepts, i.e. the keywords and/or phrases, in the research project.

When searching for literature, researchers search library databases using keyword searches. The researcher searches the databases for published research, i.e. published accounts of research conducted in the same field, on the same topic.

For example, if the researcher is developing a research project around a marketing plan for a sports club, s/he searches the databases using those keywords: 'marketing', 'marketing plan', 'sports' and 'sports clubs'. The researcher tries to source all the literature, all the published research, that has focused on one or more of these keywords and concepts.

In another example, if the researcher is developing a research project around the study of brand recognition of a big brand such as the WWF (World Wildlife Fund) the researcher does a keyword search in the library databases for the following keywords and key concepts: 'brands', 'brand recognition', 'World Wildlife Fund', 'brand recognition World Wildlife Fund'.

You will know from your previous experience in doing keyword searches in library databases that single-word searches such as 'marketing' or 'brands' or 'sports' yield too many results to be useful. As this is the case, researchers link concepts together to narrow the search, and to produce more focused results. For example, instead of searching using the concept 'marketing', the researcher might search using the concepts 'marketing' and 'brand recognition' together.

In order to generate useful and thorough keyword searches, the researcher develops a **search strategy**. The search strategy can be developed and outlined in the research diary. In the diary, the researcher devises and decides on the keyword searches. The researcher then carries out the searches and records a summary in the research diary of the results of those searches. This can help the researcher to avoid duplicate searches. This exercise also provides a record of searches that the researcher can reflect on when developing ideas for further searches, which may be more complex or more in-depth. In writing up the methodological framework for the study (contained in the research methodology chapter in a thesis/dissertation, or in the research methodology section of a research report), the researcher might outline the search strategy used. Notes on the search strategy written or recorded in the research diary are very helpful in this context.

> **search strategy** The plan the researcher makes for their search of the literature for relevant literature for their literature review.

A key objective of the search is that the researcher sources and develops an awareness of all of the literature relevant to their study. In the first place, the researcher identifies all the relevant literature. Then the researcher sources that literature and saves it in a folder on a memory stick and on their computer. It is important to make and keep back-up copies of everything. Then the researcher begins the process of reading the literature, developing an understanding of it and an understanding of the body of knowledge represented in the literature.

The researcher reads the literature with a view to developing from it a theoretical framework for their own research project.

CREATE A THEORETICAL FRAMEWORK

The theoretical framework is the second framework within the four frameworks approach to the research project. Here we reproduce the figure of the four frameworks approach that is detailed in Chapter 1 (see Figure 1.2).

Within the figure, as you can see, each of the frameworks rests on the first framework. So, the second framework, the theoretical framework, rests on, and emerges from, the conceptual framework. This process is demonstrated in Figures 6.1 and 6.2.

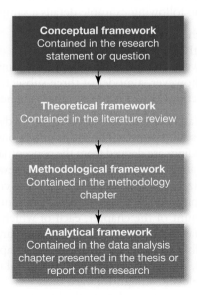

Figure 6.1   The four frameworks

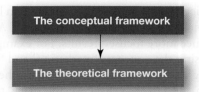

Figure 6.2 The theoretical framework emerges from the conceptual framework

As can be seen from these figures, the theoretical framework emerges from the conceptual framework. In practice, what this means is that the researcher uses the conceptual framework to provide direction and focus for their literature search and for the layout and structure of the theoretical framework.

WRITING THE LITERATURE REVIEW

When starting to write the literature review, the first thing to do is to develop a plan for its **structure**. Plan the literature review first and then write the literature review to that plan. Sketch the structure for the literature review in the research diary.

structure The structure of a chapter, or any written work, is the way in which it is organized.

For the literature review, the structure will start with an introduction followed by a number of subsections and ending with a summary.

 The introduction is an introduction to the chapter, nothing else, nothing more. The summary is a summary of the chapter, nothing else, nothing more.

It is important that the introduction and the summary are effective. The introduction should thoroughly and succinctly introduce the reader to the content of the chapter and to the main argument to be developed in the literature review.

The argument will be an argument for the research that you are about to undertake and you will develop it from your critique of the literature that is undertaken in relation to the research statement/question.

The summary should thoroughly and succinctly summarize the chapter and the main argument of the chapter.

It is a good idea to read journal articles to find brief succinct and effective chapter introductions and summaries that you may use as models for your own chapter introductions and summaries.

Each literature review chapter is divided into subsections, each of which is headed by a subheading. The subheading indicates the content of the subsection. The following example details a sample structure for a literature review:

- the first subsection in the chapter is the introduction
- the final subsection in the chapter is the summary
- there are then three subsections between the introduction and the summary. There might in fact be four or five subsections or just two subsections; however, a model of three subsections between the first subsection (which is the introduction) and the final subsection (which is the summary) generally works very well.

The subsections between the introduction and the summary represent the body of the literature review. Here, the researcher presents the theoretical framework for the research project. The main subsections of the literature review are each developed around individual subheadings. These subheadings are derived from the conceptual framework and the reading of the literature undertaken for the review. The subheadings are presented in the literature review in the order that makes most sense.

Each subheading is carefully conceptualized and developed to reflect the content of that subsection. Each subsection contains a carefully developed, cogently expressed and well-laid-out argument. Each section contains two, three, four or five paragraphs, depending on the word count of the chapter, each of which contains substantial amounts of information. Each subsequent subsection in the chapter further develops the main argument presented in the literature review.

Given this structure, it should be possible to plan the layout of the chapter in detail before actually beginning to write the chapter. With a very detailed plan, and a comprehensive and critical reading of the literature, the writing of the literature review should be a relatively simple and straightforward task.

A critical reading of the literature is a questioning reading of the literature; critical in this context does not mean negative. In a critical reading of the literature, you are questioning and evaluating everything that the researcher did, every decision that they made in relation to the research project. It is helpful to read published literature reviews to develop an understanding of a critical approach to the literature and an understanding of how a critical approach to the literature is presented in writing a literature review. Everything written must be clearly relevant to the research project that you are undertaking and explicitly related to the argument that you are developing in the chapter. Ultimately, the argument that the researcher is expressing in the chapter is an argument for the research that they are carrying out.

In the sample research project outlined in the Research in Practice box, the three subsections that form the body of Sara's literature review chapter are drawn from the conceptual framework, Sara's research statement. The focus of Sara's study is on recruitment, on recruitment practices, and on recruitment practices in a major media organization, the BBC. As you can see:

- all of the key concepts, taken from the conceptual framework, are used to guide the search for literature
- all of the key concepts are used to construct a theoretical framework for the research project
- all of the key concepts are used to structure the chapter that is the literature review.

So in the case of Sara's research project, the chapter that is the literature review could be structured, for example, as shown in Tables 6.1, 6.2, and 6.3.

Table 6.1 Example of structure for the literature review for Sara's research project (based on 5000-word count)

First section 300 words – in one paragraph	Introduction (a brief introduction to the chapter and the contents of the chapter)
Second section (first subheading) 1400 words – in four paragraphs	The internet and contemporary recruitment and selection practices
Third section (second subheading) 1400 words – in four paragraphs	The use of the internet and the company website in recruiting employees
Fourth section (third subheading) 1400 words – in four paragraphs	Issues in contemporary internet-based recruitment practices
Fifth section 500 words – in two paragraphs	Summary (a brief summary of the main points and the key argument developed throughout the chapter)

Table 6.2 Example of structure for the literature review for Sara's research project (based on 3000-word count)

First section 200 words – in one paragraph	Introduction (a brief introduction to the chapter and the contents of the chapter)
Second section (first subheading) 800 words – in three paragraphs	The internet and contemporary recruitment and selection practices
Third section (second subheading) 800 words – in three paragraphs	The use of the internet and the company website in recruiting employees
Fourth section (third subheading) 800 words – in three paragraphs	Issues in contemporary internet-based recruitment practices
Fifth section 400 words – in two paragraphs	Summary (a brief summary of the main points and the key argument developed throughout the chapter)

Table 6.3 Example of structure for the literature review for Sara's research project (based on 1000-word count)

First section 100 words – in one paragraph	Introduction (a brief introduction to the chapter and the contents of the chapter)
Second section (first subheading) 250 words – in two paragraphs	The internet and contemporary recruitment and selection practices
Third section (second subheading) 250 words – in two paragraphs	The use of the internet and the company website in recruiting employees
Fourth section (third subheading) 250 words – in two paragraphs	Issues in contemporary internet-based recruitment practices
Fifth section 150 words – in one paragraph	Summary (a brief summary of the main points and the key argument developed throughout the chapter)

Sara's research project

Sara is undertaking a degree in business management. She wants to conduct her research within the area of human resource management. She is particularly interested in recruitment practices. Sara has no way of gaining access to a human resource department within which to conduct her research. As this is the case, Sara has decided to study the recruitment practices of a major company as they are published on the company's website. Sara has developed the following research statement for her research project:

> This research project is a content analysis study of the recruitment practices of the BBC (British Broadcasting Company) as they are outlined on the BBC website.

The word count given to the literature review is dependent on the word count given to the research project. Table 6.4 details approximate word counts for literature reviews based on the word count of the research project.

Table 6.4 Approximate word count for the literature review

In a 20 000-word thesis	Literature review is 5000–7000 words
In a 15 000-word thesis	Literature review is 3500–4000 words
In a 12 000-word thesis	Literature review is 3000 words
In a 10 000-word thesis	Literature review is 2500 words

The model of the structure of the literature review chapter for the research project, based on the conceptual framework that Sara developed for her research, demonstrates the simplicity and the utility of the four frameworks approach in the construction and development of the research project. This was also demonstrated in Chapter 4 of this textbook when we considered Kate's research project, which was situated within the HR department of the SME Greene's Biscuits Ltd. This approach to the construction and development of the research project may be applied to any research project.

YOUR RESEARCH
Common research problems

The standard of writing

There is an expectation in every academic institution that the students registered in that institution can read and write fluently and properly in the language of the institution. If the language of the institution is English, there is a presumption that the students registered in the institution can write correct English. There is no tolerance of misspellings, poorly constructed sentences or grammatical errors. This rule applies regardless of whether or not English is the first language of the student. Any student who is not confident that their written English is up to the standard required should have their thesis proofread before they submit it for examination. A great many marks are needlessly lost by students to poorly written and badly presented work.

As the entire research project rests on the conceptual framework, it is critical that the conceptual framework is very well constructed. It is of the utmost importance that the researcher properly, actively and thoroughly engages with the process of conceptualizing the research project. The well-conceptualized research project facilitates the development of a good theoretical framework, a good methodological framework, a good analytical framework and, ultimately, a good research project.

When the researcher uses the conceptual framework as a guide in the literature search, the focus of the research is maintained. While meandering off on tangents through research literature is often a very pleasant and engaging pastime, it can lead to time being wasted, and, in the worst case scenario, to a loss of focus in the research. To avoid losing focus, it is useful to have a copy of the research statement/question to hand, perhaps written on the first page of your research diary, which you should always have with you when you are working on your research project. Refer to the research statement/question regularly when you are searching for and reading literature. Check that the material you are sourcing and reading is relevant to your research project. If it is not, move on from that literature to literature which is clearly relevant.

When sourcing literature, check the theoretical content of the literature. Ask the following questions:

1. Does the material you are reading clearly have a theoretical framework?
2. Does the material you are reading reference other research?

The literature that you source in or through the university or college library will be the most useful because it will be academic material, and it will almost certainly have been developed for the purpose of contributing to scientific knowledge.

A quick search of the library, using electronic means, will establish whether a great deal has been written on your chosen topic or not. It will also establish when the material was written. It is important to establish the seminal authors in any field. These are the authors who made a founding contribution to any area of knowledge. It is also important to establish which contemporary authors are writing on the topic. You need to situate your work in relation to the most up-to-date sources. Between the seminal authors and the most up-to-date authors, there may be other authors who have made a noteworthy or significant contribution to the development of the concept that you are researching.

One question that is often asked by students is 'how much literature should be reviewed?' The short answer to this question is 'a warehouse full'. While this is true, the researcher must be realistic in terms of what it is possible to accomplish, given the time available for the research. The expectation on the part of the supervisor(s) and the examiner(s) is that the work will be excellent. The student strives to reach this standard, balancing the requirements of the standard of excellence with the time available for the study.

THE VALUE OF GOOD RESEARCH

Focus on content analysis

Content analysis is a research methodology that is used when the research calls for the analysis of the content of any text or set of texts. Using content analysis, researchers search the text for the presence of particular words, phrases and concepts. Any text that is language based can be used as data in a research project using content analysis as the research methodology. Examples of texts include advertising, records, books, chapters, newspaper content, speeches and transcripts of conversations.

Content analysis can also be used within a different research methodology as an approach to data analysis. We will see an example of this in the case study at the end of Chapter 11, where Tom in his research proposal uses documentary analysis as his research methodology, and content analysis as his approach to analyzing his data. Content analysis is a technique for analyzing the content of texts. Using content analysis the researcher can compare content across different texts and analyze the content using quantitative and/or qualitative techniques. The researcher is interested in the manifest content, what can be seen/read in the text, and in the latent content, what lies beneath the surface of the text. The researcher attempts to read between the lines and tries to uncover the meaning underlying the written lines of text.

The article detailed here (Yin Zhen *et al.*, 2017) 'Promoting business schools: A content analysis of business school's magazines', *Journal of Applied Business and Economics*, 19(3): 106–116), details a study undertaken using content analysis.

The focus of this study is on analyzing the content of Business School magazines, used, as explained in the article, for promotion purposes. In the study, the researchers focused on business schools in the USA with AACSB accreditation, a hallmark of excellence in business management education.

In the journal article, the researchers present a short literature review on marketing business schools. You will very quickly read this short literature review. If you wish, you can use it to help you develop your understanding of how to write a literature review. Note that at the end of the literature review, the researchers highlight a gap in knowledge in relation to higher education branding, and they write that there is an urgent need for more research on brand development from the perspectives of higher education consumers. Does this gap in knowledge prompt you to think of ideas for a research project that you might consider undertaking for your dissertation?

The researchers go on to explain their research methodology in clear and simple terms. They explain that in the study they analyzed the content of 36 Business School magazines around the USA. They write that while some content is similar across all the magazines, such as messages from the Dean and Alumni news, some magazines present school specific content, such as news on innovations and sports news. This study is a quantitative study. The researchers present tables summarizing their data. These tables are interesting to read. If you do read them, you may find that they help you with the development of ideas about how to present quantitative data in your own research project. At the end of the article, the researchers present a short section with the subtitle Discussion and Conclusions. This section is interesting to read, it is short, so you will read it quickly, and it may help you develop ideas around how you should present the discussion and conclusions section(s) of your own research project.

It would be a useful exercise to source the original article and to examine it in relation to the different elements of the research process as they are dealt with in the article. This is a simple, relatively short journal article detailing a simple quantitative content analysis study. If you are interested in content analysis as a research methodology, you will find this article helpful.

(Continued)

If your interest is in qualitative content analysis, please see the guide presented by Erlingsson and Brysiewicz (2017), which is detailed in the list of resources below.

Some useful resources on content analysis include:

BBC World Service Trust, 'Using content analysis to measure the influence of media development interventions: elections training for journalists in Yemen', www.gov.uk/dfid-research-outputs/using-content-analysis-to-measure-the-influence-of-media-development-interventions-elections-training-for-journalists-in-yemen Colorado State University, 'Introduction to content analysis', writing.colostate.edu/guides/page.cfm?pageid=1305&guideid=61 (Accessed 14.03.2018).

Erlingsson, C. and Brysiewicz, P. (2017) 'A hands-on guide to doing content analysis', *African Journal of Emergency Medicine, 7*: 93–99. (This is a guide to qualitative content analysis.)

Krippendorff, K. (2018) *Content Analysis An Introduction to Its Methodology* (4th edn), California and London: Sage.

Neuendorf, K.A. (2017) *The Content Analysis Guidebook* (2nd edn), California and London: Sage.

Research Methods Knowledge Base, 'Unobtrusive measures (indirect measures, content analysis, and secondary analysis of data'), www.socialresearchmethods.net/kb/unobtrus.php

Schreier, M. (2012) *Qualitative Content Analysis in Practice*, California, London, New Delhi, Singapore: Sage.

The journal article by Mogaji *et al.* in the Real World Research box provides a good example of a simple and effective conceptual framework providing guidance and direction for the development of the theoretical framework for the research project. There are two pages of a literature review in the article, addressing the literature in the field. It is important that you source this article and read the content of the article. Read the literature review. It will help you develop an understanding of how you should write your literature review for your research project.

REAL WORLD RESEARCH

How theory influences research

Search for the article given here (Mogaji *et al.*, 2018, 'Emotional appeals in business-to-business financial services advertisements', *International Journal of Bank Marketing*, *36*:1, 208–227) and look through it (or if you do not have access to this article, any well-structured academic article should do). Read the abstract of the article. This provides a summary of the research project. It begins with a clear, single-sentence introduction: 'The purpose of this paper is twofold: to analyze the use of emotional appeals in business-to-business (B2B) bank advertisements and to understand business owners' perceptions of such appeals.'

The article reports the findings of two studies, or a study in two parts. In Study 1, 1834 advertisements collected from British newspapers were subjected to content analysis, and in Study 2, 17 semi-structured interviews were conducted with business owners who operate a current account with a British bank.

In the article there is a good literature review on marketing and communication in marketing. Different models of communication are considered, and one of the models, Kotler's (1967) communication model was used to guide the development of Study 1. It's interesting to think about why the authors of the study felt that this model, which is now quite dated, was the best model to use. We can think of Kotler's model as a seminal contribution to the body of knowledge. A seminal contribution to knowledge is a contribution that was so significant it is still used and referenced today even though it was published a long time ago.

The authors explain that the findings of Study 1 were further explored in semi-structured interviews in Study 2. This is an example of triangulation, where the researcher(s) examines the phenomenon under investigation from more than one perspective.

There is a good explanation of the research methodology used in the study. There is also a good explanation of the sampling approach used to develop the sample of newspaper advertisements gathered for the dataset used in the study. The authors also explain very clearly the coding framework developed for the study. If you read through this section, you will see how the authors explain their methodology, and how they justify their methodology. You will also see the concerns they expressed in relation to the validity of the work, and the ways in which they emphasized the validity of their research.

The authors go on to outline Study 2, and the methodology and sampling method used. This part of the study involved semi-structured interviews. The authors detail the way in which the interviews were carried out and explain how the gathered data were analyzed.

The journal article provides a good example of a complete research project. In the journal article you can trace the model of the research process and follow every step in the process. You will notice that at the end of the journal article the authors present a very good comprehensive list of references. When you read through the list of references you will be able to see how such a list of references is in itself a very useful resource for researchers in this field, as it points readers towards resources in the literature on the topic.

READING LITERATURE: SOME KEY POINTS

In reading literature, the researcher engages in an evaluation of the literature. The researcher is trying to establish the value of the literature in terms of their own research project. The literature review is undertaken in order to provide for the development of a theoretical framework for the research project. The literature has relevance only to the degree that it is relevant to the research being undertaken. This is the first and the most fundamental measure of value in terms of the literature being sourced, read and reviewed. How relevant is the literature to the research?

The next question is how dated is the literature sourced? If the literature is quite dated, is it from seminal sources? Is there any very up-to-date literature? The more up-to-date the literature the better and dated, or old, literature should only be referenced in the literature review if it comes from seminal sources. The next questions then relate to the author(s) of the literature. Who authored the literature? What qualifications do they have? Do they have other publications? In other words, do the authors have academic authority in the field? It is useful to establish whether or not the research is referenced by other researchers. Is the research cited by other authors? Questions such as these will help you discern the quality of the research you are reviewing.

When reading published research, it is important, as highlighted earlier, to take a critical approach or a **critical perspective**. When developing such a critical perspective it is helpful to draw on the model of the research process. Using this model, read and critically examine every element of the published research project. The following questions will be useful in helping you develop the critical perspective needed when appraising and reviewing literature.

critical perspective A reflective, thoughtful, evaluative, questioning perspective or view.

Questions for the introduction to the research

Critically examine the research question/statement, the research hypothesis:

- Does it seem useful and appropriate?
- Are the aim and objectives of the research clearly outlined?
- Do they seem reasonable and appropriate?
- Do the aim and objectives 'fit' with the research statement/question/hypothesis?

Questions for the literature review

Critically examine the literature review, the theoretical framework:

- Is it comprehensive?
- Does it include seminal authors?
- Is it up-to-date?
- Does it adequately support the research project as it is detailed in the research statement/question, in the hypothesis?

Questions for the research methodology

Examine the methodology:

- Is it appropriate? Does it 'fit' with the research project?
- Has enough detail been given on the methodology to allow for a critique of the research?
- Is the population of the study detailed?
- Was a sample used? If so, is the sampling method detailed? Is the sampling method used appropriate?
- Are the data collection methods outlined?
- How well did the data collection methods serve the research?
- Do the data collection methods 'fit' with the aim of the research?
- Is there a copy of the data collection method(s) in the appendices, e.g. the questionnaire/interview schedule?

Questions for data analysis

- How were the data analyzed?
- Was the means of analysis adequate and appropriate?

Questions for the findings of the research

- Are the findings from the data clearly drawn from the data? Is it clear that the findings did emerge from the data?
- Are the findings reasonable, useful, interesting and insightful?
- Are the findings theorized? Did the author(s) knit the findings from the research back into the body of knowledge? Did the author(s) connect the findings with the theory laid out in the literature review, in the theoretical framework for the research project constructed and presented in the literature review?

Questions for the conclusions drawn from the research

- Are there conclusions? Are they reasonable?
- Do the conclusions emerge clearly from the findings?
- Are the conclusions meaningful?
- Do they evidence a deep level of reflection on the part of the researcher?
- Are they useful, interesting and insightful?

Questions for the recommendations made at the end of the study

- Are there recommendations?
- Are the recommendations clear and simple?
- Do the recommendations make sense?
- Are the recommendations achievable? Are they do-able?
- Are there recommendations for further research?

Questions for an overall critical appraisal of the study

- Is the report of the research well written?
- Is the research well presented?
- Has the research been carried out to a high standard?
- Does the research make a contribution to knowledge?
- Is it a valid contribution to knowledge?
- Is it a valuable contribution to knowledge?

These are generic questions that may be asked of any research project. You should use these questions to develop a critical perspective on the research (and on the literature) that you are reviewing.

You can expect your supervisor(s) and your examiner(s) to take a critical perspective on your research. As this is the case, you could use the bullet points just given to critically appraise your own research before you submit it for examination. This will give you a sense of the kind of critique your supervisor and/or your examiner will develop when they are appraising or examining your research.

REFERENCING THE WORK

Referencing is critically important and much of the work of the literature review is in referencing all of the relevant research that you have used in developing the theoretical framework for your study. It is essential that the literature review be properly referenced. Establish with your lecturer and/or your supervisor which referencing system is to be used in the work and learn how to use that system. The system of referencing will be standard across the institution so the theses in the library will all have been written using that system. These theses are a good source of information regarding referencing, although it is important to take a critical perspective on them. It is often the case in academic institutions that all of the theses are placed in the library, the poorly written theses as well as the outstanding ones. Try to be discerning when you read, so that the standards you are absorbing as you read are high. Try to avoid picking up bad habits from poorly written works. Your lecturer and/or supervisor may provide you with an official guide to referencing. If not, the library may provide this. There are some useful resources in terms of referencing in Chapter 2 of this textbook, under the heading of 'plagiarism'. That chapter also explains in detail the way in which to compile a list of references.

YOUR RESEARCH
Common research problems

There are some common mistakes that students make when writing the literature review:

- Students do not review enough literature.
- Students review irrelevant literature.
- Students present unnecessary detail in their review (the case study at the end of this chapter presents an example of a poorly written literature review and an example of a better literature review).
- Students fail, in writing their literature review, to present and then develop a main argument in the review.

Try to ensure that you are reading and reviewing enough literature and that the literature you are reviewing is relevant to your research. In ensuring that the literature is relevant, be guided by the conceptual framework for the research project. The research statement or question or the research hypothesis contains the conceptual framework for the research project. The structure for the literature review should emerge from the conceptual framework.

When you are planning the writing of the literature review, decide precisely what your main point is (what your main argument is) in the review. Then outline and develop that argument throughout the chapter. The key points to remember are that:

1. You are presenting a review of the literature.
2. This review of the literature is your take on the literature, your appraisal of the literature.
3. It is your appraisal of how the literature relates to your research project, as it is detailed in the research question or statement or research hypothesis.

In accomplishing all of this, your review of the literature must be open, balanced and critical, because you cannot be seen to have any bias in relation to the literature. You must be open to contradictions and contradictory arguments. Your appraisal of the literature must be logical. Your critique must be reasonable and your argument must be clear and coherent. It will be much easier to write a reasoned and logical argument if you reflect on it critically before you start to write. You will find it helpful to clarify your argument in notes in your research diary.

It is important to try to reference as much as possible throughout the literature review. Include all of the **references** you can in writing the review. These references evidence the amount of reading you have undertaken for the research. While referencing as many theorists as possible, it is important to lead the review with your own voice. Remember, it is your take on the literature, as it pertains to or relates to your research project, that you are presenting in this chapter. This is important. Try not to begin a paragraph with a reference. Opening sentences in paragraphs should lead the reader into the paragraph. Do not deploy references in the introduction or the summary. The introduction gives the reader a broad introduction to the chapter, the summary summarizes the chapter. There should not be any new information in the summary. The summary is simply a summary of the main points and the main argument presented in the chapter.

references Details of the source of literature, see list of references for example.

CASE STUDY

Two literature reviews

In this case study, two examples of sample literature reviews are presented. The first is an example of a poorly written literature review. The second is an example of a better literature review.

In reading the two examples, try to see why one is a poor example and the other a better example. In your research diary, write down, in short phrases, why one is a poorly written review and the other a better review.

Remember to use the lessons learned in this exercise when writing the literature review for your research project. This exercise is designed to help you write a better literature review.

(Continued)

Example of a bad literature review

Induction programmes for new employees at work come in many forms. Williams and O'Brien (2018) in their study of induction programmes in SMEs found that, in general, the programmes used by the firms tended to be short 2-hour induction programmes designed simply to introduce new employees to their new workplace and their new work colleagues. They found too that employees who participated in the short induction programmes felt that the induction programmes were too short, and that sometimes, because they were too short, the programmes failed to introduce new employees to key people and key processes within the organization. Their research project was a case study, and in the case study they examined the induction programmes of 8 SMEs in the greater Middleton area. Bradley and Finch (2017), in their study of the induction programmes of five MNCs found that the induction programmes of the MNCs tended to be longer than those of the SMEs studied by Williams and O'Brien (2018), and they tended to be generic, with each MNC developing their own generic induction programme. The MNCs of the Williams and O'Brien (2018) study each had highly structured and highly detailed induction programmes, each of which was designed to thoroughly introduce new employees to their new work environment. Cooper *et al*. (2018), detail in their work three main models of induction programme: The Large model, the Medium model, and the Small model. In their work, Cooper *et al*. (2018), presented a review of the literature on induction models presented in business journals over the last 20 years. They found that, over those years, different models of induction were in vogue at different times. They state in their work that while contemporarily an integrated model of induction, encompassing elements of the Large, Medium and Small models is in vogue internationally among businesses of every size, in fact, each of the models is suited, they believe, to different kinds of businesses and different sized businesses. Frank and Lyden (2017), in a survey of 300 British firms, found that the majority of the firms (63%) had week-long induction programmes. Of the rest of the firms, 20% had 3-day induction programmes and 20% had induction programmes that lasted 3 weeks. The remaining 7% had either no induction programme (2%) or induction programmes that lasted longer than 3 weeks. Frank and Lyden (2017), used a random sampling technique in their research and only businesses with 15 or more employees were included in the sample.

Example of a better literature review

There are many different kinds of induction programmes and many different models of induction programmes currently in use in different businesses and firms; some last for a number of hours and some last for a number of weeks (Williams and O'Brien, 2018; Bradley and Finch, 2017; Frank and Lyden, 2017). The model of induction programme generally used by SMEs tends to be a short 2-hour model of induction (Williams and O'Brien, 2018). This model was established by Williams and O'Brien (2018), as being flawed. They suggest that the model is too short and, as a consequence, it does not properly address the task of induction. The model of induction used by MNCs is a long generic model, designed for use internationally across different national and cultural borders and boundaries (Bradley and Finch, 2017). A potential flaw in this model might be the lack of cultural nuance allowed for in the model.

Different models of induction have evolved over recent decades (Cooper *et al*. 2018). There are currently, as established by Cooper *et al*., (2018), three main models, Large, Medium and Small models. The model which is currently in vogue among firms internationally is a hybrid model, encompassing elements of each of the three main models. Following their extensive review of existing models, Cooper *et al*. (2018), suggest that each of the three main models has particular application in particular kinds of businesses and in different sized businesses. It is important to note that, in Britain, almost all firms have developed some kind of induction programme for new employees (Williams and O'Brien, 2018; Frank and Lyden, 2017). Only 2 per cent of the 300 firms studied by Frank and Lyden (2017), had not.

Question: Having read both of the sample literature reviews above, can you explain why one of the reviews is better than the other? (Please note that the literature used in the sample literature reviews is fictitious, created by Quinlan for the purposes of the exercise.)

END OF CHAPTER QUESTIONS

1   What is a theoretical framework in a research project?

2   What is the relationship between the conceptual framework and the theoretical framework in a research project?

3   Outline three key elements in a literature search strategy.

4   What is meant by a critical engagement with the literature?

5   Explain the role of references in the literature review.

6   What is a list of references?

7   Name and explain the referencing style used in your institution.

8   Explain why it is necessary for the researcher to plan the literature review.

9   How does the researcher develop the key argument of the literature review?

10 Demonstrate, by means of an example, an appropriate structure for a literature review for a research project.

REFERENCES

BBC World Service Trust, 'Using content analysis to measure the influence of media development interventions: elections training for journalists in Yemen', www.gov.uk/dfid-research-outputs/using-content-analysis-to-measure-the-influence-of-media-development-interventions-elections-training-for-journalists-in-yemen (Accessed 14.03.2018).

Colorado State University, 'Introduction to content analysis', writing.colostate.edu/guides/page.cfm?pageid=1305&guideid=61 (Accessed 14.03.2018).

Datablog, The Guardian, www.theguardian.com/data (Accessed 15.06.2018).

Erlingsson, C. and Brysiewicz, P. (2017) 'A hands-on guide to doing content analysis', *African Journal of Emergency Medicine, 7*: 93–99.

Krippendorff, K. (2018) *Content Analysis An Introduction to Its Methodology* (4th edn), California and London: Sage.

Mogaji, E., Czarnecka, B. and Danbury, A. (2018) 'Emotional appeals in business-to-business financial services advertisements', *International Journal of Bank Marketing, 36*(1): 208–227.

Neuendorf, K.A. (2017) *The Content Analysis Guidebook* (2nd edn), California and London: Sage.

Schreier, M. (2012) *Qualitative Content Analysis in Practice*, California, London, New Delhi, Singapore: Sage.

Yin Zhen, J., Coulson, K.R., Yu, J. and Zhou, J.X. (2017) 'Promoting business schools: A content analysis of business school's magazines', *Journal of Applied Business and Economics, 19*(3), 106–116.

RECOMMENDED READING

Bell, J. and Waters, S. (2014) *Doing Your Research Project* (6th edn), Maidenhead: Open University Press.

Collis, J. and Hussey, R. (2013) *Business Research, A Practical Guide for Undergraduate and Postgraduate Students* (3rd edn), Basingstoke: Palgrave Macmillan.

Creswell, J. and Creswell, D.J. (2018) *Research Design: Qualitative, Quantitative and Mixed Methods Approaches* (5th edn), London, California, New Delhi, Singapore: Sage.

Easterby-Smith, M., Thorpe, R. and Jackson, P. (2015) *Management and Business Research* (5th edn), London: Sage.

Hart, C. (2018) *Releasing the Research Imagination*, London: Sage.

Lee, N. and Lings, I. (2008) *Doing Business Research: A Guide to Theory and Practice*, London: Sage.

Onwuegbuzie, A. and Frels, R. (2016) *Seven Steps to a Comprehensive Literature Review*, London: Sage.

Ridley, D. (2012) *The Literature Review: A Step-by-Step Guide for Students* (Sage Study Skills Series), London: Sage.

Trochim, William M. *The Research Methods Knowledge Base* (2nd edn), socialresearchmethods.net/kb (Accessed 17.03.2018).

White, B. and Rayner, S. (2014) *Dissertation Skills for Business and Management Students*, London: Cengage.

CHAPTER 7

QUANTITATIVE RESEARCH: AN INTRODUCTION TO MEASUREMENT

LEARNING OBJECTIVES

At the end of this chapter, the student should:

- Understand quantitative research.

- Be able to define and explain quantitative research.

- Know how and when to use quantitative research in a research project.

RESEARCH SKILLS

At the end of this chapter, the student should, using the exercises on Cengage Brain, be able to:

- Determine what needs to be measured to address a research question.

- Distinguish levels of scale measurement.

- Form an index or composite measure.

- List the three criteria for good measurement.

INTRODUCTION

Not every cook or chef needs to follow a recipe to create a great dish, but most amateur chefs find one very useful. Look at Figure 7.1. The recipe shows ingredients that can produce a tasty chicken dish. However, many readers, even those with some cooking ability, may have a difficult time following this recipe. Why? First, many may have difficulty translating all the French terms. Second, even when this is done, many will have difficulty knowing just what amounts of what ingredients should be included. How many readers could easily deal with the different measures listed by the ingredients? 'How much is 50 ml?', 'What is 454 g?', 'How much is a pincée?', 'Can I use my normal measuring utensils (scales)?' The essential question is a question of measurement; what needs to be measured and what means of measurement should be used.

WHAT DO I MEASURE?

In a research project the research statement or question, which provides the conceptual framework for the research project, is used to decide what concepts need to be measured.

Recette de la Jour	
454 g	Poitrine de Poulet
50 ml	Farine Tout Usage
2 ml	De Poudre d'Ail
2 ml	De Poudre d'Oignon
1 ml	De Sel
2	Blancs d'Oeuf
50 ml	De Lait Écrémé
Pincée	De Poivre Rouge
36	Craquelins

Figure 7.1 More ways than one to measure ingredients

THE VALUE OF GOOD RESEARCH

Money matters?

Griff Mitchell is vice-president of Customer Relationship Management (CRM) for one of the world's largest suppliers of industrial heavy equipment. In this role, he oversees all sales and service operations. This year, for the first time, the company has decided to perform a CRM employee evaluation process that will allow an overall ranking of all CRM employees. Griff knows this will be a difficult task for many reasons, not least of which is that he oversees over 1000 employees worldwide.

The ranking will be used to single out the best performers. These employees will be recognized at the company's annual CRM conference. The rankings will also be used to identify the lowest 20 per cent of performers. These employees will be put on a probationary list with specific targeted improvement goals that will have to be met within 12 months or they will be fired. Griff is becoming really stressed out trying to define the performance ranking process.

Griff's key question is, 'What is performance?' Although these employees are now often referred to as CRM employees, they have traditionally performed the sales function. Griff calls a meeting of senior CRM managers to discuss how ranking decisions should be made.

One manager simply argues that sales volume should be the sole criterion. She believes that 'sales figures provide an objective performance measure that will make the task easy and difficult to refute'. Another manager counters that, for the past 22 years, he has simply used his opinion of each employee's performance to place each of them into one of three groups: top performers, good performers and underperformers. 'I think about who is easy to work with and doesn't cause much trouble. It has worked for 22 years, why won't it work now?' Another responds curtly, 'It's margin! It's margin! I don't care about sales volume; I want my guys selling things that improve my division's profit!' One of the newer managers sits silently through most of the meeting and finally summons up the courage to speak. 'Aren't we CRM? That means performance should not be tied to sales, profits, or convenience, it should be based on how well a salesperson builds and maintains relationships with customers. So, we should see how satisfied the customers assigned to the employee are and use this in the evaluation process!' After this, the meeting disintegrates into a shouting match with each manager believing the others' ideas are flawed.

Griff feels like he is back to square one. 'How do I make sure I have a valid performance measure so that all of our people are treated fairly?' He decides to seek out an opinion from a long-time friend in the research business, Robin Donald. Robin suggests that a research project may be needed to define a reliable and valid measure. She also brings up the fact that because employees from all over the world will be considered, the measure will have to maintain its reliability and validity anywhere it is used! Griff agrees to the project. He feels good about letting someone outside the company develop the measure, because he believes that they will be independent. He certainly realizes the tremendous challenges that are involved in the research.

Griff's situation in this vignette illustrates how difficult it can be to define, let alone measure, important business phenomena. While some items can be measured quite easily, others present tremendous challenges to the business researcher.

Measurement is the process of describing some property of a phenomenon of interest by assigning numbers in a reliable and valid way. The numbers convey information about the property being measured. This is quantitative research. Quantitative research is numerical research. It is research conducted by generating numerical data, or data that can readily be coded numerically.

> **measurement** The process of describing some property of a phenomenon of interest, usually by assigning numbers in a reliable and valid way.

Measurement can be illustrated by thinking about the way instructors assign students' grades. A grade represents a student's performance in a class. Students with higher performance should receive a different grade than students with lower performance. Even the apparently simple concept of student performance is measured in many different ways. Consider the following options:

1. A student can be assigned a letter corresponding to his/her performance.
   a. A – Represents excellent performance
   b. B – Represents good performance
   c. C – Represents average performance
   d. D – Represents poor performance
   e. F – Represents failing performance

2. A student can be assigned a number from 1 to 20.
   a. 20 – Represents outstanding performance
   b. 11–20 – Represents differing degrees of passing performance
   c. Below 11 – Represents failing performance

3. A student can be assigned a number corresponding to a percentage performance scale.
   a. 100 per cent – Represents a perfect score. All assignments are performed correctly
   b. 60–99 per cent – Represents differing degrees of passing performance, each number representing the proportion of correct work
   c. 0–59 per cent – Represents failing performance but still captures proportion of correct work

4. A student can be assigned one of two letters corresponding to performance.
   a. P – Represents a passing mark
   b. F – Represents a failing mark

Actually, this situation is not terribly different from that of a manager who must assign performance scores to employees. In each case, students with different marks are distinguished in some way. However, some scales may better distinguish students. Each scale also has the potential of producing error or some lack of validity. Figure 7.2 illustrates a common measurement application.

It often happens that instructors may use a percentage scale all semester long and then be required to assign a letter grade for a student's overall performance. Does this produce any measurement problems? Consider two students who have percentage scores of 79.4 and 70.0, respectively. In the USA, the most likely outcome when these scores are translated into 'letter grades' is that each receives a C (the common 10-point spread would yield a 70–80 per cent range for a C (in the USA)). Consider a third student who finishes with a 69.0 per cent average and a fourth student who finishes with a 79.9 per cent average.

Which students are happiest with this arrangement?

- The first two students receive the same grade, a C, even though their scores are 9.4 per cent apart.
- The third student gets a grade lower (D) than the first two students, even though her score differs by only 1 per cent from the second student's score.
- The fourth student who has a score only 0.5 per cent higher than the first student would receive a B.

Thus, the measuring system (final grade) suggests that the fourth student outperformed the first student (assuming that 79.9 is rounded up to 80) but the first student did not outperform the second (each gets a C), even though the first and second students have the greatest difference in percentage scores.

A strong case can be made that error exists in this measurement system. All measurement, particularly in the social sciences, contains error. Researchers, if we are to represent concepts truthfully, must make sure that the measures used, if not perfect, are accurate enough to yield correct conclusions.

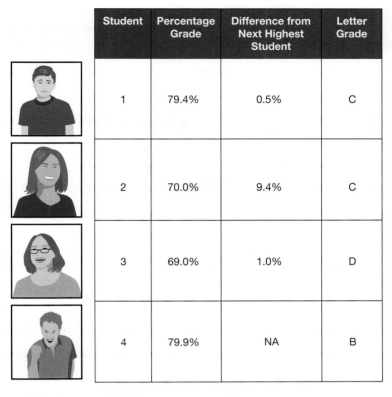

Student	Percentage Grade	Difference from Next Highest Student	Letter Grade
1	79.4%	0.5%	C
2	70.0%	9.4%	C
3	69.0%	1.0%	D
4	79.9%	NA	B

Figure 7.2 Are there any validity issues with this measurement?

REAL WORLD RESEARCH

Peer pressure and investing behaviour

How much of an influence do your friends have on what you buy? Would you be more likely to buy clothes, music or films that others approve of?

Research into peer pressure has indicated that some people are much more likely to succumb to it than others and that pressure or influence can take place when selecting almost any product or service.

Researchers measuring influence on investment decisions examined how happy various people were to accept information from someone else as fact; as well as how people attempted to create their own self-image by associating with another person or group of people.

This research noted that people with little investment knowledge but strong social needs are very likely to take advice from others. Perhaps even more interestingly, the researchers also recorded that some respondents placed more importance on showing that they agreed with their peers than on making investment returns.

Think about this research not only in the context of your daily life, but in connection with your own research project. Could peer influence be a theme you could use in your own research?

Concepts

A researcher has to know what to measure before knowing how to measure something. The concepts that must be measured are to be found in the conceptual framework for the research project. The conceptual framework is explained in detail in Chapter 2 of this textbook. A **concept** can be thought of as a generalized idea that represents something of meaning. Concepts such as age, sex, education and number of children are relatively concrete properties. They present few problems in either definition or measurement. Other concepts are more abstract. Concepts such as loyalty, personality, trust, corporate culture, customer satisfaction, value, and so on are more difficult to both define and measure. For example, loyalty in business research has been measured as a combination of customer share (the relative proportion of a person's purchases going to one competing brand/store) and commitment (the degree to which a customer will sacrifice to do business with a brand/store). Thus, loyalty consists of two components: the first is behavioural and the second is attitudinal.

> **concept** A generalized idea about a class of objects that has been given a name; an abstraction of reality that is the basic unit for theory development. Every discipline and theory is made up of concepts, e.g. key ideas, keywords, key phrases.

Operational definitions

Researchers measure concepts through a process known as **operationalization.** This process involves identifying scales that correspond to variance in the concept.

> **operationalization** The process of identifying scales that correspond to variance in a concept that will be involved in a research process.

Scales provide a range of values that correspond to different values in the concept being measured. In other words, scales provide **correspondence rules** that indicate that a certain value on a scale corresponds to some true value of a concept. Hopefully, they do this in a truthful way.

> **scales** A device providing a range of values that correspond to different values in a concept being measured.
>
> **correspondence rules** Indicate the way in which a certain value on a scale corresponds to some true value of a concept.

Here is an example of a correspondence rule: 'Imagine you are a business manager. Assign the numbers 1 through 7 according to how much trust you have in your sales representative. If the sales representative is perceived as completely untrustworthy, assign the numeral 1; if the sales rep is completely trustworthy, assign a 7.'

Variables

Variables capture different concept values. Scales capture variance in concepts.

Hypothesis testing

In the scientific method, when the research idea(s) can be stated in researchable terms, we reach the hypothesis stage. The next step involves testing the hypothesis against empirical evidence (facts from observation or experimentation). The results either support a hypothesis or do not support a hypothesis. From these results, new knowledge is generated.

In basic research, testing these prior conceptions or hypotheses and then making inferences and drawing conclusions about the phenomena leads to the establishment of facts about the phenomena.

Consider the following hypothesis:

 H1: Experience is positively related to job performance.

The hypothesis implies a relationship between two variables: experience and job performance. The variables capture variance in the experience and performance concepts. One employee may have 15 years' experience and be a top performer. A second may have ten years' experience and be a good performer. The scale used to measure experience is quite straightforward in this case and would involve simply providing the number of years an employee has been with the company. Job performance, by way of contrast, can be quite complex, as described in the opening vignette of this chapter.

Constructs

Sometimes, a single variable cannot capture a concept alone. Using multiple variables to measure one concept can often provide a more complete account of some concept than could any single variable. In the physical sciences, multiple measurements are often used to make sure an accurate representation is obtained. In social science, many concepts are measured with multiple measurements.

A **construct** is a term used for concepts that are measured with multiple variables. For instance, when a business researcher wishes to measure the customer orientation of a salesperson, several variables like these may be used, each captured on a 1–5 scale:

1. I offer the product that is best suited to a customer's problem.
2. A good employee has to have the customer's best interests in mind.
3. I try to find out what kind of products will be most helpful to a customer.

> **construct** A term used for concepts that are measured with multiple variables.

Constructs can be very helpful in operationalizing a concept.

An operational definition is like a manual of instructions or a recipe: even the truth of a statement like Christina Quinlan likes chocolate cake is dependent on the recipe for the chocolate cake. Different instructions lead to different results. In other words, how we define the construct will affect the way we measure it. An operational definition tells the investigator, 'Do such-and-such in so-and-so manner.' Figure 7.3 presents a concept definition and an operational definition from a study on a construct called susceptibility to interpersonal influence.

Concept	Conceptual definition	Operational definition
Susceptibility to interpersonal influence	Susceptibility to interpersonal influence is 'the need to identify with or enhance one's image in the opinion of significant others through the acquisition and use of products and brands, the willingness to conform to the expectations of others regarding purchase decisions, and/or the tendency to learn about products and services by observing others or seeking information from others'. Susceptibility to interpersonal influence is a general trait that varies across individuals.	Please tell me how much you agree or disagree with each of the following statements (if you wish, for the purposes of the exercise, you might substitute the word 'mobile phone' for the word 'stock'): 1. I frequently gather information about stocks from friends or family before I invest in them. 2. To make sure I buy the right stock, I often observe what other investors invest in. 3. I often consult other people to help choose the best stock to invest in. 4. If I have little experience with a (type of) stock, I often ask my friends and acquaintances about the stock. 5. I like to know what investment decisions make good impressions on others. 6. I generally purchase those stocks that I think others will approve of. 7. I often identify with other people by purchasing or selling the same stocks they sell or purchase. 8. I achieve a sense of belonging by purchasing or selling the same stocks that others purchase or sell. 9. If others can see in which stocks I invest, I often invest in stocks that they invest in.

Figure 7.3 Susceptibility to interpersonal influence: an operational definition

Levels of scale measurement

Business researchers use many scales or number systems. Not all scales capture the same richness in a measure. Not all concepts require a rich measure. Traditionally, the level of scale measurement is seen as important because it determines the mathematical comparisons that are allowable. There are four levels of measurement or types of scale measurement: nominal, ordinal, interval and ratio level scales. Each type offers the researcher progressively more power in analyzing and testing the validity of a scale.

Nominal scale

Nominal scales represent the most elementary level of measurement. A nominal scale assigns a value to an object for identification or classification purposes only. The values are simply placed in categories, they are labelled. The value can be, but does not have to be, a number because no quantities are being represented. Nominal scales are extremely useful and are sometimes the only appropriate measure, even though they can be considered elementary.

> **nominal scales** Represent the most elementary level of measurement in which values are assigned to an object for identification or classification purposes only.

Business researchers use nominal scales quite often. Suppose a soft drinks company was experimenting with three different types of sweetener (cane sugar, corn syrup or fruit extract). The researchers would like the experiment to be blind, so the three drinks that subjects are asked to taste are labelled A, B or C, not cane sugar, corn syrup or fruit extract. Or, a researcher interested in examining the production efficiency of a company's different plants might refer to them as 'Plant 1', 'Plant 2' and so forth.

Nominal scaling is arbitrary. What we mean is that each label can be assigned to any of the categories without introducing error. For instance, in the soft drink example, the researcher can assign the letter C to any of the three options without damaging scale validity. The researcher could just as easily use numbers instead of letters, as in the plant efficiency example and vice versa. If so, cane sugar, corn syrup and fruit extract might be identified with the numbers 1, 2 and 3, respectively, or even 543, 26 and 2010, respectively. The important thing to note is that the numbers are not representing different quantities or the value of the object. Thus any set of numbers, letters or any other identification is equally valid. Cane sugar might be identified as blue, corn syrup might be identified as yellow, and fruit extract might be identified as red. The labels, blue, yellow and red are assigned arbitrarily to the three options, the labels are a code that only the researcher who created the code can decipher.

We encounter nominal numbering systems all the time. Sports uniform numbers are nominal numbers. Lionel Messi playing for Barcelona is identified on the football pitch by his number 10 jersey. Bus numbers are nominal in that they simply identify a bus. In the USA, elementary school buses sometimes use both a number and an animal designation to help small children get on the right bus. So, bus number 8 may also be the 'tiger' bus, but it could just as easily be the 'horse' or the 'giraffe' bus.

The first drawing in Figure 7.4 depicts the number 7 on a horse's colours. This is merely a label to allow racing enthusiasts to identify the horse. The assignment of a 7 to this horse does not mean that it is the seventh fastest horse or that it is the seventh biggest or anything else meaningful. It is simply a number assigned to a horse so that the horse can be easily identified; particularly useful, for example, when the horse is one of a number of horses galloping around a race track.

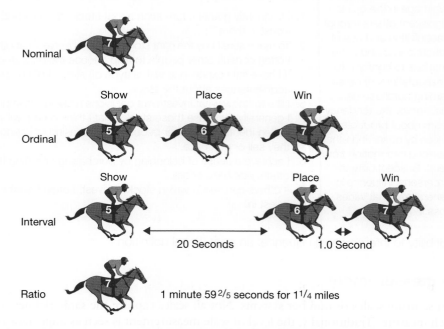

Figure 7.4 Nominal, ordinal, interval and ratio scales provide different information

To summarize, nominal scale properties mean the numbering system simply identifies things by categorizing them, labelling them. See Table 7.1 for examples of nominal scales commonly used by business researchers.

Ordinal scale

Ordinal scales allow things to be arranged in order based on how much of some concept they possess. In other words, an ordinal scale is a ranking scale. In fact, we often use the term rank order to describe an ordinal scale. When school students are ranked, we use an ordinal scale. We know that the student ranked first finished top of the class. We know that the student ranked seventh finished ahead of the student ranked eighth, who finished ahead of the ninth-ranked student. However, we do not know what the grade point average (GPA) of any student or how close these four students are to each other in overall GPA.

Table 7.1 Facts about the four levels of scales

Level	Examples	Numerical operations	Descriptive statistics
Nominal	Student ID number Yes – No Male – Female Buy – Did Not Buy East region Central region West region	Counting	• Frequencies • Mode
Ordinal	Student class rank Please rank your three favourite movies. Choose from the following: • Dissatisfied • Satisfied • Very satisfied • Delighted Indicate your level of education: • Some high school • High school diploma • Some college • College degree • Graduate degree	Counting ordering	• Frequencies • Mode • Median • Range
Interval	Student grade point average (GPA) Temperature (Celsius and Fahrenheit) Points given on an essay question 100-point job performance rating provided by supervisor	Common arithmetic operations	• Frequencies • Mode • Median • Range • Mean • Variance • Standard deviation
Ratio	Amount spent on last purchase Salesperson sales volume Number of stores visited on a shopping trip Annual family income Time spent viewing a web page	All arithmetic operations	• Frequencies • Mode • Median • Range • Mean • Variance • Standard deviation

ordinal scales Ranking scales allowing things to be arranged based on how much of some concept they possess.

Research participants are often asked to rank things based on preference. So, preference is the concept and the ordinal scale lists the options from most to least preferred, or vice versa. Five objects can be ranked from 1–5 (least preferred to most preferred) or 1–5 (most preferred to least preferred) with no loss of meaning. In this sense, ordinal scales are somewhat arbitrary, but not nearly as arbitrary as a nominal scale.

When business professors take some time off and go to the race track, even they know that a horse finishing in the 'show' position has finished after the 'win' and 'place' horses (see the second drawing in Figure 7.4). The order of finish can be accurately represented by an ordinal scale using an ordered number rule:

● Assign 1 to the 'win' position.
● Assign 2 to the 'place' position.
● Assign 3 to the 'show' position.

Perhaps the winning horse defeated the place horse by a nose, but the place horse defeated the show horse by 20 seconds. The ordinal scale does not tell how far apart the horses were, but it is good enough to let someone know the result. Typical ordinal scales in business research ask respondents to rank their three favourite brands or have personnel managers rank potential employees after job interviews, or judge investments as 'buy', 'hold' or 'sell'. Researchers know how each item, person or stock is judged relative to others, but they do not know by how much.

Interval scale

Interval scales have both nominal and ordinal properties, but they also capture information about differences in quantities of a concept. So, not only would a sales manager know that a particular salesperson outperformed a colleague, information that would be available with an ordinal measure, but the manager would know by how much. If a professor assigns grades to term papers using a numbering system ranging from 1.0–20.0, not only does the scale represent the fact that a student with a 16.0 outperformed a student with 12.0, but the scale would show by how much (4.0).

> **interval scales** Scales that have both nominal and ordinal properties, but that also capture information about differences in quantities of a concept from one observation to the next.

The third drawing in Figure 7.4 depicts a horse race in which the win horse is one second ahead of the place horse, which is 20 seconds ahead of the show horse. Not only are the horses identified by the order of finish, but the difference between each horse's performance is known. So, horses number 7 and 6 performed similarly (1 second apart), but horse number 5 performed not nearly as well (20 seconds slower).

The classic example of an interval scale is temperature. Consider the following weather:

- 6 June was 80°F
- 7 December was 40°F.

The interval Fahrenheit scale lets us know that 7 December was 40°F colder than 6 June. But we cannot conclude that 7 December was twice as cold as 6 June. Although the actual numeral 80 is indeed twice as great as 40, remember that this is a scaling system. In this case, the scale is not iconic, meaning that it does not exactly represent some phenomenon. In other words, there is no naturally occurring zero point – a temperature of 0° does not mean an absence of heat (or cold for that matter).

Since temperature scales are interval, the gap between the numbers remains constant (i.e. the difference between 20° and 30° is 10°, just as the difference between 68° and 78° is 10°). This is an important element of interval scales and allows us to convert one scale to another. In this case, we can convert Fahrenheit temperatures to Celsius scale. Then, the following would result:

- 6 June was 26.7°C
- 7 December was 4.4°C.

Obviously, now we can see that 7 December was not twice as cold as 6 June; 7 December was 40°F or 22.3°C cooler, depending on your thermometer. Interval scales are very useful because they capture relative quantities in the form of distances between observations. No matter what thermometer is used, 7 December was colder than 6 June.

See Table 7.1 for some examples of interval level scales.

Ratio scale

Ratio scales represent the highest form of measurement in that they have all the properties of interval scales with the additional attribute of representing absolute quantities. Interval scales possess only relative meaning, whereas ratio scales represent absolute meaning. In other words, ratio scales provide iconic measurement.

> **ratio scales** Represent the highest form of measurement in that they have all the properties of interval scales with the additional attribute of representing absolute quantities; characterized by a meaningful absolute zero.

Zero, therefore, has meaning in that it represents an absence of some concept. An absolute zero is the defining characteristic differentiating between ratio and interval scales. For example, money is a way to measure economic value. Consider the following items offered for sale in an online auction:

- 'Antique' 1970s digital watch – did not sell and there were no takers for free.
- Gold-filled Elgin wristwatch circa 1950 – sold for €100.
- Vintage stainless steel Omega wristwatch – sold for €1000.
- Antique rose gold Patek Philippe 'Top Hat' wristwatch – sold for €9000.

We can make the ordinal conclusions that the Patek was worth more than the Omega and the Omega was worth more than the Elgin. All three of these were worth more than the 1970s digital watch. We can make interval conclusions such as the Omega was worth €900 more than the Elgin. We can also conclude that the Patek was worth nine times as much as the Omega and that the 1970s watch was worthless (selling price = €0.00). The last two conclusions are possible because price represents a ratio scale.

The fourth drawing in Figure 7.4 shows the time it took horse 7 to complete the race. If we know that horse 7 took 1 minute 59 2/5 seconds to finish the race, and we know the time it took for all the other horses, we can determine the time difference between horses 7, 6 and 5. In other words, if we knew the ratio information regarding the performance of each horse – the time to complete the race – we could determine the interval level information and the ordinal level information. However, if we only knew the ordinal level information, we could not create the interval or ratio information. Similarly, with only the interval level data, we cannot create the ratio level information.

Using our opening Value of Good Research box as an example, Griff could decide to use a ratio measure – salesperson annual sales volume – as the indicator of performance for the CRM division. If he did this, he could create interval level data (groups of salespeople) or ordinal level data (the rank of each salesperson). However, this would be valid only if performance was truly equal to sales.

Mathematical and statistical analysis of scales

While it is true that mathematical operations can be performed with numbers from nominal scales, the result may not have a great deal of meaning. For instance, a school district may perform mathematical operations on the nominal school bus numbers. With this, they may find that the average school bus number is 77.7 with a standard deviation of 20.5 (there is a good introduction to quantitative data analysis in Chapter 19). Will this help them use the buses more efficiently or better assign bus routes? Probably not. Can a professor judge the quality of her classes by the average ID number of the students in the class? While it could be calculated, the result is meaningless. Thus, although you can put numbers into formulas and perform calculations with almost any numbers, the researcher has to know the meaning behind the numbers before a meaningful analysis can be conducted and before meaningful conclusions can be drawn.

Discrete measures

Discrete measures are those that take on only one of a finite number of values. A discrete scale is most often used to represent a classification variable. Therefore, discrete scales do not represent intensity of measures, only membership. Common discrete scales include any yes-or-no response, matching, colour choices, or practically any scale that involves selecting from among a small number of categories. Thus, when someone is asked to choose from the following responses:

- disagree
- neutral
- agree.

The result is a discrete value that can be coded 1, 2 or 3, respectively. This is also an ordinal scale to the extent that it represents an ordered arrangement of agreement. Nominal and ordinal scales are discrete measures.

 discrete measures Measures that take on only one of a finite number of values.

Certain statistics are most appropriate for discrete measures. Table 7.1 shows statistics for each scale level. The largest distinction is between statistics used for discrete versus continuous measures. For instance, the central tendency of discrete measures is best captured by the mode. When a student wants to know what the most likely grade is for a management class, the mode will be very useful. Observe the results below from the previous term:

A 3 students.
B 9 students.
C 6 students.
D 3 students.
E 1 student.

The mode is a 'B' since more students obtained that value than any other value. Therefore, the 'average' student would expect a B in that class.

Continuous measures

Continuous measures are those assigning values anywhere along some scale range in a place that corresponds to the intensity of some concept. Ratio measures are continuous measures. Thus, when Griff measures sales for each salesperson using the dollar amount sold, he is assigning a continuous measure. A number line could be constructed ranging from the least amount sold to the most, and a spot on the line would correspond exactly to a salesperson's performance.

> **continuous measures** Measures that reflect the intensity of a concept by assigning values that can take on any value along some scale range.

Strictly speaking, interval scales are not necessarily continuous. Consider the following common type of survey question:

	Strongly disagree	Disagree	Neutral	Agree	Strongly agree
I enjoy participating in online auctions	1	2	3	4	5

This is a discrete scale because only the values 1, 2, 3, 4 or 5 can be assigned. Furthermore, it is an ordinal scale because it only orders based on agreement. We really have no way of knowing that the difference in agreement of somebody marking a 5 instead of a 4 is the same as the difference in agreement of somebody marking a 2 instead of a 1. Therefore, the mean is not an appropriate way of stating central tendency and, technically, we really should not use many common statistics on these responses.

However, as a scaled response of this type takes on more values, the error introduced by assuming that the differences between the discrete points are equal becomes smaller. This may be seen by imagining a Likert scale (see Chapter 16 for a good introduction to Likert scales) with 1000 levels of agreement rather than three. The differences between the different levels become so small with 1000 levels that only tiny errors could be introduced by assuming each interval is the same. Therefore, business researchers generally treat interval scales containing five or more categories of response as interval. When fewer than five categories are used, this assumption is inappropriate.

The researcher should keep in mind, however, the distinction between ratio and interval measures. Errors in judgement can be made when interval measures are treated as ratio. For example, attitude is usually measured with an interval scale. An attitude of zero means nothing. In fact, attitude only has meaning in a relative sense. In other words, attitude takes on meaning when one person's response is compared to another or through some other comparison. A single attitude score alone contains little useful information.

The mean and standard deviation may be calculated from continuous data. Using the actual quantities for arithmetic operations is permissible with ratio scales. Thus, the ratios of scale values are meaningful. A ratio scale has all the properties of nominal, ordinal and interval scales. However, the same cannot be said in reverse. An interval scale, for example, has ordinal and nominal properties, but it does not have ratio properties (see Table 7.1 and see also Chapter 19).

Index measures

Earlier, we distinguished constructs as concepts that require multiple variables to measure them adequately. Looking back to the chapter vignette, could it be that multiple items will be required to adequately represent job performance? Likewise, a consumer's attitude toward some product is usually a function of multiple attributes. An **attribute** is a single characteristic or fundamental feature of an object, person, situation or issue.

> **attribute** A single characteristic or fundamental feature of an object, person, situation or issue.

Indexes and composites

Multiple-item instruments for measuring a construct are called index measures or composite measures. An **index measure** assigns a value based on how much of the concept being measured is associated with an observation. Indexes often are formed by putting several variables together. For example, a social class index might be based on three weighted variables: occupation, education and area of residence. Usually, occupation is seen as the single best indicator and would be weighted highest. With an index, the different attributes may not be strongly correlated with each other. A person's education does not always relate strongly to their area of residence. The American Consumer Satisfaction Index shows how satisfied American consumers are based on an index of satisfaction scores. Readers will perhaps not be surprised to read that Americans appear more satisfied with soft drinks than they are with cable TV companies, based on this index.

> **index measure** An index assigns a value based on how much of the concept being measured is associated with an observation. Indexes often are formed by putting several variables together.

Composite measures also assign a value based on a mathematical derivation of multiple variables. For example, salesperson satisfaction may be measured by combining questions such as, 'How satisfied are you with your job? How satisfied are you with your territory? How satisfied are you with the opportunities your job offers?' For most practical applications, composite measures and indexes are computed in the same way.

> **composite measures** Assign a value to an observation based on a mathematical derivation of multiple variables.

Computing scale values

Figure 7.5 demonstrates how a composite measure can be created from common rating scales. This scale was developed to assess how much a consumer trusts a website. This particular composite represents a **summated scale**. A summated scale is created by simply summing the response to each item making up the composite measure. For this scale, a respondent that judged the website as extremely trustworthy would choose SA (value of 5) for each question. Across the five questions, this respondent's score would be 25. Conversely, a respondent that thought the website was very untrustworthy would choose SD (value of 1) for each question; a total of 5. Most respondents would likely be somewhere between these extremes. For the example respondent in Figure 7.5, the summated scale score would be 13 based on his responses to the five items (2 + 3 + 2 + 2 + 4 = 13). A researcher may sometimes choose to average the scores rather than summing them. The advantage to this is that the composite measure is expressed on the same scale (1–5 rather than 5–25) as the original items. So, instead of a 13, the consumer would have a score of 2.6. While this approach might be more easily understood, the information contained in either result (13 versus 2.6) is the same.

> **summated scale** A scale created by simply summing (adding together) the response to each item making up the composite measure.

Item	Strongly disagree (SD) → Strongly agree (SA)				
This site appears to be more trustworthy than other sites I have visited.	SD	Ⓓ	N	A	SA
My overall trust in this site is very high.	SD	D	N	A	SA
My overall impression of the believability of the information on this site is very high.	SD	Ⓓ	Ⓝ	A	SA
My overall confidence in the recommendations on this site is very high.	SD	Ⓓ	N	A	SA
The company represented in this site delivers on its promises.	SD	D	N	Ⓐ	SA
Computation: Scale Values: SD = 1, D = 2, N = 3, A = 4, SA = 5					
Thus, the Trust score for this consumer is 2 + 3 + 2 + 2 + 4 = 13					

Figure 7.5 Computing a composite scale

Sometimes, a response may need to be reverse coded before computing a summated or averaged scale value. **Reverse coding** means that the value assigned for a response is treated oppositely from the other items. If a sixth item were included on the website trust scale that said, 'I do not trust this website', reverse coding would be necessary to make sure the composite made sense. For example, the respondent that judged the website is extremely trustworthy would choose SA for the first five items, then SD for the sixth. We can see that we would not want to just add these up, as this score of 21 would not really reflect someone that felt very positive about the trustworthiness of the site. Since the content of the sixth item is the reverse of trust (distrust), the scale itself should be reversed. Thus, on a five-point scale, the values are reversed as follows:

- 5 becomes 1.
- 4 becomes 2.
- 3 stays 3.
- 2 becomes 4.
- 1 becomes 5.

> **reverse coding** A method of making sure all the items forming a composite scale are scored in the same direction. Negative items can be recoded into the equivalent responses for a non-reverse-coded item; changing the value of a response to a scale so it is the opposite of the original value, e.g. a scale from 1–5 is reversed so 1 = 5, 2 = 4, 3 = 3, 4 = 2 and 5 = 1. In this way, negative items in a scale are scored in the same direction as positive items.

After the reverse coding, our respondent who felt the website was trustworthy would have a summated score of 25, which does correctly reflect a very positive attitude. If the respondent described in Figure 7.5 responded to this new item with a SA (5), it would be reverse coded as a 1 before computing the summated scale. Thus, the summated scale value for the six items would become 14.

Three criteria for good measurement

The three major criteria for evaluating measurements are: reliability, validity and sensitivity.

Reliability

Reliability is an indicator of a measure's internal consistency. Consistency is the key to understanding reliability. A measure is reliable when different attempts at measuring something converge on the same result. For example, consider an exam that has three parts: 25 multiple-choice questions, two essay questions and a short case. If a student gets 20 of the 25 (80 per cent) multiple-choice questions correct, we would expect she would also score about 80 per cent on the essay and case portions of the exam. Further, if a professor's research tests are reliable, a student should tend towards consistent scores on all tests. In other words, a student who scores 80 per cent on the first test should score close to 80 per cent on all subsequent tests. Another way to look at this is that the student who achieves the best score on one test will score close to the best score in the class on the other tests. If it is difficult to predict what students would score on a test by examining their previous test scores, the tests probably lack reliability or the students are not putting in the same amount of preparation for each test.

YOUR RESEARCH

Most computer statistical software makes scale recoding easy. For example, using Statistical Package for Social Scientists (SPSS), possibly the most widely used software package in the analysis of quantitative data, all that needs to be done to reverse code a scale is to go through the right click-through sequence described here:

1. Click on transform.
2. Click on recode.
3. Choose to recode into the same variable.
4. Select the variable(s) to be recoded.
5. Click on old and new values.
6. Use the menu that appears to enter the old values and the matching new values. Click add after entering each pair.
7. Click continue.

You would find it helpful to read Chapter 19 'Analyzing Quantitative Data' in conjunction with this chapter. There is a good introduction to SPSS in that chapter.

The concept of reliability revolves around consistency. Think of a scale to measure weight. You would expect this scale to be consistent from one time to the next. If you stepped on the scale and it read 70 kilos, then got off and back on, you would expect it to again read 70; if it read 60 the second time, while you may be happier, the scale would not be reliable.

Internal consistency

Internal consistency represents a measure's homogeneity. An attempt to measure trustworthiness may require asking several similar but not identical questions, as shown in Figure 7.5. The set of items that make up a measure is referred to as a battery of scale items. Internal consistency of a multiple-item measure can be measured by correlating scores on subsets of items making up a scale.

 internal consistency Represents a measure's homogeneity or the extent to which each indicator of a concept converges on some common meaning.

The **split-half method** of checking reliability is performed by taking half the items from a scale (for example, odd-numbered items) and checking them against the results from the other half (even-numbered items). The two scale halves should produce similar scores and correlate highly. The problem with the split-half method is determining the two halves. Should it be even- and odd-numbered questions? Questions 1–3 compared to 4–6? Coefficient alpha provides a solution to this dilemma.

 split-half method A method for assessing internal consistency by checking the results of one-half of a set of scaled items against the results from the other half; used to test equivalence reliability.

Coefficient alpha is the most commonly applied estimate of a multiple-item scale's reliability. Coefficient α represents internal consistency by computing the average of all possible split-half reliabilities for a multiple-item scale. The coefficient demonstrates whether or not the different items converge. Although coefficient α does not address validity, many researchers use α as the sole indicator of a scale's quality. Coefficient alpha ranges in value from 0, meaning no consistency, to 1, meaning complete consistency (all items yield corresponding values). Generally speaking, scales with a coefficient α between 0.80 and 0.95 are considered to have very good reliability. Scales with a coefficient α between 0.70 and 0.80 are considered to have good reliability and an α value between 0.60 and 0.70 indicates fair reliability. When the coefficient α is below 0.6, the scale has poor reliability. Most statistical software packages, such as SPSS, will easily compute coefficient α.

 coefficient alpha (α) The most commonly applied estimate of a multiple-item scale's reliability. It represents the average of all possible split-half reliabilities for a construct.

Test–retest reliability

The **test–retest method** of determining reliability involves administering the same scale or measure to the same respondents at two separate times to test for stability. If the measure is stable over time, the test, administered under the same conditions each time, should obtain similar results. Test–retest reliability represents a measure's repeatability.

 test–retest method Used to estimate reliability. A questionnaire is used in a pilot test, then later, the same test is repeated and compared for consistency; administering the same scale or measure to the same respondents at two separate points in time to test for stability.

Suppose a researcher at one time attempts to measure buying intentions and finds that 12 per cent of the population is willing to purchase a product. If the study is repeated a few weeks later under similar conditions, and the researcher again finds that 12 per cent of the population is willing to purchase the product, the measure appears to be reliable. High stability correlation or consistency between two measures at time 1 and time 2 indicates high reliability.

Let us assume that a person does not change his or her attitude about orange juice. Attitude might be measured with an item like the one shown below:

> *I prefer orange juice to all other types of fruit juice.*

If repeated measurements of that individual's attitude toward orange juice are taken with the same scale, a reliable instrument will produce the same results each time the scale is measured. Thus, one's attitude in October 2018 should tend to be the same as one's attitude in May 2019. When a measuring instrument produces unpredictable results from one testing to the next, the results are said to be unreliable because of error in measurement.

As another example, consider these remarks made by a Gillette executive about the reliability problems in measuring reactions to razor blades:

> *There is a high degree of noise in our data, a considerable variability in results. It's a big mish-mash, what we call the night sky in August. There are points all over the place. A man will give a blade a high score one day, but the next day he'll cut himself a lot and give the blade a terrible score. But on the third day, he'll give the same blade a good score. What you have to do is try to see some pattern in all this. There are some gaps in our knowledge.*

Measures of test–retest reliability pose two problems that are common to all longitudinal studies. First, the pre-measure, or first measure, may sensitize the respondents to their participation in a research project and subsequently influence the results of the second measure. Furthermore, if the time between measures is long, there may be an attitude change or other maturation of the subjects. Thus, a reliable measure can indicate a low or a moderate correlation between the first and second administration, but this low correlation may be due to an attitude change over time rather than to a lack of reliability in the measure itself.

Validity

Good measures should be both consistent and accurate. Reliability represents how consistent a measure is, in that the different attempts at measuring the same thing converge on the same point. Accuracy deals more with how a measure assesses the intended concept. Validity is the accuracy of a measure or the extent to which a score truthfully represents a concept. In other words, are we accurately measuring what we think we are measuring?

Achieving validity is not a simple matter, as made clear in the opening Value of Research box in this chapter. The job performance measure should truly reflect job performance. If a supervisor's friendship affects the performance measure, then the scale's validity is diminished. Likewise, if the performance scale is defined as effort, the result may well be a reliable scale but not one that actually reflects performance. Effort may well lead to performance but effort probably does not equal performance.

Establishing validity

Researchers have attempted to assess validity in many ways. They attempt to provide some evidence of a measure's degree of validity by answering a variety of questions. Is there a consensus among other researchers that my attitude scale measures what it is supposed to measure? Does my measure cover everything that it should? Does my measure correlate with other measures of the same concept? Does the behaviour expected from my measure predict actual observed behaviour? The four basic approaches to establishing validity are face validity, content validity, criterion validity and construct validity.

Face validity refers to the subjective agreement among professionals that a scale logically reflects the concept being measured. Do the test items look like they make sense given a concept's definition? When an inspection of the test items convinces experts that the items match the definition, the scale is said to have face validity.

face validity A scale's content logically appears to reflect what was intended to be measured.

Clear, understandable questions such as 'How many children do you have?' generally are agreed to have face validity. But it becomes more difficult to assess face validity in regard to more complicated business phenomena. For instance, consider the concept of customer loyalty. Does the statement 'I prefer to purchase my groceries at Delavan Fine Foods' appear to capture loyalty? How about 'I am very satisfied with my purchases from Delavan Fine Foods'? What about 'Delavan Fine

Foods offers very good value'? While the first statement appears to capture loyalty, it can be argued the second question is not loyalty but rather satisfaction. What does the third statement reflect? Do you think it looks like a loyalty statement?

In scientific studies, face validity might be considered a first hurdle. In comparison to other forms of validity, face validity is relatively easy to assess. However, researchers are generally not satisfied with simply establishing face validity. Because of the elusive nature of attitudes and other phenomena, additional forms of validity are sought.

Content validity refers to the degree that a measure covers the domain of interest. Do the items capture the entire scope but not go beyond the concept we are measuring? If an exam is supposed to cover Chapters 1–5, it is fair for students to expect that questions should come from all five chapters, rather than just one or two. It is also fair to assume that the questions will not come from Chapter 6. Thus, when students complain about the material for an exam, they are often claiming it lacks content validity. Similarly, an evaluation of an employee's job performance should cover all important aspects of the job, but not something outside of the employee's specified duties.

> **content validity** The degree to which a measure covers the breadth of the domain of interest.

It has been argued that shoppers receive value from two primary elements. Hedonic shopping value refers to the pleasure and enjoyment one gets from the shopping experience, while utilitarian shopping value refers to value received from the actual acquisition of the product desired. If a researcher assessing shopping value only asked questions regarding the utilitarian aspects of shopping, we could argue the measure lacks content validity since part of the domain (hedonic value) is ignored.

Criterion validity addresses the question, 'How well does my measure work in practice?' Because of this, criterion validity is sometimes referred to as pragmatic validity. In other words, is my measure practical? Criterion validity may be classified as either concurrent validity or predictive validity depending on the time sequence in which the new measurement scale and the criterion measure are correlated. If the new measure is taken at the same time as the criterion measure and is shown to be valid, then it has concurrent validity. Predictive validity is established when a new measure predicts a future event. The two measures differ only on the basis of a time dimension – that is, the criterion measure is separated in time from the predictor measure.

> **criterion validity** The ability of a measure to correlate with other standard measures of similar constructs or established criteria.

For example, a home pregnancy test is designed to have concurrent validity – to accurately determine if a person is pregnant at the time of the test. Fertility tests, by way of contrast, are designed for predictive validity – to determine if a person can become pregnant in the future. In a business setting, participants in a training seminar might be given a test to assess their knowledge of the concepts covered, establishing concurrent validity. Personnel managers may give potential employees an exam to predict if they will be effective salespeople (predictive validity). While face validity is a subjective evaluation, criterion validity provides a more rigorous empirical test.

Construct validity exists when a measure reliably measures and truthfully represents a unique concept. Construct validity consists of several components, including:

- face validity
- content validity
- criterion validity
- convergent validity
- discriminant validity.

> **construct validity** Exists when a measure reliably measures and truthfully represents a unique concept; it consists of several components including face validity, content validity, criterion validity, convergent validity and discriminant validity.

We have discussed face validity, content validity and criterion validity. Before we move further, we must be sure our measures look like they are measuring what they are intended to measure (face validity) and adequately cover the domain of interest (content validity). If so, we can assess **convergent validity** and **discriminant validity**.

convergent validity Concepts that should be related to one another are, in fact, related; highly reliable scales contain convergent validity.

discriminant validity Represents the uniqueness or distinctiveness of a measure; a scale should not correlate too highly with a measure of a different construct.

These forms of validity represent how unique or distinct a measure is. Convergent validity requires concepts that should be related are indeed related. For example, in business we believe customer satisfaction and customer loyalty are related. If we have measures of both, we would expect them to be positively correlated. If we found no significant correlation between our measures of satisfaction and our measures of loyalty, it would bring into question the convergent validity of these measures. Contrariwise, our customer satisfaction measure should not correlate too highly with the loyalty measure if the two concepts are truly different. If the correlation is too high, we have to ask if we are measuring two different things or if satisfaction and loyalty are actually one concept. As a rough rule of thumb, when two scales are correlated above 0.75, discriminant validity may be questioned. We expect related concepts to display a significant correlation (convergent validity), but not to be so highly correlated that they are not independent concepts (discriminant validity).

Multivariate procedures like factor analysis can be useful in establishing construct validity. There is a basic introduction to statistical analysis in Chapter 19. If you have a particular interest in statistics, you will find very many useful sources in the library of your college or university.

Reliability versus validity

Reliability is a necessary but not sufficient condition for validity. A reliable scale may not be valid. For example, a purchase intention measurement technique may consistently indicate that 20 per cent of those sampled are willing to purchase a new product. Whether the measure is valid depends on whether 20 per cent of the population indeed purchases the product. A reliable but invalid instrument will yield consistently inaccurate results.

Sensitivity

The sensitivity of a scale is an important measurement concept, particularly when changes in attitudes or other hypothetical constructs are under investigation. **Sensitivity** refers to an instrument's ability to accurately measure variability in a concept. A dichotomous response category, such as 'agree or disagree', does not allow the recording of subtle attitude changes. A more sensitive measure with numerous categories on the scale may be needed. For example, adding 'strongly agree', 'mildly agree', 'neither agree nor disagree', 'mildly disagree' and 'strongly disagree' will increase the scale's sensitivity.

sensitivity Measurement of an instrument's ability to accurately measure variability in stimuli or responses.

The sensitivity of a scale based on a single question or single item can also be increased by adding questions or items. In other words, because composite measures allow for a greater range of possible scores, they are more sensitive than single-item scales. Thus, sensitivity is generally increased by adding more response points or adding scale items.

YOUR RESEARCH

A comprehensive survey often involves many different types of measurement. The questionnaire used in this survey contained multiple scale measurement levels. Take a look at the questions shown below. What scale measurement level do these items represent? Each set of items is designed to capture a single construct. In the top portion, the items assess how much work–life interferes with life outside of work. In the lower portion, the scales assess self-perceived performance. What do you think of the scales? Do they give you any ideas in relation to your own research?

The opening Value of Good Research box of this chapter describes a situation in which Griff must develop a 'recipe' for distinguishing employees, based on job performance. Before the measurement process can be defined, he will have to decide exactly what it is that needs to be produced. In this case, the outcome should be a valid job performance measure.

(Continued)

The next set of items concerns how much your current job affects what you do when you are away from work. For each question, choose the response that best describes how your current job has impact on:

	Strong negative impact	Negative impact	Mild negative impact	Mild positive impact	Positive impact	Strong positive impact
your mental and physical state away from work	◉	◉	◉	◉	◉	◉
your participation in home activities	◉	◉	◉	◉	◉	◉
concern for your health	◉	◉	◉	◉	◉	◉
your personal development	◉	◉	◉	◉	◉	◉
your performance in school	◉	◉	◉	◉	◉	◉
your social life	◉	◉	◉	◉	◉	◉

Relative to the other workers at your place of employment, how would you describe your job performance?

	Strongly disagree	Disagree	Neither agree or disagree	Slightly agree	Somewhat agree	Strongly agree	Absolutely agree
I am the best at performing my particular job	◉	◉	◉	◉	◉	◉	◉
I am in the top 10 per cent of all employees	◉	◉	◉	◉	◉	◉	◉
I know more about my job than most of my coworkers	◉	◉	◉	◉	◉	◉	◉
I put in more effort than most of my coworkers	◉	◉	◉	◉	◉	◉	◉
I receive more incentive pay than most of my coworkers	◉	◉	◉	◉	◉	◉	◉

QUESTIONS FOR REVIEW AND CRITICAL THINKING

1. Indicate whether the following measures use a nominal, ordinal, interval, or ratio scale.
   a. Prices on the stock market.
   b. Marital status, classified as 'married' or 'never married'.
   c. A yes–no question asking whether a respondent has ever been unemployed.
   d. Professorial rank: assistant professor, associate professor or professor.
   e. Grades: A, B, C, D or F.
2. What are the components of construct validity? Describe each.
3. Comment on the validity and reliability of the following.
   a. A respondent's report of an intention to subscribe to *Consumer Reports* is highly reliable. A researcher believes this constitutes a valid measurement of dissatisfaction with the economic system and alienation from big business.
   b. A general interest magazine claimed that it was a better advertising medium than television programmes with similar content. Research had indicated that for a soft drink and other test products, recall scores were higher for the magazine ads than for 30-second commercials.
   c. A respondent's report of frequency of magazine reading consistently indicates that she regularly reads *Good Housekeeping* and *Gourmet* and never reads *Cosmopolitan*.

4. How is it that business researchers can justify treating a seven-point Likert scale as interval?

5. How can a researcher assess the reliability and validity of a multiple-item composite scale?

6. Describe, compare and contrast the four different levels of scale measurement.

7. Why might a researcher wish to use more than one question to measure satisfaction with a particular aspect of retail shopping?

8. Look at the responses to the following survey items that describe how stressful consumers believed a shopping trip was using a 10-point scale ranging from 1 (= no stress at all) to 10 (= extremely stressful):
   - How stressful was finding a place to park? 7
   - How stressful was the checkout procedure? 5
   - How stressful was trying to find exactly the right product? 8
   - How stressful was it to find a store employee? 6
     a. What would be the stress score for this respondent based on a summated scale score?
     b. What would be the stress score for this respondent based on an average composite scale score?
     c. Do any items need to be reverse coded? Why or why not?

9. Suppose a researcher takes over a project only after a proposal has been written by another researcher. Where will the researcher find the things that need to be measured?

10. Consider the different grading measuring scales described at the beginning of the chapter. Describe what level of measurement is represented by each. Which method do you think contains the least opportunity for error?

11. Define measurement. How is your performance in your research class being measured?

12. What is the difference between a concept and a construct?

CASE STUDY

FlyAway Airways

Wesley Shocker, research analyst for FlyAway Airways, was asked by the director of research to make recommendations regarding the best approach for monitoring the quality of service provided by the airline. FlyAway Airways is a national air carrier that has a comprehensive route structure consisting of long-haul, coast-to-coast routes and direct, non-stop routes between short-haul metropolitan areas. Current competitors include Midway and Alaska Airlines. FlyAway Airlines is poised to surpass the billion-dollar revenue level required to be designated as a major airline. This change in status brings a new set of competitors. To prepare for this move up in competitive status, Shocker was asked to review the options available for monitoring the quality of FlyAway Airways service and the service of its competitors. Such monitoring would involve better understanding the nature of service quality and the ways in which quality can be tracked for airlines.

After some investigation, Shocker discovered two basic approaches to measuring quality of airline service that can produce similar ranking results. His report must outline the important aspects to consider in measuring quality as well as the critical points of difference and similarity between the two approaches to measuring quality.

Some background on quality

In today's competitive airline industry, it is crucial that an airline does all it can to attract and retain customers. One of the best ways to do this is by offering quality service to consumers. Perceptions of service quality vary from person to person, but an enduring element of service quality is the consistent achievement of customer satisfaction. For customers to perceive an airline as offering quality service, they must be satisfied and that usually means receiving a service outcome that is equal to or greater than what they expected.

An airline consumer usually is concerned most with issues of schedule, destination and price when choosing an airline. Given that most airlines have competition in each of these areas, other factors that relate to quality become important to the customer when making a choice between airlines. Both subjective aspects of quality (food, pleasant employees, and so forth) and objective aspects (on-time performance, safety, lost baggage, and so forth) have real meaning to consumers. These secondary factors may not be as critical as schedule, destination and price, but they do affect quality judgements of the customer.

There are many possible combinations of subjective and objective aspects that could influence a customer's perception of quality at different times. Fortunately, since 1988, consumers of airline services have had access to objective information from the Department

(Continued)

of Transportation regarding service performance in some basic categories. Unfortunately, the average consumer is most likely unaware of or uninterested in these data on performance; instead, consumers rely on personal experience and subjective opinion to judge quality of service. Periodic surveys of subjective consumer opinion regarding airline service experience are available through several sources. These efforts rely on contact with a sample of consumers who may or may not have informed opinions regarding the quality of airline service for all airlines being compared.

A consumer survey approach

In his research, Shocker discovered a recent study conducted to identify favourite airlines of frequent flyers. This study is typical of the survey-based, infrequent (usually only annually), subjective efforts conducted to assess airline quality. A New York firm, Research & Forecasts, Inc., published results of a consumer survey of frequent flyers that used several criteria to rate domestic and international airlines. Criteria included comfort, service, reliability, food quality, cost, delays, routes served, safety and frequent-flyer plans. The questionnaire was sent to 25 000 frequent flyers.

The 4462 people who responded were characterized as predominantly male (59 per cent) professional managers (66 per cent) whose average age was 45 and who travelled an average of at least 43 nights a year for both business and pleasure. This group indicated that the most important factors in choosing an airline were: (1) route structure, 46 per cent; (2) price, 42 per cent; (3) reliability, 41 per cent; (4) service, 33 per cent; (5) safety, 33 per cent; (6) frequent-flyer plans, 33 per cent; and (7) food, 12 per cent. When asked to rate 20 different airlines, respondents provided the rankings in Case Table 7.1.

A weighted average approach

Shocker also discovered a newer, more objective approach to measuring airline quality in a study recently published by the National Institute for Aviation Research at the Wichita State University in Wichita, Kansas. The Airline Quality Rating (AQR) is a weighted average of 19 factors that have relevance when judging the quality of airline services (see Case Figure 7.1). If you are interested, you can check the latest reports from the AQR at this website: airlinequalityrating.com/. The AQR is based on data that are readily obtainable (most of the data are updated monthly) from published sources for each major airline operating in the USA. Regularly published data on such factors as consumer complaints, on-time performance, accidents, number of

Case Table 7.1 Ranking of major airlines: consumer survey approach

1. American	11. Lufthansa
2. United	12. USAir
3. Delta	13. KLM
4. TWA	14. America West
5. SwissAir	15. JAL
6. Singapore	16. Alaska
7. British Airways	17. Qantas
8. Continental	18. Midway
9. Air France	19. Southwest
10. Pan Am	20. SAS

Factor	Weight
1. Average age of fleet	25.85
2. Number of aircraft	14.54
3. On-time performance	18.63
4. Load factor	26.98
5. Pilot deviations	28.03
6. Number of accidents	28.38
7. Frequent-flyer awards	27.35
8. Flight problems[b]	28.05
9. Denied boardings[b]	28.03
10. Mishandled baggage[b]	27.92
11. Fares[b]	27.60
12. Customer service[b]	27.20
13. Refunds	27.32
14. Ticketing/boarding[b]	−7.08
15. Advertising[b]	−6.82
16. Credit[b]	25.94
17. Other[b]	27.34
18. Financial stability	26.52
19. Average seat-mile cost	24.49

$$AQR = \frac{w_1F_1 - w_2F_2 + w_3F_3 + \cdots - w_{19}F_{19}}{w_1 + w_2 + w_3 + \cdots + w_{19}}$$

a. The 19-item rating has a reliability coefficient (Cronbach's alpha) of 0.87.

b. Data for these factors come from consumer complaints registered with the Department of Transportation.

Case Figure 7.1 Factors included in the airline quality rating (AQR)[a]

(Continued)

Rank	Airline	AQR Score
1	American	10.328
2	Southwest	10.254
3	Delta	10.209
4	United	10.119
5	USAir	10.054
6	Pan Am	10.003
7	Northwest	20.063
8	Continental	20.346
9	America West	20.377
10	TWA	20.439

Case Figure 7.2   Airline rankings

aircraft and financial performance are available from the Department of Transportation, the National Transportation Safety Board, Moody's Bond Record, industry trade publications and annual reports of individual airlines.

To establish the 19 weighted factors, an opinion survey was conducted with a group of 65 experts in the aviation field. These experts included representatives of most major airlines, air travel experts, Federal Aviation Administration (FAA) representatives, academic researchers, airline manufacturing and support firms, and individual consumers. Each expert was asked to rate the importance that each individual factor might have to a consumer of airline services using a scale of 0 (no importance) to 10 (great importance). The average importance ratings for each of the 19 factors were then used as the weights for those factors in the AQR. Case Figure 7.1 shows the factors included in the AQR, the weight associated with each factor and whether the factor has a positive or negative impact on quality from the consumer's perspective. Using the AQR formula and recent data, rankings for the 10 major US airlines are shown in Case Figure 7.2.

What course to chart?

Shocker has discovered what appear to be two different approaches to measuring quality of airlines. One relies on direct consumer opinion and is mostly subjective in its approach to quality and the elements considered. The other relies on performance data that are available through public sources and appear to be more objective. Both approaches incorporate pertinent elements that could be used by consumers to judge the quality of an airline. Shocker's recommendation must consider the comprehensiveness and usefulness of these approaches for FlyAway Airways as it moves into a more competitive environment. What course of action should he recommend?

Questions

1. How comparable are the two different methods? In what ways are they similar? In what ways are they different?
2. What are the positive and negative aspects of each approach that Shocker should consider before recommending a course of action for FlyAway Airways?
3. What aspects of service quality does each approach address well and not so well?
4. Considering the two methods outlined, what types of validity would you consider to be demonstrated by the two approaches to measuring quality? Defend your position.
5. Which of the methods should Shocker recommend? Why?

END OF CHAPTER QUESTIONS

1   Define each of the following concepts and then operationally define each one by providing correspondence rules between the definition and the scale:

   a   a good bowler
   b   purchasing intention for an iPhone
   c   consumer involvement with cars
   d   a workaholic
   e   outstanding supervisory skills
   f   a risk-averse investor.

2   Refer back to the opening Value of Good Research box. Use a search engine to find stories dealing with job performance. In particular, pay attention to stories that may be related to CRM (customer relationship management). Make a recommendation to Griff concerning a way that job performance should be measured. Would your scale be nominal, ordinal, interval or ratio?

3   Go to www.queendom.com/tests. Click on the lists of personality tests. Take the hostility test. Do you think this is a reliable and valid measure of how prone someone is to generally act in a hostile manner?

REFERENCES

AQR Airline Quality Rating, airlinequalityrating.com (Accessed 17.03.2018).

Queendom The Land of Tests, www.queendom.com/tests/index.htm (Accessed 17.03.2018).

RECOMMENDED READING

Anderson, B.F. (1971) *The Psychology Experiment*, Belmont, CA: Brooks/Cole.

Arnold, C. (2004) 'Satisfaction's the name of the game', *Marketing News, 38*: 39–45, www.theacsi.org

Babin, B.J. and Attaway, J. (2000) 'Atmospheric affect as a tool for creating value and gaining share of customer', *Journal of Business Research, 49*: 91–99.

Babin, B.J., Darden, W.R. and Griffin, M. (1994) 'Work and/or fun: measuring hedonic and utilitarian shopping value', *Journal of Consumer Research, 20*: 644–656.

Bart, Y., Shankar, V., Sultan, F. and Urban, G.L. (2005) 'Are the drivers and role of online trust the same for all web sites and consumers? A large-scale exploratory study', *Journal of Marketing, 69*: 133–152.

Cohen, J. (1990) 'Things I have learned (so far)', *American Psychologist, 45*: 1304–1312.

Cox, K.K. and Enis, B.M. (1972) *The Marketing Research Process, Pacific Palisades*, CA: Goodyear.

Creswell, J. and Creswell, J.D. (2018) *Research Design: Qualitative, Quantitative and Mixed Methods Approaches*, Thousand Oaks, CA: Sage.

Cronbach, L.J. and Shavelson, R.J. (2004) 'My current thoughts on coefficient alpha and successor procedures', *Educational and Psychological Measurement, 64(3)*: 391–418, epm.sagepub.com/cgi/content/short/64/3/391

Hair, J.F., Black, B.C., Babin, B.J., Anderson, R. and Tatham, R. (2006) *Multivariate Data Analysis* (6th edn), Upper Saddle River, NJ: Prentice Hall.

Kerlinger, F.N. (1973) *Foundations of Behavioral Research*, New York: Holt, Rinehart & Winston.

Neuman, W.L. (2014) *Social Research Methods: Quantitative and Qualitative Approaches* (7th edn), Essex, England: Pearson Education Ltd.

Periatt, J.A., LeMay, S.A. and Chakrabarty, S. (2004) 'The selling orientation–customer orientation (SOCO) scale: Cross-validation of the revised version', *Journal of Personal Selling and Sales Management, 24*: 49–54.

Verhoef, P.C. (2003) 'Understanding the effect of customer relationship management efforts on customer retention and customer share development', *Journal of Marketing, 67*: 30–45.

Wells, C. (1980) 'The war of the razors', *Esquire*, February, 3.

CHAPTER 8

QUALITATIVE RESEARCH: AN INTRODUCTION

LEARNING OBJECTIVES

At the end of this chapter, the student should:

- Understand qualitative research.

- Be able to define and explain qualitative research.

- Know how and when to use qualitative research.

RESEARCH SKILLS

At the end of this chapter, the student should, using the exercises on Cengage Brain:

- Understand the role of qualitative research in business research.

- Be able to describe the basic qualitative research orientations.

- Recognize common qualitative research tools and know how to apply them.

THE VALUE OF GOOD RESEARCH

What's in the Van?

Is this shoe too cool? That was really the question asked by VF Corporation when they acquired Vans. Vans traditionally are synonymous with skateboarding and skateboard culture. Readers that are unfamiliar with skateboarding may well have never heard of the company. However, any reader who is part of the skateboard culture is probably looking down at his or her Vans right now!

Former Vans CEO Gary Schoenfeld pointed out that a decade before the acquisition (a $396 million deal), Vans was practically a dead brand. However, in recent years there has been a revival in skateboard interest and Vans has remained the number one skateboard shoe provider. Now, the management team has been given the task of deciding how to raise Vans' sales beyond the $2.3 billion achieved in 2016, as reported in *Fortune* (Whaba, 2017).

Where will the growth come from? Should the company define itself as a 'skateboard footwear' company, a 'lifestyle' company or as the icon for the skate culture? Answering this question will require a deeper interpretation of the meaning of the 'Van'.

Skateboarding is a dynamic activity. So, what exactly is in the mind and heart of a 'boarder'? Two important research questions involve 'What is the meaning of a

(Continued)

pair of Vans?' and 'What things define the skateboarding experience?'

Questions like these call for qualitative research methods. Not just any researcher is 'fit' for this job. One way to collect these data is to hire young, energetic research employees to become 'boarders' and immerse themselves in the culture.

They may have to 'Casper' like a 'flatland' skateboard legend in order to try to fit in, while probing for meaning among the discussion and activities of the other boarders. From such fieldwork, Vans may find that their brand helps identify a boarder and makes them feel unique in some ways.

If so, Vans may want to investigate increasing its product line with innovations attractive to skateboarders.

For the research, in-depth interviews of Vans wearers in which people describe in detail why they wear Vans, will also be useful. Vans should not be surprised if they find a significant portion of their shoes are sold to people like Mr Samuel Teel, a retired attorney from Toledo, Ohio. Sam is completely unaware of the connection between Vans and skateboarding. He likes them because he does not have to bend to tie his shoelaces! Maybe there are some secondary market segments that could bring growth to Vans. But marketing to them could complicate things – who knows?

INTRODUCTION

The focus in qualitative research is not on generating and analyzing numeric data, but on generating and analyzing non-numeric data. Qualitative research is generally focused on individual human experiences, understandings and interpretations. In qualitative research, the experience, understanding and/or interpretation of each individual and/or group participating in the research, in relation to the phenomenon under investigation, is recorded and represented to the degree possible and/or to the degree required in any report of the research. As explained in earlier chapters, qualitative research is research conducted within an interpretivist paradigm or a social constructionist paradigm, while quantitative research is research conducted within a positivist paradigm (see Chapter 4).

QUALITATIVE RESEARCH IN BUSINESS

Qualitative business research is research that addresses business objectives through techniques that allow the researcher to provide elaborate interpretations of business phenomena without depending on numerical measurement. The focus is on discovering inner meanings and new insights. Qualitative research is very widely applied in practice in business. There are many research firms that specialize in qualitative research.

> **qualitative business research** Research that addresses business objectives through techniques that allow the researcher to provide elaborate interpretations of phenomena without depending on numerical measurement; the focus is on discovering inner meanings and new insights.

Qualitative research is less structured than quantitative research. For example, it does not rely on questionnaires containing structured response formats. Instead, the researcher must extract meaning from unstructured or semi-structured responses, from a semi-structured questionnaire or from another data-gathering method, such as text from a recorded interview or perhaps a collage representing the meaning of some experience. The researcher interprets the data to extract their meaning.

Uses of qualitative research

Mechanics cannot use a hammer to fix everything that is broken. Instead, the mechanic has a toolbox from which a tool is matched to a problem. Business research is the same. The researcher has many tools available and the research design should try to match the best tool to the research. It is important to use the appropriate tool for the task in hand. However, just as a mechanic is probably not an expert with every tool, each researcher usually has special expertise with a small number of tools.

In a research project where the emphasis is on a deeper understanding or perhaps on the creative work of developing novel concepts, qualitative research is often appropriate. The following list represents common situations that call for qualitative research:

1. When the aim of the research is to develop an understanding of some phenomena in great detail and in much depth. Qualitative research tools are aimed at discovering the primary themes indicating human experience, interpretation and motivation, and the documentation of activities (the data-gathering process) is usually very complete. Often qualitative research provides richer information than quantitative approaches.

2. When it is difficult to develop specific and actionable problem statements or research objectives. For instance, if after several interviews with the research client the researcher still cannot determine exactly what needs to be measured, then qualitative research approaches may help with problem definition. Qualitative research is often useful when the researcher needs to gain further insight in order to clearly understand the research problem.

3. When the aim of the research is to learn how phenomena occur in natural settings or to learn how to express some concept in colloquial terms. For example, how do consumers actually use a product? Or, exactly how does the accounting department process invoices? While a survey can probably ask many useful questions, observing a product in use or watching the invoice process will usually be more insightful. Qualitative research produces many product and process improvement ideas.

4. When some behaviour the researcher is studying is particularly context dependent, for instance if the reasons something is liked or some behaviour is performed depends very much on the particular situation surrounding the event. For example, understanding why Goth clothing is worn is probably difficult outside the Goth subculture. So a researcher would go inside Goth culture, if allowed access, in order to study the meaning of Goth clothing within that culture.

5. When a fresh approach to studying some problem is needed, or when quantitative research has yielded less than satisfying results. Qualitative tools can yield unique insights, insights that could not be developed with the use of quantitative research, many of which may lead to new directions.

Qualitative 'versus' quantitative research

In social science, one can find many debates about the superiority of qualitative research over quantitative research and vice versa. We will begin by saying that this is largely a superfluous argument in either direction. The truth is that qualitative research can accomplish research objectives that quantitative research cannot and quantitative research can accomplish objectives that qualitative research cannot. In other words, both quantitative and qualitative research approaches are equally useful. The key to successfully using either is to match the right approach to the right research project.

Many good research projects combine both qualitative and quantitative research. For instance, developing valid survey measures requires first a deep understanding of the concept to be measured and a description of the way these ideas are expressed in everyday language. Both of these are tasks best suited for qualitative research. However, validating the measure formally to make sure it can reliably capture the intended concept will likely require quantitative research. Also, qualitative research may be needed to separate symptoms from problems and then quantitative research can follow up to test relationships among relevant variables. The Real World Research box 'Discoveries at P&G!' describes one such situation.

YOUR RESEARCH

Imagine that you have developed an online survey focused on examining perception among respondents regarding the quality of business education in your college or university. Let us say that the survey is designed to gather primarily quantitative data. However, the question that asks respondents to provide suggestions about improving the quality of business education in your college or university is qualitative in nature. Let's say that this information is elicited from respondents by means of a sentence completion exercise. So, in the questionnaire, respondents are asked to complete the following sentence: 'The quality of business education could be improved in this college/university by . . .'. Ask some of your classmates to complete the sentence. When they have done so, their completed sentences provide you with qualitative data. Look over the comments provided by the students. Then identify the major themes present in them. Based on the comments, and your thematic analysis of them, what suggestions would you offer administrators at your school for improving the educational environment?

REAL WORLD RESEARCH

Discoveries at P&G!

With literally thousands of products to manage, Procter & Gamble (P&G) finds itself conducting qualitative research almost daily. P&G never introduces a product that has not been reviewed from nearly every possible angle. Likewise, before taking a product to a new country, you can be confident that the product has been 'focus grouped' in that environment.

P&G often uses qualitative research techniques to discover potential problems or opportunities for the company's products. For example, focus groups played a major role in Herbal Essences hair care's new logo, advertising copy, reformulated ingredients and new bottle design. The redesigned bottles for shampoos and conditioners were curved in a yin and yang fashion so they can fit together.

At times, P&G seeks outside help for its research. Such was the case when P&G wanted a study of its own business problems. The researchers selected began by applying qualitative research techniques including depth interviews (or in-depth interviews), observational techniques and focus groups with P&G managers and marketing employees. This data-gathering exercise gave the researchers the idea that perhaps P&G was suffering more from a management problem than from a marketing problem. It helped form a general research question that asked whether business problems were really due to low morale among the employees. After a lot of qualitative interviews with dozens and dozens of P&G employees, a quantitative study followed up these findings and supported this idea, leading to suggestions for improving employee morale!

While **quantitative business research** can be defined as business research that addresses research objectives through empirical assessments that involve numerical measurement and analysis approaches, qualitative business research addresses research objectives through empirical assessments that involve non-numerical approaches.

> **quantitative business research** Business research that addresses research objectives through empirical assessments that involve numerical measurement and analysis.

Contrasting qualitative and quantitative methods

Table 8.1 illustrates some differences between qualitative and quantitative research. Certainly, these are generalities and exceptions may apply. However, it covers some of the key distinctions.

Table 8.1 Comparing qualitative and quantitative research

Qualitative research	Research aspect	Quantitative research
Discover ideas, used in exploratory research with general research questions	Common purpose	Test hypotheses or specific research questions
Observe and interpret	Approach	Measure and test
Unstructured, free-form	Data collection approach	Structured response categories provided
Researcher is intimately involved, findings are said to be subjective	Researcher independence	Researcher uninvolved observer, results/findings are said to be objective
Small samples – often in natural settings	Samples	Large samples to produce generalizable results (results that apply to other situations)
Exploratory research designs	Most often used	Descriptive and causal research designs

Quantitative researchers direct a considerable amount of activity towards measuring concepts with scales that either directly or indirectly provide numeric values. The numeric values can then be used in statistical computations and hypothesis testing. As will be described in detail later, this process involves comparing numbers in some way. In contrast, qualitative researchers are more interested in observing, listening and interpreting. As such, the researcher is intimately involved in the research process and in constructing, with participants, the results. For these reasons, qualitative research is said to be more **subjective.** Different researchers may reach different conclusions based on the same interview. In that respect, qualitative research is said to lack **intersubjective certifiability** (sometimes called inter-subjective verifiability), the ability of different individuals following the same procedures to produce the same results or come to the same conclusion. This should not be considered a weakness of qualitative research; rather, it is simply a characteristic that yields differing insights. In contrast, when a survey respondent provides a commitment score on a quantitative scale, it is thought to be more objective because the number will be the same no matter what researcher is involved in the analysis.

> **subjective** Findings can be said to be researcher dependent, meaning different researchers may reach different conclusions based on the same interview; the focus of the research is on the subjective understanding/perception/experience of participants in the study.
>
> **intersubjective certifiability** Different individuals following the same procedure will produce the same results or come to the same conclusion.

Qualitative research seldom involves samples with hundreds of respondents. Instead, a relatively small number of participants often provide the source of qualitative data. This is perfectly acceptable. Does a smaller sample mean that qualitative research is easier than quantitative? No, it does not. While fewer respondents have to be interviewed, the deeper involvement of the researcher in both data collection and analysis adds to the richness, depth and complexity of qualitative research.

In qualitative research, generally small samples are used, interpretive procedures are used that require subjective judgements, and unstructured or semi-structured approaches are generally used in data collection. Thus, these qualitative approaches cannot be used for drawing mathematically precise conclusions, as would be expected, for example, from causal designs involving experiments. This is no disadvantage, however, as it is the flexibility inherent in qualitative research and the depth of exploration possible with qualitative research that provide the essential utility of qualitative research.

Contrasting exploratory and confirmatory research

Most exploratory research designs produce **qualitative data**. Exploratory designs do not usually produce quantitative data, which represent phenomena by assigning numbers in an ordered and meaningful way. Rather than numbers, the focus of qualitative research is on words, on stories, on visual portrayals, on meaningful characterisations, interpretations and other expressive descriptions.

Sometimes, exploratory research may be needed to develop the ideas that lead to research hypotheses. In other words, in some situations the outcome of exploratory research is a testable research hypothesis. Confirmatory research then tests these hypotheses with quantitative data. The results of these tests help decision making by suggesting a specific course of action.

For example, an exploratory researcher is more likely to adopt a qualitative approach that might involve trying to develop a deeper understanding of how families are impacted by changing economic conditions, investigating how people suffering economically spend scarce resources. This may lead to the development of a hypothesis that during challenging economic times consumers seek low-cost entertainment such as movie rentals, but would not test this hypothesis. In contrast, a quantitative researcher may search for numbers that indicate economic trends. This may lead to hypothesis tests concerning how much the economy influences rental movie consumption.

> **qualitative data** Non-numerical data; data are textual, visual or oral; focus is on stories, visual portrayals, meaningful characterizations, interpretations and other expressive descriptions.

Some types of qualitative research can be conducted very quickly. Others take a very long time. For example, a single focus group involving a large bottling company's sales force might be conducted and interpreted in a matter of days, providing very fast results. However, other types of qualitative research, such as, for example, a participant–observer study aimed at understanding skateboarding, could take months to complete.

Orientations to qualitative research

Qualitative research can be performed in many ways using many techniques. It would be a useful exercise now to look back at Chapter 2 in order to examine again Figure 2.1, the methodological pyramid.

The methodological pyramid illustrates how the fundamental philosophies in the social sciences support the research methodologies used in social science research and how the research methodologies in turn facilitate the use of different data-gathering methods, for example, focus groups, interviews and projective techniques.

The major categories of qualitative research include:

1. Phenomenology – originating in philosophy and psychology.
2. Ethnography – originating in anthropology.
3. Grounded theory – originating in sociology.
4. Case studies – originating in psychology and in business research.

Phenomenology

What is a phenomenological approach to research?

Phenomenology represents a philosophical approach to studying human experiences based on the idea that human experience itself is inherently subjective and determined by the context in which people live. The phenomenological researcher focuses on how a person's behaviour is shaped by the relationship s/he has with the physical environment, objects, people and situations. Phenomenological inquiry seeks to describe, reflect on and interpret experiences, lived experience as detailed and explained by the person living the experience.

> **phenomenology** A philosophical approach to studying human experiences based on the idea that human experience itself is inherently subjective and determined by the context in which people live.

Researchers with a phenomenological orientation rely largely on conversational interview tools, although image-based research is also very useful (see Chapter 9 for a full introduction to research methodologies and methods). When conversational interviews are face to face, they are recorded either with video or audiotape and then the recording, or more usually a transcript of the recording, is interpreted by the researcher. The recording and/or the transcript of the recording is the data gathered. The phenomenological interviewer is careful to avoid asking direct questions and indeed is careful to avoid directing the research encounter to any discernible degree. Instead, the researcher facilitates the participant in describing and explaining the phenomenon under investigation. In addition, the researcher must do everything possible to make sure a respondent is comfortable telling his or her story. One way to accomplish this is to become a member of the group being studied (for example, becoming a skateboarder in the scenario described earlier in this chapter). The best way, of course, is to develop the necessary communication skills and degrees of empathy required of an accomplished social scientist.

A phenomenological approach to studying the meaning of skateboarding, or Goth culture, may require considerable time. The researcher may first spend weeks or months fitting in with the person or group of interest in order to establish the necessary level of trust. During this time, careful notes of conversations are made. If an interview is sought, the researcher would likely not begin by asking a Goth to describe his or her clothes. Instead, asking general questions about Goth culture, about becoming and being a Goth, may generate productive conversation. Generally, the approach is unstructured so as to allow the participant in the study to explain the meaning of the phenomenon under investigation from his or her perspective. The unstructured approach helps the researcher avoid leading questions. The unstructured approach facilitates the development in the research encounter of new insights into the phenomenon under investigation. There is more detail as well as useful references on phenomenology in Chapter 9, Table 9.2. Phenomenology is the methodology in focus in Chapter 14.

What is hermeneutics?

If you remember, back in Chapter 4 (Table 4.2) there is an introduction to philosophical frameworks. One of the frameworks listed in Table 4.2 is **hermeneutics**. Hermeneutics is defined in that table as the theory of interpretation and the study of the processes of interpretation. The term hermeneutics is important in phenomenology. Hermeneutics is an approach to understanding phenomenology that relies on analysis of texts in which a person tells a story about him or herself. Meaning is then drawn by connecting text passages to one another or to themes expressed outside the story. These connections are usually facilitated by coding the key meanings expressed in the story. While a full understanding of hermeneutics would require a substantial amount of reading beyond this textbook, it is useful to have some familiarity with the terminology as used when applying qualitative tools. For instance, a **hermeneutic unit** refers to a text passage (a quote) from a respondent's story that is linked with a key theme from within this story or provided by the researcher (in thematic coding of data – the processes of data analysis, including coding, are covered in detail in Part Four of this textbook). These text passages are important in the ways in which data are interpreted.

> **hermeneutics** Hermeneutics is defined as the theory of interpretation and the study of the processes of interpretation.
>
> **hermeneutic unit** Refers to a text passage from a respondent's story that is linked with a key theme from within this story or provided by the researcher.

Computerized software exists to assist in coding and interpreting texts and images and it is referred to as computer-assisted data analysis (CADA). ATLAS.ti is one such software package. Atlas.ti adopts the term hermeneutic unit in referring to groups of phrases that are linked with meaning. A useful component of computerized approaches is the word counter. The word counter will return counts of how many times words were used in a story. Clearly, the data generated by the word counter are quantitative, i.e. the *number* of words used; and this is an example of how quantitative data can be generated from qualitative data; it is an example of how close in practice quantitative and qualitative research approaches can be. The word counter is useful as frequently occurring words in data can suggest a key theme in data analysis.

Ethnography

Ethnography represents ways of studying cultures through methods that involve the researcher becoming a part of that culture. **Participant–observation** is a data-gathering method that typifies an ethnographic research approach. Participant–observation means the researcher becomes immersed within the culture that s/he is studying and draws data from his or her observations. A culture can be either a broad culture, like British culture, or a narrow culture, like urban gangs, Harley-Davidson owners, Goths or skateboarding enthusiasts. Netnography is a development of ethnography for the internet (Kozinets, 2015). It is used for the study of online communities and online cultures.

> **ethnography** Represents ways of studying cultures through methods that involve becoming highly active within that culture.
>
> **participant–observation** A data-gathering method carried out by the researcher when the researcher participates in the action or in the phenomenon being observed; an ethnographic research approach is where the researcher becomes immersed within and participates in the culture that s/he is observing in order to draw data from his or her observations.

Organizational culture would also be apt for ethnographic study. At times, researchers have actually become employees of an organization for an extended period of time. In doing so, they become part of the culture and over time other employees come to act quite naturally around the researcher. The researcher may observe behaviours that the employee would never reveal otherwise. For instance, a researcher investigating the ethical behaviour of salespeople may have difficulty getting a car salesperson to reveal any potentially deceptive sales tactics in a traditional interview. However, ethnographic techniques may result in the salesperson letting down his or her guard, resulting in more valid discoveries about the car-selling culture. There is more detail and useful references on ethnography in Table 9.2 in Chapter 9. Ethnography is the methodology in focus in Chapter 13.

Observation in ethnography

Observation plays a key role in ethnography. Researchers today sometimes ask households for permission to place video cameras in their home. In doing so, the ethnographer can study the consumer in a 'natural habitat' and use the observations to test new products, develop new product ideas and develop strategies in general.

Ethnographic study can be particularly useful when a certain culture is comprised of individuals who cannot or will not verbalize their thoughts and feelings. For instance, ethnography has advantages for discovering insights among children since it does not rely largely on their answers to questions. Instead, the researcher can simply become part of the environment, allow the children to do what they do naturally and record and analyze their behaviour.

The opening Value of Good Research box describing a participant–observer approach to learning about skateboarding culture represents an ethnographic approach to research, the use of an ethnographic research methodology. Essentially, ethnography is the study of a culture from within.

Grounded theory

Grounded theory is a research methodology specifically designed for the production of theory from data. Grounded theory represents an inductive investigation in which the researcher poses questions about information provided by respondents or taken from historical records. The researcher asks the questions to him or herself and then repeatedly questions the responses in order to derive deeper explanations. Grounded theory is particularly applicable in highly dynamic situations involving rapid and significant change. Two key questions asked by the grounded theory researcher are 'What is happening here?' and 'How is it different?' The distinguishing characteristic of grounded theory is that it does not begin with a theory but instead develops theory from the data gathered in the research project. There is more detail and useful references on grounded theory in Table 9.2 in Chapter 9. Grounded theory is the methodology in focus in Chapter 18.

> **grounded theory** Represents an inductive investigation in which the researcher poses questions about information provided by respondents or taken from historical records; the researcher asks the questions to him or herself and repeatedly questions the responses to derive deeper explanations.

How is grounded theory used?

Consider a company that approaches a researcher to study whether or not its salesforce is as effective as it was five years ago. The researcher uses grounded theory to discover a potential explanation. A theory is inductively developed based on text analysis of dozens of sales meetings that have been recorded over the previous five years. By questioning the events discussed in the sales interviews and analyzing differences in the situations that may have led to the discussion, the researcher is able to develop a theory. The theory suggests that with an increasing reliance on email and other technological devices for communication, the salespeople communicate with each other frequently and informally much more than they did five years previously. As a result, the salespeople have bonded into a close-knit 'community'.

Case studies

Case studies involve the in-depth study of the phenomenon under investigation. The case being studied may be as relatively simple as one incident or as complex as an entire organization. In business research, typically, a case study may describe the events of a specific company as it faces an important decision or situation, such as introducing a new product or dealing with some management crisis.

The case studies developed can be analyzed for important themes. **Themes** are identified by the frequency with which the same issue or concept or synonym arises in the narrative description. The themes may be useful in discovering variables that are relevant to potential explanations. There is more detail and useful references on case study methodology in Table 9.2 in Chapter 9. Case study is the methodology in focus in Chapter 3.

> **themes** Identified by the frequency with which the same issue or concept or term (or synonym) arises in the narrative description.

How are case studies used?

Case studies are commonly applied in business. For instance, case studies of brands that sell 'luxury' products help provide insight into what makes up a prestigious brand. A business researcher carefully conducted case studies of high-end cars (such as BMWs) including the methods of production and distribution. The findings of the analysis suggested that a key ingredient to a prestige brand may well be authenticity. When consumers know something is authentic, they attach more esteem to that product or brand.

A case study approach can be used as the research methodology in a research project and it can also be used as the means of gathering and presenting data for the research project. Case studies can be used as a means of gathering and presenting data within any research project developed using any research methodology. Hence, a research project developed using, for example, an ethnographic methodology or a phenomenological methodology, or even a survey methodology, could use one or more case studies as one means of gathering and presenting data (see Chapter 9).

A primary advantage of the case study is that an entire organization or entity can be investigated in depth with meticulous attention to detail. This highly focused attention enables the researcher to carefully study the order of events as they occur or to concentrate on identifying, analyzing and understanding the relationships among functions, individuals or entities.

Common techniques used in qualitative research

Qualitative researchers apply a nearly endless number of techniques. Table 8.2 lists characteristics of some common qualitative research techniques. Each is then described.

Table 8.2 Four common qualitative research tools

Tool	Description	Key advantages	Key disadvantages
Focus group interviews	Small group discussions facilitated by a trained moderator	Can be done quickly Gain multiple perspectives Flexibility	Results do not generalize to larger population Difficult to use for sensitive topics Can be expensive
Depth interviews (In-depth interviews)	One-on-one, probing interview between a trained researcher and a respondent	Gain considerable insight from each individual Good for understanding behaviours	Results not meant to generalize Can be expensive
Conversations	Unstructured dialogue recorded by a researcher	Gain unique insights from enthusiasts Can cover sensitive topics Less expensive than depth interviews or focus groups	Easy to get off course
Semi-structured interviews	Open-ended questions, sometimes in writing, that ask for short free flow answers from respondents	Can address more specific issues Results can be easily interpreted Cost advantages over focus groups and depth interviews	Needs particular skill in design and execution to ensure the required data are gathered
Word association/sentence completion	Records the first thoughts that come to a consumer in response to some stimulus	Economical Can be done quickly	Lacks flexibility
Observation	Recorded notes describing observed events	Can be unobtrusive Can yield actual behaviour patterns	Can be very obtrusive
Collages	Respondent assembles pictures that represent their thoughts/feelings	Flexible enough to allow novel insights	Can be difficult to interpret
Thematic apperception/cartoon tests	Researcher provides an ambiguous picture and respondent tells the story	Projective, allows researcher to get at sensitive issues Flexible	Design can be complex and complicated Can be difficult to interpret

Observation

Observation is a very important data-gathering method in the social sciences. The participant–observer approach typifies how observation can be used to explore various issues. Using an observation data-gathering method, meaning is extracted from field notes. **Field notes** are the researchers' descriptions of what actually happens in the field. These notes then become the data from which meaning is extracted. Field notes can be made in the research diary or an observation schedule can be developed for use in recording data gathered through the observation carried out.

Observation may also take place in visual form. Researchers may observe employees in their workplace, consumers in their home or try to gain knowledge from photographic records of one type or another.

Observation as a data-gathering method is explained in detail in Chapter 13.

field notes The researcher's descriptions of what actually happens in the field; these notes then become the data from which meaning is extracted.

Focus groups

A **focus group** is an unstructured, free-flowing discussion among a small group of people, usually between six and ten in number. Focus groups are facilitated by a trained moderator who follows a flexible format encouraging dialogue among respondents. In business research, common focus group topics include employee programmes, employee satisfaction, brand meanings, problems with products, advertising themes or new product concepts.

focus group An unstructured, free-flowing discussion with a small group of around six to ten people, facilitated by a trained moderator who follows a flexible format encouraging dialogue. The moderator focuses discussion on the issue under investigation, allowing data to be collected that produces new knowledge and new insights.

Participants might range from consumers talking about hair colouring, petroleum engineers talking about problems in the 'oil patch', children talking about toys or employees talking about their jobs. A moderator, or facilitator, begins by providing some opening statement to broadly steer discussion in the intended direction. Ideally, discussion topics emerge at the group's initiative, not the moderator's. It is the data generated by the interaction of the focus group participants that the focus group method is designed to provide. A focus group might be thought of as a kind of brainstorming session, with the group of participants discussing the phenomenon under investigation in order to, through the discussion, generate new insights and/or ideas.

Interactive media and online focus groups

Internet applications for qualitative exploratory research are growing rapidly and there are both formal and informal applications. Formally, the term **online focus group** refers to a qualitative research effort in which a group of individuals provides unstructured comments by entering their remarks into an electronic internet display board of some type, such as a chatroom session or in the form of a blog. Because respondents enter their comments into the computer, transcripts of verbatim responses are available immediately after the group session. Online groups can be quick and cost-efficient. However, because there is less personal interaction between participants, group synergy and the value of the snowballing of ideas may be diminished.

Several companies have established a form of informal, 'continuous' focus group by establishing an internet blog for that purpose. We might call this technique a **focus blog** when the intention is to mine the site for business research purposes. General Motors, American Express and Lego all have used ideas harvested from their focus blogs.

online focus group A qualitative research effort in which a group of individuals provides unstructured comments by entering their remarks into an electronic internet display board of some type.

focus blog A type of informal, 'continuous' focus group established as an internet blog for the purpose of collecting qualitative data from participant comments.

When operating, the Lego blog can be found at legoisfun.blogspot.com. While traditional focus group respondents are generally paid $100 or more to show up and participate for 90 minutes, bloggers and online focus group respondents often participate for no fee at all. Thus, technology provides some cost advantages over traditional focus group approaches.

Online versus face-to-face focus group techniques

A research company can facilitate a formal online focus group by setting up a private chat room for that purpose. Participants in formal and informal online focus groups feel that their anonymity is very secure. Often respondents will say things in this environment that they would never say otherwise. For example, a clothing company might want insights into how it could design products for very tall women. Online, these women may be happier to discuss more personal issues than, for example, in a face-to-face situation. Increased anonymity can be a major advantage for a company investigating sensitive issues.

Because participants do not have to be together in the same room at a research facility, the number of participants in online focus groups can be larger than in traditional focus groups. Twenty-five participants or more is not uncommon for the simultaneous chatroom format. Participants can be at widely separated locations since the internet does not have geographical restrictions. Of course, a major disadvantage is that often the researcher does not exercise as much control in precisely who participates. In other words, a person could very easily not match the desired profile and could even answer screening questions in a misleading way simply to participate.

A major drawback with online focus groups is that moderators cannot see body language and facial expressions (bewilderment, excitement, boredom, interest, and so on). As this is the case, they cannot fully interpret how people are reacting. Also, moderators' ability to probe and ask additional questions on the spot is reduced in online focus groups. Research that requires focus group members to actually touch something (such as a new easy-opening packaging design) or taste something, is clearly not suitable for an online format.

Focus groups and interviews are explained in detail in Chapter 14.

Depth interviews

Depth interviews, or in-depth interviews, are a primary source of data in qualitative research. A **depth interview** is a one-on-one interview between a professional researcher and a research respondent. In a depth interview, the researcher asks questions and/or suggests topics or items for discussion, explanation and clarification on the part of the respondent, and probes for additional elaboration.

depth interview/in-depth interview A one-on-one interview between a professional researcher and a research respondent conducted about the phenomenon under investigation.

Like focus group moderators, the interviewer's role is critical in a depth interview. They must be a highly skilled individual who can encourage the respondent to talk freely without influencing the direction of the conversation. Probing questions are critical.

Laddering is a term used for a particular approach to probing, asking respondents to compare differences between brands at different levels. What usually results is that the first distinctions are attribute-level distinctions, the second are benefit-level distinctions and the third are at the value or motivation level. Laddering could, for example, distinguish two brands of skateboarding shoes based on (1) the materials they are made of, (2) the comfort they provide and (3) the excitement they create.

laddering A particular approach to probing, asking respondents to compare differences between brands at different levels that produce distinctions at the attribute level, the benefit level and the value or motivation level.

Each depth interview may last an hour or more than an hour. It is a time-consuming process if multiple interviews are conducted. Not only does the interview have to be conducted, but each interview, when transcribed, produces about the same amount of text as does a focus group interview. This text is the data that has to be analyzed and interpreted by the researcher. A third major issue stems from the necessity of recording both surface reactions and subconscious motivations of the respondent.

Depth interviews provide more insight into a particular individual than do focus groups. In addition, since the setting is private, respondents are more likely to discuss sensitive topics than, for example, participants in a face-to-face focus group. Depth interviews are particularly advantageous when some unique or unusual behaviour is being studied. For instance, depth interviews have been usefully applied to reveal characteristics of adolescent behaviour, ranging from the ways they get what they want from their parents to shopping, smoking and even shoplifting.

Conversations

Holding **conversations** in qualitative research is an informal data-gathering approach in which the researcher engages a respondent in a discussion of the relevant subject matter. This approach is almost completely unstructured and the researcher enters the conversation with few expectations. The goal is to have the respondent produce a dialogue about his or her lived experiences. Meaning will be extracted from the resulting dialogue.

> **conversation** An informal qualitative data-gathering approach in which the researcher engages a respondent in a discussion of the relevant subject matter.

New technologies have influenced conversational research. Online communications such as, for example, the reviews posted about book purchases at www.barnesandnoble.com, can be treated as a conversation. Companies may discover product problems, as well as ideas for overcoming them, by analyzing these computer-based consumer dialogues.

A conversational approach is advantageous because each interview is usually inexpensive to conduct. Respondents often need not be paid. Conversational approaches are relatively effective at getting at sensitive issues once the researcher establishes a rapport with the respondent.

Social networking

Social networking has become an important element in social research in recent times. For many consumers, particularly younger generations, social networking sites like Facebook and MySpace have become the primary tool for communicating with friends both far and near, and contacts both known and unknown. Social networking has replaced large volumes of email and, many would say, face-to-face communications as well. While the impact that social networking will eventually have on society is an interesting topic for debate, what is most relevant to business research, arguably, is the large portion of such communication that involves discussions of marketing and consumer-related information.

Companies can assign research assistants to monitor these sites for information related to their particular brands. The information can be coded as either positive or negative. When too much negative information is being spread, the company can try to react to change opinions. In addition, many companies like P&G and Ford maintain their own social networking sites for the purpose of gathering research data. In a way, these social networking sites are a means by which companies can eavesdrop on consumer conversations and discover key information about their products. The textual data that consumers willingly put up become like a conversation. When researchers get the opportunity to react with consumers or employees through a social network site, the process can function much like an online focus group or interview.

Free-association/sentence completion method

Free-association techniques simply record a respondent's first cognitive reactions (top-of-mind) to some stimulus. The Rorschach or inkblot test typifies the free-association method. Respondents view an ambiguous figure and are asked to say the first thing that comes to their mind. Free-association techniques allow researchers to map a respondent's thoughts or memory.

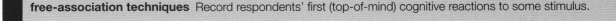

> **free-association techniques** Record respondents' first (top-of-mind) cognitive reactions to some stimulus.

The sentence completion method is based on free-association principles. You will remember that we used a sentence completion exercise in the 'Research This' box at the start of this chapter. Respondents simply are required to complete a few partial sentences with the first word or phrase that comes to mind. For example:

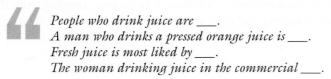

> *People who drink juice are ___.*
> *A man who drinks a pressed orange juice is ___.*
> *Fresh juice is most liked by ___.*
> *The woman drinking juice in the commercial ___.*

Answers to sentence completion questions tend to be more extensive than responses to word-association tests, and they are a very effective way of finding out what is on a respondent's mind. They can do so in a quick and very cost-effective manner. Free-association and sentence completion tasks are sometimes used in conjunction with other approaches. For instance, they can sometimes be used as effective icebreakers in focus group interviews. As we saw in the exercise in the 'Research This' box, sentence completion exercises can be, and often are, used in questionnaires.

Collages

Business researchers sometimes have respondents prepare a collage (artwork assembled from different media) to represent their experiences. The collages are then analyzed for meaning much in the same manner as text dialogues are analyzed.

Harley-Davidson commissioned research in which collages depicting feelings about Harley-Davidson were compared based on whether the respondent was a Harley owner or an owner of a competitor's brand. The collages of 'Hog' (Harley Owners' Group) members revealed themes of artwork and the freedom of the great outdoors. These themes did not emerge in the non-Hog groups. This led to confirmatory research that helped Harley continue its growth, appealing more specifically to its diverse market segments.

Like sentence completion and word association, collages are often used within some other approach, such as a focus group or a depth interview.

Projective research techniques

A **projective technique** is an indirect means of questioning enabling respondents to project beliefs and feelings onto a third party, an inanimate object or a task situation. Projective techniques usually encourage respondents to describe a situation in their own words with little prompting by the interviewer. Individuals are expected to interpret the situation within the context of their own experiences, attitudes and personalities, and to express opinions and emotions that may be hidden from others and possibly themselves. Projective techniques are particularly useful in studying sensitive issues.

> **projective technique** An indirect means of questioning enabling respondents to project beliefs and feelings onto a third party, an inanimate object or a task situation.

There is an old story about asking a man why he purchased a Mercedes-Benz car. When asked directly why he purchased a Mercedes, he responds that the car holds its value and does not depreciate much, that it gets better petrol mileage than you would expect or that it has a comfortable ride. If you ask the same person why a neighbour purchased a Mercedes, he may well answer, 'Oh, that status seeker!' This story illustrates that individuals may be more likely to give true answers (consciously or unconsciously) to disguised questions and a projective technique provides a way of disguising the question.

Thematic apperception test (TAT)

A **thematic apperception test (TAT)**, sometimes called the picture interpretation technique, presents participants with an ambiguous picture(s) and asks the participant to tell what is happening in the picture(s) now and what might happen next. Hence, themes (thematic) are elicited on the basis of the perceptual-interpretive (apperception) use of the pictures. The researcher then analyzes the contents of the stories that the subjects relate. A TAT represents a projective research technique.

> **thematic apperception test (TAT)** A test that presents participants with an ambiguous picture(s) in which consumers and products are the centre of attention; the investigator asks the participant to tell what is happening in the picture(s) now and what might happen next.

Frequently, the TAT consists of a series of pictures with some continuity so that stories may be constructed in a variety of settings. The first picture might portray a person working at her desk; in the second picture, a person that could be a supervisor is talking to the worker; the final picture might show the original employee and another having a discussion at the water cooler.

The picture or cartoon stimulus must be sufficiently interesting to encourage discussion but ambiguous enough not to disclose the nature of the research project. Clues should not be given to the character's positive or negative predisposition. A pretest of a TAT investigating why men might purchase chainsaws used a picture of a man looking at a very large tree. The research respondents were homeowners and weekend woodcutters. They almost unanimously said that they would get professional help from a tree surgeon to deal with this situation. Thus, early in pretesting, the researchers found out that the picture was not sufficiently ambiguous. The tree was too large and did not allow respondents to identify with the tree-cutting task. If subjects are to project their own views into the situation, the environmental setting should be a well-defined, familiar problem, but the solution should be ambiguous.

An example of a TAT using a cartoon drawing where the respondent suggests a dialogue in which the characters might engage is provided in Figure 8.1. This TAT is a purposely ambiguous illustration of an everyday occurrence. The two office workers are shown in a situation and the respondent is asked what the woman might be talking about. This setting could be used for discussions about the organization's management, store personnel, particular software products, and so on.

Figure 8.1 An example of a TAT picture

THE VALUE OF GOOD RESEARCH

Focus on action research

Action research is one of many research methodologies used in social science research. Action research has particular use when the focus of the research is on bringing about change and development. The research process, as outlined in Figure 1.1 in Chapter 1, is generally the same for every research project, but there are one or two exceptions. Among these exceptions is action research, where the research process is more cyclical than linear.

The model in Figure 8.2 is a simple model of the cyclical process of action research. As you can see, the process is quite different from the linear process detailed at the start of Chapter 1 in the model of the research process (see Figure 1.1). Action research is a research methodology that has particular application in the work of improving practice. It

(Continued)

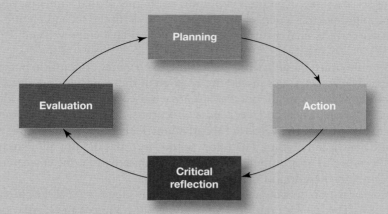

Figure 8.2 The process of action research

is an appropriate methodology if a researcher wants, through their research project, to develop some process, to improve their own work performance, the performance of a team or performance in any other setting.

As can be seen from the model the process of action research is cyclical or spiralling. The research process moves from:

- planning some change and the ways in which to measure it
- to acting, carrying out the planned change and measuring it
- to critically reflecting, thinking in a critical way about the change that was made and the data from the measurement of the change
- to evaluating the change, deciding what impact the change has had and weighing the value of the impact of the change.

When the researcher gets to the end of evaluating the change, they can, if they have time, go back to the planning stage and reiterate each of the steps in the action research process, thus further developing the research project. The cyclical process can be re-enacted as often as is necessary or as often as is practicable. There are many YouTube videos on action research that you might like to view. Participatory action research (PAR) is another methodology that is used a lot in development work. For examples of this type of research, see the case studies on the website of the organization Research

for Development (r4d.dfid.gov.uk/), supported by the UK Department for International Development (DFID).

In their journal article, Petrie, Jones and Murrell (2018) 'Measuring impact while making a difference', *Developments in Business Simulation and Experiential Learning*, 45: 42–48, detail a participatory action research project that they undertook in which a team of undergraduate business students delivered a financial literacy services learning programme. The programme was designed to develop financial literacy skills in a group of high school students. Financial literacy, the article explains, is the capacity to understand different financial products such as loans, for example, pay day loans, as well as the capacity to make wise decisions in relation to them. The article is very interesting. It draws on literature on pedagogy, that is education, and on literature on student mentorship. The article explains how participatory action research works and it shows how this research methodology was applied in the research project. The authors of the article explain how and in what ways the university students developed as they used the action research methodology to develop their financial literacy services learning programme. The study also shows how the school pupils who participated in the programme developed. This is an interesting action research project. You should source the journal article and read it. It might give you some good ideas for your own research project.

The case study that follows details a student's research proposal for a research project to be developed using an action research methodology.

CASE STUDY

Malika's action research project

Malika has a part-time job working as a weekend manager in a restaurant. She has decided that she is

going to situate her research project in the restaurant. The owner of the restaurant has given her permission to do this. Malika feels that the team she manages in the restaurant could improve their performance and she feels that such an improvement in performance would lead to an enhanced customer experience. Malika's team in the restaurant consists of ten waiting staff. They have all agreed to participate in the research.

(Continued)

Before commencing the work of developing this research proposal, Malika discussed her idea for her research project with her thesis supervisor. Her supervisor agreed that this was an interesting and useful research project and she accepted this research as appropriate in terms of the programme of study Malika is undertaking, which is for a BSc in Business Management.

Having secured this approval, Malika developed the following research proposal. She submitted this to her thesis supervisor who formally endorsed it.

A research proposal

Research statement: This research project is an action research project designed to improve the performance of a team of waiting staff at the *Bon Viveur Restaurant*.

Aim and objectives

The aim of the research is to improve the performance of a team of waiting staff at the *Bon Viveur Restaurant*. The objectives of the research are as follows:

- To measure current performance of the team of waiting staff.
- To establish which aspects of the performance warrant improvement.
- To consider the contribution of the supervisory team to the performance of the team of waiting staff.
- To design a process by which performances of both teams might be improved.
- To implement this process.
- To measure the performance of both of the teams following implementation.
- To evaluate the efficacy of the improvement process.
- To develop a model for the development of small teams in business enterprises.

The population of the study

The population of the study consists of the ten members of the team of waiting staff the researcher supervises in her work as weekend manager at the *Bon Viveur Restaurant;* six members of the supervisory team; ten members of the restaurant's management team; and 40 of the restaurant's regular customers.

Sample literature review

This research project is focused on team performance. The focus of the review of the literature for this research project is on performance, on team training and development for improved performance.

Following the work of Katzenbach and Smith (2003), this research project will provide a model for the development of small teams in business. According to Katzenbach and Smith, team performance is one of the single largest untapped resources of most organizations. Katzenbach and Smith state that 'commitment to goals' and 'shared purpose' is critical to team success; leadership, they write, is key. Yuki (2010) holds that leadership is in part about the organization of work activities and the motivation of people (the team) to meet objectives.

The use of teams has increased in organizations, as shown by Morgeson *et al.* (2010, see also McCleskey 2014). They outline how research in management has begun to focus on the role of leadership in developing teams and in team success. Vasilagos, Polychroniou and Maroudas (2017) highlight the importance of emotional intelligence, the supervisors intrapersonal and interpersonal emotional intelligence competencies and his or her transformational leadership capability. Transformational leadership is a key concept in this study.

The literature review for this research project will explore:

- the nature of teams in business organizations
- the critical issues in team success
- the nature of team leadership in relation to successful teams.

Research methodology

The methodology to be used in the study is action research (Brydon-Miller *et al.*, 2003; McNiff and Whitehead, 2009; McNiff 2017). Action research is a research methodology designed in particular to bring about change and development. As the focus of this research project is on developing the performance of a team, the methodology action research is an appropriate methodology.

Action research methodology follows a cyclical rather than a linear process, whereby the researcher first plans the research to be undertaken and then acts, putting the plans into action. When the action has been completed, the researcher critically reflects on the action and on what was accomplished by the action. Finally, the researcher evaluates the action. Having evaluated the action, the researcher may begin the cyclical process again, by planning the next stage of the research, implementing the plan, reflecting on the implementation and the impact of the implementation, and finally evaluating the effect of the process. The researcher can repeat the cyclical process as often as possible or as often as is necessary, in order to bring about the desired change.

(Continued)

The data collection methods to be used in the study are as follows:

- focus group
- observation
- questionnaire.

To begin with, the researcher will convene a focus group with the ten members of the waiting team. The purpose of the focus group is to explore the views of the team in relation to the improvements in performance needed and the improvements in performance possible. The focus group will be audio recorded. The researcher will transcribe the audio recording and, from the transcript, develop a plan for the implementation of the improvements decided on by the members of the focus group.

The researcher will then convene a focus group with the six members of the supervisory team. The researcher will prepare a focus group schedule, based in part on the data gathered in the focus group conducted with the waiting staff. The purpose of the focus group is to explore the views of the team in relation to the improvements in performance needed and the improvements in performance possible. The focus group will be audio recorded. The researcher will transcribe the audio recording and, from the transcript, develop a plan for the implementation of the improvements decided on by the members of the focus group.

During the implementation phase of the research, the researcher and both of the teams will observe the impact of the changes in performance. Two observation schedules will be developed for this purpose. The first observation schedule will be used to record the implementation of the proposed changes in performance. The second observation schedule will be used to measure the impact of the changes.

Finally, the researcher will develop a questionnaire designed to measure the impact of the changes in performance on the customer experience. This questionnaire will be administered to ten regular customers on two Saturday nights before the changes are implemented and on two Saturday nights after the changes have been implemented. In all, 40 regular customers will participate in the study. The questionnaire will also be administered to all ten members of the restaurant's management team. The data will be analyzed using SPSS. Statistical Package for Social Scientists is a computerized statistical analysis package, used for the analysis of social science data. The responses to the 'before' and 'after' questionnaires will be compared and conclusions will be drawn regarding the impact of the research on the customer experience.

Context for the research

The research is being undertaken for a BSc in Business Management. The research will be conducted as a training and development exercise with the team of ten waiting staff the researcher supervises, and the team of six supervisors the researcher works with, in her role as weekend manager at the *Bon Viveur Restaurant* in the village of Martens, in Upper Lakelands.

Rationale for the research

In undertaking the research, the researcher hopes to contribute to the development of her team and her workplace. Through the research, she hopes to develop some expertise in action research and the use of action research in training and development. Finally, she hopes through the research to make a contribution to knowledge in relation to small team management. The researcher plans to publish an account of the research in the trade magazine *Restaurants Today*. A copy of the thesis, the formal account of the research, will be placed in the university library.

Question: What do you think of Malika's research proposal? Do you think the project is researchable, using the test of researchability outlined in Chapter 1? Explain your answer. Does Malika's research proposal give you any ideas for your own research project?

This chapter has emphasized that any argument about the overall superiority of qualitative versus quantitative research is misplaced. Rather, each approach has advantages and disadvantages that make it appropriate in certain situations. The presence or absence of numbers is not the key factor discriminating between qualitative and quantitative research. Qualitative research relies more on subjective interpretations of text or other visual material. In contrast, the numbers produced in quantitative research are objective in the sense that they do not change simply because someone else computed them. Thus, we expect quantitative research to have intersubjective certifiability, while qualitative research may not. Qualitative research typically involves small samples while quantitative research usually uses large samples. Qualitative procedures are generally more flexible and produce deeper and more elaborate explanations than quantitative research.

END OF CHAPTER QUESTIONS

1 Comment on the following remark by a business consultant: 'Qualitative exploration is a tool of research and a stimulant to thinking. In and by itself, however, it does not constitute business research.'

2 What is laddering? How might it be used in trying to understand which fast food restaurant customers prefer?

3 A researcher tells a manager of a wine company that he has some 'cool focus group results' suggesting that respondents like the idea of a screw cap to top wine bottles. Even before the decision maker sees the report, the manager begins purchasing screw caps and the new bottling equipment. Comment on this situation.

4 Visit some websites for large companies like Honda, Qantas Airlines, Target, Tesco and Marriott. Is there any evidence that they are using their internet sites in some way to conduct a continuous online focus blog or intermittent online focus groups?

5 A packaged goods manufacturer receives many thousands of customer letters a year. Some are complaints, some are compliments. They cover a broad range of topics. Are these letters a possible source for qualitative research? Explain your answer.

6 What type of exploratory research would you suggest in the following situations?

   a A product manager suggests development of a non-tobacco cigarette blended from wheat, cocoa and citrus.

   b A research project has the purpose of evaluating potential names for a corporate spin-off.

   c A human resource manager must determine the most important benefits of an employee health plan.

   d An advertiser wishes to identify the symbolism associated with cigar smoking.

7 Why do exploratory research designs rely so much on qualitative research techniques?

8 What are the key differences between a focus group interview and a depth interview?

9 Define qualitative and quantitative research. Compare and contrast the two approaches.

10 Go back to the opening Value of Good Research box. What if Vans approached you to do a focus group interview that explored the idea of offering casual attire (off-board) aimed at its primary segment (skateboarders) and offering casual attire for male retirees like Samuel Teel? How would you recommend the focus group(s) proceed? Prepare a focus group outline(s) to accomplish this task.

11 Interview two people about their exercise behaviour. In one interview, try to use a semi-structured approach by preparing questions ahead of time and trying to have the respondent complete answers for these questions. With the other, try a conversational approach. What are the main themes that emerge in each? Which approach do you think was more insightful? Do you think there were any 'sensitive' topics that a respondent was not completely forthcoming about?

REFERENCES

Brydon-Miller, M., Greenwood, D. and Maguire, P. (2003) 'Why action research?', *Action Research*, 1: 9–28.

Katzenbach, J.R. and Smith, D.K. (2003) *The Wisdom of Teams: Creating the High-Performance Organization*, New York: McKinsey & Company.

Kozinets, R. (2015) *Netnography: Redefined* (2nd edn), London, California, New Delhi, Singapore: Sage.

McCleskey, J.A. (2014) 'Situational, transformational, and transactional leadership and leadership development', *Journal of Business Studies Quarterly*, 5(4): 117–130.

McNiff, J. (2017) *Action Research*, London, California, New Delhi, Singapore: Sage.

McNiff, J. and Whitehead, J. (2009) *Doing and Writing Action Research*, London: Sage.

Morgeson, F.P., Scott DeRue, D. and Karam, E.P. (2010) 'Leadership in teams: a functional approach to understanding leadership structures and processes', *Journal of Management*, 36(1): 5–39.

Petrie, J., Jones, R. and Murrell, A. (2018) 'Measuring impact while making a difference: A financial literacy service learning project as participatory action research', *Developments in Business Simulation and Experiential Learning*, Vol. 45: 42–48, journals.tdl.org/absel/index.php/absel/article/view/3133/3073 (Accessed 15.06.2018).

Research for Development, a free-to-access online database containing information about research projects supported by the Department for International Development UK, Department for International Development (DFID), r4d.dfid.gov.uk

Vasilagos, T., Polychroniou, P. and Maroudas, L. (2017) 'Relationship between Supervisors Emotional Intelligence and Transformational Leadership in Hotel Organisations', in A. Kavoura, D. Sakas and P. Tomaras (eds) *Strategic Innovative Marketing* (Springer Proceedings in Business and Economics), Cham, Switzerland: Springer.

Whaba, P. (2017) 'How Vans Skated Past a Big Retail Milestone', fortune.com/2017/03/31/vans-vfc

Yuki, G. (2010) *Leadership in Organizations* (7th edn), Upper Saddle River, NJ: Prentice Hall.

RECOMMENDED READING

Methodspace, www.methodspace.com (Accessed 17.03.2018).

Myers, M. (2013) *Qualitative Research in Business and Management* (2nd edn), London, California, New Delhi, Singapore: Sage.

Neill, J. (2009) 'Qualitative versus quantitative research: key points in a classic debate', wilderdom.com/research/QualitativeVersusQuantitativeResearch.html

Neuman, W.L. (2014) *Social Research Methods: Qualitative and Quantitative Approaches* (7th edn), Essex, England: Pearson Education Ltd.

Niemi, W. (2004) 'Schoenfeld to leave as Vans CEO; as its deal with VF Corp. closes, the skate brand gains a new president and a new focus on apparel', *Footwear News*, 5 July, 2.

RAPAR, Refugees and Asylum Seekers Participatory Action Research, www.rapar.org.uk

Robson, C. and McCartan, K. (2016) *Real World Research*, John Wiley & Sons Ltd.

Woodside, A.G., Pattinson, H.M. and Miller, K.E. (2005) 'Advancing hermeneutic research for interpreting interfirm new product development', *Journal of Business and Industrial Marketing*, 20: 364–379.

CHAPTER 9
RESEARCH METHODOLOGY AND DESIGN

LEARNING OBJECTIVES

At the end of this chapter, the student should:

- Understand, and be able to discuss and write about, research methodology.

- Understand how research methodologies are deployed in research.

- Be able to decide on the methodology most appropriate for their own research and create a methodological framework for that research.

- Be able to critique the use of methodologies in other research projects.

- Be able to explain which data-gathering methods work with which research methodologies and why.

RESEARCH SKILLS

At the end of this chapter, the student should, using the exercises on Cengage Brain, be able to:

- Evaluate the utility, value and limitations of the methodologies deployed in given research projects.

- Design a research project with an appropriate methodology and data-gathering methods.

The aim of this chapter is to introduce the student to research methodology, to give the student an understanding of how to use different research methodologies and to outline some of the key methodologies used in social science research. The chapter provides an introduction to data-gathering methods and explains which data-gathering methods are used with which research methodologies. The chapter details and explains the third framework in the four frameworks approach to research, the methodological framework. The chapter demonstrates how the researcher develops an appropriate methodological framework for any research project. The different elements of the methodological framework are introduced, highlighted and explained.

INTRODUCTION

In this chapter the focus is on **research methodology**. As you can see from the model of the research process detailed in Chapter 1 (see Figure 1.1), research methodology is situated after 'literature review' and before 'data collection' methods. As we will see in this chapter, 'data collection methods' are a major part of the methodological framework for the research project.

> **research methodology** How the research was conducted and what philosophical assumptions underpin the research.

As explained in earlier chapters, thoughts and ideas in relation to the research methodology and data collection methods to be used in the project should develop as the idea for the research project develops. This is because all of the elements of the research project have to fit together. The research methodology used must be capable of supporting the research, capable of enabling and facilitating its completion. The research methodology must be the appropriate research methodology for the research project; it must fit with the research project. The researcher must justify the research methodology and data-gathering methods used in the research project.

You will remember we discussed research methodology in Chapter 4 of this textbook, where we explored the philosophical frameworks of social research and the philosophical underpinnings of different research methodologies. As we saw in that chapter, there are many different approaches to research and a number of different philosophical frameworks within which you might situate your work. Then, in Chapters 7 and 8 we considered quantitative and qualitative approaches to research. In this chapter, there is a deeper discussion and explanation of research methodology and you will learn how to use research methodologies and data-gathering methods in research projects. This chapter will teach you how to apply all of this knowledge.

The four frameworks

- Conceptual Framework
- Theoretical Framework
- *Methodological Framework*
- Analytical Framework

Every research project is designed to make a contribution to knowledge. The process or processes through which knowledge is created, are of fundamental importance in research. A researcher poses a question and then conducts research in order to be able to answer that question. When the researcher develops some clarity in relation to the focus of the research project, they can start to develop the design of the research project. The researcher thinks about the nature and purpose of the study and begins to develop a sense of the best research methodology to use in the research project.

YOUR RESEARCH
Common research problems

Sometimes students have absolutely no idea what to focus on for their research project.

The challenge of making a decision regarding the focus of the research project often seems to students, and to beginner researchers in general, to be substantial. Sometimes students are a little in awe of the research process and feel overwhelmed by the assignment they have been set.

The best way to overcome some of these fears and issues is to practise developing ideas for research projects in your research diary.

As we know, the first thing to do when designing a research project is to decide on an area or an issue on which to focus your research. The next thing to do is to create a research statement or question around this area. This research statement or question becomes the conceptual framework for your research. The next task is to quickly detail the context for the research, where the research will take place. Then it would be helpful to write a note about the likely population of the research, if there is a human population in the research, who they are and where they are. If the research does not involve

human participants, it would be helpful to write a note on the data to be gathered for the project, what form or format the data are in and where the data are located. Then quickly estimate the kind of data-gathering method(s) required. For example, will you need to conduct interviews? Would a questionnaire be helpful? Will there be documentary evidence? How many case studies could/should you develop?

When you have this done, read quickly through the summaries of the different research methodologies listed in Table 9.1 and try to pinpoint the most appropriate methodology for your research. Then read through the summaries of the different data-gathering methods listed in Table 9.2 and try to decide the data-gathering method(s) you will use in your research project. It is important to remember that although you may use more than one data-gathering method, you will use only one research methodology in your research project.

The important thing is to get started and begin to engage with the process. When you get started, you might be surprised at how quickly the design of your research project comes together.

RESEARCH METHODOLOGIES

There are very many different methodologies in social research. You have seen examples of many of these in the accounts of published research and student projects presented in this textbook. You have also seen examples and explanations of some of the different research methodologies in the Research in Practice box. The decision on the methodology to be used in a research project is informed by the nature of the research, focus of the research, the research question or statement or the research hypothesis, and by the type of data required for the research and by the location of that data. Through your study of different research proposals, examples of which are presented in this textbook, you have seen the way in which the different elements of the research project are designed by the researcher to fit together in such a way as to properly and adequately support the research project.

Table 9.1 is a list of the main research methodologies used in social science research. As you can see, there are very many different research methodologies, all of which are interesting and all of which have been used by researchers in useful, creative and engaging research projects. It is important to read a little about these methodologies in order to develop some understanding of the ways in which they are used in research projects. This reading will help you in the work of deciding which research methodology best fits the research project you are designing. The research methodology used in the research project is the most fundamental aspect of the research project's methodological framework. You will remember that, in the four frameworks approach to the research project, the methodological framework emerges from the conceptual framework.

Table 9.1 List of research methodologies

Survey	Life history
Case study	Phenomenology
Experimental design	Narrative analysis
Ethnography (and netnography)	Semiotics
Action research	Attitude research
Grounded theory	Image-based research
Content analysis	Archival analysis
Discourse analysis	Textual analysis
Documentary analysis	Meta-analysis
Historical analysis	Feminist research

The four frameworks

- Conceptual Framework
- Theoretical Framework
- *Methodological Framework*
- Analytical Framework

Figure 9.1 illustrates the way in which the methodological framework emerges from the conceptual framework.

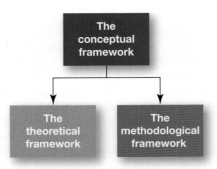

Figure 9.1 The methodological framework emerges from the conceptual framework

Figure 9.2 details the methodological pyramid. The methodological pyramid illustrates how the fundamental philosophies support research methodologies, which in turn support the different data-gathering methods.

One of the most important decisions to be made in any research project is the decision about methodology. The research methodology used must be capable of supporting the research, and of facilitating the accomplishment of the aim and completion of the research. Practised, experienced researchers can make decisions around appropriate methodologies for research projects relatively quickly. For the beginner researcher, the decision-making process is slower and needs to be supported by some study of the different research methodologies used in social science research.

The different research methodologies listed in Table 9.1 give some indication of the depth and complexity of this area of social science research. The table provides a succinct introduction to the more frequently used social science research

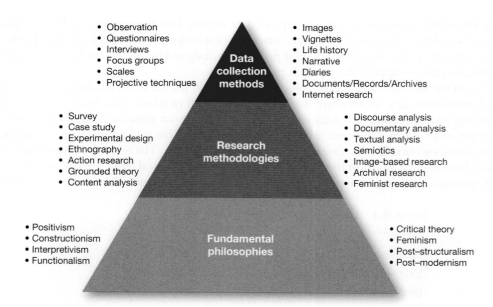

Figure 9.2   The methodological pyramid

methodologies. Reading a little about each of the methodologies listed here will help you decide which research methodology to use in your own research. Tables 9.1 and 9.2 will provide you with a knowledge base in relation to research methodology that you could use to critique the methodological choices made in the research of others. This is a valuable skill to have anyway and is a particularly useful skill to have in the workplace.

Table 9.2 contains brief summaries of each of the research methodologies listed in Table 9.1. Enough detail is given in the table on each of the methodologies to enable you to decide which of them might be a good fit for the research project you are designing. In addition, at least one reference is given for further reading on each of the methodologies. You will remember that there is an introduction to four of these methodologies (phenomenology, ethnography, grounded theory and case study) in Chapter 8.

Table 9.2 may help you clarify your thinking in relation to the decision you have to make regarding the research methodology to use in your research project. In order to confirm your decision, you will need to do further reading and engage in further reflection. You will need to do further reading in any case, in order to develop the level of expertise required by your programme of study in terms of the research methodology you decide to use in your research project.

Table 9.2   Detailed research methodologies

Survey	Surveys tend to be quantitative research projects or largely quantitative research projects, that is quantitative with some qualitative element. In general, the data collection methods that tend to be used in surveys are questionnaires and/or scales. It is often the case that the population or population sample used in surveys tend to be big, and a questionnaire and/or a scale is an effective method to use in engaging with large research populations. Sometimes the population is geographically scattered. A questionnaire can generally easily be posted or emailed or made available on the internet to a geographically scattered population. The use of the internet in survey research is very common and online surveys are commonly used. Rea and Parker (2014), have written on designing and conducting survey research. Survey methodology is the methodology in focus in Chapter 15 and questionnaires and scales are explored in detail too in that chapter.
Case study	If the research is located in a bounded entity, in a specific space or place, in a particular incident, it may be possible to conduct the research using a case study methodology. Within a case study methodology, the case to be studied could be a class in a school, a school, an office, shop or factory, an enterprise of some kind. It could be a study of a particular practice, for example, recruitment and selection processes or a marketing campaign. Case study research can involve the study of one case or the study of a number of cases. Using this research methodology, the researcher engages in an in-depth examination of the phenomenon under investigation. A case study generally does not have the substantial population in terms of numeric size or geographic spread of survey research. Instead of breadth, i.e. numeric size and geographic spread, case study research calls for depth; it calls for the deeper investigation of some bounded entity. A simple definition of case study methodology is that it is the in-depth study of a bounded entity. A case study methodology can draw on quantitative or qualitative data, or it can draw on a mixture of both. Yin (2018) has written on case study methodology. Case study methodology is the research methodology in focus in Chapter 3.

Table 9.2 Detailed research methodologies (*Continued*)

Experimental design	Experimental design is the methodology used when conducting experiments. True experiments are rarely conducted in business research or in social science research generally. This is because of the difficulties in controlling all the different variables in social science situations and phenomena. Properly designed experiments can be very effective in laboratories or in laboratory conditions. Laboratory conditions are difficult to replicate in the social world or in the study of social phenomena. Experiments which are conducted in real-life settings are called field experiments. In an experiment, two groups are established, with individuals or units being randomly assigned to both groups. The two groups are pretested, and the dependent variable is measured. Then a programme or application, the independent variable, is applied to one group, the experimental group, and not to the other group, the control group. Both groups are tested again; again the dependent variable is measured. If there is a difference in the experimental group but not in the control group, the programme or application applied to them, the independent variable, is said to account for the difference. There can be more than one dependent variable in an experiment but there should only be one independent variable. Experimental design is the methodology in focus in Chapter 19. You may also find Trochim's website 'Research Methods: Knowledge Base' useful in this context. It provides a clear introduction to experimental design: https://socialresearchmethods.net
Ethnography	Ethnographic research is used when a researcher wants to carry out an in-depth examination of a culture. Ethnographic research calls for the observation in the field of the phenomenon under investigation. Using ethnography, the researcher goes inside the culture being investigated in order to develop a very deep understanding of it. The researcher must be inside the culture enough to be able to document the culture, but also (and at the same time) outside of the culture enough to be able to document the culture. This means that when an individual is part of a culture, when they are immersed in that culture, they are in a position to properly and thoroughly document that culture and all its complexities. Yet because they are immersed in the culture they often cannot see the strangeness of the culture; the culture can appear to them to be 'natural'. In order to be able to conduct ethnographic research, the researcher must have the capacity to see the 'strangeness' of the culture they are attempting to document and analyze. The researcher needs to be outside the culture as well as being inside the culture. Netnography is an adaption of ethnography for research with online cultures and communities. This methodology can draw on quantitative or qualitative data, or a mixture of both. Jerolmack and Khan (2018) have written on ethnographic research. Kozinets (2015) has written about netnography. Ethnography is the research methodology in focus in Chapter 13.
Action research	Action research (AR) is used to bring about change, improvement and development in the quality of any organization and/or in the practice or performance of any team or group or organization. Action research follows a cyclical or spiral process of planning, action, critical reflection and evaluation. AR can be a particularly effective approach to problem solving in organizations. One form, participatory action research (PAR), is widely used in development research. PAR was developed from the teaching theories of Paulo Freire, the revolutionary twentieth-century Brazilian educator. AR was developed by MIT professor Kurt Lewin in the 1940s. This methodology can draw on quantitative or qualitative data, or on a mixture of both. McNiff (2017) has written about action research (AR). AR is the methodology in focus in Chapter 8.
Grounded theory	Grounded theory (GT) methodology is used when the specific focus of the research is on building theory from data. This methodology is very useful when researching a phenomenon about which little is known. In the thesis of a GT research project, the written account of the research project, there is sometimes a very short literature review, as little has been written on the phenomenon under investigation. In some grounded theory research projects, there is no literature review at all, this is because some methodologists hold that within a grounded theory methodology, studying the literature gives the researcher preconceived ideas about what is to be found in the data. Within the GT research project, theory is generated from data and so within a grounded theory research project, the concluding chapter in the report of the research/the thesis is theoretically very rich. This chapter contains the theory developed from the data gathered for the research project. A GT approach to data analysis involves three stages: open coding, selective coding and theoretical coding. This approach to data analysis is used frequently in research projects that have been designed using research methodologies other than GT. This is a tribute to the efficacy of this approach to data analysis. GT was developed by Barney Glaser and Anselm Strauss (1967), although they later split in their understanding of the methodology. Within Glaser's GT methodology, the methodology can draw on quantitative or qualitative data, or on a mixture of both. Strauss and Corbin (1997) have more recently written on this methodology; they presented the methodology as a qualitative methodology. Flick (2018), has written on grounded theory. GT is the research methodology in focus in Chapter 18.

(*Continued*)

Table 9.2 Detailed research methodologies (*Continued*)

Phenomenology	A phenomenological research methodology is used in the social sciences to examine lived experience. Phenomenology is the study of lived experience from the first-person point of view. It is the study of experience or consciousness. Phenomenology is one of the most qualitative of the social science methodologies. Using a phenomenological research methodology, the researcher spends a great deal of time developing accounts of lived experience from the perspective of those living the experience. The lived experience can be any lived experience: a worker in a factory, the CEO of a company, an undergraduate business student, etc. Very powerful phenomenological accounts of personal experience can be used to bring about change; phenomenological accounts of, for example, experiences of bullying in the workplace or experiences of working in a racist or a sexist workplace, can highlight and challenge such behaviours and practices in a way that can quickly lead to change. Paley (2018) has written about this research method. See also Moustakas (1994). Phenomenology is the research methodology in focus in Chapter 14.
Narrative research/analysis	This methodology is used in the gathering and analysis of narratives. The narratives gathered as data and analyzed are often narratives (or stories) of personal experience told to the researcher by the person who has had the experience. Narrative research is frequently used, for example, in marketing and consumer behaviour research in order to understand consumption and consumer behaviour. Narrative analysis can be used to analyze textual data in written or visual texts. This methodology can be used to examine and analyze the narratives or stories created or developed around products for marketing purposes. Such narratives are often developed around a character(s) real or fictional, with attributes or characteristics which the product developers want consumers to associate with their product(s). An example would be the fictional character Lara Croft and the use of her image in promoting such diverse products as computer games, magazines, credit cards and soft drinks. Narrative research and narrative analysis has been written about by Kim (2016), and by Gubrium and Holstein (2009) (see also Andrews *et al.*, 2013). Narrative analysis is the research methodology in focus in this chapter, Chapter 9.
Historical research/analysis	This methodology involves exploring and analyzing the history of some phenomenon. The subject of the research might, for example, be a particular industry, such as coalmining in Wigan, or brewing in Wiveliscombe. There might, for example, be useful lessons to be learned from the study of the history of Apple Computer Inc. or the history of the Microsoft Corporation. The different historical periods of trade, such as an aspect of colonial trading history, or a history of some aspect of globalization, might prove illuminating in terms of some issue in contemporary business studies. Some contribution to the study of the history of economic thought might be valuable, perhaps a study of the lessons of Marxist economics for contemporary society. An interesting idea for a research project might be the study of Guinness advertising over the last 50 years or perhaps a study of the most popular Guinness advertising campaign ever. It is worth remembering that recent history is as valid as ancient history in terms of historical research. There might be some aspect of recent business history that you could study that would count as a valuable contribution to knowledge. There are very many possibilities for the useful application of this methodology in business research. This methodology can draw on quantitative or qualitative data, or on a mixture of both. Danto (2008) has written about historical research, see also McDowell (2002). Connor (2004) has written about women, accounting and bookkeeping in eighteenth-century England.
Life history	Life history is used to compile life histories of different people or different companies. It can be used, for example, to understand the changes that have occurred in the lives of a group of people or the changes that have occurred in the life of a company. This methodology can draw on quantitative or qualitative data, or on a mixture of both. One particular kind of life history research is oral history. Oral history has been written about by Thompson (2000). An oral history is a vocalized account of some historical experience given by a witness or participant in that experience. An interesting and useful oral history research project might be one of the vocalized accounts of the experiences of people involved in the recent crisis in banking. The most fundamental data collection method within a life history and an oral history research methodology is the life history interview. The life history interview has been written about by Atkinson (1998), see also Cole and Knowles (2001). Life history research is the research methodology in focus in Chapter 20.
Content analysis	Content analysis is a research methodology used to analyze the content of any text. Content analysis can be used to examine the tenor of a text and both the explicit and the latent content of texts. It can be used to calculate the frequency with which particular words or phrases, or concepts or ideas. appear in the text being analyzed. It can be used to examine the placing within the text of particular aspects and elements of the communication. It can be used to examine the strength of the communication, through the force given to aspects of the communication, evident in the size of the font, in the organization of the communication, and in any highlighting, for example, through the use of colour in the text. Texts can be documents,

Table 9.2 Detailed research methodologies (*Continued*)

Content analysis (*Continued*)	interview transcripts or the transcripts of speeches, newspapers, conversations, advertising, websites and web pages, and so on. Any text that is language based can be analyzed using a content analysis approach. Content analysis is used a great deal in media analysis. An interesting research project using content analysis might be the study of the website of a company. For example, you could study a company's website to examine their positioning in the marketplace, or to examine their brand, or perhaps to examine their business ethics. Although traditionally a quantitative methodology, this methodology can draw on quantitative or qualitative data, or on a mixture of both. Content analysis has been written about by Neuendorf (2017), and by Krippendorff (2012) and Krippendorff and Bock (2009). Content analysis is the research methodology in focus in Chapter 6 of this textbook.
Discourse analysis	Discourse analysis is a research methodology that facilitates the identification of discourses in the social world and the analysis of those discourses. According to Fairclough (1995), discourses can be written texts, spoken words and/or cultural artefacts. Discourses are, he suggests, embedded in social events and social practices. Foucault (1970, 1972), believed that public discourses can be shaped by powerful individuals and groups and he also thought that such discourses have the power to shape individuals and their experience of the social world. Foucault believed that powerful discourses could bring about particular realities, they could bring those realities into being. You might, by way of an example, think about the discourses that prevailed in international economics before the recent global economic turmoil. Then think about the discourses that prevail in international economics since the recent global economic turmoil. Think about the powerful forces creating, propounding and perpetuating those discourses and think about the impact of those discourses on you, your family and your friends and on every individual on the planet. Discourse analysis calls for the identification and analysis of discourses. Fairclough (2013) has written on critical discourse analysis. Discourse analysis is the methodology in focus in Chapter 10.
Documentary analysis/research	Documentary analysis is the methodology designed to facilitate research on documents. Documentary analysis involves the systematic analysis of data in the form of documents or data drawn from documents. The documents used can be written documents, books, papers, magazines, notices, letters, records, and so on. Scott (1990) has written in detail about documentary research; see also Coffey (2014). Documentary research is the research methodology in focus in Chapter 11.
Semiotics	Semiotics is the study of signs, their form, content and expression. Semiotics is and has long been widely used in media analysis. In recent years the study of social semiotics has become prominent. Signs in society are signs because they signify something. Anything that has signifying power can be studied semiotically. If you consider, for example, the following signs, £, $, you will immediately recognize the signs and you will know immediately what each signifies, and the great complexity of meaning conveyed by these two symbols. The social world, and the world of social interaction, is full of signifying signs. Semiotics is the study of such signs. Semiotics can be used, for example, to uncover the meaning of the image of a company, or a brand, or a product. Semiotic data can be analyzed both quantitatively and qualitatively. Erving Goffman published a (now classic) study, *Gender Advertisements* (1979), in which he engaged in a semiotic analysis of advertising. Chandler (2017) has written about semiotics. Semiotics is the research methodology in focus in Chapter 17.
Attitude research	Attitude research is the methodology used in the measurement of attitudes. Attitude research can be used to measure the attitudes of people to anything: to a product, to an advertising campaign, to a company, to spending, to saving, anything. Attitude research has traditionally been a quantitative methodology or a methodology that uses quantitative data; however, qualitative data can also be used in attitude research, as can a mixture of both quantitative and qualitative data. There are many scales that have been specifically designed for attitude measurement in research. Some examples of the different scales include Likert scales, semantic differential scales and social distance scales. All of these scales, and many more, are explained in detail by Oppenheim (2000). These scales are detailed, illustrated and explained in Chapter 16 of this textbook.
Image-based research	Image-based research is the use of images in social research. Using this research methodology, a researcher can draw on data from photographs, film, videos, advertising, cartoons, drawings, maps, charts and any other kind of image. Visual data can be analyzed using a quantitative or a qualitative approach, or a mixture of both. Rose (2016), Banks and Zeitlyn (2015), Banks (2007), Pink (2006), and Prosser (1998) are among those who have written on this methodology. An interesting example of image-based research in sports management is the work of Geurin-Eagleman and Burch (2016), who studied Olympic athletes and their visual (photographic) representations of themselves on Instagram. The purpose of the study was to develop an understanding of the ways in which athletes use social media as a

(*Continued*)

Table 9.2 Detailed research methodologies (*Continued*)

Image-based research (*Continued*)	communication and marketing tool to build their personal brand. Another interesting example in business studies is the work of Pullman and Robson (2007), who, in one of their research projects, used image-based research to examine hotel guests' responses to the design of a hotel. Pullman and Robson said that because design is a visual medium, image-based research was the most appropriate research methodology for their research project. In your own research, you might think about taking some photographs of the phenomenon you are investigating. Using image-based research, the images might be the only data in the research project or they might be used to supplement data from other sources. If there is no opportunity to take photographs to use as data in your research project, you might think about using photographs, or other images, already in existence that you could draw on as data for your research project. Image-based research is the research methodology in focus in Chapter 4. In Chapter 4 there is an account of Ian's research project, which he has developed using an image-based research methodology.
Archival research	Archival research is research carried out on the content of archives. Archives are documents or stores of documents. Archives can be very small or they can be very extensive. Libraries, for example, can store archives. The stored records and/or documents of a company or a business would constitute an archive. According to the website of the National Archive of the UK (www.nationalarchives.gov.uk), archives are documents in any medium that have been created by an individual, family, business or organization during its existence and have been chosen to be kept permanently because they are considered to be of continuing value, www.nationalarchives.gov.uk/documents/archives/defining-archives.pdf. Researchers when they conduct archival research, gain access to the archive and then conduct their research on the contents of that archive. It is often the case that different data collection methods are used in archival research, for example, content analysis, documentary analysis, image-based research. The methods used, as always, depend on the data available in the archive, on the requirements of the study, and they depend on the imaginative way in which the researcher engages with the archival material. Moore *et al.* (2017) have written on archival research in the social sciences.
Textual analysis	Textual analysis is the analysis of any text. Texts can be books, magazines, other documents or images or film, TV programmes, DVDs, videos, websites and web pages, advertisements, clothes, graffiti, the décor, layout and organization of rooms, and so on. The researcher analyzes the text in order to develop some interpretation of the meaning of the text in relation to the aim of the research. The researcher analyzes and interprets the text in order to try to make some meaning of the text. There is a short introduction to textual analysis on the website of Duke University, USA (guides.library.duke.edu/text_analysis). Boréus and Bergström (2017), have written on textual analysis.
Meta-analysis	Meta-analysis is a research methodology that involves the quantitative analysis of amalgamated previously existing research data sets. It involves the bringing together of quantitative data sets from previously conducted research projects, combining them and then analyzing them. The possibility of error is quite large in using this methodology because the meta-analysis depends on the validity of the existing data sets. The researcher conducting the meta-analysis generally will not have been involved in the design or conduct of any of the research projects that produced the data sets. As this is the case, the researcher cannot guarantee the validity of the data. Another issue in terms of validity in meta-analysis is that the process of amalgamating the data sets could alter or damage in some way the data in the data sets. Despite these issues, meta-analyses are conducted. In an article published in the *International Business Review*, Kirca and Yaprak (2010) investigate how often meta-analysis techniques have been used in the international business literature over the past 30 years; they provide an overview of the process of meta-analysis research; they examine the role of meta-analysis in the synthesis of research in international business and suggest guidelines for future applications of the technique. Lipsey and Wilson (2000) have written in detail about meta-analysis, as have Borenstein *et al.* (2009).
Feminist research	Feminist research can be undertaken to highlight the experiences of women, to highlight gender inequality and as a means of leading change in relation to gender equality. Feminism, as detailed in Chapter 4, is a philosophical framework and it is an intellectual and political movement. Feminists hold a particular standpoint in relation to the nature of the social world. Feminists hold that the world is structured around gender inequality, with men holding more power than women. Feminist research is research conducted from that standpoint. Pierre Bourdieu (2001) is one of many theorists to have written on this topic. Feminist research can be undertaken using any kind of data collection methods, the requirement being that the data collection methods used fit the population and the data requirements of the study. Hesse-Biber (2014) edited a book on feminist research practice. Leavy and Harris (2018) have written on feminist research.

The Real World Research box 'How theory influences research' details a study of decision making among three entrepreneurs. The study was a **longitudinal study**; it took place over one year and six months. The aim of the study was to examine 'sense making' among entrepreneurs. The population of the study was three entrepreneurs, so, a very small population. The study involved the researchers engaging each of the three entrepreneurs in three **interviews**, so nine interviews were carried out in total. The interviews with each of the entrepreneurs were undertaken at six-monthly intervals over the time period of the study; as explained the study was a longitudinal study. The methodology used in the study was **narrative research**, sometimes called narrative analysis. This methodology calls for the analysis of different narratives (or stories) in the data gathered for the research project. In this research project, the researchers interviewed the entrepreneurs, thus gathering interview data. During the interview process, the researchers may have asked the entrepreneurs for narratives, short stories illustrating their experience of the phenomenon under investigation in the research project, or they may have themselves identified narratives in the interview data during the process of data analysis. The research methodology narrative research or narrative analysis is the research methodology in focus in the Value of Good Research box in this chapter.

longitudinal study A study of respondents at different times over a long or relatively long period of time, thus allowing analysis of response continuity and changes over time.

interviews The social science researcher develops a series of questions or a series of points of interest to discuss and explore with the interviewees.

narrative research Narrative inquiry or narrative analysis is a research methodology that is used in the gathering and analysis of narratives (stories).

REAL WORLD RESEARCH

How theory influences research

In the article presented here (Holt and Macpherson, 2010 'Sensemaking, rhetoric and the socially competent entrepreneur', *International Small Business Journal*, *28*(1): 20–42), the authors describe the research they carried out using a narrative research methodology. The research focused on the accounts that three participating entrepreneurs gave of the ways in which they negotiated uncertainty in their work.

The methodological approach to the research is laid out clearly in the journal article. The research methodology used was narrative research. The data-gathering method used was longitudinal interviews. The data gathered was triangulated by using within-method triangulation; using this method three different interviews were conducted with each of the three participants in the study.

The authors state that nine interviews in all were conducted for the study, three open-ended, in-depth interviews with each of the three manufacturing entrepreneurs. Each of the three interviews, conducted with each of the three entrepreneurs, took place at six-monthly intervals and each lasted between one and a half to two hours.

The article details that the main questions asked in the interviews were framed in terms of what Sole and Edmundson (2002) called 'significant learning episodes'; they say that significant learning episodes are an extension of the critical incident technique developed by Flanagan (1954). The authors state that, although initially a way of collecting data for quantitative analysis, critical incident technique is now commonly used to orient interviews around particular events that have meaning for the participants (Chell and Allman, 2003; Kokalis, 2007).

In the interviews, each entrepreneur was asked to recount moments at which their experience of creating and sustaining their firm changed significantly, moments within their experience which culminated in a particular insight, a change of direction, or the review and revision of existing understanding.

The interviews were recorded and fully transcribed and then sorted into accounts of learning episodes.

The interviews, according to the authors, allowed the entrepreneurs to construct stories (narratives) about their experiences and to make sense of those experiences by reflecting on them.

The brief synopsis of the journal article presented here clearly demonstrates how theory influences research. This is evident in the way in which the work of other researchers and theorists influenced and informed the way that the authors of this study designed their research project. You should source the original article and read it.

DECIDING ON THE MOST APPROPRIATE METHODOLOGY FOR YOUR RESEARCH PROJECT

It is very important that you decide as quickly as possible which methodology you intend to use in your research project. Take the time that you need to get this right, but try to get it right as quickly as you can. Again, do not hesitate to ask for guidance in selecting a research methodology and for feedback in relation to any decision you make regarding research methodology from your lecturers and your thesis supervisor.

YOUR RESEARCH

Common research problems – learning more about research methodologies

You will need to read a little more about the methodologies introduced and outlined in Table 9.2. A good way to begin would be to do an internet search using the name of the research methodologies that seem particularly relevant to your research. For example, search the internet using the words 'ethnography' or 'feminist research' or 'grounded theory'.

The next step would be to locate some textbooks on the methodology or methodologies in which you have a particular interest. In a couple of hours in the library you could have a good look at a number of different textbooks covering a number of different research methodologies. You will find the reading lists at the end of the chapters in this book very helpful in such searches.

The next step is to locate journal articles which feature the research methodology or methodologies that seem particularly relevant to your research. Research articles in academic journals are relatively short synopses of research projects that have been carried out, completed and published in journals. The first thing

to do is to identify the journals relevant to your research. You will find that there are a number of journals dedicated to every aspect of social science and business research, for example, the *International Small Business Journal, Journal of the Academy of Marketing Science, Journal of Business Communication*.

You can use the search mechanisms within journals, most if not all of which are available electronically, to search for articles detailing research projects which have used the methodology or methodologies that are relevant to your research.

You can download copies of these articles from your library's online resources. If you do not know how to do this, the librarians will help you, or they will direct you to someone who can help. Do not be afraid to ask for help and direction. If you wanted to, you could ask for a mentor. You might be able to connect with a more senior student who could support and direct you. Perhaps you could develop a research project around a mentoring system for undergraduate students. Remember, ideas for research projects are all around you.

YOUR RESEARCH

Common research problems – deciding on a research methodology

The best way to learn how to decide on an appropriate research methodology for a research project is to practise. The following exercise is a research diary exercise.

Imagine that you are a professional researcher and you have been asked to conduct a research project on the following: 'Key principles of Britain's top strategic managers'.

Using your research diary, propose three different methodologies for the research and detail the data collection methods to be used in each.

As you will see, there are usually a number of options in terms of the design of any research project. The key is to

select the best option for the project in relation to what it is that you want to accomplish with the research.

I once asked a class of 15 students to design a research project around the concept of Santa Claus. Each one of the 15 students designed a unique research project, using different research methodologies and data-gathering methods. One student designed a case study, another a ethnographic project, and another a visual methods study. There was even a project designed using a feminist methodology. From the exercise, 15 very different research projects were outlined and each of them was viable, valid and interesting.

It often happens that a research project has elements that seem to fit with more than one research methodology. It is important, however, that you make a decision and choose one methodology. If you can see aspects of more than one methodology in your work, decide which one will work best in relation to what it is that you want to accomplish with your research and work with that methodology. The decision around which research methodology to use in the research project must be a reasoned logical decision which can stand up to the critical scrutiny of other academics, readers and examiners.

The best way to learn how to design and develop research projects is to practise designing and developing research projects. The research diary exercise in the Your Research box is designed to encourage you to begin to do this. It also demonstrates that many research projects can be carried out using one of a number of different research methodologies. It is important to understand that the choice of research methodology shapes the research project; different research methodologies produce different research projects. Think of the Santa Claus example above, imagine such a project carried out using visual methods. What would that research project look like? Imagine that research carried out using historical analysis for the research methodology. Imagine what that research project would look like, and so on. You can see from this simple example how the research methodology used in the research project actually shapes the research carried out, and consequently the final written account of the research project, the thesis or the research report.

RESEARCH METHODS

The term **research methods** means data collection methods or data-gathering techniques; data collection methods are the means by which researchers gather the data required for the research project. There are very many research methods that can be used in gathering data for the research project. Commonly used research methods include: questionnaires, interviews, focus groups, scales, projective techniques, diaries, documents, records and visual methods such as photographs and/or videos. Each research method, or data-gathering technique, each questionnaire, each series of interviews, and so on, must be either designed by the researcher specifically for each research project, or borrowed (possibly adapted and always referenced) from another research project. The choice of data-gathering method(s) is dependent on the aim of the research, the population of the study, the data required for the study, and the location of those data.

> **research methods** Data collection methods.

The researcher must know what kind of data are needed and where the data are to be found before decisions can be made about how to gather data. The data could be in documents or written reports. The data could be in the attitudes and beliefs of human participants, or in the behaviours of human participants in the research. Each of these examples would require the design of a different data-gathering technique.

It might be that there is some vulnerability in the human participants in the research or that participation in the research could potentially render the population vulnerable. If this is the case, the data-gathering methods must be demonstrably sensitive to that vulnerability. If, for example, the human population of the study is made up of children, the age of the respondents and their potential vulnerability in participating in the research will require special consideration in the design of data-gathering technique(s). The researcher might be working with a population with cultural issues, with language issues or with literacy issues. Any or all of these will have an impact on the design of the data-gathering technique. The researcher must identify the data required, decide where the data are, and finally decide how best, within a framework of research ethics, to gather the data.

Researchers are very pragmatic when it comes to research methods. They use whatever method of data collection is most appropriate and whatever data collection method will work best. In deciding on the most appropriate data collection method(s) to use, some of the typical considerations of researchers are:

- whether the data can be gathered by interviewing people
- if a questionnaire and/or a scale, or a series of scales, would produce the required data
- whether or not it would be useful to conduct a focus group or a series of focus groups
- if the data required could be gathered from diaries in which participants in the research would record their experiences of the phenomenon under investigation
- if the data required are to be found in documents, in records or in archives
- if the data would best be gathered using a series of observations
- if the data could be gathered through taking a series of photographs or using an existing series of photographs
- if the data exist in media reports or in internet sources.

When the researcher knows what data are required for the research project, where those data are, and how that data can best be gathered, the researcher designs the approach to data gathering to be used. Data-gathering methods are designed in such a way as to ensure that they will yield the data required. The data gathered are the means by which the researcher establishes the thesis developed in the research, the means by which the research hypothesis is accepted or rejected. They are also the means by which the researcher proves their case, the means by which they illustrate the phenomenon under investigation. As this is the case, the data gathered must be adequate in terms of the needs of the research project and they must be valid in terms of the standards of social science research.

DATA COLLECTION METHODS

The researcher is, as stated, a pragmatist when it comes to gathering data. The techniques that provide the most useful data, the most appropriate data, are the methods used. As explained, there are very many data collection methods at the disposal of the researcher. In fact, the researcher is limited only by his/her own imagination and by the issue of validity, in terms of the data collection method(s) they use in their research project. Table 9.3 and Table 9.4 contain a list and short descriptions of different data-gathering methods. You will notice that some of the data-gathering methods listed are also listed in Tables 9.1 and 9.2. This is because these approaches to research can be used as research methodologies and/or as data collection methods. Some of them, such as discourse analysis, content analysis and narrative analysis can also be used as approaches to data analysis. We will encounter these terms again when we explore data analysis in later chapters of this textbook.

You will already be familiar with many of the data collection methods detailed here, although some will undoubtedly be new to you. It is possible that the knowledge that you have of some of the data collection methods listed is 'common sense knowledge'. This kind of knowledge can be harmful rather than helpful in scientific undertakings. The rigorous use or application of data collection methods in social science research requires sophisticated scientific knowledge. For this reason it is important that you read the brief descriptions of the data-gathering methods given. It is important too that you follow this up with further reading, guided by the references and recommended readings given in this textbook. This is particularly important in relation to the data collection methods that you intend to use in your own research project.

As stated previously, you are only limited in terms of your own imagination in relation to the ways in which you use these data collection methods and any other data collection methods you find, or devise, for your project. The only stipulations or constraints are that the data collection methods must be valid and they must fit the research. This means that they must fit the aim of the research, the population of the research and the data requirements of the research and they must accomplish what it is that they purport to accomplish.

Table 9.3   Data collection methods

Observation	Scales
Participant observation	Projective techniques
Covert observation	Content analysis
One-to-one interviews	Field diaries
Telephone interviews	Visual methods
Group interviews	Narrative analysis
Postal questionnaires	Documentary evidence
Drop and collect questionnaires	Discourse analysis
Group administered questionnaires	Semiotics
Online questionnaires	Oral history
Focus groups	Archival research
Internet research	Experiments
Secondary sources	Unobtrusive methods
Case studies	Critical incident method

Table 9.4 Detailed data collection methods

Observation	Observation is a data collection method used in order to record observations of a phenomenon. The researcher engages in observation in order to gather data on the phenomenon under investigation. In conducting an observation study, the researcher observes what is happening and records their observations. Observations can be carried out in an unstructured, semi-structured or structured manner. In an *unstructured observation*, the researcher has no pre-set criteria in terms of what it is that s/he is observing. This kind of observation is usually engaged in at the beginning of a study, when the researcher is not sure precisely what will happen, or what exactly s/he needs to be observing. Often, through unstructured observation, these things become apparent. In *semi-structured observation*, the researcher has a pre-prepared list of actions that s/he wishes to focus on through the observation. Generally, this list will contain about eight points, each of which relates to the action to be observed. The researcher notes each time the action happens and records, generally in field notes, his or her observations on and around the action. In *structured observation*, the researcher has a structured list of actions or points related to the action that s/he wishes to observe. A schedule designed for the recording of a structured observation can look like a highly structured questionnaire. The researcher ticks boxes on the schedule to record the actions s/he is observing, recording his or her thoughts in separate field notes. Chapter 13 of this textbook is focused on observation.
Participant observation	Participant observation is the same as observation, with one major difference: the researcher is a participant in the action s/he is observing. While the researcher participates in the action, s/he observes the action and records their observations on the action.
Covert observation	Covert observation is observation carried out covertly or secretly. The researcher observes the action and records their observations of the action covertly. There are substantial ethical issues in covert research. Chapter 3 of this text book is focused on research ethics.
One-to-one interviews	One-to-one interviews are interviews carried out generally face-to-face and on a one-to-one basis between the interviewer and the interviewee. One-to-one interviews or face-to-face interviews are a very common data collection method. They have very many advantages. In a one-to-one interview, the interviewer has an opportunity to establish a rapport with the interviewee. The researcher has the opportunity to explain the research in detail to the interviewee. S/he can discuss the questions and issues with the interviewee. S/he can observe the interviewee's responses to the interview questions and issues. The interviewer can probe the interviewee in terms of any responses to questions. Interviews are usually audio-recorded and transcribed later. Every interview is a social engagement and the interviewer, the researcher, must have the capacity to engage the interviewee in the interview in an empathetic way. The interviewer must have the capacity to sustain that engagement for the length of the interview. In interviews, there is a danger of interviewer bias. This is where the interviewer attempts to influence or lead the responses of the interviewee, intentionally or otherwise. Interviewing in research is a particular skill. The researcher must be empathetic, but s/he must not influence the responses in any way. Interviews can be time-consuming, and they can be exhausting for the interviewer. Interviewees can be very cooperative but sometimes they can be quite uncooperative. The interviewer must be prepared to deal with any contingency. What should s/he do if the interviewee suddenly terminates the interview? What should s/he do if a fire alarm goes off? Interviewers need to be very well prepared for the social encounter that is the interview. Any equipment needed, electronic or otherwise, must be in proper working order, prepared and ready for the interview. The interviewer must ensure that sufficient time is given to each interview, to preparation, to set-up, to debriefing and/or recovery after the interview. After the interview, there must be sufficient time for the transcribing of interview recordings. Transcribing interviews is the process through which recorded interviews are typed up into transcripts. Transcripts of interviews are complete and accurate typed records of the interviews, taken from (or transcribed from) the recordings of the interviews. The transcript becomes the data to be analyzed. Chapter 14 of this textbook focuses in detail on interviews.
Telephone interviews	Telephone interviews are interviews conducted, generally on a one-to-one basis, over the telephone. Telephone interviews can be very convenient and very time and resource efficient. They are relatively inexpensive when compared to the cost of actually visiting all of the respondents as is necessary in one-to-one interviewing. Telephone interviews can yield a substantial amount of data relatively quickly and easily. On the negative side, the interviewer in telephone interviewing is not face-to-face with the interviewee, and so cannot observe the responses of the interviewee to the interview questions and issues. Neither generally can the interviewer establish the same level of rapport with the interviewee as is possible with one-to-one interviews. It can be more difficult in telephone interviewing to discern when more information needs to be given to the interviewee; it can be more difficult to discern whether or not it would be possible or appropriate to probe an issue with a telephone interviewee. In addition, it is, generally speaking, easier for an interviewee to terminate a telephone interview or to withdraw from a telephone interview, than from a one-to-one face-to-face interview.

(Continued)

Table 9.4 Detailed data collection methods (*Continued*)

Group interviews	Group interviews are interviews conducted face-to-face between the interviewer and a group of interviewees. This type of face-to-face interview has all of the advantages of the one-to-one interview, as well as all of the issues. A key skill required in group interviewees is that of facilitating groups. Facilitating groups is a substantial and a complex task. It requires particular skill and diplomacy. A group interview is used by a researcher when the data required for the research project can best be gathered through a group interview. This means that there is something in the group processes, which generally occur naturally within group interviews, that will lead to the generation within the group interview of the data required for the research. The researcher chooses group interview as the data-gathering method when there is something in the group process which will aid generation of the data required.
Online interviews	Online interviews can be synchronous (in real time) using a chatroom or using conferencing software, or asynchronous (outside of real time) using email or message boards or discussion boards, and so on. In synchronous interviewing, the interviewer asks questions and the interviewee responds immediately. Synchronous interviews can be conducted very quickly and this can have advantages. In asynchronous interviewing, the interviewer sends questions to the interviewee and the interviewee responds at a later time. Interviewers send one question at a time or a very short number of questions at a time; a long list of questions is a questionnaire, not an interview schedule. Asynchronous interviewing can take time. This has advantages and disadvantages. One advantage is that respondents can take time to consider their responses and this can improve the quality of responses. A disadvantage can be the difficulty in keeping respondents engaged with the interview process. Online interviews are useful with geographically dispersed populations and with otherwise difficult to reach populations. Online interviews are very resource efficient, if all participants have ready access to the technology used in the interviews. The relative anonymity of the interviewee can facilitate openness and frankness in their responses to interview questions and probes. There is a possibility of respondents mistrusting online interviewing. Some people feel that chatrooms, for example, are too open. Sometimes people perform different identities online. Video links in online interviewing can intimidate respondents, and consequently inhibit the quality of their engagement in the interview. On the other hand, where there is no video link, there is reduced chance of interviewer bias. Interviewer bias occurs when the interviewer influences the responses of the interviewee in some way. Bias is dealt with in detail in Chapter 15 of this textbook.
Postal questionnaires	Questionnaires are among the most widely used data collection methods. I am sure that you have filled in a questionnaire at some point in your life. You fill in a questionnaire if you open a bank account, if you join a library. Questionnaires are generally highly structured data collection instruments. With highly structured data collection instruments, respondents are often simply required to tick boxes in order to respond to the research. This facilitates participants, and large numbers of participants, in participating in the research. The researcher in designing the data collection instrument has decided very precisely what data are required and they have structured the data collection instrument very precisely to provide those data. Questionnaires can be made up of both open and closed questions. Closed questions are questions that require a set response, for example, yes/no/don't know/not applicable. The respondent is given a set of possible responses and simply ticks a box to indicate the response that they have selected in response to the question posed. Open questions do not have a set of pre-defined responses. Open questions allow the respondent to express themselves. An example of an open question is: Please explain why you decided to introduce the new product. In response, respondents are invited to respond as they wish and they are given space in the questionnaire to respond openly to the question or issue. There are generally very few such open questions in questionnaires. This is because of the complexity posed by coding such responses. It is much easier to code the responses to closed questions. The more open questions there are in a questionnaire, the more complex and time consuming will be the coding process. Questionnaires with closed questions can be readily and quickly coded and analyzed. Questionnaires are often used with big research populations. Questionnaires can readily and easily be administered to large populations. Postal questionnaires are questionnaires that are posted to respondents. A covering letter is sent with the questionnaire and a stamped addressed envelope (SAE) to facilitate the respondents in responding. The respondent is required to fill in the questionnaire and post it back to the researcher using the SAE. Often the researcher has to post a reminder to the respondents to encourage them to respond to the questionnaire. As the researcher does not meet with the respondents or engage with the respondents in any other way, there can be an issue with low levels of response rates using this method of data collection. The cost of this data collection method is the cost of the stationery and the postage. Chapter 15 of this textbook deals in detail with survey research and questionnaires.
Drop and collect questionnaires	A drop and collect questionnaire is where a researcher drops (leaves) a questionnaire with respondents and then returns to collect it when the respondent has completed filling in the questionnaire. The method of administering the questionnaire, drop and collect, can produce good response rates.

Table 9.4 Detailed data collection methods (*Continued*)

Group-administered questionnaires	Group-administered questionnaires are questionnaires that the researcher administers to a group. When the group is gathered together, the researcher administers the questionnaire to them. It might happen that the group assembles for a meeting, or for a class, or a lecture, or for a conference or for some other purpose. The researcher takes the opportunity of the gathering to administer the questionnaire. This is a very efficient means of gathering data. The data are gathered in one go. The collective nature of the data gathering, together with the presence of the researcher, helps boost response rates. Response rates of 100 per cent are not unusual with group administered questionnaires.
Online questionnaires	Online questionnaires are questionnaires that are administered online. Such questionnaires can be sent to respondents via email or respondents can be sent a link to the questionnaire, which can be uploaded to a website, and invited to respond to the questionnaire. Response rates can be a substantial issue using online questionnaires. Questionnaires can be created online using tools such as Survey Monkey, Instant Survey or Zoomerang. The *Exploring Online Research Methods* web page of the University of Leicester is a useful resource for information (www.geog.le.ac.uk/ORM/site/home.htm).
Focus groups	In focus group research, the researcher brings groups of people together to focus on a particular issue. The optimum number of participants in a focus group is eight, the lowest is six, and the highest is 12. The group generally meets around a table, in a boardroom-like setting. This setting facilitates an even, balanced, contribution from all participants. The focus group is generally audio-recorded. The audio recording is transcribed. Transcribing focus groups is the process through which the recorded focus group is typed up into a transcript. Typed transcripts of focus groups are complete and accurate typed records of focus groups, taken from, or transcribed from, the recordings of the focus groups. The transcript becomes the data to be analyzed. In addition, the researcher, and/or any assistant researcher(s), may also record in their research diaries their observations of the focus group and their impressions of the focus group. These observations and impressions can be used to supplement the data from the transcripts. Focus groups, like questionnaires, can be unstructured, semi-structured or structured. Usually, they are semi-structured. In a semi-structured focus group, the researcher has a list of questions or issues to be explored during the focus group. The researcher moderates the focus group, or may invite another expert to moderate. The moderator facilitates the focus group. The moderation of focus groups requires particular skills. The group dynamic in focus group research often produces unique insights and perspectives, and this is the real value of this particular data-gathering method, the focus group. The onus is on the moderator to get the discussion going, to maintain it, to manage it, and to conclude it on time. Focus groups are introduced in Chapter 8 of this textbook and dealt with in detail in Chapter 14.
Internet research	Internet research is research conducted on the internet. Obviously, there is a great deal of information on the World Wide Web (www). The internet can be used to source literature and it can also be used to source both primary and secondary data. We have seen where the internet can be used to develop and administer questionnaires. Interviews can be conducted on the internet, using email, chat rooms, discussion boards or through the use of video-conferencing (see Chapter 14). The internet can be searched for information. Search engines on the www can help you find the information you need. Google is a very popular web search engine. Google Scholar is, as one of my students recently remarked, a gift for researchers. Other web search engines such as Bing and Yahoo! can also be used. Keyword searches are generally used to find information. The researcher uses the keywords, or key concepts, from the research statement/question to find information on the internet. Domain searches are also important. A domain on the internet is the home or area of authority or autonomy of an individual, an organization, an entity. You could search, for example, the domain of the OECD (Organization for Economic Cooperation and Development), or the domain of the IMF (International Monetary Fund). As explained earlier, the *Exploring Online Research Methods* web page of the University of Leicester is a useful resource for anyone interested in internet research (www.geog.le.ac.uk/ORM/site/home.htm).
Secondary sources	A secondary source is something that has been written about a primary source. A secondary source is, in a sense, a second-hand source. When a researcher creates data, they are creating a primary source. When the data they are using were created by someone else, the data are secondary data, data from a secondary source. A secondary source builds on a primary source, a secondary source interprets and analyzes a primary source. A secondary source is an account of something. The original material is the primary source. Secondary sources of data can be used, and often are used very effectively by researchers in research projects.
Case studies	A case study, as explained in this chapter, is research carried out on a bounded entity, on a specific space or place, on a particular incident, or on specific entities. Using a case study method, the researcher studies one case or a number of cases. The researcher, drawing on all of the data sources possible, engages in an in-depth examination of the case(s). Yin (2018) has written on case study methodology. Case study methodology is the research methodology in focus in Chapter 3 of this textbook. Susan Soy (2006) has produced a good simple guide to case study research which can be found at: www.ischool.utexas.edu/~ssoy/usesusers/l391d1b.htm

(Continued)

Table 9.4 Detailed data collection methods (*Continued*)

Scales	Scales and scaling techniques are used widely in attitude measurement research. Commonly used scales include Likert scales, Bogardus social distance scales and semantic differential scales. Joo *et al.* (2018) used a number of different scales in their study of attitudes of residents to tourists. Scales are used to generate quantitative data. Scales are very interesting research techniques. They appear to be quite simple, but appearances can be deceptive. The production of a valid scale involves a great deal of work and preparation. Scales are dealt with in detail in Chapter 16 of this textbook.
Projective techniques	Projective techniques are used to explore people's instinctive responses to stimuli such as, for example, advertising campaigns. Projective techniques are indirect ways of exploring attitudes. It is suggested sometimes that as the purpose of projective techniques is often less obvious than the purpose of attitude scales, projective techniques can yield truer results. One example of a projective technique is sentence completion. This is an exercise whereby the researcher gives the respondent the first part of a sentence, and asks the respondent to complete the sentence. Scales and projective techniques can be used alone or as part of other research methods. They can, for example, be built into questionnaires. They can be used in interviews, or to help start or prompt discussions in focus groups. Oppenheim (2000) has a very good chapter on projective techniques. There is an introduction to projective techniques in Chapter 8, with further details in Chapter 16.
Content analysis	Content analysis is a research method that involves the analysis of any kind of content. Content analysis is widely used in communications research. Traditionally, content analysis was used for the systematic quantitative description of the explicit content of any communication. Content analysis can also be used qualitatively. Content analysis generally means the analysis of some aspect of a particular type of communication. The communication might be a newspaper, a newsletter, or a radio or TV programme. The research is focused on a particular phenomenon and the researcher identifies that phenomenon in the communication. The researcher then examines the phenomenon within that communication. The researcher might explore, for example, how often a word or phrase is used. The researcher might analyze the content in order to come to some conclusion about the tone of the communication, about the message in the communication, about the ideologies expressed in the communication, and so on. Content analysis is the research methodology in focus in Chapter 6 of this textbook.
Field diaries	Traditionally, field notes or field diaries are the way in social research, and in particular in anthropological and ethnographical research, through which observations in the field are recorded. Field diaries are diaries in which the researcher records all of their observations in the field. The field in social research is the site, beyond the library, the desk, and/or the laboratory. It is the site where the research takes place, or the site where the research is carried out. Field diaries are particularly useful for researchers in the writing-up phase of the research. They can be used by the researcher as a prompt to memory, an aide memoir, or as a record more reliable than memory. They can be used for the descriptive passages they often contain regarding the research site. Elements of these when included in the written account of the research, the thesis or the research report, can greatly enhance a research project, adding richness and colour to the descriptions of the site, the phenomenon, and/or the participants (see Hammersley and Atkinson, 1995: Chapter 7). Research participants can be requested to keep diaries within which they record their observations and experiences of and reflections on the phenomenon under investigation. These diaries can then be used as data in the research project.
Visual methods and image-based research	Visual methods in data gathering is the use of any kind of visual image as data in the research project. Visual methods involves the analysis of visual images. Any kind of visual images can be used, maps, charts, photographs, drawings, paintings, cartoons, videos and films, and so on. The researcher can gather visual images, or s/he can create visual images, or they can ask participants in the research to give visual images to the research project, or to create visual images for the research project. As with every data collection method, data generated by the method must be valid in terms of the purpose of the research project. Visual data can be analyzed using a quantitative or a qualitative approach, or a mixture of both. Rose (2016), Banks and Zeitlyn (2015), Banks (2007), Pink (2006) and Prosser (1998) are among those who have written on visual methods and image-based research. Image-based research is the research methodology in focus in Chapter 4 of this textbook.
Narrative analysis	Narrative analysis calls for the analysis of narratives. Narratives are collected as data or narratives are identified in data and then analyzed. Narratives are stories. These stories can be oral histories or biographies; they can be folk tales or myths. They can be the stories participants tell about the phenomenon under investigation. Human beings tell stories. In fact much of human communication is accomplished through storytelling.

Table 9.4 Detailed data collection methods (*Continued*)

Narrative analysis (*Continued*)	The stories told about a culture or a phenomenon can be very revealing. People within a culture or people experiencing a phenomenon tell stories about that culture and/or that phenomenon. It is one of the ways through which people make meaning of culture and/or phenomena. The narratives that a culture develops and propagates about that culture are revealing. Such narratives can be discerned from the material published by organizations about their organization. The researcher gathers data for the research project. S/he identifies the narratives in the data and then analyzes those narratives in order to explain or illustrate the phenomenon under investigation. Narrative research and narrative analysis has been written about by Kim (2016) and by Gubrium and Holstein (2009). Narrative analysis is the research methodology in focus in this chapter.
Documentary evidence	Documentary evidence is data in the form of documents or data drawn from documents. Documentary analysis involves the systematic analysis of data in the form of documents or data drawn from documents. The documents used can be written documents, books, newspapers, notices, letters, records, and so on. Documentary research is the research methodology in focus in Chapter 11 of this textbook.
Discourse analysis	Discourse analysis is a way of analyzing the social world as it is produced and represented in language and in social practices. According to Fairclough (1995), discourses can be written texts, spoken words and/or cultural artefacts. Discourses are, he suggests, embedded in social events and social practices. Foucault (1970, 1972) was concerned with the way in which individuals could be represented within powerful discourses. You might, for example, think about the powerful discourse that a multinational corporation may develop and circulate about itself. Another way to think about discourses is to think about the individual and how the individual might be represented within the discourses of the organization. For example, how are individuals represented within marketing discourses, within HR discourses? You can see how all of these discourses would differ. Discourses are embedded in the language we use and in the way in which we use that language. Discourse analysis calls for the identification of such discourses within the ways through which we communicate, and the analysis of them. Fairclough (2013) has written on this topic. Discourse analysis is the methodology in focus in Chapter 10 of this textbook.
Semiotics	Semiotics is the study of signs in society. Signs are the words, pictures, symbols, etc. used by people in society to communicate, to make meaning. van Leeuwen (2005) explores social semiotics such as dress, everyday objects, artefacts and images. He defines semiotic resources (2005: 3) as the actions and artefacts we use to communicate. According to van Leeuwen (2005: 5), 'Studying the semiotic potential of a given semiotic resource is studying how that resource has been, is, and can be, used for the purposes of communication.' In using semiotics in research, the focus is on the way in which people use semiotic resources, language, dress, artefacts, food, images, etc. to communicate. Social semiotics are loaded with meaning and cultural significance. Semiotics is widely used in market research. There are many articles detailing research projects carried out using semiotics in journals such as the *European Journal of Marketing,* the *Journal of Consumer Marketing*, the *Journal of Consumer Research* and the *International Journal of Market Research*. Hestbaek Anderson *et al.* (2015) have written on this topic. Semiotics is the methodology in focus in Chapter 17 of this textbook.
Oral history	Oral history is a data collection method by which oral testimony is gathered from the research participants on their experience of the phenomenon on which the research project is focused. Oral history is a systematic method of gathering such data. Oral historians are focused on establishing an historic record. They do not gather anecdotes or folk tales. Oral history is a history of the present or the recent past. This is because oral historians deal with the testimonies of living individuals. The Oxford journal *Oral History Review* is a good place to look for examples of oral history research projects. The University of Winnipeg, Canada, has an Oral History Centre, www.oralhistorycentre.ca/welcome. The UCLA (University of California, Los Angeles) Center for Oral History Research has an oral history research programme called *Entrepreneurs of the West* (www.library.ucla .edu/destination/center-oral-history-research/collections/subject-areas/business-oral-histories). Oral history and life history is the methodology in focus in Chapter 20 of this textbook.
Archival research	Archival research is research carried out on the content of archives. Archives are documents or stores of documents. Archives can be very small, or they can be very extensive. Libraries, for example, can store archives. The stored records and/ or documents of a company or a business would constitute an archive. According to the website of the National Archive of the UK (www.nationalarchives.gov.uk), 'Archives are documents in any medium that have been created by an individual, family, business or organization during its existence and have been chosen to be kept permanently because they are considered to be of continuing value.' Moore *et al.* (2017) have written on archival research.

(*Continued*)

Table 9.4 Detailed data collection methods (*Continued*)

Experiments	In an experiment two groups are established, with individuals or units being randomly assigned to both groups. The two groups are pretested and the *dependent variable* is measured. Then a program or application, the *independent variable*, is applied to one group, the experimental group, and not to the other group, the control group. Both groups are tested again; again the dependent variable is measured. If there is a difference in the experimental group but not in the control group, the program or application applied to them, the independent variable, is said to account for the difference. There can be more than one dependent variable in an experiment but there should only be one independent variable. In the social world, there are so many variables it can be difficult sometimes to isolate an independent variable. It can be difficult to establish precisely which variable(s) account for changes that occur in social science research. It can be difficult in social research, to absolutely establish cause and effect, to establish precisely what/which cause brought about what/which effect. The Hawthorne experiments (1924–1933) are classical examples. Elton Mayo, a professor of Industrial Management at the Harvard Business School, studied worker behaviour at the Western Electrical Company's Hawthorne Works in Illinois, USA. The experiments Mayo carried out were designed to measure worker productivity. Mayo found that as he studied the workers, their productivity improved. What he realized was that the subjects of his experiments changed their performance in response to being observed. In other words, it was the experience of being observed that caused worker productivity to improve. This variable of being observed was an unforeseen variable in the experiments, yet it was the variable that brought about the change in worker behaviour. This discovery became known as 'the Hawthorne effect'. You can read about the experiments on the Harvard Business School website at www.library.hbs.edu/hc/hawthorne/09.html. Trochim (2006) provides a clear introduction to experimental design (www.socialresearchmethods.net/kb/desexper.php). Experimental design is the methodology in focus in Chapter 19 of this textbook.
Unobtrusive methods	Unobtrusive methods are data collection methods that can be employed by the researcher without the researcher intruding in any way on the site of the research or on the population of the research. Unobtrusive methods clearly have an important place in social research, given the impact of other methods on the behaviour of research participants, as highlighted in the Hawthorne experiments detailed earlier. Unobtrusive methods avoid the reactivity generated by other data-gathering methods. Many of the methods detailed can be used unobtrusively, secondary sources are clearly unobtrusive. Potentially unobtrusive methods include content analysis and documentary analysis. Other methods can be used unobtrusively, such as observation and photography. In his book on unobtrusive methods in social research, Lee (2000) talks about 'found data', for example data in the form of material objects found that inform the research, data in the form of environmental damage, or erosion and accretion measures whereby the data are in the form of some physical evidence, such as graffiti or garbage. Garbage-based research, garbology, the study of what people throw away, is used in consumer research. Garbage analysis was used by Cote *et al.* (1985) in their study of the disparity between stated intention and actual behaviour in relation to 15 commonly consumed food and beverage products. There are clearly ethical implications in the use of many unobtrusive methods. There may also be legal issues. It is always a good idea to get feedback on your ideas for your research before you become fixed on them or committed to them. It is essential that you seek and secure approval from your research supervisor for those ideas before you put any of them into practice.
Critical incident technique	This method involves gathering data about a critical incident or a series of critical incidents and the consequences of that/those incident(s). The researcher generally uses observation and/or interviews to explore the critical incident and its consequences. The researcher also uses official reports, media reports and any other reports and documentation available on the critical incident. The researcher gathers data on the critical incident in order to understand the incident. The researcher then applies their understanding of the critical incident to the phenomenon under investigation in order to develop further insight(s) into the phenomenon under investigation. One disadvantage of the critical incident method is that the focus on critical incidents may cause routine incidents to be overlooked. There is a chapter on critical incident (Gilbert and Lockwood, 1999) in *The Handbook of Contemporary Hospitality Management Research* (Brotherton, 1999). Kaulio and Uppvall (2009) used critical incidents to study leadership in R&D alliances. Kinnunen, Uhmavaara and Jaaskelainen (2017), used critical incident technique (CIT) in their study of the defining factors influencing a rock festival brand.

Focus on narrative research/narrative inquiry/narrative analysis

Narrative research, narrative inquiry or narrative analysis is a research methodology that is used in the gathering and analysis of narratives (stories). Human beings communicate by telling stories. They narrate their lives and their experiences; they narrate their work, their experiences, knowledge and understanding of their workplaces. According to Kohler Riessman (2008), the storytelling impulse is natural and universal across the globe. Narratives are socially situated. As Kohler Riessman (2008), states, they are composed for particular audiences at particular points in time. They draw on the taken-for-granted discourses and values circulating in the culture from which they are drawn. Consequently, they do not speak any essential truth; they do not evidence any essential reality. Based on this statement, can you say something about the philosophical framework within which a researcher is working when using narrative analysis? These issues of truth and reality are, as we know from our reading of Chapter 4 of this textbook, epistemological and ontological issues.

The researcher gathers the narratives (stories) as data, or the researcher extracts narratives from data. Data in narrative research can be in the form of texts such as diaries, interviews, letters, documents, web pages, and so on. They can also be in the form of orally told stories. The researcher explores and analyzes the narratives in the data. Kohler Riessman (2008), presents four different approaches to analyzing narratives: thematic analysis, structural analysis, dialogic/performance analysis, and visual analysis. It would be useful to read about these different approaches to narrative analysis, outlined in Kohler Riessman's (2008) book, if

you think you might use narrative research as your research methodology in your research project.

Rajan's research project

Rajan is thinking of using a narrative research methodology in his research project. He has been following media accounts of an episode of industrial unrest in the national postal service. He is thinking about using narrative research to explore, with the different parties in the dispute, the different ways in which each party is constructing and representing the dispute within their own narratives. Rajan wants to situate his research project within a regional office of the national postal service. The office is located in the city in which he lives. The different parties to the dispute, as he has identified them, are postal workers, trade unionists and postal service managers. Rajan also wants to study the dispute as it is narrated in the media. He believes that the narratives of the dispute presented in the media have had, and are having, a substantial impact on the dispute.

What do you think of Rajan's idea for his research project? Do you think his thesis supervisor will support the research?

The following are some useful resources for narrative research:

Andrews, M., Squire, C. and Tamboukou, M. (eds) (2013) *Doing Narrative Research* (2nd edn), London, California, New Delhi, Singapore: Sage.

Boje, D.M. (2001) *Narrative Methods for Organizational & Communication Research*, Sage Series in Management Research.

Colorado State University Guide to Narrative Inquiry, writing.colostate.edu/guides/page.cfm?pageid=1346&guideid=63

Fletcher, D. (2007) '"Toy Story": the narrative world of entrepreneurship and the creation of interpretive communities', *Journal of Business Venturing*, 22(5): 649–672.

Kim, J-H. (2016) *Understanding Narrative Inquiry*, London, California, New Delhi, Singapore: Sage.

Kohler Riessman, C. (2008) *Narrative Methods for the Human Sciences*, Sage.

HOW TO CREATE A METHODOLOGICAL FRAMEWORK: THE THIRD OF THE FOUR FRAMEWORKS

The methodological framework for the research project contains all of the detail in relation to how the research was carried out. It is contained in the research methodology chapter of the thesis or in the research methodology section of the research report. In this chapter/section, the researcher begins by introducing the research methodology used in the research project. Then, drawing on (and referencing) research methodology textbooks, the researcher justifies that research methodology, by explaining why it was chosen and how it was used (or how it is to be used) in the research project.

The four frameworks

- Conceptual Framework
- Theoretical Framework
- *Methodological Framework*
- Analytical Framework

In the research methodology chapter of the thesis or section in the report of the research, following an explanation and justification of the research methodology used in the research project, the researcher details and explains the population of the study and the sample drawn from that population. If a sample was used, the researcher details and explains the sample, and the size of the sample in relation to the size of the population. The sampling method used is clearly outlined and justified. Chapter 10 in this textbook explains populations and sampling in detail.

In the methodological framework, the next issue to be dealt with is data collection. The researcher thoroughly details, explains and justifies the data collection methods used in the research project. Usually a copy of each of the data collection methods, such as the questionnaire, or the **interview schedule** or the **observation schedule**, is placed in appendices in the written account of the research project, the thesis or the research report. Each of the data collection methods used is discussed, explained and justified in detail. The level of detail given is important as this allows readers and examiners to fully understand the research project, and to critically engage with it and evaluate it.

interview schedule The list of questions the researcher develops to ask participants; the list of points or the key issues the researcher develops to discuss/explore with participants.

observation schedule An observation schedule is a form, or series of forms, on which observations are recorded.

The issues of validity and reliability are then addressed. As stated in Chapter 2, perhaps the key issue in any research project is that of validity. Validity in social research is the degree to which a research project measures that which it purports to measure. This means that if, for instance, the researcher develops a research project designed to measure levels of industrial unrest in a particular workplace, then the research project must do that if it is to be valid. The data collection methods used in the research project must be valid measures of industrial unrest in the workplace and the researcher must be able to establish the validity of the data collection methods used.

The term reliability in social science research, as explained in Chapter 2, relates to the degree to which the research can be repeated while obtaining consistent results. A measurement instrument in social science research is deemed reliable if it produces consistent results again and again.

The issue of reliability has more application to quantitative than to qualitative research. Within quantitative research the data-gathering instrument is designed before the researcher goes into the field to accomplish a specific purpose. Therefore, the instrument is to a degree independent of the context for the research. Such an instrument, if used again, should yield consistent results.

On the other hand, qualitative research is context specific and the data collection methods developed for qualitative research are developed specifically for the context within which the research is situated. As this is the case, it would not be meaningful to test whether or not data collection methods developed for qualitative research would yield consistent results over time, in different contexts and with different populations. Rather than attempting to establish the reliability of their data-gathering methods, qualitative researchers focus on establishing the rigour of their research; they focus on establishing the soundness, the dependability of their research (see Guba and Lincoln, 1994; Riege, 2003; see also Table 15.1 in Chapter 15).

The next issue to be addressed in the research methodology chapter/section is the issue of triangulation. Triangulation in social science research, as explained in Chapter 2 of this textbook, is the use of more than one approach to answering the research question or responding to the research issue. It means looking at the phenomenon under investigation from more than one perspective. In Chapter 2, we outlined and explained theoretical triangulation, methodological triangulation and within- and between-method triangulation.

As we have said before, completing a research project is a bit like going into a court of law. If you were in court to win a case, you would amass and present as much evidence as you could in order to do so. It is the same in research. You want to amass and present as much evidence as possible in order to prove or establish your case.

You set out in your research project with a research question or statement, a research hypothesis that you hope to prove or disprove. In triangulating the research, you develop as many different perspectives on the phenomenon you are investigating as necessary, or as many as is feasible. In analysis, the different perspectives are compared in order to produce within the research a more comprehensive description and understanding of the phenomenon under investigation. Limits on triangulation in any research project arise from the resources at the researcher's disposal: the amount of time the researcher has in which to conduct the research; the amount of money the researcher can spend on the research, if any money is required; and, above all, the level and degree of access the researcher has to relevant data.

YOUR RESEARCH

Common research problems – the need for triangulation

Let us use as an example an HR manager working with a multi-ethnic multiracial workforce. Let us say that the manager believes there are intercultural issues and barriers to communication among the workforce. He decides to introduce training in intercultural communication in order to challenge these issues and to attempt to break down the barriers.

The manager carries out the training and then asks the employees who participated in the training to complete a questionnaire. The questionnaire was designed to establish how useful or beneficial the training was to the employees in terms of helping them overcome the intercultural barriers in their workplace relationships. The employees respond very positively to the questionnaire indicating in their responses that the training was beneficial or very beneficial.

The manager then engages in a series of observations, noting the level and nature of intercultural communication taking place among the workers. The observations establish that there has been little or no change in the situation, that the intercultural issues and barriers that the training was designed to challenge and overcome still exist.

The data are apparently inconsistent, in that the responses to the questionnaire contradict the findings of the observations. There can be a number of reasons for this.

The positive responses to the questionnaire might indicate a degree of bias in the research, with the employees who responded to the questionnaire giving what they believed to be the 'correct' response to the questions in the questionnaire. The positive responses might evidence issues of power in the organization. The employees might have been afraid to give real responses, afraid for their jobs, afraid of repercussions, afraid of presenting themselves to management in a poor light, afraid that they might be identifiable from their responses and that there might be negative repercussions for them.

It could be that the employees really did find the training helpful, but there are other issues in employee relations that need to be addressed; issues that have been highlighted by the observations carried out by the HR manager.

In research terms, using only one of the methods (either one) would not have given a valid insight into the situation. The use of two methods yielded a more complex representation of the phenomenon under investigation, a more comprehensive, a more correct, a more valid representation of the phenomenon under investigation.

As explained in Chapter 2, using between-method triangulation for example, the research question might be explored using a questionnaire and a series of interviews, or using a series of **observations** and a focus group. Using within-method triangulation the research issue or phenomenon might be explored, for example, using two different and perhaps sequential **questionnaires**, or using two different sets of interviews. The data collection method in the Holt and Macpherson (2010) study, outlined in the Real World Research box in this chapter, uses within-method triangulation, whereby three different interviews were conducted sequentially with each of the three entrepreneurs who participated in the study.

observation A data collection method where the researcher engages in observing and recording the phenomenon under investigation or some part of it.

questionnaires Questionnaires are structured means of gathering data.

Finally, it is important within the methodology chapter to have a very good reflective section on ethics which deals with the ethical issues in the design and conduct of the research project. Research ethics are dealt with in some detail in Chapter 3 of this textbook.

The end of chapter Case study details Genji's case study research project, with an outline of the structure of the methodological framework she developed for her research. As stated at the start of this chapter, the methodological framework is contained in, or is the content of, the research methodology chapter of the thesis or the research methodology section of the report of the research.

CASE STUDY

Genji's case study research project: the methodological framework

In this case study, we examine Genji's research project and the methodological framework she developed for the project.

Genji is being sponsored in her studies for her degree by an international NGO (Non Governmental Organisation). The NGO sponsoring Genji's studies has asked her to examine in her research project strategies for the promotion of the uptake of low-carbon technologies in developing countries. This is an issue which the NGO in its work is currently addressing.

Genji developed the following research statement (conceptual framework) for her research project: 'This research project is a case study designed to identify key strategies that can be used to promote the uptake of low-carbon technologies in developing countries.'

When Genji's research supervisor approved this research statement, Genji then developed the following aim and objectives for the study: 'The aim of the research project is to identify key strategies that can be used to promote the uptake of low-carbon technologies in developing countries.'

'The objectives of the study are as follows:

- To identify the different strategies used to promote the uptake of new technologies.
- To establish which of these strategies would be useful in promoting the uptake of low-carbon technologies in developing countries.
- To produce a template of key strategies that can be used to promote the uptake of low-carbon technologies in developing countries.'

Genji carried out a literature review. She constructed the theoretical framework (contained in the literature review/the content of the literature review) using the structure detailed here:

- Introduction.
- *First subsection heading* 'Promoting new technologies in developing countries'.
- *Second subsection heading* 'Strategies for the promotion of new technologies in developing countries'.

- *Third subsection heading* 'Strategies for the promotion of new low-carbon technologies in developing countries'.
- Summary.

Genji developed the following methodological framework for her project. (The word count of Genji's methodological framework, from here to the end excluding references, is 1571 words.)

Research methodology

This research project will be developed using a case study methodology (Yin, 1989 and 2018). Case study research calls for the in-depth study of the phenomenon under investigation (Yin, 2018). The phenomenon under investigation can be an issue, or a number of issues, an organization, or a number of organizations, an individual, or a number of individuals, an event or incident, or a number of events or incidences. As Yin (1989) states, the case can be an event, an entity, an individual or even a unit of analysis; 'a case study is an empirical enquiry that investigates a contemporary phenomenon within its real life context using multiple sources of evidence'.

The phenomenon under investigation in this proposed case study is the key strategies that can be used for the promotion of low-carbon technologies in developing countries. A case study approach to this research is appropriate as the research calls for the in-depth study of strategies for the promotion of particular technologies and for the development of a template of key strategies for the promotion of these technologies. A case study methodology will allow for the in-depth study of the strategies used to promote particular technologies and it will allow for the identification of key strategies. When the key strategies have been identified through this case study, a template of the key strategies will be developed and presented. This template of key strategies that can be used to promote the uptake of low-carbon technologies in developing countries will be presented in the final chapter of the thesis.

Population of the study

This case study will draw on multiple sources of data (Yin, 2018) and the study will use two different populations.

The first population will be a population of senior managers involved in the development of strategies for the promotion of low-carbon technologies. These

(Continued)

managers will be drawn from commercial companies producing low-carbon technologies.

The second population in this study will be a population of development workers engaged in the promotion of low-carbon technologies in developing countries.

Sample and sampling method

Five participants for the research will be selected from each of the two populations. A judgemental sampling method will be used in selecting participants in the research. Using a judgemental (or purposive) sampling technique (Quinlan, 2011, Quinlan *et al.*, 2015, see also Chapter 10 of this textbook), the researcher decides, or makes a judgement about, who to include in the research. The criterion for inclusion in the research lies in the capacity of the participant to inform the research. The participants chosen by the researcher must have a contribution to make to the research in terms of the focus of the research. In this study, the focus of the study is on key strategies used to promote low-carbon technologies in developing countries.

The people chosen to participate in the study will be key informants on this topic.

Data collection methods

This research project, as stated above, will involve a multi-method approach (Creswell and Creswell, 2018; Denscombe, 2017). It will involve multiple sources of data.

First, an internet search will be undertaken in order to develop a comprehensive portfolio of documents (see Duffy, 2005), detailing:

- strategies used in the promotion of new technologies
- strategies used in the promotion of low-carbon technologies
- strategies used in the promotion of low-carbon technologies in developing countries.

Second, the strategies found in the internet search will be compared with the strategies detailed in the review of the literature. The data from this exercise will help inform the engagement with the data-gathering exercise to be conducted with the ten participants in the research; that is, the five senior managers from companies producing low-carbon technologies and the five development workers engaged in promoting low-carbon technologies in developing countries.

In the next phase of data gathering for the case study, each of the ten participants in the research will be sent a short questionnaire which they will be required to complete prior to interview. The questionnaire will contain five questions on key strategies to promote low-carbon technologies in developing countries.

In order to complete the questionnaire, participants will have to compile a list of key strategies. They will give the researcher a copy of this list prior to the in-depth interview in which each will participate. The researcher will refer to the list during the interview.

Finally, in the in-depth interviews with each of the ten participants, the interview schedule will focus on the key strategies in promoting low-carbon technologies in developing countries.

A copy of the questionnaire and a copy of the interview schedule will be placed in the appendices of this thesis.

Triangulation

As stated, the study involves multiple sources of data (Yin, 1989, 2018). Data gathering for the research project involves a study of documentation of the strategies used in the promotion of low-carbon technologies available on the internet. In addition, there will be a short survey of the strategies used by the key informants in the study. The key informants will supply documentation on the key strategies they use and recommend to the researcher. Finally, the researcher will engage the ten participants in the study in in-depth interviews.

Altogether, the research will draw on two different kinds of documentary evidence, survey data and interview data. Taken together, these data will provide the research project with the in-depth and triangulated perspective necessary in case study research.

Data analysis

The data gathered for the research project will be analyzed. A thematic approach to data analysis will be used (Bryman and Burgess, 1994; see Table 18.2 in Quinlan *et al.*, 2015, for a simple example of a thematic approach to data analysis).

The core aspects of the strategies to emerge in data gathering will be identified. Key strategies will be identified. The relative strengths and weaknesses of the different strategies will be evaluated. Finally, the key strategies to be used in the promotion of low-carbon technologies in developing countries will be identified and highlighted.

New strategies will be developed from the analysis of the existing strategies, based on their core aspects, their relative strengths and weaknesses, and their utility in a developing world context.

(Continued)

Issues of validity and reliability

The issue of validity is perhaps the key issue in research (Quinlan, 2011, Quinlan *et al.*, 2015). A measurement of the validity of the research is the degree to which the research project measures what it set out to measure, the degree to which the research project accomplishes what it set out to accomplish. The validity of this research project is evident in the manner in which a strict focus on the aim of the research has been maintained throughout the research project. This strict maintenance of the focus of the research project has been facilitated by the deployment throughout the design of the research project of the four frameworks approach to the design of the research project (Quinlan, 2011 and Quinlan *et al.*, 2015). The validity of the research is evident in the multi-method approach taken to the research and outlined earlier. This case study will be triangulated using a between-method approach to triangulation (Denzin, 1970). The data collection methods used in the study include documentary research, survey data and interview data. The data collection methods are the correct data collection methods for the case study. They will yield the data required. The population of the case study is an expert population in relation to the phenomenon under investigation.

The issue of reliability in the research project (see Quinlan, 2011 and Quinlan *et al.*, 2015) relates to the degree to which the research can be repeated while obtaining consistent results. The validity of this case study has been established earlier. The case study has been well constructed. The populations used in the case study and the data-gathering methods deployed in the case study are appropriate to the case study and appropriate to the phenomenon under investigation in the case study. This case study could be repeated and the same results would be achieved. It would seem, therefore, that the case study is reliable.

Ethics

The ethical issues in this research project are substantial. The research has been requested by an NGO working in a developing country. The research, when it is completed, will go to shape the work of that NGO, and it will go to shape the experiences of development of the people of that developing country and development work in other countries. As this is so, the case study must be properly and thoroughly conducted. It must be well designed. The findings of the research, the conclusions drawn from the research and the final product of the research, the template of key strategies designed to promote the use of low-carbon technologies in developing countries, must be meaningful and useful.

There are ethical responsibilities in the conduct of this research with regard to the two populations of the research: the population of senior managers involved in the development of strategies for the promotion of low-carbon technologies, and the population of development workers engaged in the promotion of low-carbon technologies in developing countries. The participants in the research must be engaged with in a professional manner. Their contribution to the research will be acknowledged. They will be made aware of the fact that by participating in the research they will be making a substantial contribution to the international development work of the NGO. The participants will be made fully aware of the extent of the participation in the research required of them before they agree to participate.

The individual identities of the participants in the research will remain anonymous. The organizations they represent will not be identified.

The data gathered for the research will be held safely and securely. The names of the participants and their organizations will be coded and only the researcher and her supervisor will have access to the codes and access to the data.

Correct data analysis procedures will be used in the analysis of the data.

The research, when it is completed, will be presented to the NGO. An article from the research will be published on the website of the NGO. A copy of the thesis will be placed in the university library.

Questions: What do you think of Genji's research project? What do you think of the methodological framework that she developed for her research project? Using this chapter as a guide, do you think you could design a methodological framework for your own research project?

END OF CHAPTER QUESTIONS

1 The methodological framework emerges from the conceptual framework. Explain this statement.

2 Name and briefly explain five different research methodologies.

3 Name the research methodology you intend to use in your research project and explain why it is the most appropriate research methodology for your research.

4 Name two other research methodologies that you could use to develop your research project and explain why you decided not to use them.

5 Outline and briefly explain the data-gathering methods you intend to use in your research project.

6 Can you detail and defend the methodological framework developed for your research project?

7 Explain the meaning of the word triangulation and the use of triangulation in social science research.

8 Explain the key differences between survey research methodology and case study research methodology.

9 Explain the term narrative inquiry in relation to social science research.

10 What are the key ethical concerns you now have in relation to your research project?

REFERENCES

Andrews, M., Squire, C. and Tamboukou, M. (eds) (2013) *Doing Narrative Research* (2nd edn), London and Thousand Oaks, CA: Sage.

Atkinson, R. (1998) *The Life Story Interview* (Qualitative Research Methods Series 44), London: Sage.

Banks, M. (2007) *Using Visual Data in Qualitative Research*, London: Sage.

Banks, M. and Zeitlyn, D. (2015) *Visual Methods in Social Research*, London, California, New Delhi, Singapore: Sage.

Boje, D.M. (2001) *Narrative Methods for Organizational & Communication Research* (Series in Management Research), London: Sage.

Borenstein, M., Hedges, L.V., Higgins, J.P.T. and Rothstein, H.R. (2009) 'A basic introduction to fixed-effect and random-effects models for meta-analysis', *Research Synthesis Methods*, *1*: 97–111.

Boréus, K., and Bergström, G. (2017) *Analysing Text and Discourse: Eight Approaches for the Social Sciences*, London: Sage.

Bourdieu, P. (2001) *Masculine Domination*, Stanford, CA: Stanford University Press.

Brotherton, B. (ed.) (1999) *The Handbook of Contemporary Hospitality Management Research*, New York: John Wiley & Sons.

Bryman, A. and Burgess, R.G. (1994) *Analyzing Qualitative Data*, London: Routledge.

Chandler, D. (2017) *Semiotics: The Basics* (3rd edn), Oxford, New York: Routledge.

Coffey, A. (2014) 'Analysing Documents', in *The Sage Handbook of Qualitative Data Analysis*, London, California, New Delhi, Singapore: Sage.

Cole, A.L. and Knowles, G.J. (2001) *Lives in Context: The Art of Life History Research*, Altamira, a Division of Rowman & Littlefield Publishers Inc.

Colorado State University Guide to Narrative Inquiry, writing. colostate.edu/guides/page.cfm?pageid=1346&guideid=63 (Accessed 17.03.2018).

Connor, R.E. (2004) *Women, Accounting and Narrative: Keeping Books in Eighteenth-Century England*, London: Routledge.

Cote, J.A., McCullough, J. and Reilly, M. (1985) 'Effects of unexpected situations on behavior intention differences: a garbology analysis', *Journal of Consumer Research*, *12*(2): 188–194.

Creswell, J. and Creswell, J.D. (2018) *Research Design: Qualitative, Quantitative and Mixed Methods Approaches*, Thousand Oaks, CA: Sage.

Danto, E.A. (2008) *Historical Research*, Oxford: Oxford University Press.

Denscombe, M. (2017) *The Good Research Guide: For Small-scale Social Research Projects* (6th edn), Milton Keynes: Open University Press.

Denzin, N. (1970) *The Research Act in Sociology*, Chicago, IL: Aldine.

Duffy, B. (2005), 'The analysis of documentary evidence', in J. Bell (ed.), *Doing your Research Project*, Maidenhead: Open University Press.

Duke University, 'Introduction to text analysis', guides.library. duke.edu/text_analysis (Accessed 17.03.2018).

Exploring Online Research Methods, University of Leicester, www.geog.le.ac.uk/ORM/site/home.htm (Accessed 17.03.2018).

Fairclough, N. (1995) *Critical Discourse Analysis*, London: Longman.

Fairclough, N. (2013) *Critical Discourse Analysis*, Oxford, New York: Routledge.

Fletcher, D. (2007) '"Toy Story": the narrative world of entrepreneurship and the creation of interpretive communities', *Journal of Business Venturing*, *22*(5): 649–672.

Flick, U. (2018) *Doing Grounded Theory (Qualitative Research Kit)* (2nd edn), London, California, New Delhi, Singapore: Sage.

Foucault, M. (1970) *The Order of Things*, New York: Pantheon.

Foucault, M. (1972) *Archaeology of Knowledge*, New York: Pantheon.

Gilbert, D. and Lockwood, A. (1999) 'Critical incident technique', in B. Brotherton (ed.) *The Handbook of Contemporary Hospitality Managaement Research*, Chichester: John Wiley & Sons.

Glaser, B. and Strauss, A.L. (1967) *The Discovery of Grounded Theory*, Chicago, IL: Aldine.

Goffman, E. (1979) *Gender Advertisements*, New York: Harper & Row.

Guba, G.G. and Lincoln, Y.S. (1994) 'Competing paradigms in qualitative research', www.uncg.edu/hdf/facultystaff/Tudge/Guba%20&%20Lincoln%201994.pdf

Gubrium, J.F. and Holstein, J.A. (2009) *Analyzing Narrative Reality*, Thousand Oaks, CA: Sage.

Geurin-Eagleman, A.N. and Burch, L.M. (2016) 'Communicating via photographs: A gendered analysis of Olympic athletes' visual self-presentation on Instagram', *Sport Management Review*, 19, 133–145.

Hammersley, M. and Atkinson, P. (1995) *Ethnography*, London: Routledge.

Hesse-Biber, S.N. (ed.) (2014) *Handbook of Feminist Research: Theory and Practice* (2nd edn), Thousand Oaks, CA: Sage.

Hestbaek Anderson, T., Boeriis, M., Maagero, E. and Seip Tonnessen, E. (2015) *Social Semiotics: Key Figures, New Directions*, Oxford and New York: Routledge.

Holt, R. and Macpherson, A. (2010) 'Sensemaking, rhetoric and the socially competent entrepreneur', *International Small Business Journal*, 28(1): 20–42.

Jerolmack, C. and Khan, S. (2018) *Approaches to Ethnography*, Oxford University Press.

Joo, D., Tasci, A.D.A., Woosnam, K.M., Maruyama, N.U., Hollas, C.R. and Aleshinloye, K.D. (2018) 'Residents' attitude towards domestic tourists explained by contact, emotional solidarity and social distance', *Tourism Management*, 64: 245–257.

Kaulio, M.A. and Uppvall, L. (2009) 'Critical incidents in R&D alliances: uncovering leadership roles', *European Management Review*, 6(3): 195–205.

Kim, J-H. (2016) *Understanding Narrative Inquiry*, London, California, New Delhi, Singapore: Sage.

Kinnunen, M., Uhmavaara, K., and Jaaskelainen, M. (2017) Evaluating the brand image of a rock festival using positive critical incidents, *International Journal of Event and Festival Management*, 8(2): 186–203.

Kirca, A.H. and Yaprak, A. (2010) 'The use of metaanalysis in international business research: its current status and suggestions for better practice', *International Business Review*, 19(2): 160–177.

Kohler Riessman, C. (2008) *Narrative Methods for the Human Sciences*, Thousand Oaks, CA: Sage.

Kozinets, R. (2015) *Netnography: Redefined* (2nd edn), London, California, New Delhi, Singapore: Sage.

Krippendorff, K. (2012) *Content Analysis: An Introduction to its Methodology* (3rd edn), London, California, New Delhi, Singapore: Sage.

Krippendorff, K. and Bock, M.A. (2009) *The Content Analysis Reader*, London: Sage.

Leavy, P. and Harris, A. (2018) *Contemporary Feminist Research from Theory to Practice*, New York, Guilford Publications.

Lee, R.M. (2000) *Unobtrusive Methods in Social Research*, Milton Keynes: Open University Press.

Lipsey, M.W. and Wilson, D. (2000) *Practical Meta Analysis*, Thousand Oaks, CA: Sage.

McDowell, W.H. (2002) *Historical Research: A Guide*, London and New York: Routledge.

McNiff, J. (2017) *Action Research: All You Need to Know*, London, California, New Delhi, Singapore: Sage.

Moustakas, C.E. (1994) *Phenomenological Research Methods*, Thousand Oaks, CA: Sage.

National Archive of the UK, www.nationalarchives.gov.uk (Accessed 17.03.2018).

National Archive of the UK, Formal Definitions, www.nationalarchives.gov.uk/documents/archives/defining-archives.pdf (Accessed 17.03.2018).

Moore, N., Salter, A., Stanley, L. and Tamboukou, M. (2017) *The Archive Project: Archival Research in the Social Sciences*, Oxford and New York: Routledge.

Neuendorf, K.A. (2017) *The Content Analysis Guidebook* (2nd edn), London, California, New Delhi, Singapore: Sage.

Oppenheim, A.N. (2000) *Questionnaire Design, Interviewing and Attitude Measurement*, London: Pinter.

Paley, J. (2018) *Phenomenology as Qualitative Research: A Critical Analysis of Meaning Attribution*, Oxford and New York: Routledge.

Pink, S. (2006) *Doing Visual Ethnography* (2nd edn), London: Sage.

Prosser, J. (1998) *Image-based Research*, London: Routledge.

Pullman, M.E. and Robson, S.K.A. (2007) 'Visual methods: using photography to capture customers' experience with design', *Cornell Hotel and Restaurant Administration Quarterly*, 48(2): 121–144.

Quinlan, C. (2011) *Business Research Methods*, Andover: Cengage Learning EMEA.

Quinlan, C., Babin, B., Carr, J., Griffin, M. and Zikmund, W.G. (2015) *Business Research Methods*, Andover: Cengage Learning EMEA.

Rea, L.M. and Parker, R.A. (2014) *Designing and Conducting Survey Research: A Comprehensive Introduction* (4th edn), Jossey Bass, A Wiley Brand.

Riege, A.M. (2003) 'Validity and reliability tests in case study research: a literature review with "hands-on" applications for each research phase', *Qualitative Market Research*, 6(2): 75–86.

Rose, G. (2016) *Visual Methodologies*, London, California, New Delhi, Singapore: Sage.

Scott, J. (1990) *A Matter of Record: Documentary Sources in Social Research*, Oxford: Blackwell.

Soy, S. (2006) *The Case Study as a Research Method*, www.ischool.utexas.edu/~ssoy/usesusers/l391d1b.htm (Accessed 17.03.2018).

Strauss, A. and Corbin, J. (eds) (1997) *Grounded Theory in Practice*, London: Sage.

The University of Winnipeg, Canada, Oral History Centre, www.oralhistorycentre.ca/welcome (Accessed 17.03.2018).

Thompson, P. (2000) *The Voice of the Past: Oral History* (3rd edn), Oxford: Oxford University Press.

Trochim, W.M. (2006) *The Research Methods Knowledge Base*, 'Experimental design', www.socialresearchmethods.net/kb/desexper.php (Accessed 17.03.2017).

UCLA (University of California, Los Angeles) Center for Oral History Research, *Entrepreneurs of the West*, www.library.ucla.edu/destination/center-oral-history-research/collections/subject-areas/business-oral-histories (Accessed 17.03.2018).

van Leeuwen, T. (2005) *Introducing Social Semiotics*, London: Routledge.

Yin, R.K. (1989) *Case Study Research*, London: Sage.

Yin, R.K. (2018) *Case Study Research and Applications: Design and Methods* (6th edn), Thousand Oaks, CA: Sage.

RECOMMENDED READING

Bell, J. and Waters, S. (2014) *Doing Your Research Project* (6th edn), Maidenhead: Open University Press.

Bignell, J. (2002) *Media Semiotics: An Introduction*, Manchester: Manchester University Press.

Collis, J. and Hussey, R. (1997) (repr. 2003, 2009, 2013) *Business Research: A Practical Guide for Undergraduate and Postgraduate Students*, Basingstoke: Palgrave Macmillan.

Creswell, J. and Creswell, D.J. (2018) *Research Design: Qualitative, Quantitative and Mixed Methods Approaches* (5th edn), London, California, New Delhi, Singapore: Sage.

Creswell, J. (2013) *Qualitative Inquiry and Research Design: Choosing Among Five Approaches*, London, California, New Delhi, Singapore: Sage.

Deacon, D., Pickering, M., Golding, P. and Murdock, G. (1999) (repr. 2010) *Researching Communications: A Practical Guide to Methods in Media and Cultural Analysis*, Oxford: Oxford University Press.

Fowler, F.J. Jr (2013) *Survey Research Methods* (Applied Social Research Methods) (5th edn), Thousand Oaks, CA: Sage.

Marshall, J. and Adamic, M. (2010) 'The story is the message: shaping corporate culture', *Journal of Business Strategy*, 31(2): 18–23.

Neuman, W.L. (2014) *Social Research Methods: Quantitative and Qualitative Approaches* (7th edn), Essex, England: Pearson Education Ltd.

Roberts, H. (1997) *Doing Feminist Research*, London: Routledge.

Robson, C. and McCartan, K. (2016) *Real World Research*, John Wiley & Sons Ltd.

Simpson, M. and Tuson, J. (2003) *Using Observation in Small-scale Research*, Glasgow: University of Glasgow.

White, B. and Rayner, S. (2014) *Dissertation Skills for Business and Management Students* (2nd edn), London: Cengage.

CHAPTER 10

UNDERSTANDING POPULATIONS AND SAMPLING

LEARNING OBJECTIVES

At the end of this chapter, the student should be able to:

● Define a research population.

● Describe the process of identifying a target population and outlining a sampling frame.

● Identify the different types of probability and non-probability sampling and summarize their relative advantages and disadvantages.

● Select a sample from a population.

RESEARCH SKILLS

At the end of this chapter, the student should, using the exercises on Cengage Brain, be able to:

● Explain how to choose an appropriate sample design.

● Outline an appropriate population for a given research project and select a sample from that population using an appropriate sampling method.

● List and explain the challenges of internet sampling.

Research populations, samples and sampling methods are fundamental elements of the methodological framework, the third framework in the four frameworks approach to the research project. The aim of this chapter is to explain how to select a population and when and how to select a sample from a population for a research project.

INTRODUCTION

This chapter explores and explains research populations and sampling methods. The methodological framework of the research project comprises an account of all of the ways and means by which the research was actually carried out. The population used in the research and the sample selected from that population, if sampling is engaged in, are fundamental aspects of the methodological framework.

SAMPLING TERMINOLOGY

A **population (universe)** is any complete group – for example, of people, sales territories, stores or college students – that shares some common set of characteristics. The term **population element** refers to an individual member of the population.

> **population (universe)** Any complete group of entities that share some common set of characteristics.
>
> **population element** An individual member of a population.

Researchers could study every element of a population to draw some conclusion. A **census** is an investigation of all the individual elements that make up the population – a total enumeration of every element of interest. Thus, if we wished to know whether adults in Scotland played more golf or more tennis, we could contact every adult in Scotland and find out whether they play more golf or more tennis. We would then know the answer to this question definitively.

> **census** An investigation of all the individual elements that make up a population.

Typically, business researchers would not conduct a census of the population, but rather select a smaller number of population elements, a **sample**. A sample is a subset, or some part of, a larger population. The purpose of sampling is to estimate an unknown characteristic of a population. The process of sampling involves using a portion of a population to make conclusions about the whole population.

> **sample** A sample is a subset of a larger population.

WHY SAMPLE?

Sampling is carried out for pragmatic reasons. Applied business research projects usually have budget and time constraints. If the Ford Motor Corporation wished to take a census of past purchasers' reactions to the company's recalls of defective models, the researchers would have to contact millions of automobile buyers. Some of them would be inaccessible (for example, they may be travelling or they might be seriously ill in hospital) and it would be impossible to contact all these people within a short time period.

YOUR RESEARCH

Imagine that you are creating a survey designed to ask students questions related to job preferences. These data may well be of interest to prospective employers looking to hire qualified business people:

1. Describe the population of your study. Outline the key characteristics of that population.
2. What sampling method would you use, and why would you use that sampling method?

3. Can the data be stratified in a way that would allow them to represent more specific populations? Explain your answer. Do you think that a stratified sampling method would have value in this study? Explain your answer.
4. Would a quota sampling method have value in this study? Explain your answer.

You will find the answers to all of these questions, and more, in this chapter.

A researcher who wants to investigate a population with an extremely small number of population elements may elect to conduct a census rather than engage in sampling because the cost, labour and time drawbacks would be relatively insignificant. For a company that wants to assess salespersons' satisfaction with its computer networking system, circulating a questionnaire to all 25 of its employees is practical. In this case, the population of the study is relatively small, just 25 employees. In most situations, however, for practical reasons, sampling is appropriate and it may even be necessary. Populations are often very large. When working with a large population, sampling cuts costs, reduces labour requirements and gathers vital information quickly. These advantages may be sufficient in themselves for using a sample rather than a census, but there are other reasons.

Accurate and reliable results

Another major reason for sampling is that most properly selected samples give results that are quite accurate. This is particularly true if the elements of a population are similar. When this is the case, only a small sample is necessary to accurately portray the characteristic of interest. Thus, a population consisting of 10 000 year-9 students in all boys' Catholic high schools will require a smaller sample than a broader population consisting of 10 000 year-7 to year-11 students from coeducational secondary schools.

While not common, in some situations a sample may be more accurate than a census. Interviewer mistakes, tabulation errors and other non-sampling errors may increase during a census because of the increased volume of work. In a sample, increased accuracy may sometimes be possible because the fieldwork and tabulation of data can be more closely supervised. In a field survey, a small, well-trained, closely supervised group may do a more careful and accurate job of collecting information than a large group of non-professional interviewers who try to contact everyone. An interesting case in point is the use of samples by the US Census Bureau to check the accuracy of the US Census. If the sample indicates a possible source of error, the census is redone.

DESTRUCTION OF TEST UNITS

Many research projects, especially those in quality-control testing, require the destruction of the items being tested. If a manufacturer of firecrackers wished to find out whether each unit met a specific production standard, no product would be left after the testing. This is the exact situation in many research strategy experiments. For example, if an experimental sales presentation were presented to every potential customer, no prospects would remain to be contacted after the experiment. In other words, if there is a finite population and everyone in the population participates in the research and cannot be replaced, no population elements remain to be selected as sampling units. The test units have been destroyed or ruined for the purpose of the research project.

PRACTICAL SAMPLING CONCEPTS

Before taking a sample, researchers must make several decisions. Figure 10.1 presents these decisions as a series of sequential stages, but the order of the decisions does not always follow this sequence. These decisions are highly interrelated. The issues associated with each of these stages, except for fieldwork, are discussed in this chapter. Fieldwork is explored in Chapter 12 of this textbook.

Defining the target population

Once the decision to sample has been made, the first question concerns the identification of the target population. What is the relevant population? In many cases, this question is easy to answer. For example, registered voters may be clearly identifiable. Likewise, if a company's 106-person sales force is the population of concern, there are few definitional problems. In other cases, the decision may be difficult.

One survey concerning organizational buyer behaviour incorrectly defined the population as purchasing agents whom sales representatives regularly contacted. After the survey, investigators discovered that industrial engineers within the customer companies rarely talked with the salespeople but substantially affected buying decisions. For consumer-related research, the appropriate population element frequently is the household rather than an individual member of the household. This presents some problems if household lists are not available.

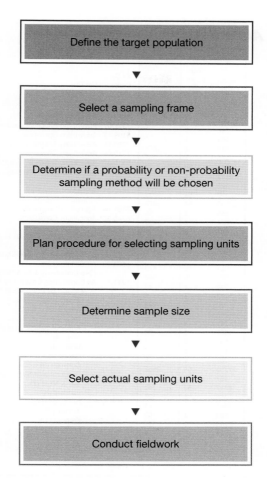

Figure 10.1 Stages in the selection of a sample

At the outset of the sampling process, the target population must be carefully defined so that the proper sources from which the data are to be collected can be identified. The usual technique for defining the target population is to answer questions about the crucial characteristics of the population. Does the term comic book reader include children under six years of age who do not actually read the words? The question to answer is, 'To whom do we want to talk?'

The sampling frame

A list of elements from which the sample may be drawn is called a **sampling frame**. The sampling frame is also called the working population because these units will eventually provide the units involved in the analysis. A simple example of a sampling frame would be the list of students from the registrar's office at a university.

> **sampling frame** A list of elements from which a sample may be drawn; also called working population.

Some firms, called sampling services or list brokers, specialize in providing lists or databases that include the names, addresses, phone numbers and email addresses of specific populations. Figure 10.2 shows a page from a mailing list company's offerings. Lists offered by companies such as this are compiled from subscriptions to professional journals, credit card applications and a variety of other sources. One sampling service obtained its listing of households with children from an ice-cream retailer who gave away free ice-cream cones on children's birthdays. The children filled out cards with their names, addresses and birthdays, which the retailer then sold to the mailing list company.

Lists Available - *Alphabetical*

S.I.C. Code	List Title	United States Total Count	United States State Count Page	Canadian Count
	A			
5122-02	Abdominal Supports	201	‡	28
8399-03	Alternatives Organizations'	946	‡	•
8093-04	Information & Services	551	‡	•
5085-23	Abrasives	1811	‡	277
5169-04	Absorbents	145	‡	•
6541-03	Abstracters	4057	58	•
6411-06	Accident & Health Insurance	2113	‡	9
8748-52	Accident Reconstruction Service	125	‡	•
8721-01	Accountants	127392	64	6933
8721-02	Accounting & Bookkeeping General Svc	27996	64	2072
5044-08	Accounting & Bookkeeping Machines/Supls	889	‡	50
5044-01	Accounting & Bookkeeping Systems	624	‡	1230
8711-02	Acoustical Consultants	381	‡	91
1742-02	Acoustical Contractors	3063	47	433
1742-01	Acoustical Materials	878	‡	210
8999-10	Actuaries	1185	‡	•
8049-13	Acupuncture (Acupuncturists)	2921	62	493
5044-02	Adding & Calculating Machines/Supplies	5524	49	648
5044-09	Addressing Machines & Supplies	345	‡	29
5169-12	Adheuives & Glues	1187	‡	4
3579-02	Adhesives & Gluing Equipment	170	‡	204
6411-02	Adjusters	6164	57	8357
6411-01	Adjusters-Public	161	‡	•
8322-07	Adoption Agencies	1621	‡	32
8059-03	Adult Care Facilities	596	‡	•
8361-08	Adult Congregate Living Facilities	170	‡	•
7319-03	Advertising-Aerial	337	‡	26
7311-01	Advertising-Agencies & Counselors	27753	59	2552
7336-05	Advertising-Art Layout & Production Svc	457	‡	101
7331-05	Advertising-Direct Mail	6347	59	540
7311-03	Advertising-Directory & Guide	2465	‡	124
7319-01	Advertising-Displays	3441	59	571
7319-11	Advertising-Indoor	209	‡	63
7311-05	Advertising-Motion Picture	143	‡	11
7311-06	Advertising-Newspaper	4274	59	404
7312-01	Advertising-Outdoor	3052	59	297
7311-08	Advertising-Periodical	817	‡	78

S.I.C. Code	List Title	United States Total Count	United States State Count Page	Canadian Count
7313-03	Advertising-Radio	2866	59	247
7311-07	Advertising-Shoppers' Guides	392	‡	4
5199-17	Advertising-Specialties	12827	52	1648
7389-12	Advertising-Telephone	120	‡	•
7313-05	Advertising-Television	1746	‡	102
7319-02	Advertising-Transit & Transportation	179	‡	38
0721-03	Aerial Applicators (Service)	1479	‡	61
3999-01	Aerosols	158	‡	•
3812-01	Aerospace Industries	426	‡	•
	Affluent Americans		73	
5191-04	Agricultural Chemicals	549	‡	210
8748-20	Agricultural Consultants	1047	‡	474
9999-32	Air Balancing	353	‡	•
5084-64	Air Brushes	219	‡	•
4512-02	Air Cargo Service	6005	48	•
5075-01	Air Cleaning & Purifying Equipment	2055	‡	342
5084-02	Air Compressors	4358	50	717
	(See Compressors Air & Gas)			
1711-17	Air Conditioning Contractors & Systems	50951	47	2667
	Available By Brands Sold			
	Airtemp (A)	187		
	Amana (B)	1450		
	Arco Aire (2)	673		
	Armstrong/Magic Chef (C)	395		
	Arvin (4)	106		
	Bryant (D)	2223		
	Carrier (E)	5927		
	Coleman (5)	1176		
	Comfortmaker/Singer (O)	989		
	Day & Night (Z)	749		
	Fedders (H)	318		
	Heli/Quaker (3)	1977		
	Janitrol (7)	587		
	Kero-Sun (W)	2		
	Lennox (K)	4390		
	Luxaire (L)	510		
	Payne (M)	553		

Figure 10.2 Mailing list directory page

A valuable source of names in the USA are city directories, such as City Town Info (www.citytowninfo.com) and City Directories (www.uscitydirectories.com). Directories such as these provide complete, comprehensive and accurate business and residential information. The reverse directory pages offer a unique benefit. A **reverse directory** provides, in a different format, the same information contained in a telephone directory. The UK reverse directory can be accessed at www.searchyellowdirectory.com/reverse-phone/44/. Listings may be by city and street address or by phone number, rather than alphabetical by last name. Such a directory is particularly useful when a researcher wishes to survey only a certain geographical area of a city or when census tracts are to be selected on the basis of income or another demographic criterion.

> **reverse directory** A directory similar to a telephone directory except that listings are by city and street address or by phone number rather than alphabetical by last name.

In practice, almost every list excludes some members of the population. For example, would a university email directory provide an accurate sampling frame for a given university's student population? Perhaps the sampling frame excludes students who registered late and includes students who have resigned from the university. The email directory also will likely list only the student's official university email address. However, many students may not ever use this address, opting to use a private email account instead. Thus, the university email directory could not be expected to perfectly represent the student population. However, a perfect representation is not always possible or necessary.

A **sampling frame error** occurs when certain sample elements are excluded or when the entire population is not accurately represented in the sampling frame. Election polling that used a telephone directory as a sampling frame would be contacting households with listed phone numbers, not households whose members are likely to vote. A better sampling frame might be voter registration records. Another potential sampling frame error involving phone records is the possibility that a phone survey could under-represent people with disabilities. Some disabilities, such as hearing and speech impairments, might make telephone use impossible. However, when researchers in Washington State in the USA tested for this possible sampling frame error by comparing Census Bureau data on the prevalence of disability with the responses to a telephone survey, they found the opposite effect. The reported prevalence of a disability was actually higher in the phone survey. These findings could be relevant for research into a community's health status or the level of demand for services for disabled persons.

> **sampling frame error** An error that occurs when certain sample elements are not listed or are not accurately represented in a sampling frame.

As in this example, population elements can be either under- or over-represented in a sampling frame. A savings and loan association defined its population as all individuals who had savings accounts. However, when it drew a sample from the list of accounts rather than from the list of names of individuals, individuals who had multiple accounts were over-represented in the sample.

Sampling frames for international research

The availability of sampling frames around the globe varies dramatically. Not every country's government conducts a census of population. According to the UK Office for National Statistics (www.ons.gov.uk/census/index.html), a national census is a count of all people and households in the country. The 2011 census of England and Wales covers around 25 million households.

In some countries, telephone directories are incomplete, no voter registration lists exist and accurate maps of urban areas are unobtainable.

In Taiwan, Japan and other Asian countries, a researcher can build a sampling frame relatively easily because those governments release some census information. If a family changes households, updated census information must be reported to a centralized government agency before communal services (water, gas, electricity, education, and so on) are made available. This information is then easily accessible in the local Register of Inhabitants.

Sampling units

During the actual sampling process, the elements of the population must be selected according to a certain procedure. The **sampling unit** is a single element or group of elements subject to selection in the sample. For example, if an airline wishes to conduct a study of passenger satisfaction, it may take every 25th name on a complete list of all passengers. In this case, the sampling unit would be individual passengers, the same as the element. Alternatively, the airline could first select certain flights as the sampling unit and then select either all of the passengers or certain passengers on each selected flight. In this case, the sampling unit would be flights rather than individual passengers.

> **sampling unit** A single element or group of elements subject to selection in the sample.

If the target population has first been divided into units, such as airline flights, additional terminology must be used. A unit selected in the first stage of sampling is called a **primary sampling unit (PSU)**. A unit selected in a successive stage of sampling is called a **secondary sampling unit** or (if three stages are necessary) **tertiary sampling unit**. When there is no list of population elements, the sampling unit generally is something other than the population element. In a random-digit dialing (RDD) study, the sampling unit will be telephone numbers.

> **primary sampling unit (PSU)** A term used to designate a unit selected in the first stage of sampling.
>
> **secondary sampling unit** A term used to designate a unit selected in the second stage of sampling.
>
> **tertiary sampling unit** A term used to designate a unit selected in the third stage of sampling.

RANDOM SAMPLING AND NON-SAMPLING ERRORS

An advertising agency sampled a small number of shoppers in grocery stores that used Shopper's Video, an in-store advertising network. The agency hoped to measure brand awareness and purchase intentions. Investigators expected this sample to be representative of the grocery shopping population. However, if a difference exists between the value of a sample statistic of interest (for example, the sample group's average willingness to buy the advertised brand) and the value of the corresponding population parameter (the population's average willingness to buy), a statistical error has occurred. Two basic causes of differences between statistics and parameters are described here:

1. random sampling errors
2. systematic (non-sampling) error.

Random sampling error

Random sampling error is the difference between the sample result and the result of a census conducted using identical procedures. Random sampling error occurs because of chance variation in the scientific selection of sampling units. The sampling units, even if properly selected according to sampling theory, are not likely to perfectly represent the population, but generally they are reliable estimates. Our discussion on the process of randomization (a procedure designed to give everyone in the population an equal chance of being selected as a sample member) will show that, because random sampling errors follow chance variations, they tend to cancel one another out when averaged. This means that properly selected samples, while perhaps not perfect, are generally good approximations of the population. The true population value almost always differs slightly from the sample value, causing a small random sampling error. Every once in a while, an unusual sample is selected because too many atypical people are included in the sample and then a large random sampling error can occur.

random sampling error A statistical fluctuation that occurs because of chance variation in the elements selected for a sample; difference between the sample result and the result of a census conducted using identical procedures.

Random sampling error is a function of sample size. As sample size increases, random sampling error decreases. It is possible to estimate the random sampling error that may be expected with various sample sizes. Suppose a survey of approximately 1000 people has been taken in Fresno, California, to determine the feasibility of a new soccer franchise. Assume that 30 per cent of the respondents favour the idea of a new professional sport in town. The researcher will know, based on the laws of probability, that 95 per cent of the time a survey of slightly fewer than 900 people will produce results with an error of approximately plus or minus 3 per cent. If the survey were conducted with only 325 people, the margin of error would increase to approximately plus or minus five percentage points. This example illustrates random sampling errors.

Systematic sampling error

Systematic (non-sampling) errors result from non-sampling factors, primarily the nature of a study's design and the correctness of execution. These errors are not due to chance fluctuations. For example, highly educated respondents are more likely to cooperate with mail surveys than respondents with low levels of education, for whom filling out forms is more difficult and intimidating. Sample biases such as these account for a large portion of errors in business research. The term sample bias is somewhat unfortunate, because many forms of bias are not related to the selection of the sample.

systematic (non-sampling) error Error resulting from non-sampling factors, primarily the nature of a study's design and the correctness of execution. These errors are not due to chance fluctuations.

Errors due to sample selection problems, such as sampling frame errors, are systematic (non-sampling) errors and should not be classified as random sampling errors.

Less than perfectly representative samples

Random sampling errors and systematic errors associated with the sampling process may combine to yield a sample that is less than perfectly representative of the population. Figure 10.3 illustrates two non-sampling errors (sampling frame error and non-response error) related to sample design. The total population is represented by the area of the largest square. Sampling frame errors eliminate some potential respondents. Random sampling error (due exclusively to random, chance fluctuation) may cause an imbalance in the representativeness of the group. Additional errors will occur if individuals refuse to be interviewed or cannot be contacted. Such non-response error may also cause the sample to be less than perfectly representative. Thus, the actual sample is drawn from a population different from (or smaller than) the ideal.

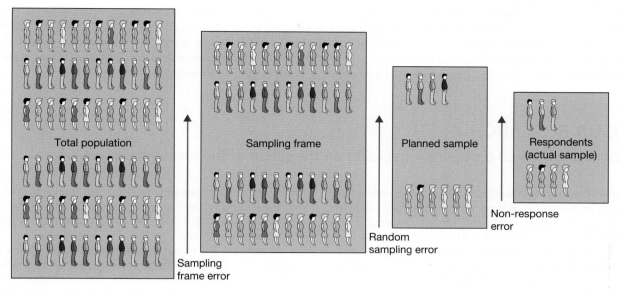

Figure 10.3   Errors associated with sampling

The role of the researcher in populations and sampling

The researcher designing the research project decides on and defines the parameters of the population of the study. If, for example, the researcher is interested in disposable income levels among undergraduate students at university, then the population of that research will be university undergraduates. As the global population of university undergraduates is enormous, the researcher uses some means to limit and more narrowly define that population.

The population could be defined, for example, as all of the students in one undergraduate class at university or all of the undergraduate students in one school or faculty, or all of the undergraduate students at one particular university, or all of the undergraduate students at university in one town or city. The researcher might choose two different universities to work with, or all of the undergraduate students in the country. An EU-based researcher might decide to study only undergraduate students from EU countries or only undergraduate students from non-EU countries. The researcher might decide to compare levels of disposable income:

- among EU and non-EU undergraduate students at the University of Liverpool
- or among undergraduate students at university in Liverpool
- or among undergraduate students at university in England
- or among undergraduate students at university in the UK.

The researcher may decide to focus on the population of undergraduates in UK universities, the population of undergraduates in the University of Westminster, or the University of Edinburgh or Cardiff University. The researcher may decide to focus on the population of undergraduates in all three universities. All of these populations are valid. The key point is that the researcher defines the population of the study, based on the requirements of the study. The researcher has to make a judgement about the population of the study, and s/he makes this judgement in relation to the requirements of the study. The question the researcher asks is this: in order to properly carry out and complete this study, what population is necessary and appropriate?

The researcher defines the population of the study precisely, in order to ensure that the research project is researchable, as outlined in Chapter 1 of this textbook. The researcher must limit the scope of the research to what it is possible to do, given the resources of the research project. As explained earlier, the resources required are:

1. the time needed to conduct the study
2. the money required to conduct the study, if any money is required
3. access to the data necessary for the research project.

The research must be valid. So the researcher endeavours, within whatever constraints exist, to gather the data necessary for the research.

The researcher defines the scope of the research to suit the resources available to the project. If the researcher is an undergraduate student in a university, and the research project is one of many projects the student is charged with completing for a degree programme, then clearly the resources available will be quite constrained. In such a situation, the student researcher should be very concise in terms of the scope of the research project. As well as time and money, access to data is also a key resource. In order to access data, it is often necessary to access research sites and research populations. Such access frequently requires formal and/or informal permission(s). All of this takes time. The researcher is above all concerned with making a contribution to knowledge. With that in mind, the researcher conceptualizes a research project that they will be able to carry out and complete given the resources available, a project that is useful and one that makes a very specific, clearly outlined and detailed, contribution to knowledge.

YOUR RESEARCH
Common research problems – deciding on the scope of the research project

Remember that the researcher devises the research project, and in so doing s/he designs the mountain they must climb. That mountain should not be too high, too challenging. Great care is needed in the design of the research project.

For the student researcher learning new research skills, it is important to keep the scope of the research project relatively narrow. Ensure that the research project is properly focused. Keep the project design simple. The project will grow in complexity naturally. This will happen through the researcher's scholarly engagement with the literature, through their scholarship in research methodology, through their work on data gathering, and analyzing the data gathered for the project, and through the insights and conclusions they draw from the analyzed data.

To reiterate, the research project as designed should be simple. The research project that develops from that simple design will be complex. It will become complex through each step of the research process and through the scholarship the researcher brings to each step of that process as s/he develops and completes their research project.

There are many examples of research projects in this textbook. You can read back through the examples you have already examined to study the different populations of those projects. Table 10.1 provides examples of populations of research projects. Table 10.2 provides examples of research projects focused on entities rather than people.

The important issue to note from the lists that follow is the necessity to define a population very clearly.

Table 10.1 Examples of human research populations

For the purpose of a national census, the entire population of a country is included in the research as the population of the research.
All graduates of the BA Business Studies at the University of Exeter (2015–2018).
All mothers of toddlers attending the 'Mothers and Toddlers Group' at the Village Community Club, Fernfield, Greater Heaton, Manchester, Thursday, 9 July 2018.
All members of the 2017–2018 final year undergraduate class BA Business Studies, the University of Exeter, who have played the video game *Grand Theft Auto V*.
All diners at Angie's Happy Haven Café, Friday, 8 August 2018.
All operational staff in Thompson's Conveyors and Elevators Ltd.
All HR managers in Hinton's Ltd.

Table 10.2 Examples of research projects without human populations

All businesses employing less than ten employees in the town centre, Oaklands, Sheffield.
All advertisements shown during the commercial breaks in the soap opera *Coronation Street* for the month of October, 2018.
The advertisements used in TV advertising for Guinness in the year 2018.
The legislation governing the import and export of goods in the UK in 2018.
Levels of output in Milton's Joinery for the six months from January to June 2018 inclusive.
The HR policies of the multinational corporation *Bright Com*.

It often happens in the course of conducting the research project that the research shifts a little. Such a shift might involve a change in the scope of the research, perhaps the population becomes defined in a slightly different way, or the aim of the project changes slightly, perhaps the research question becomes a little clearer or changes slightly. Such changes are appropriate. They simply reflect the natural organic shifts a research project goes through as it develops. The researcher must be flexible enough to allow these changes to occur and s/he should be competent enough to incorporate such shifts and changes into the design of the research project.

It often happens that the population of the research forces a shift or a change in the research. This can happen as a result of access issues. It can happen that the gatekeepers, the people in charge of access to the site of the research, withhold access from the researcher. They may do this officially and explicitly, or perhaps tacitly or even covertly. The role of gatekeepers in research is considered in detail in Chapter 3 of this textbook. Part of the responsibility of the researcher is to obtain access to the data required and the data sources, and then, most importantly, to maintain that access for the duration of the research project, from the beginning of the research to publication of the research. Remember that placing a copy of a dissertation in a university library is deemed to be a publication of that research. If access to data and data sources is not secured, or if access is withdrawn, the design of the research project will necessarily change and those changes will have to be managed and accommodated in the design of the entire research project.

Figure 10.4 illustrates the population, the sample and the unit/the individual/or the case. As can be seen from the figure, the population is all of the units in the figure. The sample is a small subset of the population. The population is made up of many individual units, cases or individuals.

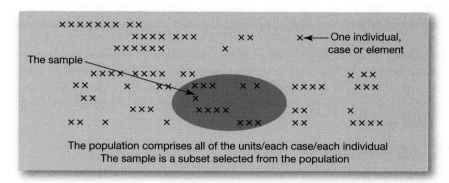

Figure 10.4 Population and sample

When using a sample of a population in a research project, the researcher must clearly describe the sample. Then s/he they must explain why that sample was selected and clearly describe the sampling method, the means by which that sample was selected. In describing the sampling method, the researcher aims to establish how *representative* the sample is of the research population. The key issue in sampling is this notion of **representation**. The concept of representation relates to the degree to which a sample drawn from a population can be said to be representative of the population. Another issue to be addressed is that of the **inclusion and exclusion criteria**. The inclusion criteria are the criteria potential participants must meet in order to be included in the study. Exclusion criteria are the criteria on which potential participants will be excluded from participation in the study. Outlining clear inclusion and exclusion criteria is a good way of achieving clarity in terms of what potential participants could and would contribute to the research.

> **representation** The degree to which a sample selected from a population can be said to be representative of that population.
>
> **inclusion and exclusion criteria** The criteria potential participants must meet in order to be included in the study. Exclusion criteria is the criteria on which potential participants will be excluded from participation in the study.

There are two kinds of sampling, **probability sampling** and **non-probability sampling**.

> **probability sampling** A sampling technique in which every member of the population has a known, non-zero probability of selection.
>
> **non-probability sampling** A sampling technique in which units of the sample are selected on the basis of personal judgement or convenience; the probability of any particular member of the population being chosen is unknown.

Probability sampling

Using probability sampling, the sample selected from the population is claimed by the researcher to be representative of the population. It is of fundamental importance that the sample selected is representative of the population of the study. This is because the researcher using a probability sampling technique wants to claim that the findings of research conducted with the sample are generalizable to the entire population of the study. Probability sampling is based on the theories of mathematics of probability. Probability sampling techniques include **simple random sampling**, **stratified sampling**, **systematic sampling** and **cluster sampling**. If used properly, probability sampling techniques yield precise results while working with samples a fraction the size of the original populations of research.

> **simple random sampling** A probability sampling procedure that assures each element in the population an equal chance of being included in the sample.
>
> **stratified sampling** A probability sampling procedure in which simple random subsamples that are more or less equal on some characteristic are drawn from within each stratum of the population.
>
> **systematic sampling** A probability sampling procedure in which a starting point is selected by a random process and then every nth number on the list is selected.
>
> **cluster sampling** An economically efficient probability sampling technique in which the primary sampling unit is not the individual element in the population but a large cluster of elements; clusters are selected randomly.

The basic rule of probability sampling holds that each member of the population has an equal probability of being selected for inclusion in the sample. As this is the case, the researcher, in order to engage in probability sampling, must have a complete list (or map or chart) of every member of the population. This list is known as a sampling frame. The sample is drawn from this list. Each member or item in the sample is randomly selected from the population for inclusion in the study, using the sampling frame.

Probability sampling techniques

The following paragraphs explain the different sampling techniques used in probability sampling. Each of the sampling techniques is simply and clearly explained, with enough detail to enable you, the student, to make a decision with regard to which sampling technique to use in your research project.

Simple random sampling

Simple random sampling involves selecting a sample at random from a sampling frame. Let us say that you want to study the population of your class and there are 30 students in your class. As it is a simple thing to get a complete list of the names of the students in your class (a complete sampling frame), it is possible to engage in simple random sampling with this population. Make a list on a sheet of paper of the names of all of the people in your class. Then tear off each name one by one and place each one into a hat or a box. Then select one name at a time from the hat or box. You are now engaging in simple random sampling. Every time you select a name, note the name and then replace it in the hat or box. Each time you select a name, you are selecting from a complete population. This is known as *sampling with replacement*. You continue this process until you have the complete sample required, the number of names required to complete the sample.

National lotteries use a system of simple random sampling to compile the numbers in each game. In the game, all of the numbers are placed into the machine and they are selected one at a time until the complete set of numbers is drawn. This is *sampling without replacement*, i.e. the balls after they have been selected and the numbers on them noted are not placed back into the machine in order that the next number drawn is drawn from a complete set of numbers.

In social science research, in order to generate random samples, researchers often use tables of random numbers. Books of mathematical tables contain tables of random numbers. Tables of random numbers can also be computer generated. The case study at the end of this chapter focuses on random numbers, on the process by which random numbers can be produced in Microsoft Excel, and on the way in which a researcher would use such random numbers to generate a sample for a research project.

Systematic sampling

Systematic sampling involves selecting items at systematic or regular intervals from the sampling frame. For example, you might be working in a housing estate trying to establish which brand of washing powder is used in each house. Your sampling frame is made up of all of the houses in the housing estate. Let us suppose there are 500 houses in the estate, and you begin at a random starting point and then sample every third house, or every fifth house, or whatever interval of house you decide on, until you complete your sample. Your complete sample is the number of houses or households you have decided to include in the study. You are engaging in systematic sampling. Alternatively, you might spin a pen on the ground, and then begin at the house toward which the pen is pointing when it stops spinning, and then call at every third house, or every fifth house, or whatever interval you have decided on, in order to complete your sample. The random starting point is important. This is an example of a systematic sampling technique.

Stratified sample

A stratified sample is a sample selected based on some known characteristic of the population, a characteristic that will have an impact on the research. Using stratified sampling the researcher divides, or stratifies, the sample selected for use in the research using the characteristic which s/he knows will have an impact on the research. In the Real World Research box 'The need for and the use of stratified sampling', the researcher uses first a simple random sampling technique and then a systematic sampling technique before finally deciding that a stratified sampling technique is really required for this particular study with this particular population. This example provides a good and simple explanation of stratified sampling.

Cluster sampling

Cluster sampling is used when the units or the people who make up the population of the study are to be found in groups or clusters. Sampling is carried out by randomly selecting a sample of the clusters to study, rather than randomly selecting from the population. Cluster sampling is particularly efficient with populations that are geographically spread in clusters. Rather than randomly selecting from all of the members of the population, the researcher identifies all of the clusters of units or individuals within the population and then randomly selects units or individuals from all of the clusters to include in the study.

When the researcher is designing the research project, s/he should take note of any characteristics of the population that are or that might be significant in terms of the proposed research. In particular, the researcher should be alert to patterning in those characteristics. It may be that the age range of the population has some significance for the research, or the work and employment of the population is organized in some significant way, or it might be that the gender or racial makeup of the population is significant. There may be some patterning in some characteristic in the population that will necessitate the use of a systematic sampling method. The task of gathering this kind of information would form part of the preliminary work conducted for a research project. The information gathered in this preliminary phase can be recorded in the research diary. The notes the researcher makes for themselves in the research diary can lead to insights that fundamentally shape the design, and the validity, of the research project.

Another key figure is the **response rate** to the research. A high response rate is important to ensure that the research is representative. While the sample drawn may be relatively easily established as being representative, the research will falter if the response rate from the sample is not sufficiently high. It is very important in reporting research to include the response rate. This gives the reader of the research an understanding of the scale, the scope and the validity of the research. The most carefully designed research can be undermined by a low or a poor response rate.

response rate A count of the number of valid responses received to a data-gathering exercise.

Non-probability sampling

In non-probability sampling, the sample is selected to *represent* the population, but it cannot be said to be *representative* of the population in any statistical sense. The emphasis in non-probability sampling is on the capacity of a relatively small number of cases to clearly and comprehensively illustrate the phenomenon under investigation.

It often happens with social science research projects that it is not possible to produce a complete list of the population; when this is the case, it is not possible to develop a sampling frame. For example, a researcher might be asked to examine brand loyalty among consumers of *Cosmopolitan* magazine. It would not be possible to compile a complete list of consumers of *Cosmopolitan* magazine. Without a complete sampling frame, it is not possible to engage in probability sampling, as without a sampling frame it is not possible to guarantee that every member of the population has an equally likely chance of being included in the study. The sampling approach used in such circumstances is non-probability sampling.

Non-probability sampling techniques include **judgemental sampling, quota sampling, snowball sampling** and **convenience sampling**.

judgemental sampling A non-probability sampling procedure whereby the researcher decides (makes a judgement) as to who to include in the sample. Those included in the sample must be key informants on the phenomenon under investigation.

quota sampling A non-probability sampling procedure that ensures the sample will comprise the different quotas required to represent various subgroups of a population.

snowball sampling A non-probability sampling procedure in which initial respondents are selected by probability methods and additional respondents are obtained from information provided by the initial respondents.

convenience sampling A non-probability sampling procedure in which the sample obtained comprises those people who are most conveniently available.

REAL WORLD RESEARCH

The need for and the use of stratified sampling

A study of religious practice among your classmates

Suppose you as a researcher decided to examine religious practice among your classmates. Let us say that there are 30 students in your class.

You decide to select a sample of ten students from this population of 30 using a simple random sampling technique.

You obtain or create a list of the names of all of the students in your class. This is your sampling frame. You write all of the names on individual pieces of paper, put all of them into a box or a hat, and select pieces of paper at random, until you have selected ten names. This technique is a simple random sample technique. Now you have the ten names you need. All seems well.

Alternatively, carrying out the same study you decide to use a systematic sampling technique. For this technique, use your original list of 30 names, select a random start and then select every third name on the list until you have your sample of ten names. Again, all seems well.

In both of these examples, you have used different sampling techniques and you have used them properly. However, your research could still go sadly awry.

What would happen if, for example, using either of these sampling techniques the ten students you selected, unknown to you, just happened to be devout Jehovah's Witnesses, practising Buddhists or Sikhs, Muslims or Catholics or Jews?

What if the other 20 students in the class, none of whom was selected to be part of the sample for the study, just happened to be non-religious, atheists or agnostics? Well, certainly the sample that you have chosen to work with will not be in any way representative of religious practice among your classmates.

What you have here is an example of random sampling error. The sample drawn is not and cannot be representative of your population in terms of the phenomenon that you are investigating.

It is important for researchers to know enough about the population of their study before they begin to sample that population to know if there is something significant about the population in terms of the research being conducted.

In the case of the study of religious practice described here, the researcher might overcome the issues in sampling by conducting a census, in which case all 30 students are included in the study. In this way, the religious practice of all of the members of the class will be explored in the research.

Alternatively, the researcher might overcome the issues by using a stratified sample. Using a stratified sampling technique, the researcher produces two lists of names, one list contains the names of the practising students, students who engage in religious practice, the other list contains the names of the non-practising students, students who do not engage in religious practice. The researcher puts all the names from one list into a hat and selects five names. Then the student puts the names from the other list into a hat and selects five names. Now the student has ten names, the ten names required for the sample. This sample is a stratified sample. It is stratified along religious lines. The sample has been stratified in order to ensure that the sample selected is representative of religious practice in the population being studied, i.e. the population of 30 students in your class.

Non-probability sampling techniques

The following paragraphs explain the different sampling techniques used in non-probability sampling. As with the probability sampling techniques explained earlier, each of these sampling techniques is simply and clearly explained. Enough detail is given to enable you, the student, to make a decision with regard to which sampling technique to use in your research project.

Judgemental (judgement) or purposive sampling

Using a **judgemental** or purposive sampling technique the researcher decides, or makes a judgement, about who to include in the sample. The criterion for inclusion in the research is the capacity of the participant to inform the research. Each person, or unit, chosen to be included must have a contribution to make to the research. People chosen to be included in such a sample would be key informants on the topic under investigation. For example, Genji in her research, detailed in the case study at the end of Chapter 9 in this textbook, used a judgemental sampling technique in order to compile the sample for her study. Genji was researching key strategies used in the promotion of low-carbon technologies in developing countries. Her judgemental sample comprised five senior managers from companies producing low-carbon technologies and five development workers engaged in promoting low-carbon technologies in developing countries.

> **judgemental** Using a judgemental or purposive sampling technique the researcher decides, or makes a judgement, about who or what to include in the sample.

Quota sampling

Using a quota-sampling technique the researcher develops a sample of participants for the research using different quota criteria. One student, Jack, in his research project, used a quota-sampling method in order to compile the sample for his survey research. Jack wanted to develop an online weekly newsletter detailing all of the events on campus. He decided to conduct a survey on campus, among staff and students, to test the market for such a product. The population of the study was all the students and staff at his university, in total about 15 000 people. Jack decided that he needed 100 participants in his survey. He decided that 100 participants would be sufficient for the purposes of his research. Jack decided to use a quota sampling method, which would comprise of four quotas. The first quota was to be made up of 25 female students, the second quota was to be made up of 25 male students, the third quota was to be made up of 25 female members of staff and the fourth and final quota was to be made up of 25 male members of staff. In this way, Jack used a quota sampling method to develop, using four different quotas, the sample for his research. Please note all the decisions that Jack had to make in relation to this aspect of his research project. As explained earlier in this book, the ability to make decisions is a critical skill in research.

Convenience sampling

Using a convenience sampling technique the researcher engages those participants in the research whom it is easiest to include, for example, people in the newsagents, people in the supermarket, people attending a conference, and so on. The researcher knows how many people to include in the sample, then continues to engage people in the research until the sample has been filled. Another example is when a student at university goes into a lecture (with the permission of the lecturer/professor) and asks all of the students in the lecture to complete their questionnaire. In such a data-gathering exercise, typically, all of the students will complete the questionnaire. So, there is a good chance of a 100 per cent response rate in such a data-gathering exercise. This is an example of convenience sampling. The sample is a convenient sample because it comprises all of the students attending a lecture.

Snowball sampling

Using a snowball sampling technique the researcher finds one participant in the research, conducts the research with that participant and then asks that participant to recommend the next participant. Participants must fit the inclusion criteria for the research project. The researcher goes through the procedure with the second participant and when finished, asks that participant to recommend another participant to be included in the research. The researcher continues in this manner until the sample is complete.

In some qualitative research projects, the research is allowed to unfold and so the population or the samples used are sometimes not defined from the outset. One frequently asked question in such circumstances is: When does the researcher stop engaging participants in the research? The answer is when the researcher reaches **saturation point**. Saturation point is reached when the researcher, although continuing to explore the phenomenon with participants in the research, no longer hears any new thoughts, feelings, attitudes, emotions, intentions, etc. This is saturation point, the researcher is 'saturated' with knowledge on the topic and continuing to engage participants would not be useful, necessary or ethically sound, as it will not add in any way to the knowledge generated.

> **saturation point** Saturation point is reached when the researcher gathering data for the project no longer hears any new thoughts, feelings, attitudes, emotions, intentions, etc. At this point continuing to engage participants would not be useful, necessary or ethically sound, as further participants will not add to the knowledge being generated.

There are substantial ethical issues involved in engaging some populations in research; in particular, vulnerable populations such as children, people with impairments, and socially, culturally and/or materially disadvantaged people. Particular care should be taken in the design of research projects involving such participants.

It is a well-established fact that social research tends to be conducted with less powerful populations. This is because more powerful individuals and populations are in a position to deflect research or refuse to participate. They are powerful enough to do so. Less powerful individuals and populations are less likely to refuse to engage in research, less likely to opt out of research. This is often because they do not possess the social capital (see Bourdieu, 1986) that such action would require. Power and powerlessness raise particular ethical issues for social science researchers.

Internet sampling is unique

Internet surveys allow researchers to reach a large sample rapidly – this can be both an advantage and a disadvantage. Sample size requirements can be met overnight, or in some cases almost instantaneously. A researcher can, for instance, release a survey one morning and have data back from around the globe by the next morning. If rapid response rates are expected, the sample for an internet survey should be metered out across global regions and/or across all time zones. In addition, it might be that people in some populations are more likely to go online during the weekend than on a weekday. If the researcher can anticipate a day-of-the-week effect, the survey should be kept open long enough so that all sample units (in this situation, invited participants) have the opportunity to participate in the research project.

The ease and low cost of an internet survey also has contributed to a flood of online questionnaires, some more formal than others. As a result, frequent internet users may be more selective about which surveys they bother answering; they may be suffering from survey fatigue.

Researchers investigating college students' attitudes toward environmental issues found that those who responded to an email request that had been sent to all students tended to be more concerned about the environment than students who were contacted individually through systematic sampling. The researchers concluded that students who cared about the issues were more likely to respond to the online survey.

Another disadvantage of internet surveys is the lack of computer ownership and internet access among certain segments of the population. This is particularly true in regions of the world where internet availability is limited. A sample of internet users is representative only of internet users, who tend to be younger, better educated and more affluent than the general population. This is not to say that all internet samples are unrepresentative of all target populations. Nevertheless, when using internet surveys, researchers should be keenly aware of potential sampling problems that can arise due to systematic characteristics of heavy computer users.

Website visitors

As noted earlier, many internet surveys are conducted with volunteer respondents who visit an organization's website intentionally or by chance. These unrestricted samples are clearly convenience samples. They may not be representative, because of the haphazard manner by which many respondents arrived at a particular website, or because of self-selection bias.

A better technique for sampling website visitors is to randomly select sampling units. ComScore (www.comscore .com), a company that conducts internet surveys and focus groups, can collect data by using its 'pop-up survey' software. The software selects web visitors at random and 'pops up' a small JavaScript window asking the person if s/he wants to participate in an evaluation survey. If the person clicks yes, a new window containing the online survey opens up. The person can then browse the site at his or her own pace and switch to the survey at any time to express an opinion.

Randomly selecting website visitors can cause a problem. It is possible to over-represent frequent visitors to the site, and thus represent site visits rather than visitors. Several programming techniques and technologies (using cookies, registration data or prescreening) are available to help accomplish more representative sampling based on site traffic.

This type of random sampling is most valuable if the target population is defined as visitors to a particular website. Evaluation and analysis of visitors' perceptions and experiences of the website would be a typical survey objective with this type of sample. Researchers who have broader interests may obtain internet samples in a variety of other ways.

Panel samples

Drawing a probability sample from an established consumer panel or other pre-recruited membership panel is a popular, scientific and effective method for creating a sample of internet users. Typically, sampling from a panel yields a high response rate because panel members have already agreed to cooperate with the research organization's email or internet surveys. Often panel members are compensated for their time with a sweepstakes, a small cash incentive or redeemable points. Further, because the panel has already supplied demographic characteristics and other information from previous questionnaires, researchers are able to select panelists based on product ownership, lifestyle or other characteristics relevant to their research project.

Consider Harris Interactive, an internet survey research organization that maintains a panel of millions of individuals in countries around the globe. In addition, Harris Interactive has different specialty panels such as Americans with Disabilities, Technology Decision Makers, and Sports. A database this large allows the company to draw simple random samples, stratified samples and quota samples from its panel members. You should access Harris Interactive on the internet, and browse their website to develop an understanding of the services and facilities they provide for researchers. You can access Harris Interactive at the following website: harris-interactive.com/.

Recruited ad hoc samples

Another means of obtaining an internet sample is to obtain or create a sampling frame of email addresses on an ad hoc basis. Researchers may create the sampling frame offline or online. Databases containing email addresses can be compiled from many sources, including customer/client lists, advertising banners on pop-up windows that recruit survey participants, online sweepstakes and registration forms that must be filled out in order to gain access to a particular website. Researchers may contact respondents by 'snail mail', that is by mail (post), or by telephone to ask for their email addresses and obtain permission for an internet survey. Using offline techniques, such as random digital dialling (RRD) and short telephone screening interviews to recruit respondents can be a very practical way to get a representative sample for an internet survey. Companies anticipating future internet research can develop a valuable database for sample recruitment by including email addresses in their customer relationship databases (by inviting customers to provide that information on product registration cards, in telephone interactions, through onsite registration, etc.).

Opt-in lists

Research Now Survey Sampling International (SSI) specializes in providing sampling frames and scientifically drawn samples. The company offers more than 17 million panelists in more than 90 countries around the globe. You should visit their website and explore it in order to develop an understanding of the company and the services and facilities they provide for researchers. You can access their website at the following website: www.surveysampling.com/. They have thousands of lists of high-quality, targeted email addresses of individuals who have given permission to receive email messages related to a particular topic of interest. Research Now Survey Sampling International's database contains millions of internet users who **opt in** for limited participation. An important feature of Research Now Survey Sampling International's database is that the company has each individual confirm and reconfirm interest in communicating about a topic before the person's email address is added to the company's database.

opt in To give permission to receive selected email, such as questionnaires, from a company with an internet presence.

By whatever technique the sampling frame is compiled, it is important not to send unauthorized email to respondents. If individuals do not opt in to receive email from a particular organization, they may consider unsolicited survey requests to be spam. A researcher cannot expect high response rates from individuals who have not agreed to be surveyed. Spamming is not tolerated by experienced internet users and can easily backfire, creating a host of problems – the most extreme being complaints to the internet service provider (ISP), and this may result in the shut-down of the survey site.

As well as creating knowledge, every researcher is charged with disseminating the knowledge that they have created. In other words, researchers are obliged to publish their research. As a matter of course, students generally publish their work in theses libraries. In addition to this, you might think about other ways of publishing your research. It might be possible to publish a synopsis of your research in a student newsletter or newspaper, in a trade newsletter or journal. You should consider submitting an article from your research to an academic journal. The Reinvention Centre for Undergraduate Research at Warwick University in the UK publishes an online peer-reviewed journal of undergraduate research, *Reinvention: A Journal of Undergraduate Research* (www.warwick.ac.uk). It would be a useful exercise to locate

REAL WORLD RESEARCH

Detailing the population and sample

Both the population and the sample used in the research project raise issues of validity. In order for the research to be valid, the population used in the research must be a valid population in terms of the phenomenon under investigation. The research population must be the appropriate population, in terms of the focus of the research. It is a good idea to use your research diary to record your reflections on these issues and the decisions that you make in relation to them.

In your research diary, describe the population of your research. Do this in the first instance in broad terms. Then do this in as insightful a manner as possible in order to highlight any potential issues with the population or characteristics in the population likely to influence your research and

the design of your research project. The diary should record background details, and first and fresh impressions of the population. Background knowledge of the population is very useful to the researcher when making decisions on population, samples and sampling methods. First impressions can provide insights that can contribute substantially to the richness of a research project, when included in the written account of the research project.

Decide whether you are going to work with the entire population or a sample of that population. Record these decisions in your research diary and write clear and detailed explanations, justifications, for these decisions.

In writing up the research, the researcher must clearly outline the population of the study, the sample selected if sampling is used, and the sampling technique used. The researcher records and explains the decisions made with regard to the population and sample and the rationale for those decisions. The size of the population and the size of the sample must be clearly and unambiguously stated in the report of the research and the decisions made in relation to the population and sample must be outlined, explained and justified.

THE VALUE OF GOOD RESEARCH

Focus on discourse analysis

Discourse analysis (DA) is a research methodology and a means of analyzing data. Discourse analysis means simply the analysis of discourses. Traditionally, discourses have been understood to be language based, and found in conversation, in written texts and in spoken words. More recently, discourses have been accepted as being more broadly based, and, in fact, contemporarily, any kind of communication can be said to be discursive, to have different discourses embedded in it. For example, included among the different discourses studied by Christina Quinlan in her work are historic discourses, managerial discourses, architectural discourses and media discourses.

In the detail on discourse analysis presented in Table 9.4, discourse analysis is said to be a way of analyzing the social world, as the social world is produced and represented in language. As detailed in that table, according to Fairclough, 1995 (see also Fairclough, 2013), discourses can be written texts, spoken words and/or cultural artefacts, discourses are embedded in social events and social practices.

In their study of the impact of personal attitudes on the growth ambitions of small business owners, Braidford, Drummond and Stone (2017), carried out a telephone survey, the

results of which were used to inform the development of two focus groups and 29 in-depth interviews.

These researchers used discourse analysis to explore the data gathered. Their findings are very interesting. If you have an interest in discourse analysis, you should source the article and read it through. It might give you an idea for your own research project. The researchers present a useful literature review focused on small business growth. They draw on the theories of French sociologist and philosopher Pierre Bourdieu, and they give a good, interesting and very short introduction to his work. This use of Bourdieu's work in the journal article provides a particularly good example of the use of theory in the development of a research project. The researchers also give a succinct outline of the data-gathering exercises undertaken for the research. It would be useful to source the original article and to read it through.

In the study, using a discourse analysis approach, the researchers found orientations among small business owners that were either towards or against business growth. They found that the growth-inclined business owners were strategic in outlook, prepared to accept small returns in the short term for long-term benefit. Growth-resistant owners, they found, were inclined to see barriers to growth as insurmountable. One example of this, presented and discussed by the researchers, was the propensity of growth-resistant owners to highlight bank lending practices as an obstacle to growth. Growth-inclined business owners, the researchers reported, in response to restrictive bank lending practices, were more likely to seek alternative funding sources.

Another interesting research project is that of Wang (2006). Wang explored the use of questions as a means of

(Continued)

exercising power in both casual conversation and institutional dialogue. Wang writes of power being overt in institutional dialogue, for example in business, and covert in casual conversation, and he writes that questions are used to exercise power differently in both forms of verbal interaction. He writes that questions are powerful in conversation and in dialogue because unequal distribution of questions leads to unequal turn-taking in conversation and dialogue. He writes that dominant questions control the conversation or dialogue, and questions that demand a 'yes' or 'no' answer and the 'wh' questions (who, what, where, why) exercise power in different degrees.

In his review of the literature, Wang explores the nature of power, the definition of a question and the phenomenon of power in questions. If you examine the structure of Wang's literature review (his theoretical framework) you will clearly see how the structure for the literature review emerged from the conceptual framework of the research project.

For his data on conversational analysis, Wang used ten real casual conversations between college roommates and talks between close friends from two film scripts, *Sleepless in Seattle* and *Notting Hill*. For his analysis of institutional dialogue, Wang carried out analyses on five different kinds of encounter:

medical encounters, courtroom cross-examinations, classroom encounters, news interviews and service encounters.

It would be useful to source this article and study how Wang uses discourse analysis in his exploration of power in questions. As much research involves researchers posing questions, this is an interesting article for all researchers in relation to the power they have in shaping and asking questions in research, the ways in which they use that power and the implications of that.

The website of CADAAD (Critical Approaches to Discourse Analysis Across Disciplines) is a useful resource (www.cadaad.org/).

You will remember that we read about critical theory in Chapter 4 of this textbook. We discovered that critical theory is a philosophical framework that calls for a critical engagement with society and in particular with the way in which power operates in society.

There are a number of journals that specialize in research focused on discourses and discourse analysis. Among these journals are *Discourse Studies*, *Discourse and Society* and *Discourse and Communication*. See also van Dijk (2011) *Discourse Studies: A Multi Disciplinary Introduction*, and Fairclough (2013) *Critical Discourse Analysis*.

REAL WORLD RESEARCH

How theory influences research

The research project detailed here (Dermody and Scullion, 2004, 'Exploring the value of party political advertising for youth electoral engagement: an analysis of the 2001 British General Election advertising campaigns', *International Journal of Nonprofit and Voluntary Sector Marketing*, 9(4): 361–79) explored youth electoral engagement. It is a multi-method research project. As well as the *questionnaires* used and *focus groups* conducted with young people, the researchers *interviewed* personnel from advertising agencies and they engaged in a *content analysis* of election posters. Read the synopsis that follows and then find the original article online. Use this article to develop your knowledge of sampling methods and data collection methods. In particular, read the 'research design' section of the journal article. This section provides a good example of the level of detail required in writing up the research methodology chapter in the thesis or the research methodology section in the report of the research.

The authors of the article wrote that one of the key issues in the later days of the 2001 British General Election was the issue of encouraging the electorate to vote.

They wrote that turnout at British elections was in decline, particularly among young people. They said that British democracy appeared to be facing a crisis and stated that election advertising campaigns had been accused of failing to engage a disinterested young electorate.

The aim of their research was to explore youth attitudes to electoral advertising and to explore the value of electoral advertising for public servants tasked with increasing voter engagement and voter turnout.

Research design

A multi-method approach was taken to the research. This included a *survey* and *focus group* interviews with potential first-time voters aged 18–22. The population for the survey comprised British citizens who were eligible to vote for the first time. They were aged between 18 and 22 at the time of the 2001 British General Election. The *focus group* respondents also conformed to this pattern. The sample contained a mix of students. Some were employed and some were unemployed. There was an equal gender mix. There was a bias towards 21- to 22-year-olds. A greater proportion of the respondents said that they voted. The majority of the participants classified themselves as 'white British'. They were educated to GCSE standard, with a large cluster also holding A/AS qualifications. The students in the sample were typically studying for their first degree. When the authors compared the sample with the national profile of 18- to 22-year-olds, there was a slight bias towards students, young people who

(Continued)

claimed they voted and were alleged Labour supporters. The authors felt that, overall, the respondent 'fit' was 'reasonably tight' and they felt that this close fit helped to confirm 'the robustness of findings from the data'.

We are told that both the *survey* and *focus group* data were collected during the three-week period immediately following the election on 1 June 2001. The authors state that five *focus groups* were conducted in a variety of regions over that time period. They detail that each of the *focus groups* typically consisted of six-to-ten respondents and on average lasted two and a half hours each. All *interviews* were taped and the analysis conducted on the *interview* data was based on verbatim transcripts. The *interviews* explored respondents' attitudes to advertising generally before moving on to explore their attitudes to the election advertising and the election itself. Two *pilot focus groups* and a review of pertinent literature informed both the content and structure of the *focus group* interviews.

The authors state that a quasi-random sampling approach was adopted for the *survey*. A filtering system was used to ensure all respondents fitted the sampling criteria – the interview was terminated if they did not. The data collection method was a *survey* involving *street intercept interviews,* using an *interviewer-administered questionnaire. Street intercept interviews* are *interviews* conducted in the street with people passing by. The researcher intercepts the passers-by

and engages them in an interview. The *street intercept interviews* took place in large towns throughout the UK. A total of 867 usable *questionnaires* were completed. The two *pilot focus groups* and literature review also informed the content and structure of the *questionnaire.* The *questionnaire* focused on the attitudes of the respondents to the election generally, before moving on to ask each of the respondents specifically about three advertisements used to encourage voting before the election. The respondents' attitudes to the three advertisements were measured using *semantic differential scales.* The Statistical Package for the Social Sciences (SPSS) was used to analyze the data. SPSS is a computerized data analysis package used for the analysis of quantitative data. The analysis of quantitative data and the use of SPSS in analyzing quantitative data are dealt with in detail in this textbook in Chapter 19.

What sampling method was used in this study? Could you write a short critique of that sampling method?

What population was used in the study? How well do you think the sample selected represents the population?

Do you agree with the authors' claim that there was a close fit between the population of the study and the sample of that population included in the study?

What do the authors mean when they state that this close fit helped to confirm the robustness of findings from the data?

the journal online and read some of the articles published in it. In due course, you might think of submitting an article based on your own research to the journal for publication.

In writing up your research it is important that you clearly detail as fully as possible all of the elements of the methodological framework. The methodological framework, as you know, is contained in, or it is the content of, the research methodology chapter of the thesis, or the research methodology section of the research report (Figure 10.5).

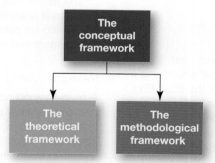

Figure 10.5 The methodological framework emerges from the conceptual framework.

The four frameworks

- Conceptual Framework
- Theoretical Framework
- *Methodological Framework*
- Analytical Framework

In the research methodology chapter in the thesis or in the research methodology section of the report of the research, you must detail and explain the methodology used and the rationale for choosing that methodology. You have to clearly outline the population of the study and sample used (if a sample is used). The sampling technique used and the manner in which the technique was operationalized or used in the research project must be explained. You must name and explain the data collection methods; you must explain why those particular data collection methods were used, how they were designed, and how they were used. It is also important to clearly present the response rates to the different data collection methods used in the research. You should detail the ethical issues in your research, and explain how you dealt with them. You should detail the ethical frameworks that you used for guidance in the research, for example, you might highlight the ethical guidance provided by your own university. You might refer to the ethical guidelines provided in the research methods textbook(s) you are using in your studies.

YOUR RESEARCH

Common research problems – understanding the difference between quantitative and qualitative research and data

It is sometimes the case that students have difficulty in grasping the difference between quantitative and qualitative research and data. The following research diary exercise is designed to help you develop an understanding of both quantitative and qualitative research and data. Record this exercise in your research diary.

For this exercise, we will revisit the table on research methodologies in Chapter 9 (Table 9.2). From your reading of the descriptions of the methodologies in the table, can you name the methodologies in which only quantitative data can be used? Can you name the methodologies in which only qualitative data can be used? Can you name the methodologies which can draw on a mixture of quantitative and qualitative data?

Now think about your own research project. Think about the research methodology you are using in your research. Think about the data collection methods you are using, and look again at the table on data-gathering methods in Chapter 9 (Table 9.4). In your research diary, write a short paragraph on the contribution of both quantitative and qualitative data to your research. In your writing, respond to the following questions:

- What do you think of the contribution to research generally of both the quantitative and qualitative data?
- In your research project, do you think one is more useful than the other?
- Why do you think that?

Capture your answers and thoughts in notes in your research diary. You will find these notes are useful to look back on when you are designing your research project, when you are writing the research methodology chapter or section of your thesis, and when you are explaining the choices that you made in relation to the design of your research project.

CASE STUDY

How to use a table of random numbers to randomly select a sample

1. Let us say that we have a population of 90 students and in our study we want a sample of 30 students from that population of 90.
2. We get access to, or we compile, a complete list of the names of the 90 students. This is our sampling frame.
3. We assign each student on the list a number, between 1 and 90 (see Case Table 10.1).
4. As we have a population of 90 and 90 is a two-digit number, we need to use the first two

Case Table 10.1 Part of a table of random numbers

13245	12908	10987	63689	65789
90876	45387	66754	88975	22234
34512	76894	24674	34577	34688
20137	23144	23557	13567	98799
42378	34556	76889	32412	57886
76890	44321	35669	54678	35467
34667	78665	21332	23123	87923

digits of the numbers in the table of random numbers in Case Table 10.1.

5. To begin, we randomly point to a number on the table. This number becomes our starting point.
6. Let us say we pointed to the number 44321. We use the first two digits of this number, and the number becomes 44. The student who has been allocated

(Continued)

the number 44 in our sampling frame becomes the first student to be included in our sample.

7. We then continue down that column to the end, selecting the first two digits of each number and including the student to whom that number has been assigned in our sample of 30 students.

8. Then we move onto the next column, selecting the first two digits of each number and including the student to whom this number has been assigned in our sample.

9. We continue this process until our sample is complete, until we have selected the 30 students from the population of 90 students to be included in the sample for our study.

You will find tables of random numbers in maths books and in the appendices of books on statistics.

The web tutor Stat Trek (stattrek.com) has a very simple, easy-to-use *random number generator* that you can use to generate any amount of random numbers.

You can use Excel to generate random numbers using a mathematical formula, the RAND function. The RAND function in Excel generates a random number which is greater than or equal to 0 and less than 1. The syntax for the RAND function is: = RAND (). Every time you use the command, Excel will generate a new random number. You continue generating random numbers until you have enough.

Question: The sampling method used in the exercise in this case study is systematic sampling. Can you define this sampling method and explain how it works?

END OF CHAPTER QUESTIONS

1 Explain what is meant by the term the population of the research project.

2 Detail and explain the reasons why a researcher would engage in sampling with a research population.

3 Explain the difference between probability and non-probability sampling.

4 What is simple random sampling and how is it used?

5 Outline an example of a research project that should be developed using a stratified sampling technique. Explain why a stratified sampling method should be used in this research project.

6 What is meant by the term judgemental sampling method and how and when is such a method used in research?

7 Describe the process of identifying a target population and selecting a sampling frame.

8 Compare random sampling and systematic (non-sampling) errors.

9 Identify the types of non-probability sampling, including their advantages and disadvantages.

10 Summarize the advantages and disadvantages of the various types of probability samples.

11 Discuss how to choose an appropriate sample design, and explain in your answer the challenges for internet sampling.

12 What are random numbers? How are random numbers used in sampling in research projects?

REFERENCES

Bourdieu, P. (1986) 'The forms of capital', in J. Richardson (ed.) *Handbook of Theory and Research for the Sociology of Education*, New York: Greenwood Press.

Braidford, P., Drummond, I. and Stone, I. (2017) 'The impact of personal attitudes on the growth ambitions of small business owners', *Journal of Small Business and Enterprise Development*, 4(4): 850–862.

CADAAD (Critical Approaches to Discourse Analysis Across Disciplines), cadaad.net/. (Accessed 17.03.2018).

City Directories, www.uscitydirectories.com. (Accessed 17.03.2018).

City Town Info, www.citytowninfo.com (Accessed 17.03.201).

ComScore, www.comscore.com (Accessed 17.03.2018).

Dermody, J. and Scullion, R. (2004) 'Exploring the value of party political advertising for youth electoral engagement: an analysis of the 2001 British General Election advertising campaigns', *International Journal of Nonprofit and Voluntary Sector Marketing*, 9(4): 361–379.

Fairclough, N. (1995) *Critical Discourse Analysis*, London: Longman.

Fairclough, N. (2013) *Critical Discourse Analysis: The Critical Study of Language*, Oxon and New York: Routledge.

Reinvention: An International Journal of Undergraduate Research, The University of Warwick, warwick.ac.uk/fac/cross_fac/iatl/reinvention (Accessed 17.03.2018).

Research Now Survey Sampling International (SSI), www.
surveysampling.com/(Accessed 17.03.2018).
Stat Trek, Teach Yourself Statistics, stattrek.com (Accessed
17.03.2018).
UK Office for National Statistics, www.ons.gov.uk/census/
index.html (Accessed 17.03.2018).

van Dijk, T.A. (ed.) (2011) *Discourse Studies: A Multi Disciplinary
Introduction* (2nd edn), London, California, New Delhi,
Singapore, Sage.
Wang, J. (2006) 'Questions and the exercise of power', *Discourse
and Society*, *7*(4): 529–548.

RECOMMENDED READING

Blair, E. and Blair, J. (2015) *Applied Survey Sampling*, London,
California, New Delhi, Singapore: Sage.
Daniel, J.N. (2012) *Sampling Essentials: Practical Guidelines for
Making Sampling Choices*, London, California, New Delhi,
Singapore: Sage.
Emmel, N. (2013) *Sampling and Choosing Cases in Qualitative
Research: A Realist Approach*, London, California,
New Delhi, Singapore: Sage.
Deacon, D., Pickering, M., Golding, P. and Murdock, G.
(1999) (repr. 2010) *Researching Communications:
A Practical Guide to Methods in Media and Cultural
Analysis*, Oxford: Oxford University Press.
Levy, P.S., Lemeshow, S., Hade, E.M. and Ferketich, A.K.
(2009) *Sampling of Populations Solutions Manual: Methods*

and Applications, (Wiley Series in Survey Methodology) (4th
edn), Wiley.
Marshall, J. and Adamic, M. (2010) 'The story is the message:
shaping corporate culture', *Journal of Business Strategy*, *31*(2):
18–23.
Neuman, W.L. (2014) *Social Research Methods: Quantitative and
Qualitative Approaches* (7th edn), Essex, England: Pearson
Education Ltd.
Sudman, S. (1976) *Applied Sampling*, New York: Academic Press.
Wodak, R. and Krzyzanowski, M. (eds) (2008) *Qualitative
Discourse Analysis in the Social Sciences*, Basingstoke: Palgrave
Macmillan.

CHAPTER 11

WRITING THE RESEARCH PROPOSAL

LEARNING OBJECTIVES

At the end of this chapter, the student should be able to:

- Generate ideas for research projects.

- Develop research questions/statements, research hypotheses, define and refine them.

- Provide a sample literature review for a research proposal.

- Outline a methodological framework for a research proposal.

- Write a research proposal.

RESEARCH SKILLS

At the end of this chapter, the student should, using the exercises on Cengage Brain, be able to:

- Generate research ideas.

- Outline researchable problems.

- Develop research proposals.

In this chapter, the focus is on the development of research proposals. This is a very important chapter. As well as teaching you how to develop formal proposals for research projects, this chapter looks again at how to generate ideas for research and how to critically evaluate those ideas in order to make sure they are researchable.

INTRODUCTION

As a social science researcher, the first thing you need to be able to do is to generate ideas for research projects. As you have probably gathered from your reading of this textbook, ideas for research projects are all around you. You just need to be able to identify them as potential research projects.

The model of the research process, detailed in Chapter 1, shows that the first step in the process calls for an idea for the research project; once the researcher has an idea for a research project, s/he starts refining that idea. The process of refining the idea should result in the researcher being able to state the research project in one sentence. This one sentence can be phrased as a statement or a question and, most importantly, as we know, it contains the conceptual framework for the research project. The conceptual framework is the first framework in the four frameworks approach to the research project.

YOUR RESEARCH

Ideas for research projects are all around you. Perhaps you have an interest in the music industry. If so, you might read Gamble, Brennan and McAdam's (2017) study which explores how crowdfunding affects the music industry using an interpretive epistemological approach to research methodology. Do you know what these researchers mean by an interpretive epistemological approach to research methodology? We read about interpretivism and epistemology in Chapter 4 of this textbook. You might perhaps have an interest in digital games. If so, you might read the study carried out by Nucciarelli *et al.* (2017), designed to study the effects of crowdfunding in the digital games industry. This study was developed using a case study research methodology. Do you think there might be some scope from your reading of one or both of these journal articles for the development of an idea for your own research project?

Think about your use of different web-based social networking products. Is there, do you think, scope for developing a research project around the study of any of those products? Think about Instagram. What is the business rational underpinning Instagram? How does Instagram make money? It might be interesting to develop a research project on the means through which revenue is, or might be, generated from or by Instagram. Think about celebrities and the ways they use Instagram. Many use the platform to help them develop their brand and their brand image. It might be interesting to study a celebrity and their use of Instagram for your research project.

Questions that you have about people that interest you, or businesses, or aspects of business that interest you, provide good starting points in the search for an idea for a research project.

The four frameworks

- *Conceptual Framework*
- Theoretical Framework
- Methodological Framework
- Analytical Framework

The research statement or question, which is, or which contains, the conceptual framework for the research project, drives every element of the research process. All of the decisions made for every element of the research process are determined by the research statement/question.

GENERATING IDEAS FOR RESEARCH PROJECTS

As we have seen, there are good ideas for potential research projects all around us. It is important to begin to develop some skills in identifying potential research projects, because you will have to do so to satisfy the requirements of your course of study. Remember, 'ideas' are simply new ways of thinking about things. Developing your capacity to think in new ways will help you become innovative, a key skill.

You can generate ideas for research projects from:

- everything you have studied so far in your work toward your qualification
- everything you have seen, watched and experienced in your work and in your life
- everything that interests or intrigues you about the business world
- every person you have encountered in the business world.

The problem should not be one of having no ideas; the problem should be in deciding on which idea, of the many ideas you have, to focus on for your research project.

Think about all that you have studied so far in your work for your qualification(s). Are there any thoughts that come to you straightaway about ideas for research projects? If there are, jot them down in your research diary; try to capture them right away, before you forget them. Think about the subjects and topics you studied that really interested you and/or the subjects you did well in, and jot them down. Now think about any issues, or unanswered questions, or downright problems that you came across in your reading for your studies. Was there anything that particularly interested you? Was there anything that might be worth thinking about in more detail? If there is, write it down in your research diary.

The next step is to begin to think critically about your ideas for research projects. Think about them in terms of the kinds of problem you might encounter trying to develop these into research projects. Some of the questions you need to ask yourself at this point are detailed next.

Questions in relation to the proposed research idea/research project

- Are there any particular problems, sensitivities, issues, about this **research idea** that stand out from the start?
- Do you think that these problems, issues and sensitivities would be substantial enough to stop such a research project, or to substantially delay such a research project? If the answer is yes to this, you may need to move on quickly from this idea.

research idea The broad area within which you want to situate your research.

Questions in relation to the literature in the area or field of the proposed research

- Is there anything written about this issue or topic: is there any literature, any published research, on this research or topic? There may be a great deal, there may be little – indeed, there may be none at all. If there is little literature on the topic, you should seek advice as to whether or not you should continue with the topic. It is likely that you will be advised against continuing if there is little literature.
- Who has been writing on this topic? When did they write on this topic? Recently?
- Where is the topic being written about? In journals? In newspapers? Online?
- What is being written about the topic?
- If the topic has been or is being written about in journal articles, this is really useful. This means that the topic has been addressed and developed theoretically. This would be particularly helpful for a beginner researcher working within an academic institution.
- Try to locate the journal articles online.
- Make a file on your computer and in that file save copies of the journal articles that you have found on this topic.
- When you have saved the journal articles to your computer, scan them quickly, and then read them closely. As you read, record the thoughts and ideas that come to you in your research diary.
- What are the authors of those journal articles saying about the topic? What is known about the topic? What issues and aspects have been thoroughly explored? What issues, aspects, questions do the authors of the journal articles recommend for further research? What issues are yet to be explored?
- Is there any issue among those issues that you would/could/should explore in your research project?

You should record your answers to the above questions in your research diary. If you do take the time to answer the questions above, it is likely that you will develop a sophisticated understanding of your idea for your research project. If this is so, you will be able to communicate your idea for your research project in a very informed academic manner to your lecturer in research methods and/or to your dissertation supervisor.

The questions below are designed to help you think critically about your ideas for the research methodology and the data-gathering methods you might use in the research project you are now thinking about.

Questions in relation to research methodology and methods for the proposed research

- What methodologies did the researchers in the literature you have read use in their study of this issue/phenomenon?
- Did they study human populations? If so, what populations did they work with? Were they big populations or small? Did the researchers encounter any particular problems in working with these populations?
- Did the researchers use a sample? If so, what sampling method was deployed? Were there any issues in the population, the sample and/or the sampling method used?
- What kind of data collection methods (data-gathering methods) did they use?
- If you were to conduct research on this topic, where would you conduct the research? Do you have access to a site, an organization, a population, where or with whom you could conduct your research on this topic?

- What kind of data would you look for to produce new knowledge in this field?
- Where are these data? Are they in records and reports? Are they, for example, in the testimony of people? If the data are in the testimony of people, how would you gather that data. Would you gather the data through interviews or focus groups?
- Explain how would you go about gathering the data.
- Why would you gather the data in that manner? Why is this the best way to gather the data required?

Try to answer these questions. Scribble your notes in response to these bullet points, statements and questions into your research diary. Then, in your research diary, quickly organize your notes. Think about the ideas and insights you have had during this exercise. Using more scribbles, arrange them and rearrange them. Are more ideas coming to you through this process? Try to put your thoughts, ideas and insights into some kind of order.

Now quickly analyze your notes. What are they telling you about this possible research project? Is there potential in your notes for more than one idea for a research project or does one idea stand out? How does this idea strike you? Does it seem reasonable and do-able? As you think about it, is this research project becoming more and more interesting? Perhaps your notes are warning you in some way about this research project. What do you now feel about this research project? Do you think that this is something on which you would like to spend some more time, or should you move on to another idea? If your instincts are telling you that this is not the way to go with your research project, then perhaps you should listen to your instincts. Do not be afraid to ask for advice. Talk to your research supervisor or your lecturer in research methods. You may have an opportunity to run your idea very quickly by your lecturer at the end of a lecture. If there is a major issue or problem with your idea, they may be able to spot it right away. If they do, this can save you a lot of time and work.

It is important not to become too attached to an idea for a research project until you have been given some indication that, in general, the idea you are developing is viable and that your proposed research idea is acceptable. There is no point in getting attached to an idea for a research project that, for one reason or another, is not acceptable to your supervisor/potential examiner. It may be that there is some ethical issue, or perhaps the scope of the research idea may not be broad enough or deep enough for the standard required by the programme of study. Perhaps the area has been studied too much. Perhaps it has not been studied enough and consequently there really is nothing written on the topic. While such a research idea can be an intriguing and engaging challenge for experienced researchers, it is not a good starting point for beginner researchers.

In addition to the ideas just detailed, there may be some other experience or area in your life that you can explore with the view to generating an idea or ideas for research projects. The media, TV, the internet, newspapers and magazines, are all very useful areas of exploration in terms of ideas for research projects. Hobbies and pastimes as well as sporting and social endeavours, clubs and organizations, are all potentially fruitful too in terms of ideas for research projects.

THE VALUE OF GOOD RESEARCH

Focus on documentary research/ documentary analysis

Documentary research or documentary analysis, as it is often called, is research focused on analyzing documents. Examples of the kinds of documents used in documentary analysis include company reports, government reports, archives, files, records of meetings, other records, memoranda and diaries. Documentary research can be used in internet research, in researching websites and web pages and other documents on the internet. Any document can be used as the focus of documentary research. Both quantitative and qualitative approaches can be used to analyze data in documentary research.

Documentary research can be used as the methodology in the research project and/or it can be used as a data collection method in the research project. The journal article detailed here (Kennelly, Corbett, and Toohey (2017) 'Leveraging ambitions and barriers: Glasgow universities and the 2014 Commonwealth Games', *Marketing Intelligence & Planning*, 35(6): 822–38), provides an interesting example of a case study in which documents were gathered and used as data.

In the article, the researchers explain that they set out to discover why and how universities in the Glasgow region of Scotland used the 2014 Commonwealth Games to achieve benefits.

They explain that in recent years universities have become more entrepreneurial. Many universities now operate like businesses in a competitive global marketplace. The Commonwealth Games, according to the authors, are second

(Continued)

only to the Olympic Games in terms of the number of competing countries and athletes, and the range of sports.

Every research project is tasked with making a contribution to knowledge. This is the most fundamental requirement of all research. The researchers in this journal article clearly state the contribution to knowledge that they believe this research makes in extending the theoretical knowledge on sports events leveraging and the production of events benefits. The research is of benefit to other universities in other locations seeking to strategically leverage sports events for their benefit.

There is a good literature review covering the key concepts in the research project, leveraging major sports events, and the changing role of universities in society.

The researchers explain their research methodology in some detail. The study is a qualitative case study. They explain what a case study is, and they reference a key research methodology textbook on case study research (Yin, 2014), for support.

They explain that two qualitative data-gathering techniques were used in the research: document analysis and semi-structured interviews. They use Yin again to support and justify their choice of these data-gathering methods for their case study. They explain that in total 63 documents mentioning the Commonwealth Games and the universities in and around Glasgow were used in the study. They give more detail on the types of documents collected, including reports and administrative documents, press releases and new reports.

They explain that the documentary evidence was analyzed using NVivo 10, a software package used by qualitative researchers and mixed methods researchers to help them manage, organize and analyze their data. We explore NVivo in more detail in Chapter 18 of this textbook.

The researchers explain that they supported the data from documentary sources with data from interviews with 16 key informants who had knowledge of or a role in the interactions between the universities and the Commonwealth Games.

The research provides insight into how events like sporting events can be used for the benefit of the broader community. You should source this article and read it through. What do you think about this research project? Does it give you any ideas for your own research project? Focus in particular on the methodology section. What do you think of the methodology used in the research project? Does it give you any ideas for a research project that you might undertake?

Some useful resources on documentary research include:

Bowen, G.A. (2009) 'Document analysis as a qualitative research method', *Qualitative Research Journal*, 9(2): 27–40.

Denscombe, M. (2017) *The Good Research Guide for Small-scale Social Research Projects* (6th edn), Maidenhead: Open University Press.

McCulloch, G. (2004) *Documentary Research in Education, History and the Social Sciences*, Oxon and New York: Routledge.

Scott, J. (1990) *A Matter of Record: Documentary Sources in Social Research*, Oxford: Blackwell.

World History Sources, *Scholars Analyzing Documents*, George Mason University, chnm.gmu.edu/worldhistorysources/whmdocuments.html

The last of the five resources is a history resource. It would be interesting to think about a research project focused on some aspect of business history. There are a number of academic journals dealing with business history, among them *Business History*, *Business History Review*, *Business and Economic History*, *Management and Organization History*, and *Accounting History Review*. The US Library of Congress provides a very good guide to business history resources: www.loc.gov/rr/business/guide/guide1/businesshistory/intro.html

The case study presented at the end of this chapter contains a research proposal for a research project to be carried out using a documentary analysis methodology.

Figure 11.1 details some ideas for research projects developed around a (fictitious) cricket club. If you belong to any kind of club, is there any research that you could conduct in the club and/or for the club that would be useful? Four ideas have been jotted down in the spidergram for research projects for this particular cricket club. You may find some inspiration in the spidergram in terms of ideas of your own. Perhaps you can think of other potential research projects for this club or for another club or for a different enterprise or organization. Figure 11.2 is another spidergram that presents five ideas for potential research projects all focused on the World Wildlife Fund (WWF).

The five (scribbled) ideas for the WWF are as follows:

- a study of the brand recognition
- a study of the web presence of the WWF, by this we mean a **critical analysis** of the website of the WWF
- a new marketing campaign for the WWF
- a marketing campaign for the WWF aimed specifically at third-level students
- a study of new fundraising models for the WWF or perhaps the development of a fundraising model designed specifically for the WWF.

critical analysis A questioning analytical approach to any phenomenon.

Figure 11.1 Research diary research project ideas: Willowbrook Cricket Club

Figure 11.2 Research diary research project ideas: World Wildlife Fund (WWF)

It may be that one or more of these ideas appeals to you and perhaps gives you an idea for your own research project. If so, that is good. It may be that reading this chapter and reflecting on the ideas presented here helps you to decide that you would like to go in a different direction entirely in developing your own research idea(s). This is good too. The important thing is that you take some action and actively engage with the development of your research project. Figure 11.3 shows two spidergrams copied from a research diary.

The first spidergram in Figure 11.3 is a study of a (fictitious) high street. The student who prepared this spidergram is thinking about conducting his research project on the local high street. In this spidergram, there are ideas for five potential research projects:

- A proposal for a new business venture for the high street.
- A study of the key attractions on the high street.
- A study of perceptions of the high street. (It does not say whose perceptions. It might be the perceptions of shoppers, or shopkeepers, perhaps the perceptions of both, or perhaps the perceptions of another group entirely.)
- A critical analysis of the provision for shoppers on the high street.
- A study of footfall or pedestrian flows on the high street.

In the second spidergram of Figure 11.3, we can see that the student who created it is thinking about designing a research project around developing a new product. This student is interested in new product development. The five ideas depicted in the spidergram are as follows:

- An idea for a research project based on the development of a new business model for web-based products.
- A proposal for the development of a farmers' market for Illingford High Street.
- An idea for the development of a marketing campaign for a new (fictitious) girl band, 'It Glitters'.

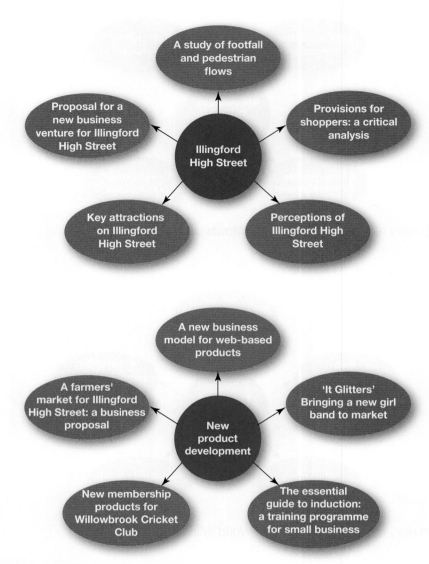

Figure 11.3 Two spidergrams from a research diary

- An idea for a research project focused on the development of new membership products for the (fictitious) Willowbrook Cricket Club (Figure 11.1).
- An idea for a research project focused on the development of a generic induction programme for small businesses, 'The essential guide to induction: a training programme for small businesses'.

Having read through all of these ideas for research projects, are there any ideas that appeal to you? If not, perhaps the ideas presented here suggest to you ideas for research projects that you do find interesting.

A CONCEPTUAL FRAMEWORK: THE FIRST STEP

The conceptual framework is the first of the four frameworks in the four frameworks approach to research, as explained previously. The conceptual framework is contained in the research statement or research question. In a properly conceptualized research statement or question, the entire conceptual framework for the research project should be stated in one sentence. This one sentence should contain all of the key concepts of the research project.

Drawing on the spidergrams detailed earlier, it is useful here to explore the conceptual frameworks of the ideas for research projects presented in them.

In the cricket club example (Figure 11.1), a useful conceptual framework might be as follows:

> *This research project is a case study designed to examine the branding of Willowbrook Cricket Club.*

Another example might be:

> *This research project is a case study designed to produce a new marketing campaign for Willowbrook Cricket Club.*

Yet another example might be:

> *This research project is a survey designed to explore perceptions of the members of Willowbrook Cricket Club of the image and branding of the club.*

As can be seen from these examples, each research project is expressed in one sentence, and that one sentence captures all of the key concepts and issues in the project, and it also contains an expression of the methodology to be used. As you can see, in one of the research statements, the proposed methodology is a survey, a survey methodology, while in the other two the proposed methodology is a case study.

Each of the three research statements details a relatively simple research project. As has been explained many times in this textbook, it is a good idea to begin with a very clear simple research statement or question. Each or any of the research projects outlined earlier would be a useful starting point for any student. Through engagement with the relevant literature, and development of a methodological framework for the project, as well as analysis of the data gathered, the simple project just outlined would develop into a complex and scholarly work.

Figure 11.2 attempts to develop those research ideas into conceptual frameworks for research projects. This spidergram is concerned with the WWF. The ideas that emerged were:

- issues of awareness of the fund
- issues of perceptions of the fund
- the branding of the fund
- the market presence of the fund.

Appropriate conceptual frameworks for these issues and ideas are as follows:

> *This research project is an image-based research project designed to measure brand awareness of the brand WWF among undergraduates at Hazelbrook University.*

Another example might be:

> *This research project is a survey of perceptions of the WWF among 50 shoppers in Hazelbrook Shopping Centre, Illingford.*

Another example might be:

> *This research project is a case study designed to critically examine the web presence of the WWF.*

Another example might be:

> *This research project is a survey examining awareness of and perceptions of the WWF among students at Hazelbrook University.*

Once again, each of the research statements detailed above contains all of the key concepts in the research project and each provides an appropriate conceptual framework for the research project. Each of the research statements contains a statement of the methodology to be used in the research and each statement is simple and concise.

Let us consider Figure 11.3 spidergram which focused on developing ideas for a research project around a study of a high street. An example of a research statement for such a project might be as follows:

> *This research project is a case study of Illingford High Street with a view to producing a new development plan for that high street.*

Each of the sample research statements outlined represents an appropriate research statement for a research project for business studies. You could adapt any of these research statements to your own research idea and, in this way, produce a good, simple and clear statement for your own research project.

REFINING RESEARCH IDEAS

Every research idea needs to be properly defined and refined. It often happens that students have really great ideas for their research projects, but those ideas are too big, too broad or too ambitious. Telling yourself, and your thesis supervisor, that you want to examine your cricket club, or you want to study the WWF, or you want to study your home town for your research project is great. It means that you know at least what it is you want to study and this is often a big first step forward. However, this is just your research idea. You now need to get from your research idea to a properly defined and refined research project. For example, where studying your hometown is your research idea, 'a case study of Illingford High Street with a view to producing a new development plan for that high street' could be a model for your specific research statement.

It is important to understand clearly the difference between research ideas and research projects. Your research idea is the broad area within which you want to work. Your research project is your carefully defined and refined research statement or question. It is the conceptual framework for your research project and it contains all of the key ideas, all of the key concepts of your research project. Use the research statement/question to help you maintain your focus. This is not to say that your research will not grow or develop. It will and it should. But every shift and change in the research must be reflected in a shift and change in the research statement/question.

It is worth spending as much time as is necessary at the conceptualizing stage of a research project, because this will save you time in the long run. It is better to spend time thinking about it and reflecting on it at the start to ensure that when you start work on the research, you are working on the right research project.

This level of engagement with your research project will facilitate the development of a research project of the depth and complexity appropriate to your course of study. This reflective engagement will help to ensure that, from the start, you design and develop the right research project for you. Remember it is essential that you have the support of your thesis supervisor for your research idea, your research statement/question, for your research project.

LIMITING THE SCOPE OF A RESEARCH PROJECT

One of the most critical steps in any research project is the process of limiting its scope. The critical question is whether or not the research is do-able, given the resources available. In Chapter 1, we defined a researchable problem as one where the researcher has the time, money and the access to the data required to complete the project. If the research project is one assignment of many to be completed in the course of the academic year, then there are implications in terms of the amount of time available for the research project. This will obviously have implications for the scope and size of the project.

The word count allowed for the research project is a useful indicator of the expected scope of the project. Clearly, a research project of 10 000 words will be of a different magnitude to a research project of 20 000 words or 50 000 words. It is useful, in developing a sense of the scope of a project, to have some sense of what is expected from the research. You should be able to answer the following questions:

- What is the word count allocated to the work?
- Is the research for an undergraduate degree or a postgraduate degree?
- Are you tasked with simply designing a research project or do you have to also conduct the research, to gather and analyze data and produce findings?
- Are you restricted in any way in terms of the kind of research you can undertake? Are you, for example, expected to engage in survey research?

It is important to be very clear on the standard expected, the magnitude or scope expected, and any expectations or requirements in terms of populations, methodologies and data-gathering techniques.

It is also important to know what it is that you, as the researcher, want to accomplish with the research. Once you know what is expected, and what it is that you want to do, it often becomes somewhat easier to decide on which particular research project to develop.

AIMS AND OBJECTIVES

When you have the fully and properly conceptualized research statement or question, the next step is to develop aims and objectives. For the sake of simplicity and clarity, you can restate your research statement/question as an aim. Your project then has one aim.

For example, your research statement reads as follows:

> *This research project is a case study of Illingford High Street with a view to producing a development plan for that high street.*

Then the aim of your research reads as follows:

> *The aim of this research is to develop a case study of Illingford High Street with a view to producing a development plan for that high street.*

Another example of restating the research statement or question as the aim of the project is as follows. First detail the research statement:

> *This research project is a survey examining awareness of and perceptions of the WWF among students at Hazelbrook University.*

Then state the **aim of your research** as follows:

> *The aim of this research is to examine awareness of and perceptions of the WWF among students at Hazelbrook University.*

> **aim of your research** To keep things simple, the aim of your research is your research statement/question restated as an aim.

This simple approach of restating the well-conceptualized research statement or question as the aim of the research project helps to maintain the focus of the research.

The **objectives of the research** flow from the aim of the research. They are not additional aims, but the steps you, as the researcher, are going to take in order to accomplish the aim of the research. An example of an aim and objective is as follows:

> *The aim of this research is to develop a case study of Illingford High Street with a view to producing a new development plan for that high street.*

> **objectives of the research** The steps the researcher takes in order to accomplish the aim of the research.

The objectives of the research are as follows:

- In the first place, Illingford High Street will be mapped and all of the businesses on the high street will be detailed on the map.
- An analysis will then be undertaken of the nature of all of the businesses on the high street, any gaps in retail and service provision will be identified.
- The perspectives of the owners and managers of the businesses on the high street will be gathered in terms of the development needs of the high street.
- The perspectives of the local government representatives will be gathered in terms of the development needs of the high street and in terms of any development plans already in existence for the high street.
- The perspectives of the general population of the high street will be gathered in terms of thoughts and/or ideas they might have for the development of the high street.
- Finally, following a detailed analysis of the data gathered, a new development plan for the high street will be developed and presented.

As you can see, six objectives were conceptualized and outlined and all six of the objectives flow from the aim.

Let us now consider the idea for research on the WWF. An example of the aim and objectives of one of the studies is as follows:

> *The aim of the research is to examine awareness of and perceptions of the WWF among students at Hazelbrook University.*

The objectives of the research are as follows:

- To examine levels of awareness of the WWF among students at Hazelbrook University.
- To examine perceptions of the WWF among students at Hazelbrook University.

As you can see, this research project has only two objectives. Two objectives are enough for this research project. They will allow the researcher to accomplish the aim of the research.

In general, it is a good idea to have no fewer than two objectives and no more than six objectives.

Sometimes conceptualizing the objectives of the research project can take as long as conceptualizing the research statement. It is important to take time and to engage actively and reflectively with the process of developing appropriate objectives for the research. Remember, the objectives of the research are essentially the steps you are going to undertake in order to accomplish the aim of the research. You should not include reviewing literature as an objective of the research, or outlining an appropriate methodology or creating and developing a list of references. These are all aspects of the research process that, generally, every researcher must complete. The objectives of any research project are specific to that project.

In an academic environment, the researcher is relatively free to decide on the topic of the research. It is important not to be overly ambitious. Remember that the researcher must accomplish whatever s/he sets out to achieve. It is important that the researcher creates for him or herself an acceptable research project that is meaningful to him or her and which he or she can comfortably accomplish within the time constraints of the project.

The four frameworks

- Conceptual Framework
- Theoretical Framework
- *Methodological Framework*
- Analytical Framework

Clarity in research questions and hypotheses

Sometimes the conceptual framework for the research project is expressed as a statement, and sometimes it is stated as a question. Research questions take a business problem or decision statement and express it in terms of a question or statement that invites research. A research question is the researcher's translation of the business issue into a specific inquiry.

A good research question makes doing useful research much more likely, much more feasible. However, writing a good research question is not that easy. For instance, sometimes in quantitative research a research question can be too general, leading to vagueness in what the researcher should study, for example, 'Is advertising copy 1 better than advertising copy 2?' Advertising effectiveness can be measured in a number of ways: by sales, by recall of sales message, by brand awareness, by intention to buy, by recognition or knowledge, to name a few possibilities. Asking a more specific research question such as, 'Does advertising copy 1 or advertising copy 2 have a higher day-after recall score?' helps researchers design a study that will produce useful and actionable results. The entire process of business problem definition involves stating research questions clearly, as explained in terms of the conceptual framework for the research project, and if needed, translating those into well-formulated and specifically focused hypotheses.

A sales manager may hypothesize that salespeople who show the highest job satisfaction will be the most productive.

A researcher might develop this hypothesis: the number of Facebook likes for a product relates positively to annual product sales.

Hypotheses are statements that invite an empirical test. In an empirical test, the researcher gathers the necessary data to examine the hypothesis, to prove or disprove it:

- A formal hypothesis has considerable practical value in planning and designing research. It forces researchers to be clear about what they expect to find through the study and it raises crucial questions about data required.

Figure 11.4 summarizes how a decision statement (corresponding to a business research problem) leads to research objectives that become a basis for the research design. Researchers extract broad research objectives from that statement. Each research objective can be matched to a research question(s) and possibly hypotheses. This in effect, creates the research design. Once the research has been conducted, the results may show an unanticipated aspect of the problem and suggest a need for additional research to satisfy the main objective. A research project almost always uncovers additional aspects of a particular problem that can lead to refinement of the original business problem statement or the creation of a new problem statement.

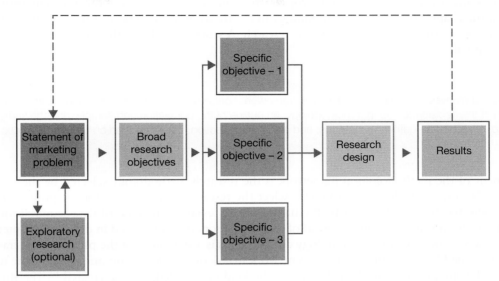

Figure 11.4 Influence of decision statement of marketing problem on research objectives and research designs

HOW TO CREATE A THEORETICAL FRAMEWORK FOR A PROJECT AND PROVIDE A SAMPLE LITERATURE REVIEW

The second framework of the four frameworks approach to the research project is the theoretical framework. The theoretical framework for the research project is contained in the literature review (see Chapter 6).

The conceptual framework for the research project, contained in the well-conceptualized research statement or question, gives the researcher direction in terms of their reading for the literature review. The researcher starts by developing a search strategy that is based on the key concepts in the conceptual framework. If your research statement reads 'This research project is a case study of Illingford High Street with a view to producing a development plan for that high street', your key concepts are: high street; small town (Illingford); development plan; development plan for a high street; development plan for a high street in a small town.

These key concepts are the focus of your research, and consequently of your literature search. They become the keywords that you use in keyword searches for literature for your literature review.

A sample literature review, which you are required to write for a research proposal, is a sample, or a small example, of the actual or proposed literature review. A sample literature review is a short literature review and in general it would consist of 300–800 words, depending on the overall word count given for the research proposal. If you wish to know what a literature review looks like, you can read any of the journal articles presented and discussed throughout this textbook. They all have good literature reviews. Remember that a literature review is not a listing of relevant literature; it is a review of relevant literature. Reviewing literature in the context of a research project involves reading the literature relevant to the research project, critically evaluating it and writing a critical review of that literature.

It is really not possible to finally outline a research statement for a research project until you have undertaken some reading of the literature. Until you have undertaken some reading around a topic, you cannot know what is known and what is not known on a topic and where the focus of your research should be. When you are familiar with the literature, then you can create and develop a useful research project, one that makes a meaningful contribution to knowledge.

The four frameworks

- Conceptual Framework
- *Theoretical Framework*
- Methodological Framework
- Analytical Framework

OUTLINING A METHODOLOGICAL FRAMEWORK FOR A RESEARCH PROJECT

The **methodological framework** for the research project is the third framework within the four frameworks approach. It is fully detailed in the chapter on research methodology in the thesis or in the report of the research. In general, this is Chapter 3 of the thesis, or the written account of the research. A synopsis of the methodological framework is presented in the research proposal.

> **methodological framework** The methodological framework contains detail of the methodology used in the research, and a justification of the decision to use that methodology; an outline of the population and sample, and the sampling method; a detailed description of data-gathering methods; and an ethical reflection, i.e. a reflection on the ethical issues in the research.

The first element of the methodological framework is the research methodology selected by the researcher for the research project. The researcher does not arbitrarily select the research methodology for the project. The appropriate methodology is indicated to the researcher by the nature of the research, the kind of data required for the study, the population of the study and the geographic spread of the population. As is explained in detail in Chapter 4 of this textbook, implicit in the statement of the methodology and methods is a statement of the philosophical framework within which the study is embedded. The philosophical framework makes ontological assumptions about the nature of reality and epistemological assumptions about knowledge and the kind of knowledge to be created by the study. If you have any difficulty understanding this last sentence, you should read Chapter 4 of this textbook.

YOUR RESEARCH
Common research problems

Beginner researchers are often confused as to what is required of them in producing a research project. A template or a guide for your research can help resolve a lot of this confusion.

It is always a good idea to try to find a published research project, or two or three such projects, in books or in journal articles, focused on the phenomenon you intend to research. You can then use these published research projects as guides or templates for your own research. From these research projects, you will get a good example of a literature review, some good insights into research design and some useful ideas for the methodology for your own research. You will also get ideas for data-gathering methods and guidance on the issue of triangulation, as well as guidance on dealing with the issues of validity and reliability, some helpful insights into the proper approach to data analysis, and some guidance in terms of writing up findings, drawing conclusions and making recommendations.

The templates will also help you by providing a guide to the writing, structuring and referencing of a research project.

If the study has a human **population** this will have a substantial influence on the design of the study. If the population of the study is big, a sample may be drawn from the population. A sample is a small subset of a population, said to be representative in some way of the population. The process of selecting a population for a research project and the different sampling methods are dealt with in detail in Chapter 10 of this textbook. In the research proposal, what is needed is a statement of the research methodology, a description of the population of the study, the number of people in the population, and the size of the sample drawn from the population, as well as an outline of the sampling method used (see Chapter 10).

> **population** Every person, or every entity, that could be included in the research.

Some detail of the data collection methods to be used in the research is given in the research proposal. The data collection methods are named and explained. The questions asked in data gathering are detailed, explained and justified.

Four important things to bear in mind when writing a research proposal are the issues of validity and reliability, the concept of triangulation and the ethical issues and potential ethical issues in the proposed research. The concept of validity in research, as defined in Chapter 2 of this textbook, is a question of how valid the research is, how logical, how truthful, how robust, how sound, how reasonable, how meaningful and how useful. The term reliability in research (see Chapter 2) relates to the degree to which the research can be repeated while obtaining consistent results. Triangulation in research (Chapter 2) involves the use of more than one approach to the research. Chapter 3 of this textbook deals in detail with research ethics.

DEVELOPING A RESEARCH PROPOSAL

Preparation of a research proposal forces the researcher to think critically about each stage of the research process. Vague plans, abstract ideas and sweeping generalizations about problems or procedures must become concrete and precise statements about specific processes and events. Data requirements and research procedures must be specified clearly so others may understand their exact implications. All ambiguities about why and how the research will be conducted must be clarified before the proposal is complete.

The following is a template for the research proposal. The case study at the end of this chapter provides an actual example of a research proposal. You can use both the template and the example as guides to help you write your own research proposal.

The researcher submits the research proposal to the research supervisor or the research clients (in the case of a professional researcher) for acceptance, modification or rejection. The supervisor(s) or the client(s) evaluate the proposed study with particular emphasis on: whether or not it will accomplish what it sets out to accomplish, that is, the aim of the research; whether it will provide useful information; and whether or not it will do so within a reasonable resource budget. Research proposals are almost always revised after the first review.

TEMPLATE FOR A RESEARCH PROPOSAL

This research project is a case study of Illingford High Street with a view to producing a new development plan for that High Street.

Aim and objectives

The aim of this research is to conduct a case study of Illingford High Street with a view to producing a development plan for that High Street. The objectives of the research are as follows:

1. In the first place, Illingford High Street will be mapped, and all of the businesses on the High Street detailed on the map.
2. An analysis will be undertaken of the nature of all of the businesses on the High Street with a view to exploring possible areas for development.
3. The perspectives of the owners and managers of the businesses on the High Street will be gathered in terms of the development needs of the High Street.
4. The perspectives of the local government representatives will be gathered in terms of the development needs of the High Street and in terms of establishing if any development plans already exist for the High Street.

5. The perspectives of the general population of the High Street will be explored in terms of any thought or ideas they might have for the development of the High Street.
6. Finally, following an analysis of the data gathered, a new development plan for the High Street will be developed and presented.

Sample literature review

Read Chapter 6 of this textbook for guidance on writing a sample literature review, and examine the sample literature review in the case study presented at the end of this chapter.

Research methodology

The research methodology proposed for this research project is a case study. In this section of the research proposal, you must detail, explain and justify the research methodology proposed for the research. In this proposal, for example, you would explain what a case study is and why it is the appropriate research methodology for this research project. In order to be able to do this, you have to read about this methodology in the research methodology textbooks. In your writing you have to try to demonstrate your scholarship in

(Continued)

relation to this methodology. In your writing, you apply the theoretical knowledge you have developed from your reading about case study methodology to the research project you are undertaking.

For an example, please read the research methodology section of the case study at the end of this chapter.

When you have fully explained and justified your choice of research methodology, you then explain, outline and justify the population of the study, the sample and the sampling method, as follows:

- Detail, explain and justify the population of the study, if the study has a human population.
- Detail, explain and justify the proposed sample and sampling method, if you propose to engage in sampling in the study.

Data-gathering methods

You then describe and justify the data collection methods to be used in the study. If you are proposing to use a questionnaire, a copy of the questionnaire should be presented in an appendix of the research proposal. Similarly, if you are proposing to use scales, projective techniques, observations, interviews and/or focus groups, copies of these, or the schedules for these (interview schedule and/or focus group schedule), should be presented in the appendices of the research proposal. All of these data-gathering methods are dealt with in detail in the following chapters of this textbook.

Research ethics

In this section you outline the ethical issues in the research that you are proposing, and you explain in detail how you plan to deal with and overcome these issues. Every research project has potential ethical issues, so don't fall into the trap of stating in the research proposal that there are no ethical issues in your research. Such a statement in a research proposal simply serves to establish that the researcher has an underdeveloped understanding of research and research methods, and consequently, that more work is needed.

In this section you should also detail the research ethics framework that you are using for guidance. This might be the research ethics standards of the university/college where you are studying. It might be the research ethics framework of a professional body, for example, The Market Research Society of New Zealand (MRSNZ). You might perhaps write about how you have been guided by both of these. Yallop and Mowatt (2016) studied codes of ethics in practice in marketing and their effect on ethical behaviour among market research practitioners in New Zealand. You should source this article online and read it. Reading the article will give you very many ideas and insights that you will find helpful when considering the ethical issues in your research project. This will be very useful when you are writing about those ethical issues in your research proposal, and indeed in the final written account of your research project, the thesis or research report.

Describe the context for the research

The context for the research would read, for example, as follows:

> This research project is being undertaken for the award of BSc in Management at the University of Newforge. The focus of the research is on Illingford High Street. Illingford is a town in Castleward County. The town has a population of 20 000 people. The High Street in the town has grown a little in the past five years. Five years ago, there were 20 businesses on Illingford High Street. Currently there are 25 businesses on the High Street. While there are signs of growth and development in the town and on the High Street, there is scope for further growth and development. This research project is designed to produce a new development plan for Illingford High Street.

(See also context for the research in the case study detailed at the end of this chapter.)

Finally the rationale for the research

See rationale for the research detailed in the case study outlined at the end of this chapter.

The proposal helps the research supervisor (or the client) decide if the proposed research will accomplish what is desired. If the issue or problem has not been adequately translated into an appropriate research statement/question, a research aim and a set of specific research objectives and a research design, the supervisor's (or the client's) assessment of the proposal will help the researcher in revising the proposal. An effective proposal communicates exactly what research is to be conducted, how it is to be conducted, where or with whom it is to be conducted, why it is to be conducted, and what the research is designed to accomplish.

Table 11.1 presents an overview of some of the basic questions that researchers typically must answer when planning a research design.

Decisions to make	Basic questions
Problem definition	What is the purpose of the study? How much is already known? Is additional background information necessary? Should research be conducted? Can/should a hypothesis be formulated?
Selection of basic research design	What types of questions need to be answered? What is the source of the data? How quickly is the information needed? What research methodology and what data-gathering methods could/should be used?
Selection of sample	Who or what is the source of the data? Can the target population be identified? Is a sample necessary? How accurate must the sample be? Is a probability sample possible/necessary? How large a sample is necessary? How will the sample be selected?
Data gathering	How will the data be gathered? Who will gather the data? How long will data gathering take? How much supervision is needed? What procedures will data collectors need to follow? Will research assistants be used to help gather data? If research assistants are to be used, what training needs to be provided for them? Who will train the research assistants?
Data analysis and evaluation	What is the nature of the data? What questions need to be answered? How will the data be analyzed? Will computerized data analysis be used? If so, what package/packages? What, if any, qualitative data analysis processes should be used? What, if any, statistical tools are appropriate?
Type of report	Who will read the report? What will be the format of the written report?
Overall evaluation	How much will the study cost? Is the time frame acceptable? Is outside help needed? Will this research design attain the stated research aim and objectives? When should the research begin?

Table 11.1 Basic points addressed by research proposals

The proposal as a contract

When the research will be conducted by a consultant or an outside research supplier, the written proposal serves as that person's bid to offer a specific service. Typically, a client solicits several competitive proposals and these written offers help management judge the relative quality of alternative research suppliers.

A wise researcher will not agree to do a research job for which no written proposal exists. The proposal also serves as a contract that describes the product the research user will buy, the final written account of the research project, the research report. Misstatements and faulty communication may occur if the parties rely only on each individual's memory of what occurred at a planning meeting. The proposal creates a record, which greatly reduces conflicts that might arise after the research has been conducted. Both the researcher and the research client should sign the proposal indicating agreement on what will be done.

The proposal then functions as a formal, written statement of agreement between clients and researchers. As such, it protects the researcher from criticisms such as, 'Shouldn't we have had a larger sample?' or 'Why didn't you use a focus group approach?' As a record of the researcher's obligation, the proposal also provides a standard for determining whether the research was conducted as originally planned.

Funded business research generally refers to basic research usually performed by academic researchers and supported by some public or private institution. A very detailed proposal is usually needed for research grants and the agreement for funding is predicated on the research actually delivering the research described in the proposal.

> **funded business research** Refers to basic research usually performed by academic researchers that is financially supported by some public or private institution.

One important comment needs to be made about the nature of research proposals. Not all proposals follow the same format. A researcher can adapt his or her proposal to the target audience or situation. An extremely brief proposal submitted by an organization's internal research department to its own executives bears little resemblance to a complex proposal submitted by a university professor to a government agency to research a basic business issue.

Anticipating outcomes

The proposal describes the data collection, data analysis and so forth, in the future tense. In the report, the actual findings or the results are presented. In this sense, the proposal anticipates the research outcome.

Experienced researchers know that research sometimes fails because the problem–definition process breaks down, or because the research client never truly understood what a research project could or could not do. While it probably seems as though the proposal should make this clear, any shortcoming in the proposal can contribute to a communication failure. Thus, any tool that helps communication become as clear as can be is valued very highly.

Dummy tables

In quantitative research, one such tool that helps to establish exactly what kind of results will be produced by research is the dummy table. **Dummy tables** are placed by quantitative researchers in research proposals and are exact representations of the actual tables that will show results in the final report with one exception: the results presented in dummy table are hypothetical. These tables get their name because the researcher fills in, or 'dummies up', the tables with likely but fictitious data. Dummy tables presented in research proposals are linked directly to the research project's aim and objectives.

> **dummy tables** Tables placed in research proposals that are exact representations of the actual tables that will show results in the final report, with the exception that the results presented in dummy tables are hypothetical (fictitious).

A research analyst can present dummy tables to the decision-maker in the research project and ask, 'Given findings like these, will you be able to make a decision?' If the decision-maker says yes, the proposal may be accepted. However, if the decision-maker cannot see how results like those in the dummy tables will help make the needed decision(s), it may be back to the drawing board with the research proposal.

In other words, the client and researcher need to rethink what research results are necessary to solve the problem. Sometimes, examining the dummy tables may reveal that a key variable is missing or that some dependent variable is really not relevant. In other words, the problem is clarified by deciding on action standards or performance criteria and recognizing the types of research finding necessary to make specific decisions.

While some tables may require additional explanation from the researcher, every effort should be made to allow tables to stand alone and be interpreted by someone who is not an experienced researcher. In other words, the user should be able to understand the results and outline and surmise any implications that the results imply. When the final report is compiled, these tables will be included with the dummy results replaced with the actual research results.

The case study that follows presents Tom's research proposal. Tom is studying part-time for a degree in business. He plans to submit the research proposal to his research supervisor at university. He plans to undertake this research for his degree. Read through Tom's research proposal. Read the aim and the objectives of the research. Read the sample literature review. Read the proposed research methodology. You should use Tom's research proposal as a model for your own research project.

CASE STUDY

Tom's research project (using a documentary analysis research methodology)

Tom is undertaking a part-time degree in business studies. He works full time for a recruitment agency. Tom has decided to focus his research project on the agency's business plans. He has been given access to the most recent business plans of the company, which cover the past three years. Tom intends to use these three business plans as data in his research project. He has decided that documentary analysis is the most appropriate research methodology for his research project. Tom has prepared the following research proposal.

This research project will critically examine the business plans of the past three years of Company A (the name has been changed in order to maintain confidentiality), a recruitment agency with 10 offices throughout England. The methodology to be used in the study is documentary analysis.

Aim and objectives

The aim of the study is to critically examine the business plans of the past three years of Company A.

The objectives of the study are as follows:

- To detail the key elements of the business plans.
- To examine any changes and/or developments in the plans over the three years.
- To highlight any shortcomings in the business plans.
- To highlight any particular strengths in the business plans.
- To determine the effectiveness of the business plans.
- To provide recommendations for the drawing up of business plans in the future.

Sample literature review

There are many different kinds of business plans. Business plans are written for many purposes and for many audiences. The business plans this research is concerned with are business plans written as guides for the management of the business, an SME which is a recruitment agency. Business plans are important. They provide a complete guide to the strategic management of the business. They signal important messages about care, diligence and effective management within the company.

This literature review will focus in particular on business plans for SMEs. The review will consider the determinants of good business plans as they are presented in the literature. The review will focus on strategies for effectiveness in business plans, and will highlight in particular those strategies deemed in the literature to be most effective.

The ultimate purpose of developing a business plan, according to Abrams (2014) and Barringer (2014), is to have a successful business. DeThomas and Derammelaere (2015), see also McKeever (2014) and Vaughan (2016) suggest that the components of a complete business plan should include an industry analysis, a market and sales analysis, a marketing plan, an operating plan, an organization plan and a financial plan. These key components of the business plan have been reduced by Prinson (2013), to three elements: the organizational plan, the marketing plan and the financial plan.

The well-written business plan, according to Prinson (2013) and Vaughan (2016), provides a pathway to profit for any new business. Prinson (2013) states that the business plan, to be of value, must be up-to-date and it must provide detailed information on the company's operations, as well as its projections (see also Johnson, 2003; Blackwell, 2017). According to DeThomas and Derammelaere (2015), the business plan's assumptions, forecasts and projections should be clearly stated and they should be supported with evidence, explanations and detail as to their basis.

In a study of owner–managers of small firms in Sheffield in the UK, Richbell et al. (2006) found a correlation between high levels of education and possession of a business plan. In addition, they found that possession of a business plan had a positive association with a growth orientation. In other words, those business managers with business plans also had an orientation towards growth for their businesses. Raj (2018), explained that by developing a business plan, a business can be prepared for unanticipated events and outcomes, and consequently, be in a position to act proactively instead of reactively to challenges and challenging environments. Business plans, according to Raj (2018), are all about being prepared.

There clearly are advantages in having business plans. However, in order to be effective, business plans must be well-written, comprehensive and thorough, and the assumptions, forecasts and predictions

(Continued)

outlined in business plans must be supported with detailed, accurate and up-to-date data.

The research proposed here is a critical analysis of the business plans for the past three years of Company A.

Research methodology

The proposed methodology for this research project is documentary analysis. Documentary analysis is a relatively unobtrusive form of research (Quinlan, 2011, Quinlan *et al.*, 2015, Bohnsack, 2014), as it does not require engagement with human participants; it is also one that provides opportunities for valuable and often unique insight into organizational policy and practice. Jameson (2009), citing research on Enron and Lehman Brothers, highlighted the utility of documentary analysis in providing important insights into the role that communication plays in major business events. Any document, (Prior, 2011), such as journals, letters, records, can provide the data for a documentary analysis methodology. In this study, the documents to be analyzed are the business plans for the past three years of Company A. The data from the documents will be analyzed using a content analysis approach.

According to Neuman (2014), content analysis is a technique for analyzing the content of texts. The texts in this case are the documents detailed earlier. The content within a content analysis approach to data analysis is any content, texts, images, figures, tables, charts, graphs, etc. in the documents.

The proposed methodology is an appropriate methodology for this research project. The project is designed to critically examine the business plans for the past three years of Company A. Therefore the study is a study of different documents. As this is the case, a documentary analysis methodology is an appropriate methodology.

Context for the research

The research is being undertaken for a BSc in Business Studies. The research will be undertaken in Company A. Company A is the workplace of the researcher. Permission to carry out the research has been formally given by the CEO of the company.

Rationale for the research

The research is being undertaken in order to provide a critical assessment of the business plans over the past three years of Company A. The research will provide insight into the effectiveness of the business plans of Company A. The research will also produce recommendations for the development of business plans in the future for Company A. A copy of the completed thesis will be placed in the University Library and will be available to other researchers. The hope for the research is that it will make a valid contribution to knowledge in relation to the writing of business plans for SMEs.

Question: Based on your reading of the methodology and methods outlined in the research proposal here, what can you say about the epistemological and ontological assumptions underpinning this research? (You may need to read Chapter 4 of this textbook to be able to answer this question.)

END OF CHAPTER QUESTIONS

1 What are the key elements of a research proposal?

2 What constitutes a viable research project?

3 Outline three research statements/questions for three viable research projects.

4 Explain why these research projects are 'viable'.

5 Develop an aim and a series of objectives for each of the research projects, outlined in response to Question 3.

6 Propose a research methodology for each of the three research projects.

7 Explain why these proposed methodologies are appropriate.

8 Explain what is meant by literature in the context of a research project.

9 What is a theoretical framework in the context of a research project?

10 Which framework of the four frameworks approach to the research project provides direction for the theoretical framework?

11 Develop and detail a search strategy for literature for the literature review for your research project.

REFERENCES

Abrams, R. (2014) *The Successful Business Plan, Secrets and Strategies*, California: Planning Shop, Rhonda Inc.

Barringer, B.R. (2014) *Preparing Effective Business Plans: An Entrepreneurial Approach*, Harlow: Pearson Education.

Blackwell, E. (2017) *How to Prepare a Business Plan: Your Guide to Creating an Excellent Strategy, Forecasting your Finances and Producing a Persuasive Plan*, (6th edn), London, New York and New Delhi: Kogan Page.

Bohnsack, R. (2014) *Documentary Method*, in *The SAGE Handbook of Qualitative Data Analysis*, London, California, New Delhi, Singapore: Sage.

Bowen, G.A. (2009) 'Document analysis as a qualitative research method', *Qualitative Research Journal*, 9(2): 27–40.

Denscombe, M. (2017) *The Good Research Guide for Small-scale Social Research Projects* (6th edn), Maidenhead: Open University Press.

DeThomas, A. and Derammelaere, S. (2015) *Writing a Convincing Business Plan* (Barron's Business Library), New York: Barron's Business Library.

Gamble, J.R., Brennan, M. and McAdam, R. (2017) 'A rewarding experience? Exploring how crowdfunding is affecting music industry business models', *Journal of Business Research*, 70: 225–36.

Jameson, D.A. (2009) 'Economic crises and financial disasters: the role of business communication', *Journal of Business Communication*, 46: 499–509.

Johnson, R. (2003) *The Perfect Business Plan: All You Need To Get It Right First Time*, London: Century Business.

Kennelly, M., Corbett, H. and Toohey, K. (2017) 'Leveraging ambitions and barriers: Glasgow universities and the 2014 Commonwealth Games', *Marketing Intelligence & Planning*, 35(6): 822–838.

McCulloch, G. (2004) *Documentary Research in Education, History and the Social Sciences*, Oxon and New York: Routledge.

McKeever, M.P. (2014) *How to Write a Business Plan*, Berkeley, CA: Nolo.

Neuman, W.L. (2014) *Social Research Methods: Qualitative and Quantitative Approaches* (7th edn), England: Pearson Education Ltd.

Nucciareli, A., Lib, F., Fernandes, K.J., Goumagias, N., Cabras, I., Devlin, S., Kudenko, D. and Cowling, P. (2017) 'From value chains to technological platforms: The effects of crowdfunding in the digital games industry', *Journal of Business Research*, 78: 341–352.

Prinson, L. (2013) *Anatomy of a Business Plan: The Step-by-Step Guide to Building a Business and Securing Your Company's Future* (8th edn), Tustin, CA: Out of Your Mind . . . and into the Marketplace Publishing Company.

Prior, L. (ed.) (2011) *Using Documents and Records in Social Research*, SAGE Benchmarks in Social Research Methods.

Quinlan, C. (2011) *Business Research Methods*, Andover: Cengage Learning EMEA.

Quinlan, C., Babin, B., Carr, J., Griffin, M. and Zikmund, W.G. (2015) *Business Research Methods*, Andover: Cengage Learning EMEA.

Raj, A. (2018) '3 New Year's resolutions for small business success in 2018', *CPA Practice Advisor, Ft Atkinson*, 28(1): 20.

Richbell, S.M., Watts, H.D. and Wardle, P. (2006) 'Owner-managers and business planning in the small firm', *International Small Business Journal*, 24(5): 496–514.

Scott, J. (1990) *A Matter of Record: Documentary Sources in Social Research*, Oxford: Blackwell.

US Library of Congress, Guide to business history resources, www.loc.gov/rr/business/guide/guide1/businesshistory/intro.html (Accessed 17.03.2018).

Vaughan, E. (2016) *The Financial Times Essential Guide to Writing a Business Plan: How to Win Backing to Start Up or Grow Your Own Business*, Harlow: Pearson.

World History Sources, *Scholars Analysing Documents*, George Mason University, chnm.gmu.edu/worldhistorysources/whmdocuments.html (Accessed 17.03.2018).

Yallop, A.C. and Mowatt, S. (2016) 'Investigating market research ethics: An empirical study of codes of ethics in practice and their effect on ethical behaviour', *International Journal of Market Research*, 58(3): 381–400.

RECOMMENDED READING

Bell, J. and Waters, S. (2014) *Doing your Research Project: A Guide for First Time Researchers*, Maidenhead: Open University Press.

Collis, J. and Hussey, R. (2013) *Business Research: A Practical Guide for Undergraduate and Postgraduate Students* (4th edn), Basingstoke: Palgrave Macmillan.

Punch, K.F. (2016) *Developing Effective Research Proposals* (3rd edn), London, California, New Delhi, Singapore: Sage.

Robson, C. and McCartan, K. (2016) *Real World Research* (4th edn), John Wiley & Sons Ltd.

Shankar, A., Elliot, R. and Fitchett, J.A. (2009) 'Identity, consumption, and narratives in socialisation', *Marketing Theory*, 9(1): 75–84.

White, B. and Raynor, S. (2000) *Dissertation Skills: For Business and Management Students* (2nd edn), London: Cengage.

PART THREE
DATA GATHERING

CHAPTER 12

FIELDWORK

LEARNING OBJECTIVES

At the end of this chapter, the student should be able to:

- Understand the nature of fieldwork.

- Describe the role of fieldworkers.

- Outline the skills required in fieldwork.

- Describe the activities involved in training and managing fieldworkers.

- Explain how fieldwork supervisors can minimize errors in the field.

RESEARCH SKILLS

At the end of this chapter, the student should, using the exercises on Cengage Brain, be able to:

- Draw up a plan for the fieldwork for a given research project.

- Create a training programme for inexperienced fieldworkers.

REAL WORLD RESEARCH

Software for fieldwork? Ask Askia

Fieldwork can best be described as collecting data 'out there'. Whether it be in a mall or customer service location or even in remote towns and villages, fieldwork requires a researcher to often directly interact with consumers and households to gather specialized or detailed data. Fieldworkers have long used notebooks and clipboards to gather data, capturing information by hand as they interact with each respondent. Once the information is collected, the fieldworker often returns to the research organization to arduously code the handwritten notes into a database or statistical package. New technologies have of course made this process significantly easier.

One example of a company that has specialized in fieldwork software is Askia, (www.askia.com). Askia provides a range of services, including questionnaire design. They provide a range of supports for data gathering, including face-to-face data gathering, telephone and mobile data gathering, and data gathering via the internet.

Askiaface is a mobile data collection solution for face-to-face interviews available across a range of devices such as notebooks, tablets and smartphones. Their system (askia**face**) represents an important advantage to field research, since the interface allows the researcher to include a wide range of data sources in fieldwork, data sources such as images and film, as well as interview data and data from questionnaires. With the askia**face** system, fieldworkers can have their research applications updated without having to return to their research base. Users can use multimedia to present products or services or provide illustrations for the respondent, the participant in the study. Askia have developed client relationships with companies around the world and have grown their customer base each year.

The ability to capture and integrate field notes and information through askia**face** is one example of how technology has assisted fieldwork research. So, if you are challenged by your own fieldwork data needs, perhaps you too should 'Ask Askia'!

INTRODUCTION

Fieldwork, as the name suggests, is work that is conducted in the field. The work in this instance is data gathering and the field is any setting beyond the desk, the library and/or the laboratory in which the required data can be gathered. Fieldwork is one aspect of data gathering. Look again at the model of the research process outlined in Figure 1.1 at the start of Chapter 1. In the model, data gathering comes after research methodology and devise data-gathering methods. When the research methodology has been decided on, outlined and justified, and when the data-gathering methods have been devised and validated, the researcher commences data gathering, and data gathering often involves fieldwork.

DATA NEEDS OF THE RESEARCH PROJECT

Data are the evidence necessary for the research project and they can be found or created in many forms. The data gathered for the research project are used to establish the case of the research, to answer the research question, to explain and illustrate the research statement or to prove/disprove the research hypothesis/hypotheses.

The researcher must decide on where the data for the research project are to be found and then how best to gather the data.

THE NATURE OF FIELDWORK

Fieldwork is the work of the researcher, or research assistant, gathering data in the field. The field in any research project is the setting within which the data are to be found or created. Fieldwork might involve conducting an observation in the field, administering a questionnaire or facilitating a focus group.

A **fieldworker** is a researcher, or a research assistant, working in the field gathering data. A fieldworker may, for example, be a personal interviewer administering a questionnaire door-to-door, a telephone interviewer calling from a central location, an observer counting pedestrians in a shopping mall or another involved in the collection of data and the supervision of that process. The activities fieldworkers perform vary substantially. The supervision of data collection for a mail or postal survey differs from that for an observation study as much as the factory production process for cereal differs from that for a pair of ski boots. Yet, just as quality control is basic to each production operation, the same basic issues arise in the various types of fieldwork. For ease of presentation, this chapter focuses on the interviewing process conducted by personal interviewers. However, many of the issues apply to all fieldworkers, no matter what their specific settings or their data-gathering method(s).

> **fieldworker** An individual who is responsible for gathering data in the field.

Who conducts the fieldwork?

The data-collecting stage is crucial, because the research project is no better than the data collected in the field. The student undertaking a research project for a degree at college or university is generally responsible for every aspect of the research project, including fieldwork. The student must find the data necessary for the research project. This might involve identifying key informants on the research topic, on the phenomenon to be investigated in the research process. Then, when the key informants have been identified, the researcher must decide on the best method to use to gather the required data. The researcher decides on whether to use a questionnaire, or perhaps an interview method, or a focus group method, or some other data-gathering method(s). The data collection method to be used must be capable of providing the required data.

Once the source of the data has been identified, and the data collection method designed for use, the researcher then requests permission to enter the field. If the data are in an organization, a business for example, the researcher must formally write to the organization, introducing themselves and their research and request permission to conduct the research in that organization. The researcher explains what it is that the research is designed to accomplish. S/he explains what data-gathering methods are being proposed and who in the organization they wish to invite to participate in the study. This process of entering the field is very delicate and must be properly managed. The researcher must have access to the required data and so s/he must have access to the field. The researcher may have to develop a relationship with one or more gatekeepers in the field in order to enter the field. The role of gatekeepers in research is explained in Chapter 1 of this textbook.

The researcher must manage relationships in the field to maintain the level of access necessary to stay in the field and to gather the required data. In the work of developing, building and maintaining relationships, the researcher must establish the value of the research, the need for the research and the contribution that the research will make to knowledge. The researcher must establish the ethical standards of both the research and the researcher, to create and maintain the level of trust needed in order to be able to carry out the fieldwork.

When leaving the field, the researcher ensures that the good relationships established throughout the fieldwork are maintained. If they are not, the professional standards of the researcher and the research, and the institution (college or university or work organization) with which the researcher is affiliated may be called into question. It might also happen that permission to use the data gathered is withdrawn. It could happen that the field might be closed to the researcher in the future. For all of these reasons, and for the sake of proper ethical standards and professionalism, the researcher needs to leave the field on good terms with all stakeholders and gatekeepers.

The process of interviewing for research is described in detail by de Wit (2013), in a very interesting journal article about interview techniques learned while conducting a study of the topic of sense of place on the American High Plains. If you read this journal article, you will learn a great deal about the process of interviewing for a research project.

Contract fieldworkers

Among professional researchers, the actual data collection process is rarely carried out by the person who designs the research. Fieldworkers are generally hired to do this work. These fieldworkers have to be trained in the fieldwork process, the process to be used in the research project for which they have been hired. They have to be managed throughout the fieldwork process, and the research administrator/manager is generally responsible for this.

Much fieldwork is conducted by research suppliers who specialize in data collection. For example, a company may subcontract the fieldwork to a **field interviewing service**. Various field interviewing services and full-service research agencies perform all manner of personal surveys including central location telephone interviewing, mall/street intercept interviews and other forms of fieldwork for a fee. These agencies typically employ field supervisors who train and monitor interviewers, gather and sort completed questionnaires in the field and telephone or recontact respondents to confirm that interviews have indeed been conducted.

> **field interviewing service** A research supplier that specializes in gathering data.

Whether the research administrator hires an **in-house interviewer** or selects a field interviewing service, fieldworkers should ideally meet certain job requirements. Although the job requirements for different types of research vary, as a rule fieldworkers should be in general good health, they should be friendly and professional and appropriately dressed. An essential part of the interviewing process is establishing rapport with the respondent. An ability to engage participants in the fieldwork, to establish a rapport with them, will help fieldworkers ensure respondents' full cooperation.

> **in-house interviewer** A fieldworker who is employed by the company conducting the research.

Researcher bias may occur if the fieldworker's clothing or physical appearance appears strange or unusual to the interviewees. So, for example, in ethnographic research, the interviewer should dress to blend in with the group being studied and if jeans and a T-shirt are the appropriate dress, then that is what the interviewer should wear.

Fieldworkers generally are paid hourly rates or per interview conducted. Often fieldworkers are part-time workers from a variety of backgrounds, for example, homemakers, graduate students and schoolteachers. Some research projects require special knowledge or skills, such as familiarity with the topic they are asking about. For example, in a survey investigating whether health education improves the likelihood that people who have suffered a stroke will quit smoking, the researchers used trained nurses to administer questionnaires to patients that included a section on each patient's medical history. Taking an accurate medical history is a skill that requires more training than most fieldworkers are likely to have.

In-house training for inexperienced interviewers

After personnel are recruited and selected, they must be trained. Suppose a woman who has just sent her youngest child off to school decides to seek a part-time job as a professional interviewer. The training she will receive after being hired may vary from virtually no training to an extensive, multiple-day programme if she is selected by one of the larger research companies. Almost always, trainees will receive a **briefing session** on the particular research project being undertaken.

> **briefing session** A training session to ensure that each interviewer is provided with common information.

The core objective of training is to ensure that each respondent or participant in the study is provided with common information and the data collection instrument, for example, the questionnaire or interview schedule, is administered in a uniform fashion by all fieldworkers. If the data are collected in a uniform manner from all respondents, the training session will have succeeded.

More extensive training programmes are likely to cover the following topics:

- How to make initial contact with the respondent and secure the interview.
- How to ask questions.
- How to probe.
- How to record responses.
- How to end the interview.

Typically in training, recruits engage in role-playing activities and record answers on a practice questionnaire during a simulated training interview.

Making initial contact and securing the interview
Personal interviews

Personal interviewers may carry a letter of identification or an ID card to indicate that the study is a bona fide research project and not a sales pitch. Interviewers are trained to make appropriate opening remarks that will convince the respondent that his or her participation is important, as in the following example.

RESEARCH IN PRACTICE

Interviewing in telephone surveys

Along with the big-name national and international research firms such as Yankelovich, Nielsen and Gallup, many smaller research companies offer interviewing and other services to clients in their city or region. Such companies serve local organizations including businesses, banks and hospitals. These companies typically provide a range of research services including conducting focus groups and telephone surveys.

In telephone surveys, one of the most significant challenges of an interviewer's job is simply to keep the respondent from hanging up. In the first few seconds of the phone call, fieldworkers quickly reassure the person that the call is for research, not to sell them something. After that, retaining respondents becomes a matter of reinforcing that they are 'doing a good service [because] it's for research'.

Telephone interviewers often recruit people to participate in focus groups. This can be quite hard work. Typically, a company needs four telephone interviewers to spend about three hours just to fill a 12-person focus group. Finding willing individuals who meet the project's specifications may require up to 600 phone calls! Each call might begin as follows:

Good afternoon, my name is ___, and I'm with [insert name of firm], an international business research company. Today, we are conducting a survey concerning ___. I would like to get a few of your ideas. It will take [insert accurate time estimate] minutes.

Telephone interviews

For the initial contact in a telephone interview, the introduction might be something like this:

> *Hello, my name is ___. I am not trying to sell anything. I'm calling from [insert name of firm] in Liverpool, UK. We are seeking your opinions on some important matters and it will only take [insert accurate time estimate] minutes of your time.*

Giving the interviewer's name personalizes the call. The name of the research agency is used to underline the caller's trustworthiness. The respondent must be given an accurate estimate of the time it will take to participate in the interview. If someone is told that only three minutes will be required for participation and the interview proceeds to five minutes or more, the respondent may well hang up before completing the interview. Providing an accurate estimate of the time not only helps secure participation, it is also the ethically correct thing to do.

Internet surveys

A similar approach should be used for an internet survey. Potential respondents should receive an email briefly explaining the project and requesting participation, as in the following example:

> *We are researchers working for [insert name of organization]. We are contacting you because of your interest in [subject matter inserted here]. We would like to invite you to participate in a survey that asks your opinion on matters related to [subject matter inserted here]. In return for your participation, we will [insert incentive here]. To participate, click on this URL: www.clickhere.com*

Gaining participation

The Survey Research Center at the University of Michigan www.src.isr.umich.edu/ once had an interviewer manual that suggested avoiding questions that ask permission for the interview, such as 'May I come in?' and 'Would you mind answering some questions?' Instead of asking permission, the researcher should introduce themselves and the research in as positive and as engaging a manner as possible.

Some people will refuse to participate and some people will object to being interviewed. Interviewers should be instructed on handling such objections. For example, if the respondent says, 'I'm too busy right now', the interviewer might be instructed to respond, 'Will you be in at four o'clock this afternoon? I would be happy to schedule a time with you.'

In some cases, client companies will not wish to offend any individual. If this is the case, the interviewer will be instructed in response to resistance or an outright refusal to merely say, 'Thank you for your time.'

The **foot-in-the-door compliance technique** and the **door-in-the-face compliance technique** can be useful in some circumstances in securing interviews. Foot-in-the-door theory attempts to explain compliance with a large or difficult task on the basis of respondents' earlier compliance with a smaller initial request. One experiment has shown that compliance with a minor telephone interview (that is, a small request that few people refuse) will lead to greater compliance with a second, larger request to fill out a long mail questionnaire. An interviewer employing door-in-the-face technique begins by making a substantial initial request that most people will reject (that is, slams the door in his or her face). When this happens, the interviewer can then request a smaller favour, such as asking a respondent to participate in a 'short' survey of a few questions.

> **foot-in-the-door compliance technique** A technique for obtaining a high response rate, in which compliance with a large or difficult task is induced by first obtaining the respondent's compliance with a smaller request.
>
> **door-in-the-face compliance technique** A two-step process for securing a high response rate. In step 1, an initial request, so large that nearly everyone refuses it, is made. Next, a second request is made for a smaller favour; respondents are expected to comply with this more reasonable request.

This technique does present an ethical issue if the respondent is deceived by the first request, or indeed in any other way. Thus, the initial request should also be a legitimate request.

Asking the questions

The purpose of an interview is, of course, to ask questions and record a respondent's answers, or, in qualitative interviewing, to introduce a topic or issue and invite the respondent to outline their feelings, beliefs and/or experiences in relation to it. Training in the art of interviewing can be extremely beneficial, because interviewer bias can be a source of considerable error in research.

In interviewing, there are five major rules:

1. Ask questions, or introduce the issues, exactly as they are worded in the questionnaire or interview schedule.
2. Read each question/statement very carefully and clearly.
3. Ask the questions, introduce the issues in the specified order.
4. If using a questionnaire, ask every question specified in the questionnaire; if using an interview schedule, introduce every issue in the schedule.
5. Repeat any questions or statements of issues that are misunderstood or misinterpreted.

Interviewers are generally trained to know these rules, but when working in the field, many do not follow these procedures exactly. Inexperienced interviewers may not understand the importance of strict adherence to the instructions. Even professional interviewers can develop a tendency to take shortcuts when the task becomes monotonous.

Interviewers may, for example, shorten questions or rephrase unconsciously when they rely on their memory of the question, rather than reading the question as it is worded. Even the slightest change in wording may inject some bias into a study. By reading the question, the interviewer may be reminded to concentrate on avoiding slight variations in tone of voice on particular words or phrases.

If respondents do not understand a question or an issue, they usually will ask for some clarification. The recommended procedure is to repeat the question/issue. If the person does not understand a word or a term or a phrase in the question, the interviewer should respond with a standard description. If the respondent still does not understand, interviewers are tempted to supply their own personal definitions and ad lib clarifications and they may include words that are not free from bias.

One reason interviewers sometimes do this is that field supervisors tend to reward people for submitting completed interviews and they tend to be less tolerant of interviewers who leave questions blank because of alleged misunderstandings. However, researchers should very strictly stay with a standardized definition when clarification is needed in order to minimize bias.

Often, respondents volunteer information relevant to a question or issue that is supposed to arise at a later point in the interview. In this situation, the response should be recorded under the question/issue that deals specifically with that subject. Then, rather than skip the question that was answered or the issue discussed out of sequence, the interviewer should be trained to say something like, 'We have briefly discussed this, but let me ask you . . .'. By asking every question, or raising every issue for discussion, the interviewer can be sure that complete answers are recorded. Omission errors can occur when questions and issues are raised and answered/discussed out of sequence.

THE VALUE OF GOOD RESEARCH

Why is 'why' important?

The use of field interviews to answer specific research questions has many logistic and quality management challenges, but in many ways field interviews are unique in the ability to really capture what a respondent is thinking about. This is due to the very nature of the field interview – the ability to follow up and probe deeper on a respondent's initial response. A key way that interviewers can capture this is through asking 'why' follow-up questions.

Calo Research Services makes asking 'why' its business. Whether it is for consumer research or for managerial strategy, Calo Research Services (www.caloresearch.com) has adopted a philosophy from the top down that stresses the importance of asking why. For example, a company that was a participant in a professional trade show determined that capturing the number of visitors to their booth would help them evaluate the success of their presentation. However, it became clear that counting visitors does not really determine success – visitors can stop by for any number of reasons – the real question is why they stopped by the booth.

Calo assisted the company by conducting a short interview that asked why the visitor to the booth was there and what got their attention when they first appeared. This allowed the company to understand what was really connecting visitors to their booth, and allowed them to build on what was successful for their other presentations around the country.

The face-to-face interview is one of the best tools that researchers have when fieldwork calls for in-depth data from respondents (or participants) on the phenomenon being investigated. The face-to-face interview can be used to probe responses, to ask respondents why, why they have responded to a question or issue as they have.

Probing when no response or an incomplete response is given

Sometimes an interviewer needs to probe, to encourage a response or a more elaborate response. Similar to the approach for qualitative interviews discussed in Chapter 8, interviewers should be provided with instructions on how to probe when respondents give no answer, incomplete answers, or answers that require clarification. As demonstrated in the Value of Good Research box, probing questions can help in the clarification of a question within the interview process. By asking 'why' carefully, the researcher can gain additional insight into the thoughts, attitudes and behaviours of the respondent.

First, probing is necessary when a respondent must be motivated to expand on, clarify, explain or complete his or her answer. Interviewers must encourage respondents to clarify or expand on answers by providing a stimulus that will not suggest their own ideas or attitudes. An ability to probe with neutral stimuli is a mark of an experienced and effective interviewer.

Second, probing may be necessary when a respondent begins to ramble or lose track. In such cases, a respondent must be led to focus on the specific content of the interview and to avoid irrelevant and unnecessary information.

Interviewers have several possible probing tactics to choose from, depending on the situation:

- Repeating the question. When the respondent remains completely silent, s/he may not have understood the question or they may not have decided how to answer it. Mere repetition may encourage the respondent to answer in such cases. For example, if the question is, 'What do you like about apple pie?' and the respondent does not answer, the interviewer may probe: 'Just to check, what is it that you like about apple pie?'
- Using a silent probe. If the interviewer believes that the respondent has more to say, a silent probe – that is, an expectant pause, an encouraging smile or nod of the head – may motivate the respondent to gather his or her thoughts and give a complete response.
- Repeating the respondent's reply. As the interviewer records the response, they may repeat the respondent's reply verbatim. This may stimulate the respondent to expand on the answer.
- Asking a neutral question. Asking a neutral question may specifically indicate the type of information that the interviewer is seeking. For example, if the interviewer believes that the respondent's motives should be clarified, they might say 'Tell me more about that', or, 'Tell me about this feeling'. If the interviewer feels that there is a need to clarify a word or phrase, s/he might say, 'What do you mean by ___?' Table 12.1 gives some examples of common interview probes.

Interviewer's probe
What do you mean by . . .?
Can you tell me more about . . .?
Could you provide an example of . . .?
I am not sure I understand. Can you be more specific about . . .?
What exactly do you mean by . . .?
It seems that you are saying . . . Is that correct?
How would you feel if . . .?
Why do you feel that way?
Why is that important?
What would that look/feel/taste/sound/smell like?
What would your friends say about . . .?
How does this differ from . . .?
Is there anything else you want to tell me about that?

Table 12.1 Commonly used probes

The purpose of asking questions as probes is to encourage responses. Such probes should be neutral and not leading. Probes may be general (such as 'Anything else?') or they may be questions specifically designed by the interviewer to clarify a particular statement by the respondent.

Recording the responses

An analyst who fails to instruct fieldworkers in the techniques of properly recording respondent answers rarely forgets to do so a second time. Although recording an answer seems extremely simple, mistakes can occur in this phase of the research. Each fieldworker should use the same recording process.

Rules for recording responses vary with different interviews. A general rule however, with a questionnaire, is to place a check mark in the box that correctly reflects the respondent's answer.

All too often, for example, interviewers do not bother recording the answer to a filter question because they believe the subsequent answer will make the answer to the filter question obvious. However, editors and coders do not know how, or even if, the respondent actually answered a question.

The general instruction for recording responses to open-ended questions is to record the response verbatim, a task that is difficult for most people. Inexperienced interviewers should be given an opportunity to practice verbatim recording of answers before being sent into the field. Some suggestions for recording open-ended answers include:

- Record responses during the interview.
- Use the respondent's own words.
- Do not summarize or paraphrase the respondent's answer.
- Include everything that pertains to the question objectives.
- Include all of your probes.

Especially for sensitive topics, decisions about how to record responses may be more difficult than these guidelines suggest.

In a survey that included open-ended questions about sexual behaviour, researchers found that some decisions about how to record answers affected the way responses were later interpreted. For example, they defined notation that would indicate pauses and vocal emphasis, which helped researchers identify answers that involved confusion or strong emotions. However, recording every non-verbal behaviour led researchers to speculate about whether one respondent was crying

REAL WORLD RESEARCH

Probing for deeper meaning at Olson Zaltman Associates

At Olson Zaltman Associates (olsonzaltman.com/) highly trained interviewers probe for the deeper thinking that underlies attitudes toward brands or product categories. One of the research firm's methods is called ZMET (for Zaltman Metaphor Elicitation Technique). According to the firm's website, ZMET 'qualitatively elicits conscious and unconscious thoughts by exploring people's non-literal or metaphoric expressions'. Interviewers using the technique begin by asking each respondent to come to a one-on-one interview, bringing along a set of photographs, perhaps eight to ten photographs, related to their thoughts and feelings about the interview's topic. The interviewer uses the photos as a starting point for the interviews. The photographs in the data-gathering exercise provide clues about the associations the person makes with the product or brand.

A typical interview lasts two hours. The interviewer's challenge is to ask questions that reveal what is behind the selection of the photographs without actually suggesting the interviewer's own ideas. The interviewer begins by asking the respondent to describe the topic-related thoughts and feelings that each picture illustrates. The interviewer then probes to uncover a deeper meaning by asking the respondent to elaborate on the initial statements. This process requires well developed interview skills, and many of the interviewers working at Olsen Zaltman Associates will have qualifications in fields such as psychotherapy or sociology. Finally, the respondent may work with an associate to create a computerized collage that illustrates the respondent's thoughts and feelings about the topic.

Researchers then use computer software to identify response patterns that suggest 'metaphors' for the product – a general theme that describes respondents' attitudes. In a study of air fresheners, people want to avoid having odours in their home that alienate them from visitors (an underlying desire for connection with others); they also want an air freshener to seem natural, rather than masking something (an underlying desire to evoke nature). Based on these ideas, the client developed Breeze air freshener. In another project, Motorola hired Olson Zaltman to help it market a high-tech security system. Many research participants brought in images of dogs, signifying the protection that dogs give their owners. As a result, Motorola avoided brand names emphasizing technology, instead they called the new system the Watchdog.

The ZMET approach has proven to be useful across a wide variety of situations and cultures. In fact, Olson Zaltman Associates have conducted ZMET studies in many different languages in countries all around the world.

or using drugs (he had a cold). Likewise, when transcriptions recorded the respondent's exact words and pronunciation, including dialects and mistakes in grammar and word usage, researchers were tempted to speculate about demographic characteristics, such as a speaker's educational level. As the researchers evaluated the effects of these decisions about how to record answers, they concluded that such decisions should be made very carefully, and in light of the research objectives.

Terminating the interview

The final aspect of training is to instruct interviewers on how to close the interview. Fieldworkers should wait to close the interview until they have secured all pertinent information. The interviewer who departs hastily will be unable to record the spontaneous comments respondents sometimes offer after all formal questions have been asked. Merely recording one of these comments may result in a new idea or creative interpretation of the results. Avoiding hasty departures is also a matter of courtesy. The fieldworker should also answer any respondent questions concerning the nature and purpose of the study to the best of their ability.

Finally, it is extremely important to thank the respondent for his or her time and cooperation. Not only is this the polite thing to do, but the fieldworker may be required to re-interview the respondent at some future time. So, the respondent should be left with a positive feeling about having cooperated in a worthwhile operation.

Principles of good interviewing

One of the top research organizations in the USA is Yankelovich Partners. One reason for its success is its careful attention to fieldwork. This section presents the organization's principles of good interviewing. These principles apply no matter what the nature of the specific data-gathering exercise; they are universal and represent the essence of sound data collection for business research purposes. For clarity, they have been divided into two categories: the basics (the interviewing point of view) and required practices (standard inquiry premises and procedures).

The basics

Interviewing is a skilled occupation and not everyone can do it – even fewer can do it extremely well. A good interviewer observes the following basic principles:

1. Have integrity and be honest. This is the cornerstone of all professional inquiry, all research, regardless of its purpose.
2. Have patience and tact. Interviewers ask for information from people they do not know. Thus, all the rules of human relations that apply to inquiry situations – patience, tact and courtesy – apply even more to interviewing. You should at all times follow the standard business conventions that control communications and contact.
3. Pay attention to accuracy and detail. Among the greatest interviewing 'sins' are inaccuracy and superficiality, for the professional analyst can misunderstand, and in turn mislead, a client. A good rule to follow is not to record a response unless you fully understand it yourself. Probe for clarification and for rich, full answers. Record responses verbatim: never assume you know what a respondent is thinking or jump to conclusions as to what s/he might have said but did not.
4. Exhibit a real interest in the inquiry at hand, but keep your own opinions to yourself. Impartiality is imperative – if your opinions were wanted, you would be asked for them. It is the opinions of the respondent that matter. You are an asker and a recorder of other people's opinions, not a contributor to the study data. (That is, unless you are engaging in co-constructed fieldwork, where the researcher and the participant in the study together co-construct data.)
5. Be a good listener. Too many interviewers talk too much, wasting time when respondents could be supplying more pertinent facts or opinions on the study topic.
6. Keep the inquiry and respondents' responses confidential. Do not discuss the studies you are doing with relatives, friends or associates; it is unacceptable to both the research agency and its clients. Above all, never quote one respondent's opinion to another – that is the greatest violation of privacy.
7. Respect others' rights. Business research depends on people's willingness to provide information. In obtaining this information, you must follow a happy medium path, between the undesirable extremes of failure to get the information, and unnecessary coercion of respondents or potential respondents to provide information. This middle road is one of clear explanation, friendliness and courtesy, offered in an interested and persuasive tone. Gently impress on prospective respondents that their cooperation is important, valuable and valued.

Required practices

Here are practical rules of research inquiry that should be followed and used without exception:

1. Complete the number of interviews according to the sampling plan assigned to you. Both are calculated precisely so that when responses are returned, the study will benefit from having available the amount and type of data or information originally specified.

2. Follow the directions provided. Remember that many other interviewers may be working on the same study in other places. Lack of uniformity in procedure can spell disaster for later analysis. Each direction has a purpose, even though it may not be completely evident to you.

3. Make every effort to keep timetables and schedules. Comments from research managers regarding schedules can range from 'hurry up' to 'there should be plenty of time'. Whatever the comment, you should be as responsive as possible. If you foresee problems, call and explain.

4. Keep control of each interview you do. It is up to you to determine the pace of a particular interview, keeping several points in mind:

   a. There is an established average length of an interview from the time you start to talk to the respondent to the time you finish. It represents a guideline, but some interviews will be shorter and some longer.

   b. Always get the whole story from a respondent, and write it all down in the respondent's own words. You may be able to audio record the interview. If so, the audio recording will have to be transcribed, that is typed up. The transcription then becomes the data to be analyzed. Also, remember to keep the interview focused on the subject at hand and prevent it from wandering off into unnecessary small talk.

   c. Avoid offending the respondent by being too talkative yourself. Avoid humour. People's views of what is funny vary greatly, and what might amuse you might perhaps be perceived as an affront or even an insult by someone else. In any case, research is serious business, and a certain degree of gravitas is necessary in professionalism.

5. Complete the questionnaires meticulously:

   a. Follow exactly all instructions that appear directly on the questionnaire. Before you start interviewing, learn what these instructions direct you to do.

   b. Ask the questions from the first to the last in the exact numerical order (unless directed to do otherwise in some particular instances). Much thought and effort go into determining the order of the questioning to avoid bias or to set the stage for subsequent questions.

   c. Ask each question exactly as it is written. The cost of not doing so is lack of uniformity; the research agency would never know whether all respondents were replying to the same question or replying to 50 different interviewers' interpretations of the question.

   d. Never leave a question blank. It will be difficult to tell whether you failed to ask it, whether the respondent could not answer it because of lack of knowledge or certainty, or whether the respondent refused to answer it for personal reasons. If none of the answer categories provided proves suitable, write in what the respondent said, in his or her own words.

   e. Use all the props provided to aid both interviewers and respondents: show cards, pictures, descriptions, sheets of questions for the respondents to answer themselves, and so on. All have a specific interview purpose. Keys to when and how to use them appear on the questionnaire at the point at which they are to be used.

6. Check over each questionnaire you have completed. This is best done directly after it has been completed. If you find something you did wrong or omitted, correct it. Often you can call a respondent back, admit you missed something (or are unclear about a particular response) and then straighten out the difficulty.

7. Compare your sample execution and assigned quota with the total number of questionnaires you have completed. Do not consider your assignment finished until you have done this.

8. Clear up any questions with the research agency. At the start of an assignment or after you have begun, if you have questions for which you can find no explanatory instructions, call the agency to get the matter clarified.

Fieldwork management

Research managers preparing for the fieldwork stage should consider the meaning of the following stanza from Robert Burns' poem 'To a Mouse':

> The best laid schemes o' mice and men
> Gang aft a-gley;
> An' lea'e us nought but grief and pain,
> For promis'd joy.

In other words, the best plans of mice and men – as well as business researchers – may go astray. An excellent research plan may get sidetracked if the fieldwork is performed incorrectly. A proper research design will minimize numerous sources of error, but careful execution of the fieldwork is necessary to produce results without substantial error. For these reasons, fieldwork management is an essential part of the research process.

Fieldwork managers select, train, supervise and manage fieldworkers. Our discussion of fieldwork principles mentioned selection and training. This section investigates the tasks of the fieldwork managers in greater detail.

Briefing session for experienced interviewers

Whether interviewers have just completed their training in fundamentals or are already experienced, they always need to be informed about the individual project. Both experienced and inexperienced fieldworkers must be briefed on the background of the sponsoring organization, broad research focus, sampling techniques, asking of questions, callback procedures and other matters specific to the particular project.

If there are any special instructions – for example, about using show cards or video equipment or restricted interviewing times – they should also be covered during the training session. Instructions for handling certain key questions are always important. For example, the following fieldworker instructions appeared in a questionnaire designed for institutional investors who make buy-and-sell decisions about stocks for banks, pension funds, and so on:

Questions 13a, 13b
These questions will provide verbatim comments for the report to the client. Probe for more than one- or two-word answers and record verbatim. Particularly, probe for more information when respondent gives a general answer – e.g., 'Poor management', 'It's in a good industry'. Ask, 'In what ways is management poor?' 'What's good about the industry?' And so on.

A training session for experienced interviewers might go something like this: all interviewers report to the central office, there they receive a brief explanation of the firm's background and the general aims of the study. Interviewers are provided with minimal information about the purpose of the study to ensure that they will not transmit any preconceived notions to respondents. For example, in a survey about the banks in a community, the interviewers would be told that the research is a banking study but not the name of the sponsoring bank. To train the interviewers in the use of the interview schedule or the questionnaire, a field supervisor conducts an interview with another field supervisor who acts as a respondent. The trainees observe the interviewing process, after which they each interview and record the responses of another field supervisor who acts as a respondent. After the practice interview, the trainees receive additional instructions.

Training to avoid procedural errors in sample selection

The briefing session also covers the sampling procedure. A number of research projects allow the interviewer to be at least partially responsible for selecting the sample. These sampling methods offer the potential for selection bias. For example, in probability sampling in which every nth house is selected, an example of systematic sampling, the fieldworker uses his or her discretion in identifying housing units. Avoiding selection bias may be more difficult than it sounds. For example, in an old, exclusive neighbourhood, a mansion's coach house or servants' quarters may have been converted into an apartment that should be identified as a housing unit. This type of dwelling and other unusual housing units (river barges, lake cottages, boarding houses) may be overlooked, giving rise to selection error. Errors may also occur in the selection of random-digit dialling samples. Considerable effort should be expended in training and supervisory control to minimize these errors.

Supervision of fieldworkers

Although briefing and training interviewers will minimize the probability of their interviewing the wrong households or asking biased questions, there is still considerable potential for errors in the field. Direct supervision of face-to-face interviewers, telephone interviewers and other fieldworkers is often necessary to ensure that the techniques communicated in the training sessions are implemented in the field.

Total quality management for interviewing

Interviewers and their supervisors can improve the process of data collection to minimize errors. One popular method, total quality management (TQM), seeks continuous improvement by getting everyone involved in measuring performance and looking for ways to improve processes:

- Measure response rates and improve interviewer training to improve response rates. To do this, researchers must describe the procedure for contacting subjects and consider alternatives, such as letters of introduction, the timing of contacts, and the number of attempts to make before a subject is classified as a non-respondent. Interviewers should be taught about the impact on research quality of interviewing only the people who are easiest to contact and they should be trained to, gently, persuade people to participate.

- Measure defects in terms of measurement errors and improve interviewer techniques and respondent behaviour. Researchers should measure the pattern of response rates by interviewer, looking for interviewer variance (a tendency for different interviewers to obtain different answers). To measure respondent behaviour, researchers can ask interviewers for objective information such as the presence of a third person, as well as for an evaluation of each interview's success; the data may signal respondent behaviours with a potential to bias responses from certain segments.

- Measure the interview process, including the training provided, the application of principles from training and feedback about the interviewer. The training should be aimed at specific, measurable objectives, with a plan for measuring whether the interviewers' performance shows that training objectives were met. For a standardized interview, one way to tell whether the interviews are following the guidelines is to measure whether they all last about the same amount of time. Verification by re-interviewing a subsample provides insight into the accuracy of recording responses. Where variances occur, the supervisor and interviewers should investigate the cause, looking for ways to improve training and interviewing.

Supervision of interviewers, like other forms of supervision, refers to controlling the efforts of workers. Field supervision of interviewers requires checking to see that field procedures are being properly followed. A supervisor checks field operations to ensure that the interviewing schedule is being met. Supervisors collect the questionnaires or other data-gathering measures daily and check them for completeness and legibility. If problems arise, supervisors discuss these problems with the fieldworkers, providing guidance and further training when necessary.

As seen in the Value of Good Research box earlier, quality control is important. In addition to quality control, continual training may be provided. For example, if a telephone supervisor notices that interviewers are allowing the phone to ring more than ten times before considering the call a 'no answer', the supervisor can instruct interviewers not to do so, as the person who eventually answers is likely to be annoyed.

Sampling verification

Another important job of a supervisor is to verify that interviews are being conducted according to the sampling plan rather than with the sampling units most accessible to the interviewer. An interviewer might be tempted to go to the household next door for an interview rather than record the sampling unit as not at home, which would require a callback. Carefully recording the number of completed interviews will help ensure that the sampling procedure is being properly conducted. Supervisors are responsible for motivating interviewers to follow the sampling plan carefully.

Closer supervision of the interviewing procedure can occur in central location telephone interviewing. Supervisors may, using telephone technology, be able to listen in on the actual interview.

Supervisors must also make sure that the right people within the household or sampling unit are being contacted. One research project for a children's cereal required that several products be placed in the home and that children record their daily consumption and reactions to each cereal in a diary. Although the interviewers were supposed to contact the children to remind them to fill out the diaries, a field supervisor observed that in almost half the cases the mothers were filling out the diaries after the children left for school because their children had not done so. The novelty of the research project had worn off after a few days; eating a specific cereal each day was no longer fun after the first few times and the children had stopped keeping the diaries. Similar issues with data gathering can occur with any research participants.

Interviewer cheating

The most blatant form of **interviewer cheating** occurs when an interviewer falsifies interviews, merely filling in fake answers rather than contacting respondents. This is sometimes referred to as **curbstoning**. Although this situation does occur, it is not common and if the job of interviewer selection has been properly accomplished, it should not happen. However, less obvious forms of interviewer cheating occur with greater frequency. Interviewers often consider quota sampling to be time-consuming, so an interviewer may stretch the requirements a bit to obtain seemingly qualified respondents. In the interviewer's eyes, a young-looking 36-year-old may be the same as a 29-year-old who fits the quota requirement; checking off the under-30 category thus is not *really* cheating. Consider the fieldworker who must select only heavy users of a certain brand of hand lotion that the client says is used by 15 per cent of the population. If the fieldworker finds that only 3 per cent qualify as heavy users, they may be tempted to interview an occasional user to stretch the quota somewhat. In research, any cheating is unethical.

> **interviewer cheating** The practice by fieldworkers of filling in fake answers or falsifying interviews.
>
> **curbstoning** A form of interviewer cheating in which an interviewer makes up the responses instead of conducting an actual interview.

An interviewer may fake part of a questionnaire to make it acceptable to the field supervisor. In a survey on automobile satellite radio systems, suppose an interviewer is requested to ask for five reasons why consumers have purchased this product. If s/he finds that people typically give two or perhaps three reasons and even with extensive probing cannot think of five reasons, the interviewer might be tempted to cheat. Rather than have the supervisor think s/he was being lazy, the interviewer may fill in five reasons based on past interviews. It would, of course, be a very significant finding of the research if consumers could think of only two or three reasons. It might perhaps indicate a need for a new, more thorough, marketing and communications campaign in relation to the product and its features.

In other cases, the interviewer may cut corners to save time and energy. Interviewers may also fake answers when they find questions embarrassing or troublesome to ask because of sensitive subjects. Thus, the interviewer may complete most of the questionnaire but leave out a question or two because they found it troublesome. For example, in a survey among physicians, an interviewer might find questions about artificial insemination donor programmes embarrassing, skip these questions and fill in the gaps later.

These examples are all, to some degree, intentional forms of interviewer cheating. What appears to be interviewer cheating can also be unintentional, most often a result of improper training or perhaps fieldworker inexperience. A fieldworker who does not understand the instructions may skip or miss a portion of the questionnaire or interview schedule, or may misuse or underuse some other aspect or element of the data-gathering procedure.

Fieldworkers are often instructed to conclude each interview with a comment such as, 'Thank you for your time. By the way, my supervisor may call you to ask about my work. Please say whatever you wish.' This or a similar statement not only increases the number of respondents willing to cooperate with the verification process but also helps to assure the quality of fieldwork.

Verification by re-interviewing

Supervision for quality control attempts to ensure that interviewers are following the sampling procedure and to detect falsification of interviews. Supervisors verify approximately 10–15 per cent of the interviews by re-interviewing. Normally the interview is not repeated; rather, supervisors recontact respondents and ask about the length of the interview and their reactions to the interviewer; then they collect basic demographic data to check for interviewer cheating. Such **verification** does not detect the more subtle form of cheating in which only portions of the interview have been falsified. A validation check may simply point out that an interviewer contacted the proper household but interviewed the wrong individual in that household – which, of course, can be a serious error.

> **verification** Quality control procedures in fieldwork intended to ensure that interviewers are following the sampling procedures and to determine whether interviewers are cheating.

CASE STUDY

The Thomas and Dorothy Leavey Library

The library serves the students and faculty of the University of Southern California. Staff at the busy library wanted to know more about their users, what library resources they find helpful, and whether they are satisfied with the library's services. However, like many libraries, this organization had a tiny budget for research. As a result, the goal was to conduct exploratory research while spending less than $250.

Staff members studied surveys conducted by other libraries to get ideas for a one-page printed questionnaire. Colleagues on the library staff provided suggestions and a few undergraduates tested the survey for clarity. Next, the survey schedule or time frame was chosen: 36 continuous hours that did not conflict with any holidays or exams.

The fieldwork involved setting up and staffing a table offering the survey and then inviting library patrons to stop and fill out a questionnaire. Possible locations included space near an elevator, stairs or computers, but the lobby area offered the greatest opportunity, because everyone passed through the lobby when using the facility's only entrance. The survey's planners divided the time into 60 slots and recruited students with jobs at the library to serve as the fieldworkers. Other members of the library staff also volunteered to fill time slots. The students in particular were enthusiastic about inviting library users to complete questionnaires. A bowl of candy for participants was a small incentive, combined with a raffle for donated prizes.

Questions:

1. Imagine that you were asked to help prepare for this survey. What fieldwork challenges would you expect to arise in a survey such as this, to be carried out by inexperienced fieldworkers?
2. What training would you recommend for the students and other library staffers conducting this survey? Suggest topics to cover and advice to give to these fieldworkers.

Fieldworkers should be aware of supervisory verification practices. Knowing that there may be a telephone or postcard validation check often reminds interviewers to be conscientious in their work. The interviewer who is conducting quota sampling and needs, for example, an upper-income German male will be less tempted to interview a middle-income German man and falsify the income data in this situation.

Certain information may allow for partial verification without recontacting the respondent. Computer-assisted telephone interviewers often do not know the phone number dialled by the computer or other basic information about the respondent. Thus, answers to questions added to the end of the telephone interview to identify a respondent's area code, phone number, city, postal code, and so on may be used to verify the interview. The computer can also record every attempted call, the time intervals between calls, and the time required to conduct each completed interview – data that may help in identifying patterns related to unethical behaviour by interviewers.

END OF CHAPTER QUESTIONS

1 Comment on the following field situations:

a After conducting a survey with ten people, an interviewer noticed that many of the respondents were saying, 'Was I right?' after a particular question.

b A questionnaire asking about a new easy-opening can has the following instructions to interviewers:

(Hand respondent can and matching instruction card.) Would you please read the instructions on this card and then open this can for me? (Interviewer: Note any comments respondent makes. Do not under any circumstances help him or her to open the can or offer any explanation as to how to open it. If respondents ask for help, tell them that the instructions are on the card. Do not discuss the can or its contents.)

c A researcher gives balloons to children of respondents to keep the children occupied during the interview.

d When a respondent asks how much time the survey will take, the interviewer responds, '15 to 20 minutes'. The respondent says, 'I'm sorry, I have to refuse. I can't give you that much time right now.'

2 A fieldworker asks respondents whether they will answer a few questions. However, the interviewer also observes each respondent's race and approximate age. Is this ethical?

3 Write some interviewer instructions for a street intercept interview.

4 An interviewer finds that when potential respondents ask how much time the survey will take, most refuse if they are told 15 minutes. The interviewer now says ten minutes and finds that most respondents enjoy answering the questions. Is this the right thing to do? Is it ethical?

5 A fieldworker conducting a political poll is instructed to interview registered voters. The fieldworker interviews all willing participants who are eligible to vote (those who may register in the future) because allowing their opinions to be recorded is part of her patriotic duty. Is s/he doing the right thing?

6 What qualities should fieldworkers possess?

7 When should interviewers probe? Give some examples of how probing should be done.

8 What forms does interviewer cheating take? How can such cheating be prevented or detected?

9 An interviewer has a rather long telephone interview. The estimate suggests that fully completing the survey will take 30 minutes. What do you think the response rate will be if people are told ahead of time that it will take 30 minutes to finish participating in the survey? Should the interviewer fudge a little and state that the survey will take only 15 minutes? Explain.

10 Why is it important to ensure that fieldworkers adhere to the sampling procedure specified for a project?

11 What should the interviewer do if a question is misunderstood? If a respondent answers a question before encountering it in the questionnaire?

12 How should the fieldworker terminate the interview?

13 How should respondents' answers to open-ended questions be recorded?

REFERENCES

Askia, www.askia.com. (Accessed 17.03.2018).

Calo Research Services, www.caloresearch.com (Accessed 17.03.2018).

Olson Zaltman Associates, olsonzaltman.com (Accessed 17.03.2018).

Survey Research Center, University of Michigan, www.src.isr. umich.edu (Accessed 17.03.2018).

de Wit, C.W. (2013) 'Interviewing for a sense of place', *Journal of Cultural Geography*, 30(1): 120–144.

RECOMMENDED READING

Bell, J. and Waters, S. (2014) *Doing Your Research Project*, Maidenhead: Open University Press.

Creswell, J. and Creswell, D.J. (2018) *Research Design: Qualitative, Quantitative and Mixed Methods Approaches* (5th edn), London, California, New Delhi, Singapore: Sage.

Denscombe, M. (2017) *The Good Research Guide: For Small-scale Social Research Projects* (5th edn), Maidenhead: Open University Press.

Eng, S. and Gardner, S. (2005) 'Conducting surveys on a shoestring budget', *American Libraries*, 36: 38–39.

Hammersley, M. and Atkinson, P. (2007) *Ethnography*, London: Routledge.

Jones, M. (2014) *Researching Organisations: The Practice of Organisational Fieldwork*, London: Sage.

Neuman, W.L. (2014) *Social Research Methods: Qualitative and Quantitative Approaches* (7th edn), England: Pearson Education Ltd.

Oliver, D.G., Serovich, J.M. and Mason, T.L. (2005) 'Constraints and opportunities with interview transcription: towards reflection in qualitative research', www.ncbi.nlm.nih.gov/pmc/articles/PMC1400594 (Accessed 17.03.2018).

Robson, C. and McCartan, K. (2016) *Real World Research*, John Wiley & Sons Ltd.

Simpson, M. and Tuson, J. (2003) *Using Observation in Small-scale Research*, Glasgow: University of Glasgow.

Smith, M. (2015) *Research Methods in Accounting*, London, California, New Delhi, Singapore: Sage.

CHAPTER 13

USING OBSERVATION

LEARNING OBJECTIVES

At the end of this chapter, the student should:

- Understand the concept of observation in research and be aware of the different kinds of observation undertaken by researchers.

- Know how to use observation in data gathering and be able to design a data-gathering exercise using observation.

- Be able to identify ethical issues in observation studies.

- Understand the need for rigour in observation.

- Be able to discuss the role of observation as a research method.

- Be able to critique the use of observation in research.

RESEARCH SKILLS

At the end of this chapter, the student should, using the exercises on Cengage Brain, be able to:

- Design a small observation study.

- Create an observation schedule for that small study.

- Complete an ethical reflection on that observation study.

The aim of this chapter is to introduce the student to the data-gathering method observation. Observation is a key data collection method in social science research. It involves the observation of the phenomenon under investigation, the recording of that observation and the subsequent analysis of the data gathered. The different kinds of observation used in data gathering are participant observation, non-participant observation (or simply observation) and covert observation. This chapter explores and explains the ways in which observation can be used in business research.

INTRODUCTION

In business research, **observation** is a systematic process of recording behavioural patterns of people, objects and occurrences as they happen. No questioning of, or communicating with, people is needed. Researchers who use observation as a method of data collection either witness and record information while watching events take place, or take advantage of some tracking system such as checkout scanners or internet activity records. These tracking systems can observe and provide data, for example, data on how many products were sold, or data on how many products were sold at a discount and how many products were sold at full price.

> **observation** A data collection method where the researcher engages in observing and recording the phenomenon under investigation, or some part of it.

Data-gathering techniques are part of the methodological framework, the third framework in the four frameworks approach to the design of the research project. The four frameworks approach to the research project is useful because the process of developing the research project from the research statement or question, the conceptual framework, helps the researcher develop a coherent, fully integrated research project. The first three frameworks of the four frameworks approach to research are laid out again in the model in Figure 13.1.

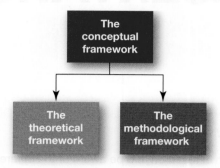

Figure 13.1   Three frameworks of the four frameworks approach to research

The four frameworks

- Conceptual Framework
- Theoretical Framework
- *Methodological Framework*
- Analytical Framework

The epistemological and ontological perspectives of the research project are, as we know from our reading of Chapter 4, embedded in the philosophical framework of the research project and they are implicit in the project's research methodology. As stated in Chapter 4, embedded in each statement of methodology are implicit statements or assumptions about the nature of reality (ontological assumptions) and about the kind of knowledge that will be generated by the research (epistemological assumptions).

Observation studies can be designed to produce both quantitative and qualitative data. Qualitative research is undertaken within a social constructivist or an interpretivist framework. The ontological perspectives within such philosophical frameworks hold reality to be multiple, individually interpreted or socially constructed.

Qualitative data are generated by observation when semi-structured or unstructured observation schedules are used. Quantitative data are generated when highly structured observation schedules are used, and/or when large numbers of observations are carried out. Quantitative research is situated within a positivist philosophical framework. The ontological perspective within this framework holds reality to be singular, objective and apart from the individual. We will see, as we read through this chapter, how the researcher designs observations to fit within one or other of these different philosophical perspectives.

Observation as a data collection method must be used, as must all data-gathering methods, in a rigorous and **systematic** manner. This means that the observation must be properly designed and there must be a system in place designed to facilitate the methodical collection of data.

> **systematic** Systematic means there must be a system in place and the action is carried out in a systematic manner, using the system.

In any data-collection exercise, the first, and arguably the most critical decision to be made, is the decision about what data to collect. The data gathered must answer, at least to some degree, the research question, or explain or illuminate in some way the research statement.

If you look back at the model of the research process in Chapter 1 (see Figure 1.1) you will see that the stage in the research process that we are currently exploring is that of devising data-gathering methods. We are at the stage of deciding on the data collection methods to use in the research project and we are about to start gathering data.

Observation as a data collection method is a traditional method in ethnographic research. Ethnography is the research methodology in focus in this chapter. Ethnography was introduced in Chapter 8 and some more detail and useful references on ethnography were given in Chapter 9 (see Tables 9.1 and 9.2). Ethnography involves the researcher going into a culture to observe and explore the culture from within. **Participant observation** is a data collection method in which the researcher participates in the action being observed. Observation, or non-participant observation, is a data collection method in which the researcher simply observes without participating in the action being observed. **Covert observation** is hidden observation.

---

participant-observation Carried out by the researcher when the researcher does participate in the action or in the phenomenon being observed; an ethnographic research approach where the researcher becomes immersed within and participates in the culture that s/he is observing in order to draw data from his or her observations.

covert observation Carried out without the knowledge of those being observed.

The Value of Good Research feature details a book called *Middletown*, written by two social scientists, Robert and Helen Lynd, and published in 1959, This feature is useful in that it details some of the different sources of data used by the Lynds in their study and the article explains that the research published by the Lynds prepared the way for a new methodology for social science research, mass observation research. As you will note from your reading of this feature, the Lynds carried out the research for the study outlined in the book *Middletown* by participating in community life and by recording the observations they gathered about life within that community through their participation in it.

Mass observation research was popular, particularly in the UK, in the mid-twentieth century. There was a mass observation social research organization in the UK from 1937 to the early 1950s. The archive of that organization is held by the University of Sussex, in Brighton (www.massobs.org.uk). You may be interested in going onto the website and reading some of the resources on the topic of mass observation.

THE VALUE OF GOOD RESEARCH

In the book *Middletown*, research was conducted by the Lynds, husband and wife social scientists who set out to study everyday life in average America. They chose the town of Muncie, Indiana, as the site of their research. The two researchers entered into the community and became a part of community life. They lived in the community and participated along with everyone else in community life, working and socializing, observing every aspect of everyday life in the community and writing up those observations. As well as their own observations, they used census data, surveys, local records, business reports, local histories; newspapers and the minutes of various meetings. Some of these sources provided them with statistical data. They drew on diaries, scrapbooks and casual conversations as data sources for personal perspectives. The publication of this study, the book entitled *Middletown: A Study in American Culture* (1959) was the first popular social analysis of everyday life in America. The study carried out by the Lynds sparked interest in mass observation research. The book was groundbreaking in social science research in terms of the way in which it examined different aspects of social life such as gender, class and age, as well as social and religious belief and practice and other aspects of everyday life.

UNDERSTANDING OBSERVATION

Observation in the context of research means watching or observing some action, activity or phenomenon, and recording it in some manner. Observation in research is very simply watching or observing. The researcher observes the action or activity or phenomenon and records their observation(s). Observation is a field research method, i.e. the researcher undertakes this data-gathering method themselves, in the field. Thus observation yields *primary data*. Primary data are data that are observed or gathered first hand, or directly, by the researcher. Observation yields empirical data, which are data gathered by observation or experience. Observation data are data gathered directly by the researcher in the field, which is the site or context of the research. The context for the research might, for example, be a business, or a classroom or an organization.

Table 13.1 lists seven kinds of observable phenomenon: physical actions, such as shopping patterns (in store or via a web interface) or television viewing; verbal behaviour, such as sales conversations or the exchange between a worker and supervisor; expressive behaviour, such as tone of voice, facial expressions; spatial relations and locations, such as traffic patterns; temporal patterns, such as amount of time spent shopping, driving, or making a business decision; physical objects, such as the amount of newspapers recycled or number of soft drink cans in the rubbish bin; and verbal and pictorial records, such as the content of advertisements.

Table 13.1 Examples of what can be observed

Phenomenon	Example
Physical action	A worker's movement during an assembly process
Verbal behaviour	Statements made by airline travellers while waiting in line
Expressive behaviour	Facial expressions, tones of voices, and forms of body language
Spatial relations and locations	Proximity of middle managers' offices to the president's office
Temporal patterns	Length of time it takes to execute a stock purchase order
Physical objects	Percentage of recycled materials compared to trash
Verbal and pictorial records	Number of illustrations appearing in a training booklet

The decision to use observation as a data collection method in any research project is taken in response to the data requirements of the research project and the location of those data. The data may be in the action or activity of some person, or some people, or some organization or entity. The researcher identifies the action or activity or phenomenon to be observed and then designs the means by which to carry out the observation. In order to do this, the researcher must gain **access** to the people who are carrying out the action or activity. Usually, the researcher must ask for permission to enter the field and to carry out the observation. This almost always involves writing formal letters to the people in charge of the field, asking their permission to enter and to carry out the observation. When the researcher has secured access, the researcher can begin the observation of the activity.

access Access to data and access to the field of the research project.

The researcher's recorded observations of the phenomenon are the data that the researcher has created or developed on the phenomenon under investigation. Now that we know what observation is, we now need to know how to carry out an observation in the field. As explained earlier, the researcher decides what to observe and where to observe it. When possible, the researcher will visit the field several times before commencing the observation in order to become familiar with the field before finally deciding on precisely which action(s) or what parts of the action(s) to observe. The researcher can then design the means by which to carry out the observation.

The preliminary visits to the field involve 'informal observations'. These are used by researchers to help them design the formal observation and to alert them to anything in the field that might interfere with, obstruct or delay the observation or indeed the fieldwork generally. If the researcher can identify potential obstructions or delays, s/he may be able to design the formal observation and the fieldwork in such a way as to circumvent or avoid these problems. Having said that, it is neither possible nor desirable that the researcher attempt to control the environment of the observation; the researcher simply needs to be familiar enough with the environment, and secure enough in it, to be able to carry out the observation. There are essentially seven steps in the process of carrying out an observation, and these seven steps are laid out in Table 13.2.

Table 13.2 Conducting an observation study

Identify the data required for the research
Gain access to the data
Decide on observation as an appropriate data collection method to be used to gather data
Design the means by which the observation will be carried out and recorded
Carry out the observation, by observing the action or the phenomenon and recording that observation
The record of the observation is the data gathered
Analyze the data

THE DIFFERENT KINDS OF OBSERVATION

In general, researchers engage in three kinds of observation, the first kind is called 'observation' or **'non-participant observation'**; the second kind is called 'participant observation'. The third kind of observation is called 'covert observation'. Covert observation can raise substantial ethical issues and so it is used by researchers with caution.

> **non-participant observation** Carried out when the researcher does not participate in the action or in the phenomenon being observed.

Table 13.3 details the three kinds of observation, all of which can be used formally or informally. An informal study is less rigorously designed than a formal study. Informal studies can be used to inform, supplement and/or support formal studies.

Table 13.3 The different kinds of observation

Observation/non-participant observation	Participant observation Formal/informal	Covert observation Formal/informal
The first kind of observation that researchers engage in is called observation or non-participant observation. Using this kind of observation, the researcher observes some activity or action or phenomenon in the field and records that observation. The recorded observation is the data gathered.	Using participant observation, the researcher is part of the action or the activity or the phenomenon in the field. While participating in, or being part of, the action, activity or phenomenon, the researcher observes the action, activity or phenomenon and records that observation. The recorded observation is the data gathered.	Using covert observation, the researcher observes the action, activity or phenomenon in a covert manner. In other words, the fact that the action, activity or phenomenon is being observed is kept from the people who are part of, or who are generating, the action, activity or phenomenon. The observation is kept secret. It is covert. Such observations raise substantial ethical issues. The researcher records the observation. The recorded observation is the data gathered.

There are three critical decisions that must be made in any observation study. The researcher must decide what exactly is to be observed, how to conduct the observation and how to record the observation:

- Deciding what exactly is to be observed.
- Deciding how to conduct the observation.
- Deciding how to record the observation.

The Real World Research box 'Covert participant observation in management research' is an extract from a research project that was carried out using covert participant observation. The project is interesting for many reasons. In the article, the literature review consists of a review of the literature on the ethics of covert participant observation. The journal article details two case studies, both of which were developed using covert participant observation as the data collection method. In the journal article, which you should source and read, both of the case studies are outlined in detail. The aim, the design of the research, the context within which it was undertaken, the data collection method, the data gathered for each study, the findings and the conclusions are all discussed and explained.

This study is particularly useful in that it was a covert research project carried out using participant observation and, as explained earlier, the authors of the article engage in an in-depth consideration of the ethical issues in covert research.

It is unlikely that as a student researcher you will get permission to use a covert method in your research project. If you are thinking about using such a method you should get advice and guidance from your thesis supervisor and/ or your lecturer in research methods. There are substantial ethical issues in covert observational studies and it is important to have some knowledge and understanding of them.

REAL WORLD RESEARCH

How theory influences research

Covert participant observation in management research

The authors of the study examined here (Oliver and Eales, 2008, 'Re-evaluating the consequentialist perspective of using covert participant observation in management research', *Qualitative Market Research: An International Journal*, 11(3): 344–57), write that the primary purpose of using participant observation in management research is to gain insight into and knowledge of organizational phenomena. They state that the critical issue in the research process is the need to collect data in an appropriate manner. They express their concern about the possibility of the method of data collection being unethical or creating difficult personal or emotional issues for the researcher. In the paper, they ask whether engaging in extended periods of covert participant observation is an ethical way to learn about organizational problems.

They write that most of the literature regarding this research method concentrates on the epistemological methodological relationship (the relationship the method has with knowledge creation and the kind of knowledge created by the method) and the associated problems of researcher subjectivity, impressionism, bias and research outputs that are often idiosyncratic descriptions of the phenomena being investigated. However, they state that when this research method is considered in ethical terms, the debate shifts from being one of distance and objectivity in the method to one of invasion of privacy, informed consent and deception. As a result, the higher principled debate concerning covert participant research is one based on research morals, not methodological validity.

The researchers state that while the ethics of management research and the research ethics involved in investigating organizational phenomena have been dealt with in the literature, little attention has been paid to the ethical considerations and consequences for the researchers that pertain to the collection and use of data. They state that their paper makes a contribution to the growing debate concerning the ethical nature of covert participant observation in management research. They suggest that researchers need to consider the consequences for themselves when choosing to conduct management research in a covert way.

An extensive review of the literature on the use of observation, participant observation and covert observation in business, management and organizational research is presented.

The researchers state that the ethical debate about the use of covert participant observation demonstrates real tensions between obtaining often exploratory and in-depth data in a covert way and obtaining these data in a way that is not deceptive, that does not infringe on the rights of participants and that does not result in unforeseen consequences and harm to participants.

In the journal article, the researchers go on to outline two case studies. The first case study details a covert participant observation study carried out in a small family business. The second case study details a covert participant observation study carried out with a national leisure service provider. The aim of both case studies is detailed. The findings from both research projects are outlined.

Read the journal article and, in your research diary, make a note of the way in which the participant observation was carried out. Then write a short paragraph on the ethical issues, as you see them, in the study.

YOUR RESEARCH
Using observation in your research

Think about your own research project. Is there any way that you could use observation as a data-gathering technique (data-gathering method) in your research project? If you think that you could use observation in your research project, which of the three observation methods would you use? In your research diary, write a note detailing how, where, when and why you would use this means of observation.

In your research diary, write a short paragraph about covert observation. Use the internet to search for examples of covert research projects. One of the most famous (or perhaps infamous) covert social science research projects is the Milgram Study. You can read about the Milgram Study at: www.simplypsychology.org/milgram.html

Another interesting example of covert research is Derren Brown's TV programme *The Heist*, first broadcast in the UK on Channel 4, 4 January 2006. In the programme, the presenter Derren Brown invited a group of businesswomen and men to participate in a documentary about motivational speaking. This was pretence. He was, in fact, using his engagement with the group of businesspeople to examine whether or not he could persuade these people to participate in a real bank robbery. Use the internet to search for information on the TV programme *The Heist*. From your reading of this information, in your research diary describe the covert observation being undertaken by Derren Brown. Write a short summary on the ethics of that observation; critically examine the observation and in your short summary detail the ethical issues, if any, that you can see in that observation.

DIFFERENT WAYS OF USING OBSERVATION

There are a number of different ways in which observation can be used in data collection. As previously discussed, observation can be participant or non-participant, covert or open. A researcher can engage in human or mechanical observation. Mechanical observation is observation undertaken through the use of some kind of technology, such as mobile phone technology. A researcher can engage in natural observation, which is observation in a natural setting, or in contrived observation, which is observation in a setting that has been contrived by the researcher.

An example of a contrived observation would be if participants in the research read a text or watched a film or video while the researcher observed and recorded their reactions and responses. In this case, the situation is not natural but has been contrived by the researcher.

A researcher can engage in direct observation, where participants know that the researcher is watching them. In such observations, participants tend to react to being watched. As a result, this kind of observation is sometimes known as reactive observation.

A researcher can also engage in **unobtrusive observation**, where the observation is carried out without the researcher being present at the site of the activity. Perhaps the researcher is nearby, or observing through a window or screen, or perhaps the observation is conducted when the human actors have left the site. The researcher carries out the observation in an unobtrusive manner.

unobtrusive observation Carried out unobtrusively, with or without the knowledge of the research participants.

Mechanical observation

In many situations, the primary – and sometimes the only – means of observation is mechanical rather than human. Video cameras, traffic counters, checkout scanners and other machines help observe and record behaviour. Some unusual observation studies have used motion-picture cameras and time-lapse photography. An early application of this observation technique photographed train passengers and determined their levels of comfort by observing how they sat and moved in their seats. Another time-lapse study filmed traffic flows in an urban square and this study resulted in a redesign of the streets. Similar techniques may help managers determine how to better organize and arrange items in a warehouse or improve the design of store layouts to enhance traffic flow. Mechanical devices can also be utilized to observe employees and their actions when they cannot be observed in person as illustrated in the Real World Research box.

REAL WORLD RESEARCH

ATTI shadows the fleet

Advanced Tracking Technologies, Inc. (ATTI) (www.advantrack .com/contact-us/) develop sophisticated monitoring and tracking devices for fleet vehicles. While managers cannot directly observe their driver's actions, ATTI's Shadow Tracker Vision II modular vehicle tracking system provides detailed information about what is happening on the road. This electronic device can pinpoint the location of any equipped vehicle through its global positioning system (GPS), as well as record detailed trip information, including start and end times, distance travelled, average and top speed, idle time, off-hour usage and the operator's driving habits.

Not only is this observation technique useful to manage drivers, but it can assist fleet managers with many of their responsibilities. For example, they can monitor vehicle usage, and wear and tear on vehicles; they know which driver is closest to the next service call; they can easily download data for route analysis and mileage reports and they have data that they need for required taxation reports.

Monitoring website traffic

Computer technology makes gathering detailed data about online behaviour easy and inexpensive. The greater challenges are to identify which measures are meaningful and to interpret the data correctly. For instance, most organizations record the number of hits at their websites – mouse clicks on a single page of a website. If the visitor clicks on many links, that page receives multiple hits. Similarly, they can track page views, or single, discrete clicks to load individual pages of a website. Page views more conservatively indicate how many users visit each individual page on the website and may also be used to track the path or sequence of pages that each visitor follows.

Click-through rates

A **click-through rate (CTR)** is the percentage of people exposed to an advertisement who actually click on the corresponding hyperlink that takes them to the company's website. Counting hits or page views can suggest the amount of interest or attention a website is receiving, but these measures are flawed. First, hits do not differentiate between a lot of activity by a few visitors and a little activity by many visitors. In addition, the researcher lacks information about the meaning behind the numbers. If a user clicks on a site many times, the person may have found a lot of useful or enjoyable material, or it may be that the user tried unsuccessfully to find something by looking in several places. Additionally, some hits are likely made by mistake. The consumers may have had no intention of clicking through the ad or may not have known what they were doing when they clicked on the ad.

> **click-through rate (CTR)** The ratio of the number of users who view a web page and then click on a link on the web page to go through to another web page, to the total number of users who view the web page.

A more refined count is the number of unique visitors to a website. This measurement counts the initial access to the site but not multiple hits on the site by the same visitor during the same day or week. Operators of websites can collect the data by attaching small files, called cookies, to the computers of visitors to their sites and then track those cookies to see whether the same visitors return. Some research companies, notably Jupiter Research and Nielsen, specialize in monitoring this type of internet activity. A typical approach is to install a special tracking program on the personal computers of a sample of internet users who agree to participate in the research effort. Nielsen studies consumers in more than 100 countries and it has its software installed in thousands of computers in homes and workplaces. Internet monitoring enables these companies to identify the popularity of websites. In recent years, accurate measurement of unique visitors has become more difficult, because over half of computer users have deleted cookies and many users block cookies to make themselves anonymous.

As online advertising has become commonplace, business research has refined methods for measuring the effectiveness of the advertisements. The companies that place these ads can keep count of the CTR. Applying the CTR to the amount spent on the advertisement gives the advertiser a cost per click. These measures have been hailed as a practical way to evaluate advertising effectiveness. It is important to remember, however, that getting consumers to click on an ad is not the objective; the objective is, of course, sales.

Scanner-based research

Lasers performing optical character recognition and barcode technology such as the universal product code (UPC) have accelerated the use of mechanical observation in business research. This technology allows researchers to investigate questions that are demographically or promotionally specific. Scanner research has investigated the different ways consumers respond to price promotions and the effects of those differences on a promotion's profitability. One of the primary means of implementing this type of research is through the establishment of a **scanner-based consumer panel** to replace consumer purchase diaries. In a typical scanner panel, each household is assigned a barcoded card, like a frequent shopper card, which members present to the clerk at the register. The household's code number is matched with the purchase information recorded by the scanner. In addition, as with other consumer panels, background information about the household is obtained through survey questionnaires.

> **scanner-based consumer panel** A type of consumer panel where participants record purchases using a barcode scanner.

Aggregate data, which are grouped data or data combined from a number of sources, such as actual store sales as measured by scanners, are available to clients and industry groups. Data may also be aggregated by product category. To interpret the aggregated data, researchers can combine them with secondary research and panel demographics.

Demographic data are data that describe the common characteristics of a population, characteristics such as age, gender, income and geographic location. For example, data from Information Resources Inc. (IRI) (www.iriworldwide.com/en-US) indicated a downward trend in sales of hair-colouring products. Demographic data suggested that an important reason was the aging of the population; many consumers who had dyed their hair, reached an age at which they no longer wished to cover their grey hair. A smaller segment of the population was at an age where consumers typically began using hair colouring.

Data from scanner research can have advantages, such as:

1. The data measure observes actual purchase behaviour.
2. Substituting mechanical for human recordkeeping can improve accuracy.
3. Observation is unobtrusive.
4. Mechanical observation eliminates the possibility of social desirability or other bias on the part of respondents.
5. More extensive purchase data can be collected, because all UPC categories are measured.
6. Because all UPC-coded items are measured, brand loyalty and switching rates can be measured and the performance of own brands and rival brands can be tracked.
7. The data collected from computerized checkout scanners can be combined with data about the timing of advertising, price changes, displays and special sales promotions. The data gathered can be analyzed using powerful analytical computer software provided by the scanner data providers.

Scanner data can show a researcher week by week how a product is doing, even in a single store, and track sales in response to changes of sales personnel, local advertising or price promotions. Also, several organizations have developed scanner panels and expanded them into electronic test-market systems. One such company is Information Resources Inc. You should log onto this company's website and explore the work that it is doing in marketing research (www.iriworldwide.com/).

Table 13.4 details these different ways in which researchers use observation.

Table 13.4 Ways in which researchers use observation

Participant observation	Non-participant observation
Direct observation	Indirect observation
Human observation	Mechanical observation
Covert observation	Overt observation
Natural observation	Contrived observation
Direct (reactive) observation	Unobtrusive observation

As with every data collection method, the researcher makes a decision about which observation method to use based on the aim of the research, the population of the research, the data requirements of the research, the best way in which to gather the data required for the research, and the ethical issues in conducting the proposed observation.

Unstructured observations are sometimes undertaken when the researcher is unsure about precisely which aspects of the phenomenon under investigation need to be explored or examined. Unstructured observations are sometimes used by researchers in the early stages of a research project. Often an unstructured observation leads to a more **structured observation**. The researcher uses the unstructured observation to get to know the field and/or the phenomenon under investigation. Then the researcher designs a semi-structured or structured observation in order to focus the observation on the precise phenomenon being investigated (see Table 13.5).

unstructured observations Carried out when the researcher is unsure about precisely which aspects of elements of the action or the phenomenon should or could be observed or when the researcher wants to carry out a general observation of the phenomenon.

structured observation Carried out when the researcher knows precisely what aspects or elements of the phenomenon should or could be observed.

Table 13.5 Unstructured, semi-structured and structured observation

Unstructured observation	In an unstructured observation, the researcher goes into the field and observes the action or the phenomenon under investigation in the research project. The researcher records their observations of the phenomenon. The recorded observations are the data to be analyzed. An unstructured observation can be recorded in a field diary.
Semi-structured observation	In a semi-structured observation, the researcher knows which aspects or elements of the action or the phenomenon s/he wishes to observe and so s/he designs a semi-structured observation schedule in order to facilitate that observation. The researcher observes the elements or aspects of the action or the phenomenon and then records those observations in the semi-structured observation schedule s/he has designed for the research
Structured observation	In a structured observation, the researcher knows very precisely which aspects or elements of the action or phenomenon s/he wishes to observe and so s/he designs a structured observation schedule in order to facilitate that observation. A structured observation schedule can look like a questionnaire. A questionnaire is an example of structured data-gathering instrument. The researcher designs the structured observation schedule or they use and acknowledge (reference), a structured observation schedule they have found in their reading of the literature.

Figure 13.2 is an example of a schedule for a **semi-structured observation**.

semi-structured observation Carried out when the researcher knows, broadly speaking, what aspects or elements of the research should or could be observed.

Health and Safety Research/Textile Resources Ltd

(Record every incidence of the following:)
Date _____

Infringement of Health and Safety Regulations	Notes Record detail of infringement	Number of times infringement occurs

Figure 13.2 Example of a semi-structured observation schedule

THE VALUE OF GOOD RESEARCH

Focus on ethnography

The research methodology ethnography is used when the researcher wants to carry out an in-depth study of a culture.

The researcher goes inside the culture in order to develop an in-depth view of the culture. Although inside the culture, the researcher has to maintain, simultaneously, an outsider perspective on the culture. This is in order to ensure that the researcher does not become acculturated, totally part of the culture, and so much a part of the culture that they can no longer critically engage with it. Ethnographers are said to be methodological pragmatists. They use any data-gathering method that will provide the necessary data on the phenomenon under investigation. The phenomenon under

(Continued)

investigation in ethnographic research will be a culture or some aspect or element of a culture.

Ken Anderson is an anthropologist who works at Intel Research. In 2009 he wrote about ethnographic research as a key to strategy in the *Harvard Business Review*. Anderson wrote that corporate ethnography is not just for innovation any more, it is central to gaining a full understanding of customers and the business itself. The ethnographic work at his company Intel and other firms, he wrote, now informs functions such as strategy and long-term planning. In the article, Anderson states that ethnography is the branch of anthropology that involves trying to understand how people live their lives. He wrote of researchers visiting consumers in their homes and offices to observe and listen in non-directed ways. The goal, he stated, is to see people's behaviour on their terms, not on ours. While this observational method might seem inefficient, in fact it informs the company about the context within which customers would use a new product and about the meaning the new product might hold for them in their lives.

Some of the research questions ethnographers engaged with included: how long particular markets will play out; if and how television and personal computer technologies will converge; whether or not consumers shift comfortably to new media; and whether smartphones will take over most of the functions of personal computers.

Anderson wrote that Intel can analyze data on the latest buying patterns and data from customer surveys, but customers often cannot articulate precisely what it is that they want in products and services. A company such as Intel employs ethnographers so that it can study how people live, in order to discover trends that will be used to inform the company's future strategies. You can read Anderson's article at hbr .org/2009/03/ethnographic-research-a-key-to-strategy/ar/1.

In a more recent paper (2017), Anderson *et al.* present a case study on how ongoing ethnographic research within Intel led to the re-segmentation of a market. The paper details the value of cumulative ethnographic work from within an organization and the role of ethnography in shifting the perspectives of stakeholders, driving impact with a new segmentation. This is a very interesting paper and it presents in detail the research carried out by Ken Anderson and the team at Intel. The paper outlines the research methodology used in the study, the findings from the study, and the value of the study for Intel.

The Sage journal *Ethnography* has many articles detailing business research projects carried out using ethnography as the research methodology. In an article published in the journal in 2009, Lee wrote about the professionalizing of the rap career. Lee's research involved four years of ongoing ethnographic fieldwork with inner-city men who rap at an 'open mic' venue in South Central Los Angeles in California. In the article, Lee explains that the rappers in the study view the venue as a place to develop their skills and earn the respect of their peers, but they hope to move beyond the venue, develop their careers as rappers and make money in the music industry. The data for the article came from observations and interviews. In the article, Lee provides an interesting account of the ethnographer's journey into that culture (2009: 480–84), a journey he had to make in order to be able to engage in ethnographic research.

Another Sage journal, the *Journal of Contemporary Ethnography*, also has many articles detailing business research projects carried out using ethnography as the research methodology.

An interesting and potentially useful website is that of Ethnographic Research, Inc. (www.ethnographic-research.com). This company provides an ethnographic research service, and their website is a useful research for anyone interested in learning more about ethnography and ethnographic research.

Colorado State University provides a writing guide on ethnography, observational research and narrative inquiry at: writing.colostate.edu/guides/guide.cfm?guideid=63.

Kozinets (2015) has written an interesting book on netnography. Netnography, as explained earlier in this textbook, is an adaptation of ethnography for use in the study of online cultures and communities. Kozinets provides a good introduction to designing and carrying out netnography, that is ethnographic research conducted on the internet.

A structured observation schedule can be a great deal more structured even than Figure 13.3. Figure 13.3 is an example of a schedule for a structured observation. Think of the degree of structure and design in questionnaires you have seen, some of which you may have completed. A structured observation schedule is designed in a similar way. The key to designing a data-gathering instrument is to design it to meet the data requirements of the research project. The data-gathering instrument is designed specifically for the job it is required to do.

THE NEED FOR RIGOUR IN OBSERVATION

One of the most basic principles in research is the principle of rigour. For a research project to be rigorous, as explained in Chapter 1, it must adhere to the scientific principles of research. The research must be systematic and it must be valid. The aim and objectives of the research must be clearly stated and they must be valid. The researcher has to design a methodology for the research that will facilitate the accomplishment of the aim and objectives. The methodology must be the appropriate methodology for the proposed research. The population of the research must be clearly defined and appropriate for the proposed research. If a sample is drawn from the population, the sampling method must be

Customer relations research/Willow Music Store
(Every occurrence observed of the activities listed below will be recorded.)

Date _____
Place a tick in box to record occurrence.

Engaging customers in conversation									
Active selling									
Smiling at customers									
Product promotion									
Good customer service									
Poor customer service									
Missed sales opportunities									

Figure 13.3 Example of a structured observation schedule

detailed. If a sampling frame is used, it must be detailed and it must be valid. The sample size must be clearly stated. The limitations of the research must be explored and outlined. If possible and appropriate, attempts to overcome the limitations of the research must be made and then detailed and explained. The data collection methods designed and used must be appropriate and valid. The **fieldwork** undertaken for the research must be systematic, rigorous and valid. The data gathered must be properly managed and stored, and, in due course, properly analyzed. The researcher must have the scholarship, the skills and the competencies necessary for the conduct of the research. This should be evident in the manner in which the researcher engages with the research project and in the manner in which the researcher writes up the research.

> **fieldwork** The work of data gathering in the field of the research project. The data gathered in fieldwork is primary data, data specifically created for the research project. The field is any setting beyond the desk, the library and/or the laboratory in which the required data can be gathered.

It is not the case that one kind of observation, for example, is more rigorous than another. It is the way in which the observation is designed and carried out by the researcher that establishes the rigour of the observation. Similarly, no one data-gathering method is any more rigorous than any other. It is the way in which the researcher uses the data-gathering method that establishes the rigour of the method. Research methodologies and data-gathering methods are flexible and can be used in different ways to accomplish many different things in social research. We have seen this in detail in Chapter 9 of this textbook. Rigorous research uses appropriate methods systematically and consistently in order to thoroughly accomplish the aim and objectives of the research project.

An aid to improving the rigour and the validity of the research project is the **pilot study**. The researcher undertakes a pilot study to test the design of the research project. A pilot study can also be undertaken to test the data-gathering method(s) designed for the research project. In a pilot study, the researcher tests the instrument to see how it works. For example, to test an observation schedule, the researcher engages in a practice observation to see how well the observation schedule records the data required for the study. This is a pilot study. Following the pilot study, the researcher can amend the data-gathering instrument in order to improve the instrument. The improved instrument will provide better quality data for the study being undertaken.

pilot study An aid to improving the rigour and the validity of the research. This is a test of the data-gathering instrument designed for the research.

As can be seen, the researcher is required throughout the research process to make decisions regarding the design and development of the research project. A beginner researcher needs a good deal of guidance in making these decisions. Therefore it is important to have access to a research supervisor or a lecturer in research methods whose expertise in this area you can call on as you develop your research project.

HOW TO CRITIQUE THE USE OF OBSERVATION IN RESEARCH

It is important, as a student, to learn how to critically engage with research, how to critique research. As a researcher, when you critique the use of observation in someone else's research you should consider the validity of the observation proposed or carried out as a means of gathering data for that particular study. You should also consider the rigour with which the observation was designed, constructed and carried out. You should be concerned with the manner in which observation, as a means of data gathering, serves the data requirements of the study. You are also concerned with the means by which the data were analyzed.

You should be concerned with the aim and objectives of the study and whether, or to what degree, the observation carried out served to accomplish them. You should consider whether or not the observation data collection method used was the most appropriate data collection method, in terms of the data requirements of the study. You might suggest that other data collection methods may have served the research better. You should consider the population of the study and whether or not observation was the best means of data collection with that population. If the study does not have a human population, you should consider the context for the study and whether or not observation was the most appropriate means of data collection in that context.

In reading such a research project, you should think about the way in which the observation was designed. The observation should be as thorough, systematic and consistent as possible. Even when a data collection method is designed to be unstructured, it should be systematic; the observation should be clearly and thoroughly organized, and that organization should be thoroughly detailed, outlined and explained in the written report of the research. The thorough, indeed meticulous, reporting of the manner in which the observation was carried out facilitates the researcher in establishing the validity and the rigour of the observation.

When you critique an observation, you should examine the observation schedule, a copy of which should be included in the appendices of the study, in terms of the appropriateness and thoroughness of the observation. You should check what was included in the observation and note what, if anything, was omitted. Decide whether or not there was an error in what was included or omitted. Examine when, where and with whom the observation was conducted. Explore the manner in which the observation was conducted. Decide whether or not the conduct of the observation was appropriate to the needs of the study, and appropriate in terms of proper and appropriate ethical standards. Examine the manner in which the observation was recorded, and whether the recording of the observation was rigorous. Examine and critique the evidence presented in terms of the validity and rigour of the observation.

This is how you critique an observation study in a research project and this is how any observation that you may design and carry out in the course of your own research will be critiqued. It is important to be aware of all of these points when designing and carrying out an observation as part of a research project.

It is most important to remember too that many if not all of these issues are relevant to most data collection methods.

DESIGNING AN OBSERVATION STUDY

When designing an observation study, it is important to be sure that observation is an appropriate data-gathering method for the study. The researcher does not arbitrarily select the data collection method(s) for the research project. The data collection method(s) used in the research project is dictated by the data requirements of the study. The location of that data, the kind(s) of data available and the level of access possible to that data, the aim and objectives of the research, the population of the research, the location of the population and the context for the research are also important.

The researcher builds the research project, step by step, and each step taken in the design of the research project must be congruent with all of the previous steps taken. In other words, each step taken must fit with all of the other steps already taken in the process of designing the research project. The example that follows provides an outline of Iona's research project in which observation was used as a data-gathering method. What do you think of Iona's research and the methodology and data-gathering methods she has proposed for it?

Iona has developed a very interesting research project. The methodology and the data collection methods designed for the project are congruent with the aim and the objectives of the research. The data-gathering methods fit well with the population of the study and they are appropriate in terms of the data requirements of the research project. The project is simple but comprehensive. The research, when completed, will provide a rich insight into employee relations within the firm. Iona's project is situated within a social constructivist philosophical framework. Her data-gathering methods will provide predominantly qualitative data. Through the data-gathering methods she is using in the project, Iona will be able to develop an account of how employee relations within the company are socially constructed.

RESEARCH IN PRACTICE

Proposed research methodology for Iona's research project

This research project is a case study examining employee relations in Techtron Ltd. Techtron Ltd. is an SME with 50 employees situated in the East Midlands in the UK. Almost half of the employees are technicians, the rest are management and administrative staff. The focus of this study is on employee relations within and between these three groups of employees.

Aim and objectives

The aim of this research project is to examine employee relations in the company Techtron Inc.

The objectives of the research are as follows:

- To examine employee relations in Techtron Inc. in relation to the three groups of employees in the company: management, administrative staff and technicians.
- To examine within and between group employee relations in Techtron Inc.
- To document both within and between group employee relations in Techtron Inc.

This research project is a case study. The methodology used for the research is case study methodology.

Two different data collection methods will be used in this research, observation and interviews. The data collection methods will be used sequentially. First, a series of observations will be undertaken in order to facilitate the recording and documentation of employee relations in the firm. Second, issues in employee relations evidenced in the observations will be further explored in a series of in-depth interviews. It is anticipated that the interviews will allow the researcher to probe and further examine or examine in more detail the findings of the observations. The in-depth interviews will also allow participants in the study to explain employee relations in the firm, as they are evidenced in the observations.

With the use of two different data collection methods in the research, triangulation can be accomplished. Triangulation in research is the examination of the phenomenon under investigation from more than one perspective. In this research project, the findings of the observation will be triangulated with the findings from the in-depth interviews. The data from the two different data collection methods will together provide a richer, deeper, more nuanced and more complex insight into employee relations in the firm.

Observations

As the observations are to be conducted with all 50 employees in the firm, there is no sampling in this element of the fieldwork. To begin with there will be a series of unstructured observations in the workplace. These observations will take place over a two-week period, from 10 June to 24 June. Each of these observations will take place in two-hour slots. Over the two-week period there will be two of these observations each day. These unstructured observations will be recorded in the field diary of the researcher in the following manner:

Unstructured observation schedule
Date
Time
Venue
Population
Record observation

Semi-structured observations

Following these unstructured observations, there will be four weeks of semi-structured observations.

The first week of these semi-structured observations will be spent observing within-group employee relations among the technicians in the firm.

The second week will be spent observing within-group employee relations among administrative staff in the firm.

The third week will be spent observing within-group employee relations among managers in the firm.

The fourth and final week will be spent studying between-group employee relations among the three groups of employees in the firm.

(Continued)

As explained, the findings from the unstructured observation and the issues in employee relations in the firm evidenced by those observations will be used to structure the semi-structured observations.

The semi-structured observation schedule to be used to record these observations is detailed as follows:

Semi-structured observation
Date
Time
Venue
Observing

Evidence of good employee relations
Apparent causes
Evident consequences
Evidence of bad employee relations
Apparent causes
Evident consequences

Finally, a series of in-depth interviews will be undertaken with a sample of employees from each of the three groups of employees in the firm. A purposive sampling technique will be used, whereby the researcher will select the employees to be included in the sample for interview:

- Technicians – there are 24 technicians in the company. Twelve of these technicians will be interviewed for the research.
- Administrators – there are 12 administrators in the company. Six of these administrators will be interviewed for the study.
- Managers – there are 14 managers in the company. Seven managers will be interviewed for the research.

In all, 25 in-depth interviews will be conducted. The interview schedule will be semi-structured, as was the second observation schedule. The findings of both series of observations will be used to inform the construction of the interview schedule. It is anticipated that the interviews will shed light on the history of employee relations in the firm, as well as explaining and clarifying the firm's employee relations, as they were evidenced in the observations. The completeness of the proposed methodology for this research establishes in part the validity of the research. The rigour with which the research was carried out will be evident in the completeness of the data gathered for the research.

In the case study that follows, the researcher, Dabir, develops his research project idea from his reading of a research project published in a journal article. As you read the case study, think about how you might develop a research project of your own from your reading of journal articles.

CASE STUDY

Dabir's research idea

Dabir is doing a degree in business management. He has decided to travel around Ireland over the summer holidays. He plans to conduct his research for his thesis while on that trip. Following his reading of Russell's (2008) journal article 'Nostalgic tourism', Dabir decided to model his research project for his thesis on Russell's research.

In his article, Russell wrote that the global tourism industry was experiencing unprecedented growth, as more people seek its services and as more competition enters the marketplace. Russell wrote that both the UK and the Republic of Ireland had experienced steady growth in tourism. Due to increased competition, tourism companies had to reassess their business models in order to look for new niche opportunities.

These niche opportunities would, he explained, positively benefit the tourism industry as a whole. One such niche opportunity, according to Russell, was to cater to nostalgic tourists. Such tourists are in search of authentic cultural experiences through which they can experience their ancestral roots. In order to conduct his research, Russell participated in a 23-day bus tour. He used a multi-method approach to the research. The data-gathering methods used were observation, interview and survey.

(For the purposes of this chapter, with its focus on observation, in this case study we will focus on the observation data-gathering method used by Russell in the research project.)

Using participant observation, Russell made an effort to observe all the activities participated in by the tourists on the tour. He observed what they ate, what they bought and what they did. He also made a record of what they said when speaking aloud. He did not engage in eavesdropping. Observation was conducted at all times in public places, on the bus, during visits to cultural sights, during and after meals.

(Continued)

Russell also conducted brief interviews with the tourists before the tour commenced and he administered a questionnaire, comprising ten questions, to the group when the tour had ended and before everyone left. While he engaged in participant observation on the tour, he did not speak of the research on the tour. In this way, he managed to conduct the research relatively unobtrusively.

In the article, Russell wrote that nothing is more fundamental to a sound marketing strategy than understanding and catering to the needs and desires of consumers. He suggested that such understanding is important in order for travel companies to better target tourist subsets and to more appropriately position their travel package offerings, especially at a time when the global tourism market faces more intense competition.

The ancestral tourism experience, he wrote, involves sustained immersion and active interpretation that continues even after conclusion of the tour. His research demonstrated that the perception of authenticity and the fulfilment of cultural experiences are important determinants in fostering repeat business and soliciting favourable recommendations from customers. He suggested that, in order to improve customer satisfaction, tour companies should consider integrating what are now supplemental tour options into the regular package offering, in an effort to improve authentic experience perceptions.

Dabir has decided to build on Russell's work. He is going to take a bus tour around Ireland. While on the tour he will explore the tourists' engagement with heritage tourism and he will consider the response of the heritage tourism industry to heritage tourists.

Dabir plans to engage in participant observation on the tour. He will observe his fellow tourists in the manner in which they engage with and respond to the different elements of the tourist product offered to them. He will also observe the manner in which the providers of the tourist product engage with and respond to the tourists.

Dabir also plans to use documentary sources in his research. He will examine the heritage tourist product as it is presented in tour company literature and on their websites.

From all of these data, Dabir hopes to provide an analysis of the needs of heritage tourists and the degree to which those needs are met by heritage tourism providers.

What do you think of Dabir's research idea? It seems like a good idea. It is simple and interesting. An area of concern would be the validity of the research. Dabir must take great care in designing and carrying out his observations. He must ensure that the observations are conducted and recorded in a systematic and consistent manner. He must clearly make a contribution to knowledge with his research. He should clearly and explicitly establish that contribution when writing up his research.

The following exercise is based on Russell's journal article 'Nostalgic tourism'. You will find the exercise useful in terms of developing your understanding of the research process.

Read the journal article and examine the use of observation in the study. Detail in your research diary the manner in which observation was used in the study. Write a short note in your research diary about the contribution that the observation element of data collection made to the study. In your reflection on the study in your research diary, engage with and respond to the following:

1. How was the observation conducted?
2. What data were gathered through observation?
3. What contribution, if any, did the observation data make to the findings?
4. Could another method of data gathering have been substituted for the observation method? If yes, state the method(s). If no, explain why not.
5. Give five reasons why the observation data collection method, as it was deployed in this study, was useful.

Take particular note of the manner in which theory is deployed in the writing of this journal article.

In the journal article, try to identify three of the four frameworks from the four frameworks approach to the research process:

The conceptual framework
The theoretical framework
The methodological framework.

Read how the researcher clearly defines what it is that they are trying to do. Can you see how the researcher creates, from the literature, a theoretical framework for the research that they are proposing to carry out?

Examine the way in which the researcher clearly outlines the methodology for the research, detailing the population of the study and the data-gathering methods to be used in the study. Can you see how the data gathered evidences the phenomenon under investigation?

Examine the way in which the researcher uses the data gathered.

Read how the researcher theorizes the data gathered.

Can you see how, through theorizing the data gathered, the researcher knits their research into the body of knowledge? It is through theorizing the data gathered, through knitting their research into the body of knowledge, that the researcher makes a contribution to knowledge.

END OF CHAPTER QUESTIONS

1 Explain what is meant by observation in field research.

2 What is meant by the term rigour in social research?

3 Name the three main types of observation engaged in by researchers.

4 What are the three critical decisions to be made in any observation study?

5 Why would a researcher use unstructured observation as an observation method?

6 Why would a researcher use semi-structured observation as an observation method?

7 Why would a researcher use structured observation as an observation method?

8 What is unobtrusive observation in research?

9 Explain mechanical observation with the use of three examples.

10 What is covert observation in research and what are the main ethical issues in such research?

11 Detail and explain how you would critique an observation study.

REFERENCES

Advanced Tracking Technologies, Inc. (ATTI) www.advantrack.com/contact-us/ (Accessed 17.03.2018).

Anderson, K. (2009) 'Ethnographic research: a key to strategy', hbr.org/2009/03/ethnographic-research-a-key-to-strategy (Accessed 17.03.2018).

Anderson, K., Faulkner, S., Kleinman, L. and Sherman, J. (2017) 'Creating a Creators' Market: How Ethnography Gave Intel a New Perspective on Digital Content Creators', Ethnographic Praxis in Industry Conference Proceedings, Cases 3 – New Ventures and New Markets, anthrosource.onlinelibrary.wiley.com/doi/epdf/10.1111/1559-8918.2017.01162 (Accessed 17.03.2018).

Colorado State University, 'Writing guide: ethnography, observational research, and narrative inquiry', writing.colostate.edu/guides/guide.cfm?guideid=63

Ethnographic Research, Inc. www.ethnographic-research.com (Accessed 17.03.2018).

Information Resources Inc. (IRI) www.iriworldwide.com/en-US (Accessed 17.03.2018).

Kozinets, R. (2015) Netnography: Redefined (2nd edn), London, California, New Delhi, Singapore: Sage.

Lee, J. (2009) 'Open mic: professionalizing the rap career', Ethnography, 10(4): 475–495.

Lynd, R.S. and Lynd, H.M. (1959) Middletown: A Study in Modern American Culture, New York: Mariner Books.

Mass Observation Archive, The Library, University of Sussex, Brighton www.massobs.org.uk (Accessed 17.03.2018).

Oliver, J. and Eales, K. (2008) 'Re-evaluating the consequentialist perspective of using covert participant observation in management research', Qualitative Market Research: An International Journal, 11(3): 344–357.

Russell, D.W. (2008) 'Nostalgic tourism', Journal of Travel and Tourism Marketing, 25(2): October, 103–116.

RECOMMENDED READING

Berger, J. (2008) Ways of Seeing, Penguin Modern Classics, London: The British Broadcasting Company, and Harmondsworth: Penguin.

Collis, J. and Hussey, R. (2013) Business Research: A Practical Guide for Undergraduate and Postgraduate Students (4th edn), Basingstoke and New York: Palgrave Macmillan.

Denscombe, M. (2017) The Good Research Guide: For Small-scale Social Research Projects (5th edn), Maidenhead: Open University Press.

Easterby-Smith, M., Thorpe, R. and Jackson, P.R. (2008) Management Research (3rd edn), London: Sage.

Gill, J. and Johnson, P. (2010) Research Methods for Managers (4th edn), London, California, New Delhi, Singapore: Sage.

Hammersley, M. and Atkinson, P. (2007) Ethnography: Principles in Practice (3rd edn), Oxon and New York: Routledge.

Lee, R. (2000) Unobtrusive Methods in Social Research, Milton Keynes: Open University Press.

van Leeuwen, T. (2005) Introducing Social Semiotics, London: Routledge.

Miles, M.B., Huberman, A.M. and Saldana, J. (2014) Qualitative Data Analysis: A Methods Sourcebook, London Thousand Oaks, CA, New Delhi, Singapore: Sage.

Neuman, W.L. (2014) Social Research Methods: Qualitative and Quantitative Approaches (7th edn), Essex, England: Pearson Education Ltd.

Paterson, M. (2018) Consumption and Everyday Life (2nd edn), Oxon and New York: Routledge.

Prosser, J. (1998) Image-based Research, London: Routledge.

Robson, C. and McCartan, K. (2016) Real World Research, John Wiley & Sons Ltd.

Rose, G. (2016) Visual Methodologies, London, California, New Delhi, Singapore: Sage.

Simpson, M. and Tuson, J. (2003) Using Observations in Small-scale Research: A Beginner's Guide, The SCRE Centre, Glasgow: University of Glasgow.

University of Pennsylvania, Center for Urban Ethnography, www.gse.upenn.edu/cue (Accessed 17.03.2018).

Yin, R.K. (2018) Case Study Research and Applications: Design and Methods (6th edn), Thousand Oaks, CA: Sage.

CHAPTER 14

USING INTERVIEWS AND FOCUS GROUPS

LEARNING OBJECTIVES

At the end of this chapter, the student should be able to:

- Decide on the most appropriate use and design of interviews and/or focus groups for particular research projects.

- Use interviews and/or focus groups in their own research.

- Design and develop appropriate interview and focus group schedules for their own research.

- Critique the use of interviews and focus groups in research.

RESEARCH SKILLS

At the end of this chapter, the student should, using the exercises on Cengage Brain, be able to:

- Decide when to use interviews and when to use focus groups to gather data.

- Design an interview schedule and a focus group schedule for a sample project.

- Critique the design of a proposed interview and focus group.

The aim of this chapter is to explain in detail two data collection methods, interviews and focus groups. You will remember that these data-gathering methods were introduced in Chapter 8. In this chapter, the ways in which to structure and carry out interviews and focus groups are explained in detail. Both face-to-face (F2F) focus groups and interviews, and focus groups and interviews conducted using computer-mediated communication (CMC), are explored. The different types of interview, one-to-one interviews, depth interviews (or in-depth interviews), telephone interviews, group interviews, photo elicitation interviews and online interviews are described, along with their relative advantages and disadvantages.

The four frameworks

- Conceptual Framework
- Theoretical Framework
- *Methodological Framework*
- Analytical Framework

INTRODUCTION

Data-gathering techniques are part of the methodological framework, the third framework in the four frameworks approach to the design of the research project. The four frameworks approach to the research project facilitates the researcher in developing a logical and coherent fully integrated research project. The first three frameworks of the approach to research are laid out again in Figure 14.1.

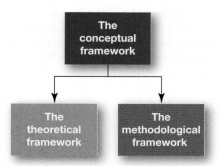

Figure 14.1   Three frameworks of the four frameworks approach to research

The epistemological and ontological perspectives of the research project are, as we know from Chapter 4, embedded in the philosophical perspective informing the research project, and consequently in the project's research methodology. As explained in Chapter 4, embedded in each statement of methodology are implicit statements or assumptions about the nature of reality (ontological assumptions), and about the kind of knowledge that will be generated by the research (epistemological assumptions). Focus groups and interviews are often used in research undertaken within a social constructivist or interpretive philosophical framework. The ontological perspectives within such philosophical frameworks hold reality to be multiple, individually interpreted or socially constructed.

Focus groups and interviews are most frequently used to generate **qualitative research**. Quantitative data can be generated when a highly structured interview schedule is used, and/or when a large number of interviews and/or **focus groups** are carried out. **Quantitative research** is situated within a positivist philosophical framework. The ontological perspective of this framework holds reality to be singular, objective and apart from the individual.

qualitative research Research that produces non-numeric data. Qualitative research focuses on words rather than numbers in the collection of data. Qualitative research as a research strategy is inductive and subjective, constructivist and/or interpretivist.

focus group An unstructured, free-flowing discussion with a small group of around six to ten people. Focus groups are facilitated by a trained moderator who follows a flexible format encouraging dialogue among respondents.

quantitative research Research that focuses on the gathering of numeric data or data in numerical form, i.e. data in the form of numbers. Quantitative research is deductive and positivistic and it is said to be objective.

We will see, as we read through this chapter, how the researcher designs their interviews and focus groups to help accomplish the aim of the research. S/he does this by engaging the population of their study in a data-gathering exercise that will provide the data required for the study. The philosophical perspective within which the project is situated is indicated in the aim of the research and confirmed in the methodology used to carry out the research.

It is likely that you have at some time participated in an interview and perhaps you have participated in a focus group. This chapter explores these two data-gathering methods in detail and explains how they are used in business research projects. As explained in the previous chapter, in any data-gathering exercise the most critical decisions to be made are the decisions on exactly what data to gather and how to gather that data.

THE VALUE OF GOOD RESEARCH

A good example of the use of interviews and focus groups is provided by the UK's TV station Channel 4. In 2000 Channel 4 developed a new programme for television called *Big Brother*. This programme became very popular with television audiences and the show is still one of the UK's top rated shows (www .bigbrotherauditions.com/). According to Doug Wood (2017), of Endemol Shine Group, a global production company for all platforms, (www.endemolshinegroup.com/about/) *Big Brother* was the UK's most tweeted TV show of 2016. The show is now a global phenomenon, and currently, CBS in the USA is running a version of the show entitled *Celebrity Big Brother*.

Throughout the lifetime of this programme in the UK, Channel 4 has engaged in audience research. The approach used for this research is a multi-method approach, in other words multiple data-gathering methods are used. Channel 4 carries out such research in order to find out what its audiences really think about the TV programmes it broadcasts.

A market research organization carried out research for *Big Brother*. In order to develop a real and in-depth understanding of the audience, it used qualitative research methods. Three different qualitative data-gathering methods were used: diaries, interviews and focus groups. Audience members were asked to keep media diaries in which they recorded their viewing habits and their thoughts and feelings about the programming they viewed. They were also invited to participate in focus groups and interviews.

This is interesting because it is often the case that quantitative data are gathered in audience research. For example, the television ratings produced by organizations such as the Broadcasters' Audience Research Board (BARB) (www.barb .co.uk) are quantitative data. However, as those in charge at Channel 4 were clearly aware, it is qualitative data that are required for a real understanding of what audience members think and feel about programming.

Doug Wood is currently Group Director of Research & Insight for Endemol Shine Group (Wood, 2017). He set up the group's global research and insight function. He is said to be an expert on global trends for the TV industry and in his work he oversees all research on the company's global hit formats such as *Big Brother*, *The Island*, and many more. He has worked on TV programmes as diverse as *Masterchef*, *The Bridge* and *Broadchurch*. Interestingly, Doug Wood began his career with the UK broadcaster Channel 4.

If you refer back to Figure 1.1 in Chapter 1, you will see where in the research process the researcher uses data-gathering methods. As can be seen from the figure, when the researcher has selected a methodology s/he begins to devise data collection methods. The data-gathering methods we focus on in this chapter are interviews and focus groups.

INTERVIEWS AND FOCUS GROUPS

Interviews and focus groups, as stated earlier, are data-gathering methods. They are ways through which data can be gathered for a research project.

Interviews are generally used when the researcher can identify key respondents in relation to the phenomenon under investigation and can engage these respondents in an interview process.

Focus groups are generally used when the researcher wants the participants to focus on a particular phenomenon and, through that focus, generate some ideas about and/or insights into that phenomenon. Focus groups are efficient ways of gathering data simultaneously from a range of participants. Focus groups are also used when a **group dynamic** would be useful to the research agenda. A group dynamic can drive a conversation to powerful levels of depth and complexity. Such conversations can generate very valuable insights into the phenomenon being researched.

> **group dynamic** Energy that develops naturally within a group. It can be positive or negative and is often affected by strong personalities.

Interviews

There are essentially five different types of interview in research: the one-to-one interview, the group interview, the telephone interview, the online interview and the photo-elicitation interview. Interviews and focus groups and other data-gathering methods are listed and explained in Chapter 9 in Table 9.2. The five different types of interview are briefly explained below:

- The one-to-one interview: this is usually a depth interview, (an in-depth interview) where the researcher, generally one researcher interviewing one interviewee, explores the phenomenon under investigation in depth with the interviewee (the person being interviewed).
- The group interview: this is where the researcher interviews a group of people at the same time, two or more people. This is not, as will be seen, the same as a focus group. In a focus group, a moderator or facilitator facilitates the group discussion. In an interview, the interviewer asks questions or poses topics and the interviewees respond. The interviewer controls the interview. The focus group moderator or facilitator facilitates the discussion in the focus group. In practice, there is quite a substantial difference.
- The telephone interview: this is where the researcher (the interviewer) interviews the interviewee (the participant or respondent) over the telephone.
- The online interview: this is where the researcher conducts the interview using the internet or an intranet (an intranet is a private network of computers within an organization).
- In a photo-elicitation interview, the interviewer engages the interviewee in a discussion and analysis of a photograph or a series of photographs.

Photo-elicitation interview

In a **photo-elicitation interview**, the researcher engages participants in their research in an exploration and analysis of a photograph or a series of photographs. As Harper (1998: 35, see also Harper, 2012) states, in the photo-elicitation interview, the interview, and the discussion in the interview, is stimulated and guided by images. These images can be photographs taken by the researcher and/or the participants in the research, or they can be other photographs or images. Becker (1974) said that photo elicitation is a method whereby the researcher uses photographs to engage the informants in verbal commentary. Collier and Collier (1986) and Harper (1996, 1998, 2012) refer to this method as the photo interview.

> **photo-elicitation interview** The researcher takes the interviewee through an exploration and analysis of a series of photographs.

Photo-elicitation research has been used to explore many aspects of the world of work, for example to document the experiences of migrant workers, dairy farmers, industrial workers and child labourers. Liu, Sparks and Coghlan (2017) used photo elicitation to study customer experiences of a food and wine event. They encouraged customers participating in the event to take photographs, and then, with the participants, they analyzed the content of the photographs and the meaning of the photographs for the participants in terms of their experience of the event. Bates, Kaye and McCann (2017) used photo elicitation to explore student satisfaction with the student experience at university. Venkatraman and Nelson (2008) used photo elicitation in their research when they asked young urban Chinese consumers to photograph their experiences in Starbucks in Beijing. The researchers used the photographs in in-depth interviews to explore those experiences with the young people. You might think about the possibility of using photo-elicitation interviews in your own research. (Image-based research is the research methodology in focus in Chapter 4 of this textbook.)

One-to-one interviews

In the **one-to-one interview**, or face-to-face (F2F) interview, the researcher has the opportunity to develop a rapport, or comfortable communicative relationship, with the interviewee. This rapport helps the researcher engage the interviewee in the interview process. In one-to-one interviewing, the interview process calls for confidential, formal, open and honest communication between the interviewer and interviewees.

> **one-to-one interview** The researcher interviews each participant, one at a time and in great depth and detail.

During a one-to-one interview, the researcher has the opportunity to observe the interviewee, including the manner in which they engage with, and respond to, the research questions/issues. The interviewer records those observations, and the recorded observations are further data for the research project. The researcher also has the opportunity to probe the responses. This probing is not usually done in any challenging way. The researcher uses gentleness, skill, discretion and respect to question the responses of the interviewee, asking for clarification where necessary, or perhaps prompting the interviewee for a more detailed or more elaborate response.

In the one-to-one interview the interviewee becomes the sole focus of the interviewer. This means that, during the interview, the interviewee has the space and the time to express their individual perspective on, and/or their individual experience of, the phenomenon under investigation. The one-to-one interview gives the researcher the opportunity to gather in detail the testimony of the one research respondent who is participating in the interview. This may be useful, or even essential, in terms of the data requirements of the research project. Or it may not. The researcher must decide how best to gather the data required for the research. The main disadvantage of one-to-one interviews is that they are time-consuming. There is also potential in a one-to-one interview situation for the interviewer to influence or lead the responses of the interviewee in some way. Such action is a source of **bias** in interview data (the issue of bias in research is explored in detail later in this chapter).

> **bias** Anything that contaminates or compromises the research or data.

Group interviews

In a group interview, the researcher conducts the interview with a group of respondents/participants. Here, the same opportunities do not exist for the building of rapport with each respondent or for each respondent to express at length and in depth their own perspective on, or experience of, the phenomenon under investigation. The group interview has its own unique advantages. The group dynamic may produce data that would not be produced through a one-to-one interview process. The group setting may also serve to protect the interviewer and the interviewees. There is safety in numbers. The group setting may provide a sense of security for participants and the group dynamic may encourage the participants to engage more fully and more freely in the process of creating data. However, the researcher must exercise caution. The group dynamic can also have completely the opposite effect. Participants can feel constrained or even intimidated by the group setting, and may as a consequence be less inclined to engage with the process. Once again, the researcher must make a decision about the optimum method to use to gather the data required within the constraints of the resources available. Figure 14.2 provides an excerpt from a transcript of a one-to-one interview. This excerpt from a one-to-one interview conducted with a member of a hillwalking club is useful in that it demonstrates the amount of data and the depth of data that it is possible to gather in such a research encounter. Obviously, the excerpt detailed is a short piece from a longer interview. Clearly, a very substantial amount of detailed, rich data were gathered in the interview.

An interviewer (I) talks with an interviewee (Daniel (D)) about his hobbies. Daniel talks about outdoor pursuits. He is particularly keen on hillwalking. He is a member of a hillwalking club and he spends a great deal of his free time participating in club activities:

D   We walk every Sunday, in some part of Ireland. As the club is based in Dublin, we walk a lot in Wicklow National Park.

I   Do you ever travel longer distances to walk?

D   Oh yes, we walk in many different parts of Ireland. We walk in Donegal, in Connemara, in West Cork and in Kerry. Actually some of my favourite walks are in Kerry.

I   Have you ever walked outside Ireland?

D   Yes, three or four times. I walked in Snowdonia National Park in North Wales, and in Scotland, on the island of Iona, and I've walked part of the Camino de Santiago de Compostela. I enjoy going abroad on walking trips with the club and I would go more often, if I had the time.

I   Can I ask you, why is it, do you think, that you enjoy hillwalking so much?

D   Emmm, I just love being out on the hills. I love the freedom. I love the fact that you get to see places that you could never see if you didn't go hillwalking.

I   Can you think of any other reasons?

D   Well, I do like being in the club, the hillwalking club. It's very sociable. You meet a lot of people. I made a lot of new friends when I joined and I get a lot of invitations through the club, invitations to parties and other social events. So, yes, being a member of the club has made an enormous difference to me in terms of my social life. I have, I suppose I have a lot of friends now, friends I made through the club and, you know, I socialize with them all the time. The club is not just about walking; it's about the friends you make as well. That's important too. Yeah, mmmmm, I suppose I would say that I've become more confident, you know, socially, since I joined the club.

Figure 14.2   Excerpt from a depth interview

The excerpt might give you some ideas of how you might use in-depth one-to-one interviews in your own research. You should read the excerpt and think about how you would design and conduct a one-to-one interview, or a series of interviews. Think about the possible contribution one-to-one interviews might make to your research.

Telephone interviews

In a telephone interview, the researcher conducts the interview over the telephone. Usually this is done on a one-to-one basis, with one interviewee/participant/respondent. The telephone interview does not afford the researcher any opportunity to observe the interviewee. However, the telephone does offer convenience for both the interviewer and the interviewee. The researcher does not have to travel to where the interviewee is in order to conduct the interview and the interviewee can take part in the interview in any location with a telephone or access to a signal for a mobile phone. The use of the telephone also allows for some degree of privacy and anonymity, because the researcher cannot see the interviewee. Sometimes there is a requirement in the research for privacy and/or anonymity and sometimes there is simply a distinct benefit for the research in the researcher conducting the interviews by telephone; for example if the population of the research is scattered over a large geographic area or if there is some sensitivity in the research question. It is important to remember that many people do not have telephones and also that many people who do have telephones have unlisted telephone numbers. This can, in some research projects, have substantial implications for population sampling.

Online interviews

Online interviews can be synchronous or asynchronous. Synchronous interviews are interviews undertaken in real time, for example, interviews carried out in chatrooms, when the interviewer asks a question and the interviewee responds immediately. Asynchronous interviews are interviews that are conducted out of real time, for example using email or online discussion forums, bulletin boards, message boards, and so on. An email interview involves the interviewer in sending the interviewee a question or a short series of questions to which the interviewee responds; a long list of questions sent via email is a questionnaire (questionnaires are dealt with in detail in Chapter 15). Asynchronous interviews can be carried out over extended periods of time. Using web-conferencing software, both synchronous and asynchronous one-to-one and **group interviews** can be carried out. You can learn a lot about gathering data online from the Exploring Online Research Methods web page of the University of Leicester. This is a very useful resource: (www2.le.ac.uk/departments/geography/projects/tri-orm).

> **online interviews** Interviews conducted online. Can be synchronous or asynchronous.
>
> **group interviews** A researcher interviews the participants in a group.

How to conduct interviews

The researcher must decide on which interview technique to use and then plan the interviews. It is a useful exercise to do this step-by-step and the research diary should be used for this work, so that a secure record is kept of the planning process. The planning process will help you to prepare properly for the interviews and it will help ensure that you spot any potential issues or problems in the interview process. The notes from your research diary will be of help when you write up this process in the research methodology chapter of your thesis, or in the research methodology section of the report of your research.

Interviews are conducted differently in quantitative and qualitative research. There are substantial epistemological and ontological reasons for this. As you know from Chapter 4, epistemology relates to the nature of knowledge, to what is known and to how we know what we know, while ontology relates to the nature of being and reality. As explained in Chapter 4, the philosophical framework of positivism holds that there is one objective reality. The philosophical framework of constructivism holds that reality is subjective, that individuals construct their own (multiple) realities. The philosophical framework of interpretivism (which is related to constructivism) holds that social reality is a subjective construction based on interpretation and interaction, the individual creates their own reality through interpretation and interaction.

In quantitative research, the researcher decides what needs to be known and designs a very precise data-gathering instrument to gather data in order to create that knowledge. In designing such a precise instrument, the researcher controls and even shapes the information that is gathered and consequently the knowledge generated by the research project. Quantitative research is said to be objective and situated within a framework of positivism.

In qualitative research, the researcher loosely designs the research instrument. This is in order to allow the research participants to control and shape the information that is gathered and, consequently, the knowledge generated by the research project. This is because in qualitative research, the focus is on developing insight into and an understanding of the thoughts, ideas, experiences, and so on, of the participants in the study. It is the participants' realities (plural) that qualitative research is designed to record. Qualitative research is said to be subjective and situated within a framework of constructivism and/or interpretivism.

In quantitative research, interviews are conducted in a structured systematic manner. The researcher designs a structured interview schedule, which is like a questionnaire, and follows it rigidly, asking each interviewee the same questions in the same order. The interview schedule is the list of questions to be asked or issues to be explored in the interview(s). If the interview schedule is long, questions are grouped into sections so that the issues raised can be dealt with thoroughly, efficiently and systematically. The interview schedule begins with background questions, with demographic questions, then more general questions, before finally moving to specific questions on the phenomenon under investigation. Standardized probes are written into the interview schedule. This is to ensure that if probing is used, the same probing is used with each interviewee. You will remember this from Chapter 12 and the discussion in that chapter on the work of training and managing fieldworkers for a research project. When probing an interviewee, interviewers say things like 'could you tell me a little more about that' or 'could you say a little more about that' or the interviewer might simply make an encouraging noise, such as 'hmmmm'. The interviewer does not want to bias the interview by leading the interviewee in their responses. Such bias is known as interviewer bias or researcher bias (see separate section on bias later in this chapter).

In quantitative research, the interview schedule guides the interview, so that every interviewee is asked the same questions. This is necessary to ensure that the data are gathered in a rigorous systematic manner. Structured interview schedules are comprised mostly of **closed questions**. These are questions that provide respondents with a restricted set of options in terms of possible answers, for example 'yes/no', or 'sometimes/often/regularly'. Closed questions elicit short responses and are often used to gather factual data. The possible responses to closed questions can be pre-coded to ensure that the data gathered can be easily and quickly analyzed. The work of coding data is dealt with in detail in Part Four of this textbook.

> **closed questions** Questions that elicit a defined limited range of responses, e.g. yes/no. Often used to establish factual information.

Open questions are questions that do not anticipate particular responses; they are questions to which the respondents may answer in any unique and individual way. Open questions are used to explore respondents' understandings, feelings and beliefs. They often require thought and reflection on the part of respondents and they usually generate long responses.

> **open questions** Used to explore understandings, feelings and beliefs. Usually require thought and reflection on the part of respondents. Tend to generate relatively long responses.

In qualitative research, the interviews are more loosely structured. The interview schedule is either unstructured or semi-structured and the interview is conducted in a flexible manner. The focus of the interview in qualitative research is on exploring the interviewees' perspectives and the emphasis is on allowing or facilitating the interviewee to open up and express their ideas and thoughts on the phenomenon being explored. These interviews are more like conversations, where the interviewee is allowed to take the discussion in any direction they wish in order to explain or illustrate their perspective. The interviewer can probe responses, ask interviewees to elaborate or to illustrate an answer with an example. This loose structure and flexible approach to interviews in qualitative research allows for the production of rich and complex data. In general, such interviews are audio recorded and the recording is transcribed after the interview. The transcript becomes the data gathered.

Table 14.1 takes you step-by-step through the process of planning and conducting interviews for your research project.

Bias in research

As explained earlier, bias in research is anything that contaminates or compromises the research. Bias can be introduced to a research project at any stage, at the design stage, during sampling, data gathering or data analysis, or at the stage of developing findings and coming to conclusions about the research. Bias can refer to a particular perspective that the research takes which highlights some aspects or findings of the research while ignoring or even hiding others. Bias can also refer to some systematic error that has somehow been introduced into the research.

Table 14.1 How to conduct interviews

Decide on interview method	The first thing the researcher must do is decide on the interview method: one-to-one, group telephone, online interview or other.
Devise interview schedule	The researcher must devise the interview schedule. The interview schedule is highly structured in interviews in quantitative research. It is generally either unstructured or semi-structured in interviews in qualitative research.
Select interviewees using appropriate sampling method (see Chapter 10)	The researcher must decide on whom to interview. The researcher selects a sampling method for the interviewees based on the population of the study and the needs of the research. For example, if the population of the study is a large population and the researcher wants a sample representative of the population, the researcher will likely use a probability sampling method, and may engage in simple random sampling in order to select the sample of interviewees. Sometimes the researcher knows precisely who in the population s/he needs to interview. In such a case, the researcher uses a judgemental or purposive sampling technique to select key informants on a topic to interview. Judgemental, or purposive, sampling is a non-probability sampling method. It is important to select the appropriate sampling technique for your research.
Contact interviewees and invite them to participate	When you have compiled a list of potential interviewees and their contact details, you should contact them in order to invite them to participate in the interview. Remember that they are free to refuse to participate, and there must be no repercussions for them, and no evidence of disappointment on the part of the researcher, when and if a potential respondent declines an invitation to participate in a study.
Provide interviewees with formal information on the research	Provide potential participants with information on your research. The decision they make with regard to whether or not to participate in your research is likely to be made based on this information. As this is the case, it is important to develop a good information sheet, one which properly, and clearly and succinctly, explains your research. The information sheet should clearly identify you and your organization and/or college or university. If you are undertaking the research in order to qualify for a diploma or degree, this should be stated on the information sheet. If the research is funded, this should be stated and the source(s) of the funding should be acknowledged. The information sheet should clearly and simply explain your research, the background to it, the context for it, and it should briefly explain why you are conducting the research and what you hope to learn/gain from it. It is a good idea to explain in the information sheet the benefits of participation to the participants. The benefits may be related to them making a contribution to knowledge through their participation. You can also offer to provide feedback to them on the findings of the research. This may be beneficial for them in terms of their business and/or their career. With a little reflection, you may come up with other benefits to your participants that may accrue to them from participation in your research. It should be noted on the information sheet that their participation in the research is voluntary. Participants should be guaranteed anonymity as far as is legally and practically possible. They should be guaranteed confidentiality, and they should be guaranteed that they will not in any way be harmed or disadvantaged through participation. The issue of informed consent is considered in detail in Chapter 3 of this textbook.
Set up interviews	The work of setting up the interviews may, depending on the interview method, involve deciding on a mutually convenient location and time. If so, the location is critical. It must be suitable. It must be comfortable, quiet, reasonably private and if possible free from interruption. A noisy background will have a negative impact on any audio recording of the interview. It may even render parts of, or even the entire, recording of the interview inaudible. If you are audio recording the interviews you should ensure that the system you are using is dependable. You should test it and you should ensure that you have two power supplies, usually mains electricity and batteries, in case one runs out or suddenly becomes unavailable. It is important to have a back-up recording device. You need two recording devices, in case one of them doesn't work when you start the interview. It is appropriate usually to provide a copy of the interview schedule to participants before the interviews. This gives participants the opportunity to prepare in advance. It also reassures participants that they are not going to be surprised by the interview questions/issues or find themselves unprepared for the interview questions/issues. Providing participants with the interview schedule before the interview signals frankness, openness and honesty, and this can help the researcher in the work of establishing rapport with interviewees.
Conduct one-to-one interviews/face-to-face (F2F) interviews	Remember that you are being judged as a researcher as soon as you enter the location for the interview. It is important that you behave accordingly. Dress appropriately and present yourself in a professional manner. Be prepared for things to go wrong, allow that things may not go according to plan. When you are prepared for this, you will react appropriately. Allow the interviewee the time they need to settle down to the interview. Take the time needed to complete the interview properly and get the data required. Be patient. As soon as the interview does begin, it is a good idea to switch the recorder on, if the interview is being audio recorded. Test the recorder to make sure that it is recording. Then start the interview process. The interviewee usually quickly forgets that the interview is being recorded. Both the interviewer and the

(Continued)

Table 14.1 How to conduct interviews (*Continued*)

Conduct one-to-one interviews/ face-to-face (F2F) interviews (*Continued*)	interviewee should have copies of the interview schedule. You should allow the interviewee the time s/he needs to answer each question, to discuss each issue. Remember that the responses the interviewees make to the questions and/or issues discussed in the interview become the data gathered for the research project. Ensure that you use the opportunity of the interviews to gather as much data as you can. The data you gather should be good and useful data, pertinent to the research project.
Conduct telephone interviews	When conducting telephone interviews ensure that the interviewee has the time to engage properly with the interview. Ensure as much as you can that the interviewee has the privacy necessary to engage properly with the interview. Allow them the time they need to prepare. Be ready for things not to go according to plan. Be prepared to be patient. Be prepared to ring back at another time or on another day if necessary. When the interview does commence, work systematically down through the interview schedule with the interviewee. Allow them the time they need to express themselves. If the interview is interrupted, wait patiently for the interview to resume.
Conduct group interviews	Ensure that the venue is suitable. Remember that the group dynamic is what makes the group interview unique. Use the group dynamic to help generate the data you need. You do this by encouraging the development of group interaction. You can ask a direct question. You can give the members of the group a minute or two of silence to think about their answers, you can then encourage them to confer in groups of two or three before encouraging them to speak out. It is often the case that the issue in facilitating groups is that of discouraging one or two individuals from speaking too much and dominating the group, rather than any difficulty with generating energy or a dynamic within a group. Sometimes a group will police itself in this regard and the dominant voices will be checked by members of the group. Sometimes the facilitator has to check the dominant voices. This must be done skilfully and diplomatically. You do not want to offend or alienate any member of the group. Even when you are checking a dominant member, you must make it clear that their contribution is very much valued. As a last resort, you can use a system of allocating imaginary cards to each member of the group. Each member is given a number of imaginary cards, for example five cards. Every time they speak, they use up a card. When all the cards are used up, they have to stop participating in the discussion. This method is not ideal, but as a last resort it is effective.
Conduct online interviews	When conducting interviews online, you must first establish that your population and/or sample are online or can get online, and that they have the information and communication technology (ICT) skills necessary to engage in an online interview. You must also establish that your population and/or sample is willing to engage in an interview online with you. In asynchronous interviews, you post a question one at a time, or a short series of questions, to your interviewees, and you allow them to respond in their own time. You can repeat this exercise until the interview is completed. Using synchronous interviewing, the interview is in real time, you ask the questions and the interviewee(s) respond immediately. Online communication differs from F2F communication. It tends to be faster and more informal. Written online communication tends to have a lot of abbreviations, like texting, and lots of spelling and grammatical errors. An advantage in written online communication is the immediate provision of a transcript of the interview. Keeping interviewees engaged in online interviews can be difficult. Participants can be distracted and the interviewer is not there with them and consequently cannot anticipate distraction or witness distraction and so cannot take action to keep the participant engaged. The interviewer should be prepared for this and have a plan to deal with it. The researcher has to motivate the interviewee to stay engaged. They may be able to do this by persuading the interviewee of the importance of the research, it may be possible to coax the interviewee to stay engaged, or the interviewee might be provided with some incentive to stay engaged. It is important to remember that exercising, or attempting to exercise, too much control over participants or potential participants raises ethical issues.
What to do if things go wrong	If the interview breaks down for any reason, try to establish why this has happened. It may be because there has been some loss of trust on the part of the interviewee. It can happen accidentally and it can happen without the interviewer knowing or understanding why it happened. Do not insist on completing the interview. If the interviewee wants the interview to stop, allow that to happen. Try, if you can, to establish why this has happened. Offer to make adjustments. Offer to provide further information on the research. Offer apologies for any offence or upset that you may have unknowingly caused. Be ready if necessary to accept that the interview has broken down irretrievably. If you feel it is necessary, explain to the interviewee that you will write to them apologizing for any upset or offence you might have unwittingly caused and outlining an account of what happened. Such a letter serves as a formal record of your perspective on what happened. Explain what happened to your thesis supervisor and ask for their advice. Do not worry unduly. Researchers are very pragmatic people. If one approach to a research issue does not work, another approach will. If you do happen to lose one interviewee, replace this interviewee with

Table 14.1   How to conduct interviews (*Continued*)

What to do if things go wrong (*Continued*)	another, assuming that you yourself, through your manner or behaviour, are not the cause of the breakdown in the interview. If you do lose a participant in your research, learn what you can from the experience. One of the most important lessons to learn following such a setback is how to get back on track, how to move your research forward.
Conclude interview	When concluding interviews it is important to ask the interviewee if they have anything more that they would like to say, or if there is anything that they would like to add. Often in these final moments of an interview, interviewees will sum up their thinking on the phenomenon being investigated in a clear, succinct and useful manner. Sometimes interviewees will at this point remember and articulate something critical. Always allow interviewees the opportunity to do this. It is important to note in your research diary any promise you make to the interviewee, for example, in terms of feedback on the findings of the research. It is important to thank the interviewee for their participation. Be polite. Express your gratitude for the help and support you have been given with your research. Be open and communicative but careful. Do not identify or discuss other participants in the research, or anything they said throughout their engagement with the research. Do not engage in speculation with respondents about the possible findings, conclusions or implications of the research. Ensure that you have packed up all your equipment safely before you leave the venue. In particular, ensure that the data are secured.
Manage data	The proper management of data is an ethical issue in every research project. The security of data is a fundamental aspect of the proper management of data. Data can be lost, misplaced or even stolen. Ensure that you have a mindful, careful plan in place for the secure transport and storage of data. The safety and security of your data is one of your main priorities.

Researcher bias

Researchers can themselves be the cause of bias. For example, researchers can be biased in favour of a particular result or finding in their research. They can have a particular view and want that view confirmed by the study, rather than keeping an open mind as to what the study might confirm. They can influence the findings of the research through the design of the study. Through the use of what are known as leading questions, the researcher can influence participants in the study, through the wording of the questions, the emphasis they place on the different words and concepts in the questions and through encouraging and/or affirming particular responses. Sometimes in qualitative research, the researcher is said to be the research instrument. The data gathered for the research project are filtered through their perceptions of the phenomenon under investigation, through their engagement with and experience of the phenomenon. In such research, there are not more possibilities for bias than there are in other kinds of research, but there are different opportunities for bias. All researchers are in control of their own research. It is their responsibility as competent and ethical researchers to guard against bias.

Conducting interviews
Sampling bias

Sampling bias occurs when the sampling procedure used in the research is flawed or compromised in some way. Researchers can introduce sampling bias into their study if the population or sample used is biased in favour of a particular population or sample population. Population samples that under-represent some members of the population will bias research. Bias can be introduced through non-responses, when the non-respondents in the study differed in some significant way to respondents. When respondents are self-selecting, voluntary response bias can occur if the respondents have a particular agenda in the research. The population and/or the sample selected for the study should be appropriate for that study, and appropriate sampling methods should be used when selecting samples from study populations. Sampling methods are dealt with in detail in Chapter 10. The online 'teach yourself statistics' website Stat Trek provides a simple tutorial on bias in survey sampling (stattrek.com/survey-research/survey-bias.aspx).

Respondent bias

Respondents can bias research in a number of ways. They can respond in a patterned way to each question, perhaps answering 'yes' to every question, or 'no' to every question. This is known as a response set. Acquiescence bias happens when a respondent agrees with everything the researcher says. Social desirability bias occurs when a respondent gives the socially desirable or the politically correct response, rather than an honest response. Prestige bias occurs when the respondent is influenced in responding by their perception of the prestige of a group or individual, for example, the use of words such as 'doctor', 'president' or 'excellent' might introduce prestige bias.

Researchers try to eliminate bias from their research. If they find that, in spite of their best efforts, they have not managed to eliminate bias from their research, they acknowledge that their study is biased or that it may be to some degree biased. Researchers try to identify possible sources of bias in their research, although it is not always possible to do this. When researchers do identify a possible source of bias in their research, they acknowledge it.

YOUR RESEARCH
A common research problem

Sometimes, beginner researchers go to extraordinary lengths in planning and organizing their fieldwork, their interviews, focus groups or observations. Then when they are at home or back at their desks examining the data gathered in the field, they find that the data are not adequate. The data do not address the phenomenon under investigation, they do not address it in the detail required for the research or they do not address every aspect of the phenomenon as the researcher had hoped.

This is very common and it is a serious problem. The way to counter this problem is to ensure that you design the most appropriate data collection method(s) for your research project. Then, when you are in the field carrying out your data collection, you must ensure that the data you are collecting really do address the phenomenon you are investigating, the phenomenon detailed in your research statement/question

and in the aim and objectives of your research. The data gathered must address the phenomenon under investigation and they must do this thoroughly. When you are planning and designing your fieldwork, you must keep the research statement/question close to hand and you should check constantly that your plan and design for data gathering really will allow you to accomplish and complete this research.

It is always a good idea to ask for support and guidance from your supervisor and/or lecturer in research methods when undertaking an exercise as critical as the design and conduct of the fieldwork for your research project. It is worth remembering too that beginner researchers often panic unnecessarily over the data that they have gathered in the fieldwork. If the fieldwork has been properly prepared and carried out, it is likely that the process will produce a great deal of good, relevant data.

Focus groups

A focus group is used in research as a data collection method when there is some advantage, in terms of data gathering or data collection, in bringing a group of people together and facilitating this group in a focused discussion of the phenomenon under investigation in the research project. Clearly, the people invited to participate in the focus group must be expert in some way on the phenomenon under investigation.

THE VALUE OF GOOD RESEARCH

Domino's Pizza and focus group research

In the Domino's Pizza 'Pizza Turnaround' advertising campaign, the company acknowledged that it had problems with its product. The company engaged in research, including focus group research, with its customers. The

research established that the company's customers wanted changes in the company's product. Domino's Pizza demonstrated its commitment to customers by changing and improving its product. After this had been achieved, the company introduced a new advertising campaign to launch the improved product. The new advertising campaign was called 'Pizza Turnaround'. The TV commercials in the 'Pizza Turnaround' advertising campaign featured some footage from the focus groups. This footage was also featured in a documentary the company made about the process of changing the product. The documentary is called *The Pizza Turnaround Documentary* and you can view it at pizzaturnaround.com/.

In order to conduct focus group research, the researcher must have the capacity to properly facilitate the discussion, to ensure that the discussion stays focused and to ensure that the discussion is fruitful in terms of the data required for the research. In any group discussion, focus can easily be lost. The researcher must have the confidence, ability and diplomatic skills necessary to facilitate the discussion and to ensure that the group maintains the necessary focus in order to gather useful and pertinent data. Figure 14.3 provides an example of an excerpt from a focus group transcript.

Thank you for agreeing to participate in this focus group. Let me explain how it works and then please do ask questions if you would like me to clarify anything.

This is a focus group and in this focus group we are going to focus on newspaper readership. We would like you to read the information sheet provided. This explains the focus group, the research and the extent of your participation in the research. The focus group will be audio recorded and the recording will be transcribed. You will not be identified in any way in any publication of the research and your contribution will, outside of this room, remain confidential.

When you have read the information sheet, if you are happy to do so, please sign the consent form and pass the signed consent form to me.

Now that you have all signed the consent form, we can take a look at the focus group schedule. This schedule will guide our discussion.

Please do contribute to the discussion where and when you can. It is your views, your ideas and your perspectives that we want to explore. As we are recording the focus group, it would be helpful if just one person speaks at a time and please do project your voice a little when you speak, for the benefit of the group and the audio recording.

The subject is newspaper readership. Some of you may read a daily newspaper. Some of you may read more than one daily newspaper. Perhaps some of you read a newspaper once or twice a week, perhaps at the weekend, when you have enough free time to really enjoy reading a newspaper. Perhaps some of you occasionally or very rarely read a newspaper. We would like you now to tell us about your newspaper reading habits.

1. OK, so who would like to begin? We'll go around the table to start with so that everybody gets to talk about their own experience.
2. OK, so can you now tell us why you read the newspapers that you do read?

(PROBE: SO SOME OF YOU HAVE SAID THAT YOU USED TO READ A DAILY NEWSPAPER BUT YOU NO LONGER DO SO. I WONDER IF THOSE OF YOU WHO SAID THAT COULD EXPLAIN WHY THAT IS SO?)

3. OK, now can you tell me why you read the newspapers that you do read? Perhaps we can go around the table again and hear from everyone.
4. Can I ask now, does anyone read an international newspaper, such as, for example, *The Times of India, The Wall Street Journal* or *Bild*?

(PROBE: SO ONE OR TWO OF YOU DO READ AN INTERNATIONAL PAPER. CAN YOU TELL ME ABOUT THAT? TELL ME WHICH PAPER YOU READ, AND HOW OFTEN YOU READ IT, AND TELL ME TOO WHY YOU READ THAT PAPER.)

5. Now I'd like you to talk about reading newspapers online. Do any of you read newspapers online? Can we go around the table again? It would be very helpful if you would each talk about your experience, if any, of reading newspapers online.
6. Thank you for that. That's most helpful. Can I now ask you, those of you who do read or who have read a newspaper online, did you pay to access the newspaper or was the newspaper and/or the content you read freely available online?
7. It's interesting that some of the newspapers were freely available. That leads me now to the next issue on the focus group schedule. Would you be prepared to pay to access a newspaper online, in the same way as you pay for a newspaper if you buy it in a shop or from a kiosk? Can we go around the table again to hear how everyone feels about that?
8. Right. So, I'm beginning to develop an understanding now of how you feel about that. I think we can move the discussion along. The next issue on the schedule is the issue of price. Can you please think about this for a moment and then perhaps we can go around the table again. How much should an online newspaper cost? How much would you be prepared to pay for access to an online newspaper?
9. That's very interesting. We are coming to the end now. I just have one more issue that I'd like you to discuss. I would like to hear any thoughts or ideas you might have in relation to the kind of content that you would be prepared to pay for in an online newspaper?

(PROBE: SO A LOT OF VERY USEFUL THOUGHTS AND IDEAS. THANK YOU FOR THAT. BEFORE WE MOVE ON, CAN ANYBODY THINK OF ANY OTHER CONTENT THAT YOU MIGHT BE PREPARED TO PAY FOR IN AN ONLINE NEWSPAPER?)

10. Before we finish, is there anything that you would like to add to the discussion? Is there any issue you would like to revisit or is there any issue that hasn't come up in the discussion that you would like to raise now, that you would like to comment on now?

OK, thank you very much for your help. Does anybody want to ask a question or make a comment? Well, we'll be here for a little while longer, so if any of you would like clarity on any point or issue, please do feel free to talk to me or to my colleague here. Please do take your copy of the information sheet away with you. My contact details are on it; do contact me if you have any questions you'd like to ask or any comment you'd like to make about the focus group or the research.

Figure 14.3 Discussion guide for a focus group

You should read the excerpt and think about how you would design and then carry out a focus group. Think about the contribution that focus groups might make to your research.

Focus groups can be F2F or they can be online. Online focus groups (OFG) can be synchronous, in real time, or asynchronous, out of real time. In synchronous OFG, the focus group happens in real time using chatrooms or focus group software. Using conferencing software, the participants in the focus group can see one another; using suitable software, the typed contributions of participants are visible to all participants.

In asynchronous OFG, the focus group happens out of real time, using listservs, mailing lists or discussion groups. The focus group issues and/or questions are posted for participants and participants engage with the issues and questions and respond to the focus group facilitator/moderator in their own time.

Table 14.2 sets out the key advantages and disadvantages of online interviews and focus groups.

Table 14.2 Advantages and disadvantages of online interviews and focus groups

Advantages	Disadvantages
No access issues if the population is online or can go online	Potential participants must have access to the technologies and capability to use them
Participants located anywhere in the world, with access to the technologies, can participate	Recruitment can be difficult
Very large numbers can participate	Authentic participant identification can be an issue
No time limits	Different levels of skill and ease with the technologies can disadvantage some participants
Can be very inexpensive	It can be difficult to establish and/or maintain rapport with participants
Without video link participants cannot be seen and consequently may engage more openly	Without video link participants cannot be observed so data on non-verbal cues/facial cues/body language cannot be gathered
Can provide many data very quickly	Quality of data may not be adequate to research requirements
Very convenient for participants	Participants may be easily distracted
Can be structured to guarantee participants anonymity and privacy	Level and quality of participant engagement can be problematic
Participants less likely to be intimidated/controlled/controlling	Participants can easily/suddenly disengage from the research
Participants in asynchronous interviews and focus groups have more time to respond	Lack of depth in data compared to data gathered from in-depth F2F interviews and F2F focus groups
No recording necessary, so no recording issues or errors	Asynchronous interviews and focus groups can take a long time to complete
Accurate transcript provided, transcripts can readily be used in computerized data analysis	The facilitator/moderator may have to work very hard at facilitating and maintaining interaction
Safe and secure environment for researcher and participants	Technology can break down/the connection can be lost

Online focus groups have particular advantages and are useful in some research projects. For other research projects, the traditional F2F focus group is the most suitable method. This was the finding of Reid and Reid (2005), who, using experimental design as their methodology, carried out a comparison of focus groups using CMC (Computer Mediated Communication) and conventional F2F focus groups. According to Reid and Reid, the results of their experiment suggest that CMC is a viable alternative to F2F focus groups for certain purposes. Experimental design is the methodology in focus in Chapter 19.

Traditional F2F focus groups ideally take place around a table, ideally a boardroom table or a table like a boardroom table. Figure 14.4 outlines the processes involved in undertaking a F2F focus group.

Interview and focus group schedules

Data-gathering instruments, whether they are observation schedules, as explored in the previous chapter, interview or focus group schedules, as discussed in this chapter, or questionnaires and scales as discussed in the following chapters, are designed to provide the necessary data for the research project. As this is the case, the overall aim of the research and the objectives of the research inform the content of the data-gathering instrument. In addition, the review of the literature conducted by the researcher will inform the development of the research instrument and its content.

Using the research diary, the researcher gathers together all of the issues they would like to explore, or all of the issues they believe should be explored in the research. A long list of these issues can be developed in the research diary. Then the researcher groups together the issues that appear to belong together. The researcher begins to reduce the long list by continuing to group together issues that belong together and by collapsing together issues that are really about the same thing, perhaps conceptualizing a new concept (a new word or new phrase) to cover these issues. This is a process of conceptualization and reduction.

Decide on participants

The population of the study should be clearly outlined. If necessary, a sample of participants should be drawn from this population. An appropriate sampling method should be used. Ideally each **focus group** should comprise eight to 12 participants. Participants must be capable of making a useful contribution to discussion of the phenomenon under investigation. Participants should be contacted, and invited to participate in the focus group. They should be provided with an information sheet and an informed consent form (see Chapter 3). The information sheet should succinctly explain the research, the background to it, the context for it, and it should briefly explain why you are conducting the research and what you hope to learn/gain from it. It is a good idea to explain in the information sheet the benefits of participation in the interviews to the participants. In order to participate in the research, participants must read and sign the informed consent form, indicating that they freely participate in the research, that they understand the research and that they consent to the data generated by their participation in the research being used by the researcher(s) for the purposes of the research.

↓

Decide on venue

The venue should be convenient for participants. The **focus group** should take place in a comfortable room with a boardroom-style table. This style of table facilitates equal participation. The room should be properly heated and ventilated. The room should be neither too big nor too small. In a very big room, electronic recording can become compromised.

↓

Prepare focus group schedule

The **focus group** schedule should be semi-structured. This structure will allow the researcher to guide the focused discussion of the group while allowing for **group** discussion. There is an example of a focus group schedule below in the box feature titled Research Project.

↓

Prepare recording mechanism

Focus groups should be recorded electronically, usually audio recorded. If the **group dynamic** is of interest or if the physical, facial and/or bodily responses of participants are relevant, the **focus group** will be video recorded. There is too much discussion in a **focus group** for the discussion to be recorded adequately by hand. The transcript of the recorded **focus group** is the data gathered from the **focus group**. These data can be supplemented by any notes the researcher and/or research assistant(s) make during the **focus group**.

↓

Convene the focus group

The participants in the **focus group** should sit together around the table, in a boardroom table format. Drinking water and fresh drinking glasses or paper cups should be provided for participants. There should be no hierarchy. The participants should participate in the **focus group** as equals. The recording device should be switched on and checked to ensure that it is recording properly. There should be a back-up, a second recording device. When everyone is seated comfortably, the researcher introduces themselves and the research, and any research assistants. The researcher explains the process, what will happen and what s/he hopes to accomplish in terms of data collection through the process. The researcher might ask the members of the group to introduce themselves and to say a little about themselves. The researcher passes around copies of the focus group schedule. There should be one for every participant. Then the researcher takes the participants through the **focus group** schedule, familiarizing the participants with the schedule and answering any questions and queries they might have. The facilitator or moderator of the focus group (usually the researcher) starts the **focus group** discussion.

↓

(Continued)

Figure 14.4 Conducting a F2F focus group

Starting the focus group

Ideally, when the **focus group** begins, everyone in the room should be sitting at the table. There should be room at the table for the researcher and any researcher assistant(s). When the researcher(s) sit with the group as part of the group, this has the effect of neutralizing their presence in the room. They become participants in the **focus group** rather than observers of the **focus group**. If participants in research feel that they are being observed, they may feel uncomfortable, and, more problematically, they may begin to perform, and in doing so, they may introduce bias into the research. When research participants 'perform' for research, they try to give the researcher what it is that they think the researcher really wants, rather than clearly and simply, openly and honestly, engaging with the research questions and issues. This kind of **bias**, as explained above, is known as social desirability **bias**.

The focus group discussion

The **focus group** discussion should be very tightly focused on the phenomenon under investigation. The **focus group** facilitator or moderator controls and directs the discussion, using the **focus group** schedule and working methodically down through each of the different points and/or issues in the schedule. The facilitator should ensure proper time management of the group. If **the focus group** runs over time, members of the group may leave before the **focus group** is completed. The purpose of the **focus group** discussion can vary, according to the aim of the focus group and the overall aim of the research project. The outcome of the discussion should be an in-depth perspective on the phenomenon under investigation with some new understanding, new knowledge and/or new insight into that phenomenon.

Managing the group dynamic

The use of the **focus group** allows the researcher, as with a group interview, to benefit from group dynamics. When a group of people get together, any group of people, a natural dynamic develops between them and this dynamic will help drive the discussion within the group. It might happen that participants in the research are a little shy of each other or of the research process. In this case, the group dynamic may be a little slow to develop and the researcher must encourage the development of the **group dynamic**. The researcher may pose a simple question or present a simple or slightly provocative statement to encourage the discussion to begin and to facilitate the development of the **group dynamic**. **Group dynamics** can be very tricky. Groups can naturally develop good dynamics, and they can just as easily develop poor dynamics. The researcher should be sensitive to the nature of the dynamic within the group and should manage the group accordingly.

Concluding the focus group

At the end of the **focus group** discussion, the facilitator gives participants an opportunity to voice any further comments they wish to make. Then the facilitator thanks the participants for the contribution they have made to the research and the help and support they have given to the researcher. The researcher briefly informs the participants of the likely date of completion of the research. The researcher should not be drawn into speculating about the findings or conclusions of the research or the possible implications of the research. The researcher does not comment on any participant in the research, or their contribution to the research, whether or not they are present. The researcher ensures that the data are secure. S/he packs up all the equipment and leaves the room. The room should be clean and tidy when the researcher leaves. The safe and secure transport of the data from the venue to the researcher's desk, office or home is a key priority now for the researcher.

Figure 14.4   Conducting a F2F focus group (*Continued*)

Sometimes researchers convene a panel to help in this process. This panel could comprise fellow researchers, researchers with expertise in the area, senior researchers or a mixture of such individuals. A three-person panel is sufficient. Engaging such a panel in this exercise can help in establishing the validity of the research. Through repetitions and reiterations of the process of conceptualization and reduction, the key issues to be examined in the data collection phase of the research begin to emerge. The researcher, working alone or with the help of a panel, decides on the key issues to explore in the schedule and the different aspects of those key issues; decisions are also made on the order in which the issues should be explored in the schedule. The interview, focus group or observation schedule is designed in accordance with these decisions.

A focus group schedule is the list of questions to be asked, or the series of points or issues to be discussed, during a focus group or a series of focus groups. As explained previously, data-gathering schedules, whether they are used in observation, interviews or focus groups, can be unstructured, semi-structured or structured.

Semi-structured interview and focus group schedules allow participants more scope to express themselves with regard to the phenomenon under investigation. The semi-structured design of the schedules provides an open approach to the research encounter. Using such an approach, the researcher does not, through the design of the research instrument, impose on participants their own perspective, or understanding of, the phenomenon under investigation. The meaning of the phenomenon for participants and their personal experience and understanding of it are allowed to emerge in the interviews or focus groups through the semi-structured or unstructured design of the data-gathering exercise.

The following research project contains an example of a semi-structured focus group schedule, used in a study of brand loyalty among third-level students. The focus group schedule is simple, but the simplicity of the structure belies the amount of work and preparation that goes into the construction of such a schedule.

RESEARCH PROJECT
Brand loyalty among third-level students

Focus group schedule

Date ___ Venue ___ No. of participants ___

1. Introductions
2. The aim of the focus group
3. The focus group schedule – the conduct of the focus group, one speaker at a time, balanced discussion, the views of all participants, recording mechanisms

Issues for discussion

4. Brand loyalty
5. Loyalty to particular brands
6. Brands that tend to prompt loyalty among third-level students
7. Why these brands prompt loyalty
8. Key elements and aspects of the brands
9. Ways of prompting and/or promoting brand loyalty among third-level students
10. Summing up
11. Thanks and feedback

A structured interview schedule is like a questionnaire. It is comprised mostly of closed questions. As explained earlier, closed questions are often used to establish facts, for example, a respondent's age, or gender, or to establish whether or not a respondent uses a particular product. Often closed questions can be answered with yes or no answers.

There are often one or two, or a few, open questions in a questionnaire or in a structured interview schedule. Open questions are designed to allow the respondent to answer in any way they choose and they tend to generate long answers. Respondents usually have to think and reflect on the issue raised in an open question in order to answer the question. Asking a respondent why they do something, for example, 'Why do you use that product?' will generate a long, and probably unique, response from every respondent. The question 'Why do you use that product?' is an open question. The respondent may respond in any way to that question and their response cannot be anticipated by the researcher. We will explore open and closed questions in more detail in the following chapters.

Structured interview schedules are useful where the interviewer has a limited amount of time for the interview, for example, in street intercept interviews, or shopping centre intercept interviews, where the interviewer intercepts passers-by on the street or in a shopping centre and engages them in interviews. Structured interview schedules are also useful where the interviewer is not audio recording the interview, but recording the responses by hand.

Audio recorded F2F interviews are transcribed, then typed up, and these typed transcripts become the data to be analyzed. Where the responses to the interview questions are recorded by hand, these handwritten responses become the data to be analyzed. Obviously the quality of interview transcripts is of fundamental importance.

It is common for researchers to give interviewees a copy of the transcript of their audio recorded interview. When this happens, the interviewees are asked to read the transcript and verify that the transcript is an accurate account of the interview. This is known as **interviewer verification**.

interviewer verification An interviewer gives each of the interviewees a transcript of their interview. Each interviewee then verifies that the transcript is an accurate record of their interview.

Interviewee verification is an aid to establishing the validity of the data and, consequently, the validity of the research. Having read their interview transcript, interviewees can also provide the researcher with feedback on the data gathered during the interview and can clarify points and correct errors.

Interview schedules and focus group schedules can be subjected to pilot studies. As explained in the previous chapter, a pilot study is a test of the design of the research project or a test of the data-gathering instrument(s) designed for the research. An interview schedule is piloted by engaging in interview a small number of interviewees, perhaps three, four or five interviewees, depending on the size of the study, in order to pilot, or test, the interview schedule. The people interviewed in the pilot study are not those who will be interviewed in the study, but they are similar to the people who will be interviewed in the study itself. The pilot study demonstrates to the researcher how the interview schedule will work in a real interview. Based on the experience of the pilot, the researcher may amend the interview schedule.

YOUR RESEARCH
Common research problems

It sometimes happens that students and/or beginner researchers use the 'wrong' data collection method or an inappropriate data collection method in their research project. When this happens, it is usually because the student has some preconceived notion or idea about the data-gathering method they wish to use in their research project. Often the student feels comfortable for some reason with their preferred data-gathering method. It may be that the student has used the data-gathering method before or has participated in a research project that required him or her to use that data-gathering method. For whatever reason, the student has some degree of familiarity with that data-gathering method. This familiarity leads the student to favour this data-gathering method and, potentially problematically, to favour the use of this data-gathering method in their research project.

There are many ways of gathering data, as we saw in Chapter 9. The data-gathering method used should be the most appropriate method for the research project. The aim of the research gives an indication of the data required for the research project. The location of those data is the key to the kind of data-gathering method to use. If the data can best be gathered by engaging in one-to-one interviews, then this is the method to use. If the data can best be gathered by facilitating a group of experts on the phenomenon under investigation in a focused group discussion, then a focus group or a series of focus groups is the method to use.

In order to be able to make good decisions about the method(s) to use in your research, you must have some knowledge of a variety of data-gathering methods and the data that can be gathered using these methods.

Similarly, a focus group schedule can be piloted by engaging in a pilot focus group. Three or four participants are enough in a focus group pilot. Alternatively, the researcher might engage a panel, as described earlier, to critique the design of the focus group schedule.

It is important to try out or test data-gathering methods before using them to generate data for a research project. Many unanticipated issues and problems can emerge in piloting and when they do they can then be dealt with before data gathering commences for the research project. In addition, and as explained in the previous chapter, a pilot study is an aid to establishing the rigour and the validity of the data-gathering methods and the research project.

VALIDITY AND RELIABILITY IN QUALITATIVE AND QUANTITATIVE RESEARCH

The issues of validity and reliability are engaged differently in qualitative and in quantitative research (see Chapter 15 for a discussion of the issues of validity and reliability in quantitative research). Many researchers object to the application of quantitative measures of quality to qualitative research. Indeed, Corbin (Corbin and Strauss, 2008: 301–2), suggests that even the words 'validity' and 'reliability' do not fit well with qualitative research; Corbin believes that they carry with them too many quantitative implications. Even the word 'truth' is too dogmatic for Corbin in relation to evaluations of the quality of qualitative research; she prefers to use the word 'credibility' (Glaser and Strauss, 1967; Lincoln and Guba, 1985). Lincoln and Guba's terms for naturalistic inquiry (qualitative research) are laid out in Table 14.3 in relation to the comparable term in conventional inquiry (quantitative research). These terms, as they are used in qualitative research, are explained and explored in more detail in Table 14.4.

Table 14.3   Lincoln and Guba's (1985) terms for naturalistic inquiry

Conventional inquiry (Quantitative research)	Naturalistic inquiry (Qualitative research)
Internal validity	Credibility
External validity	Transferability
Reliability	Dependability
Objectivity	Confirmability

Table 14.4   Issues of validity and reliability in qualitative research

Validity	Reliability
The term validity in research, as defined in Chapter 2, is a question of how valid the research is, how logical, how truthful, how robust, how sound, how reasonable, how meaningful and how useful. Qualitative researchers are concerned with the credibility, the honesty and the truthfulness of their research. Above all, they want their research to be trustworthy and authentic (see Lincoln and Guba, 1985; Guba and Lincoln, 1994). Qualitative researchers regard qualitative data as being co-constructed, constructed by the researcher and the research participants together in the data-gathering processes used in the research project.	The term reliability in research, as defined in Chapter 2, relates to the dependability of the research, to the degree to which the research can be repeated while obtaining consistent results. Rather than reliability in the quantitative research sense of achieving consistent results over time and with different populations (see Chapter 15), qualitative researchers (Chapter 8), focus on establishing the rigour of their research. They focus on establishing the soundness, the dependability of their research (see Guba and Lincoln, 1994; Riege, 2003).
Qualitative researchers gather empirical data in the field and they use that data to present authentic, vivid and detailed accounts of the experiences of the people participating in their research. Qualitative researchers use a wide variety of data-gathering methods. The focus is on developing a 'thick description' (Geertz, 1973) of the experiences of the social world that are the focus of the research. Guba and Lincoln (1994) argue that this thick description allows for judgements to be made in relation to whether or not the findings of the research are transferable to other contexts, rather than generalizable to other contexts in a quantitative research sense.	While rejecting standardized structured approaches to data gathering, qualitative researchers do try to gather data in a consistent manner. In order to help establish the dependability of the research, Guba and Lincoln (1994) recommend that an audit approach be adopted by the researcher (see Bowen, 2009). Using such an approach, every decision made in the research project should be documented, explained and justified. Using Guba and Lincoln's approach to auditing, evaluators of the research (advisors, examiners and readers) then become auditors of the research, auditing the decisions made.
Respondent verification (interviewee verification as outlined earlier in the chapter is an example) is a method used to help establish the validity of the research project; the researcher encourages research participants to verify the findings of the research. In qualitative research, the fundamental aim of research is to illustrate the experiences of the participants in the research of some aspect of the social world. The ontological position of qualitative researchers is that there is no objective reality in terms of experiences of the social world; rather, there are individually constructed or individually interpreted experiences of reality. The work of the qualitative researcher is to create in their research credible, i.e. truthful and authentic, accounts of the experiences of research participants.	An alternative approach to auditing can be developed using the research diary. The qualitative researcher can record an audit trail in their research diary. The audit trail is a documented trail of their experiences, insights, knowledge development, and decision making, throughout the research project. The researcher can use this audit trail to help establish the dependability of the research project. A dense account of this audit trail can be included in the research methodology chapter of the thesis, or in the research methodology section of the report of the research. This account can be used to clearly document, outline, explain and justify the decisions the researcher made in relation to the research. Such an account can form part of the 'thick description' necessary in the writing up and reporting of qualitative research. It can provide for confirmability of the research.

Qualitative researchers are generally not concerned with measurement and often they do not support a scientific perspective that holds that the social world can be studied in a similar fashion to the ways in which the natural world is studied. They reject positivist approaches to social science and their approach to the study of the social world is either constructivist or interpretivist. They hold the philosophical perspective of experiences of the social world as being constructed and/or experienced and interpreted uniquely by every individual. Thus, they hold that every individual has their own reality, their own experience of reality. There are multiple realities.

Qualitative researchers see data gathering as an interactive process, often as a co-constructed process, a process that the researcher co-constructs with the participants in their research. For qualitative researchers, their engagement with their fieldwork tends to be prolonged and in-depth. They often use more multi-method approaches, and more varied approaches to fieldwork. While they tend not to use fixed or standardized measures of any phenomenon, they do produce deeply complex and rich accounts of the phenomena they investigate.

In both quantitative and qualitative research, validity can be established through the depth and complexity of the research project; through the researchers prolonged engagement with the field and with the participants in the research; through the scholarship evident in the written account of the research; through the detailed description of the methodology and methods used in the research project; through the expert analysis of the data carried out by the researcher; through the knowledge the researcher has of the phenomenon being investigated; and through the contribution to knowledge the researcher makes through the publication of the research.

REAL WORLD RESEARCH

Differences in quantitative and qualitative research

Quantitative and qualitative researchers engage differently in research. Sometimes beginner researchers fail to adequately respect the differences, both in the way in which they conduct their research and in the way in which they write up their research.

Quantitative and qualitative researchers make different assumptions about the social world and they expect different results from their researches. Whereas quantitative researchers are generally in search of facts, qualitative researchers explore experiences and perceptions and understandings. Very often, research projects will have elements of both kinds of research, both quantitative and qualitative research.

A problem that can arise is in the different languages used by the two different perspectives. Quantitative research generally employs a technicist, instrumental language, using words like instrument and subject. Qualitative research generally employs a softer language, using words like participant or respondent rather than subject, and data collection methods rather than data collection instruments.

A quantitative researcher will never refer to 'I' or 'me' or 'the researcher' in writing up their research. As the research in qualitative research is filtered through the perceptions of the researcher, because the researcher carried out the research, the researcher will position themselves in the research. They will explain in detail who they are, and why they are carrying out the research. They will do this in order to provide an understanding of the perspective(s) they bring to the research project. It would be a useful exercise to find an example of a qualitative study in an academic journal and read it for the ways in which the researcher positions themselves in the research.

A skilled researcher is able to use the appropriate language and approach to both quantitative and qualitative research. Really skilled researchers have studied and understand the different philosophical traditions underpinning both approaches.

Beginner researchers have to develop a capacity to nuance the language they use in writing up their research as appropriate, depending on whether the research being written about is quantitative or qualitative or a mixture of both.

A good way to begin to develop this skill is to read reports of research published in academic journals. Find and read a report of a quantitative study and a report of a qualitative study and compare the different language used in both. Then find a report of a study that used a mixed-methods approach, drawing on both quantitative and qualitative data, and consider the way in which language was used in that report. In your research diary, note the differences in the style and language used in the reporting of quantitative and qualitative research.

The qualitative researcher is reflexive. This means that they engage in a continuous process of reflection on the research. They examine their own assumptions and preconceptions regarding the research, the phenomenon under investigation, the population of the study, the questions asked, the concepts used and the concepts developed, and so on. They are keen to understand and explain their own reality and their engagement with the research in order to provide a clearer understanding of the way in which they, as the researcher, shaped the research, the design of the research, the findings of the research, and ultimately the contribution to knowledge made by the research.

Remember, from your reading of Chapter 4, that epistemology is a founding philosophical principle of research. Epistemology is concerned with knowledge and with knowledge creation. The concern is with what is known, and with how what is known is known. Who creates knowledge? Who has the power to create knowledge? What do we accept as 'knowledge'? There are critically important issues of power in this. Can you think of what some of these issues might be? Think about this, for example, in terms of culture, gender, race and class. Does this give you any ideas in relation to your own research project?

The project detailed in the journal article in the Real World Research box is a study of UK environmental entrepreneurs, and their mindset. As you read the synopsis of the methodology used in the research project, you will see how the researchers used one focus group and a series of 20 in-depth interviews with social and commercial environmental entrepreneurs to develop an understanding of environmental entrepreneurs, their beliefs, their understandings of the world, and their drivers. The researchers explain that their study is located within the naturalistic paradigm, it involves a qualitative research strategy. Through the research, they explain, they provide a social constructivist perspective on the environmental entrepreneurial mindset. Based on your reading of this chapter, can you explain what these researchers mean by the terms naturalistic paradigm, qualitative research strategy, and a social constructivist perspective?

It is important to read the synopsis and to source the original article and read it through. The article provides an interesting literature review as well as an overview of the methodology used in the research. When you read the article, look in particular for the justification the researchers provide for the methodology. As you read, critique their methodology and their justification of it.

REAL WORLD RESEARCH

How theory influences research

In this study (Outsios and Kittler, 2017) 'The mindset of UK environmental entrepreneurs: A habitus perspective', *International Small Business Journal: Researching Entrepreneurship*: 1–22), the researchers explore how environmental entrepreneurship has emerged as a significant subdomain of entrepreneurship research. The purpose of the research was to understand how environmental entrepreneurs are formed and shaped. As the researchers explain, the aim of the article is 'To examine the way environmental entrepreneurs start to form their distinctive way of thinking, the way they start to develop their environmental entrepreneurial mindset'. Mindset, the researcher's state, is 'ultimately an outcome of an individual's past, subject to alterations by new information and experiences'.

The researchers provide a very good and very interesting literature review, covering (i) the emergence of environmental entrepreneurs, (ii) the entrepreneurial mindset, and (iii) environmental entrepreneurs and the entrepreneurial mindset. If you think about the four frameworks approach to the research project, you can clearly see in the structure of this literature review in this journal article, (the subheadings in the literature review), how the researchers used the conceptual framework for the research project (the research statement/the aim of the research), to develop the theoretical framework for the research project. Remember, the theoretical framework is, or is contained in, the literature review.

The researchers develop a very interesting theoretical perspective drawing on the work of French sociologist Pierre Bourdieu and his concept 'habitus'. You should read through the journal article and examine how the researcher's use this concept habitus to help them conceptualize, shape and develop their research project.

As detailed above, the study is located within the naturalistic paradigm, it involves a qualitative research strategy. Through the research, a social constructivist perspective on the environmental entrepreneurial mindset was produced. Based on your reading of this chapter, you should be able to explain the meaning of these two sentences.

In carrying out the research, a focus group was conducted with, we are told, four environmental entrepreneurs, a moderator, and one additional discussant. A thematic analysis approach was used to analyze the focus group data. Key themes and observations from the focus group were used to develop the interview schedule used in in-depth interviews with 20 environmental entrepreneurs. The researchers explain that their goal in undertaking 20 in-depth interviews was to achieve saturation point, 'the stage where no new themes emerge from any additional interviews'. Saturation point is explained and defined in Chapter 10 of this textbook.

We are told that the interviews lasted on average one hour. They were recorded, transcribed and then analyzed using the qualitative data analysis software package NVivo. We will learn more about qualitative data analysis and NVivo in Chapter 18, 'Analyzing Qualitative Data' of this textbook.

The researchers present a good defence of their study, the robustness and the rigour of their study. In this they provide us with a good practical example of how to justify and defend qualitative research. In accomplishing this, as you will see, they draw on Guba and Lincoln (1989). They go on to highlight and explain the key factors, as indicated in their research, that help shape the mindsets of environmental entrepreneurs.

Those factors are education, environmental movements, parenthood and travel experiences.

The study is a relatively simple yet useful study. The study might help you develop ideas for your own research project. As you can see, it is possible to conduct important research, research that will be published and widely read, using relatively small scale resources. The authors of the study conceptualized a relatively simple research project, a study of the mindset of environmental entrepreneurs. Through the scholarly way in which they engaged with the literature in the field and research methodology theory, they developed a research project that has made a substantial contribution to knowledge.

There are, however, potential weaknesses in this study. Can you identify them? What do you think of the decision the researchers made to conduct just one focus group? What do you think of the sample and sampling method used? Was sampling carried out properly in the study? What do you think of the focus group in relation to the participants selected to participate in it? Do you think the focus group approach to data gathering was appropriate? The researchers do not provide copies of the interview or focus group schedules used in the study. Providing copies in the appendices to the study would allow readers a closer and a more precise perspective on the study.

The Value of Good Research box feature focuses on the research methodology phenomenology. A brief introduction to phenomenology was provided in Chapter 8 and phenomenology is explained in Table 9.2 in Chapter 9. This box feature provides a further introduction to that research methodology along with some useful references.

THE VALUE OF GOOD RESEARCH

Focus on phenomenology

Phenomenology, in social science research, is the study of lived experience from the perspective of those living the experience. The aim of a phenomenological study is to examine and highlight the essences of the everyday lived experiences studied. Phenomenological research is situated within an interpretivist philosophical perspective.

The philosophical perspective of the research project, as we know, is embedded in the methodological framework of the research project. Embedded in each statement of methodology are implicit statements or assumptions about the nature of reality (ontological assumptions) and implicit statements or assumptions about the kind of knowledge that will be generated by the research (epistemological assumptions).

Phenomenological research is in-depth research. Phenomenological researchers often work at great depth with relatively small numbers of research participants. The kind of knowledge generated in phenomenological studies is knowledge about individual and unique lived experiences. The focus on individual lived experience within phenomenological research renders the one-to-one depth interview a preferred method of gathering data within that research methodology.

Any everyday lived experience is an appropriate topic for a phenomenological study. In business research, among the very wide variety of topics studied using phenomenology are: time management and productivity (Abugre, 2017); work–life balance for entrepreneurs (Ezzedeen and Zikic, 2017); how graduates in the agricultural sector experienced entrepreneurial learning (Zamani and Mohammadi, 2017); and the factors influencing HR managers, evaluations of applicants with a criminal history (Griffith and Jones Young, 2017). Phenomenological research is widely used in management (see for example Phillips et al., 2017, and Chan et al., 2010) and it is also used in sports management (see for example Hemme et al., 2017; see also Edwards and Skinner, 2016).

In an interesting study of career anxiety among college students, Pisarik, Clay Rowell and Thompson (2017), used a phenomenological research methodology to investigate the experiences of seven traditional-aged college students

at different levels in their undergraduate education. The authors explain that they wanted to qualitatively examine the experience of career anxiety. They provide a theoretical framework (a literature review) on the issues of anxiety and career anxiety. They explain that grounding the phenomenon theoretically can help guide future research and other approaches to studying the issue. They also state that their research will inform practitioners, including counsellors, about the lived experience of career anxiety for college students. As you know from your reading of this research, phenomenology is used to study lived experience. The lived experience focused on in the research is career anxiety for college students.

The authors explain their research methodology, their sample, seven college students, and their data-gathering method, in-depth interviews. The authors present a good and a very useful description of their approach to data analysis. They outline and describe in helpful detail the key themes that emerge from their study. If you read through the journal article, you will develop an understanding of phenomenological research, how a phenomenological research methodology is used and what can be accomplished with it. You might consider developing a similar study for your research project, using phenomenology to explore experiences of career anxiety among business college students. If you did decide to do this, you could use this study as a guide. You could even base your research on this study. You may remember the case study at the end of the previous chapter, Chapter 13. In that case study, Dabir developed his research idea from a journal article that he read. It would be a good idea to read that case study again and think about how you might develop your idea for your research project.

In relation to phenomenological research, the resources listed here are also helpful:

Finlay, L. (2009) 'Debating phenomenological research methods', *Phenomenology & Practice*, 3(1): 6–25, ejournals.library.ualberta.ca/index.php/pandpr/article/viewFile/19818/15336

Groenewald, T. (2004) 'A phenomenological research design illustrated', *International Journal of Qualitative Methods*, 3(1): 1–26, www.ualberta.ca/~iiqm/backissues/3_1/pdf/groenewald.pdf

Walters, J. (2017), Phenomenological Research Guidelines, Capilano University, www.capilanou.ca/psychology/student-resources/research-guidelines/Phenomenological-Research-Guidelines

HOW TO CRITIQUE THE USE OF INTERVIEWS AND FOCUS GROUPS IN OTHER RESEARCH PROJECTS

The first question to consider when critiquing research is whether the data-gathering method used, interviews or focus groups, is the most appropriate data-gathering method in terms of the data requirements of the project. When this question has been answered, the critique moves on to an examination of the data collection method as it was used in the research project. At issue is the design of the data collection method(s) and the manner in which the method(s) were used. Questions asked and issues considered in this critique would include those detailed in Table 14.5.

Table 14.5   Critique an interview or focus group

How many interviews/focus groups were conducted?
How were the interviews/focus groups conducted? Was this appropriate?
Where did the interviews/focus groups take place?
Was the population appropriate? If sampling was used, how was the sample selected? Was the sampling method used appropriate?
How many interviews were completed? How many people participated in each focus group?
How long did the interviews/focus groups last?
Were they audio recorded? If so, how were they audio recorded?
Were they video recorded? If so, was a reasonable rationale given for this?
Were the recordings transcribed? If so, how were they transcribed? Who had access to the data? Did any individuals, other than the researcher and research supervisor, have access to the data? Is there an ethical issue in this?
Was there an interview/focus group schedule?
Has the interview/focus group schedule been included in appendices in the published account of the research?
Were the issues/themes detailed for consideration and the questions asked in the interview/focus group schedule appropriate to the research? Were they likely to provide the data required for the research project?
Is there evidence of scholarship in the construction of the interview/focus group schedule?
Was the interview/focus group schedule appropriately structured?
Was anything omitted from the interview/focus group schedule? Could there have been useful additions to the schedule?
Was the presentation of the interview/focus group schedule of an appropriate professional standard?
Were the interviews/focus groups conducted in a professional manner?

The list of questions in Table 14.5 is useful in terms of developing a critique of any research that used interviews and focus groups. They also provide guidance in terms of the critique likely to be levelled at any interviews and/or focus groups you might carry out for your own research.

When you decide to use a series of interviews, a focus group or a series of focus groups in your research, it is a good idea to source sample interviews and focus groups in theses and in journal articles and examine how the interviews and focus groups were designed. Look at the interview and/or focus group schedules. Copies of these should be presented in the appendices of the research. In examining these written accounts of interviews and focus groups, pay particular attention to:

- The appropriateness of the population of the study and/or the sample of that population, and the sampling method used in the interviews and/or focus group(s).
- The length of the interview or focus group schedule and the level of complexity in the structure of the interview and/or focus group schedule. In general, such schedules should be neither long nor complex.
- The areas and issues explored with participants in the interviews/focus group(s).
- The relevance of the areas explored in the interview/focus group schedule to the research question/statement and to the aim and objectives of the research.
- The capacity of the participants in the research to engage with and respond to the questions asked and/or the issues discussed.

Remember, the most important issue is the capacity of the data collection instrument to facilitate production of the data required for the research. The participants in the research must be capable of participating fully and usefully in the research.

The ethical aspects of every element of every research project are of fundamental importance. When you are reading through the examples of interviews and focus groups you have located in the literature, pay particular attention to the manner in which the researchers dealt with the ethical issues they were dealing with in designing and carrying out their research. In your critique of the ethical standards they brought to their work, try to see if there is anything in those standards that you might bring to your own work. In addition, consider whether there are any ethical concerns that you can see that those researchers did not properly or thoroughly address.

YOUR RESEARCH
Common research problems

Every researcher engaged in a research project is vulnerable to charges and accusations of inappropriate and/or unethical behaviour. Beginner researchers and/or student researchers should ensure that their research supervisor and/or research methods lecturer reads and signs off on every aspect and element of the research process as it develops.

If a researcher has any grounds for concern about this, for example, if you are conducting your research with particularly vulnerable people or engaging research participants on a particularly sensitive issue, it is a good idea to use a research assistant. This research assistant can be a classmate or colleague. Your research assistant simply accompanies you, the researcher, through the potentially vulnerable encounter. They provide a chaperone service to the research, ensuring that the researcher and the research participants are not alone together while the research is being conducted. They provide witness to the correct and ethical conduct of the research.

Remember too that the audio or visual recording of the research encounter evidences the professionalism and appropriateness of any encounter in the field. As well as providing evidence in terms of data, the recording can provide evidence of the professional and ethical conduct of the fieldwork for the research.

Such caution and foresight is another aspect of the level of preparedness every researcher needs when engaging in field with human participants.

CASE STUDY

The museum shop as a marketing tool for the Imperial War Museum

The research outlined here was an exploratory study undertaken by Kent (2010), to assess the role of the museum shop in extending the learning experience in the museum.

In his journal article, Kent explains that the research is situated in the theoretical framework of museum experiences and learning. He presents in the article a review of the literature on the role of museums, their commercial, educational and recreational orientations and the provision of visitor experiences. He explores the issues in marketing the museum, the tensions between the commercial aspect of the museum and the museum's educational remit, and the desire on the part of consumers for authentic museum experiences.

A mixed methods approach was used in the research to examine visitors' knowledge and experience of museums and their shops. Data collection for the study was undertaken at the Imperial War Museum (IWM) in London.

In the first phase of the research, in-depth interviews were undertaken to examine the experience of museum shops and their contribution to learning. We are told that for the in-depth interviews, six respondents were selected for interview using a purposive sampling approach. Each of the six respondents was a regular museum visitor. A semi-structured interview schedule was used to guide respondents through the interview. In the interviews, respondents were asked questions about their visits to the museum and in particular their visits to and experiences of the museum shop.

In the second phase of the research, a convenience sample of museum visitors was asked to complete a semi-structured questionnaire. A semi-structured questionnaire was devised, using different types of question (open and closed), and a semantic scale assessment on store atmospherics. A semantic scale, or a semantic differential scale, uses opposite adjectives, such as hot/cold, good/bad, interesting/dull, and

(Continued)

asks respondents to indicate which of the adjectives better describes the phenomenon under investigation. Questionnaires and scales are the focus of Chapters 15 and 16 of this textbook, and an example of a semantic differential scale is given in Chapter 16.

We are told that 150 completed questionnaires were obtained during weekdays by intercepting visitors leaving the museum shop. The researcher noted that respondents appeared to have a positive relationship with the museum and were therefore willing to take part in the study because they wanted to help.

Finally, the researcher states that observations were undertaken about the ambience of the ground floor, in which the main hall and shop are located.

As you can see, a substantial amount of data were gathered for the research project using observations, in-depth one-to-one interviews, and a questionnaire that incorporated a semantic differential scale.

You will notice that the researcher made notes to himself during the data-gathering phase of the research and those notes were used to supplement the data gathered. Researchers engaged in data gathering make notes to themselves in a field diary, or in the research diary of the research project.

We are told in the journal article what sampling methods were used in the study. For the in-depth interviews, a purposive sampling method was used. For the questionnaires, a convenience sampling method was used.

Following your reading of Chapter 10 of this textbook, can you explain these two sampling methods? Can you outline the differences between them? Do you think that these sampling methods were the appropriate sampling methods to use? Why do you think that? The researcher presents a useful analysis of the data gathered. Reading this analysis will help you prepare for the following chapters in this textbook which are focused on data analysis.

In his discussion of the data analysis undertaken, Kent provides an interesting and a complex insight into the role of the museum shop. He concludes that the museum shop is a significant destination for museum visitors. The museum shop is, he holds, a commercial space, a recreational space, and a space which supports informal learning.

Kent's research, as it is outlined in the journal article, provides a good model for a research project. When you read the article, read it in conjunction with the model of the research project outlined at the start of Chapter 1 in this textbook. You will see in Kent's research how the different elements of that model come together in a real life research project.

Now update your interactive research diary with your notes and findings on Cengage Brain. Complete the activities provided to reinforce your understanding of this chapter.

END OF CHAPTER QUESTIONS

1   Name and briefly explain five types of interview.

2   Outline the advantages and disadvantages of one-to-one in-depth interviews.

3   Devise a simple flow chart for the design and conduct of a series of telephone interviews.

4   Detail and explain the reasons why a researcher would decide to conduct group interviews.

5   What are the key issues in conducting structured interviews?

6   What is a focus group and how is it different from a group interview?

7   Outline the key advantages and disadvantages of online interviews and focus groups.

8   Design a simple research project with a focus group data-gathering method conducted using CMC.

9   Design a simple research project using a FTF focus group.

10   What is bias in research? Name and explain three different kinds of bias.

REFERENCES

Abugre, J.B. (2017) 'A phenomenological study of time concept and management and productivity in a sub-Saharan African context', *International Journal of Cross Cultural Management*, *17*(2): 197–214.

Bates, E.A., Kaye, L.K. and McCann, J.J. (2017) 'A snapshot of the student experience: exploring student satisfaction through the use of photographic elicitation', *Journal of Further and Higher Education*, DOI: 10.1080/0309877X.2017.1359507

Broadcasters' Audience Research Board (BARB), www.barb .co.uk. (Accessed 17.03.2018).

Becker, H.S. (1974) 'Photography and sociology', *Studies in the Anthropology of Visual Communication*, *1*(1): 3–26.

Big Brother 2018, www.bigbrotherauditions.com (Accessed 17.03.2018).

Bowen, G.A. (2009) 'Supporting a grounded theory with an audit trail: an illustration', *International Journal of Social Research Methodology*, *12*(4): 305–316.

Chan, G., Benner, P., Brykcynski, K.A. and Malone, R.E. (2010) *Interpretive Phenomenology in Health Care Research: Studying Social Practice, Lifeworlds, and Embodiment*, Sigma Theta Tau Intl, catalog.sit.edu/cgi-bin/koha/opac-detail. pl?biblionumber=86905

Collier, J. Jr and Collier, M. (1986) *Visual Anthropology: Photography as a Research Method*, Albuquerque, NM: University of New Mexico Press.

Corbin, J. and Strauss, A. (2008) *Basics of Qualitative Research*, Thousand Oaks, CA: Sage.

Dominos Pizza, *The Pizza Turnaround Documentary*, pizzaturnaround.com/ (Accessed 17.03.2018).

Edwards, A. and Skinner, J. (2016) *Qualitative Research in Sports Management*, Routledge.

Endemol Shine Group, www.endemolshinegroup.com/about (Accessed 17.03.2017).

Exploring Online Research Methods, University of Leicester, www2.le.ac.uk/departments/geography/projects/tri-orm (Accessed 17.03.2018).

Ezzedeen, S.R. and Zikic, J. (2017) Finding balance amid boundarylessness: An interpretive study of entrepreneurial work-life balance and boundary management, *Journal of Family Issues*, *38*(11):1546–1576.

Finlay, L. (2009) 'Debating phenomenological research methods', *Phenomenology & Practice*, *3*(1): 6–25, ejournals.library.ualberta.ca/index.php/pandpr/article/ viewFile/19818/15336 (Accessed 17.03.2018).

Geertz, C. (1973) *The Interpretation of Cultures*, New York: Basic Books.

Glaser, B. and Strauss, A. (1967) *The Discovery of Grounded Theory*, Chicago, IL: Aldine.

Groenewald, T. (2004) 'A phenomenological research design illustrated', *International Journal of Qualitative Methods*, *3*(1), 1–26, www.ualberta.ca/~iiqm/backissues/3_1/pdf/ groenewald.pdf (Accessed 17.03.2018).

Guba, E. G. and Lincoln, Y. S. (1989) *Fourth Generation Evaluation*. Newbury Park, CA and London: Sage Publications.

Guba, E.G. and Lincoln, Y.S. (1994) *Competing Paradigms in Qualitative Research*, www.uncg.edu/hdf/facultystaff/ Tudge/Guba%20&%20Lincoln%201994.pdf

Harper, D. (1996) 'Seeing sociology', *The American Sociologist*, *37*(3): 69–78.

Harper, D. (1998) 'An argument for visual sociology', in J. Prosser (ed.), *Image-based Research*, London: Routledge Falmer.

Harper, D. (2012) *Visual Sociology*, Oxon and New York: Routledge.

Hemme, F., Morias, D., Bowers, M.T. and Todd, J.S. (2017) 'Extending sport-based entrepreneurship theory through phenomenological inquiry', *Sport Management Review*, *20*(1): 92–104.

Griffith, J.N. and Jones Young, N.C. (2017) 'Hiring ex-offenders? The case of ban the box', *Equality, Diversity and Inclusion: An International Journal*, *36*(6): 501–518.

Kent, T. (2010) 'The role of the museum shop in extending the visitor experience', *International Journal of Nonprofit and Voluntary Sector Marketing*, *15*(1): 67–77.

Lincoln, Y.S. and Guba, E.G. (1985) *Naturalistic Inquiry*, Newbury Park, CA: Sage.

Liu, W., Sparks, B. and Coghlan, A. (2017) 'Event experiences: Through the lens of attendees', *Event Management*, *21*(4): 463–479.

Outsios, G. and Kittler, M. (2017) 'The mindset of UK environmental entrepreneurs: A habitus perspective', *International Small Business Journal: Researching Entrepreneurship* 6(3): 285–306.

Phillips, C.R., Haase, J.E., Broome, M.E., Carpenter, J.S. and Frankel, R.M. (2017) 'Connecting with healthcare providers at diagnosis: adolescent/young adult cancer survivors' perspectives', *International Journal of Qualitative Studies on Health and Well-being*, *12*(1). DOI: 10.1080/17482631.2017.1325699

Pisarik, C.T., Clay Rowell, P. and Thompson, L.K. (2017) 'A phenomenological study of career anxiety among college students', *The Career Development Quarterly*, *65*(4): 339–352.

Reid, D.J. and Reid, F.J.M. (2005) 'Online focus groups: an in-depth comparison of computer mediated and conventional focus group discussions', *International Journal of Market Research*, *47*(2): 131–262.

Riege, A.M. (2003) 'Validity and reliability tests in case study research: a literature review with "hands-on" applications for each research phase', *Qualitative Market Research*, *6*(2): 75–86.

Stat Trek, Teach yourself statistics, 'Tutorial on bias in survey sampling', stattrek.com/survey-research/survey-bias.aspx (Accessed 17.03.2018).

Venkatraman, M. and Nelson, T. (2008) 'From servicescape to consumptionscape: a photo-elicitation study of Starbucks in the New China', *Journal of International Business Studies*, *39*(6): 1010–1026.

Walters, J. (2017) Phenomenological Research Guidelines, Capilano University, www.capilanou.ca/psychology/ student-resources/research-guidelines/Phenomenological- Research-Guidelines (Accessed 17.03.2018).

Wood, D. (2017) *What's Hot in Global Entertainment*, hub.editiondigital.com/whats-hot-in-global-entertainment (Accessed 17.03.2017).

Zamani, N. and Mohammadi, M. (2017) 'Entrepreneurial learning as experienced by agricultural graduate entrepreneurs', *Higher Education*, 1–16, doi.org/10.1007/s10734-017- 0209-y (Accessed 17.03.2018).

RECOMMENDED READING

Bell, J. and Waters, S. (2014) *Doing Your Research Project* (6th edn), Maidenhead: Open University Press.

Collis, J. and Hussey, R. (2013) *Business Research: A Practical Guide for Undergraduate and Postgraduate Students* (4th edn), Basingstoke and New York: Palgrave Macmillan.

Denscombe, M. (2017) *The Good Research Guide: For Small-scale Social Research Projects* (5th edn), Maidenhead: Open University Press.

Easterby-Smith, M., Thorpe, R. and Jackson, P.R. (2008) *Management Research* (3rd edn), London: Sage.

Hammersley, M. and Atkinson, P. (2007) *Ethnography: Principles in Practice* (3rd edn), Oxon and New York: Routledge.

Kvale, S. and Brinkmann, S. (2014) *InterViews: Learning the Craft of Qualitative Interviewing* (3rd edn), London, California, New Delhi, Singapore: Sage.

Neuman, W.L. (2014) *Social Research Methods: Qualitative and Quantitative Approaches* (7th edn), Essex, England: Pearson Education Ltd.

Oppenheim, A.N. (2000) *Questionnaire Design, Interviewing and Attitude Measurement* (2nd edn), London: Pinter.

Robson, C. and McCartan., K. (2016) *Real World Research*, John Wiley & Sons Ltd.

Wengraf, T. (2009) *Qualitative Research Interviewing*, London, California, New Delhi: Sage.

CHAPTER 15

SURVEYS AND QUESTIONNAIRES

LEARNING OBJECTIVES

At the end of this chapter, the student should be able to:

- Define surveys and explain their advantages.

- Describe the type of information that may be gathered in a survey.

- Identify sources of error in survey research.

- Design questionnaires for different research projects.

- Discuss and explain the issues of validity and reliability in relation to questionnaire design.

RESEARCH SKILLS

At the end of this chapter, the student should, using the exercises on Cengage Brain, be able to:

- Design a questionnaire for a given research project.

- Explain the significance of decisions about question design and wording in a questionnaire.

- Demonstrate how the proper sequence of questions may improve a questionnaire.

- Describe the process of pretesting a questionnaire.

- Explain the value of pretesting a questionnaire.

The aim of this chapter is to explain the use of surveys and questionnaires in business research. The purpose of survey research is to collect primary data – data gathered specifically for the research project being carried out. This chapter discusses typical research objectives that may be accomplished with surveys and various advantages of the survey method. The chapter details the various data-gathering methods used in survey research.

INTRODUCTION

As explained in previous chapters, data-gathering techniques are part of the methodological framework, the third framework in the four frameworks approach to the design of the research project. The four frameworks approach to the research project facilitates the researcher in developing a logical and coherent, fully integrated research project. The first three frameworks of the four frameworks approach to research are laid out again in Figure 15.1.

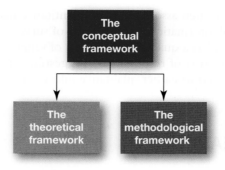

Figure 15.1   Three frameworks of the four frameworks approach to research

The four frameworks

- Conceptual Framework
- Theoretical Framework
- *Methodological Framework*
- Analytical Framework

The epistemological and ontological perspectives of the research project are, we know from our reading of Chapter 4 of this textbook, embedded in the philosophical perspective informing the research project, and they are implicit in the project's research methodology. As stated in Chapter 4 and in the previous two chapters, embedded in each statement of methodology are implicit statements or assumptions about the nature of reality (ontological assumptions) and implicit statements or assumptions about the kind of knowledge that will be generated by the research (epistemological assumptions).

When engaging a large population in a research project, it is often not possible to engage every member of the population in in-depth research. When this is the case, the researcher engages in sampling, s/he selects a sample from the population, and conducts the research with that sample. The researcher must design a research instrument which facilitates a broad approach to researching the phenomenon, using the sample respondents. A survey research methodology is an appropriate research methodology in such research. Survey research is situated within a framework of positivism, it is deductive and it is used primarily to generate quantitative data. Questionnaires are appropriate data-gathering instruments in such research.

Questionnaires are used to collect data through the post (mail), by telephone, online perhaps using email or online survey software such as SurveyMonkey (www.surveymonkey.com), or in face-to-face interviews, for example, in street intercept or (shopping) centre intercept interviews. Thus, a survey is defined as a method of collecting primary data based on communication with a representative sample of individuals. Surveys provide a snapshot at a given point in time. The more formal term, **sample survey**, emphasizes that the purpose of contacting respondents is to obtain a representative sample, or subset, of the target population.

> **sample survey**   A more formal term for a survey.

USING SURVEYS

The type of information gathered in a survey varies considerably depending on the research objectives. Examples of the kinds of business research for which surveys are typically used include studies to identify the characteristics of target markets; studies designed to measure customer attitudes; and studies describing consumer purchase patterns. Although consumer surveys are a common form of business research, not all survey research is conducted with the ultimate consumer. Survey research is used very widely in business research. A survey could be used, for example, to determine an organization's commitment to the environment.

Most business surveys have multiple objectives; few gather only a single type of factual information. A study commissioned by eBay provides an example of the information that can be gathered using survey research. eBay learned in its survey that almost 60 per cent of respondents receive unwanted gifts and 15 per cent of them had sold an unwanted gift online, suggesting a possible source of demand for eBay's auction services. In addition, the survey indicated that selling unwanted gifts online was more common among 25 to 34-year-olds. This is useful demographic data.

The term survey, as explained, is most often associated with quantitative data and findings. Although most surveys are conducted to quantify certain factual information, some aspects of surveys may also be qualitative. In new product development, for example, a survey often has a qualitative objective of refining product concepts; stylistic, aesthetic or functional changes may be made on the basis of respondents' suggestions. In an example of an organization's environmental attitudes, a survey might be used to gather qualitative information regarding activities that could make the company more 'green'.

ERRORS IN SURVEY RESEARCH

There are two major sources of error in survey research: random sampling error and systematic error. Figure 15.2 outlines the various forms of survey error. Study this figure and try to memorize the different kind of bias and their sources.

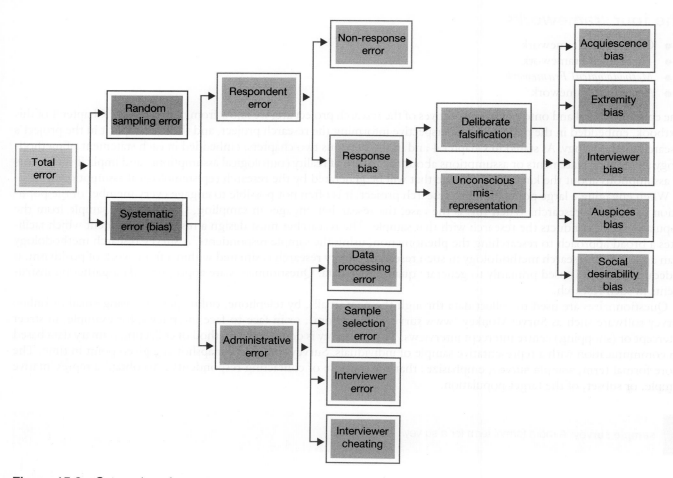

Figure 15.2 Categories of survey errors

Random sampling error

Most surveys try to portray a representative cross-section of a particular population. Even with proper random probability samples, however, statistical errors will occur because of chance variation in the sample selected. These statistical problems are unavoidable without very large samples (> 400). However, the extent of **random sampling error** can be estimated.

> **random sampling error** A statistical fluctuation that occurs because of chance variation in the elements selected for a sample; difference between the sample result and the result of a census conducted using identical procedures.

YOUR RESEARCH

This chapter introduces survey research and details several different types of error and bias that may be present in survey research. Following your study of Figure 15.2, address the following questions:

1. Identify the two main sources of survey error and in your research diary write an explanation of both of them.

2. Imagine that you are training a team of research assistants to work in the field, prepare an exercise on interviewer bias for them.

3. Consider the issue of administrative error in survey research. In your research diary, write a short paragraph on each of the four types of administrative error highlighted in Figure 15.2.

Systematic error

The other major source of survey error, **systematic error**, results from some imperfect aspect of the research design or from a mistake in the execution of the research. Because systematic errors include all sources of error other than those introduced by the random sampling procedure, these errors or biases are also called non-sampling errors. A **sample bias** exists when the sample is different in some way from the population. The many sources of error can be divided into two general categories: respondent error and administrative error.

> **systematic error** Error resulting from some imperfect aspect of the research design that causes respondent error or from a mistake in the execution of the research.
>
> **sample bias** A persistent tendency for the results of a sample to deviate in one direction from the true value of the population parameter.

Respondent error

Surveys ask people for answers. If people participate in the survey and give truthful answers, a survey will probably accomplish its goal. If these conditions are not met, non-response error or response bias, the two major categories of **respondent error**, may cause sample bias.

> **respondent error** A category of sample bias resulting from some respondent action or inaction such as non-response or response bias.

Non-response error

Few surveys have 100 per cent response rates. In fact, surveys with relatively low response rates may still accurately reflect the population of interest. However, to use the results, the consumers who responded to the questionnaire must be established in the study as being representative of all consumers, including those who did not respond. Non-response rates can be high in mail/postal and internet surveys. Non-response rates can also threaten telephone and face-to-face interviews.

People who are not contacted or who are contacted but decline to participate in the survey are called **non-respondents**. For example, a non-response occurs if no one answers the phone at the time of both the initial call and any subsequent callbacks. In recent years, the number of **no contacts** in telephone survey research has been increasing, because of the proliferation of answering machines and growing use of caller ID to screen telephone calls. **Refusals** occur when people are unwilling or unable, for whatever reason, to participate in the research.

> **non-respondents** People who are not contacted or who refuse to cooperate in the research.
>
> **no contacts** People who are not at home or who are otherwise inaccessible on the first and second contact.
>
> **refusals** People who are unwilling to participate in a research project.

Response bias

A **response bias** occurs when respondents tend to answer questions with a certain slant. People may consciously or unconsciously misrepresent the truth, intentionally or inadvertently. The resulting sample bias will be a response bias.

> **response bias** A bias that occurs when respondents either consciously or unconsciously tend to answer questions with a certain slant that misrepresents the truth.

Occasionally people deliberately give false answers. It is difficult to assess why people knowingly misrepresent answers. A response bias may occur when people misrepresent answers to appear intelligent, conceal personal information, avoid embarrassment, and so on. Sometimes respondents become bored with the interview and provide answers just to get rid of the interviewer. At other times respondents try to appear well informed by providing the answers they think are expected of them. On still other occasions, they give answers simply to please the interviewer.

One explanation for conscious and deliberate misrepresentation of facts is the so-called average-person hypothesis. Individuals may prefer to be viewed as average, so they alter their responses to conform more closely to their perception of what the average person 'looks like'.

Even when a respondent is consciously trying to be truthful and cooperative, response bias can arise from the question format, the question content or some other stimulus such as the environment within which the questionnaire is administered. Respondents who misunderstand questions may unconsciously provide biased answers. Or they may be willing to answer but unable to do so because they have forgotten the exact details. A bias may also occur when a respondent has not thought about an unexpected question. Many respondents will answer questions even though they have given them little thought.

THE VALUE OF GOOD RESEARCH

Focus on survey methodology

Survey methodology is a very popular methodology with business students. Basically, surveys involve researchers asking questions of research participants. In survey research, information is gathered using standardized means. This is in order to ensure that every participant is asked the same questions in the same way. The requirement for standardization means that, usually, survey research involves the use of simple question formats. Questions are either closed or open. Using a closed format, the respondent is required only to give a set response, perhaps a 'yes' or 'no' or 'not applicable' response to questions. For example, the question 'Do you use this product?' requires a 'yes' or 'no' response. Using an open format, the respondent is required to briefly explain something in response to questions. For example, the question 'Why do you use this product?' requires quite an elaborate response, as the respondent explains why they use the product. Survey questionnaires can be very short or very long.

Surveys tend to involve big or relatively big populations and samples; 30 respondents would be a very small number of respondents in a survey. As surveys tend to engage large populations of respondents, and as they tend to gather terse responses to questions (a lot of questions in survey research simply require the respondents to tick a box in order to answer the question), surveys are useful ways of generating quantitative data. Surveys can be carried out in different ways: online, by email, by mail/post, by telephone or in person.

A census of a population is a survey in which every member of the population is included in the study. In general, when carrying out survey research, a sample of the population (a small subsection of the population), rather than the entire population, participates in the research. The sample is selected using an appropriate sampling method, such as simple random sampling. Using a simple random sampling method, if the sampling method is used correctly, the sample can be said to be representative of the entire population and the findings of such a survey can be said to be applicable to, or generalizable to, the entire population of the study. Sampling and sampling methods are dealt with in detail in Chapter 10 of this textbook.

(Continued)

In general, surveys tend to use questionnaires and/or structured interviews as data-gathering methods. Questionnaires are effective in engaging with large populations. If the population is geographically scattered, a questionnaire can be easily and relatively cheaply emailed or mailed/posted. Telephone interviews can be used relatively easily and cheaply with geographically scattered populations. Surveys can also be developed using one-to-one in-depth interviews. One-to-one in-depth interviews may be possible with geographically scattered populations, if the population of the study is not too big, and/or if the researcher has the resources needed (time and money) to travel to interview all of the members of the population.

Many survey questionnaires are now created online, using tools such as SurveyMonkey (www.surveymonkey.com) or Instant Survey (www.instantsurvey.com) or Checkbox (www.checkbox.com). All of these tools are quite easy to use and you can learn a lot about survey research from logging onto these websites and making attempts at developing questionnaires using the basic tools that are freely available on the websites.

There are very many resources on the web for students of survey research. One of the most useful is the Princeton University Survey Research Center (PSRC) (www.princeton.edu/~psrc/). This Center provides a lot of information on how to conduct survey research. The PSRC refers students to the American Statistical Association's online guide 'What is a survey?' (www.whatisasurvey.info/). This is a free booklet that contains ten chapters, each of which deals with an aspect of survey research.

Another good resource on the web is the Research Methods Knowledge Base, 2nd edn (Trochim, 2006) (www.socialresearchmethods.net/).

Methodspace (www.methodspace.com) is also a good resource for research and researchers generally, as well as for those particularly interested in survey research.

QUESTIONNAIRES

Questionnaires tend to be very precisely structured data-gathering instruments; they are widely used in survey research. Questionnaires are used primarily in quantitative research to generate quantitative data, although qualitative data can be generated by questionnaires through the use of open questions. Quantitative data are factual data. The gathering of quantitative data in a research project indicates a positivistic perspective in the research and a positivistic philosophical framework for the research.

You will at some time in your life have filled in a questionnaire. You cannot open a bank account or join a library without filling in a questionnaire, so you will know that, usually, it is an easy process. In order to fill in a questionnaire, typically, you read down through it, ticking boxes or putting numbers into boxes as you go. The simplicity of the design of the questionnaire, from the respondent's point of view, is a tribute to the amount of work and reflection the researcher engaged in while compiling the questionnaire.

The model of the research process, detailed in Figure 1.1 in Chapter 1, demonstrates where in the research process questionnaires are used. Questionnaires, like observation, interviews and focus groups, explored in the previous two chapters, are data-gathering methods. As Figure 1.1 shows, the selection and design of the data-gathering methods for the research project generally takes place after the literature review has been substantially completed and decisions around methodology have been made.

The researcher may have some ideas around data collection from the start of the project. However, these ideas are likely to change and/or develop over the course of the conceptualization of the research statement, the conduct of the literature review and the design of the methodological framework for the research project. It is only at the point at which the methodology for the project and the population and sample are finally decided on, that the data-gathering methods for the research project are finally selected and designed.

When the data collection methods are devised, the researcher then proceeds to use them to gather the data needed for the research project.

The Value of Good Research box 'Access to the internet' details different research projects related to internet usage globally. Among the sources quoted is a survey carried out for the BBC World Service. As you will see as you read through the extract presented, the data gathered through the survey were primarily quantitative data. The survey was very big. More than 27 000 people across 26 different countries participated in the research. It is interesting to consider this study, to consider how it was conducted as well as what it accomplished. As well as presenting the findings of the research in terms of the entire population of the study, some of the findings from individual countries were also presented. It is interesting to consider the different sources quoted in the box, the data they present and the concerns they articulate. When you read through the feature, as well as learning something about global current key concerns in relation to internet access, you may develop some ideas of your own for research project.

THE VALUE OF GOOD RESEARCH

Access to the internet

On 1 July, 2016, the United Nations declared internet access to be a basic human right. Article 19 of the Universal Declaration of Human Rights (UDHR) states: 'Everyone has the right to freedom of opinion and expression; this right includes freedom to hold opinions without interference and to seek, and receive, and impart information and ideas through any media and regardless of frontiers', (see UN Declaration of Human Rights, www.un.org/en/universal-declaration-human-rights/)

The 2010 study conducted for the BBC World Service on the topic of internet access, which engaged with more than 27 000 adults across 26 countries, found strong support across all the participating countries for internet access. The survey uncovered substantial disagreements regarding the issue of government control of some aspects of the internet. (see 'Internet Access is a "fundamental right"', BBC News).

The survey reported that 87 per cent of internet users (this rose to 90 per cent in Turkey) believed that access to the internet was a basic right, while more than 70 per cent of non-users believed that they should have access to the internet.

The United Nations (UN) is continuously pushing for universal web access. Former Secretary General of the UN, Ban Ki-moon, regularly spoke against attempts to suppress internet access. In his Millennium Report (2000), the Secretary General listed, among other priorities, the building of digital bridges as a priority. The call in the Millennium Report was specifically for the removal of regulatory and pricing impediments to internet access.

In 2016, The Brookings Institution (www.brookings.edu/about-us/), a non-profit public policy institution based in Washington DC, published a TechTank blog on their website (Howell and West, 2016, The internet as a human right, www.brookings.edu/blog/techtank/2016/11/07/the-internet-as-a-human-right/). The blog reported on Article 19, detailing that Section 32 highlights 'the promotion, protection and enjoyment of human rights on the internet', along with another 15 recommendations that cover the rights of people working with and relying on internet access. The blog highlights the difficulties of those people impacted by the digital divide. The authors point out that although the UN resolution is not enforceable, it does hold weight internationally.

According to the BBC news article, countries such as Finland and Estonia have already ruled that internet access is a human right for their citizens. The article explains that the findings of the survey showed that the web users in South Korea and Nigeria who participated in the study strongly believed that governments should never be involved in regulation of the internet. By the same token, a majority of those in China and participants in many European countries disagreed; we are told, for example, that over half of those surveyed in the UK believed that there is a case for some government regulation of the internet.

Finland was the first country to declare that broadband internet access is a legal right (CNN, 15 October, 2009). The CNN news article quotes Finland's Minister of Transport and Communications who said that internet access is something that people cannot live without in a modern society; the minister likened internet access to access to banking, electrical and water services.

Internet access as a basic human right is an issue that is considered, discussed, debated and researched globally. Perhaps there is an aspect to internet access, or an issue in it, that you might be interested in focusing on in your research project. If you think about the issue of access to the internet, and jot down your reflections in your research diary, you might come up with a number of ideas for viable research projects.

A survey research methodology works well in large-scale research projects. As explained, surveys are often used in research conducted with large and/or geographically spread populations. Questionnaires can be easily mailed/posted or emailed to such populations, or placed on the internet to allow for easy access globally. Online methods are commonly used, and they are very effective where the survey population has access to the required technologies and the skills necessary to use those technologies.

As explained in the Value of Good Research box, Focus on survey methodology, there are very many software packages that facilitate the creation of questionnaires to be used in survey research, including online research. Among these packages are SurveyMonkey, Qualtrics (www.qualtrics.com), Surveyspro (www.surveyspro.com), Snap Surveys (www.snapsurveys.com) and Question Pro (www.questionpro.com). They are all useful and they all give help and direction in terms of question and questionnaire design. For example, SurveyMonkey allows for the use of a number of different kinds of questions, among them open and closed questions, multiple-choice questions, **sentence completion exercises** and **rating scales**. The use of an online software package is also helpful in the aesthetics of a questionnaire, providing different options in terms of organization and style. As well as providing for the design of the data-gathering instrument, an online package facilitates the administration of the instrument and the collation of results.

sentence completion exercise A projective technique. The researcher starts a sentence and asks the respondent to complete it.

rating scales The researcher asks participants to rate different aspects or elements of the phenomenon under investigation.

Questionnaires can be used in drop-and-collect situations where they are left with respondents and collected when the respondent has completed them. Questionnaires can be administered to respondents in structured interviews conducted F2F, by telephone or online. Questionnaires, as stated earlier, are structured data-gathering methods. They are structured to ensure that each respondent is asked the same simple, clear, concise and precise questions, and to ensure that the responses made to those questions/issues are also simple, clear, concise and precise.

The data gathered by researchers engaged in very large studies tend to be mostly or entirely quantitative data. Quantitative data are precise and concise, while qualitative data tend to be complex, dense and, quite often, voluminous. Researchers tend not to gather much qualitative data from very large studies because if they did, there would just be too many data to manage and analyze. So, in studies with large numbers of participants, researchers tend to restrict the amount of qualitative data gathered by only including very few open questions in the data-gathering instrument, or by engaging a small sample from the overall sample to participate in a small qualitative study which will form a part of the overall research project.

In Figure 15.3, an extract from a sample questionnaire, you will note that the questionnaire has been designed to allow for the coding of responses to the questionnaire. The coded responses are detailed on the right-hand side of the questionnaire. (We will explore the coding of data and the analysis of data, both quantitative and qualitative data, in Part Four of this textbook.)

		Code
Q1. What is your age? Please state	22 yrs	22
Q2. What is your level of formal education? Please circle Primary school Secondary school University/college		3
Q3. What is your annual income? Please tick		
Less than £10 000	☐	
More than £10 000, less than £20 000	☑	2
More than £20 000, less than £30 000	☐	
More than £30 000, less than £40 000	☐	

Figure 15.3   A sample questionnaire

In the first question, the respondent is asked to indicate their age; obviously the response to this question is always a number. We can see from the response to the question that the respondent to this questionnaire is 22 years old. In the second question, the respondent is asked to indicate their level of formal education. Three options are given, first level, second level and third level. The respondent is asked to circle one of the three levels in order to indicate their level of education. In the next question, the respondent is asked for information regarding level of income. As you can see, to encourage respondents to respond to the question, levels of income have been grouped (aggregated) into four bands. The respondent to this questionnaire has indicated that s/he earns between £10 000 and £20 000 annually.

In the sample questionnaire the numeric values of two of the responses are real, while one has been assigned by the researcher. Can you tell which is which? If you said that the numeric value (code) 22 is real, while the numeric values (codes) 2 and 3 have been assigned by the researcher, you are correct. Coding assigned by the researcher is always assigned using a simple logic. In response, for example, to question three, the respondent selected the second option, so in coding this response the researcher assigned the number 2 as the code to signify this response. Codes and coding and the analysis of quantitative data are explored in detail in Chapter 19.

THE ISSUES OF VALIDITY AND RELIABILITY

As explained in Chapter 14, the issues of validity and reliability are treated differently in quantitative research and qualitative research. In quantitative research, the researcher is primarily concerned with measurement and with the precision of the data-gathering instruments they use or develop for use in their research projects. The issues of validity and reliability in quantitative research are explored in Table 15.1.

Table 15.1 Validity and reliability in quantitative research

Validity	Reliability
The term validity in research, as defined in Chapter 2, is a question of how valid the research is, how logical, how truthful, how robust, how sound, how reasonable, how meaningful and how useful. The issue of validity in relation to data collection methods is measurement validity. *Measurement validity* refers to the degree to which the data collection methods, as they are designed, can accomplish what it is that they are designed to accomplish. There are different ways of establishing measurement validity: content validity, face validity, criterion-related validity and construct validity.	The term reliability in research, as defined in Chapter 2, relates to the dependability of the research, to the degree to which the research can be repeated while obtaining consistent results. A data collection instrument in social science research is deemed reliable if it produces the same result again and again, over time and in different circumstances. A ruler, for example, is a reliable measure. If you use a ruler to measure the length and breadth of one of your shoes, you will get a particular result. If tomorrow you use the same ruler in the same measurement exercise, you will get the same result. If one of your friends uses a ruler to measure the length and breadth of the shoe you measured, they will get the same result. The ruler is a dependable measure, it produces consistent results; it is a reliable instrument.
Using content validity, the researcher establishes the validity of the data-gathering method by ensuring that the phenomenon under investigation, as defined, or as outlined in the conceptual framework for the research project, is fully represented in the data-gathering instrument(s). Using face validity, the researcher establishes that the data-gathering instrument seems a reasonable measure of the phenomenon under investigation. The researcher can improve the face validity of a data-gathering instrument by asking people with some expertise on the phenomenon to judge whether or not the instrument is valid. The data-gathering instrument can be changed and developed following their feedback.	There are three different kinds of reliability: 1. *Stability reliability* (sometimes referred to as the test-retest reliability) relates to whether or not the data collection instrument produces the same result over time. 2. *Representative reliability* relates to whether or not the data collection instrument produces the same result when applied to different subgroups in a population. Testing the instrument on a subpopulation of the population can establish whether or not the instrument has representative reliability. 3. *Equivalence reliability* relates to whether or not when a lot of different items are used in a questionnaire, they all measure the phenomenon consistently. The *split-half method* is used to test for equivalence reliability. Using this method, the researcher divides the questionnaire into two halves, by randomly assigning all of the measures in the questionnaire to one half or the other, and then tests whether or not both halves yield consistent results.
Using criterion-related validity, also known as instrumental validity, the researcher uses some standard or criterion to measure the data-gathering instrument against. For example, the researcher could use another data-gathering instrument developed and validated by another (perhaps more established) researcher. Construct validity is applicable to data-gathering instruments that have multiple indicators (questions/issues). In attempting to establish construct validity, the researcher demonstrates how all of the indicators are consistent with each other and consistent with the phenomenon under investigation. The researcher ensures that the questions asked are relevant and pertinent to the phenomenon under investigation; that the data collection method designed is a complete and comprehensive examination of/reflection on the phenomenon under investigation.	Using the test-retest means of estimating reliability, the data-gathering instrument (questionnaire or scale) is used in a pilot test, then, on another later occasion, the same pilot test is carried out with the same people. The two sets of responses are then compared for consistency. One problem with this method is that respondents may reflect on the first responses they gave and, as a consequence, they may give different, perhaps more mature responses the second time. Researchers sometimes use a method called *inter-coder reliability*. This is where there is more than one researcher, observer or coder. A measure is reliable if the observers or coders consistently agree with each other. This method of reliability is used often in content analysis. Inter-coder reliability is tested by having two or more researchers, observers or coders measure the same phenomenon and then compare their results. If their results are consistent, inter-coding can be deemed reliable. Measuring at the most precise level possible will help improve reliability. Using clearly, precisely and simply defined items will help improve reliability.

Table 15.1 Validity and reliability in quantitative research (*Continued*)

Validity	Reliability
The questionnaire designed by the researcher must be a valid measure of the phenomenon under investigation. Every item in the questionnaire must be relevant. Every item in the questionnaire must be essential. The data-gathering instrument must provide the data required for the research project. A pilot test can help improve the validity of a data-gathering instrument. Replicating and/or building on data-gathering instruments developed by other researchers (these are to be found in the literature, in published books, journal articles, reports) helps improve validity.	Using each item to measure only one concept will help improve reliability. Using more than one item to measure each concept will help improve reliability. A pilot test can help improve the reliability of the data collection instrument. Replicating and/or building on the data-gathering instruments developed by other researchers (these are to be found in the literature) helps improve reliability.

DESIGNING QUESTIONNAIRES

The researcher works hard at producing a questionnaire that will be valid and reliable, that will provide the data needed for the research project, a questionnaire that will be simple for the respondent to complete. In order to produce such a precise yet simple data-gathering instrument, the researcher studies examples of questionnaires in textbooks and in the literature and s/he considers the data requirements of the research project.

When you are designing a questionnaire for your research project, along with your study of survey research and questionnaires in this and other textbooks, you should examine examples of questionnaires used in other research projects. You will find these detailed and explained in journal articles outlining research projects conducted using a survey research methodology. When you have collected a number of such questionnaires, examine them:

1. Study the way in which they are presented in terms of both organization and aesthetics.
2. Study the structure and sequence of questions and items.
3. Take note of which questions were asked first and which questions came later.
4. Study the words, concepts and language used.
5. Examine the manner in which questions are presented.
6. Take note of the manner in which the respondent was required to respond to the questions, ticking boxes, inputting words and/or numbers, writing phrases and/or sentences.
7. Note the structure and presentation of the closed questions and the way in which the respondent is required to respond to them.
8. Note the structure and presentation of the open questions and the way in which the respondent is required to respond to them.
9. Note all of the different question formats in the questionnaires.
10. Note **skips and filters** and the ways in which they are used.
11. Note the length of the questionnaires. Questionnaires are designed to be concise and precise data-gathering methods; they should be as long as is necessary, and as short as is possible.

skips and filters Devices used in questionnaires to allow respondents to skip over questions that do not relate to them.

The key issues when designing a questionnaire are:

- the content of the questions
- the construction and presentation of each of the questions
- the order of the questions
- the length of the questionnaire.

The best guide to the design of an appropriate question, to begin with, is the conceptual framework of your research project. The conceptual framework of the research project is contained in the research question or statement of your project and it is the question or statement driving your research. If it is phrased as a question, you will need to find an answer to this question through your research. If it is phrased as a statement, you will need to respond fully to this statement through your research. If you are testing hypotheses, you will need to gather the data necessary to prove or disprove your hypotheses.

When you begin to design a questionnaire for your research, you look at your research statement/question and from that you decide what it is precisely that you need to know. Look next at the aim and objectives of your research. Then consider the literature you have reviewed for the research project. Drawing on the literature, you set about designing the series of questions that will elicit responses that will provide you with the data you need to complete your research.

As you think of possible research questions, imagine posing those questions to a member of your research population. Then try to imagine the kinds of responses that person might make to those research questions. This is a useful exercise when attempting to generate research questions. When you have done this for a series of questions, examine the likely responses to see how well they fit with the data requirements of the research. This is an exercise in critical reflection. It is a good idea to record such critical reflections in your research diary. You will be able to use them in writing up your research and in particular in writing the research methodology chapter of your thesis, or the research methodology section of your research report.

The politics and practicalities of asking a question

As explained, in quantitative research the researcher decides what needs to be known and designs a very precise data-gathering instrument to gather data in order to create knowledge. In such a data-gathering exercise, the researcher is the 'expert' and it is the researcher's understanding of and/or perspective on the phenomenon that is explored or examined in such research. In designing the precise instrument, the researcher controls and even shapes the information that is gathered, and consequently the knowledge generated by the research project.

Critiques of such approaches to research stem from what are perceived as power issues. The researcher has all the power in designing the research project and the researched (the participants in the study) are powerless. The researcher outlines and explains the experiences and concerns of those researched from within their own understanding of those experiences and concerns, instead of allowing those researched to themselves outline and explain their experiences and concerns. This is the essence of the politics of asking a question. Who is asking the question, from what or from whose perspective was the question created, developed, framed, and why is the question being asked? These are all substantial questions in social science research and they raise important issues.

Clearly a research project initiated and designed by a CEO in a company will be quite different from a research project initiated and designed by a trade union official in the same company. These two individuals hold different perspectives and are concerned with different issues with regard to the same company. Each has their own perspectives on the world. The issues they choose to study, the perspective within which they construct the study, their motives for conducting the study, will all shape the study and, consequently, the findings of the study. Issues of power such as these provide some of the reasons why researchers work hard to justify the choices and decisions, e.g. methodological decisions, made in a research project.

Quantitative research is said to be objective. To try to ensure that your research is objective, you must avoid bias. Bias in research, as defined in Chapter 14, is anything that contaminates or compromises the research. There is a general introduction to bias and error in survey research at the start of this chapter. As you know from your reading of this chapter and the preceding chapter, it is possible to bias research through the wording of the questions used in questionnaires and through the way in which respondents can be influenced in responding to those questions and items.

The researcher tackles these issues through the design of the data collection methods used in the research project, through the design of the questions asked of participants and through the organization and management of data gathering for the research. There are very many issues in designing questions and some of the key issues are considered here (see Table 15.2). When you are designing a questionnaire you must critically engage with the words, concepts and language you use in the questions in your questionnaire.

The presentation of the questionnaire should be simple, succinct and professional. The spacing of the questions should be logical and aesthetically pleasing. In other words, the questionnaire should be attractive. This is important because the appearance of the questionnaire will influence people in terms of whether or not they respond to it. Questionnaires are often sent to respondents by post or by internal mail/post or by email. When this happens, obviously the researcher is not at hand to encourage the respondent to respond to the questionnaire. So the questionnaire must appeal to the respondent, aesthetically as well as in terms of its content, and it must appeal in terms of the rationale for the questionnaire and the research. Creating aesthetically pleasing questionnaires takes a considerable amount of time and skill, but it is important to invest time in this creative endeavour. As stated earlier, software designed to facilitate the creation of questionnaires is very helpful in terms of producing clear, well formatted and aesthetically pleasing questionnaires.

Table 15.2 Issues in designing questions and items for questionnaires and scales

Leading responses	The possibility of leading participants to a particular response through the way in which the question is framed: for example, 'Nike and Adidas are two of the most popular brands among third-level students in the UK. What brands would you name as being your top five favourite brands?' The use of two brand names in the research question works as a prompt for respondents. As these two brands have been introduced by the researcher into the research encounter, it is likely that the respondents will name these two brands as being among their five favourite brands. It is also possible that the naming of the brands by the researcher might prompt respondents to deliberately avoid using these particular brand names as they name their top five. This is equally problematic. The problem is that the researcher has contaminated the research by prompting respondents through the use of particular brand names. For example, 'It has been established, in research and in the media, that the "Fantastic Jersey" company uses child labour in the manufacture of its products. Do you support the brand "Fantastic Jersey"'? It is unlikely that any respondent will admit to supporting a brand that uses child labour. So the researcher has contaminated responses to the research through the design of the question.
Ambiguous questions	These are questions that have an unclear meaning or questions that can have more than one possible meaning.
Complicated questions	Questions should be short, simple and clear, concise and precise.
Asking two questions, or more, in one question	For example, 'Please name your top five favourite brands, and explain why they are your favourites.' Here we have two questions in one. Always check that you have not done this when you are compiling a questionnaire, and if you have, rephrase your question, turning that one question into two or more questions.
Potentially embarrassing questions and/or questions which you have no right to ask	Examples might be questions about how much money someone earns, questions about a person's sexual orientation, and so on. If you need to ask potentially sensitive questions, such as how much money the respondent earns, or how old the respondent is, it is helpful to aggregate the possible answers and then ask the respondent to indicate which range they belong to, rather than respond with a precise figure.
Asking unnecessary questions	Ensure that your questionnaire, or schedule of questions and/or issues to be explored, is succinct and relevant, and absolutely to the point. Do not gather unnecessary data.
Loaded words	Loaded words are words with a particularly strong emotional impact. For example, class is a loaded word, lower class is a loaded concept. Other words are loaded, too, and perhaps they are not so apparent, e.g. poor is a loaded word.
Unclear or vague concepts	Concepts that are not clearly defined are problematic. 'Fat' is such a concept. By what standard can a person be described as being fat? Even medical definitions of obesity are contested. Another such concept is 'old'. Again, what is old? By what definition or standard can something or someone be described as old?
Insulting words	Some words and phrases are simply insulting or even degrading. They should not be used. It is important to remember that a word or phrase that is perfectly acceptable in one culture may be quite unacceptable in another.
Humour	As a rule, it is best to avoid humour completely, unless humour is the topic of your research. Perceptions of what is funny vary from person to person, as well as from culture to culture, so it is best to avoid it completely.
Slang and colloquialisms	Many of the words and phrases we use every day are, in fact, either colloquial expressions, peculiar to who we are and where we have come from, or they are slang. While such language can be charming and colourful, the standard for language in a written account of a research project is formal. So a simple formal language should be used throughout. Avoid slang and colloquial words and expressions.
Ethnocentrism	Ethnocentrism means viewing the world, and in this context consequently organizing and designing data collection for your research, from your own ethnic or cultural perspective. Ensure that your questionnaire is not ethnocentric. Ensure that the words, concepts, language you use in your questionnaire are not ethnocentric.

(Continued)

Table 15.2 Issues in designing questions and items for questionnaires and scales (*Continued*)

Classist, sexist, racist, ageist or disablist language	Do not use classist, sexist, racist, ageist or disablist words, concepts or language in your questionnaire. Ensure that you are not, through the language you use, discriminatory towards or displaying prejudice against any class, race or gender; younger people or older people; or people with different physical and/or intellectual abilities.
Abbreviations and jargon	Do not use abbreviations or jargon. Make each question as simple and clear as possible. Use words, concepts and phrases that will be familiar to your respondents.
Respondent bias	The different kinds of response bias are detailed in Figure 15.2.
Talking down to respondents	Do not 'talk down' to respondents by treating them disrespectfully or by patronizing them.
Double negatives	Double negatives in a question or sentence can be confusing. Avoid using the word 'not' in a question, e.g. 'is it not true that . . .'. Avoid negative questions.
Ask simple, easy-to-answer questions	Ask questions that the respondent will be easily able to answer. Do not ask too much of respondents; keep to a minimum the effort they have to make in order to respond to the questionnaire.
Give clear instructions	Ensure that you give clear instructions to respondents. Make sure that respondents have all the instructions, direction and guidance they need in order to be able to properly and fully respond.

RESPONSE RATES

Researchers are very fundamentally concerned with response rates because non-responses, as explained earlier, can cause error. A response rate in a research project is a count of the number of valid responses received in a data-gathering exercise, for example the number of properly completed and returned questionnaires and/or completed interviews. The higher the response rate the better. If every member of the study population or sample responds, then the study will have a very complete data set. In F2F data-gathering exercises, it is not unusual to achieve 100 per cent response rates, in telephone interviews it is not unusual to achieve 80 per cent response rates. In mail/postal surveys and in online surveys, response rates are often considerably lower than this. If the response rate is, for example, 75 per cent, then there are no data on the attitudes or experiences of 25 per cent of the study population or sample. If the response rate is 25 per cent, then there are no data on the attitudes or experiences of 75 per cent of the study population or sample. The problem is that it is possible that the non-respondents vary in some way from the respondents in terms of their attitudes and experiences of the phenomenon being studied. Non-responses change the nature of the study and the claims that can be made about the study. If everyone responds, you can apply your findings confidently to the population of the study. The fewer the number of valid responses, the less confident you can be.

One claim that researchers sometimes make about their research is that it is generalizable. **Generalizability** in research is the application of the findings of a research project beyond the specific context of the study. In claiming that the findings of their research are generalizable, what the researcher means is that the findings and conclusions drawn from their study can be applied more generally. So, for example, if the researcher has studied the attitudes of financial controllers in companies in the UK to risk taking, they may claim that the findings of their study can be applied to financial controllers generally, i.e., to financial controllers across and perhaps even beyond the UK. The rule is, the bigger the sample population of the study, the more you can generalize. This is the reason why only quantitative research is said to be generalizable, if sound design and sampling procedures have been used. Qualitative research is said to be transferable rather than generalizable (see Chapter 14, Table 14.4). Researchers tend to be very focused on getting good response rates in their research, and active in encouraging as many responses as possible in order to be able to claim that their research is generalizable.

> **generalizability** The application of the findings of a research project beyond the specific context of the study.

There are a number of ways through which response rates can be improved. Respondents can be contacted and encouraged to respond. Incentives can be given in order to improve response rates, although the value of the research, when clearly explained, is often incentive enough. Clear and persuasive information sheets and informed consent forms (see Chapter 3) can improve response rates, as can the presentation, format and layout of questionnaires. People can be encouraged to respond by clarity, simplicity and brevity in the design of the data-gathering instrument. With postal questionnaires, the use of a covering letter, sending stamped addressed envelopes and addressing the envelopes containing postal questionnaires to a specific person, can all help improve response rates. It is generally not a good idea to attempt to engage people in data-gathering exercises during public or religious holidays. Being courteous with respondents and potential respondents will improve response rates.

REAL WORLD RESEARCH

Setbacks and surprises in data gathering

One time, I was conducting research on the experiences of pupils in primary school education. I very carefully designed my research project and my research questions. One aspect of the classroom experience I was anxious to explore in the study was that of participation in class. I decided that I would ask the pupils participating in the study, as a measure of participation in class, how many times they raised their hands in class. I stood in front of a classroom full of ten-year-olds and I asked them how many times they put their hands up in class. They looked at me blankly. They did not know what I was talking about. They were not familiar with the concept of putting your hand up in class to indicate that you had something you wished to say, something to contribute to the class. When I was at primary school, if you had something to say in the classroom, you indicated this by putting up your hand. That was then. Things have changed, perhaps classroom culture has changed, or perhaps the culture of the class I was standing in front of was different from the culture of the classes I attended when I was at primary school.

Whatever the case, the important point is that things often do not work in the field in the way that you imagine they will. It is important to be prepared for this. It can be very disconcerting for a researcher when data gathering does not go the way they anticipated it would. It is important to be flexible, to be able to respond to and accept the experience of fieldwork as it actually happens in the field.

Whatever happens in the field should be recorded in your research diary. It is important to record what happens in as much detail as is possible and reasonable. It is important to examine what happens in the field and to attempt to understand what happens in the field. Reporting such experiences in the thesis or in the report of the research will add to the value of your research. Record what is happening when it happens. You can interpret what has happened later.

A PILOT STUDY

A pilot study or pretest, as defined in Chapter 13, is a test of the design of the data-gathering instrument(s) designed for the research. In general, all data-gathering methods should be tested, and in your reading for the literature review and for the research methods element of your research, you will notice that almost every data collection method you come across will be subjected to a pilot study. This is because the assumptions researchers make about how research participants will respond to the questions and items presented to them in the data-gathering methods designed for the research project are not always correct. Therefore, researchers test the data collection methods they design to find out how, in reality, participants will respond.

A pilot study, as explained, is carried out using a small number of respondents. These respondents should be similar to the actual respondents in the study, but they should not be respondents in the study. Usually, pilot studies are carried out with five to 15 respondents, depending on the size of the study. In piloting a questionnaire, the researcher wants to establish how respondents will respond to the questionnaire. Will they clearly understand each item and question in the questionnaire and will the responses they give be the responses required?

Any issues that the pilot study throws up can be dealt with before the real study takes place. For example, the pilot study might establish that the respondents do not understand some element(s) of the data collection instrument. It might also reveal that respondents interpret some element(s) of the data collection instrument in a way other than the way the researcher had anticipated. The pilot study will show if there is any resistance among the respondents to responding to any aspect of the data collection instrument.

How much pretesting and revising are necessary?

Many novelists write, rewrite, revise and rewrite again certain chapters, paragraphs, or even sentences. The researcher works in a similar world. Rarely – if ever – does s/he write only a first draft of a questionnaire. Usually the questionnaire is written, revised, shared with others for feedback and then revised again. After that, it is tried out (tested) on a group, selected on a convenience basis, which is similar in makeup to the one that ultimately will be sampled. Although the researcher should not select a group too divergent from the target market – for example, selecting business students as surrogates for businesspeople – pretesting does not require a precise sample. The pretesting process allows the researcher to determine whether respondents have any difficulty understanding the questionnaire and whether there are any ambiguous or biased questions.

For example, in one study involving the use of a questionnaire investigating student teacher experiences with web-based instruction, the researcher had the questionnaire reviewed first by university faculty members to ensure the questions were valid and s/he then asked 20 student teachers to try answering the questions and indicate any ambiguities they noticed. The feedback received prompted changes in the format and wording of the questionnaire. Pretesting was especially helpful in this study because the English-language questionnaire was used in a school in the United Arab Emirates, where English, although spoken, is not the primary language.

CASE STUDY

Strategy of celebrity endorsement

The research project outlined in this journal article (Samman *et al.*, 2009, 'The role of celebrity in endorsing poverty reduction through international aid', *International Journal of Nonprofit and Voluntary Sector Marketing*, *14*(4): 137–48), was designed to explore the strategy of celebrity endorsement which, the authors state, is gaining momentum in attempts to develop public awareness around the issue of poverty. An understanding of public perceptions is important for international organizations intending to use celebrity endorsement in order to further their causes.

In the journal article, Samman *et al.* (2009), report the results of a preliminary survey conducted among 100 members of the Irish public. The survey, as stated, was carried out 'to evaluate levels of awareness of celebrity involvement in international development work and the public's opinions about such involvement'.

The survey instrument, we are told, was semi-structured with some open-ended questions.

The focus of the survey, according to the article, was on respondents' ability to identify celebrities associated with international development work and to elicit their opinions on those celebrities' perceived aims and knowledge of international development. The survey was designed to elicit data on whether or not such celebrity involvement influenced the respondents. The survey also sought the opinions of the respondents on the value of celebrity involvement generally.

Most of the respondents found celebrity involvement to be valuable in raising the profile of charities, although only a small number claimed to be personally influenced by such activity.

Methodology

In the methodology section of the journal article, we are told that a brief survey was conducted among 100 respondents randomly selected from the Irish public.

The research was carried out using a survey methodology. The questionnaire, the data collection instrument used in the research project, is very simple and it was used effectively. If you read the original article, you will see the great use the researchers made of the data generated by this questionnaire. It is important to remember that the study was a preliminary, exploratory study. This generally means that the researchers are planning to develop a larger more robust study based on the experience and findings of this study.

The population of the research was a simple population, consisting of Dublin commuters who were accessing the DART (Dublin Area Rapid Transit) service commuter train in Dublin city centre.

In the methodology section, we are told that the sample of 100 participants was selected randomly. Can you critique that statement? Was the sample a random sample or a convenience sample? Can you provide a short description of both sampling methods and briefly outline the differences between them?

The questionnaire contains examples of both open and closed questions. Can you identify the open and the closed questions?

Both quantitative and qualitative analyses of findings are presented in this journal article. Read these different approaches to data analysis and document in your research diary the issues apparent to you and the ideas that come to you as you read.

Examine the article:

1. for the manner in which the researchers constructed a theoretical framework for the project
2. for the manner in which the project emerged from the theoretical framework
3. for the way in which the quantitative data are presented in tables (in tabular form)
4. for the way in which the findings of the research are knitted into the body of knowledge in this field.

Tabulating the results of a pretest (putting the results into a table) can facilitate insight into the data (the results). In this context, a **preliminary tabulation** might, for example, show that although respondents can easily comprehend and answer a given question, the question is inappropriate because it does not provide the required data.

Designing questionnaires for global markets

Now that business research is being conducted around the globe and people are so mobile, researchers must take cultural factors into account when designing questionnaires. The most common problem involves translating a questionnaire into other languages. A questionnaire developed in one country may be difficult to translate because equivalent language concepts do not exist. Although Spanish is spoken in both Mexico and Venezuela, one researcher found that the Spanish translation of the English term 'retail outlet' works in Mexico but not in Venezuela. Venezuelans interpreted the translation to refer to an electrical outlet, an outlet of a river into an ocean, or the passageway onto a patio.

Counting on an international audience to speak a common language such as English does not necessarily bridge language and cultural barriers, even when the respondents actually do speak more than one language. Cultural differences incorporate many shades of meaning that may not be captured by a survey delivered in a language used primarily for, say, business transactions.

International marketing researchers often have questionnaires back translated. **Back translation** is the process of taking a questionnaire that has previously been translated from one language to another and having it translated back again by a second, independent translator. The back translator is often a person whose native tongue is the language that will be used for the questionnaire. This process can reveal inconsistencies between the English version and the translation. For example, when a soft drink company translated its slogan, 'Baby, it's cold inside' into Cantonese for research in Hong Kong, the result read 'Small mosquito, on the inside, it is very cold'. In Hong Kong, small mosquito is a colloquial expression for a small child. Obviously the intended meaning of the advertising message had been lost in translation.

Literacy influences the designs of self-administered questionnaires and interviews. Knowledge of the literacy rates in foreign countries, especially those that are just developing modern economies, is vital. Clearly, if there are literacy issues in the research population or sample, gathering data through the use of questionnaires will be problematic, if not impossible.

Classifying surveys and questionnaires

Surveys may be classified in terms of the method of communication, the degrees of structure and disguise in the questionnaire, and the time frame in which the data are gathered (temporal classification). Many surveys are classified according to method of communicating with the respondent, e.g. personal interviews, telephone interviews, mail/postal surveys and internet surveys.

Questionnaires can be classified in terms of their degree of structure. A structured questionnaire provides respondents with a limited number of allowable responses. Questionnaires may have **undisguised questions** or **disguised questions**. A straightforward, or undisguised, question such as, 'Do you have dandruff problems?' assumes that the respondent is willing to reveal the information. However, researchers know that some questions are threatening to a person's ego, prestige or self-concept. So, they have designed a number of indirect techniques of questioning to disguise the purpose of the study.

Questions can be structured and **unstructured** (open and closed questions). An open, unstructured question such as, 'Why do you shop at Tesco?' allows the respondent considerable freedom in answering.

Cross-sectional studies

The key characteristic of cross sectional research is that it focuses on gathering data at one point in time. Although most surveys are individual research projects conducted only once over a short time period, some projects require multiple surveys carried out over a long period, this is longitudinal research.

Cross-sectional studies can, for example, sample various segments of the population to investigate relationships among variables by cross-tabulation. A typical method of analyzing a cross-sectional survey is to divide the sample into appropriate subgroups. For example, if a manager thinks that length of time an employee has been with the organization will influence their attitudes toward corporate policies, employees might be broken into different groups based on tenure (e.g. less than 5 years, 5–9 years, 10–14 years and 15 years or more) so their attitudes can be examined. Length of tenure is cross tabulated with attitude to corporate policy.

Cross tabulation is a statistical process and it is explored in detail in Chapter 19.

Longitudinal studies

In a **longitudinal study**, respondents are surveyed at multiple points in time. The purpose of longitudinal studies is to examine continuity of response and to observe changes that occur over time. Many syndicated polling services, such as Gallup, conduct regular polls. For example, in the USA, the Bureau of Labor Statistics conducts the National Longitudinal Survey of Youth, interviewing the same sample of individuals repeatedly since 1979 (respondents, who were 'youth' at the beginning of the study, are now in their 40s). The Yankelovich MONITOR is a survey that has been tracking American values and attitudes for more than 30 years. This survey is an example of a longitudinal study that uses successive samples; its researchers survey several different samples at different times. Longitudinal studies of this type are sometimes called cohort studies, because similar groups of people who share a certain experience during the same time interval (cohorts) are expected to be included in each sample. Figure 15.4 illustrates the results of a longitudinal study by Harris Interactive, which since 1966 has been asking five questions related to powerlessness and isolation to create an 'alienation index'.

> **longitudinal study** A survey of respondents at different times, thus allowing analysis of response continuity and changes over time.

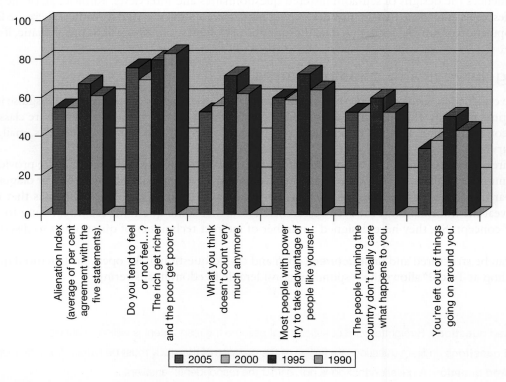

Figure 15.4 Longitudinal research from a Harris poll

THE VALUE OF GOOD RESEARCH

Overestimating patient satisfaction

When companies conduct surveys to learn about customer satisfaction, they face an important challenge: Do the responses represent a cross section of customers? Maybe just the happiest or most angry customers participate. This problem also occurs when the 'customers' are the patients of a health-care provider.

To investigate this issue, a group of researchers in Massachusetts studied data from patient satisfaction surveys that rated 6681 patients' experiences with 82 primary-care physicians (internists and family practitioners) at a health maintenance organization (HMO). These ratings represented response rates ranging from 11 to 55, depending on the physician being rated. The researchers compared their information about response rates with a set of simulated data for which they knew the underlying distribution of responses. They found that the actual data closely matched simulated data in which responses were biased so that responses were more likely when satisfaction was higher.

The researchers concluded that there was a significant correlation between the response rate and average (mean) satisfaction rating. In other words, more satisfied patients were more likely to complete and return the survey. Thus, if the HMO were to use the data to evaluate how satisfied patients are with their doctors, it would overestimate satisfaction. Also, it would have less information about its lower performing doctors. The researchers therefore concluded that it is important to follow up with subjects to encourage greater response from less satisfied patients.

In applied business research, a longitudinal study that uses successive samples is called a **tracking study** because successive waves are designed to compare trends and identify changes in variables such as consumer satisfaction, brand image or advertising awareness. These studies are useful for assessing aggregate trends but do not allow for tracking changes in individuals over time.

> **tracking study** A type of longitudinal study that uses successive samples to compare trends and identify changes in variables such as consumer satisfaction, brand image or advertising awareness.

Conducting surveys in waves with two or more sample groups avoids the problem of response bias resulting from a prior interview. A respondent who was interviewed in an earlier survey about a certain brand may become more aware of the brand or pay more attention to its advertising after being interviewed. Using different samples eliminates this problem. However, researchers can never be sure whether the changes in the variable being measured are due to a different sample or to an actual change in the variable over time.

CONSUMER PANELS

A longitudinal study that gathers data from the same sample of individuals or households over time is called a **consumer panel**. Consider the packaged-goods marketer that wishes to learn about brand-switching behaviour. A consumer panel that consists of a group of people who record their purchasing habits in a diary over time will provide the manager with a continuous stream of information about the brand and product class. Diary data that are recorded regularly over an extended period enable the researcher to track repeat-purchase behaviour and changes in purchasing habits that occur in response to changes in price, special promotions or other aspects of business strategy.

> **consumer panel** A longitudinal survey of the same sample of individuals or households to record their attitudes, behaviour or purchasing habits over time.

Panel members may be contacted by telephone, in a personal interview, by mail/postal questionnaire or by email. Typically, respondents complete media exposure or product purchase diaries and mail/post them back to the survey organization. If the panel members have agreed to field test new products, face-to-face or telephone interviews may be required.

Because establishing and maintaining a panel is expensive, panels often are managed by contractors who offer their services to many organizations. A number of commercial firms specialize in maintaining consumer panels. In recent years internet panels have grown in popularity.

The first questionnaire a panel member is asked to complete typically includes questions about product ownership, product usage, pets, family members and demographic data. The purpose of such a questionnaire is to gather the behavioural and demographic data that will be used to identify heavy buyers, difficult-to-reach customers, and so on for future surveys. Individuals who serve as members of consumer panels usually are compensated with cash, attractive gifts or the chance to win a sweepstake.

REAL WORLD RESEARCH

Intuit gets answers to satisfy customers

Intuit, manufacturer of Quicken, QuickBooks and Turbo Tax software for accounting and tax preparation, has enjoyed years of growth and profits, thanks in part to its efforts to learn what customers want. One of its most important marketing research tools is called a 'net promoter survey'. That survey is extremely simple. Researchers simply ask customers, 'On a scale of 0 to 10 [with 10 being most likely], how likely is it that you would recommend our product to your friends or colleagues?' Customers who respond with a 9 or 10 are called 'promoters', and customers who respond with 0 to 6 are called 'detractors'. Subtracting the percentage of respondents who are detractors from the percentage who are promoters yields the net promoter score.

Intuit's CEO, Steve Bennett – who says he believes that 'anything that can be measured can be improved' – encourages the ongoing collection of net promoter scores as a way to improve products and customer service and thereby build revenues and profits. Of course, making improvements requires that the company not only know whether customers are satisfied or dissatisfied but also know why. To learn more, the company asks survey respondents who are promoters to go online and provide more detailed opinions. For example, Intuit learned that claiming rebates was an annoying process (the company has simplified it) and that discount stores were offering some products for less than the prices offered online to frequent buyers (the company plans to adjust prices).

For even more in-depth information, Intuit supplements survey research with direct observation of customers. One year the company sent hundreds of employees, including CEO Bennett, to visit customers as they worked at their computers. The observers learned that a significant number of small business owners were struggling with the accounting know-how they needed to use QuickBooks and were mystified by terms such as accounts payable and accounts receivable. In response, the company introduced QuickBooks: Simple Start Edition, which replaces the financial jargon with simple terms like cash in and cash out. In the first year after its launch, Simple Start Edition sold more copies than any other accounting software except the standard QuickBooks.

This study not only illustrates Intuit's reliance on survey research to enhance products and monitor customer satisfaction and loyalty, but also shows the close relationship between qualitative and quantitative research. As we discussed previously, qualitative research is often used in exploratory business research to set the stage for quantitative research, such as surveys. Qualitative research can also be used to provide richer information and to bring the quantitative research numbers to life. Intuit recognizes the value of both research approaches.

Total quality management and customer satisfaction surveys

Total quality management (TQM) is a business strategy that emphasizes market-driven quality as a top priority. Total quality management involves implementing and adjusting the firm's business activities to assure customers' satisfaction with the quality of goods and services.

> **total quality management (TQM)** A business philosophy that emphasizes market-driven quality as a top organizational priority.

Internal and external customers

Organizations that have adopted the total quality management philosophy believe that a focus on customers must include more than external customers. They believe that everyone in the organization has customers, and that the development of sound, comprehensive customer relationships is a key factor to business success.

Implementing total quality management

Implementing a total quality management programme requires considerable survey research. A firm must routinely ask customers to rate it against its competitors. It must periodically measure employee knowledge, attitudes and expectations. It must monitor company performance against benchmark standards. It must determine whether customers found any delightful surprises or major disappointments. In other words, a total quality management strategy expresses the conviction that to improve quality, an organization must regularly conduct surveys to evaluate quality improvement.

Overall tracking of quality improvement requires longitudinal research (shown in Figure 15.5). The process begins with a commitment and exploration stage, during which management makes a commitment to total quality assurance and researchers explore external and internal customers' needs and beliefs. The research must discover what product features customers value, what problems customers are having with the product, what aspects of product operation or customer service have disappointed customers, what the company is doing right and what the company may be doing wrong.

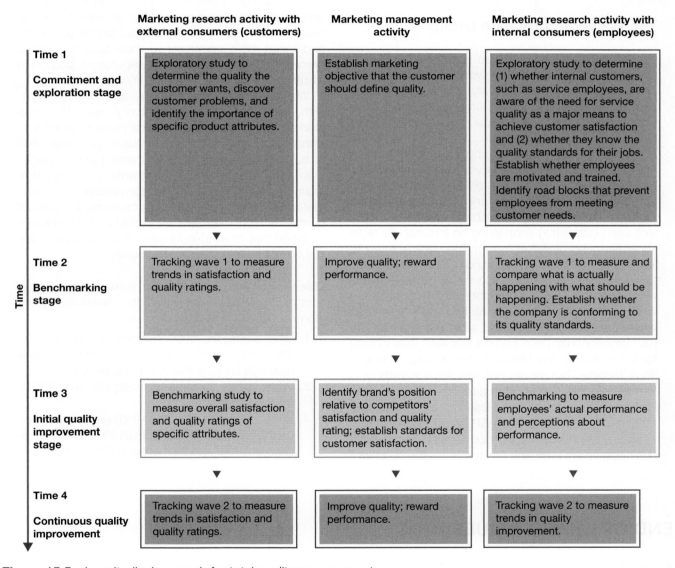

Figure 15.5 Longitudinal research for total quality management

After internal and external customers' problems and desires have been identified, the benchmarking stage begins. Research must establish quantitative measures that can serve as benchmarks or points of comparison against which to evaluate future efforts. The surveys must establish initial measures of overall satisfaction, of the frequency of customer problems and of quality ratings for specific attributes. Researchers must identify the company's or brand's position relative to competitors' quality positions.

In organizations that wish to improve service quality, managers must identify and analyze customer service needs and then establish specifications for the level of service. They must then train frontline personnel and give them the responsibility for quality service. Front line personnel need to be motivated and encouraged to deliver the service that goes beyond consumer expectations. Finally, regular surveys with both external customers and internal employees measure results against standards.

CASE STUDY

The Walker Information Group

The Walker Information Group is among the largest research companies in the world. Walker's clients include many Fortune 500 and blue chip industry leaders such as Cummins Engine Company, Lenscrafters, Continental Cablevision, Florida Power and Light and Oglethorpe Power Corporation.

The Indianapolis-based company was founded in 1939 as a field interviewing service by Tommie Walker, grandmother of Steven F. Walker, the current chairman and chief executive officer of the organization. In the 1920s Tommie Walker's late husband worked for a bank that was considering sponsoring an Indianapolis radio show featuring classical music. The bank wanted to know who was listening to this show. Tommie was hired to do the interviewing and she threw herself into the work. After that, referrals brought her more interviewing work for surveys. During an interview with a woman whose husband was a district sales manager for the A&P grocery chain, she learned that A&P was looking for a surveyor in the Midwest. A&P's sales manager liked Tommie, but would not hire anyone without a formal company, a field staff and insurance. Tommie founded Walker Marketing Research on 20 October 1939 and her business with A&P lasted 17 years.

Today, the Walker Information Group specializes in business, health care and consumer research, as well as database marketing. The company is organized around several services that it provides to its clients.

Walker Information conducts traditional market research services that range from questionnaire design and data collection to advanced analysis and consultation. Walker has expertise in helping companies measure how their actions are perceived by the audiences most important to them and how these perceptions affect their image, reputation, corporate citizenship, recruiting, sales and more.

Walker Global Reach spans across the globe, with partnerships in virtually every major business market. It is the first international network of professional research and consulting businesses dedicated to customer satisfaction measurement and management. The Global Reach programme assures that multi-country customer satisfaction research is consistent by taking into account local conditions and cultural norms. Network members are trained to use consistent methods that allow standardization and comparability of information from country to country.

Questions What type of custom survey research projects might Walker Information, Inc. (www.walkerinfo.com) conduct for its clients?

1. What stages are involved in conducting a survey? For which stages might a client company hire a research supplier like Walker Research?
2. What is the purpose of customer satisfaction measurement?
3. What measures, other than findings from surveys, might a company use to evaluate the effectiveness of a total quality management programme?

END OF CHAPTER QUESTIONS

1 What is survey research?

2 Why are questionnaires the key data-gathering method in survey research?

3 Why are questionnaires particularly useful with large, geographical spread populations?

4 List and explain the four key issues in designing a questionnaire.

5 Develop a checklist of things to consider in questionnaire construction.

6 List and explain ten key issues in question design.

7 How might the wording of a question about income influence respondents' answers?

8 What is meant by the term response rate?

9 What is the difference between a leading question and a loaded question?

10 A client tells a researcher that he wants a questionnaire that evaluates the importance of 30 product characteristics and rates his brand and ten competing brands on these characteristics. The researcher believes that this questionnaire will induce respondent fatigue because it will be far too long. How should the researcher respond?

11 Design eight questions that assess how effective an undergraduate college business course has been.

12 What is the typical process for developing questionnaires for markets where consumers speak a language other than English?

13 Explain the issues of validity and reliability in relation to quantitative research.

14 Go to SurveyMonkey (www.surveymonkey.com). Then, visit My Survey (www.mysurvey.com). Are there any differences between the two websites in terms of the services they provide to users?

REFERENCES

American Statistical Association online guide, 'What is a survey?', www.whatisasurvey.info (Accessed 17.03.2018).

BBC News, 'Internet access is "a fundamental right"', news.bbc.co.uk/2/hi/technology/8548190.stm (Accessed 17.03.2018).

Checkbox, www.checkbox.com. (Accessed 17.03.2018).

CNN (2009) 'Fast internet access becomes a legal right in Finland', 15 October, edition.cnn.com/2009/TECH/10/15/finland.internet.rights/index.html?_s=PM:TECH (Accessed 17.03.2018).

Howell, C. and West, D.M. (2016) *The Internet as a Human Right*, www.brookings.edu/blog/techtank/2016/11/07/the-internet-as-a-human-right (Accessed 17.03.2018).

Instant Survey, www.instantsurvey.com (Accessed 17.03.2018).

Methodspace, www.methodspace.com (Accessed 17.03.2018).

Millennium Report of the Secretary General (2000) 'We The Peoples: the Role of the United Nations in the 21st century' www.un.org/en/events/pastevents/we_the_peoples.shtml

Princeton University Survey Research Center (PSRC), www.princeton.edu/~psrc (Accessed 17.03.2018).

Qualtrics, www.qualtrics.com (Accessed 17.03.2018).

Question Pro, www.questionpro.com (Accessed 17.03.2018).

Samman, E., McAuliffe, E. and MacLachlan, M. (2009) 'The role of celebrity in endorsing poverty reduction through international aid', *International Journal of Nonprofit and Voluntary Sector Marketing*, 14(4): 137–148.

Snap Surveys, www.snapsurveys.com (Accessed 17.03.2018).

Survey Monkey, www.surveymonkey.com (Accessed 17.03.2018).

Surveyspro, www.surveyspro.com (Accessed 17.03.2018).

The Brookings Institution, www.brookings.edu/about-us (Accessed 17.03.2018).

Trochim, W.M. (2006) *The Research Methods Knowledge Base* (2nd edn), www.socialresearchmethods.net (Accessed 17.03.2018).

UN Declaration of Human Rights, www.un.org/en/universal-declaration-human-rights (Accessed 17.03.2018).

RECOMMENDED READING

Bell, J. and Waters, S. (2014) *Doing Your Research Project* (6th edn), Maidenhead: Open University Press.

Collis, J. and Hussey, R. (2013) *Business Research: A Practical Guide for Undergraduate and Postgraduate Students* (4th edn), Basingstoke and New York: Palgrave Macmillan.

Creswell, J. and Creswell, D.J. (2018) *Research Design: Qualitative, Quantitative and Mixed Methods Approaches* (5th edn), London, California, New Delhi, Singapore: Sage.

Denscombe, M. (2017) *The Good Research Guide: For Small-scale Social Research Projects* (5th edn), Maidenhead: Open University Press.

Easterby-Smith, M., Thorpe, R. and Jackson, P.R. (2008) *Management Research* (3rd edn), London: Sage.

Gill, J. and Johnson, P. (2010) *Research Methods for Managers* (4th edn), London, California, New Delhi, Singapore: Sage.

Neuman, W.L. (2014) *Social Research Methods: Qualitative and Quantitative Approaches* (7th edn), Essex, England: Pearson Education Ltd.

Oppenheim, A.N. (2000) *Questionnaire Design, Interviewing and Attitude Measurement* (2nd edn), London: Pinter.

Robson, C. and McCartan, K. (2016) *Real World Research*, John Wiley & Sons Ltd.

de Vaus, D. (ed.) (2013) *Surveys in Social Research* (6th edn), London: Routledge.

CHAPTER 16
ATTITUDE MEASUREMENT

LEARNING OBJECTIVES

At the end of this chapter, the student should be able to:

● Identify basic approaches to measuring attitudes.

● Discuss the use of rating scales for measuring attitudes.

● Represent a latent construct by constructing a summated scale.

● Summarize ways to measure attitudes with ranking and sorting techniques.

● Discuss the major issues involved in the selection of a measurement scale.

RESEARCH SKILLS

At the end of this chapter, the student should, using the exercises on Cengage Brain, be able to:

● Explain what a Likert scale is and design a ten-item Likert scale to measure attitudes to a new product.

● Explain what a rating scale is and design a ten-item rating scale for a training programme.

● Explain a semantic differential scale with the use of an example.

● Explain what is meant by the term 'sentence completion exercise', with the use of an example.

● Explain what vignettes are and briefly outline a small research project to be carried out using vignettes.

INTRODUCTION

For social scientists, an **attitude** is an enduring disposition to respond consistently to specific aspects of the world, including actions, people or objects.

> **attitude** An enduring disposition to consistently respond in a given manner to various aspects of the world, composed of affective, cognitive and behavioural components.

One way to understand an attitude is to break it down into its components. Consider this brief statement: 'Kayleigh believes Tesco is clean, conveniently located and has low prices. She likes Tesco and enjoys shopping there. She intends to shop there every Thursday.' This simple example demonstrates an attitude's three components: cognitive, affective and behavioural.

A person's attitudinal feelings are typically driven directly by their beliefs or cognitions. This cognitive component represents an individual's knowledge about attributes and their consequences. One person might feel happy about the purchase of a car because she believes the car 'gets great mileage' or because she knows the person selling the car.

The affective component refers to an individual's general feelings or emotions toward an object. Statements such as, 'I really like my iPod', 'I enjoy reading Harry Potter books', and 'I hate cranberry juice' reflect the emotional character of attitudes.

The behavioural component of an attitude reflects a predisposition to action based on intentions.

ATTITUDES AS HYPOTHETICAL CONSTRUCTS

Business researchers often pose questions involving psychological variables that cannot directly be observed. For example, someone may have an attitude toward working on a commission basis. We cannot actually see this attitude. Rather, we can measure an attitude by making an inference based on the way an individual responds to multiple scale indicators. Because we cannot directly see these phenomena, they are known as latent constructs, **hypothetical constructs** or just simply, constructs. Common constructs include job satisfaction, organizational commitment, personal values, feelings, role stress, perceived value and many more. The Research in Practice box talks about measuring love. Is love a latent construct?

hypothetical constructs Variables that are not directly observable but are measurable through indirect indicators, such as verbal expression or overt behaviour.

RESEARCH IN PRACTICE

Is it positive emotionality, or is it LOVE?

Love is a four-letter word. Or is it more than that? Psychologists and cognitive scientists view love as just one example of positive emotionality and they have developed numerous definitions to describe what love is and how it works. In fact, a recent study found there are nine different ways love can be defined and/or measured! The concept of love is a hypothetical construct – that is, a term that psychologists use to describe or explain a particular pattern of human behaviour. Love, hate, learning, intelligence – all of these are hypothetical constructs. They are hypothetical in that they do not exist as physical entities; therefore, they cannot be seen, heard, felt or measured directly. There is no love centre in the brain that, if removed, would leave a person incapable of responding positively and affectionately towards other people and things. Love and hate are constructs in that we invent these terms to explain why, for instance, a young man spends all his time with one young woman while completely avoiding another. From a scientific point of view, we might be better off if we said that this young man's behaviour suggested that he had a relatively enduring, positive approach attitude towards the first woman and a negative avoidance attitude towards the second! (Based on Myers and Shurts, 2002).

Importance of measuring attitudes

Most managers hold the intuitive belief that changing consumers' or employees' attitudes towards their company or their company's products or services is a major goal. Because modifying attitudes plays a pervasive role in developing strategies to address these goals, the measurement of attitudes is an important task. For example, after Whiskas cat food had been sold in Europe for decades, the brand faced increased competition from new premium brands and consumers had difficulty identifying with Whiskas (Anhalt, 1998). The company conducted attitude research to determine how people felt about their cats and their food alternatives. The study revealed that cat owners see their pets both as independent and as dependent fragile beings. Cat owners held the attitude that cats wanted to enjoy their food but also needed nutrition. This attitude research was directly channelled into managerial action. Whiskas' marketers begin positioning the product as having 'Catisfaction', using advertisements that featured a purring silver tabby – a pedigree cat – which symbolizes premium quality but also presents the image of a sweet cat. The message: 'Give cats what they like with the nutrition they need. If you do, they'll be so happy that they'll purr for you.' This effort reversed the sales decline the brand had been experiencing.

Techniques for measuring attitudes

A remarkable variety of techniques has been devised to measure attitudes. This variety stems in part from lack of consensus about the exact definition of the concept. In addition, the cognitive, affective and behavioural components of an attitude may be measured by different means.

Research may assess the affective (emotional) components of attitudes through physiological measures such as galvanic skin response (GSR), blood pressure and pupil dilation. These measures provide a means of assessing attitudes without verbally questioning the respondent. In general, they can provide a gross measure of likes or dislikes, but they are not really sensitive to the different gradients of an attitude.

Obtaining verbal statements from respondents generally requires that the respondents perform a task such as ranking, rating, sorting or making choices. A **ranking** task requires the respondent to rank order a small number of stores, brands, feelings or objects on the basis of overall preference or some characteristic of the stimulus. **Rating** asks the respondent to estimate the magnitude or the extent to which some characteristic exists. A quantitative score results. The rating task involves marking a response indicating one's position using one or more cognitive or attitudinal scales. A **sorting** task might present the respondent with several different concepts printed on cards and require the respondent to classify the concepts by placing the cards into groups (stacks of cards). Another type of attitude measurement is **choice** between two or more alternatives. If a respondent chooses one object over another, the researcher assumes that the respondent prefers the chosen object, at least in this setting. The following sections describe the most popular techniques for measuring attitudes.

RESEARCH THIS!

This chapter focuses on different ways to assess respondent attitudes. One popular way is to use a multi-attribute model. The process begins by asking respondents in one way or another to evaluate the attributes that help form an attitude toward the activity involved. For example, in our survey, we assess attitudes towards working in a specific business career (marketing, management, finance, accounting). Each respondent's attribute evaluation is multiplied by the corresponding belief about whether or not the particular activity is associated with the attribute. This process is described here. After reading the chapter, see if you can compute respondents' attitudes towards working in a business career (just consider each of the four disciplines a business career). Later, we'll actually revisit these attitude scores to see which business area is truly preferred.

Many things can influence whether or not a career is best for you. The items below describe characteristics associated with different jobs. Complete the statements 'A career where ___' using the list of phrases shown on the left. Rate each phrase using the provided scale based on whether the statement describes a relatively bad or good thing compared to the others (you may wish to review the list before making the first response).

A career where . . .	Very bad	Bad	Poor	Fair	Good	Very good	Excellent
the work is easy	⦿	⦿	⦿	⦿	⦿	⦿	⦿
one has to work more than 40 hours a week	⦿	⦿	⦿	⦿	⦿	⦿	⦿
one's pay is tied to his or her job performance	⦿	⦿	⦿	⦿	⦿	⦿	⦿
one has to learn new things to be successful	⦿	⦿	⦿	⦿	⦿	⦿	⦿
people have no fear of losing their job	⦿	⦿	⦿	⦿	⦿	⦿	⦿
one has to travel more than once a month	⦿	⦿	⦿	⦿	⦿	⦿	⦿
the work does not interfere with your personal life	⦿	⦿	⦿	⦿	⦿	⦿	⦿

ranking A measurement task that requires respondents to rank order a small number of objects on the basis of overall preference or some characteristic of the stimulus.

rating A measurement task that requires respondents to estimate the magnitude of a characteristic or quality that an object possesses.

sorting A measurement task that presents a respondent with several objects or product concepts and requires the respondent to arrange the objects into piles or classify the product concepts.

choice A measurement task that identifies preferences by requiring respondents to choose between two or more alternatives.

Attitude rating scales

Perhaps the most common practice in business research is using rating scales to measure attitudes. This section introduces and explains many rating scales designed to enable respondents to report the intensity of their attitudes.

Simple attitude scales

In its most basic form, attitude scaling requires that an individual agrees or disagrees with a statement or responds to a single question. For example, respondents in a political poll may be asked whether they agree or disagree with the statement 'The President should run for re-election'. Or an individual might indicate whether they like or dislike jalapeño bean dip. This type of self-rating scale merely classifies respondents into one of two categories, thus having only the properties of a nominal scale. The types of mathematical analysis that may be used with this basic scale are limited.

Despite the disadvantages, simple attitude scaling may be used when questionnaires are extremely long, when respondents have little education, or for other specific reasons. A number of simplified scales are merely checklists: a respondent indicates past experience, preference, and so on, simply by checking an item. In many cases the items are adjectives that describe a particular object. In a survey of small business owners and managers, respondents indicated whether they found working in a small firm more rewarding than working in a large firm, as well as whether they agreed with a series of attitude statements about small businesses. For example, 77 per cent said small and midsized businesses 'have less bureaucracy', and 76 per cent said smaller companies 'have more flexibility' than large ones.

Most attitude theorists believe that attitudes vary along continua (the plural of continuum). Early attitude researchers pioneered the view that the task of attitude scaling is to measure the distance from 'bad' to 'good', 'low' to 'high', 'dislike' to 'like', and so on. Thus, the purpose of an attitude scale is to find an individual's position on the continuum. However, simple scales do not allow for fine distinctions between attitudes. Several other scales have been developed for making more precise measurements.

REAL WORLD RESEARCH

Students ask – are you responsible?

Businesses today face an increasing need to be perceived as having an interest in social responsibility. In many instances, products and services have been promoted based on the fact that the product or service is environmentally friendly or has a tie to improving the social environment. Companies such as The Body Shop (with an emphasis on environmental protection) and Yoplait (with its commitment to reducing the company's carbon footprint) highlight a trend that showing interest in improving the world can also have bottom-line implications. The Alloy Eighth Annual College Explorer study, conducted within the USA with the assistance of the Harris Group, recently surveyed 1554 college students to determine their opinions about corporate social responsibility. Results indicate that 41 per cent of college students consciously prefer products and services from companies they *perceive* as having a social role. Large companies such as Toyota and smaller companies like Burt's Bees were ranked as highly socially responsible brands.

The implications for business leaders are quite interesting. Increasingly, perceptions of the company itself, and not just its products, drive purchasing decisions among this important demographic. Based on Bush (2008).

Category scales

The simplest rating scale described earlier contains only two response categories, such as yes/no or agree/disagree. Expanding the response categories provides the respondent with more flexibility in the rating task and the ability to more precisely indicate his/her attitude. Even more information is provided if the categories are ordered according to a particular descriptive or evaluative dimension. Consider the following question:

How often do you disagree with your partner about how much to spend on holiday?				
Never	Rarely	Sometimes	Often	Very often
☐	☐	☐	☐	☐

This **category scale** is a more sensitive measure than a scale that has only two response categories. By having more choices for a respondent, the potential exists to provide more information. Compare this question to one that asks the respondent, 'Do you disagree with your partner about how much to spend on a holiday?' And offers only yes/no as possible responses. The benefits of additional points in the measurement scale should be obvious. However, if the researcher tries to represent something that is truly bipolar or dichotomous (yes/no, female/male, member/non-member, and so on) with more than two categories, error may be introduced.

> **category scale** A rating scale that consists of several response categories, often providing respondents with alternatives to indicate positions on a continuum.

Question wording is an extremely important factor in the usefulness of these scales. Figure 16.1 shows some common wordings used in category scales.

Quality				
	Poor	Fair	Good	Excellent
Not good at all	Not very good	Neither good nor bad	Fairly good	Very good
Well below average	Below average	Average	Above average	Well above average
Importance				
Not at all important	Not so important	Neutral	Fairly important	Very important
Interest				
Not very interested		Somewhat interested		Very interested
Satisfaction				
Completely dissatisfied	Somewhat dissatisfied	Neither satisfied nor dissatisfied	Somewhat satisfied	Completely satisfied
	Not at all satisfied	Somewhat satisfied	Quite satisfied	Very satisfied
Frequency				
Hardly ever	Sometimes	Often	Very often	All of the time
Never	Rarely	Sometimes	Often	Very often
	Just now and then	Some of the time	Most of the time	All of the time
Truth				
	Definitely no	Probably no	Probably yes	Definitely yes
Uniqueness				
	Not at all different	Slightly different	Somewhat different	Very different
Not at all unique	Slightly unique	Somewhat unique	Very unique	Extremely unique

Figure 16.1 Selected category scales

Method of summated ratings: the Likert scale

A method that is simple to administer and therefore extremely popular is business researchers' adaptation of the method of summated ratings, developed by Rensis Likert. With the **Likert scale**, respondents indicate their attitudes by checking how strongly they agree or disagree with carefully constructed statements, ranging from very negative to very positive attitudes toward some object. Individuals generally choose from approximately five response alternatives – strongly disagree, disagree, uncertain, agree and strongly agree – although the number of alternatives may range from three to ten or more. In the following example, there are five alternatives.

> **Likert scale** A measure of attitudes designed to allow respondents to rate how strongly they agree or disagree with carefully constructed statements, ranging from very positive to very negative attitudes towards some object.

I really enjoy my business research class.				
Strongly disagree	Disagree	Uncertain	Agree	Strongly agree
☐	☐	☐	☐	☐
(1)	(2)	(3)	(4)	(5)

Researchers assign scores, or weights, to each possible response. In this example, numerical scores of 1, 2, 3, 4 and 5 are assigned to each level of agreement, respectively. The numerical scores, shown in parentheses, are typically not printed on the questionnaire or computer screen. Strong agreement indicates the most favourable attitude on the statement and a numerical score of 5 is assigned to this response.

Reverse coding

The statement given in this example ('I really enjoy my business research class') is positively framed. A student who loves her research class would choose 'strongly agree', with a scale value of 5. If a second statement used to measure attitude about your business research class is framed negatively (such as 'My business research class is my least favourite class'), the same student would choose 'strongly disagree', with a scale value of 1. To make these questions consistent, the numerical scores would need to be reversed. This is done by reverse coding the negative item so that a strong agreement really indicates an unfavourable response rather than a favourable attitude and vice versa. In the case of a five-point scale, the recoding is done as follows:

Old value	New value
1	5
2	4
3	3
4	2
5	1

Recoding in this fashion turns agreement with a negatively worded item into a mirror image, meaning the result is the same as disagreement with a positively worded item. The computerized software package SPSS, which is used for analyzing quantitative data, has a recode function that allows simple recoding to be done by entering 'old' and 'new' scale values. Alternatively, a simple mathematical formula can be entered. For a typical 1–5 scale, the following formula would result in the same recoding:

$$X_{new\ value} = 6 - X_{old\ value}$$

Composite scales

A Likert scale may include several scale items to form a **composite scale**. Each statement is assumed to represent an aspect of a common attitudinal domain. For example, Figure 16.2 shows the items in a Likert scale for measuring attitudes towards bank staff. The total score is the summation of the numerical scores assigned to an individual's responses. Note that item 3 is negatively worded and therefore it must be reverse coded prior to being used to create the composite scale. In other words, a person that felt extremely positively about the bank's staff would indicate 'strongly agree' with items 1, 2 and 4, and 'strongly disagree' with item 3. If we use the typical five-point 'strongly disagree' to 'strongly agree' scale, the possible scores for each respondent's composite would range from 4 (extremely negative) to 20 (extremely positive) after recoding.

> **composite scale** A way of representing a latent construct by summing or averaging respondents' reactions to multiple items each assumed to indicate the latent construct.

In Likert's original procedure, a large number of statements are generated and an item analysis is performed. The purpose of the item analysis is to ensure that the final items evoke a wide response and discriminate among those with negative and positive attitudes. Items that are poor because they lack clarity or elicit mixed response patterns are eliminated from the final statement list. Scales that use multiple items can be analyzed for reliability and validity. Only a set of items that demonstrates good reliability and validity should be summed or averaged to form a composite scale representing a hypothetical construct. Unfortunately, not all researchers are willing or able to thoroughly assess reliability and validity. Without this test, the use of Likert scales can be disadvantageous because there is no way of knowing exactly what the items represent or how well they represent anything of interest. Without valid and reliable measures, researchers cannot guarantee they are measuring what they say they are measuring.

> 1. The staff at my bank take an interest in me.
> 2. The staff at my bank are polite and very friendly.
> 3. The staff at my bank are more interested in looking after the bank's interest than they are in looking after me.
> 4. The staff at my bank are always professional in their dealings with me.

Figure 16.2 Likert-scale items for measuring attitudes towards customers' interaction with a bank's service staff

Semantic differential

The **semantic differential** is actually a series of attitude scales. This popular attitude measurement technique consists of getting respondents to react to some concept using a series of seven-point bipolar rating scales. Bipolar adjectives – such as 'terrible' and 'excellent', 'cramped' and 'spacious' or 'dirty' and 'clean' – anchor the beginning and the end (or poles) of the scale. The subject makes repeated judgements about the concept under investigation on each of the scales. Figure 16.3 shows seven of 18 scales used in a research project that measured attitudes towards supermarkets.

> **semantic differential** A measure of attitudes that consists of a series of seven-point rating scales that use bipolar adjectives to anchor the beginning and end of each scale.

Inconvenient location	_ _ _ _ _ _ _	Convenient location
Low prices	_ _ _ _ _ _ _	High prices
Pleasant atmosphere	_ _ _ _ _ _ _	Unpleasant atmosphere
Modern	_ _ _ _ _ _ _	Old-fashioned
Cluttered	_ _ _ _ _ _ _	Spacious
Fast checkout	_ _ _ _ _ _ _	Slow checkout
Dull	_ _ _ _ _ _ _	Exciting

Figure 16.3 Semantic differential scales for measuring attitudes toward supermarkets

The scoring of the semantic differential can be illustrated using the scale bounded by the anchors 'modern' and 'old-fashioned'. Respondents are instructed to check the place that indicates the nearest appropriate adjective. While only the anchors are included on the survey, the scale intervals are assumed to be interpreted as something like 'extremely modern', 'very modern', 'slightly modern', 'both modern and old-fashioned', 'slightly old-fashioned', 'very old-fashioned' and 'extremely old-fashioned':

Modern _ _ _ _ _ _ _ Old-fashioned

The semantic differential technique originally was developed as a method for measuring the meanings of objects or the 'semantic space' of interpersonal experience. Researchers have found the semantic differential versatile and useful in business applications. However, the validity of the semantic differential depends on finding scale anchors that are semantic opposites, which can sometimes prove difficult. In attitude or image studies, simple anchors such as very unfavourable and very favourable work well.

For scoring purposes, a numerical score is assigned to each position on the rating scale. Traditionally, score ranges such as 1, 2, 3, 4, 5, 6, 7 or –3, –2, –1, 0, +1, +2, +3 are used. Many business researchers find it desirable to assume that the semantic differential provides interval data. This assumption, although widely accepted, has critics who argue that the data have only ordinal properties because the numerical scores are arbitrary. Practically speaking, most researchers will treat semantic differential scales as metric (at least interval). This is because the amount of error introduced by assuming the intervals between choices are equal (even though this is uncertain) is fairly small.

Figure 16.4 illustrates a typical **image profile** based on semantic differential data. Because the data are assumed to be interval, either the arithmetic mean (average) or the median (middle value) will be used to compare the profile of one company, unit, product, brand, store, or so forth with that of another.

image profile A graphic representation of semantic differential data for competing brands, products or stores, or other, to highlight comparisons.

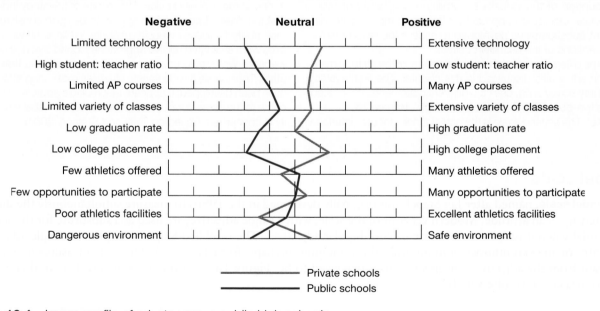

Figure 16.4 Image profile of private versus public high schools

Numerical scales

A **numerical scale** simply provides numbers rather than a semantic space or verbal descriptions to identify response options or categories (response positions). For example, a scale using five response positions is called a five-point numerical scale. A six-point scale has six positions and a seven-point scale seven positions, and so on. Consider the following numerical scale:

Now that you've had your car for about one year, please tell us how satisfied you are with your Volkswagen Jetta.

Extremely Dissatisfied 1 2 3 4 5 6 7 Extremely Satisfied

> **numerical scale** An attitude rating scale similar to a semantic differential except that it uses numbers, instead of verbal descriptions, as response options to identify response positions.

This numerical scale uses bipolar adjectives in the same manner as the semantic differential, but replaces the blanks with numbers.

In practice, researchers have found that a scale with numerical labels for intermediate points on the scale is as effective a measure as the true semantic differential. The Real World Research box demonstrates that a variety of scales can be helpful in assessing website usability.

REAL WORLD RESEARCH

Measuring website usability

How good is a website? There are a lot of factors that go into answering that question, but one of the most important is the usability of the site. There are a variety of ways to assess website usability. From an objective perspective, the time required by research subjects to complete a task can be recorded. However, subjective evaluations – a respondent's perception of the website's usability – can be as or more effective. One study approached this by comparing five different questionnaires developed to assess the respondents' perceptions of the usability of sites.

The different questionnaires use several of the attitude measurement scales discussed in this chapter. The first, system usability scale (SUS), uses ten different statements, each rated on a five-point Likert scale from 'strongly disagree' to 'strongly agree'. The second scale is the questionnaire for user interface satisfaction (QUIS), which consists of 27 questions rated on a ten-point semantic differential scale with bipolar adjectives such as 'terrible' and 'wonderful'. The third approach is the computer system usability questionnaire (CSUQ) developed at IBM. The CSUQ has 19 questions rated on a seven-point Likert scale. The fourth scale is derived from a series of 118 words used by Microsoft on product reaction cards. The respondent places a check by each word they feel describes their interaction with the website well. The final approach is a questionnaire comprising nine statements evaluated on a scale, ranging from −3 to +3, which is somewhat of a combination of a Likert statement and a Stapel scale (see later).

Respondents were asked to perform two different tasks on two financial websites, finance.yahoo.com and kiplinger.com. After interacting with the website, each respondent reacted to one of the usability scales. The results of the study indicate that the different approaches appear to be quite consistent in their ability to assess website usability. While only two websites were evaluated, all five approaches found that one of the websites was viewed as significantly more useable than the other. Thus, while a wide variety of scales measuring attitudes have been developed, it appears that multiple approaches can come to the same conclusion, at least as far as website usability is concerned. Based on Tullis and Stetson (2004).

Stapel scale

The **Stapel scale**, named after Jan Stapel, was originally developed in the 1950s to measure simultaneously the direction and intensity of an attitude. Modern versions of the scale, with a single adjective, are used as a substitute for the semantic differential when it is difficult to create pairs of bipolar adjectives. The modified Stapel scale places a single adjective in the centre of an even number of numerical values (ranging, perhaps, from +3 to −3). The scale measures how close to or distant from the adjective a given stimulus is perceived to be. Figure 16.5 illustrates a Stapel scale item that could be used to measure a website's usability.

	−3
	−2
Please select a *plus* number for words or terms that you think describe this website accurately. Select a *minus* number for words or terms that you think do not describe this website accurately. You can choose any number from +3, for words you think are very accurate, to −3, for words you think are very inaccurate.	−1
	Easy to navigate
	+1
	+2
	+3

Figure 16.5 A Stapel scale for measuring a website's usability

Stapel scale A measure of attitudes that consists of a single adjective in the centre of an even number of numerical values.

The advantages and disadvantages of the Stapel scale are very similar to those of the semantic differential. However, the Stapel scale is markedly easier to administer, especially over the telephone. Because the Stapel scale does not require bipolar adjectives, it is easier to construct than the semantic differential. Research comparing the semantic differential with the Stapel scale indicates that results from the two techniques are largely the same.

Constant-sum scale

A **constant-sum scale** requires respondents to divide a fixed number of points among several attributes corresponding to their relative importance or weight. Suppose United Parcel Service (UPS) wishes to determine the importance of the attributes of accurate invoicing, delivery as promised and price to organizations that use its service in business-to-business settings. Respondents might be asked to divide a constant sum of 100 points to indicate the relative importance of those attributes:

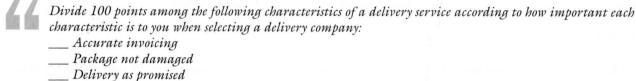

> *Divide 100 points among the following characteristics of a delivery service according to how important each characteristic is to you when selecting a delivery company:*
> ___ *Accurate invoicing*
> ___ *Package not damaged*
> ___ *Delivery as promised*
> ___ *Lower price*
> ___ *100 points.*

constant-sum scale A measure of attitudes in which respondents are asked to divide a constant sum to indicate the relative importance of attributes; respondents often sort cards, but the task may also be a rating task.

The constant-sum scale works best with respondents who have high educational levels. If respondents follow the instructions correctly, the results will approximate interval measures. As the number of stimuli increases, this technique becomes increasingly complex.

This technique may be used for measuring brand preference. The approach, which is similar to the paired-comparison method (discussed later), is as follows:

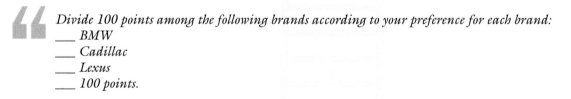

> *Divide 100 points among the following brands according to your preference for each brand:*
> ___ *BMW*
> ___ *Cadillac*
> ___ *Lexus*
> ___ *100 points.*

In this case, the constant-sum scale is a rating technique. However, with minor modifications, it can be classified as a sorting technique. Although the constant-sum scale is widely used, strictly speaking the scale is flawed because the last response is completely determined by the way the respondent has scored the other choices. While with only three brands this is not a serious issue as the respondent can make adjustments, we can see that if a large number of brands were included, the constant-sum scale becomes a rather challenging mental task.

Graphic rating scales

A **graphic rating scale** presents respondents with a graphic continuum. The respondents are allowed to choose any point on the continuum to indicate their attitude. Figure 16.6 shows a traditional graphic scale, ranging from one extreme position to the opposite position. Typically, a respondent's score is determined by measuring the length (in millimetres) from one end of the graphic continuum to the point marked by the respondent. Web surveys can also use a graphic rating scale by asking the respondent to click on the line or drag and drop a line across the screen.

Many researchers believe that scoring in this manner strengthens the assumption that graphic rating scales of this type are interval scales. Alternatively, the researcher may divide the line into predetermined scoring categories (lengths) and record respondents' marks accordingly. In other words, the graphic rating scale has the advantage of allowing the researcher to choose any interval desired for scoring purposes. The disadvantage of the graphic rating scale is that there are no standard answers.

> **graphic rating scale** A measure of attitudes that allows respondents to rate an object by choosing any point along a graphic continuum.

Please evaluate each attribute in terms of how important it is to you by placing an X at the position on the horizontal line that most reflects your feelings.		
Seating comfort	Not important _____ Very important	
In-flight meals	Not important _____ Very important	
Airfare	Not important _____ Very important	

Figure 16.6 Graphic rating scale

Graphic rating scales are not limited to straight lines as sources of visual communication. Picture response options or another type of graphic continuum may be used to enhance communication with respondents. A variation of the graphic ratings scale is the ladder scale shown in Figure 16.7. This scale also includes numerical options:

> *The diagram below represents the 'ladder of life'. As you see, it is a ladder with 11 rungs numbered 0 to 10. Let us suppose the top of the ladder represents the best possible life for you as you describe it, and the bottom rung represents the worst possible life for you as you describe it.*
>
> *On which rung of the ladder do you feel your life is today?*
> *0 1 2 3 4 5 6 7 8 9 10*

Figure 16.7 A ladder scale

Research to investigate children's attitudes has used happy face scales (see Figure 16.8). The children are asked to indicate which face shows how they feel about sweets, a toy, or some other concept. Research with the happy face scale indicates that children tend to choose the faces at the ends of the scale. Although this may be because children's attitudes fluctuate more widely than adults' or because they have stronger feelings both positively and negatively, the tendency to select the extremes is a disadvantage of the scale.

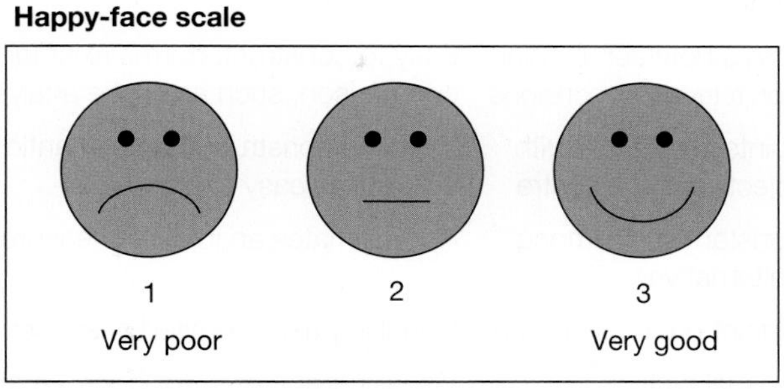

Happy-face scale

1	2	3
Very poor		Very good

Figure 16.8 Graphic rating scale with picture response categories stressing visual communication

Thurstone interval scale

In 1927 attitude research pioneer Louis Thurstone developed the concept that attitudes vary along continua and should be measured accordingly. The construction of a **Thurstone scale** is a fairly complex process that requires two stages. The first stage is a ranking operation, performed by judges who assign scale values to attitudinal statements. The second stage consists of asking subjects to respond to the attitudinal statements.

> **Thurstone scale** An attitude scale in which judges assign scale values to attitudinal statements and subjects are asked to respond to these statements.

THE VALUE OF GOOD RESEARCH

How much is a healthy home worth?

Homebuilders need to know what consumers like, but before they invest in a lot of expensive features, they should know what consumers will pay for. If consumers' budgets require some hard choices, the homebuilder needs to know which features are extremely valued, which are nice but not important and which are difficult to trade off because they are so close in buyer's minds. When a group of researchers at the University of British Columbia wanted to measure attitudes towards features of 'healthy houses', they compared the scores with a Thurstone scale.

A healthy house refers to one built with materials and a design affording superior indoor air quality, lighting and acoustics. The researchers mailed a survey asking respondents whether they would be willing to pay extra if the builder could guarantee better indoor air quality, lighting systems and acoustics. The survey also presented nine attributes associated with superior indoor air quality and energy efficiency. These were presented in every combination of pairs and the respondents were directed to choose which item in each pair they considered more important. Responses to the paired-comparison questions generated a ranking, which the researchers used to create a Thurstone scale. The highest ranked attribute (energy efficiency) appears at the top of the scale, with the next attribute (natural light) significantly below it. Thicker insulation, anti-allergic materials and airtightness are grouped close together below natural light, and artificial light falls noticeably below the other features. Based on Spetic, Kozak and Cohen (2005) and Bower (1999).

The Thurstone method is time-consuming and costly. From a historical perspective, it is valuable, but its current popularity is low. This method is rarely used in applied research settings. Figure 16.9 summarizes the attitude-rating techniques discussed in this section.

Rating measure	Subject must	Advantages	Disadvantages
Category scale	Indicate a response category	Flexible, easy to respond to	Items may be ambiguous; with few categories, only gross distinctions can be made
Likert scale	Evaluate statements on a scale of agreement	Easiest scale to construct	Hard to judge what a single score means
Semantic differential and numerical scales	Choose points between bipolar adjectives on relevant dimensions	Easy to construct; norms exist for comparison, such as profile analysis	Bipolar adjectives must be found; data may be ordinal, not interval
Stapel scale	Choose points on a scale with a single adjective in the centre	Easier to construct than semantic differential, easy to administer	Endpoints are numerical, not verbal, labels
Constant-sum scale	Divide a constant sum among response alternatives	Approximates an interval measure	Difficult for respondents with low education levels
Graphic scale	Choose a point on a continuum	Visual impact, unlimited scale points	No standard answers
Graphic scale with picture response categories	Choose a visual picture	Visual impact, easy for poor readers	Hard to attach a verbal explanation to a response

Figure 16.9 Summary of advantages and disadvantages of rating scales

REAL WORLD RESEARCH

Focus on attitude research

The research methodology in focus in this chapter is attitude research. Attitude research, as the name suggests, is used in researching the attitudes of respondents to the phenomenon that is the focus of the research, for example the attitudes of respondents to an organization(s), to a product(s), to a service(s). The importance of attitudes and the value of studying attitudes lies primarily in the assumption that attitudes facilitate intention forming and thus behaviour. Ajzen and Fishbein (1980), in their classic study in social psychology, modelled individual behaviour using four variables: beliefs, attitudes, intentions and behaviour. The way in which a person behaves, according to this model, is an outcome of their beliefs, attitudes and intentions. As this is the case, the study of beliefs, attitudes and intentions is a means of predicting likely behaviours. According to Eagly and Chaiken (1993), because attitudes are believed to actually cause perceptions and behaviours, they have become a fundamental construct for social scientists. Clearly, the ability to predict likely behaviour is very useful in business and management. Attitude research has a wide application in market research and in research in human resources.

Daniel's research project

Daniel is studying for a degree in business management. In his research for his thesis, he has focused on the Scotland Rural Development Programme (SRDP) and the work within that programme of development officers helping farmers and others in rural Scotland to diversify into alternative enterprises. The alternative enterprises these officers are mostly concerned with are food production, tourism, forestry and fishing enterprises. Daniel's methodology is attitude research. His population is the entire population of development officers working on the SRDP. There are in total 100 officers. The aim of Daniel's research is to examine attitudes to alternative enterprises among these officers. His data-gathering method is a one-to-one F2F interview using a structured questionnaire. He is developing a Likert scale that he intends to use as part of his study. The scale, as it has been developed to date, is detailed here:

Scotland's agricultural development managers and alternative enterprises

My clients are interested in alternative enterprises
agree __;__;__;__;__; disagree

I regularly advise people on alternative enterprises
agree __;__;__;__;__; disagree

Many of my clients would like to be involved in alternative enterprises
agree __;__;__;__;__; disagree

Many of my clients are involved in alternative enterprises
agree __;__;__;__;__; disagree

I am fully confident that alternative enterprises are a viable means to security for rural dwellers
agree __;__;__;__;__; disagree

My organization is fully confident that alternative enterprises are a viable means to security for rural dwellers
agree __;__;__;__;__; disagree

The alternative enterprises my clients engage with are fully and thoroughly researched
agree __;__;__;__;__; disagree

(Continued)

My organization is committing the necessary resources for research
agree __;__;__;__;__; disagree

I have access to the most up-to-date data on alternative enterprises
agree __;__;__;__;__; disagree

Alternative enterprises strengthen the economic base of rural communities
agree __;__;__;__;__; disagree

Daniel is proposing to use this scale as part of a questionnaire. The questionnaire is made up of mostly yes/no type questions, i.e. questions to which the respondent will answer either 'yes' or 'no'. The questionnaire also contains a semantic differential scale. In addition, Daniel is going to use projective techniques. He is going to use a sentence completion exercise and he is also proposing to use a vignette. The vignette he is proposing to use is a photograph that depicts a farm bed and breakfast enterprise. Daniel proposes asking his respondents to explain to him during the F2F interview what is happening in the photograph. While Daniel is proposing just one encounter with each respondent in his research, he is triangulating his research using 'between-method triangulation'. The between-method triangulation is accomplished with the use of a questionnaire, scales and projective techniques. In analyzing his data, Daniel will be able to compare the findings from the questionnaire with the findings from the scales and the findings from the projective techniques. As defined in Chapter 2, triangulation in social science research calls for more than one approach to answering the research question or responding to the research issue. What do you think of Daniel's research project? Does it give you any ideas for your own research project?

In relation to attitude research in particular, and survey research generally, you will find the following resources helpful:

QuestionPro: Online Research Made Easy. This website provides online surveys and attitude research. On the 'survey questions' page are examples of different kinds of questions and scales (www.questionpro.com/survey-questions.html).

Survey Resources Network (SRN): SRN is a service funded by the UK's Economic and Social Research Council (ESRC). The website provides extensive online resources for survey research (surveyresearch.weebly.com/survey-resources-network.html).

Surveyspro. This website provides examples of different kinds of questionnaires in its survey templates (www.esurveyspro.com).

What is an Employee Attitude Survey? This website provides information on human resources surveys and attitude research (www.hr-survey.com/EmployeeAttitude.htm).

MEASURING BEHAVIOURAL INTENTION

The behavioural component of an attitude involves the behavioural expectations of an individual towards an attitudinal object. The component of interest to researchers might be turnover intentions, a tendency to make business decisions in a certain way or plans to expand operations or product offerings. For example, category scales for measuring the behavioural component of an attitude ask about a respondent's likelihood of purchase or intention to perform some future action, using questions such as the following:

How likely is it that you will purchase an iPad Air 2?

- *I definitely will not buy.*
- *I probably will not buy.*
- *I might buy.*
- *I probably will buy.*
- *I definitely will buy.*

How likely are you to write a letter to your representative in government in support of this company if it were in a dispute with government?

- *Absolutely unlikely*
- *Very unlikely*
- *Somewhat unlikely*
- *About a 50–50 chance*
- *Somewhat likely*
- *Very likely*
- *Extremely likely*

The wording of statements used in these scales often includes phrases such as 'I would recommend', 'I would write' or 'I intend to buy' to indicate action tendencies.

Expectations also may be measured using a scale of subjective probabilities, ranging from 0 for 'absolutely no chance' to 100 for 'absolutely certain'. Researchers have used the following subjective probability scale to estimate the chance that a job candidate will accept a position within a company:

0%	(Certainly not) I will accept
10%	(Almost certainly not) I will accept
20%	(Very small chance) I will accept
30%	(Smaller chance) I will accept
40%	(Small chance) I will accept
50%	(About even) I will accept
60%	(Not so big a chance) I will accept
70%	(Big chance) I will accept
80%	(Very big chance) I will accept
90%	(Almost sure) I will accept
100%	(Absolutely certain) I will accept

Behavioural differential

A general instrument, the **behavioural differential,** is used to measure the behavioural intentions of subjects towards an object or category of objects. As in the semantic differential, a description of the object to be judged is followed by a series of scales on which subjects indicate their behavioural intentions toward this object. For example, one item might be something like this:

A 25-year-old female sales representative
Would not __ __ __ __ __ __ __ Would
ask this person for advice.

> **behavioural differential** A rating scale instrument similar to a semantic differential, developed to measure the behavioural intentions of subjects towards future actions.

Ranking

Consumers often rank order their preferences. An ordinal scale may be developed by asking respondents to rank order (from most preferred to least preferred) a set of objects or attributes. Respondents easily understand the task of rank ordering the importance of product attributes or arranging a set of brand names according to preference. Like the constant-sum scale, technically the ranking scale also suffers from inflexibility in that if we know how someone ranked five out of six alternatives, we know the answer to the sixth. In other words, the rankings are not all independent, but rather dependent on the other objects to be ranked.

Paired comparisons

Paired comparisons is a technique that allows all possible combinations of options to be compared and contrasted. The respondent is asked their preference between each pair of options. The following question illustrates the typical format for asking about paired comparisons:

> *I would like to know your overall opinion of two brands of adhesive bandages. They are Curad and Band-Aid.*
> *Overall, which of these two brands – Curad or Band-Aid – do you think is the better one? Or are they the same?*
>
> *Curad is better*
> *Band-Aid is better*
> *They are the same*

paired comparisons A measurement technique that involves presenting the respondent with two objects and asking the respondent to pick the preferred object; more than two objects may be presented, but comparisons are made in pairs.

Consider a situation in which a chainsaw manufacturer learned that a competitor had introduced a new lightweight (2.5 kilo) chainsaw. The manufacturer's lightest chainsaw weighed 4 kilos. Executives wondered if they needed to introduce a 2.5 kilo chainsaw into the product line. The research design chosen was a paired comparison. A 2.5 kilo chainsaw was designed, and a prototype built. To control for colour preferences, the competitor's chainsaw was painted the same colour as the 4 and 6 kilo chainsaws. Thus, there are four chainsaws of the same colour, two 2.5 kilo models and two 4 kilo models. Respondents were presented with two chainsaws at a time and asked to pick the one they preferred. Three pairs of comparisons were required to determine the most preferred chainsaw.

If researchers wish to compare four retirement investment plans on the basis of employee attractiveness, six comparisons $[(n)(n-1)/2]$ will be necessary. In each case, the employee would be asked their preference between two of the retirement plans. In the end, each plan would have been compared to each of the other plans.

When comparing only a few items, ranking objects with respect to one attribute is not difficult. As the number of items increases, the number of comparisons increases geometrically. If the number of comparisons is too large, respondents may become fatigued and no longer carefully discriminate among them.

Sorting

Sorting tasks ask respondents to indicate their attitudes or beliefs by arranging items on the basis of perceived similarity or some other attribute. One advertising agency has had consumers sort photographs of people to measure their perceptions of a brand's typical user. Another agency used a sorting technique in which consumers used a deck of 52 cards illustrating elements from advertising for the brand name being studied. The study participants created a stack of cards showing elements they recalled seeing or hearing, then the interviewer asked the respondent to identify the item on each of those cards. National City Corporation, a banking company, has used sorting as part of its research into the design of its website. Consumers participating in the research were given a set of cards describing various parts of processes that they might engage in when they are banking online. The participants were asked to arrange the cards to show their idea of a logical way to complete these processes. This research method shows the website designers how consumers go about doing something – sometimes very differently from the way bankers expect.

Sorting techniques can be applied in a wide variety of environments. A variant of the constant-sum technique uses physical counters (such as coins or poker chips) to be allocated among the alternatives. In an airline study of customer preferences, the following sorting technique could be used:

 Below is a list of several airlines. Next to the name of each airline is a pocket. Here are ten cards. I would like you to put these cards in the pockets next to the airlines you would prefer to fly with on your next trip. Assume that all of the airlines fly to wherever you would choose to travel. You can put as many cards as you want next to an airline or you can put no cards next to an airline.

	Cards
Emirates	___
British Airways	___
Air France	___
Qantas	___
Singapore Airlines	___
easyJet	___

Other methods of attitude measurement

Attitudes, as hypothetical constructs, cannot be observed directly. We can, however, infer a person's attitude by the way they respond to multiple attitude indicators. A summated rating scale can be made up of three indicators of attitude.

Consider the following three semantic differential items that may capture a person's attitude towards their immediate supervisor:

Not supportive _ _ _ _ _ _ _	Very supportive
Very favourable _ _ _ _ _ _ _	Very unfavourable
Very negative _ _ _ _ _ _ _	Very positive

Notice that the middle question would need to be reverse coded before a composite scale is calculated. The terminology is such that the scores from these measures would reflect the latent (unobservable) construct of attitude towards a supervisor.

Selecting a measurement scale: some practical decisions

Now that we have looked at a number of attitude measurement scales, the question arises: 'Which is most appropriate?' As in the selection of a basic research design, there is no single best answer for all research projects. The answer to this question is relative and the choice of scale will depend on the nature of the attitudinal object to be measured, the problem definition, and the other choices made with regards to the steps in the research process (see Figure 1.1 in Chapter 1), and particularly choices made in relation to methodology. However, several questions will help focus the choice of a measurement scale:

1. Is a ranking, sorting, rating or choice technique best?
2. Should a monadic or a comparative scale be used?
3. What type of category labels, if any, will be used for the rating scale?
4. How many scale categories or response positions are needed to accurately measure an attitude?
5. Should a balanced or unbalanced rating scale be chosen?
6. Should an even or odd number of response categories be provided?
7. Should a scale that forces a choice among predetermined options be used?
8. Should a single measure or an index measure be used?

The scales and scaling techniques considered in each of these questions are discussed briefly below.

Ranking, sorting, rating or choice technique?

The decision whether to use ranking, sorting, rating or a choice technique is determined largely by the problem definition and especially by the type of statistical analysis desired. For example, ranking provides only ordinal data, limiting the statistical techniques that may be used. In general, more information is gained from a rating approach than from ranking, sorting or choice. However, if the researcher feels that little variance would be generated from a rating approach, then an alternative may be preferred. For example, if a researcher was trying to determine how important salary, opportunities for advancement and an enjoyable work environment were on the selection of a career opportunity, a rating scale might not generate much variance as all three factors are likely to be considered 'very important'. If a ranking or sorting approach is used, at least the relative importance of each factor could be determined.

Monadic or comparative scale?

If the scale to be used is not a ratio scale, the researcher must decide whether to include a standard of comparison in the verbal portion of the scale. Consider the following rating scale:

Please indicate how satisfied you are with the amount of authority you are given in your present position.

Completely dissatisfied	Dissatisfied	Somewhat satisfied	Satisfied	Completely satisfied
☐	☐	☐	☐	☐

This is a **monadic rating scale**, because it asks about a single concept (level of authority) in isolation. The respondent is not given a specific frame of reference. A person who is dissatisfied with their level of authority could feel so because they have either too little or too much responsibility. A **comparative rating scale** asks a respondent to rate a concept, such as a specific amount of responsibility or authority, in comparison with a benchmark – perhaps another similar concept – explicitly used as a frame of reference. In many cases, the comparative rating scale presents an ideal situation as a reference point for comparison with the actual situation. For example:

Please indicate how the amount of authority in your present position compares with the amount of authority that would be ideal for this position.
Too little ☐   About right ☐   Too much ☐

> **monadic rating scale** Any measure of attitudes that asks respondents about a single concept in isolation.
>
> **comparative rating scale** Any measure of attitudes that asks respondents to rate a concept in comparison with a benchmark explicitly used as a frame of reference.

What type of category labels, if any?

We have discussed verbal labels, numerical labels and unlisted choices. Many rating scales have verbal labels for response categories because researchers believe they help respondents better understand the response positions. The maturity and educational levels of the respondents will influence this decision. The semantic differential, with unlabelled response categories between two bipolar adjectives and the numerical scale, with numbers to indicate scale positions, often are selected because the researcher wishes to assume interval scale data. It is more challenging to identify a series of verbal labels (i.e. extremely disappointed, very disappointed, disappointed, and so on) that have a consistent gap than to use numbers (i.e. 1, 2, 3, and so on) that we assume have an equal gap.

How many scale categories or response positions?

Should a category scale have four, five or seven response positions or categories? Or should the researcher use a graphic scale with an infinite number of positions? The original developmental research on the semantic differential indicated that five to eight points is optimal. However, the researcher must determine the number of meaningful positions that is best for the specific project. This issue of identifying how many meaningful distinctions respondents can practically make is basically a matter of sensitivity, but at the operational rather than the conceptual level. In general, more scale points (7–10) seem to perform better than fewer (3–4). Often a ten-point scale is very effective as it is easy for respondents to think in those terms.

Balanced or unbalanced rating scale?

The fixed-alternative format may be balanced or unbalanced. For example, the following question, which asks about parent–child decisions relating to television programme watching, is a **balanced rating scale**:

Who decides which television programmes your children watch?	
Child decides all of the time	☐
Child decides most of the time	☐
Child and parent decide together	☐
Parent decides most of the time	☐
Parent decides all of the time	☐

> **balanced rating scale** A fixed-alternative rating scale with an equal number of positive and negative categories; a neutral point or point of indifference is at the centre of the scale.

This scale is balanced because a neutral point, or point of indifference, is at the centre of the scale.

Unbalanced rating scales may be used when responses are expected to be distributed at one end of the scale. Unbalanced scales, such as the one shown here, may eliminate this type of 'end piling':

Completely dissatisfied	Dissatisfied	Somewhat satisfied	Satisfied	Completely satisfied
☐	☐	☐	☐	☐

unbalanced rating scale A fixed-alternative rating scale that has more response categories at one end than the other, resulting in an unequal number of positive and negative categories.

Notice that there are three 'satisfied' responses and only two 'dissatisfied' responses here. The choice of a balanced or unbalanced scale generally depends on the nature of the concept or the researcher's knowledge about attitudes toward the stimulus to be measured.

Even or odd number of scale points?

The researcher needs to decide if an even or odd number of response categories should be provided. The issue here is should there be a 'neutral' point in the scale? With an odd number of scale points there is often a middle ground that is non-committal. An even number of scale points forces the respondent to commit to a 'pro' or 'contra' response on the issue. If the researcher feels that respondents can truly hold a neutral attitude regarding the subject of investigation, an odd number of scale points is appropriate. However, issues that tend to evoke strong opinions, for example political candidates or social issues such as legalization of marijuana, are probably better captured by an even number of scale points where a respondent is forced to come down on one side of the issue.

Use a scale that forces a choice among predetermined options?

In many situations, a respondent has not formed an attitude towards the concept being studied and simply cannot provide an answer. If a **forced-choice rating scale** compels the respondent to answer, the response is merely a function of the question. If answers are not forced, the midpoint of the scale may be used by the respondent to indicate unawareness as well as indifference. If many respondents in the sample are expected to be unaware of the attitudinal object under investigation, this problem may be eliminated by using a non-forced-choice scale that provides a 'no opinion' category, as in the following example:

How does the Bank of Commerce compare with the First National Bank?

☐ *Bank of Commerce is better than First National Bank*
☐ *Bank of Commerce is about the same as First National Bank*
☐ *Bank of Commerce is worse than First National Bank*
☐ *Can't say*

forced-choice rating scale A fixed-alternative rating scale that requires respondents to choose one of the fixed alternatives.

Asking this type of question allows the investigator to separate respondents who cannot make an honest comparison from respondents who have had experience with both banks. The argument for forced choice is that people really do have attitudes, even if they are unfamiliar with the banks and should be required to answer the question. However, the use of forced-choice questions is associated with higher incidences of item non-response (no answer). Internet surveys make forced-choice questions easy to implement because the delivery can be set up so that a respondent cannot go to the next question until the previous question is answered. It is important to realize, however, that if a respondent truly has no opinion and the no opinion option is not included, s/he may simply quit responding to the questionnaire.

Single measure or an index measure?

Whether to use a single measure or an index measure depends on the complexity of the issue to be investigated, the number of dimensions the issue contains and whether individual attributes of the stimulus are part of a holistic attitude or are seen as separate items. Very simple concepts that do not vary from context to context can be measured by single items. However, most psychological concepts are more complex and require multiple-item measurement. Additionally, multiple-item measures are easier to test for reliability and construct validity. The researcher's conceptual definition will be helpful in making this choice.

The researcher has many scaling options. Generally, the choice is influenced by plans for the later stages of the research project. As with virtually all decisions in the research process, problem definition becomes a determining factor influencing the research design.

CASE STUDY

Heat and smoke – what keeps them happy?

The history of steel factories and the challenges of the furnace workers who work in those factories is well documented. While many people are familiar with the stories of the great steel industrialists such as Carnegie and Frick of the nineteenth century, few people realize that the job of the furnace worker continues to this day. It is hard and difficult work – despite the great advances in technology and an ever increasing focus on safety, furnace workers still face dangerous work environments filled with heat and smoke. The molten metal must be carefully managed within the furnace, with temperatures in the vessel exceeding thousands of degrees. The possibility of critical injury or death is ever present, either through the long-term exposure to metallic fumes or from the immediate effects of a furnace explosion.

A company that specializes in making high-grade metals knew how important these furnace workers were to its success and was keenly interested in what kept them satisfied with their company. Several of its furnace employees had been with the company for over 20 years and the skills and expertise of these experienced employees were invaluable to the training of new furnace workers and the manufacturing process itself.

A team of business researchers was asked to do an assessment of furnace employee attitudes, with the goal of identifying what aspects of their work environment contributed to their overall satisfaction. Using a survey questionnaire, a series of statements related to the company's benefits, supervisory relationships and general work-related conditions was developed. These researchers asked the furnace workers to indicate their level of agreement, on a scale that ranged from strongly disagree to strongly agree, to these statements. Examples of these statements included:

1. Our company has a health plan that addresses the needs of my family.
2. My experiences with the health plan coordinator have been good.
3. My supervisor sees me as an asset to the company.
4. My supervisor encourages me to contribute ideas that can make our work space better.
5. My company puts safety as a top priority.

For each of the statements, the researchers compiled responses from the furnace workers to see if these areas were positively related to the overall work satisfaction of the furnace employees. Results showed some interesting outcomes. While the furnace workers viewed company health benefits and the company's safety programme as important to overall work satisfaction, the opportunity to have a supervisor whom they perceived as valuing their input and who saw them as important assets to the company was a very important factor related to their satisfaction.

In a nutshell, the very dangerous work environment of the furnace floor did require a focus on safety and health benefits in their minds. But not unlike workers in safer environments, it was the positive and supportive relationship with their immediate supervisor that really made the difference.

Measurement of attitudes is a common objective in business research.

END OF CHAPTER QUESTIONS

1 Describe how business researchers think of attitudes.

2 Identify basic approaches to measuring attitudes.

3 Discuss the use of rating scales for measuring attitudes.

4 Represent a latent construct by constructing a summated scale.

5 Summarize ways to measure attitudes with ranking and sorting techniques.

6 Discuss major issues involved in the selection of a measurement scale.

7 What is the difference between a measured variable and a latent construct?

8 If a Likert summated scale has ten scale items, do all ten items have to be phrased as either positive or negative statements or can the scale contain a mix of positive and negative statements?

9 Should a Likert scale ever be treated as though it had ordinal properties?

10 If a semantic differential has ten scale items, should all the positive adjectives be on the right and all the negative adjectives on the left?

11 What is an attitude? Is there a consensus concerning its definition?

12 A researcher thinks many respondents will answer 'don't know' or 'can't say' if these options are printed on an attitude scale along with categories indicating level of agreement. The researcher does not print either 'don't know' or 'can't say' on the questionnaire because the resulting data would be more complicated to analyze and report. Is this proper?

13 Distinguish between rating and ranking. Which is a better attitude measurement technique? Why?

14 What advantages do numerical scales have over semantic differential scales?

15 How would you perform reverse coding using statistical software like SAS or SPSS?

16 Identify the issues a researcher should consider when choosing a measurement scale.

17 A researcher wishes to compare two hotels on the following attributes: convenience of location, friendly personnel, value for money:

a Design a Likert scale to accomplish this task.
b Design a semantic differential scale to accomplish this task.
c Design a graphic rating scale to accomplish this task.

REFERENCES

Ajzen, I. and Fishbein, M. (1980) *Understanding Attitudes and Predicting Social Behaviour*, Englewood Cliffs, NJ: Prentice Hall.

Anhalt, Karen, Nickel (1998) 'Whiskas campaign recruits a tiny tiger', *Advertising Age International*, (October 19): 41.

Bower, J. (1999) *Healthy House Building for the New Millennium*, Bloomington, IN: Healthy House Institute.

Bush, M. (2008) 'Students Rank Social Responsibility', *Advertising Age*, 79(Aug 4): 11.

Eagly, A.H. and Chaiken, S. (1993) *The Psychology of Attitudes*, Forth Worth, TX: Harcourt Brace and Company.

Myers, J. and Shurts, M. (2002) 'Measuring positive emotionality: A review of instruments assessing love', *Measurement and Evaluation in Counseling and Development, 34*: 28–254.

QuestionPro, www.questionpro.com (Accessed 17.03.2018).

Spetic, W., Kozak, R. and Cohen, D. (2005) 'Willingness to pay and preferences for healthy home attributes in Canada', *Forest Products Journal, 55*(Oct): 19–24.

Survey Resources Network, surveyresearch.weebly.com/survey-resources-network.html (Accessed 17.03.2018).

Surveyspro, www.esurveyspro.com (Accessed 17.03.2018).

Tullis, T.S. and Stetson, J. 'A Comparison of Questionnaires for Assessing Website Usability', citeseerx.ist.psu.edu/viewdoc/download?doi=10.1.1.396.3677&rep=rep1&type=pdf (Accessed 17.03.2018).

What is an Employee Attitude Survey? (www.hrsurvey.com/EmployeeAttitude.htm). (Accessed 17.03.2018).

RECOMMENDED READING

Oppenheim, A.N. (2000) *Questionnaire Design, Interviewing and Attitude Measurement* (2nd edn), London: Pinter.

PART FOUR
DEALING WITH DATA

CHAPTER 17

MANAGING DATA AND INTRODUCING DATA ANALYSIS

LEARNING OBJECTIVES

At the end of this chapter, the student should be able to:

- Develop an analytical framework for a research project.

- Outline, describe and explain the four stages of data analysis.

- Begin to analyze data, ask critical questions of data and engage in descriptive data analysis.

- Explain the importance of grounding both data analysis and research findings in the data gathered for the research project.

RESEARCH SKILLS

At the end of this chapter, the student should, using the exercises on Cengage Brain, be able to:

- Propose an analytical framework for a given research project.

- Explain and defend the proposed analytical framework.

The aim of this chapter is to introduce the student to data sets and to the management and analysis of data. The chapter introduces the student to the different ways of analyzing quantitative and qualitative data, to the ways in which to begin the process of data analysis and the different ways of organizing data analysis.

INTRODUCTION

In carrying out a research project, the researcher is attempting to explore or establish some phenomenon by gathering data (evidence) on that phenomenon. There are, as we know, essentially two different kinds of data: quantitative and qualitative data. Quantitative data are numerical data, data in the form of numbers or data that can readily be transformed into numerical form. Qualitative data are non-numerical data. A data set (dataset) is a complete collection of data gathered for a research project.

As there are essentially two different orders of data, quantitative data and qualitative data, there are, in effect, two different approaches to data analysis.

Quantitative data analysis is the analysis of numerical data using statistical methods. The computer software package **SPSS,** Statistical Package for the Social Sciences, is useful in the analysis of quantitative data.

SPSS Statistical Package for the Social Sciences. A computer software package designed for the analysis of quantitative data.

Qualitative data analysis does not draw on statistics or statistical methods; this is because qualitative data are non-numerical data. Qualitative data can be analyzed in a number of different ways:

- in terms of content, textually, discursively, thematically and/or semiotically
- systematically and categorically as in a grounded theory approach to data analysis (Strauss and Corbin, 1990, 1998)
- in terms of significant statements and meaning units, as in, for example, Moustakas' (1994) approach to analyzing phenomenological data.

Computer-assisted qualitative data analysis software (**computer-assisted qualitative data analysis software (CAQDAS)**) is a relatively recent development. Among the software packages available for qualitative data analysis are Atlas.ti and NVivo.

computer-assisted qualitative data analysis software (CAQDAS) Computer software designed to support qualitative data analysis.

In this chapter, as well as beginning to explore data analysis, we will learn a little about how to manage data: **data management**. Gathering the right data for the research project in a professional and scholarly manner takes considerable time and effort. It is important that the data gathered be properly managed when they have been gathered. Some of the aspects of proper data management are fairly evident. For example, it is important not to lose data or to allow them to be stolen, which could happen if the data were stored on a laptop computer and the computer was stolen.

data management The correct, safe and secure management of data while data are being gathered, stored and analyzed.

When researchers apply to a research ethics committee for ethical approval for a research project, one of the guarantees they are obliged to make is for the safe and secure management of data. In such applications, it is not enough for researchers to provide guarantees; they must also clearly and in detail explain how they will safely and securely manage the data gathered.

If you look back at Figure 1.1 in Chapter 1, the figure modelling the research process, you will see that data analysis happens towards the end of the research process. Once the data have been analyzed, all that remains in the research process is to draw conclusions from the research, make recommendations where appropriate, and finally write up and present the thesis or the written account of the research.

The Value of Good Research box that follows references the research institute, the Institute for New Economic Thinking (www.ineteconomics.org/), and refers to an article in *The Times* by Anatole Kaletsky (Kaletsky, 2009), which claimed that 'old' economics had died a death and its demise was to be celebrated; as a consequence of its passing, a new economics had to take its place. Hope for such a new economics, according to the article, was supported by the establishment of the Institute for New Economic Thinking (INET). The article Kaletsky published in *The Times* considered the way in which orthodox economic theory failed the world, by not predicting the global economic downturn. The article, as you will see, was quite critical of experimental approaches to social research. Experimental design is the research methodology in focus in Chapter 19 of this textbook.

One of the major roles of research is the generation of theory. The theory generated in research emerges from the data gathered for the research project, which comes from the questions asked in the data-gathering process. These questions are generated by the researcher from their reading of the literature in the field and from their very well-conceptualized research statement or question, the conceptual framework, that supports the entire research project. So, the data gathered emerge from theory and, in turn, the data gathered make a contribution to theory. And this, in a sense, is the full circle of the research project and the research process (see Figure 1.1). As explained throughout this textbook, the four frameworks approach is a useful guide for the researcher to the research process.

THE VALUE OF GOOD RESEARCH

Three cheers for the death of old economics

It seems that we are moving towards a new way of thinking about economics. In an interesting article in *The Times* (Kaletsky, A., 2009, 'Three cheers for the death of old economics', *The Times*, 28 October), Anatole Kaletsky stated that one of the few benign consequences of the recent financial crisis was the exposure of modern economics as an emperor with no clothes on. He wrote that many people, among them Nobel laureate economists, believe that economics has to be urgently re-invented. He believes that there is a possibility of new thinking in economics with the help of the Institute for New Economic Thinking (INET). INET (ineteconomics.org/) was founded in 2009 with a $50-million pledge from billionaire US investor, George Soros. The non-profit organization is based in New York City and it is dedicated to developing new ideas and insights into economics and economic theory.

The need for new theory in economics is driven, according to the detail on INET's website, by a recognition of the failings of the current economic system and our ways of thinking about the recent global economic crisis. The mission of INET is 'to create an environment nourished by open discourse and critical thinking where the next generation of scholars has the support to go beyond our prevailing economic paradigms and advance the culture of change'.

A report by Alan Purkiss in *Bloomberg News* (2010) detailed that Soros is also helping to establish an economics institute at Oxford University. This initiative, according to Purkiss, is part of a campaign by Soros to push economic theory away from thinking that markets should be left to themselves. Such thinking, Soros believes, led to the recent global financial crisis. Purkiss quotes Robert Johnson, a former managing director at Soros Fund Management LLC who took charge of INET, as saying that in the future a broader approach to economics is needed, an approach that will take into account the works of historians, sociologists, psychologists and political theorists, among other disciplines, when producing economic theory.

The hope for INET, according to Kaletsky, is that it might encourage original thinking in a profession where creativity has been stymied by intellectual and academic dogmas. In particular, he is critical of economic models and he writes of the failure of economic models. He says that when policymakers turned to academic economists for guidance in the recent global financial crisis, they were essentially told that the economic models the academics were working with could not cope with the reality of the global crisis.

The three key problems with economic theory as highlighted by Kaletsky were (1) the idea known as 'rational expectations', which held that capitalist economies with competitive labour markets do not need stabilizing by governments. (2) The idea of 'efficient markets', which holds, as Kaletsky explains, that competitive finance always allocates resources in the most efficient way, reflecting all the best available information and forecasts about the future. (3) The idea that economics, which had for a long time been a largely descriptive study of human behaviour, had become a branch of mathematics. The application of mathematics and mathematical formulae to economics ensured, Kaletsky explains, that only the simplest and clearest conceptualizations of human behaviour could be used in mathematical models, as these are the only ones that fit in the mathematical models. Anything that did not fit was ignored.

The worst political effects of the dogma of rational and efficient markets and the mathematical reductionism of economic modelling, as explained by Kaletsky, was that theoretical economics seemed to legitimize the most unjust effects and impacts of the markets. Huge levels of income inequality, for example, were readily explained and justified. They also became depoliticized. They were simply one result of the efficient workings of rational markets.

At the inaugural conference of INET, held in King's College, Cambridge in April 2010. George Soros in his address concluded that it is not enough to study history, we must also learn the lessons of it. He said that we need to abandon rational expectations and the efficient market hypothesis and build our theory of financial markets on the recognition that imperfect understanding, i.e. fallibility, is the human condition.

In the news article in *The Times*, Kaletsky concluded that if the next generation of academic economists aspire to succeed Smith, Keynes and Hayek, rather than as he says ineffectually aping Euclid, Newton and Einstein, then the venture that is INET will be worthwhile.

The INET was developed to provide new research and new theory in economics. Described in *The Economist* (2013) as 'George Soro's attempt to shake up the dismal science' (economics), the hope for the Institute is that, in light of the recent global economic crisis, better and more accurate or more useful research and theories in economics can and will be developed. In 2017, INET unveiled a new initiative, 'The Commission on Global Economic Transformation', led by Nobel laureates Joseph Stiglitz and Michael Spence (Goodman, 2017).

Within the four frameworks approach to the research project, the researcher conceptualizes the research statement or question for the research project. Each of the important words and phrases in the research statement or question is a key concept in the research project. The key concepts in the conceptual framework guide the researcher, they provide direction in terms of the areas of literature that need to be explored and examined for the literature review. The key concepts provide the words and phrases needed for keyword searches of the literature. In addition, the key concepts can be used by the researcher to develop a framework of subheadings and sections in the literature review (see Chapter 6). If the researcher does use the key concepts in this way, this will ensure that the literature review is properly focused on the research statement/question and on the aim of the research project.

The methodological framework for the research project is the detailed account that the researcher writes of the way in which the research was carried out. Each research project has its own unique methodology (see Chapter 9). In developing the research methodology for the research project, the researcher draws on their knowledge, including their reading of research methodology textbooks and methodologies used in other, published, research projects. Using all of these sources and supports, the researcher creates the unique methodological framework for their own research project.

The final framework in the four frameworks approach is the **analytical framework**. The researcher presents the written formal account of the analytical framework for the research project in the chapter (or section) on data analysis. This chapter (or section) contains a full account of the analysis carried out on the data and a complete presentation of the findings that emerge from that data analysis. The work of data analysis is a major project, which is undertaken at your desk. What goes into the data analysis chapter is a synopsis of all that analysis. As the work of data analysis is so substantial, there would simply be too much material to present it all in the data analysis chapter (with its limited word count). Therefore, the researcher presents a synopsis of the data analysis in the chapter. In this synopsis, the researcher presents the key findings, the key data and the key interpretations made in relation to the data.

> **analytical framework** In the four frameworks approach to the research project, the analytical framework emerges from the conceptual framework, the theoretical framework and the methodological framework. The analytical framework is presented in the data analysis chapter in the thesis or in the data analysis section of the report of the research.

The data analysis presented must respond to the research question/statement, the aim of the research. Therefore, the key concepts in the conceptual framework, which have guided the development of the theoretical framework and the methodological framework, now guide and direct the researcher as s/he designs and then constructs the analytical framework (the synopsis of the data analysis carried out) in the data analysis chapter of the thesis or in the data analysis section in the report of the research. This is how the four frameworks approach to the research project guides the researcher throughout the research process.

DATA AND DATA MANAGEMENT

Data management is an important issue. Data are the evidence that the researcher gathers for the research project and data management is concerned with the security and protection of data and the proper management of data. There are many safety and security concerns in relation to data when they are being gathered, stored and analyzed.

The four frameworks

- Conceptual Framework
- Theoretical Framework
- Methodological Framework
- *Analytical Framework*

If your data are electronically or digitally stored, you should make copies of the files. You need to back them up so that should anything happen to the originals, you have copies. It is of course important to ensure that the data and any copies of the data are secured.

Data can be lost or stolen. This can happen, for example, if you decide to move the data from your home to the university. Your car could be stolen or the bag in which you are carrying the data could be lost or stolen. You might leave the bag behind on the bus, the train or taxi. A sudden strong gust of wind might blow away some of your questionnaires. As well as being careful not to lose data, it is important to ensure that data are not damaged in any way. If, for example, a questionnaire were torn or stained, the damage might render the questionnaire illegible. As these examples demonstrate, moving data from one location to another creates risks to the security and integrity of the data. So, in order to properly manage data, it is best not to move it. If moving the data is unavoidable, it is wise to make a plan which anticipates any potential risks or dangers posed to the data. Such a plan may simply involve some reflection on the risks involved in moving your data, followed by taking steps to avoid or circumvent those risks.

Every researcher should have a plan in place for the organization, safety and security and management of the data to be gathered for the research project. This can be quite a simple plan, detailing how the data are to be recorded, where and how the data are to be stored, what precautions will be taken if the data are to be moved, and what plan is in place for the backup of the data. You should record your reflections and develop your plan in your research diary. If you do this, you can use these notes to help you write a paragraph in your research methodology chapter to evidence the level of reflection you engaged in regarding the safety and security of your data. A record (a list) should be kept of all of the data gathered for the project. The research diary is the best place for this.

Each completed and returned questionnaire should be numbered and properly stored. Similarly, each interview or focus group should be numbered, stored electronically or digitally and transcribed (typed up). The transcripts should be numbered and properly stored. For confidentiality purposes, the identities of the participants in the study should be concealed, if concealment is necessary. It will be necessary if the participants have been given a guarantee by the researcher that their participation in the research will remain anonymous. If this is the case, each of the questionnaires and interviews should have the real identity of the participant removed from the record and replaced with a coded identity for the participant. The researcher keeps a list of all of the real names of the participants and their code names and only the researcher and the supervisor of the research should have access to this list.

Every research project has its own unique ethical issues and concerns, in relation to data management as well as in relation to every other aspect of the research process. It is important to reflect on the uniqueness of your own research project and to consider the unique ethical issues in the management of your data.

The extract from the journal article that follows considers the issue of research integrity within the context of a proposal for international standards for research integrity. As you read through the synopsis, think about the conduct and management of your own research project and, in particular, think about your management of the data you have gathered for your research project. When you have read the synopsis of the article, source the original article and read it through. It contains a lot of information on the issue of research integrity and some interesting examples of ethical issues in relation to the integrity of research.

REAL WORLD RESEARCH

How theory influences research

In the article detailed here (Resnik, 2009) 'International standards for research integrity: an idea whose time has come?', *Accountability in Research*, 16(4): 218–228), the author states that research integrity encompasses a wide range of topics relating to the ethical conduct of research, among them the topics of data management and data analysis.

International standards for the ethical conduct of research with human participants have, he writes, been in place since the adoption of the Nuremberg Code after the end of World War II. The Nuremberg Code was used in the Nuremberg trials of Nazi doctors and scientists accused of war crimes committed against prisoners in concentration camps.

In 2007 the Office of Research Integrity (ORI) and the European Science Foundation (ESF) held the first global forum on research integrity. The aim of the forum was to consider ways of harmonizing policies dealing with research misconduct and fostering ethical research. One of the reasons put forward in support of clear international integrity standards is that such standards can encourage the development of local standards. Resnik (2009), explains that countries that lack local standards for the conduct of research can use international standards as a model for the development of their own rules and policies.

Some countries have used the Helsinki Declaration, adopted in 1964 by the World Medical Association and revised many times since, as a guide to developing their own policies.

Different countries, we are told, have different definitions of research misconduct. The US federal government, for example, defines research misconduct as fabrication, falsification or plagiarism (FFP). Norway defines research misconduct as FFP as well as other serious breaches of good scientific practice. Finland differentiates between fraud, which is defined as FFP, and research misconduct, which is defined as gross negligence and irresponsibility in the conduct of research.

There is a focus in the article on the issue of conflict of interest (COI). A conflict of interest can arise in research where a researcher has a vested interest in the findings of their research, for example, if a researcher will materially benefit from a particular set of findings, perhaps through direct payment, through other funding such as grants and bursaries, and/or through career advancement. A conflict of interest issue can raise serious questions about a research project and about the gathering, the management and the analysis of data for that research project and the findings and conclusions drawn in it.

The final issue the author discusses is the issue of social responsibility, i.e. promoting good consequences for society and avoiding harmful ones. The author states that some of the most important ethical questions in scientific research have to do with social responsibility and he identifies several professional organizations with codes of ethics that encompass the social responsibilities of researchers.

Resnik believes that the development of international standards of research integrity is an idea whose time has come. In fact, he concludes that such standards are long overdue.

The issue of plagiarism is dealt with in detail in Chapter 2 of this textbook, and ethics in research, including the codes of ethics of different professional bodies, is explored in detail in Chapter 3. The proper management of data is clearly an ethical issue and the way in which data are managed is a reflection of the integrity of the researcher.

AN INTRODUCTION TO DATA ANALYSIS

In social research, data are either quantitative or qualitative. Some research projects generate quantitative data, some generate qualitative data and some generate a mixture of both.

Quantitative data are numeric; they are data in the form of numbers or data that can readily be coded numerically. For example, you might ask research participants how old they are. In response they will tell you, for example, that they are 21 years old, 22 years old or 32 years old, and so on. The data you gather in response to this question are numeric and therefore they are quantitative data.

If you asked the same research participants to tell you how they celebrated their twenty-first birthdays, you would get in response very many different accounts of twenty-first birthday celebrations. These responses are qualitative and the data you gather in response to such a question are qualitative data. It is possible, however, that there might be a quantitative element to these responses. For example, a respondent might say, 'I invited 30 friends to a party to celebrate my twenty-first birthday.' In this response, we have a number, 30. Therefore, there is a quantitative element to the response. Whether or not that quantitative element is in any way useful or meaningful in the research depends on what it is the researcher is trying to explore or establish in the research project. One number does not constitute data, it is just detail. If very many or all of the respondents said that they had twenty-first birthday parties to which they invited a specific, stated number of guests/ friends, then the researcher has a range of quantitative data with which to work. This is more useful, and such a range of numbers does constitute data, rather than just detail. Whether or not these data are useful in the research project, again depends on the focus of the research project. The qualitative responses of participants to such a question will be rich and complex and very individual. The stories they tell you, the researcher, in response to that question of how they celebrated their twenty-first birthdays, will be rich and personal and full of meaning for each one of them. The responsibility of the researcher is to gather the responses properly, to manage them properly, keeping them safe and secure, to adequately and expertly analyze them for the research project and to report them thoroughly in the findings of the research.

Sometimes researchers gather both quantitative and qualitative data for their research project; this is known as a mixed-methods research project or a mixed-methods approach to the research. As discussed earlier, there are many decisions to be made by the researcher in determining what data are required for the research project, where those data are or might be, and how best to gather that data. As explained in previous chapters, the researcher designs the data collection methods for the research project. They are designed to suit the data requirements of the project, the data sources and/ or the participants in the research project.

When you design the data-gathering methods for the research project, you develop at the same time a sense of how the data will be analyzed. In your research diary you begin to develop a plan for data analysis, whether the data to be gathered are quantitative, qualitative or mixed. Your approach to data analysis will be determined by the kind of data you have to analyze.

Sample size, as well as the kind of data gathered, has implications for the ways in which data can be analyzed. Large quantities of data are best analyzed using a computer and, as explained above, there are different software packages specifically designed for the analysis of both quantitative and qualitative data. These software packages will be considered in detail in the following paragraphs and chapters.

Analyzing quantitative data – an introduction

Simple and small quantitative data sets can be analyzed by simply counting the numbers and calculating simple statistics in relation to them. Numbers can easily be counted, and the summaries of counted numbers can be meaningful. For example, let us consider again our small study of gym/fitness centre membership, as detailed in Chapter 4. Let us imagine that in response to this research we obtained the following data (see Table 17.1).

From this simple study, we have gathered a lot of quantitative data and have calculated the **summarizing statistics** as detailed in Table 17.1. The exercise was very simple, yet we have an impressive table of quantitative data. In calculating these data, we could simply use a pen and paper exercise. If we had more data, we might need to use a calculator. We might even use a spreadsheet. This is a very simple exercise, even with the use of a calculator or a spreadsheet, and yet it is a very useful one in terms of generating summarizing statistics.

summarizing statistics Summarizing statistics are examples of descriptive statistics. Descriptive statistics are statistics that are used to describe data.

Table 17.1   Data gathered in response to gym/fitness centre use study

There are 30 students in the class in total
Of the 30 students, ten are gym/fitness centre users
There are 16 female and 14 male students in the class
Of the 16 female students, six are gym/fitness centre users
Of the 14 male students, four are gym/fitness centre users
Of the six female gym/fitness centre users, one said that she had been a member for five years, two said that they had been members for four years and three said that they had been members for three years
Of the four male gym/fitness centre users, one said that he had been a member for five years, one said that he had been a member for three years, and two said that they had been members for two years

If we had many quantitative data, we might need to use a dedicated software package. As mentioned previously, one software package designed specifically for the analysis of quantitative data is SPSS. The Statistical Package for the Social Sciences (SPSS), is a very powerful tool in quantitative data analysis. It is particularly useful in analyzing larger data sets. In fact, it would be very difficult to analyze a very large set of quantitative data without SPSS or similar software. SPSS works very well in the analysis of survey data. Using SPSS, the researcher first codes each response to each question in each questionnaire. Each response is coded as a number. The numeric code (the number) is then loaded (or inputted), into SPSS. As each completed questionnaire is returned, the researcher codes the data in the questionnaire and then loads the data, or inputs the data, from the questionnaire into SPSS. When all the completed questionnaires have been loaded or inputted, the researcher then uses the software to analyze the data.

The questionnaire that follows (Figure 17.1) is the sample questionnaire used in Chapter 15, with one added question, the question on gender. You can see the coding of the responses on the right-hand side of the sample questionnaire.

			Code
Q1. What is your age? Please state	22 yrs		22
Q2. What is your level of formal education? Please circle	Primary school Secondary school University/college		3
Q3. What is your annual income? Please tick			
Less than £10 000		☐	
More than £10 000, less than £20 000		☑	2
More than £20 000, less than £30 000		☐	
More than £30 000, less than £40 000		☐	
Q4. Please indicate your gender	Female ☐ Male ☑ Trans ☐		2

Figure 17.1   A sample questionnaire

Coding assigned by the researcher is always assigned using a simple logic. In response to question 3, the respondent selected the second option, so in coding this response the researcher assigned the number 2 as the code to signify this response. Codes, coding and the analysis of quantitative data are explored in detail in Chapter 19.

In coding each response as a number, the researcher assigns a numeric label, called a value label, to each value. For example, in the sample questionnaire, the question 4 relates to gender. The respondents to the questionnaire are asked to indicate in their response to the question whether they are male or female or transgender. The respondent ticks the appropriate box to respond to the question. The researcher in preparing these data for analysis, codes the response.

Sometimes, rather than coding responses in the questionnaire, researchers develop separate **coding keys** to go with the questionnaire. The coding key in Table 17.2 relates to the sample questionnaire above. The coding key becomes the researcher's key (or guide) to the data in SPSS.

coding keys A guide to all of the codes used in coding data for input into a computer software program.

Each question in the sample questionnaire relates to one variable. Age, gender, level of education and level of income are all variables. The third column in the coding key in Table 17.2 is used to describe the variable. Variables have more than one value. Gender, for example, as coded in this questionnaire and coding key, has three values, female, male and transgender.

Table 17.2   Coding key: sample questionnaire

Question number	Variable name	Variable description	Value labels
Q1	Age	Age	Record number
Q2	Level of education	1st level	1
		2nd level	2
		3rd level	3
Q3	Level of income	< than £10 000	1
		> £10 000 < £20 000	2
		> £20 000 < £30 000	3
		> £30 000 < £40 000	4
		(the four levels of income are aggregate measures)	
Q4	Gender	Female	1
		Male	2
		Transgender	3

Level of education, as coded in this questionnaire and coding key, has three values, 1st, 2nd and 3rd. Level of income, as coded in this questionnaire and coding key, has four values. The fourth column in the coding key is used to detail the labels (or codes) assigned to each value in each variable. When each value in each variable in the questionnaire has been labelled or coded, the questionnaire can be loaded, or inputted, into SPSS. The analysis of quantitative data using SPSS is considered in detail in Chapter 19.

When a researcher uses a pen and paper to analyze data and to calculate statistics, there can be issues with regards to data management. The researcher may simply make a mistake in their calculations, which could lead to a false reading and a false reporting of data. Mistakes can also happen when the researcher uses a calculator. However, using a calculator may improve the accuracy of the calculations. Using a calculator can make the calculations less laborious, which may mean that checking and rechecking the accuracy of the calculations will be relatively simple. This encourages checks on calculations. The correct and proper analysis of data is a key aspect of good data management and a fundamental aspect of valid research.

When a researcher uses a computerized software package to aid data analysis, the computer, following the instructions of the researcher, conducts the analysis. This is known as computer-assisted data analysis (CADA). CADA is a substantial aid in the analysis of large data sets. The computer has the capacity to store the analysis and the results of analysis, and with large data sets this is particularly invaluable. The computer stores data safely and securely, assuming that the computer itself is safe and secure. A computerized software package facilitates the cleaning of data. In checking accuracy in data and the way in which data were loaded, researchers engage in cleaning data. Data are 'cleaned' in the software package to ensure that they are accurate.

REAL WORLD RESEARCH

Ensuring proper management and analysis of data

Miscalculating statistics, at the most basic level, simply means calculating the maths incorrectly; such mistakes evidence very poor work and they can lead to misinterpretations and misrepresentations of data. Through the publication of research, misrepresentations of data become more than misrepresentations of data, they become misrepresentations of the phenomenon investigated in the study.

If a researcher is not competent enough to analyze the data correctly, s/he may mismanage data and may, as a result, misrepresent the data and the phenomenon that is the focus of their research.

Imagine, for example, that you are employed as a researcher in your university. Let us say that the management of the university engages you to carry out research on overall levels of student satisfaction with the sports and leisure facilities at the university.

(Continued)

You decide to conduct a survey. You design a questionnaire to measure levels of satisfaction among the student body. You decide to study a sample of one-third of the students registered in the university; this is 3000 students. This is quite a big, seemingly robust study. Your questionnaires are completed and returned. Because there is a great deal of interest among the students on campus in relation to the sports and leisure facilities in the university, you get a 70 per cent response rate. You code the responses and you load the data into SPSS.

However, in loading the data, you made a simple mistake and you did not take the time to check and clean the data. As a result of this simple mistake, your correct reading of the incorrectly loaded data leads you to the conclusion that overall student satisfaction levels with the sports and leisure facilities are high. In fact, overall student satisfaction levels are low in relation to the sports and leisure facilities at the university.

The simple mistake that occurred in loading the data into SPSS has rendered the research useless. Actually, the research is worse than useless. It is damaging, it is causing harm. It may be that policy in the university around the provision of sports and leisure facilities for students will be based for some time to come on this research. But the research is flawed. It misrepresents the situation.

This is a simple example of the way in which mismanaged research and improperly and incorrectly analyzed data can cause harm.

Qualitative data

As stated earlier, qualitative data are non-numeric data. As such, qualitative data can come in almost any form. They can take the form of stated or articulated feelings, beliefs, opinions and perspectives. Qualitative data can be in the form of narratives or stories, images, drawings, maps, cartoons, paintings or photographs. As with quantitative data, there are a number of different ways in which qualitative data can be analyzed.

A simple approach to analyzing qualitative data

One simple approach to qualitative data analysis is to read through all the data and, while reading, make a list of all of the themes that occur in the data. The themes would be the key ideas or the key issues in the data. Some or even all of these key themes will be related to the aim of the research, the conceptual framework developed for the research, and the concepts and themes that feature in the literature review carried out for the research project (the theoretical framework developed for the research project).

The researcher continues reading the transcripts and recording themes until no new themes emerge. Then the researcher takes the complete list of themes and explores them with a view to collapsing themes together. In other words, the researcher tries to condense the list of themes by fitting themes together that seem to fit logically. In this way, the list of themes becomes shorter and more manageable. When the researcher collapses themes together, it is sometimes necessary to conceptualize a new theme that will encompass all the themes collapsed together. This is a process of abstraction and, through the process of abstraction, the researcher takes a step away from the raw data and a step towards an abstract or abstracted understanding of the data.

Through a continuing and deepening process of abstraction, the researcher comes closer to the meaning of the data in relation to the overall aim of the research. As the researcher continues to collapse themes together, s/he move to deeper levels of abstraction in relation to the data, moving further and further away from the raw data. The researcher can colour code the themes, perhaps assigning the colour red to the first theme, the colour yellow to the second theme, the colour green to the third theme, and so on. The researcher reads through the transcripts assigning the colours to the parts of the data that represent each of the themes. In this way, the researcher can see at a glance each of the themes as they are represented in the data. The researcher then decides how to tell the story of the data, based on this thematic analysis, in the written account of the analysis.

The decisions the researcher makes in relation to the story to be told are based on the overall aim of the research, the research statement or question and the objectives of the research project. The researcher must maintain an appropriate focus while telling the story (the narrative) of the analyzed data. In thoroughly outlining the narrative, the researcher brings the research project full circle. At the start of the research project, the researcher asked a question (the research question) or created a research statement. Now, when coming to the end of the research project, the researcher must answer that question, or respond to the statement. At the start of the research project, the researcher outlined a specific aim and a number of objectives. Now, in the narrative of the data analysis chapter, the researcher must begin to complete the accomplishment of that aim and those objectives. By maintaining a focus on the research question or statement and on the research aim and objectives, the researcher is not closed to any new important issue or aspect of the phenomenon under investigation to emerge from the data and the analysis of the data. Any such new and probably unanticipated finding or insight must be accommodated within the research project. If the new finding is very substantial, it may require a shift in the focus of the project. If you find yourself in this position, you would need to seek direction from your research supervisor and/or your lecturer in research methodologies. It may be possible to accommodate this new insight at the end of the study as a recommendation for further research.

REAL WORLD RESEARCH

Shifts and changes in the research project

It is possible that the focus of your research will shift slightly as the research develops. If this happens, and it often does happen, then every aspect of the research project must shift slightly to accommodate these changes.

If you find that your research shifts or changes in a major way, then either your research project was not well conceptualized to begin with, or in the course of your reading and/or reflection on the research, you encountered something substantial that you had not anticipated, and possibly could not have anticipated. It could happen that as you reflect on your research you have a major light bulb moment, a flash of insight that leads you to substantially develop your research. If such a major shift occurs in your research, it is likely that you will have to go back to the start and redesign your research project to encompass this new insight. If, as this happens, you have been fortunate enough to make some substantial move forward in your thinking, then you will be on a very exciting research journey.

If you do need to make major changes, ask for advice, guidance and support from your supervisor, your lecturer in research methods. It is possible that, at a late stage in the research process, any new ideas that you have in relation to your research can be accommodated in the research project as recommendations for further research.

What we have just described is a very simple, yet valid and useful approach to qualitative data analysis. This simple approach works well with small data sets. Such an approach will, however, also work with large data sets. That said, for the most efficient management of a large qualitative data set, a computerized qualitative data analysis software package is invaluable.

Computerized data analysis software packages are particularly helpful with managing data and data analysis. The software package stores the data and the analysis of the data so there is no need for large piles of printed data or colour coded data. There is no need to move large quantities of paper about the desk in order to carry out the analysis. The analysis can be done entirely on the computer and stored and backed up there. As well as eliminating the hard (physical) work of dealing with data analysis on paper, using colour coding or some other kind of coding system, a computerized approach to data analysis is simpler and cleaner. As well as storing and analyzing the data, the computer stores a memory of the analysis conducted on the data. So the steps taken in analysis can be revisited throughout the process and later when the process of analysis has been completed. When the data analysis process is computerized, there is less likelihood of data getting lost or simply missed in the analysis process. Qualitative data analysis is explored in detail in Chapter 18.

THE VALUE OF GOOD RESEARCH

Focus on semiotics

Semiotics, as explained in Chapter 9, is the study of signs, their form, content and expression, in society. Signs in society are 'signs' because they signify something. Anything that has signifying power, the power to signify, can be studied using semiotics. While traditionally semiotics focused on linguistics, on the study of the signifying capacity of language, more recently social scientists have engaged in the study of social semiotics.

In her research, Owyong (2009) used semiotics to explore the signifying potential of clothing. She contends in this journal article that clothes do more than meet our physical and physiological needs, they convey meanings in society that are beyond the superficial, meanings that enact and even create power relations between people. The aim of her research was to study the clothes people wear as a critical semiotic resource in the social construction of power relations. In her literature review, Owyong distinguishes between clothing and fashion as follows: clothing is used generically to describe what people wear, while fashion is a style of

(Continued)

dress temporarily worn by a 'discerning' group in society. As she says, what is fashionable in one part of the world is not fashionable in another, and what is fashionable today may be considered dated or even *passé* tomorrow. To illustrate the point, she discusses the wearing of knee-high socks by Japanese teenage girls in the 1990s, which they considered chic and fashionable, while, at the same time, Singaporean teenage girls were trying hard to keep their socks hidden in their shoes, believing the appearance of shoes with no socks to be hip and trendy.

Owyong highlights the asymmetrical power relations that can be created by clothes. She points to the power relation between the hotel manager in a well-cut suit and the hotel cleaning staff in their nondescript uniforms. She highlights the power of the policeman's uniform. She demonstrates how different articles of clothing convey different messages; clothing reflects the power, or lack of power, of the wearer.

In her analysis, Owyong presents different case studies, among them a case study of the business suit. She presents a detailed analysis of the 'power suit' and the relative positions of men and women in relation to the wearing of power suits. She completes the presentation of her case studies with a consideration of the attire of superheroes such as Spiderman, Captain America and Luke Skywalker.

She concludes the article with the comment that, while Mark Twain said that 'clothes make the man', her study shows that the right clothes can make the man (and the woman) *powerful*.

The focus of Owyong's research is on clothing semiotics and the social construction of power relations. This research is relevant for human resource development, for business management as well as for marketing. You should source the article online and read it through. It may give you ideas for your own research project.

You will find the following resources useful in relation to semiotics and to the use of semiotics as a research methodology and/or a research method in your own research:

Chandler, D., 'Semiotics for beginners', visual-memory.co.uk/daniel/Documents/S4B

Koller, V. (2007) '"The world's local bank": glocalisation as a strategy in corporate branding discourse', *Social Semiotics*, *17*(1): 111–131.

Oswald, L., 'Semiotics and strategic brand management', University of Illinois, www.csun.edu/~bashforth/098_PDF/Semiotic_branding.pdf

The academic journals *American Journal of Semiotics*, *Applied Semiotics* and *Social Semiotics* are also useful.

THE FOUR STAGES OF DATA ANALYSIS

There are four stages in data analysis. The first stage is description, in which the researcher engages in a descriptive analysis of the data. The researcher describes the data, describing what it is that they see in the data.

The second stage is interpretation. In this stage, the researcher states what it is that they think the data mean.

The third stage is the conclusions stage. In this stage, the researcher draws a major or minor conclusion from the data. Conclusions are not just findings reiterated; in drawing conclusions, researchers move their thinking and reasoning along. Conclusions are decisions that researchers make about the phenomenon under investigation based on the findings of the study. Researchers are said to come to conclusions based on the study, or they are said to draw conclusions from the study. The conclusions that you draw as you go through the analysis are for the most part minor conclusions (see Table 17.3 for an example). They add up to, or they make a substantial contribution to, your major conclusion(s), which you state in the final chapter of the thesis or in the final section of the report of the research.

Table 17.3 Drawing conclusions (an example)

Describing data	Your data, for example, show clearly that the students did not enjoy the module on research methodology
Interpreting data	Your interpretation of these data is that there is some lack of fit between the research methodology module, as it is currently presented, and the needs of the students
Drawing conclusions	The conclusion you draw is that the research methodology should be changed and improved

The fourth and final stage of the **four stages of data analysis** is the theorization stage. As we know, every research project conducted within academia must make a contribution to knowledge.

four stages of data analysis Description, interpretation, conclusions and theorization.

In order to theorize their findings, the researcher looks back at their literature review and checks to see how their findings fit with the findings of the theorists detailed there. The researcher then demonstrates this in their data analysis chapter or in the section on findings in the report of the research. S/he does this by explicitly stating and explaining how their findings fit with, or contradict, the findings of other theorists, as detailed in the literature review written for the research project. Whether the findings fit with or contradict the findings of others is unimportant; there may, for example, be temporal or cultural differences that can account for the researcher's findings contradicting the findings of others. The researcher tries as much as possible to connect their work with the theory laid out in the literature review. The four stages of data analysis are demonstrated in Figure 17.2.

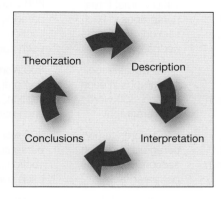

Figure 17.2 The four stages of analysis

In order to create the analytical framework for the research project, the fourth framework of the four frameworks approach, the researcher creates a structure for the chapter to contain the data analysis. This chapter is generally Chapter 4 in the thesis. The researcher constructs an analytical framework for the research project using:

- the key concepts from the conceptual framework, the research statement/question, or the overall aim of the research project
- the key concepts and key issues to emerge from the review of the literature
- the key findings from the analysis of the data gathered for the research.

The analytical framework for the research project is presented in the data analysis chapter.

The four frameworks

- Conceptual Framework
- Theoretical Framework
- Methodological Framework
- *Analytical Framework*

The analytical framework is structured around a series of chapter subsections, each of which is headed with a subtitle. The subtitles and subsections deployed in the chapter provide the structure necessary for the narrative, or story, the researcher tells of the analyzed data.

The researcher designs the data analysis chapter, before beginning to write it. S/he decides how many subsections the chapter will have, how to subtitle each subsection, what material to use in each subsection, and the order in which to present each subsection. The order in which the information is presented in the chapter is determined by the story or narrative that the researcher is developing. This narrative will be structured around the main argument, or the key point, the researcher is trying to make in the chapter. It is important, therefore, to decide precisely the key point or argument of the chapter and then structure the chapter around it. Clearly, the key point or argument will be, or will be closely related to, the research statement or question, that is, the conceptual framework for the research project. This key point or argument will be a response to the aim of the research project.

Always try to write to a structure. The structure acts as a guide and will help you focus on the overall aim of the research project. Table 17.4 provides sample structures for the data analysis chapter.

The suggested word counts in Table 17.4 are designed to be a guide for you as you begin to plan and structure your data analysis chapter. If you do use one of the structures provided (the appropriate one for the word count you are allowed), then before you begin to write the chapter, you will have:

- decided what it is that you are going to say in the chapter
- decided on the main point or key argument you wish to make in the chapter
- selected the particular aspects of your analyzed data that you wish to present in the chapter
- decided precisely where in the chapter each of these aspects fits best
- drawn up a plan for the chapter in your research diary, including a list, in order, of all of the sub-headings in the chapter.

Table 17.4   Structure of the data analysis chapter

Total word count	7000 words	5000 words	3000 words	1500 words
Introduction	300 words	200 words	200 words	100 words
First subheading	2000 words, four paragraphs in each section, 500 words in each paragraph	1400 words, three paragraphs in each section, 350 words per paragraph	800 words, three paragraphs in each section, 250 words in each paragraph	400 words, three paragraphs in each section, 125 words in each paragraph
Second subheading	2000 words, four paragraphs in each section, 500 words in each paragraph	1400 words three paragraphs in each section, 350 words per paragraph	800 words, three paragraphs in each section, 250 words in each paragraph	400 words, three paragraphs in each section, 125 words in each paragraph
Third subheading	2000 words, four paragraphs in each section, 500 words in each paragraph	1400 words three paragraphs in each section, 350 words per paragraph	800 words, three paragraphs in each section, 250 words in each paragraph	400 words, three paragraphs in each section, 125 words in each paragraph
Summary/conclusion	500 words	500 words	300 words	200 words

YOUR RESEARCH
Data reduction

It is important when writing up the data analysis chapter to remember that it is not necessary or appropriate, or even possible, to report every detail of the data or every element of data analysis. The process of data analysis is a process of data reduction. Through data reduction, data are transformed into more manageable formats. In writing up the data analysis chapter, the researcher reports only the most significant aspects of the analysis. What is presented in the data analysis chapter, in the data analysis section of the report of the research, is a synopsis of the data analysis carried out.

Raw data are data which have yet to be analyzed. In writing up the data analysis chapter, the researcher does not present raw data. The researcher carries out the analysis, and reports the key points, the key aspects, the key elements, the key themes, of the analysis of the data gathered. The key themes presented in the data analysis chapter respond to the research statement or question, that is the conceptual framework. They respond to the aim and the objectives of the research project.

Using the four frameworks approach to the research, the key concepts in the conceptual framework are used to guide and direct the literature search for the literature review. The key concepts from the conceptual framework and the key issues to emerge from the literature review, together with the aim and objectives of the research, guide and direct the analysis of the data. In turn, they guide and direct the structure of the data analysis chapter. Each of the subheadings in the data analysis chapter should reflect the key concepts of the research, as detailed in the research statement/question, in the overall aim of the research. The content of each of the subsections in the data analysis chapter is reflected in the subheading of the section.

The four frameworks

- *Conceptual Framework*
- Theoretical Framework
- Methodological Framework
- Analytical Framework

Data Analysis: Ask critical questions of data

When you have read through your data several times, you can begin the process of analyzing it. A good way to begin the process of data analysis is to ask critical questions of the data. When you have organized your data into a data set ready for analysis, whether you have a large stack of interview transcripts, a smaller stack of completed questionnaires or a data set in a computerized data analysis package (SPSS, Atlas.ti or NVivo or some other software package), you can begin to think analytically about your data.

To begin with, think about the issues that clearly and immediately emerge from your data. Think about the questions you could ask of the data in order to develop your thinking about them. The questions you ask of the data will primarily come from the conceptual framework for the project, which is contained in the research statement or question. They will come from the overall aim of the research and the research objectives, and they will come from your review of the literature. Finally, some new questions will arise from the data themselves, from your experiences in the gathering of them, what you observed while gathering your data and the insights you developed in relation to the phenomenon under investigation through your experiences in the field. From all of these sources, you will be able to generate good and useful questions with which to interrogate and analyze the data.

THE VALUE OF GOOD RESEARCH

Karl's research project

Karl works as a manager for a high street fashion company. The company has 250 retail outlets across the UK. In his research project for his degree in strategic business management, Karl has focused on the critical issues facing the company in the current economic climate. In order to examine this issue, Karl has conducted a survey. He has emailed a questionnaire to the managers of each of the 250 outlets. He has had a 90 per cent response rate to his questionnaire. He has loaded the responses to his questionnaire into SPSS and he has analyzed the data. Karl has spent six weeks analyzing his data in SPSS and he is now ready to write up his data analysis chapter.

The aim of Karl's research is as follows: 'The aim of this survey is to identify and examine the critical issues facing this company in the current economic climate.' The aim of the research project contains all of the key concepts of the research project. These key concepts were used to search for literature for the literature review. The literature review with the conceptual framework for the research project was used to develop the questionnaire used in the survey. The analysis of the questionnaire was guided by the aim of the research project, the objectives of the research, the issues that emerged from the review of the literature and the insights Karl developed from his work in analyzing the data. From all of this, Karl developed a structure for his data analysis chapter. Karl has decided on the key issues he is going to address in his presentation of his analysis of the data. He has decided what he is going to include in the chapter. He knows what data he is going to present in the data analysis chapter. He has decided on a narrative for the chapter. The word count for the chapter is 7000 words; this is given as a guide, not as an absolute word count. The structure Karl has designed for his data analysis chapter is as follows:

Introduction – (300 words)
First subheading – Critical issues facing the company (2000 words, in four paragraphs, 500 words in each paragraph)
Second subheading – The economic climate and the upturn in trade (2000 words, in four paragraphs, 500 words in each paragraph)
Third subheading – Insights and ideas from retail outlet managers across the UK (2000 words, in four paragraphs, 500 words in each paragraph)
Fourth subheading – Dealing with the issues – a way forward (2000 words, in four paragraphs, 500 words in each paragraph)
Summary/conclusion – (500 words)

What do you think of Karl's research project? Does it give you any ideas in terms of your own research project?

It is of the utmost importance that the analysis and the findings from the analysis are grounded in the data. This means that there must be evidence in the data for all of your descriptions, interpretations and conclusions. Everything that you state that you have found in your data must be clearly evident in the data. You must present data in the data analysis chapter, in tables, in figures, in matrices, in direct quotes, in images, in whatever format the data you have gathered allows, to support your claims. You cannot make claims in your research, or for your research, that your data do not or cannot support. In other words, your findings must be grounded in the data. The purpose of the data analysis chapter is to clearly and completely detail your data and the narrative you have created around and from your data. The key questions you should ask of the data analysis chapter are as follows:

1. What is the point of this chapter?
2. What point or argument am I making in this chapter?
3. How well and how clearly is this point or argument made in the chapter?
4. How well are the data used in the chapter to support this point or argument?
5. How well do the data support this main point or key argument?

You should be very clear about the argument or the point you are making in your data analysis chapter and you should make your argument or point very clearly. The argument or point you are making must also be a clear response to the overall aim of the research project.

Managing and analyzing data

In this research (Suboleski *et al.*, 2009, 'An exploratory study of multi-unit restaurant management training: a qualitative perspective', *Journal of Human Resources in Hospitality & Tourism*, 8(2): 199–214), Suboleski *et al.* studied multi-unit restaurants (MURs) and multi-unit managers (MUMs). They state that a concern in many food service organizations is the lack of consistent training provided to MUMs. In this qualitative study, they examined seven multi-unit organizations and the training they provided for their MUMs in depth.

The data collection method used in the study was an open-ended interview process which, the authors stated, allowed for a detailed examination of the ways in which training was conducted, and the specific training content delivered. Interviews were conducted with seven executives from seven of the top 100 MUR organizations in the USA. The interviews were conducted over the phone during a two-month period in 2005. The interviews were taped and the interview transcriptions underwent content analysis using the qualitative software package, Atlas.ti.

In an in-depth interview, the authors of this study state that the goal is to get as much information as possible from participants on the particular topic or subject area. They explain that for their study, using the literature review as a foundation, an open-ended interview schedule was developed. They tell us that the schedule was reviewed by 'subject matter experts' and pilot tested by several training directors in MUR organizations in order to ensure that the content was complete and the questions asked were clear and concise.

A purposive sampling approach was used in the study. Twelve executives were invited to participate. In the end, seven did participate and seven interviews in total were carried out.

The data-gathering instrument had both open-ended questions and demographic questions regarding the organization and the MUMs who work for the organization. The demographic questions, we are told, were developed to give each organization some kind of quantifiable description.

With respect to the open-ended questions, three specific dimensions of interest were addressed: the MUM's job, the MUM's employment and the training the MUM received, in relation to:

- The manager's job: questions were posed about the roles, duties, responsibilities and expectations of them.
- The manager's employment: the questions asked were concerned with the criteria used in the organization for employing, promoting and developing managers.
- The manager's training: the questions asked examined the training efforts or training programmes in place for managers. Questions were also asked about any training plans in development for future programmes for the development of current managers and new managers.

We are told that, as more than one interviewer was used (two, in fact), and they both had their own unique style of creating a conversation with the respondents, there was a need to ensure consistency in the analysis of the data. The individual interview styles of the two interviewers led to differences in the ways in which responses were generated. We are told that although the data-gathering instrument was similar for each interview, different styles of interview prompted the researchers to use content analysis as the means by which the interview data were analyzed.

The interviews were conducted over the telephone. This was done to ensure consistency in the responses and to avoid possible bias by the interviewer being led by the physical responses, the body language, of the respondent. The interviews were organized to ensure that they were all conducted at the respondent's office or workspace. The interviews lasted between 60 and 90 minutes, and they were collected over a two-month period in the spring of 2005. The seven interviews were carried out by two interviewers. Both interviewers were experienced in conducting in-depth interviews and in posing follow-up or probing questions in order to maximize the quality and depth of the responses.

We are told that, in keeping with the nature of a semi-structured interview, the goal of the interviewers was not to get all the questions in the schedule asked. Instead their focus was on gaining, through the interviews, an understanding of the participant's perspective on manager training and the role that manager training played in their organization.

A decision was made to tape all of the interviews. This was done in order to keep the data as pure and as complete as possible. Each of the seven interviews was transcribed promptly on completion by a professional transcriber. All conversations between the

(Continued)

interviewers and respondents were transcribed so that the entire interaction, including all follow-up questions and probes, could be reviewed. The transcripts were reviewed to ensure that the different interviewer styles did not affect analysis.

In their analysis of the interview transcripts, the researchers focused on the words, phrases and themes in the data. They stated that information from each participant was first analyzed separately to identify emerging themes within particular organizations. Then the themes that emerged from each respondent were compared across respondents in order to identify common beliefs or practices. The stated expectation was that such a multiple analysis approach would lead to a more sophisticated understanding of the data. Analysis was completed using the computer program Atlas.ti.

The authors explain that the three dimensions identified for the construction of the data-gathering instrument – job, employment and training – were the major themes developed from the literature and they were the major themes used in the process of coding the data. The following data were presented:

- Seven companies were interviewed ($n = 7$).
- The ages of these companies ranged from five to 51 years, with the mean being 28.5 years.
- Only two of the companies were younger than ten years old.
- Two of the companies were older than 25 years old.
- Two firms identified themselves as belonging to the quick-service hamburger market segment.
- The remaining five described themselves in terms of segment with the term 'casual'.
- Two of the companies identified themselves as part of the casual dining market segment.
- The remaining three identified themselves as fast casual, family-style casual and full-service casual.
- The companies had anywhere from 32 to 1400 units.
- Two of the respondents held positions as directors of operations.
- One was a divisional vice president of operations.

- Three of the respondents were involved in training. Their titles were regional training director, vice president of management development and training, and field training specialist.
- One respondent was a vice president of human resources and was also directly involved with training.
- All of the participants were either MUMs themselves or directly involved with the training or supervision of MUMs within their organization.
- In four of the companies, MUMs were referred to as directors of operations.
- Two of the organizations called their MUMs multi-unit managers.
- One firm referred to the position by the title company business manager.
- The companies employed from nine to 342 MUMs each.
- Two of the companies employed more than 100 MUMs, while four of the companies employed fewer than 25.
- The span of control, or number of properties for which each MUM was responsible, ranged from three to 11 per MUM.
- Three of the companies would not disclose the average age of their MUMs.
- The remaining four companies had MUMs ranging in age from 30 to 48 years of age.
- Three companies would not disclose the gender breakdown of their MUMs.
- The remaining four companies had an overwhelming majority of male MUMs, ranging from 41 to 100 per cent.
- Tenure of the MUMs in the organizations interviewed ranged from 2.5 years to 15 years.

Question: The synopsis given here of the research published by Suboleski *et al.* (2009) provides a good example of the detailed reflection on data, engagement with data, and management and analysis of data that researchers routinely undertake. Having read the synopsis, what would you say the main strengths and weaknesses of this study are?

END OF CHAPTER QUESTIONS

1   What is meant by the term data management?

2   Write a short paragraph on the key concerns in data management in a research project.

3   Describe a simple approach to quantitative data analysis.

4   Describe a simple approach to qualitative data analysis.

5   What are the four stages of the data analysis process, as explained in this chapter?

6 What is CADA and what are the key advantages of CADA in data analysis?

7 What is SPSS and what is it used for?

8 Explain in detail the acronym CAQDAS.

9 Explain the use of the analytical framework within the four frameworks approach to the research project.

10 Using the analytical framework and the sample structures for the data analysis chapter provided in this chapter, design a structure for the data analysis chapter of your research project.

REFERENCES

Chandler, D., 'Semiotics for beginners', visual-memory.co.uk/daniel/Documents/S4B (Accessed 17.03.2018).

Goodman, D. (22.10.2017) *Nobel Laureates Stiglitz and Spence to Lead New Group to Tackle World's Economic Woes*, www.bloomberg.com/news/articles/2017-10-21/nobel-laureates-lead-new-group-to-tackle-world-s-economic-woes (Accessed 17.03.2018).

Institute for New Economic Thinking (INET), ineteconomics.org/ (Accessed 17.03.2018).

Kaletsky, A. (2009) 'Three cheers for the death of old economics: the orthodox mathematical model took no account of reality. The new George Soros Institute should bring back some sanity', *The Times*, 28 October.

Koller, V. (2007) '"The world's local bank": Glocalisation as a strategy in corporate branding discourse', *Social Semiotics*, *17*(1): 111–131.

Moustakas, C.E. (1994) *Phenomenological Research Methods*, Thousand Oaks, CA: Sage.

Oswald, L., 'Semiotics and strategic brand management', University of Illinois, www.csun.edu/~bashforth/098_PDF/Semiotic_branding.pdf (Accessed 17.03.2018).

Owyong, Y.S.M. (2009) 'Clothing semiotics and the social construction of power relations', *Social Semiotics*, *19*(2): 191–211.

Purkiss, A. (2010) 'Soros plans economics institute at Oxford University, *Times* says', 5 April, www.bloomberg.com/news/articles/2010-04-05/soros-plans-oxford-university-economics-institute-on-markets-times-says (Accessed 17.03.2018).

Resnik, D.B. (2009) 'International standards for research integrity: an idea whose time has come?', *Accountability in Research*, *16*(4): 218–228.

Soros, G. (2010) 'Anatomy of crisis – the living history of the last 30 years: economic theory, politics and policy', presented at the INET Conference, King's College, 8–11 April, www.ineteconomics.org/research/research-papers/george-soros-the-living-history-of-the-last-30-years (Accessed 17.03.2018).

Strauss, A. and Corbin, J. (1990, 1998) *Basics of Qualitative Research: Techniques and Procedures for Developing Grounded Theory*, Thousand Oaks, CA: Sage.

Suboleski, S., Kincaid, C.S. and Dipietro, R.B. (2009) 'An exploratory study of multi-unit restaurant management training: a qualitative perspective', *Journal of Human Resources in Hospitality & Tourism*, *8*(2): 199–214.

The Economist, (13.04.2013) 'The Institute for New Economic Thinking: A Slipping Taboo, www.economist.com/news/finance-and-economics/21576089-george-soross-attempt-shake-up-dismal-science-arrives-asia-slipping (Accessed 17.03.2018).

RECOMMENDED READING

Bell, J. and Waters, S. (2014) *Doing Your Research Project* (6th edn), Maidenhead: Open University Press.

Collis, J. and Hussey, R. (2013) *Business Research: A Practical Guide for Undergraduate and Postgraduate Students* (4th edn), Basingstoke and New York: Palgrave Macmillan.

Creswell, J. and Creswell, D.J. (2018) *Research Design: Qualitative, Quantitative and Mixed Methods Approaches* (5th edn), London, California, New Delhi, Singapore: Sage.

Denscombe, M. (2017) *The Good Research Guide: For Small-scale Social Research Projects* (5th edn), Maidenhead: Open University Press.

Easterby-Smith, M., Thorpe, R. and Jackson, P.R. (2008) *Management Research* (3rd edn), London: Sage.

Lewins, A. and Silver, C. (2007) *Using Software in Qualitative Research: A Step By Step Guide*, London: Sage.

Miles, M.B., Huberman, A.M. and Saldana, J. (2014) *Qualitative Data Analysis: A Methods Sourcebook* (3rd edn), California, London, New Delhi, Singapore: Sage.

Neuman, W.L. (2014) *Social Research Methods: Qualitative and Quantitative Approaches* (7th edn), Essex, England: Pearson Education Ltd.

Oppenheim, A.N. (2000) *Questionnaire Design, Interviewing and Attitude Measurement* (2nd edn), London: Continuum.

Robson, C. and McCartan, K. (2016) *Real World Research*, John Wiley & Sons Ltd.

White, B. and Rayner, S. (2014) *Dissertation Skills for Business and Management Students*, London: Cengage Learning EMEA.

CHAPTER 18
ANALYZING QUALITATIVE DATA

LEARNING OBJECTIVES

At the end of this chapter, the student should:

- Understand qualitative data analysis.

- Be able to analyze qualitative data.

RESEARCH SKILLS

At the end of this chapter, the student should, using the exercises on Cengage Brain, be able to:

- Conduct an analysis of the data set presented.

- Critique the data provided in terms of the stated aim of the research project.

The aim of this chapter is to develop the focus on qualitative data and qualitative data analysis started in Chapter 17, and to teach the student how to engage in qualitative data analysis. The chapter explains the key concepts and issues in qualitative data analysis, describes some of the different approaches to qualitative data analysis, and demonstrates the processes and procedures involved. The student will learn in this chapter how to carry out qualitative data analysis.

INTRODUCTION

This chapter explains in detail what qualitative data are and how qualitative data are analyzed. The chapter outlines a simple approach to qualitative data analysis and introduces the student to more complex approaches to qualitative data analysis. The use of computer-assisted qualitative data analysis software (CAQDAS) is explored and two different software packages, NVivo and Atlas.ti, designed for qualitative data analysis are considered. The centrality of language in qualitative data and qualitative data analysis is explored and explained. Different ways to present qualitative data and qualitative research findings in the thesis, or research report, are considered. Finally, the chapter explains how to blend together the findings from quantitative and qualitative research, mixed-methods research, in the writing up of data analysis.

Once again, if you look back at the model of the research process presented at the start of Chapter 1 (Figure 1.1), you will see where in the research process data analysis occurs. As you can see from the figure, the researcher gathers data, analyzes the data and then draws conclusions from the analyzed data in order to complete the research.

The research project outlined in the following Value of Good Research box explains how a 50-year-old company used qualitative research to gain an understanding of what customers required and what they expected. In-depth qualitative research designed to examine customer needs was carried out. Through the research the purchase experience of customers was mapped out, step-by-step. Customer types were defined, different choices and behaviours on the part of customers were analyzed, and scenarios of the ideal customer experience were developed. The findings of the qualitative research provided the company with a complete rethink of the service provided for customers.

THE VALUE OF GOOD RESEARCH

Amplifon – redesigned and reinvigorated

Amplifon was founded in 1950 and its headquarters are in Milan, Italy. Amplifon is a worldwide market leader in the business of hearing aids. It has 5700 specialist centres in 20 countries.

The group was the market leader in its sector, and it wanted to stay that way. That meant selling more hearing aids. The company believed that selling more hearing aids depended on the customers' experience in the stores, and the belief was that the customer experience provided for decades was no longer fit for purpose.

There are two aspects to Amplifon's business: medical and consumer. The products Amplifon sells are medical and its 'customers' are both customers and medical patients. In the in-store sales experience provided, the medical aspect had become the dominant aspect. Walking into an Amplifon store was like walking into a medical clinic. This had to change.

In order to develop a real understanding of what customers wanted, the company hired the design consultancy firm, Continuum. Continuum conducted ethnographic research primarily in the form of in-depth qualitative research into the customer experience. The research focused on the process of buying a hearing aid. The process was mapped out, step-by-step. Customer types were defined, and customer behaviour and customer choices were analyzed. Finally, scenarios of ideal experiences were developed through the use of vignettes.

Based on the findings of the study, the stores were redesigned. Following redesign, the company achieved a 20 per cent increase in sales. Amplifon stores now provide a customer experience that fits with customer needs and expectations.

QUALITATIVE DATA ANALYSIS

Qualitative data analysis is the process through which qualitative data are analyzed. One of the main functions of qualitative data analysis is to develop as thick and rich and complete an account of the phenomenon under investigation as possible. The concept of a **thick description** was introduced by Clifford Geertz in his book *The Interpretation of Cultures* (1973). This concept of a thick description is useful in relation to qualitative data analysis. The essential aim of the process of analysis in qualitative data analysis is to accomplish this thick description of the phenomenon under investigation.

thick description Developed by Clifford Geertz, to explain the complex in-depth representation qualitative researchers attempt to accomplish when describing their research projects.

Qualitative researchers, rather than objectively studying the 'real' world, acknowledge multiple realities (the subjective realities of individuals). Qualitative research is situated within a constructivist or interpretivist paradigm. Qualitative researchers hold that we co-construct our world, our understanding of reality. We interpret the world individually and in our own way. In qualitative research, it is these subjective experiences and expressions of reality that the qualitative researcher tries to understand and describe.

The language of qualitative research and qualitative data analysis tends to be softer than the language of quantitative research and quantitative data analysis. In some respects, the language of quantitative research and quantitative data analysis is a technicist instrumentalist language. The vocabulary of quantitative research, for example, tends to include words such as 'instrument', 'subject', 'experiment' and 'test'. In qualitative research, by way of contrast, the word 'method' is often used instead of instrument. Rather than research subjects, qualitative researchers talk about research participants; rather than experiment or test, qualitative researchers tend to 'explore', 'describe', 'detail' and 'construct'. In qualitative research there is an emphasis on signaling throughout the research process and the writing of the research, an acknowledgement of and respect for the basic humanity of research participants and the circumstances of their lives.

Another striking difference in the reporting of quantitative and qualitative research is the presence of the researcher. In the reporting of quantitative research, there is no space for the researcher; the researcher is completely written out of the analysis. Qualitative research is very different. While the fundamental aim of qualitative research is to uncover the subjective meanings participants make of the phenomenon under investigation, there is an acknowledgement of the role that the researcher plays in creating meaning, through their essential selection, description and interpretation of the data they gather for the research project. This is because, within qualitative research, there is an explicit acknowledgement that data gathered are filtered through the consciousness of the researcher. In qualitative data analysis, the researcher becomes subjectively immersed in the data. The researcher does not stand objectively apart from the data. As this is the case, there is a call within qualitative research for the researcher to provide a reflexive account of themselves within the research project.

Reflexivity

In qualitative research, reflexivity calls for an acknowledgement on the part of the researcher of their role in the research project. The essential role of the researcher in interpreting the experiences of others in the qualitative research process, calls for the perspective of the researcher in this process to be made explicit. This is done through a reflexive process in which the researcher makes explicit the perspectives, understandings and decisions that guide them through the process of data analysis to the findings and conclusions of the research.

This is important because of the explicit acknowledgement in qualitative research that who we are in relation to the phenomenon we are investigating impacts on how we study the phenomenon, how we interpret and make sense of it, and the conclusions we come to in relation to it. As this is the case, within qualitative research there is a need for reflexivity on the part of the researcher. Reflexivity in qualitative research is the account that the researcher provides of themselves and their role in the construction of meaning in the gathering and analysis of data.

Within qualitative data analysis, the researcher and the role of the researcher are evident and made evident, in a reflexive manner, in the way in which the report of the data analysis is written. It is a good exercise to use your research diary to develop notes of your ideas and thoughts on your reflexive engagement with your research project. These notes can be drawn on when you are writing a reflexive account of your engagement with your research project in the formal account of the research. We will explore this process further in the final chapter of this book.

When reading journal articles, it is useful to identify any differences in the language used in accounts of quantitative research projects and qualitative research projects, and to highlight the reflexive accounts that researchers in qualitative research projects give of themselves and their role(s) in the research. This will help you develop your own knowledge and understanding of how to write quantitative and qualitative research, and mixed-methods research. Mixed-methods research, as you know, has both quantitative and qualitative elements.

Language

Language is particularly important in qualitative data and qualitative data analysis, as it is frequently through the study and analysis of the language of the participants that qualitative researchers carry out their research. The thick description that the researchers attempt to develop through data analysis is generated from and generated with the language of the participants in the study. In qualitative data analysis, rather than analyzing and reporting numbers, researchers analyze language which they use to give expression to their analyses. Many of the data collection methods used in qualitative research produce data that are language based, for example, interview and focus group transcripts of the oral testimony of participants.

In qualitative data analysis, there are different approaches to the process of analysis, depending on the needs and design of the study. Qualitative data can be analyzed thematically, in terms of themes, or discursively, in terms of discourses. Qualitative data can be analyzed using a content analysis approach. Content analysis has application in both quantitative data analysis and qualitative data analysis. It means, simply, analyzing the content of some phenomenon, such as a photograph or a series of photographs, a cartoon, drawing, newspaper, magazine, film interview, or focus group transcript and so on. Qualitative data can be analyzed using a phenomenological approach, if the research project has been developed using a phenomenological methodology. Sometimes an argument can be made for using a phenomenological approach to data analysis in a research project that has not been developed using this methodology. Similarly, qualitative research can be analyzed using a grounded theory approach, if the research project has been developed using a grounded theory methodology. Sometimes this approach to data analysis can be appropriate in a research project which has not been developed using a ground theory methodology. **Narrative analysis** in qualitative data analysis calls for an analysis of narratives in the data. Textual analysis calls for an analysis of data as texts; data can be in the form of films, videos, television programmes, magazines, advertisements, photographs, clothes and graffiti, which can all be considered texts for the purposes of textual analysis. The key to selecting or developing an appropriate approach to qualitative data analysis is to select or develop an approach which best suits, which best fits, the research project.

narrative analysis The analysis of data in the form of narratives or through the use of narratives.

THE FOUR STAGES OF DATA ANALYSIS

The four stages of data analysis (see Figure 18.1), as explained in the previous chapter, are description, interpretation, conclusions and theorization:

1. In the first stage of data analysis, we describe what is there in the data, what is evident in the data. This first stage of data analysis is known as descriptive analysis.
2. In the second stage, the interpretive stage, we try to interpret what is in the data. In interpreting the data, the researcher tries to uncover the meaning of the data, and tries to articulate that meaning. The researcher asks themselves: 'If this is what is in the data, if this is what the data say, then what does that mean?'
3. The third stage is the conclusions stage. In this stage, the researcher draws minor conclusions from the data, as the process of data analysis unfolds. The question the researcher asks themselves is: 'If this is what the data say and these are the possible meanings of that, what are the implications of that?' The researcher tries to tease out the implications of the data. The data may have different implications for different constituents in the research (different stakeholders in the research). These may include the participants in the research, the broader population of the study and the discipline, if there is a discipline, the area of business, if the research is situated within a particular area of business, and so on. The researcher tries to tease out the implications of the data for all of those constituents.
4. The final stage in the four stages approach to data analysis is theorization. In this stage, the researcher looks back at the theoretical framework outlined in the literature review chapter, or section, of the study. The researcher examines the literature review to see if and how the findings of their study fit with or contradict the findings of the studies and the theorists as they have presented them in their literature review. The researcher, in writing the data analysis stage of the research, demonstrates how their findings fit with, or contradict, the findings of other (published) research projects. The researcher shows how, in the writing of the data analysis section or chapter of the research project, the research they are carrying out fits with the research published in the field or area. This is the process of theorization and it is the way in which the researcher knits their research into the body of knowledge. This is the way in which the researcher makes a contribution to the body of knowledge.

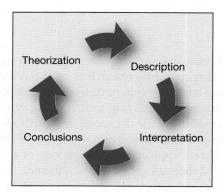

Figure 18.1 The four stages of analysis

The analytical framework

In the four frameworks approach to the research project, the fourth and final framework is the analytical framework. This framework takes its focus and direction from the conceptual framework for the research project. The conceptual framework for the research project is contained in the research statement or question. It contains all of the key concepts in the research project and it informs the development of the theoretical framework. Both the conceptual framework and the theoretical framework inform the methodological framework. They inform the selection and design of the methodology for the study and this methodology, with the conceptual and theoretical frameworks, informs the data collection methods used in the study, the questions asked and the areas explored in the data-gathering phase of the study. The methodological framework comprises the methodology, the data collection methods used in the project and all of the aspects of the process of carrying out the research. Finally, the analytical framework for the study is informed by the three preceding frameworks, the conceptual, theoretical and methodological frameworks.

If the methodology used in the research is phenomenology, then the data analysis process will be phenomenological. Similarly, if the methodology is grounded theory, then the data analysis process will be a grounded theory process. If the methodology calls for the study of texts, then the process of analysis is likely to be textual analysis, and if the methodology calls for the gathering of narratives, then the process of analysis is likely to be narrative analysis. Sometimes the process of analysis to be used in the study is as clearly indicated as this, sometimes it is not. When the process of analysis is not so clearly indicated, the researcher develops an approach to analysis that best fits the research project.

The approach to analysis, as well as being informed by the methodological framework, is informed by the conceptual framework. The conceptual framework guides the design and development of the process of data analysis for the research project. Along with the theoretical and methodological frameworks, it guides the design and development of the analytical framework for the project. The analytical framework is presented in the data analysis chapter of the thesis or in the data analysis section of the report of the research. The structure of the data analysis chapter, the subheadings in the chapter and the content of the subsections under each of the subheadings, are informed by the conceptual framework, the theoretical framework, and the data gathered and analyzed for the research project. Thus the four frameworks approach ensures that focus is maintained throughout the research process, and it helps to ensure that the research project, as it develops, remains properly and thoroughly integrated (see Table 18.1).

Table 18.1 The four frameworks

The conceptual framework	Contained in the research statement/question and in the stated aim of the research. The entire research project rests on the conceptual framework for the research project. The conceptual framework contains all of the key concepts in the research. The key concepts in the conceptual framework inform and guide the search for literature for the literature review, and they help structure the literature review.
The theoretical framework	Contained in the literature review. The literature review contains the theoretical framework for the research project. The structure and development of the literature review is guided and directed by the conceptual framework.
The methodological framework	The methodological framework is contained in the methodology chapter of the thesis or in the methodology section of the report of the research. The methodological framework contains all of the detail on how the research was carried out. The conceptual framework, the aim and objectives of the research and the theoretical framework inform and direct data collection for the research. They inform, guide and direct the questions asked in the fieldwork/data gathering for the research.
The analytical framework	The analytical framework is contained in the data analysis chapter of the thesis or in the data analysis section of the report of the research. Data are gathered for the research project in order to respond to the research statement/question, the overall aim and the objectives of the research project. The focus of data analysis is on responding to the research statement/question and the overall aim and objectives of the research. This helps ensure that the research project maintains focus, and it ensures that the researcher accomplishes what s/he set out to accomplish in undertaking the research, as formally stated in the research aim and objectives.

The four frameworks

- Conceptual Framework
- Theoretical Framework
- Methodological Framework
- *Analytical Framework*

A simple approach to qualitative data analysis

Basic qualitative data analysis begins with a close reading of the data. In order to achieve this, the researcher will read through the data over and over again. The researcher must become familiar with the data and eventually become immersed in the data. This close reading brings the researcher into the nuances of the data. The researcher must know and understand the data before they can begin to describe and analyze them.

In qualitative data analysis (as in quantitative data analysis), the researcher engages in coding the data. In qualitative research, the codes used by the researcher are words or concepts which the researcher identifies in the data as relevant to or even key or critical to the study. When the researcher has become immersed in the data through their close reading of the data, they begin this process of coding the data. Table 18.2 outlines the simple approach to qualitative data analysis presented in Chapter 17. (Please note that this is the data analysis process that Lian used in analyzing her qualitative data – see Lian's research project in Chapter 19.)

Table 18.2   A simple approach to qualitative data analysis

One simple approach to qualitative data analysis is to read through all of the data and, while reading, make a list of all of the themes that occur in the data. The themes will be the key ideas and the key concepts that the researcher considers important and relevant to the research, as s/he reads through the data transcripts. The researcher continues reading the transcripts and recording themes until no new themes emerge. Then the researcher takes the complete list of themes and explores them with a view to collapsing themes together. In other words, the researcher tries to condense the list of themes by fitting themes together that seem to logically fit together. In this way, the list of themes becomes shorter and more manageable.

When the researcher collapses themes together s/he needs to conceptualize a new theme, a theme that will encompass all the themes collapsed together. This process is a process of abstraction. Through this process, the researcher takes a step away from the raw data and a step towards an abstract or abstracted understanding of the data. Through this process of abstraction, the researcher comes closer to the meaning of the data, the meaning of the data in relation to the overall aim of the research. The researcher moves to deeper levels of abstraction in relation to the data, moving further and further away from the raw data, as s/he continues to collapse themes together. The researcher can colour code the themes; in colour coding the themes, s/he assigns colours arbitrarily, for example, red to the first theme, yellow to the second theme, and so on. The researcher reads through the transcripts assigning the colours to the parts of the data that represent each of the themes. In this way, the researcher can see at a glance each of the themes as they are represented in the data. The researcher then decides how to tell the story of the data, based on this thematic analysis, in the written account presented in the data analysis chapter of the thesis or in the data analysis section of the report of the research.

In engaging in qualitative data analysis, the researcher is above all concerned with the key concepts, the key words or key phrases in the data. It is important to remember that concepts are the building blocks of theory. It is from the work of connecting concepts together that theories are developed and/or extended:

1. The researcher engages in a process of attempting to group concepts together around key or core concepts.
2. Then the researcher groups the key or core concepts together in themes.
3. The researcher groups the themes together around key themes.
4. The researcher identifies the key themes in the data.

This process of analysis takes considerable reflection and engagement with the raw data. Eventually, the researcher presents an account of the project of data analysis, using the key themes that emerged in data analysis.

The research project should be fully integrated. The four frameworks approach to the research project is designed to facilitate the researcher in accomplishing this. Each aspect of the research process helps to build the next aspect. As this is the case, the themes that emerge from the process of data analysis should fit with the conceptual framework of the research project and they should fit with the theoretical framework constructed by the researcher for the research project. This is not to say that the researcher should be closed to new and unanticipated concepts, themes and ideas that emerge from the data. The researcher should, of course, be open to new ideas, fresh insights and unanticipated concepts and themes in the data. These ideas, insights and concepts and themes, if and when they are discovered, can be incorporated into the research project. If they are substantial, they can be used to extend the focus of the research project and, if they are less substantial, they can be integrated into the structures that the researcher has provided for the analytical framework of the research project.

Other approaches to data analysis

In **discourse analysis**, instead of themes, the researcher is focused on identifying and interpreting different discourses. The approach taken to analysis is the same or similar to the approach detailed earlier, but the focus is on discourses rather than themes. In narrative analysis, the researcher is focused on describing and interpreting the different narratives in the data. In semiotics, the researcher is focused on identifying signs in the data and on describing and interpreting the way in which signs are used in the data and the meanings of the signs in the data. Within semiotics the researcher uncovers the denotative (explicit) and the connotative (implicit) meanings of the data (see Chandler, 2017). In image-based research, the images can be analyzed using **thematic analysis**, using discourse analysis, narrative analysis, textual analysis, content analysis or semiotic analysis. Image-based research could be used as the data-gathering method, or as one of the data-gathering methods, in many methodological approaches. For example, in a case study, in a phenomenological study, in a grounded theory research project, in an action research project or in feminist research. As stated, the most appropriate approach to data analysis is based on what it is that the research project is attempting to accomplish, the methodology used in the research, the data collection methods used and the data gathered.

> **discourse analysis** A way of analyzing the social world as it is produced and represented in language.
>
> **thematic analysis** The analysis of data through the use of themes.

When the overall aim of a research project is to explore and describe how language is used in relation to a particular phenomenon, appropriate methodologies for such projects are methodologies that particularly focus on language. These include discourse analysis and narrative analysis. When the overall aim of a research project is to create a representation of some experience or culture, an appropriate methodology for such research is ethnography. Ethnography is the methodology in focus in Chapter 13. Data in ethnographic research can be analyzed thematically, discursively or semiotically; they can be analyzed using discourse analysis, content analysis, and so on. The key, as always, is that the approach to data analysis used in the research project must fit with the research project. Sometimes the overall aim of a research project is specifically to develop theory. Grounded theory is an appropriate methodology for such projects. A particular approach to data analysis has been developed within grounded theory. The Value of Good Research box describes grounded theory and a grounded theory approach to data analysis.

A grounded theory approach to data analysis, as detailed earlier, is a good approach to data analysis within different methodological approaches. It facilitates in-depth data analysis. Adaptations of the grounded theory approach to data analysis are used in many research projects. Grounded theory is the methodology in focus in this chapter.

THE VALUE OF GOOD RESEARCH

Focus on ground theory methodology

Grounded theory (GT) methodology, as explained in Chapter 9, is used when the specific focus of the research is on building theory from data. GT methodology is situated within a social constructivist paradigm, and it is rooted in symbolic interactionism. Very simply, symbolic interactionism is the formation of meaning between individuals through the ways in which they interact with each other.

GT was developed by Barney Glaser and Anselm Strauss (1967). Glaser and Strauss later split in their understanding of the methodology, a rift developed between them in terms of the understanding of the methodology. This is further evidence of the great debates that exist, and are ongoing, in relation to research and research methodologies in the social sciences. Within Glaser's GT methodology, the methodology can draw on quantitative or qualitative methods or both. Corbin and Strauss (2014), in their work on GT, present the methodology as a qualitative methodology.

In an interesting journal article, Murphy, Klotz and Kreiner (2017), provide an overview of the research methodology, GT. They explain that GT research has been carried out for 50 years in sociology, but it is only in recent years that business researchers have become interested in it. The authors explain that the primary goal of GT research is to build theory that is deeply informed by data, the data gathered for the research project. This is done in order to ensure that the theory that emerges from the research project can be said to be 'grounded' in data.

The authors explain in detail what grounded theory is. They also explain variations in the grounded theory approach. They explain in relatively simple terms the different philosophical frameworks within which GT research projects are developed. They make it clear that the different approaches can be differentiated in the first place in terms of their positivist (i.e. deductive) or interpretivist/constructivist (i.e. inductive) assumptions. We covered research philosophy in some detail in Chapter 4 of this textbook. This journal article provides an opportunity to revisit this topic.

The authors compare a GT approach to research with other inductive research methodologies, among them ethnography, discourse analysis and content analysis. This provides you with an opportunity to deepen your knowledge of these research methodologies. You will remember that these research methodologies, and many more, were introduced and explained in Chapter 9 of this textbook.

The authors present a succinct and very useful guide to 'doing' GT. They provide an overview of a GT approach, and they present a very useful flow chart, a visual representation of the process. They also provide a good introduction to data analysis in GT research. If you have an interest in GT research, you should source this journal article online and read it through. The journal article represents an excellent aid to learning about GT research. It provides a thorough introduction to GT methodology and GT research in a business context.

Data analysis in phenomenological research: an introduction

The focus of phenomenological research is on the study of lived experience from the perspective of those living the experience. A phenomenological inquiry tries to uncover the meaning, the structure and the essence of lived experience of the person or the group, or the community living the experience. Phenomenology is the research methodology in focus in Chapter 14. The main stages in data analysis in phenomenological research are shown in Table 18.3.

Table 18.3   Data analysis in phenomenological research

First stage	In the first stage, the researcher examines their own beliefs, views, perspectives and assumptions regarding the phenomenon under investigation. Then the researcher sets those aside. This process is also known as *bracketing*. This is a way in phenomenological data analysis of performing the essential reflexivity of the qualitative research project.
Second stage	In the second stage of phenomenological data analysis, the researcher lists all of the significant statements in the data. This is called, in Moustakas' (1994) terms, horizontalization of the data. The final list eliminates repetitive and overlapping statements. The statements will be significant in terms of the areas considered, examined and/or explored in the data-gathering phase of the research. The researcher then clusters statements together in meaning units.
Third stage	In the third stage, using the meaning units the researcher develops a textual description of the phenomenon. Then the researcher develops a structural description of how the phenomenon was experienced. The researcher does this first to develop their own account of the experience. The researcher then does this for each participant in the research. After this, a description of the phenomenon is written which encompasses all of the experiences. Through this process, the researcher develops a thick description of the meaning, structure and essence of the experience.

The process of analysis for phenomenological research, detailed in Table 18.3, has been developed specifically for this methodology. As can be seen, it is a quite distinct approach to data analysis. It is important that the researcher uses, and fully understands, the most appropriate approach to analysis for the data they have gathered. A great deal has been written about the different approaches to qualitative data analysis. You should source and read detailed and reliable material on the approach to data analysis you propose using in your research project. This chapter is simply a general basic introduction to qualitative data analysis.

Data analysis in case study research: an introduction

In case study research, data analysis involves developing a thick description of the case being studied. Case study research generally calls for the analysis of multiple streams of data. The data may be quantitative or qualitative, or both. There is a good introduction to quantitative data analysis in Chapter 19 of this textbook.

Within a case study methodology, a thematic approach to qualitative data analysis (as detailed earlier in this chapter) would be appropriate (see Table 18.2). Content analysis or discourse analysis, or documentary analysis, where appropriate, can be used in case study research. The important thing is that the approach to data analysis used should be the approach best suited to the data. The important issues in data analysis are the comprehensiveness and the validity of the data gathered on the case(s) and the quality of the analysis conducted with the data. De Massis and Kotlar (2014) provide a good and relatively simple overview of case study research, including analysis in case study research, in their journal article on the case study in family business research. If you have an interest in case study research, you should source this journal article online. You will find it interesting and very helpful. It's a useful guide for qualitative research developed using a case study research methodology.

Data analysis in qualitative content analysis: an introduction

Content analysis has application in both quantitative and qualitative research. In qualitative research the focus is on developing a deep understanding of some aspect of human experience. Data gathered in a qualitative research project, or qualitative data gathered in a mixed methods research project, are gathered for the purpose of providing that deep understanding. In data analysis, the researcher reduces a large amount of data into a succinct and deeply informative account of the key findings to emerge from the analysis of the data. The findings of the analysis conducted must relate to the aim of the research. It is in this way that the conceptual framework development for the research project guides and directs the development of the analytical framework for the research project.

In their journal article, Erlingsson and Brysiewicz (2017), provide a good introduction to qualitative content analysis. This journal article represents a good learning aid in relation to qualitative content analysis. The authors provide a succinct glossary of the terms used in the approach to data analysis they present in the journal article, and they present a flow chart detailing an example of analysis in practice. If you have an interest in qualitative content analysis, you should source this article online and read it through. You will learn a great deal from it about qualitative content analysis, and if you decide to use qualitative content analysis in your research project, you can use this article as a guide.

The Value of Good Research box contains an interesting study of the role of branded products in nostalgia. The data-gathering methods used consisted of two sets of interviews and a projective technique. The projective technique involved showing pictures of the products and brands to interviewees, during interviews, in order to explore the thoughts and memories the products and brands evoke for them.

Using a content analysis approach to data analysis, the researchers analyzed the content of the interview transcripts in three different and distinct stages:

1. In the first stage, the transcripts were analyzed discursively (data analysis focused on the discourses in the data).
2. In the second stage, they were analyzed using a computer software package specifically designed to analyze words/vocabulary.
3. In the third stage, a semiotic analysis of the texts (the interview transcripts) was carried out.

It would be a good idea to access this article online and to read it through. As you can see, a very thorough analysis was carried out. The three stages in the data analysis process undertaken in the research enabled the researchers to immerse themselves in the data. The three stages provided different perspectives on the data and different insights into the data. You can see in the extract how and where the researchers theorized their work, how and where they knitted the findings of their research into the findings of other researchers. The process of theorization is the fourth stage in data analysis in the four stages approach to data analysis.

THE VALUE OF GOOD RESEARCH

In their research (Kessous and Roux, 2008, 'A semiotic analysis of nostalgia as a connection to the past', *Qualitative Market Research, 11*(2): 192–212), the authors focused on a semiotic analysis of the meaning of nostalgia related to products and brands. Their research involved a two-stage interview process, each interviewee was interviewed twice. The interviews took place at one-year intervals. Informants were interviewed about products and brands connected to nostalgic feelings. Pictures of products and brands evoked in the first interview were shown again in the second interview. Informants were asked to explain what came to mind for them when they looked at the pictures.

The interviews were taped and transcribed and based on the transcripts of the interviews, a three-step content analysis was performed.

The researchers state that content analysis was performed in three stages. First, all of the interviews were reviewed to identify discernable patterns as they emerged from the texts and to define a coding criterion. From this stage, the researchers distinguished first-time nostalgia from longstanding nostalgia. In the second stage, the vocabulary the interviewees used when expressing nostalgic experiences was examined. In order to do this, a software package called Sphinx Lexica was used. This software, according to the researchers, enabled a fast key-word search of the transcripts. This, they said, made it possible to select the products/brands that were the most frequently mentioned and these could then be related to their spatial-temporal-emotional-personal context. The researchers state that 'the simple description and quantification' of data quickly becomes sterile if not completed by a willingness to understand the meaning and the origin of frequency, textual structures, lexical associations or categories. It was decided, we are told, that in a third stage in analysis a complementary semiotic approach was to be used to overcome this limitation.

The results of this study showed that some individuals are attached to special possessions, 'either replaceable (e.g. food) or irreplaceable (e.g. family jewels), which are rooted in a specific period of time, place or social situation'. The researchers state that 'nostalgia connects objects, individuals and events across time and place'. They said that 'in each case, some symbolic reminder is sought so that the memories attached to the object will remain vivid and real'. They said that, 'furthermore, possessions derive their value by expressing or reinforcing the sense of self'.

Through their analysis of the data gathered in the interviews, the researchers established that the interviewees experienced four nostalgic moments: (1) everyday past, (2) uniqueness, (3) tradition and (4) transition, and these were linked to specific brands and objects. In conclusion, the researchers suggested that these four distinct moments can provide a better understanding of the emotional attachment of consumers to brands and products.

PRESENTING QUALITATIVE DATA

The key to the presentation of data is the story or the narrative the researcher is trying to tell in relation to the data. The narrative presented will be the one that best, and most completely, responds to the research question/statement, the aim and the objectives of the research. The researcher decides, based on the narrative, how to present the analysis of the data, and in what order the analyzed data should be provided. The data should be presented in the order in which the reader will best be able to make sense of it. As explained in Chapter 17, the researcher constructs a framework for the data analysis chapter based on the key issues/themes in the narrative to be presented. The researcher creates a structure for the data analysis chapter. The researcher then presents the analysis within that structure. Table 18.4 provides a succinct overview of the key issues in presenting the analysis of qualitative data.

Table 18.4 Issues in presenting the analysis of qualitative data

The process of analyzing data is a substantial and often a protracted process. The process of data analysis tends to generate very substantial amounts of material, i.e. the results of the analysis. It would not be possible to report all of the results of the analysis or all of the findings from the analysis. What is reported is a synopsis of the analysis. This synopsis is presented in the data analysis chapter of the thesis or in the data analysis section of the report of the research.

Clearly, the structure of the chapter will reflect the process of analysis undertaken. For example, a thematic analysis will be presented in themes.

The structure of a chapter on a phenomenological data analysis process will reflect the complexity of the lived experiences examined in the research. Analyzed data in a phenomenological study are presented in a natural fashion, in order to best describe the experience or phenomenon studied.

The structure of a grounded theory data analysis process will evidence the GT process of data analysis and the emerging theory that the process is designed to generate. Analyzed data in a GT project will be presented in terms of the theory generated, with the core category presented first and the other categories then related to it.

The key to presenting data is to remain faithful in the presentation of the data to the methodology used in the research project. The manner in which analyzed data are presented in the thesis or report of the research should fit with research methodology used in the research project. The research methodology used in the research project will guide the process of analysis used in data analysis. The methodology and the data analysis procedure or process used should inform the manner in which the data are presented in the chapter.

Within the structure decided on for the data analysis chapter/section, analyzed data may be presented in terms of the most simple to the most complex, with the simplest elements of the data being presented first, followed by progressively more complex elements of the analysis. It may be presented in terms of the least important to the most important, with the least important data being presented first, followed by progressively more important data. It may be presented in terms of the most important data to the least important, with the most important aspects of data analysis being presented first, followed by progressively less important aspects of the data.

Data from a narrative analysis project will be presented in terms of narratives. The process of presenting data in narratives can be used in other research projects where narratives can be discerned in the data and where there is sense and logic in presenting data in this manner.

Data from a discourse analysis project will be presented in terms of discourses. The process of presenting data in discourses can be used in other research projects where discourses can be discerned in the data and where there is sense and logic in presenting the data in this manner.

In quantitative research the researcher uses numbers to support the analysis. In qualitative research, the researcher uses words and concepts and images to support the analysis. These words, concepts and images are drawn from the raw data, as numbers in quantitative analysis are drawn from the raw data. The words, concepts and images drawn from the raw data may be presented in the written account of the analysis in terms of direct quotes, or in the form of photographs or other still images or drawings, etc. Aspects of raw data are presented in the data analysis chapter to support the narrative unfolding in that chapter. This is done in the same way as numbers, statistics, graphs and charts are presented in the chapter on data analysis to support the narrative unfolding in that chapter about the quantitative data gathered for the research project.

In presenting an analysis of qualitative data, the researcher details the process of analysis and the outcome of the analysis and supports all of this with reference to the raw data, the quotes and/or images. In the writing of the analysis, the researcher goes through the four stages of data analysis: description, interpretation, conclusion and theorization.

Data reduction and data display in quantitative data analysis are accomplished through the presentation of frequencies and other statistical presentations, through the presentation of tables, charts and figures. In qualitative analysis, data reduction and data display is accomplished through the presentation of direct quotes and/or taken from the data. Data reduction can be accomplished by displaying and presenting data in matrices.

Matrices

A matrix (plural **matrices**) is a display that the researcher creates with their data. Like a table or a figure in quantitative data analysis, the construction of a matrix in qualitative data analysis can provide the researcher with new and fresh insights into their data. When data are presented in a matrix, or in a table, or in a figure, it can be easy to see patterns and trends in the data. Patterns and trends in the data can become evident when data are presented in such a format.

> **matrices** Data displays that the researcher creates for the purposes of reduction of qualitative data.

The researcher decides, based on their requirements and based on the data available, how to construct the matrix, what form it should take, how many columns, rows and cells it should have, and so on. The researcher constructs a matrix for the data in order to reduce and display the data. Through such displays it may be possible to develop new insights into the data, into trends and patterns in the data, and into different relationships in the data.

The case study at the end of this chapter details the research of Götze *et al.* (2009), who used diaries to study the impact that children have on their parents' purchase decisions. The article on which the case study is based provides an interesting example of the use of a matrix of qualitative data. In addition, in their textbook Miles and Huberman (2014) provide substantial guidance and support in terms of qualitative data analysis and the presentation of such data. They provide guidance in terms of presenting data in matrices.

MIXED-METHODS RESEARCH

'Mixed methods' means that both quantitative and qualitative approaches are used in the research project. Quantitative and qualitative research methodologies have different philosophical foundations and different epistemological and ontological assumptions. Arguments against the use of mixed methods usually hold that these distinctions are not, or perhaps cannot, be observed in mixed methods research. You will notice as you read accounts of different research projects, that different methodologies and data-gathering methods are used in different ways, to different effect, all of the time.

If a researcher decides to undertake mixed-methods research, then that researcher should have the necessary skills in both quantitative and qualitative research in order to undertake, carry out and present mixed methods research. Grafton, Lillie and Mahama (2011) provide good guidance on mixed methods research. Their focus is on the use of mixed methods research in accounting.

While it is possible, and indeed often advisable, to use mixed methods in research, it is important to understand the paradigmatic issues involved in such approaches. It is, as always, necessary to know what it is you are trying to accomplish with your research, and how the research methodologies and methods you employ in your research project will facilitate this.

REAL WORLD RESEARCH

A thorough engagement with data analysis

It sometimes happens that instead of engaging in an appropriately scholarly way and detailing in the written account of their research their scholarship in relation to qualitative data analysis, students simply describe in the most basic way possible the data that they have gathered. Clearly, this is not acceptable.

In the preceding pages, there are introductions to some of the main approaches to analyzing qualitative data. Enough detail is given to introduce you to the different approaches to qualitative data analysis and to signal to you some of the differences in those approaches. When a particular approach to qualitative data analysis has been decided on, it will be necessary to read substantial detailed accounts of that process. In fact, the student researcher is expected to become quite expert on the methodology and processes of data analysis they use in their research project, in the same way as they are expected to become quite expert on the phenomenon that is the focus of their research.

If you have gathered and analyzed both quantitative and qualitative data, then both types of data will be presented in the data analysis chapter. Some researchers choose to present the findings of quantitative and qualitative data separately, presenting one first and then the other, and some choose to present them together. Either way, the key to presenting the analyzed data is always the narrative to be told of the data. To support the narrative, the researcher presents data, in the form of statistics, in tables and figures, in direct quotes, in images and in data matrices.

It is important when mixing or blending quantitative and qualitative data that the language used is sensitive and nuanced to the different kinds of data described, and the various kinds and depths of experience presented. As we know, the researcher is present in the presentation of the qualitative data, and absent in the presentation of the quantitative data. The researcher presents an objective account of quantitative data (although whether or not any data or any research can be said to be really objective is debatable) and a subjective account of experiences that are documented and explored in qualitative data. The researcher must subtly blend both kinds of data and present them in ways that are sensitive to the underlying epistemological and ontological perspectives and concerns of both.

Cremer and Ramasamy (2009) in their study of strategies for small internationalizing firms in China, understood very clearly what they could and could not accomplish with quantitative research and what they would accomplish with qualitative research. Their study encompassed a survey of senior managers in New Zealand, and a focus group discussion with executives in China. It would be a good idea to source the article detailing their research and read it through. As you read, make a note of how and to what effect the authors used mixed methods in this study.

In the journal article detailed in the Real World Research box, 'The rise and relevance of qualitative research', Alasuutari (2010) explores the rise and relevance of qualitative research. This is a very useful journal article. In it, the author presents a very accessible account of quantitative and qualitative research and an analysis of the growth of interest in recent decades in mixed methods research.

REAL WORLD RESEARCH

How theory influences research

In this journal article (Alasuutari, 2010, 'The rise and relevance of qualitative research', *International Journal of Social Research Methodology, 13*(2): 139–155), the author considers the rise of qualitative research. The article provides a brief history of quantitative research and qualitative social research and this is followed by a detailed discussion of the evolution of qualitative research.

The article highlights a growth of interest, from the 1980s, in mixed-methods research. The author highlights a new journal launched in 2007, the *Journal of Mixed Methods Research*. The author writes about the fact that many qualitative researchers have incorporated different quantitative approaches, such as cross-tabulation of their research (Alasuutari, 1995). He states that texts have appeared that go beyond the traditional qualitative–quantitative distinction. He says that there is increasingly in the social sciences a willingness to engage in different types of research practice.

The increased demand for quantitative research, he writes, is due in particular to the need for increased accountability in public expenditure and a requirement that research should serve policy ends. He says that the obligation that public policies and practices be grounded in evidence-based, scientifically validated research has grown in momentum since the early 1990s. This has led to developments in the social sciences, among them the systematic review process.

He writes that while one faction of qualitative researchers rejects the idea of qualitative research as representations of truth and its policy relevance (and he references Denzin and Lincoln, 2000 here), another faction has responded by trying to develop more rigorous and convincing arguments for their evidence and criteria against which such studies can be measured. He writes that the increased interest in mixed methods can be seen as part of the same developments, where researchers use both quantitative and qualitative methods in their research in order to improve overall the validity of their research.

Cremer and Ramasamy (2009) provide an interesting example of mixed-methods research in their study of strategies for small internationalizing firms in China (detailed earlier).

It is possible, Alasuutari believes, that the interest in and increased employer need for quantitative methods might make us miss the fact that qualitative methods have been consistently growing in strength. He says that a recent study (Payne *et al.*, 2004), shows that only about one in 20 published papers in mainstream British journals uses quantitative analysis. He says the figures are the same for Finland, the country in which he is based, and that a similar trend can be seen from the 1990s onward in Canada and the USA.

The paper asks why qualitative research has achieved such a strong position in social science research, in particular when the default assumption often is that scientifically sound research is research based on quantification and statistical analysis as in, for example, the randomized controlled trial (RCT), a methodology adopted from medicine. It is this question that Alasuutari addresses in his paper.

(Continued)

In an interesting insight he asserts that social science is more about running commentaries on changing societies than the accumulation of knowledge about a stable system. In other words, realities are not fixed but are fluid and ever changing.

It would be a useful exercise for you to source this article and read it through. The article clearly explains the development of both quantitative and qualitative social science research, the different contributions both make, and the issues in engaging in mixed-methods research.

From your reading of the article, can you outline the relative strengths of quantitative and qualitative research? Can you explain the issues, as they are detailed in the article, in engaging in mixed-methods research?

Computer-assisted qualitative data analysis software (CAQDAS)

CAQDAS is particularly helpful with large data sets. Using CAQDAS, the computer software stores and manages the data. This is particularly important, as discussed in Chapter 17, in terms of data management. When all of the qualitative data gathered for a research project is kept within a file in a computer software package, the data are relatively safe and easily secured. In addition, the management of the data throughout the process of data analysis is simple and safe. The process of analysis itself is highly organized within the structure of the data analysis package. Using a computer software package for qualitative data analysis, the data are coded using the software, making the process more organized and less liable to error. When analyzing large quantities of qualitative data by hand, it is too easy to make mistakes, to overlook data and to miss relevant issues or even critical issues within the data.

Atlas.ti is one of the main qualitative data analysis software packages. This software package has its own website (www.atlasti.com). The website contains a lot of useful and interesting information about the software package and, most importantly, it provides tutorials and a free trial.

Using Atlas.ti, each project is a distinct hermeneutic unit (HU). All of the files associated with the project are held within each HU. As well as the data files, there are files of quotes, codes and memos. These files are the means by which data are coded within Atlas.ti. Documents, which are the transcripts of interviews, focus groups, etc. are assigned to the HU by the researcher. When they have been assigned, they can be coded and quotations can be developed within them.

Another software package designed for the analysis of qualitative data is NVivo (www.qsrinternational.com). The website provides many different free online tutorials on the software. A further introduction to the use of CAQDAS is provided by Quinlan (2011).

If you have a substantial amount of qualitative data, you should use a software package to help you analyze your data. If you are interested in developing your research skills, whether or not you have substantial amounts of qualitative data, it is important to learn how to use the software packages designed for the analysis of qualitative data. It is likely that your university or college provides one or more of these software packages and it probably provides tutorials on how to use the software package. You should avail yourself of any such facilities and opportunities for training and up-skilling whenever you can.

CASE STUDY

A qualitative study using a diary method

The research project outlined here is a study of the influence that children have on their parents' purchasing behaviour (Götze, Prange and Uhrovska, 2009). The data collection method used in the study is the diary. In the study, 14 parents of young teenage children were asked to keep a diary for two weeks. They were asked to record in the diary purchase decisions they made in relation to innovative products and the impact their young teenage children had on those decisions. The research project is interesting in terms of the data-gathering method used and the data gathered using this method. The researchers suggest that the diary method is a good way of investigating phenomena that occur partly subconsciously. The diary is a method that eliminates a number of biases, for instance interviewer bias, respondent bias and retrospection bias. The data in the diaries, the researchers contend, could not have been gathered using a questionnaire or in an interview. The synopsis presented here provides a good overview of the research. There is a great deal more useful and interesting detail on this study in the original article.

The researchers in this research project studied the impact that children have on their parents' purchasing

(Continued)

behaviour. To gather data for the research project the researchers asked 14 parents to keep a diary in which they recorded their experiences in relation to their children influencing their purchasing behaviour. The value of the research, according to the researchers, is primarily in the insights for marketers that this study provides.

We are told that, over time, the influence of children has received increasing attention and studies have largely concentrated on the nature and extent of children's influence on parental consumer behaviour. The literature reviewed for the study showed that children not only influence overall family decision making, they are presumed also to impact the purchase of innovative products. As they are often more knowledgeable on certain novel products like consumer electronics or multimedia, they participate in the innovation-buying process quite actively. The researchers show that children's influence on parental spending is a vast market. The researchers state that it is absolutely vital for companies to know whether and how children influence their parents with regard to the purchase and use of innovative products, and while it might be presumed that companies already know about children's impact, current research provides evidence to the contrary.

The researchers present the diary method as an excellent instrument for studying activities, events, behaviour and other phenomena that occur on a daily basis and in situ, i.e. within the context of a given situation. They hold that, in particular, activities that cannot be remembered or are not executed day-by-day are difficult to measure by conventional survey questions. They say that the diary method allows people to express themselves in their own words and frequently report on the subject under investigation; and as respondents write their diary entry shortly after the activity to be recorded occurs, diaries can provide relevant and real records of experience. They say that although the diary method is not as common in research as other data-collecting techniques, the number of scientific disciplines that use the diary method is wide and ranges from sociology to medicine and psychology. They do say however, that studies in marketing and market research that apply the diary method are still sparse.

This diary study was carried out in June 2005, in Austria. A total of 14 respondents were recruited by means of a snowball sampling method. A prerequisite for a participant to be recruited was that s/he was a parent of at least one 10- to 15-year-old child. The researchers tell us that this age group was chosen as adolescents of this age have gained full cognitive development, they understand the concept of money and they have already developed skills related to information processing. Compared to younger children, they have more experience with products and they have acquired some knowledge on consumer roles.

All 14 parents in the sample agreed to keep the diary for two weeks. The diaries were booklets of A5 size. They were unstructured because the researchers wanted to give the parents as much freedom in reporting as possible. Before starting their diary, each family was visited personally and the method of diary writing explained using a set of instructions.

The researchers decided that the first section of the diary was to focus on parent–child interaction related to consumerism. Purchase decisions were to be described in detail, i.e. discussions, planning or execution of purchases. Participating parents were asked to report if the child expressed requests for any products, directly or indirectly, and they were asked to describe the circumstances of such requests. Parents were asked to note their reaction to such requests. In the second section of the diary, parents were asked to record the family's contact with products that were novel to the family, e.g. consumer electronics. In this section, the researchers were interested in the children's influence on parental decision on the adoption of innovations. They also wanted to see if parents learned new skills from their children regarding new technology products.

The researchers stressed the importance of making entries daily and of also reporting seemingly minor or unimportant events and activities.

The data were analyzed using content analysis and an overview of the diary data is presented in the article in a tabular format.

According to the diary entries, children applied various strategies to influence their parents. However, children seemed to stick with a specific strategy if it worked before. So the strategy used seemed to depend on the child's characteristics as well as the (expected) parental response to it. Most often (for approximately one-third of the products), the children used persuasion strategies, mainly reasonable requests or they provided their opinion on an innovation. Sometimes they would try to persuade their parents referring to 'everybody else', e.g. friends who owned the innovative product, and sometimes they would simply beg for the product in question.

The researchers concluded that the diary reports showed that children influence parent's decisions on the adoption of innovation and that their influence is strongest in problem recognition (knowledge stage). They found that children who are more knowledgeable on certain products than their parents, or have mutual hobbies with their parents, exert considerable influence also in the information search (persuasion stage) and evaluations of alternatives stage (decision stage).

(Continued)

Finally, they concurred with other researchers that it would be very useful to develop consumer decision-making typologies that specifically account for children's influence in these different phases.

You should source the original article and read it through. As you read the original article, note in particular the matrix presented of the data collected and the direct quotes from respondents that are presented in the matrix. The researchers have done this, we are told, to maintain the 'individualism and subjectivity of each diary'.

Question: What do you think of diaries as a means of gathering data? Why were the researchers concerned with maintaining the individualism and subjectivity of each diary?

END OF CHAPTER QUESTIONS

1 Outline a simple approach to qualitative data analysis.

2 What are matrices and how are they used in qualitative data analysis?

3 Explain the fundamental importance of language in qualitative data analysis.

4 Explain the role of the researcher in qualitative data analysis.

5 Name and explain four different approaches to qualitative data analysis.

6 Sketch a model of the four stages in data analysis and explain how the model works.

7 What is the analytical framework in the four frameworks approach to the research project and how does it fit with the other frameworks in the four frameworks approach?

8 What is meant by the term mixed-methods research?

9 Outline and explain the key issues and potential problems in mixed-methods research.

10 Explain what is meant by the term CAQDAS and name two qualitative data analysis software packages. What are the key advantages to using CAQDAS?

11 Explore the advantages of computerized software such as ATLAS.ti. www.atlasti.com. How do you think it might assist in coding something like a depth interview or a collage created by a respondent?

12 Design an interview schedule to explore student satisfaction with your college bookstore. Interview five classmates and then arrange the data gathered into a data matrix.

REFERENCES

Alasuutari, P. (1995) *Researching Culture: Qualitative Method and Cultural Studies.* London: Sage.

Alasuutari, P. (2010) 'The rise and relevance of qualitative research', *International Journal of Social Research Methodology*, 13(2): 139–155.

Chandler, D. (2017) *Semiotics: The Basics*, Oxon and New York: Routledge.

Corbin, J. and Strauss, A. (2014) *Basics of Qualitative Research: Techniques and Procedures for Developing Grounded Theory* (4th edn), Thousand Oaks, CA: Sage.

Cremer, R.D. and Ramasamy, B. (2009) 'Engaging China: strategies for the small internationalizing firm', *Journal of Business Strategy*, 30(6): 15–26.

De Massis, A. and Kotlar, J. (2014) 'The case study method in family business research: Guidelines for qualitative scholarship', *Journal of Family Business Strategy*, 5: 15–29.

Denzin, N.K. and Lincoln, Y.S. (2000) *Handbook of Qualitative Research*, Thousand Oaks, CA: Sage.

Erlingsson, C. and Brysiewicz, P. (2017) 'A hands-on guide to doing content analysis', *African Journal of Emergency Medicine*, 7: 93–99.

Geertz, C. (1973) *The Interpretation of Cultures*, New York: Basic Books.

Glaser, B. and Strauss, A. (1967) *The Discovery of Grounded Theory: Strategies for Qualitative Research*, Chicago, IL: Aldine.

Götze, E., Prange, C. and Uhrovska, I. (2009) 'Children's impact on innovation decision making: a diary study', *European Journal of Marketing*, 43(1/2): 264–295.

Grafton, J., Lillis, A.M. and Mahama, H. (2011) 'Mixed methods research in accounting', *Qualitative Research in Accounting & Management*, 8(1): 5–21.

Kessous, A. and Roux, E. (2008) 'A semiotic analysis of nostalgia as a connection to the past', *Qualitative Market Research*, 11(2): 192–212.

Miles,.B. and Huberman, A.M. (2014) *Qualitative Data Analysis: A Methods Sourcebook*, London, California, New Delhi, Singapore: Sage.

Moustakas, C.E. (1994) *Phenomenological Research Methods*, Thousand Oaks, CA: Sage.

Murphy, C., Klotz, A.C. and Kreiner, G.E. (2017) 'Blue skies and black boxes: The promise and practice of grounded theory in human resource management research', *Human Resource Management Review*, 27: 291–305.

Payne, G. and Payne J. (2004) *Key Concepts in Social Research*. London: Sage

Quinlan, C. (2011) *Business Research Methods*, South Western Cengage.

RECOMMENDED READING

Ball, M.S. and Smith, G.W.H. (1992) *Analyzing visual data* (Paper), Qualitative Research Methods, Series 24, London: Sage.

Banks, M. and Zeitlyn, D. (2015) *Visual Methods in Social Research*, London, California, New Delhi, Singapore: Sage.

Bell, J. and Waters, S. (2014) *Doing Your Research Project* (6th edn), Maidenhead: Open University Press.

Creswell, J. and Creswell, D.J. (2018) *Research Design: Qualitative, Quantitative and Mixed Methods Approaches* (5th edn), London, California, New Delhi, Singapore: Sage.

Denscombe, M. (2017) *The Good Research Guide: For Small-scale Social Research Projects* (5th edn), Maidenhead: Open University Press.

Denzin, N.K. and Lincoln, Y.S. (eds) (2018) *The SAGE Handbook of Qualitative Research* (5th edn), California, London, New Delhi, Singapore: Sage.

Fairclough, N. (2013) *Critical Discourse Analysis: The Critical Study of Language*, Oxon and New York: Routledge.

Flick, U. (2014) *An Introduction to Qualitative Research* (5th edn), London: Sage.

Gray, D.E. (2018) *Doing Research in the Real World*, London, California, New Delhi, Singapore: Sage.

Hesse-Biber, S.N. (2010) *Mixed Methods Research: Merging Theory with Practice*, New York: Guilford Press.

Lewins, A. and Silver, C. (2014) *Using Software in Qualitative Research: a step-by-step guide* (2nd edn), London, California, New Delhi, Singapore: Sage.

Neuman, W.L. (2014) *Social Research Methods: Qualitative and Quantitative Approaches* (7th edn), Essex, England: Pearson Education Ltd.

Prosser, J. (2001) *Image-based Research: A Sourcebook for Qualitative Researchers*, London: Routledge.

Robson, C. and McCartan, K. (2016) *Real World Research*, John Wiley & Sons Ltd.

Rose, G. (2016) *Visual Methodologies*, London, California, New Delhi, Singapore: Sage.

Seale, C. (2007) *The Quality of Qualitative Research*, Thousand Oaks, CA: Sage.

Silverman, D. (2004) *Interpreting Qualitative Data: Methods for Analysing Talk, Text and Interaction* (2nd edn), London, California, New Delhi: Sage.

Silverman, D., (2017), *Doing Qualitative Research* (5th edn), London, California, New Delhi, Singapore: Sage.

Simpson, M. and Tuson, J. (2003) *Using Observation in Small-scale Research, a Beginner's Guide*, The SCRE Centre, Glasgow: University of Glasgow.

Van Leeuwen, T. (2005) *Introducing Social Semiotics*, Oxon and New York: Routledge.

CHAPTER 19

ANALYZING QUANTITATIVE DATA

LEARNING OBJECTIVES

At the end of this chapter, the student should:

- Understand what descriptive statistics are and why they are used.

- Understand what inferential statistics are and why they are used.

- Be able to create and interpret simple tabulation tables.

- Understand how cross-tabulation can reveal relationships.

- Be able to test a hypothesis about an observed mean compared to some standard.

- Recognize when a particular bivariate statistical test is appropriate.

RESEARCH SKILLS

At the end of this chapter, the student should, using the exercises on Cengage Brain, be able to:

- Carry out an analysis of the data set presented.

- Critique the data provided in terms of the stated aim of the research project.

The aim of this chapter is to develop the focus on quantitative data and quantitative data analysis started in Chapter 17 and to teach you, the student, how to engage in quantitative data analysis. The chapter explains quantitative data analysis and the key concepts in quantitative data analysis. It demonstrates the processes involved in quantitative data analysis and basic statistical analysis. The use of visual displays of quantitative data analysis, charts and graphs is explored and the importance of visual displays of quantitative data is explained.

INTRODUCTION

Quantitative data are numerical data and quantitative data analysis is the analysis of quantitative data using statistical methods. As you know from your reading of Chapter 17, basic quantitative data analysis can be carried out by simply adding up or summarizing the numbers in a data set. More complex quantitative data analysis can be carried out using a calculator or a spreadsheet, for example an Excel spreadsheet. Large quantitative data sets can be analyzed using a computer software package such as SPSS. The software packages Excel, SAS, STATA, EViews, and SPSS account for most of the statistical analysis conducted in business research. University students may also be exposed to MINITAB, which is sometimes said to be preferred by economists. However, MINITAB has traditionally been viewed as being less user friendly than other choices.

The model of the research process, outlined at the start of Chapter 1 (Figure 1.1) illustrates where in the research process data analysis occurs. The researcher gathers data for the research project and then analyzes those data. In the process of analyzing data, the researcher interprets the data and comes to some conclusion(s) about them. Finally, the researcher theorizes the data, i.e. knits the findings of their research into the findings of other research projects as they are detailed in the theoretical framework constructed for the research project.

The research detailed in the Value of Good Research box recommends to business owners and managers the use of an eco-survey to establish how much energy their business uses and the cost of that energy. An eco-survey allows you to gather data on the ecological impact of your business. To help you analyze the data, you can plot the data on a graph or chart. Creating a graph or a chart from quantitative data is a useful and efficient way of presenting data. It often happens that a visual representation of data, in a graph and/or a chart, yields new insights into data. Patterns and trends in data are often rendered visible through the visual display of data.

THE VALUE OF GOOD RESEARCH

Eco-surveys can be used in a number of ways. They can be used to monitor the environment. They can be used to monitor environmental impact. They can be used for environmental assessment and environmental management. In addition, eco-surveys can monitor the cost of energy use.

There is now a great deal of concern for the environment. This concern is international, indeed it is global. According to NASA (National Aeronautics and Space Administration), the Earth's climate has changed throughout history and in the last 650 000 years there have been seven cycles of glacial advance and retreat. NASA explains that the last ice age ended about 7000 years ago, its end marking the beginning of the modern climate era and the beginning of human civilization. The current global warming trend, according to NASA, is particularly significant because the evidence points to it as being man-made, and with the speed of warming in this current trend, climate change is proceeding at an unprecedented pace.

An eco-survey can establish how much energy a business is using and how the business could cut down on its energy usage. An eco-survey can provide good data, data on which policy and practice in a business can be planned for, developed and implemented. Following an eco-survey, a company can cut energy usage and wastage, save money on energy bills and at the same time reduce the company's carbon footprint, its impact on the environment. For more information on climate change see NASA Global Climate Change, climate. nasa.gov

The four frameworks

- Conceptual Framework
- Theoretical Framework
- Methodological Framework
- *Analytical Framework*

Good research is the key to insight and understanding. Rather than relying on guesswork, carry out the research, gather good data and analyze them. The analysis of data and the presentation of that analysis, as explained in the previous chapters, provide the analytical framework for the research project. The analytical framework is the fourth and final framework in the four frameworks approach to the research project. The researcher presents the analytical framework for the research project in the chapter on data analysis in the thesis or in the section on analysis in the report of the research. The chapter on data analysis contains a full account of the analysis carried out on the data and a complete presentation of the findings that emerge from that data analysis. The four frameworks are detailed in Figure 19.1.

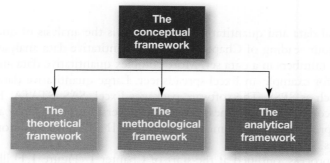

Figure 19.1 The four frameworks

Data analysis is in itself, as explained in the previous chapters, a major project. The work of analyzing data for the research project goes on for as much time as necessary, or as much time as can be allowed. If you are using Computer Assisted Data Analysis (CADA), then the work of analyzing your data takes place on your computer. This usually makes the management of data a relatively simple and secure task. If you are not using CADA, you will be analyzing your data by hand. If this is the case, the work of analyzing your data will take place at your desk, which may make the management of data a complex and relatively insecure task. Wherever the work takes place, it is in-depth work, and it is complex and time-consuming. What is presented in the data analysis chapter, the written report of the analysis of the data gathered, is a synopsis of this work.

The researcher presents a synopsis of their data analysis in the data analysis chapter, s/he presents the key findings, the key data and the key interpretations they have made in relation to the data. The researcher, steeped in the analysis of the data, plans the data analysis chapter for the thesis, the data analysis section of the research report, and constructs a framework for this chapter or section. This framework is the analytical framework for the research project, the fourth framework in the four frameworks approach to the research project.

WORKING WITH QUANTITATIVE DATA

In this section, we will consider working with secondary data, data that already exist, such as government statistics. We also consider working with data that you, the researcher, create yourself. Data created for the research project is primary data. Secondary data are data from secondary sources: data that already exists. The distinction between primary and secondary sources can be ambiguous. For a good introduction to secondary sources see Quinlan 2011, Chapter 9 'Using Secondary Data and Archival Sources'.

As an exercise, it is a good idea to browse through data relevant to your research that is available on the websites of national and international organizations. This will give you a sense of what data are available and may give you an idea for your research project. Working with an existing set of data is easier in one way than working with data you have created yourself; you don't have to go through the process of actually creating the data.

Take a look at the data presented on the website of the UK Office for National Statistics (ONS), for example, the quantitative data on the rise in internet access in the UK, between the years 1998 and 2017. Data of this kind could be useful for an assignment in which you need a data set with which to demonstrate your ability to analyze data. This historical period might be of significance if, for example, the focus of the study was on employment in the UK over that time period. The period might be useful in terms of providing background to a study, for example, of changing patterns and trends in employment in the UK. For a contemporary study, the data detailed in the example are too dated. In general, for a contemporary study, it is important to have the most up-to-date data possible.

The research conducted by one student, Lian, is presented in The Value of Good Research box 'Lian's research project'. As you will see when you read through the feature, Lian gathers both quantitative and qualitative data for her research project. An outline of the data-gathering exercise engaged in by Lian is presented, along with detail of the data gathered and the approach used to analyze that data.

THE VALUE OF GOOD RESEARCH

Lian's research project

Lian decided that she wanted a career working with one of the main high street fashion companies. She was particularly interested in high street chains. She decided to use the opportunity of undertaking a research project for her degree in marketing to study these companies.

Lian's research statement was as follows: This research project is a case study of six high street fashion shops with a focus on their current market positioning; the six shops are Zara, Topshop, Miss Selfridge, French Connection, Monsoon and Oasis.

The aim of the study was to develop six case studies of six different high street fashion shops focused on the current marketing positioning of each of the shops.

The objectives of the study were as follows:

● To examine the branding of each of the shops.
● To explore, using secondary sources, the market positioning of each of the six shops.
● To examine customer perceptions of each of the six brands.
● To examine the current market positioning of the six brands through the attitudes and perceptions of customers.

(Continued)

Using a case study methodology, Lian developed six cases, one for each of the six shops that interested her. She used secondary sources to gather data on the six cases. Among other facts, she established that Topshop and Miss Selfridge are both part of the Arcadia group; that French Connection, which was founded in 1972 by Stephen Marks, has stores worldwide; that Oasis is continuing store development in existing and new markets with an international franchise; that Monsoon, founded in 1973 by Peter Simon in London, currently operates 400 Monsoon and Accessorize stores in the UK, and over 1000 worldwide, and has expansion plans for the Americas involving joint ventures; that the Spanish Inditex Group, which owns Zara, has over 4600 stores worldwide, 2000 of them are Zara stores, 860 are Pull & Bear stores and 673 are Massimo Dutti stores.

Initially, Lian had wanted to engage in primary research with each of the companies. She had hoped to conduct interviews with managers in each of the shops. However, she got no helpful or encouraging responses whenever she contacted the shops or the companies.

Lian decided, as an alternative, to interview customers of the shops. Using street intercept interviews, she engaged 120 customers in interviews, 20 customers for each of the six shops. She intercepted customers as they left the shops and invited them to participate in her study. She used a quota sampling method. Using this sampling method she continued to invite customers to engage in interview with her until she

had her quota of 20 completed interviews with customers of each of the six shops. Lian used a structured questionnaire in the interviews that she developed herself. The focus of the questionnaire, which was informed by her reading of the literature, was on customer brand perceptions, favourite stores and shopping habits and patterns.

Lian's questionnaire is shown here. As you will see, Lian used a mixture of open and closed questions in the questionnaire. She gathered mostly quantitative data with the questionnaire, but she did gather some qualitative data. There is an explanation in Chapter 18 of the approach to data analysis that Lian used in analysing the qualitative data gathered. When you read through the questionnaire, try to identify the closed questions and the open questions. Can you identify the questions designed to generate qualitative data?

Lian developed a coding key to go with her questionnaire, which is included on the right-hand side of the questionnaire. Also presented here is an extract from Lian's data set. When she had gathered her data, she loaded it into SPSS, which was used to analyze her data.

Lian found the process of loading the data into SPSS quite complex. To help ensure that she loaded the data correctly, she decided to develop a separate coding key for her data. A copy of this coding key, developed as a separate document, is also shown here. When you examine this separate coding key, can you explain why Lian found it helpful?

QUESTIONNAIRE USED IN STREET INTERCEPT INTERVIEWS WITH HIGH STREET FASHION SHOPPERS

High street fashion – shoppers' questionnaire (Lian's research project)		Code
Date: ___		
1. Location: ___		**1 2 3 4 5 6**
2. How often do you visit high street fashion shops like Zara and Topshop?		
Every day	☐	**1**
Once or twice a week	☐	**2**
Once or twice a month	☐	**3**
Only when I must	☐	**4**
Other (please explain)	☐	**5**
3. When you visit these shops, do you tend to spend money in them?		
All the time	☐	**1**
Sometimes	☐	**2**
Occasionally	☐	**3**
Never	☐	**4**
4. Do you ever shop online with any of these retailers?		
Yes	☐	**1**
No	☐	**2**

code This side of the questionnaire contains the coding key for the questionnaire.

High street fashion – shoppers' questionnaire (Lian's research project)		Code
5. With which of these shops have you shopped online?		
Zara	☐	1
Topshop	☐	2
Miss Selfridge	☐	3
French Connection	☐	4
Monsoon	☐	5
Oasis	☐	6
Not applicable		
6. Would you describe the experience generally as		
Very good	☐	1
Good	☐	2
OK	☐	3
Not good	☐	4
Bad	☐	5
Very bad	☐	6
Not applicable	☐	7
7. Please elaborate ___		
8. On average, how much money do you spend per month in these shops?		
Less than £20		1
More than £20–less than £50		2
More than £50–less than £100		3
More than £100–less than £200		4
More than £200		5
9. In the coming 12 months, do you anticipate spending more money, less money, or about the same amount of money in these shops?		
More		1
Less		2
About the same amount		3
10. Please elaborate ___		
11. When you do shop, do you tend to buy mostly		
Work clothes	☐	1
Party clothes	☐	2
Casual clothes	☐	3
Other, please elaborate	☐	4

12. Which of the following adjectives would you apply to the six shops?

	Exciting	Fresh	Adventurous	Tired	Old	Safe	
Zara:	☐	☐	☐	☐	☐	☐	1 2 3 4 5 6
Topshop:	☐	☐	☐	☐	☐	☐	1 2 3 4 5 6
Miss Selfridge:	☐	☐	☐	☐	☐	☐	1 2 3 4 5 6
French Connection:	☐	☐	☐	☐	☐	☐	1 2 3 4 5 6
Monsoon:	☐	☐	☐	☐	☐	☐	1 2 3 4 5 6
Oasis:	☐	☐	☐	☐	☐	☐	1 2 3 4 5 6

(Continued)

High street fashion – shoppers' questionnaire (Lian's research project)	Code
13. Please rank the shops in order, 1 = favourite, 6 = least favourite	
Zara	☐ **1 2 3 4 5 6**
Topshop	☐ **1 2 3 4 5 6**
Miss Selfridge	☐ **1 2 3 4 5 6**
French Connection	☐ **1 2 3 4 5 6**
Monsoon	☐ **1 2 3 4 5 6**
Oasis	☐ **1 2 3 4 5 6**
14. Why is ___ your favourite of these shops?	
15. Do you have any other favourite high street fashion shop, other than those named in this questionnaire?	
Yes	**1**
No	**2**
16. Please elaborate: ___	
17. Please complete the following sentences:	
I would describe the brand Zara as: ___	
I would describe the brand Topshop as: ___	
I would describe the brand Miss Selfridge as: ___	
I would describe the brand French Connection as: ___	
I would describe the brand Monsoon as: ___	
I would describe the brand Oasis as: ___	

CODING KEY FOR HIGH STREET SHOPPERS' QUESTIONNAIRE: LIAN'S RESEARCH

The coding key in Table 19.1 is the separate coding key that Lian developed to help her load her data into SPSS. Detailed in the coding key (see the top line, reading from left to right) is the question number, which is taken from the questionnaire; the variable number, which is the number of the variable in SPSS; the variable name, which is simply the name of the variable; the variable description, which is a description of the variable; and the value labels, which are the codes assigned by the researcher to the different values in each of the variables. You will note from the coding key that the variable number does not track the question number (see question number 5).

It is important that you study this coding key. Try to understand the logic of the coding key. Read down through the coding key. Read it one question at a time. When you understand a question, move on to the next question. Ask for help with this exercise if you need it. Table 19.2 contains all the data, as they appear in SPSS, for the first nine questionnaires of the 120 completed questionnaires Lian gathered for her research.

Take a moment to study the data set. The numbers, 1–9, down the left side of the data set relate to the questionnaire number. The number 1 signals that this line of data is from the first questionnaire, the number 2 signals that this line of data is from the second questionnaire, and so on. As you can see, the data set contains all of the data from the first nine questionnaires.

The line of data is read from left to right. Can you read the data? Use the questionnaire and the coding key to read the data. What does var00001 relate to? If you said location, you are correct. What does var00005 relate to? If you said that it relates to the question 'With which of these shops have you shopped online?' you are correct.

It is important to remember that the variable number does not track the question number. This is sometimes because there are open questions in the questionnaire and the researcher, Lian in this case, has decided not to code these open questions for SPSS. This decision is made generally when there are too many different answers to the open questions. The answers to the open questions in Lian's project were analyzed using a qualitative data analysis process (see Chapter 18).

Table 19.1 Coding key for high street shoppers' questionnaire (Lian's research)

Question number	Variable number	Variable name	Variable description	Value labels
1	V00001	Location	Zara Topshop Miss Selfridge French Connection Monsoon Oasis	1 2 3 4 5 6
2	V00002	How often do you visit high street fashion shops such as Zara and Topshop?	Every day Once or twice a week Once or twice a month Only when I must Other/please explain	1 2 3 4 5
3	V00003	When you visit these shops do you tend to spend money in them?	Always Sometimes Occasionally Never	1 2 3 4
4	V00004	Do you ever shop online with any of these retailers?	Yes No	1 2
5	V00005 V00006 V00007 V00008 V00009 V00010	With which of these shops have you shopped online?	Zara Topshop Miss Selfridge French Connection Monsoon Oasis Not applicable	1 2 3 4 5 6 7
6	V00011	Would you describe the experience generally as:	Very good Good OK Not good Bad Very bad Not applicable	1 2 3 4 5 6 7
7		Please elaborate		
8	V00012	On average, how much money do you spend per month in these shops?	Less than £20 More than £20, less than £50 More than £50, less than £100 More than £100, less than £200 More than £200	1 2 3 4 5
9	V00013	In the coming 12 months, do you anticipate spending more money or less money, or about the same amount of money in these shops?	More money Less money About the same amount	1 2 3
10		Please elaborate		
11	V00014	When you do shop, do you tend to buy mostly:	Work clothes Party clothes Casual clothes Other, please elaborate	1 2 3 4

(Continued)

Table 19.1 Coding key for high street shoppers' questionnaire (Lian's research) (*Continued*)

Question number	Variable number	Variable name	Variable description	Value labels
12	V00015	Which of the following adjectives would you apply to the six shops?	Exciting/fresh/ adventurous/ tired/ old/safe	
	V00016		Zara	**1 2 3 4 5 6**
	V00017		Topshop	**1 2 3 4 5 6**
	V00018		Miss Selfridge	**1 2 3 4 5 6**
	V00019		French Connection	**1 2 3 4 5 6**
	V00020		Monsoon	**1 2 3 4 5 6**
	V00021		Oasis	**1 2 3 4 5 6**
	V00022			
	V00023			
	V00024			
	V00025			
	V00026			
	V00027			
	V00028			
	V00029			
	V00030			
	V00031			
	V00032			
13	V00033	Please rank the shops in order, 1 = favourite, 6 = least favourite	Zara	**1 2 3 4 5 6**
	V00034		Topshop	**1 2 3 4 5 6**
	V00035		Miss Selfridge	**1 2 3 4 5 6**
	V00036		French Connection	**1 2 3 4 5 6**
	V00037		Monsoon	**1 2 3 4 5 6**
	V00038		Oasis	**1 2 3 4 5 6**
14		Why is _____ your favourite of these shops?		
15	V00039	Do you have any other favourite high street fashion shop, other than those named in this questionnaire?	Yes No	**1** **2**
16		Please elaborate:		
17		Sentence completion exercise		

Table 19.2 Extract from the high street shoppers' data set (Lian's research project)

	var00001	var00002	var00003	var00004	var00005	var00006	var00007	var00008	var00009	var00010
1	2	3	1	1	7	7	7	7	7	**7**
2	3	2	1	1	1	2	3	4	5	**6**
3	4	1	1	1	1	2	3	7	7	**7**
4	1	4	2	1	5	3	1	2	6	**7**
5	2	5	1	1	4	2	3	1	9999	**9999**
6	6	3	3	2	7	7	7	7	7	**7**
7	5	2	1	1	4	3	5	1	2	**9999**
8	4	2	1	1	3	2	1	4	9999	**9999**
9	2	4	4	2	7	7	7	7	7	**7**

Table 19.2 Extract from the high street shoppers' data set (Lian's research project) (*Continued*)

	var00011	var00012	var00013	var00014	var00015	var00016	var00017	var00018	var00019	var00020
1	7	1	1	2	1	2	3	1	2	3
2	3	3	2	2	1	2	3	1	2	3
3	2	2	2	1	1	2	3	1	2	3
4	1	4	3	2	1	2	3	1	2	3
5	1	3	3	3	4	5	6	4	5	6
6	7	4	1	1	9999	9999	9999	9999	9999	9999
7	2	5	2	4	1	2	3	9999	9999	9999
8	3	2	3	1	1	2	3	1	2	3
9	7	1	3	4	1	2	3	1	2	3

	var00021	var00022	var00023	var00024	var00025	var00026	var00027	var00028	var00029	var00030
1	1	2	3	1	2	3	1	2	3	1
2	1	2	3	1	2	3	1	2	3	1
3	1	2	3	1	2	3	1	2	3	1
4	1	2	3	9999	9999	9999	9999	9999	9999	9999
5	4	5	6	4	5	6	4	5	6	4
6	9999	9999	9999	1	2	3	1	2	3	1
7	9999	9999	9999	9999	9999	9999	9999	9999	9999	9999
8	9999	9999	9999	9999	9999	9999	1	2	3	9999
9	9999	9999	9999	1	2	3	9999	9999	9999	4

	var00031	var00032	var00033	var00034	var00035	var00036	var00037	var00038	var00039
1	2	3	1	2	6	5	4	3	2
2	2	3	1	2	6	5	4	3	1
3	2	3	1	3	5	4	6	2	2
4	9999	9999	1	2	3	6	5	4	1
5	5	6	1	2	3	4	5	6	2
6	2	3	6	5	4	1	2	3	1
7	9999	9999	2	3	4	5	1	6	2
8	9999	9999	2	3	4	5	1	6	2
9	5	6	1	2	3	6	5	4	1

It is sometimes possible to code qualitative data for SPSS. The question the researcher must ask their self is whether it is meaningful and useful to code the qualitative data for SPSS. If, for example, there were a relatively small number of respondents to the questionnaire, let us say less than 30, then it would be relatively easy to assign a numeric **value** to each of the responses. Or, if the researcher found on initially reading the responses to the question that there were a limited range of responses, then the responses could easily be categorized, and the categories could easily be coded for SPSS.

value The different values in a variable.

There is another reason why the variable number does not track the question number. This is because some questions require more than one response. For example, as demonstrated in the coding key above, question 12 in Lian's question-naire could, possibly, elicit 18 responses. This would happen if a respondent responded that each of the three positive adjectives or the three negative adjectives could be used to describe each of the six stores. It is important when loading data into SPSS that every response is included in the data set. When you are loading data into SPSS, ensure, as you load the data from the first questionnaire, that you leave a variable space along the line of data for every possible answer.

Loading the data is simple, but it does take time, and it involves very precise, some would say tedious, work. This is because the data must be loaded correctly or they will be rendered meaningless. Loading data correctly into any software package is a data management task. An example was given in Chapter 17 of one possible consequence of incorrectly coded data. Once the data are loaded into the software package, analysis of the data is relatively simple.

When analyzing the data, the researcher uses the coding key with each of the questionnaires in order to decode the data. The top line in the SPSS Data Editor contains commands very much like the commands in Microsoft Word or Excel. The commands are as follows: File, Edit, View, Data, Transform, Analyze, Graphs, Utilities, Window, Help. The command 'Analyze' is used to run an analysis on the data in the data set. There is also a command called 'Graphs'. This command is used to generate graphs from the data in the data set.

Missing data

Sometimes respondents do not answer all the questions when they fill in a questionnaire. It is possible that a question asked in the questionnaire might not be applicable to some respondents. When this is the case, there should be some means in the questionnaire for the respondent to indicate this; the respondent should be given a 'not applicable' option in the range of responses possible to that question or to those questions. It is important that respondents respond to each question. If respondents have not responded to questions in the questionnaire, for reasons other than the question asked not being applicable to them, then the researcher when coding the data must code the non-responses.

In coding for non-responses in SPSS, a good approach is to consistently use the same number to indicate non-responses. It is important to use a number that is not likely to be used otherwise in coding, so that the non-responses are immediately apparent. Using the number 7777, for example, is a good approach to coding for non-responses. When this is done, every time the researcher sees the number 7777 in the data set, they know straight away that that number indicates a non-response.

Similarly, in coding the response 'not applicable', the researcher might choose, for example, the number 9999. Then every time the researcher sees the number 9999 in the data set, they know immediately that that question was not applicable to that respondent. If you look back at Lian's data set, you will see that the numbers 7777 and 9999 appear in the data set. Now you know what those numbers mean.

Once the data have been loaded into SPSS, and the data in SPSS have been cleaned, the analysis of the data is a very simple task. The researcher simply asks SPSS to analyze the data. The researcher taps one or two keys on the keyboard and the requested analysis is generated by SPSS and presented in an output file. A simple request for frequencies in SPSS will immediately generate frequencies on each variable in the data set.

The data presented in the frequency table (Table 19.3) are the data on gender. In the frequency table:

Table 19.3 VAR00001

	Frequency	%	Valid %	Cumulative %
Valid				
1.00	56	61.5	61.5	61.5
2.00	35	38.5	38.5	100.0
Total	91	100.0	100.0	

- There are in the first column, two values, 1 and 2. Value 1 represents female and value 2 represents male.
- The second column is labelled 'Frequency'. This refers to the number of times (the frequency) with which both of the values are represented in the data set. There are 56 females and 35 males. In total, 91 people participated in this study.
- The third column is labelled '%'. The output in this column presents the values as percentages. As you can see, females account for 61.5 per cent of respondents, and males account for 38.5 per cent of respondents.
- The fourth column is labelled 'Valid %'. This column is the most widely used column in the frequency table. The output in this column presents the valid per cent, i.e. the percentage breakdown of respondents who actually answered the question.
- The fifth column is labelled 'Cumulative %'. The output in this column is a cumulative presentation of the valid per cents. The first per cent, 61.5 per cent is added to the second per cent, 38.5 per cent and this gives a total of 100 per cent.

This is the format for every frequency table generated in SPSS. As explained in the previous chapter, it is neither necessary nor useful to detail all data when writing up data analysis. The researcher must decide what to report from all of the data available. The researcher reports the key aspects of the data and the most relevant data, in terms of the phenomenon under investigation.

Data management with SPSS

As well as helping the researcher analyze data, SPSS also serves as a tool for managing data. The data are secure within the software and may be password protected. The data within SPSS are held within one folder, which can and should be backed up. In order to load the data into SPSS, the researcher codes the data. Coding the data serves to anonymize the data, which helps protect the identities of respondents. While loading the data into SPSS, the researcher cleans the data. In cleaning the data, the researcher checks that the data are correct and that they are loaded correctly. Any errors in loading the data are corrected in cleaning the data. The data within SPSS must be accurately coded and loaded and rigorously checked, rechecked and cleaned. Within the software the data can be easily, safely and securely stored, moved and used, as long as the computer and/or memory stick containing the data is secure. For ethical reasons, this level of data management is necessary.

YOUR RESEARCH
Guides to SPSS

There are a number of online guides to SPSS and to the use of SPSS. For example, UCLA (University of California, Los Angeles), through its Institute for Digital Research and Education, presents different statistical tests (see later for definitions and explanations) and when to use them in SPSS, STATA and SAS: see Which Statistical Test?, under the Resources tab: www.ats.ucla.edu/stat/spss/modules/descript.htm

Harvard MIT Data Center also presents a guide to SPSS. This is available at www.hks.harvard.edu/fs/pnorris/Classes/A%20SPSS%20Manuals/SPSS%20Statistcs%20Base%20User's%20Guide%2017.0.pdf

There are also many books available which are guides to SPSS. These will be available in your university library. Your university may also provide the software along with tutorials. Enquire about this, and ask for a tutorial if none is provided. Your lecturer in research methods may be able to organize a tutorial in SPSS.

REAL WORLD RESEARCH

Presenting the analyzed data

It is important in data analysis to maintain a focus on the narrative to be told about the data. It is essential that the story, or narrative, told be logical and reasonable. Sometimes students fall into the trap of reporting the statistics, rather than the narrative. In reporting the narrative of the data, it is the data which are central to the narrative, and the capacity of the data to respond to and/or illustrate the overall aim of the research that must be the focus, not the statistical analysis conducted on the data. Statistical analysis is simply a tool with which data may be investigated and analyzed. Statistical analyses are reported in the data analysis section of the thesis or report to support the narrative, the story the researcher is presenting about the analyzed data.

Whether you are using CADA or a pen and paper (with or without a calculator), it is important to keep a record of your thoughts, your reflections and your insights into your analysis of your data as they form and develop. These notes, which you should for safety and security reasons make and keep in your research diary, will provide you with many ideas in terms of the final story or narrative of the analysis to be presented in the data analysis chapter. Chapter 17 contains a detailed example of how to structure a data analysis chapter (see Table 17.4).

The ideas and insights that you get in relation to your data as you immerse yourself in the data analysis phase of the research project will provide you with the narrative that you will present in the data analysis chapter in your thesis or in the report of the research. You will be able to discern, from your notes, from the analysis conducted on the data, and from the research statement or question, the research hypothesis, the overall aim of the research project, precisely what narrative to present (what story to tell) about your data.

THE VARIABLE IN QUANTITATIVE DATA ANALYSIS

In quantitative analysis, as we have seen, the unit of measurement is the variable. In conducting quantitative research, we measure, control and/or manipulate variables. A variable is a characteristic with more than one value. As explained earlier, gender, for example, is a variable. There are two values (generally) in gender, male and female. Level of education is a variable. There are, let us say, three levels of education, primary, secondary and tertiary, and so in coding the values in the variable education, there would be three values to code.

Variables are explained in detail in Chapter 7. To recap briefly, there are different level variables: **nominal variables**, **ordinal variables** and **interval variables** (see Table 19.4). The different levels are important because they determine the kind of analysis that can be carried out on, or with, each variable.

> **nominal variables** Each value is a distinct category and serves simply as a label. Categories cannot be ranked, e.g. gender, nationality, race.
>
> **ordinal variables** Values are ranked according to criteria, e.g. social class (upper, middle, working).
>
> **interval variables** Data with a meaningful and measurable distance between values, e.g. age.

A **dichotomous variable** is one that has only two values. Gender is (or it used to be) a dichotomous variable. Questions that elicit yes/no responses are dichotomous questions. The responses to such questions are dichotomous responses.

> **dichotomous variable** A variable with only two values.

The effect is called the dependent variable. The assumed cause is called the **independent variable**. An **intervening variable** is the means by which the independent variable affects the dependent variable. See the Value of Good Research box on experimental design for further explanation of dependent, independent and intervening variables.

> **independent variable** In examining the relationship between two variables, the assumed cause is the independent variable.
>
> **intervening variable** The means by which the independent variable affects the dependent variable.

Table 19.4 Nominal, ordinal and interval variables

Nominal is the lowest level of measurement. No assumptions can be made about relations between the values of a nominal level variable. The categories cannot be ranked. Each value is a distinct category and serves simply as a label. Examples of nominal level variables include gender, nationality, race, religion, type of business. A nominal scale simply involves putting the data into categories. A yes/no scale is an example of a nominal scale.
Ordinal is the intermediate level of measurement. Values in ordinal level variables are ranked according to some criteria, in other words there is distance between the different values in the scale. While there is distance between the values, it is not possible to calculate or quantify the distance between the values. Level of education is an ordinal level variable. There are, let us say, three levels of education. While we understand the distances between the different levels of education, it is not possible to mathematically measure those distances. The simplest ordinal level scale is a ranking. If you ask respondents to rank the tasks they undertake in their daily work in some order, from the most important to the least important, you are asking them to create an ordinal scale of preference. In your questionnaire, if you ask respondents to rate their satisfaction with their job on a five-point scale from very satisfied to very dissatisfied, you are using an ordinal scale.
Interval is the highest unit of measurement. Interval-level variables are distributed in an even, continuous manner. In interval-level variables, as well as scale there is meaningful and measurable distance between the values. Age is an example of an interval-level variable. Income, when it is disaggregated, is an interval-level variable. The difference between an interval-level variable and an ordinal-level variable is that there is meaningful distance between the values in an interval-level variable. The distance between the values is equal. The distance between the values can be measured or quantified. A wide range of statistical analyses can be carried out on interval-level data.

THE VALUE OF GOOD RESEARCH

Focus on experimental design

Experimental design, as explained in Chapter 9, is the methodology used when conducting experiments. Field experiments are experiments that are conducted in real-life settings.

In true experiments, the independent variable is manipulated to test whether or not it has an effect on the dependent variable. The dependent variable is what is measured in an experiment; it is the variable that responds to the independent variable. The independent variable is the variable that is introduced or acted on in some way in the experiment in order to produce some effect on the dependent variable. In a simple experiment, two groups are established, with individuals or units being randomly assigned to both groups. The two groups are pretested, and the dependent variable is measured. Then a programme or application, the independent variable, is applied to one group, the experimental group, and not to the other group, the control group. Both groups are tested once more; again the dependent variable is measured. If there is a difference in the experimental group but not in the control group, the programme or application applied to them, the independent variable, is said to account for the difference.

In an experiment, there can be more than one dependent variable (the variable(s) that are being acted on) but there should only be one independent variable (the variable that is manipulated). In real life, in the social world, there are so many variables it can be difficult to establish precisely what variable(s) account for which changes. It can be difficult in social research to absolutely establish cause and effect, to establish precisely what/which cause brought about what/ which effect. For example, you might want to study the impact of a training programme designed to bring about better communication in a company. You could establish two groups within the company, an experimental group and a control group. You pretest both groups. You then administer the training to the experimental group but not to the control group. Then you test both groups again. You may suggest that any change evident in terms of communication in the experimental group is as a result of the training in communications given. However, this may not be the case. It could be simply that the time the group spent together (while undertaking the training), brought about improved communication in the group. In that case, the training itself is not responsible for the improved communication. Rather, it was the opportunity of spending time together in a training environment that facilitated the improved communications.

The Hawthorne experiments (1924–1933) are classic examples. Elton Mayo, a professor of Industrial Management at the Harvard Business School, studied worker behaviour at the Western Electrical Company's Hawthorne Works in Illinois. The experiments Mayo carried out were designed to measure worker productivity. Mayo found that as he studied the workers, their productivity improved. What he realized was that the subjects of his experiments changed their performance in response to being observed. In other words, it was the experience of being observed that caused worker productivity to improve. This variable of being observed was an unforeseen variable in the experiments, yet it was the variable that brought about the change in worker behaviour. This discovery became known as 'the Hawthorne effect'. You can read about the Hawthorne experiments on the Harvard Business School website at www.library.hbs.edu/hc/hawthorne/09.html

Trochim's Web Center for Social Research Methods is a useful resource, as it provides a clear introduction to experimental design: socialresearchmethods.net

The website of Science Olympiad also provides a good introduction to experimental design: scioly.org/wiki/index.php/Experimental_Design

BASIC STATISTICAL ANALYSIS

Statistics are used in quantitative data analysis for two purposes: description, using **descriptive statistics**, and prediction, using **inferential statistics**.

> **descriptive statistics** Used to describe variables in the data such as gender, education, income, age, etc. Presented as percentages, ratios, ranges, averages and standard deviations.
>
> **inferential statistics** Inferential statistics infer, based on a study of a sample population, what the entire population might think or do.

Descriptive statistics

Descriptive statistics are used to describe the data gathered. Summarizing statistics are examples of descriptive statistics. Each variable in the data gathered, gender, level of education, income, age, and so on, can be described using descriptive statistics. Using descriptive statistics, each variable can be described in a number of different ways. The most generally used descriptive statistics are frequencies, ranges, means, modes, medians and standard deviations. Table 19.5 names and explains the different descriptive statistics.

Descriptive analysis is the elementary transformation of data in a way that describes the basic characteristics such as central tendency, distribution and variability. For example, consider the business researcher who takes responses from 1000 American consumers and tabulates their favourite soft drink brand and the price they expect to pay for a six pack of that product. The mean, median and mode for favourite soft drink and the average price across all 1000 consumers would be tabulated and the data analyzed.

> **descriptive analysis** The elementary transformation of raw data in a way that describes the basic characteristics such as central tendency, distribution and variability.

Table 19.5 Descriptive statistics

Measures of central tendency	
Mean	The mean is the arithmetic average. To calculate the mean, add up all the values and divide the total by the number of values.
Mode	The mode is the most commonly occurring value in a range of values.
Median	The median is the middle value of a range of values.
Measures of dispersion	
Range	The range is the minimum and maximum values in a range of data. For example, the age range was 21 years old to 39 years old. The youngest respondent was 21 years old and the oldest was 39 years old. In another example, the turnover ranged from £300 000 to £40 000. The highest turnover was £300 000, the lowest was £40 000.
Interquartile range (IQR)	The interquartile range (IQR) is a robust measure of sample dispersion. It eliminates outliers by focusing on the difference between the first and third quartiles. Outliers are extreme measures that skew a distribution.
	The median, as explained, is the middle value, and the IQR is the middle value of the lower and the upper halves of the data. For example, let us say that your population or sample ranges in age from 21 to 27 years, but you have one person who is aged 39. This one age is an extreme value, it is an outlier and it will skew the distribution of the data. Using the IQR instead of the range eliminates such outliers, and in doing this, eliminates *skew* generated by outliers.
Standard deviation (SD)	The standard deviation measures the spread of data about the mean. It is used to compare sets of data that have the same mean but a different range of data. The standard deviation is calculated as the square root of the variance. Variance in a data set is the extent to which the values in the data set differ from the mean. A calculator that handles statistics will calculate standard deviation. To calculate the standard deviation by hand: 1. Establish the mean in the range of data. 2. Subtract the mean from each of the values to establish the deviation of the values from the mean. 3. Square each deviation. 4. Sum all the squares (add them up). 5. Divide the sum by the number of data points, minus 1. 6. Take the square root of that value. This is the standard deviation.
Other measures	
Percentages	Percentages are a particular kind of scale with measures of 1 to 100.
Ratios	A ratio can be calculated as follows, the ratio of number A to number B is defined as A divided by B.
Proportions	Proportions are a type of ratio in which the denominator is the total number of cases.
Frequency distributions	A frequency distribution condenses information into a simple format which will allow the reader to picture the way in which the variable is distributed.

Figure 19.2 shows how the level of scale measurement influences the choice of descriptive statistics. Remember that all statistics appropriate for lower order scales (nominal and ordinal) are suitable for higher order scales (interval and ratio), but the reverse is not true.

The bottom part of Figure 19.2 displays example descriptive statistics for interval and ratio variables. In this case, the chart displays results of a question asking respondents how much they typically spend on a bottle of wine purchased in a store. The mean and standard deviation are displayed beside the chart as 11.7 and 4.5, respectively. Additionally, a frequency distribution is shown with a **histogram**. A histogram is a graphical way of showing a frequency distribution in which the height of a bar corresponds to the frequency of a category. Histograms are useful for any type of data, but with continuous variables (interval or ratio) the histogram is useful for providing a quick assessment of the distribution of the data. A normal distribution line is superimposed over the histogram, providing an easy comparison to see if the data are skewed or multi-modal.

> **histogram** A graphical way of showing a frequency distribution in which the height of a bar corresponds to the observed frequency of the category.

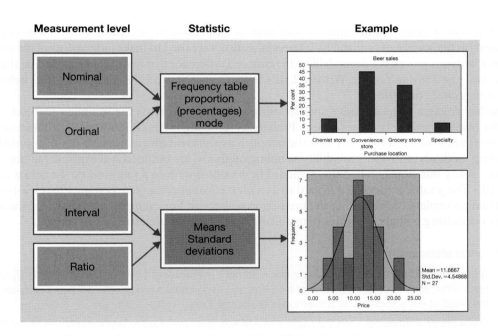

Figure 19.2 Levels of scale measurement and suggested descriptive statistics

Simple tabulation tells the researcher how frequently each response occurs. This starting point for analysis requires the researcher to count responses or observations for each category or code assigned to a variable. A frequency table showing where consumers generally purchase beer can be computed easily. The tabular results that correspond to the chart would appear as follows:

Response	Frequency	Per cent	Cumulative percentage
Chemist store	50	10	10
Convenience store	225	45	55
Grocery store	175	35	90
Specialty	35	7	97
Other	15	3	100

The frequency column shows the tally result or the number of respondents listing each store, respectively. The per cent column shows the total percentage in each category. From this chart, we can see the most common outlet – the mode – is convenience store since more people indicated this as their top response than any other. The cumulative percentage keeps a running total, showing the percentage of respondents indicating this particular category and all preceding categories as their preferred place to purchase beer. The cumulative percentage column is not so important for nominal or interval data, but is quite useful for interval and ratio data, particularly when there are a large number of response categories.

Inferential statistics

With inferential statistics, the researcher is trying to reach conclusions that extend beyond the data. Inferential statistics are used to infer, based on the study of a sample of a population, what the entire population might think, or do. **Statistical inference** uses the data gathered on a sample population to draw conclusions (or inferences) about the population from which the sample was drawn.

 statistical inference Uses the data gathered from a sample population to draw conclusions about the population.

Inferential statistics are also used in quantitative data analysis for prediction (see Table 19.6). Prediction in quantitative data analysis is based on the science of probability. Inferential statistics are used to make judgements of the probability that an observed difference between groups is a dependable difference or a difference that may have happened by chance in the study.

You may also find the Purdue Online Writing Lab's resource on 'Basic Inferential Statistics' helpful: owl.english .purdue.edu/owl/resource/672/05/.

When a researcher engages in quantitative analysis using inferential statistics, the sampling method used in selecting participants for the research project becomes critical. Probability sampling methods must be used. These sampling methods are designed to minimize biases and to ensure that the sample is as representative as possible of the population of the study. Probability sampling methods (and non-probability sampling methods) are outlined and explained in detail in Chapter 10.

The probability of any outcome is called the p value. The p value is written p followed by the actual value in brackets. For example $p = (0)$. The p value is measured from 0 to 1, with 0 equalling complete certainty that the prediction will not occur and 1 equalling complete certainty that the prediction will occur. For example, $p = 0.6$ would mean the likelihood of the prediction's occurring is slightly greater than a likelihood of the prediction's not occurring.

Table 19.6 Inferential statistics

T-tests	A t-test is used to decide if the means (the arithmetic averages) of two groups are statistically different from each other, for example the means of a control and experimental group. You will find a detailed explanation of the t-test at www.socialresearchmethods.net/kb/stat_t.php
ANOVA test (analysis of variance)	There are similarities between the t-test and ANOVA. Both are used to test hypotheses about the differences (the variance) in the means in groups. While the t-test is used to test two means, ANOVA can be used to test the differences among the means of many groups at once. The purpose of one-way ANOVA is to test whether the means of different groups are common or different. Two-way ANOVA is used when the groups tested have two different defining characteristics, rather than one. MANOVA is a multivariate version of analysis of variance (MANOVA multiple analysis of variance). You will find a detailed explanation of ANOVA at www.stat.columbia .edu/~martin/W2024/R3.pdf
Correlation tests	This is an often used statistic. A correlation, according to Trochim's Research Methods Knowledge Base, is a single number that describes the degree of relationship between two variables. Correlation tests measure the extent to which an independent variable predicts a dependent variable. As well as explaining correlation tests, The Research Methods Knowledge Base works through a correlation example at www.socialresearchmethods .net/kb/statcorr.htm
Simple linear regression	Simple linear regression is like correlation, in that it too determines the extent to which an independent variable predicts a dependent variable. However, the simple linear regression also tells how well the line fits the data. The smaller the distance of the data from the regression line, the better the fit. According to the statistics guide of the Colorado State University, regression analysis attempts to determine the best 'fit' between two or more variables (writing.colostate.edu/guides/guide.cfm?guideid=67)
Multiple linear regression	Multiple linear regression measures how well multiple independent variables predict the value of a dependent variable. You will find a detailed explanation of multiple linear regression at cnmtl.columbia.edu/projects/qmss/ about_multiple_regression.html

Hypothesis testing is commonly used in research in drawing inferences about a population based on **statistical analysis** of data drawn from a sample of that population. In hypothesis testing, a null hypothesis is a statement about the population of the study that the researcher wants to test. An alternative hypothesis is a challenging statement, or an alternative statement, against which the null hypothesis can be tested. In the first place, the hypotheses are stated and they must be mutually exclusive, i.e. if one is true the other must be false. Then the sample data are tested, using means, or *t*-tests, ANOVA or some other statistic. The results are interpreted, and the hypotheses are accepted or rejected (see Markova, 2009, for an example of a research project carried out using hypothesis testing). The online *teach yourself statistics* website Stat Trek is helpful in relation to learning how to conduct statistical analyses and how to test hypotheses: stattrek.com. Also helpful is the Quantitative Methods in Social Sciences project on the Columbia University website: ccnmtl.columbia.edu/projects/qmss/home.html

> **statistical analysis** Analysis of quantitative data through the use of statistics.

Data analysis can be carried out using **univariate analysis**, the use of one variable in analysis; **bivariate analysis**, the use of two variables in analysis; and **multivariate analysis**, the use of three or more variables in analysis.

> **univariate analysis** Analysis conducted on only one variable, e.g. frequencies.
>
> **bivariate analysis** Analysis conducted on two variables e.g. chi-square tests, one-way ANOVA, *t*-tests, correlation and simple regression.
>
> **multivariate analysis** Analysis conducted on more than two variables, e.g. examples of multivariate statistics include multiple regression analysis.

Univariate analysis is analysis of one variable. Using univariate analysis, each variable in the data set is analyzed individually. Methods for univariate analysis include: frequencies, **measures of central tendency** and **measures of dispersion**. Table 19.7 is an example of a frequency table generated in SPSS. It is an example of univariate analysis. You will remember that we explored this table in detail earlier in this chapter.

> **measures of central tendency** The mean: the arithmetic average; the mode: the most commonly occurring value; the median: the middle value of a range of values.
>
> **measures of dispersion** The interquartile range (IQR); the standard deviation; variance.

Table 19.7 VAR00001

	Frequency	%	Valid %	Cumulative %
Valid				
1.00	56	61.5	61.5	61.5
2.00	35	38.5	38.5	100.0
Total	*91*	*100.0*	*100.0*	

Bivariate analysis is analysis conducted on two variables. Examples of the statistical analysis that can be carried out in bivariate analysis include **cross-tabulation**, one-way ANOVA, *t*-tests, correlation tests and simple linear regression (see Table 19.8). Cross-tabulation is explained in more detail later in this chapter.

> **cross-tabulation** The appropriate technique for addressing research questions involving relationships among multiple less-than-interval variables; results in a combined frequency table displaying one variable in rows and another in columns.

Table 19.8   Cross-tabulating gender with level of education

	Male	Female
1 level	4	5
2 level	25	30
3 level	55	60
Descriptive analysis (there follow three sentences outlining a typical analysis of the table)		
From the table, it is clear that more than half of the respondents have third-level education, to be precise, 55 male respondents and 60 female respondents. Twenty-five male respondents and 30 female respondents have been educated to second level. Only five female and four male respondents completed their formal education after first level		

Independent samples *t*-test

Most typically, the researcher will apply the **independent samples *t*-test**, which tests the differences between means taken from two independent samples or groups. So, for example, if we measure the price for some designer jeans at 30 different retail stores, of which 15 are internet-only stores (pure clicks) and 15 are traditional stores, we can test whether or not the prices are different based on store type with an independent samples *t*-test. The *t*-test for difference of means assumes the two samples (one internet and one traditional store) are drawn from normal distributions and that the variances of the two populations are approximately equal (homoscedasticity).

> **independent samples *t*-test** A test for hypotheses which compares the mean scores for two groups comprising some interval- or ratio-scaled variable using a less-than interval classificatory variable.

Paired-samples *t*-test

What happens when means need to be compared that are not from independent samples? Such might be the case when the same respondent is measured twice – for instance, when the respondent is asked to rate both how much s/he likes shopping on the internet and how much s/he likes shopping in traditional stores. Since the liking scores are both provided by the same person, the assumption that they are independent is not realistic. Additionally, if one compares the prices the same retailers charge in their stores with the prices they charge on their websites, the samples cannot be considered independent because each pair of observations is from the same sampling unit. A **paired-samples *t*-test** is appropriate in this situation.

> **paired-samples *t*-test** An appropriate test for comparing the scores of two interval variables drawn from related populations.

Analysis of variance (ANOVA)

So far, we have discussed tests for differences between two groups. However, what happens when we have more than two groups? For example, what if we want to test and see if employee turnover differs across our five production plants? When the means of more than two groups or populations are to be compared, one-way **analysis of variance (ANOVA)** is the appropriate statistical tool. ANOVA involving only one grouping variable is often referred to as one-way ANOVA because only one independent variable is involved. Another way to define ANOVA is as the appropriate statistical technique to examine the effect of a less-than interval independent variable on a less-interval-dependent variable. Thus, a categorical independent variable and a continuous dependent variable are involved. An independent samples *t*-test can be thought of as a special case of ANOVA in which the independent variable has only two levels. When more levels exist, the *t*-test alone cannot handle the problem.

> **analysis of variance (ANOVA)** Analysis involving the investigation of the effects of one treatment variable on an interval-scaled dependent variable – a hypothesis-testing technique to determine whether statistically significant differences in means occur between two or more groups.

Simple correlation coefficient

The most popular technique for indicating the relationship of one variable to another is correlation. A **correlation coefficient** is a statistical measure of covariation, or association between two variables. **Covariance** is the extent to which a change in one variable corresponds systematically to a change in another. Correlation can be thought of as a standardized covariance.

> **correlation coefficient** A statistical measure of the covariation, or association, between two at-least-interval variables.
>
> **covariance** The extent to which two variables are associated systematically with each other.

When correlations estimate relationships between continuous variables, the Pearson product-moment correlation is appropriate. The correlation coefficient, r, ranges from -1.0 to $+1.0$. If the value of r equals $+1.0$, a perfect positive relationship exists. Perhaps the two variables are one and the same! If the value of r equals -1.0, a perfect negative relationship exists. The implication is that one variable is a mirror image of the other. As one goes up, the other goes down in proportion and vice versa. No correlation is indicated if r equals 0.

A correlation coefficient indicates both the magnitude of the linear relationship and the direction of that relationship. For example, if we find that $r = -0.92$, we know we have a very strong inverse relationship – that is, the greater the value measured by variable X, the lower the value measured by variable Y.

Figure 19.3 illustrates the correlation coefficients and scatter diagrams for several sets of data. Notice that in the no-correlation condition, the observations are scattered rather evenly about the space. In contrast, when correlations are strong and positive, the observations lie mostly in quadrants II and IV formed by inserting new axes though $\bar{X}$ and $\bar{Y}$. If correlation were strong and negative, the observations would lie mostly in quadrants I and III.

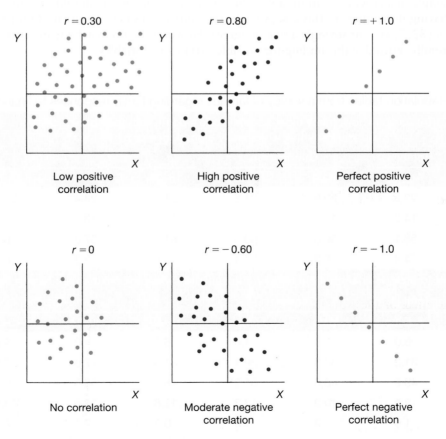

Figure 19.3 Scatter diagram to illustrate correlation patterns

Regression analysis

Regression analysis is another technique for measuring the linear association between a dependent and an independent variable. Although simple regression and correlation are mathematically equivalent in most respects, regression is a dependence technique whereas correlation is an interdependence technique. A dependence technique makes a distinction between dependent and independent variables, specifying the cause and the effect. An interdependence technique does not make this distinction and simply is concerned with how variables relate to one another.

Thus, with simple regression, a dependent (or criterion) variable, Y, is linked to an independent (or predictor) variable, X. Regression analysis attempts to predict the values of Y, a continuous, interval-scaled dependent variable from specific values of the independent variable.

Cross-tabulation

A frequency distribution or tabulation can address many research questions. As long as a question deals with only one categorical variable, tabulation is probably the best approach. Although frequency counts, percentage distributions and averages summarize considerable information, simple tabulation may not yield the full value of the research. Cross-tabulation is the appropriate technique for addressing research questions involving relationships among multiple less than interval variables. We can think of a cross-tabulation as a combined frequency table. Cross-tabs allow the inspection and comparison of differences among groups based on nominal or ordinal categories. One key to interpreting a cross-tabulation table is comparing the observed table values with hypothetical values that would result from pure chance. Here, we focus on constructing and interpreting cross-tabs.

Table 19.9 summarizes several cross-tabulations from responses to a questionnaire on how families would respond to financial hardship or instability associated with their children. Panel A presents results on whether grown children should be allowed to share a home with their parents. The cross-tab suggests this may vary with basic demographic variables. From the results, we can see that more men (24 per cent) than women (22 per cent) reported they consider it a 'good idea'. Further, it appears that there is a slight increase when comparisons are made between very young (18–29) and middle-class respondents, although this trend decreases substantially for those respondents over 60 years of age. Panel B provides another example of a cross-tabulation table. The question asks if parents should provide financial help to their children if they are having difficulties. In this case, we see some differences between men (38.6 per cent strongly agree or agree) and women (33.7 per cent strongly agree or agree). However, before reaching any conclusions based on this survey, one must carefully scrutinize this finding for possible extraneous variables.

Table 19.9 Cross-tabulation tables from a survey of families regarding family responses to financial hardships

(A) As you know, many older people share a home with their grown children. Do you think this is generally a good idea or a bad idea?							
	Total (%)	Gender (%)		Age (%)			
	Adults	Male	Female	18–29	30–44	45–59	60+
Good idea	22.8	23.9	21.8	21.2	24.4	27.4	18.4
Bad idea	14.2	14.4	14.0	12.2	13.1	11.8	18.3
It depends	58.1	56.5	59.8	61.1	57.3	56.4	58.8
Don't know	4.8	5.3	4.4	5.5	5.2	4.3	4.6
(B) Parents ought to provide financial help to their adult children when the children are having financial difficulty.							
	Total (%)	Gender (%)		Age (%)			
	Adults	Male	Female	18–29	30–44	45–59	60+
Strongly agree	5.0	5.3	4.6	6.1	4.0	4.2	5.7
Agree	31.2	33.3	29.1	31.6	27.6	29.0	36.0
Neither	49.9	48.6	51.2	48.7	53.6	50.8	46.6
Disagree	12.1	10.9	13.3	12.8	12.6	13.6	9.9
Strongly disagree	1.9	1.9	1.9	0.8	2.1	2.5	1.8

Contingency tables

Table 19.10 shows an example of cross-tabulation results using contingency tables. A **contingency table** is a data matrix that displays the frequency of some combination of possible responses to multiple variables. Two-way contingency tables, meaning they involve two less than interval variables, are used most often. A three-way contingency table involves three less than interval variables. Beyond three variables, contingency tables become difficult to analyze and explain. For all practical purposes, a contingency table is the same as a cross-tabulation.

> **contingency table** A data matrix that displays the frequency of some combination of possible responses to multiple variables; cross-tabulation results.

Table 19.10 Possible cross-tabulations of one question

(A) Cross-tabulation of question 'Do you shop at Target?' by sex of respondent			
	Yes	No	Total
Men	150	75	225
Women	180	45	225
Total	330	120	450
(B) Percentage cross-tabulation of question 'Do you shop at Target?' by sex of respondent, row percentage			
	Yes	No	Total (Base)
Men	66.7%	33.3%	100% (225)
Women	80.0%	20.0%	100% (225)
(C) Percentage cross-tabulation of question 'Do you shop at Target?' by sex of respondent, column percentage			
	Yes		No
Men	45.5%		62.5%
Women	54.5%		37.5%
Total	100%		100%
(Base)	(330)		(120)

Two variables are depicted in the contingency table shown in panel A:

- Row variable: Biological sex ___ M ___ F
- Column variable: 'Do you shop at Target? YES or NO'

Several conclusions can be drawn initially by examining the row and column totals:

1. 225 men and 225 women responded, as can be seen in the row totals column.
2. Out of 450 total consumers responding, 330 consumers indicated that 'Yes' they do shop at Target and 120 indicated 'No', they do not shop at Target. This can be observed in the column totals at the bottom of the table. These row and column totals often are called **marginals** because they appear in the table's margins.

> **marginals** Row and column totals in a contingency table, which are shown in its margins.

Researchers usually are more interested in the inner cells of a contingency table. The inner cells display conditional frequencies (combinations). Using these values, we can draw some more specific conclusions:

3. Out of 330 consumers who shop at Target, 150 are male and 180 are female.
4. Alternatively, out of the 120 respondents not shopping at Target, 75 are male and 45 are female.

This finding helps us know whether the two variables are related. If men and women equally patronized Target, we would expect that hypothetically 165 of the 330 shoppers would be male and 165 would be female. Because we have equal numbers of men and women, the 330 would be equally male and female. The hypothetical expectations (165m/165f) are not observed. What is the implication of this finding? Target shoppers are more likely to be female than male. Notice that the same meaning could be drawn by analyzing non-Target shoppers.

A two-way contingency table like the one shown in part A is referred to as a 2×2 table because it has two rows and two columns. Each variable has two levels. A two-way contingency table displaying two variables, one (the row variable) with three levels and the other with four levels, would be referred to as a 3×4 table. Any cross-tabulation table may be classified according to the number of rows by the number of columns (R by C).

Percentage cross-tabulations

When data from a survey are cross-tabulated, percentages help the researcher understand the nature of the relationship by making relative comparisons simpler. The total number of respondents or observations may be used as a **statistical base** for computing the percentage in each cell. When the objective of the research is to identify a relationship between answers to two questions (or two variables), one of the questions is commonly chosen to be the source of the base for determining percentages. For example, look at the data in parts A, B and C of Figure 19.4. Compare part B with part C. In part B, we are considering gender as the base – what percentage of men and of women shop at Target? In part C, we are considering Target shoppers as the base – what percentage of Target shoppers are men? Selecting either the row percentages or the column percentages will emphasize a particular comparison or distribution. The nature of the problem the researcher wishes to answer will determine which marginal total will serve as a base for computing percentages.

> **statistical base** The number of respondents or observations (in a row or column) used as a basis for computing percentages.

Quadrant analysis is a variation of cross-tabulation in which responses to two rating scale questions are plotted in four quadrants of a two-dimensional table. A common quadrant analysis in business research portrays or plots relationships between average responses about a product attribute's importance and average ratings of a company's (or brand's) performance on that product feature. The term **importance-performance analysis** is sometimes used because consumers rate perceived importance of several attributes and rate how well the company's brand performs on that attribute. Generally speaking, the business would like to end up in the quadrant indicating high performance on an important attribute.

> **quadrant analysis** An extension of cross-tabulation in which responses to two rating-scale questions are plotted in four quadrants of a two-dimensional table.
>
> **importance-performance analysis** Another name for quadrant analysis.

Data transformation (also called data conversion) is the process of changing the data from their original form to a format suitable for performing a data analysis that will achieve research objectives. Researchers often modify the values of scalar data or create new variables. For example, many researchers believe that less response bias will result if interviewers ask respondents for their year of birth rather than their age. This presents no problem for the research analyst, because a simple data transformation is possible. The raw data coded as birth year can easily be transformed to age by subtracting the birth year from the current year.

> **data transformation** Process of changing the data from their original form to a format suitable for performing a data analysis addressing research objectives.

Tables are useful in presenting data because they provide a means through which a great deal of data can be presented in a very succinct manner. Tables are a simple and an effective way of communicating, often, complex data. They are useful too in that tabulating data, like graphing data, can produce fresh insights into the data.

GRAPHING DATA

Graphing data is an important facility in quantitative data analysis. Graphing data, like tabulating data, allows for the communication of large quantities of data in a very succinct manner. In addition, graphing data, or visually displaying data, can make trends and patterns in the data apparent. It does sometimes happen that researchers do not see particular trends or patterns in their data until they visually display the data by graphing them. Graphing data is as important to the process of data analysis as it is to the process of communicating data analysis. It is easy to graph data, for example, a graph can be created in Microsoft Excel and then imported into the data analysis chapter in Microsoft Word. There is also, as explained earlier, a facility in SPSS for graphing data. It would be a useful exercise to spend time exploring the graphing facilities in Excel and in SPSS. Through a casual exploration of the facilities you will learn a lot about how they work, and you will get some good ideas about how you might use them in reporting your research. There are very many different kinds of graph typically used with social science data. Some examples are presented in the following paragraphs.

Line graphs

A line graph is used to visually display a line of data. Line graphs are useful in discerning trends in data and particularly trends over time. Figure 19.4 displays data on club membership over time, from 2000 to 2009. The graph on the right provides a gender breakdown on the data. In this graph, we can see the relative rise in club membership of female and male members over the years 2000–2009. As you can see from the graph, while membership rates have risen consistently for both genders, the rise in female membership rates has been consistently higher than the rise in rates of male membership.

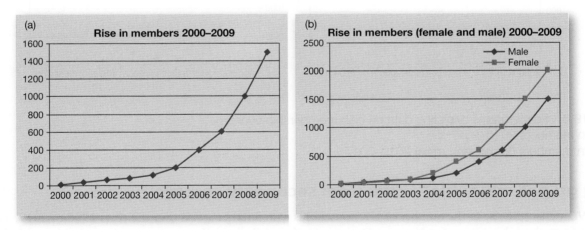

Figure 19.4 Line graphs depicting data on club membership over time
(a) Rise in members 2000–2009
(b) Rise in members (female and male) 2000–2009

Bar chart

A bar chart graphs data in tabular form. In Figure 19.5 the data on club membership are shown in bar charts. If you study both the line graphs, and the bar charts, you will clearly see that both sets of visual data representations present the same data.

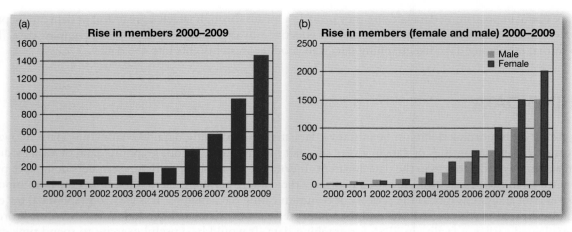

Figure 19.5 Bar charts depicting data on club membership over time
(a) Rise in members 2000–2009
(b) Rise in members (female and male) 2000–2009

Scattergrams

The data on club membership are also presented in the scattergrams in Figure 19.6. A scattergram is a useful way of visually summarizing bivariate data. A scattergram gives a good representation of the relationship between two variables.

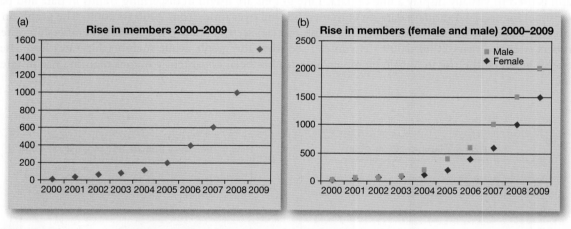

Figure 19.6 Scattergrams depicting data on club membership over time
(a) Rise in members 2010–2017
(b) Rise in members (female and male) 2010–2017

Using graphs and tables taken from secondary sources

Figure 19.7 details the rise in the number of UK households with internet access over the years 1998 to 2017. The data are taken from the UK's Office for National Statistics Statistical Bulletin 'Internet access households and individuals 2017'. This bulletin contains many data on internet access in the UK.

Figure 19.8 was taken from the UK's Office for National Statistics, their statistical bulletin entitled Annual Survey of Hours and Earnings. As you can see, the chart shows the change in median hourly pay, for all employees and those in continuous employment in the UK, April 2005–2017. As we know, the median is the middle value of a range of values.

Clearly, there is a wealth of data in national and international databases that can be accessed and used as the sole source of data in a research project, or as supplementary sources of data in a research project. The key is to find data that are useful in terms of the research you are carrying out and then to find a way to integrate those data in a meaningful way into your research.

A good way of learning how to present data is to examine how other researchers present data. You can do this by reading the theses in your library and by finding journal articles that feature research similar to your own. Look at how these other researchers present their data. If you find one or more useful models, in terms of data presentation, try to model your own presentation of your data, or some aspects of your presentation of your data, on them. Reading the work of other researchers is one of the best ways of learning how to conduct and present research.

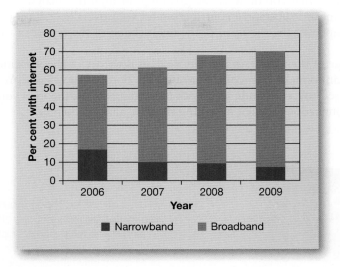

Figure 19.7 Rise in internet access, UK households and individuals, 1998–2017

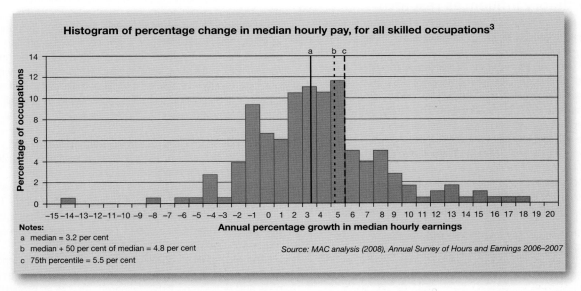

Figure 19.8 Annual percentage change in median full-time gross weekly earnings for all employees and those in continuous employment, UK, April 2005 to 2017

The research project presented in the Real World Research box is a study of the research methodologies used in small business and entrepreneurial research and published in three journals over the time period 2001 to 2008. The journal article provides a critique of the research methodologies used in the research projects. The key issues in research methodology which are focused on in the article are sampling methods and issues of validity and reliability.

THE FOUR STAGES OF DATA ANALYSIS

It is important in quantitative data analysis, as it is in qualitative data analysis, to remember the four stages of the data analysis process, detailed and explained in detail in Chapter 17:

- The first stage calls for descriptive analysis. This is, very simply, describing what it is that you see in the data.
- The second stage is interpretation. Interpreting the data involves attempting to explain the meaning of what it is that you see in your data, as you have described it in the descriptive analysis.

- The third stage is the conclusions stage. In the conclusions stage, you move the interpretation along from stating what it is that you see in the data and what you think that means, to drawing some kind of minor conclusion about that. The conclusions that you draw as you go along through the analysis are generally minor conclusions. They add up to, or they make a substantial contribution to, your overall conclusion(s). Your overall conclusion(s) are stated in the final chapter of the thesis, or in the final section of the report of the research project in the final chapter of the thesis.

- The fourth and final stage of the four stages of data analysis is theory or theorization. It is with this theorizing of the analysis that you begin to make your contribution to the body of knowledge. You look back at your literature review and you check to see how your findings fit with the findings of the theorists you have detailed in that chapter. Then you make those connections explicit in writing the data analysis chapter.

REAL WORLD RESEARCH

How theory influences research

This article (Mullen *et al.*, 2009, 'Research methods in the leading small business– entrepreneurship journals: a critical review with recommendations for future research', *Journal of Small Business Management*, 47(3): 287–307), details a critique of the research methodologies used by small business and entrepreneurship researchers. The study gathered data from reports of research projects published in journal articles in three different journals: the *Journal of Small Business Management*, the *Journal of Business Venturing* and *Entrepreneurship Theory and Practice*. The analysis carried out by Mullen *et al.* includes all of the articles published in the three journals between 2001 and 2008. There were in all 665 articles.

The stated objectives of the study were as follows:

- To discuss key methodological issues.
- To assess recent methodological practice.
- To identify current trends.
- To provide guidance for researchers in adopting existing and emerging research technologies.

Following a study by Chandler and Lyon (2001), Mullen *et al.* (2009) break their sample of articles into two broad categories: empirical and conceptual. Empirical studies are, they state, studies that include data and/or data analysis in the study, while conceptual papers include theory/conceptual development, literature reviews and other treatments that do not gather or use data. Content analysis was the methodology used by Mullen *et al.* to examine the journal articles.

They found that there were in all 478 empirical studies and 187 conceptual papers. Of the 478 empirical papers, 50 were carried out using qualitative methods, case studies, interviews and observations. The qualitative studies accounted for 7 per cent of all of the empirical research.

Almost three-quarters of all of the studies were quantitative (*n* = 428). In critiquing the quantitative studies, Mullen *et al.* focused on the sampling methods used, issues of validity and reliability and the statistical methods used.

Across the three journals included in the study, there were in all 273 primary data studies. This represented 64 per cent of all quantitative studies, and 41 per cent of all small business/entrepreneurship research.

The primary data studies were divided into two groups: those carried out using a survey methodology, and those carried out using experimental design. Of the 273 primary data studies, only 13 studies, or 5 per cent of the primary data studies, had been carried out using experimental design. The remaining 260 studies were conducted using a survey methodology. Ninety-five per cent of all primary data studies, 61 per cent of all empirical studies, and 39 per cent of all small business/entrepreneurship studies, relied on data gathered from surveys.

Secondary data, the researchers stated, were used in 155 papers, 36 per cent of all quantitative research and 24 per cent of all small business/entrepreneurship research.

Mullen *et al.* found that the researchers had used a wide range of statistical procedures to analyze their data. These statistical procedures included descriptive statistics, comparisons of means, the use of *t*-tests, correlation analysis, regression analysis and ANOVA and MANOVA.

The Mullen *et al.* (2009), study is interesting in terms of the focus on the research methodologies used in small business and entrepreneurship research. As well as providing an analysis of the different methodological approaches used, the Mullen *et al.* (2009), study is interesting in terms of the critique it provides of those methodologies.

In conclusion, Mullen *et al.* (2009), state that their review of all 655 studies published in the field of small business–entrepreneurship over the years 2001 to 2008 identifies improvements in the research methods used in the field of small business and entrepreneurship research, but also substantial methodological weaknesses.

Question: Can you determine, from your reading of the journal article, the reasoning behind this conclusion? Based on your reading of the journal article, do you agree with this conclusion? Based on your reading of the journal article can you draw further conclusions? What further conclusions have you drawn?

The means by which you draw findings from data, interpret those findings and draw conclusions from them are considered in detail in Chapter 20.

As stated earlier in this chapter, you do not report every detail of your data. You select from your data (and your analysis of your data) the key issues and aspects that you decide to present when writing up your analysis. The narrative (or story) that you tell about your data and your analysis of your data is dictated by your research statement or question, by the overall aim of your research, by the issues that emerged from your review of the literature, as well as by the data you gathered.

The four frameworks approach is designed to help the researcher maintain the focus of the research throughout the research process. The focus of the researcher should be on the research statement or question, the research hypothesis or the overall aim of the research project. The manner in which the four frameworks approach to the research process works is detailed once more in Figure 19.10.

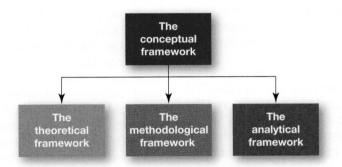

Figure 19.10   The four frameworks

The researcher must ensure that the data, the analysis of the data, and the data presented, all answer the research question, or all respond to the research statement, the research hypothesis, the overall aim of the research and the objectives of the research. Table 19.11 explains once again the logic of the four frameworks approach.

Table 19.11   Logic of the four frameworks approach to the research project

The conceptual framework	Contained in the research statement/question and repeated again in the stated aim of the research. The entire research project rests on the conceptual framework for the research project. The conceptual framework contains all of the key concepts in the research. The key concepts in the conceptual framework inform and guide the search for literature for the literature review and they help structure the literature review.
The theoretical framework	The literature review contains the theoretical framework for the research project. The structure and development of the literature review is guided and directed by the conceptual framework.
The methodological framework	The methodological framework is contained in the methodology chapter of the thesis or in the methodology section of the report of the research. The methodological framework contains all of the detail on how the research was carried out. The conceptual framework guides and directs the development of the theoretical framework. The conceptual framework with the theoretical framework guides and directs the development of the methodological framework. The conceptual framework, the aim and objectives of the research and the theoretical framework inform, guide and direct the questions asked in the fieldwork/data gathering for the research.
The analytical framework	The analytical framework is contained in the data analysis chapter of the thesis or in the data analysis section of the report of the research. Data is gathered for the research project in order to respond to the research statement/question, the overall aim and the objectives of the research project. The focus of data analysis is on responding to the research statement/question and the overall aim and objectives of the research. This ensures that the research project maintains focus and it ensures that the researcher accomplishes what s/he set out to accomplish in undertaking the research as formally stated in the research aim and objectives.

CASE STUDY

A survey: consumption of charity bracelets

In this study (Yurchisin *et al.*, 2009, 'Consumers of charity bracelets: cause-supporters or fashion-followers?', *Journal of Fashion Marketing and Management*, 13(3): 448–457), the researchers carried out a survey designed to compare the personal characteristics of buyers of rubber charity bracelets with those of non-buyers. The aim of the study was to develop a deeper understanding of the market success of rubber charity bracelets.

The survey was carried out on a convenience sample of 244 individuals in Texas and Iowa in the USA. The questionnaire used was divided into three sections. The first section was designed to assess participants' level of fashion involvement and celebrity involvement; the second section was designed to assess participants' attitudes toward the consumption of cause-related fashion products; and the third and final section was designed to facilitate the gathering of demographic data.

The authors state that the study provides useful information to manufacturers and sellers of cause-related products. They say that efforts to manufacture and sell cause-related products should focus on developing products that incorporate fashion trends with celebrity endorsers.

The article explains that one of the most popular fashion accessories in the USA in 2005 was a cause-related product: the silicone rubber charity bracelet (Dodes, 2005; Webster, 2005). These inexpensive, colourful rubber bracelets, we are told, were sold by a variety of businesses (e.g. Nike, 7-Eleven, Hot Topic), and the proceeds or a portion of the proceeds of these sales were donated to specific charities (e.g. Hot Topic Foundation to support programmes and organizations that encourage youth involvement in art and music).

With the overwhelming success of the rubber bracelet cause-related fashion product, the article explains, both for-profit and non-profit organizations located in the USA and around the globe are trying to develop new cause-related products that will be similarly popular in the upcoming seasons.

Thus, the authors suggest, a need exists among practitioners for information related to the consumers of rubber charity bracelets. They say that while general information has been collected about the consumers of ethical products and cause-related products, the unusually massive appeal of the rubber charity bracelet as a cause-related fashion product seems to warrant further investigation into the consumption of this particular product. The suggestion the authors make is that if practitioners can understand the reasons why consumers purchased the rubber charity bracelets, perhaps they can use this information to create similarly successful cause-related fashion products in the future.

They tell us that the purpose of their research was to survey rubber charity bracelet consumers by exploring their purchasing behaviour.

The demographic data presented in the article detail that most of the participants in the research were female (86 per cent). Most participants indicated that they were either Caucasian American (76 per cent) or Hispanic American (17 per cent). The participants had a mean age of approximately 28 years, with a range of 18 to 65. We are told that although an attempt was made to obtain non-student participants, most participants were currently enrolled as undergraduate students (72 per cent). The number of rubber charity bracelets owned by participants ranged from 0 to 50, with a mean of 1.88. The price paid by participants for each bracelet ranged from $0.00 to $20.00, with a mean of $2.55. The number of retail outlets where the bracelets were purchased ranged from one to seven, with an average of 2.71 outlets. The participants in the research indicated that they had purchased their bracelets most frequently from department stores (16.2 per cent); followed by speciality stores (15.3 per cent), discount retailers/mass merchandisers (14.7 per cent), internet websites (14.7 per cent) and boutiques (13.8 per cent).

In conclusion, the authors state that the results of their study indicate that the success of the rubber charity bracelet was based on different factors. They said that first, the rubber charity bracelet is consistent with larger fashion trends, and second, it has an association with popular celebrities. These two factors, the authors report, appeared to have contributed to the mass appeal of the rubber charity bracelet, particularly among individuals who were highly involved with fashion and celebrities.

The authors state that future efforts to manufacture cause-related products should focus on developing products that incorporate fashion trends. They also recommend that sellers of cause-related products could consider celebrity endorsers for effective marketing of their products.

The results of the study indicate that attitude toward purchasing a cause-related fashion product is not a good predictor of behaviour. The authors suggest that there may have been a social desirability bias where respondents showed support for particular causes and positive attitudes toward cause-related purchasing to please the researcher.

Question: Can you explain what is meant by bias in research? Can you name and explain the main sources of bias in research?

END OF CHAPTER QUESTIONS

1 What is a variable?

2 Explain the differences between nominal, ordinal and interval level variables.

3 What is a coding key and what is it used for?

4 Explain the value of tabulating research.

5 Explain what is meant by the terms univariate, bivariate and multivariate analysis.

6 Explain the differences between descriptive and inferential statistics.

7 Name and explain ten descriptive statistics commonly used in quantitative data analysis and briefly outline how they are used in data analysis.

8 Name and explain five different inferential statistics and briefly outline how they are used in data analysis.

9 Explain why graphs and tables are used for the display and analysis of data.

10 Outline and explain the key advantages to using SPSS in quantitative data analysis.

11 What is the analytical framework in the four frameworks approach to the research project? Explain how it helps the researcher maintain focus in the research project.

12 What is the ideal climate? Fill in the following blanks: The lowest temperature in January should be no lower than ___ degrees. At least ___ days should be sunny in January:

    a List at least 15 places in which you would like to live. Using the internet, find the average low temperature in January for each place. This information is available through various weather-related websites such as www.weather.com or through each community's local news website. Record the data in a spreadsheet or statistical package such as SPSS. Using the benchmark (preferred population low temperature) you filled in above, test whether the sample places that you would like to live in have an ideal January minimum temperature.

    b Using the same website, record how many days in January are typically sunny. Test whether or not the number of sunny days meets your standard.

    c For each location, record whether or not there was measurable precipitation yesterday. Test the following hypothesis:

    H_1: *Among places you would like to live, there is less than a 33.3 per cent chance of rain/snow on a given day (five days out of 15).*

REFERENCES

Colorado State University, 'Writing guide: introduction to statistics', writing.colostate.edu/guides/guide.cfm?guideid=67 (Accessed 17.03.2018).

Chandler, G. & Lyon, D. (2001) 'Issues of Research Design and Construct Measurement in Entrepreneurship Research: The past Decade', www.researchgate.net/publication/308059361_Issues_of_Research_Design_and_Construct_Measurement_in_Entrepreneurship_Research_The_past_Decade

Harvard MIT Data Center, 'Guide to SPSS', www.hks.harvard.edu/fs/pnorris/Classes/A%20SPSS%20Manuals/SPSS%20Statistcs%20Base%20User's%20Guide%2017.0.pdf (Accessed 17.03.2018).

Hawthorne Experiments, Harvard Business School, www.library.hbs.edu/hc/hawthorne/09.html (Accessed 17.03.2018).

Markova, G. (2009) 'Can human resource management make a big difference in a small company?', *International Journal of Strategic Management*, 9(2): 73–80.

Mullen, M.R., Budeva, D.G. and Doney, P.M. (2009) 'Research methods in the leading small business–entrepreneurship journals: a critical review with recommendations for future research', *Journal of Small Business Management*, 47(3): 287–307.

NASA (National Aeronautics and Space Administration), climate.nasa.gov (Accessed 17.03.2018).

Office for National Statistics, Statistical Bulletin 'Internet access households and individuals 2017', www.ons.gov.uk/peoplepopulationandcommunity/householdcharacteristics/homeinternetandsocialmediausage/bulletins/internetaccesshouseholdsandindividuals/2017 (Accessed 17.03.2017).

Office for National Statistics, Statistical Bulletin, 'Annual Survey of Hours and Earnings: 2017 Provisional and 2016 Revised Results', www.ons.gov.uk/employmentandlabourmarket/peopleinwork/earningsandworkinghours/bulletins/annualsurveyofhoursandearnings/2017provisionaland2016revisedresults#average-earnings (Accessed 17.03.2018).

Purdue Online Writing Lab, 'Basic inferential statistics', owl.english.purdue.edu/owl/resource/672/05 (Accessed 17.03.2018).

Quinlan, C. (2011) *Business Research Methods*, South Western Cengage.

Science Olympiad, 'Experimental design', scioly.org/wiki/index.php/Experimental_Design (Accessed 17.03.2018).

Stat Trek, 'Teach yourself statistics', stattrek.com (Accessed 17.03.2018).

Trochim, W.M. (2006) *The Research Methods Knowledge Base*, socialresearchmethods.net (Accessed 17.03.2018).

UCLA 'Which Statistical Test?', www.ats.ucla.edu/stat/spss/modules/descript.htm (Accessed 17.03.2018).

Yurchisin, J., Yoo Jin, K. and Marcketti, S.B. (2009) 'Consumers of charity bracelets: cause-supporters or fashion-followers?', *Journal of Fashion Marketing and Management*, 13(3): 448–457.

RECOMMENDED READING

Babbie, E. (1990) *Survey Research Methods* (2nd edn), Belmont, CA: Wadsworth Publishing.

Bell, J. and Waters, S. (2014) *Doing Your Research Project* (6th edn), Maidenhead: Open University Press.

Collis, J. and Hussey, R. (2013) *Business Research: A Practical Guide for Undergraduate and Postgraduate Students* (4th edn), Basingstoke and New York: Palgrave Macmillan.

Creswell, J. and Creswell, D.J. (2018) *Research Design: Qualitative, Quantitative and Mixed Methods Approaches* (5th edn), London, California, New Delhi, Singapore: Sage.

Curwin, J. and Slater, R. (2007) *Quantitative Methods: A Short Course*, London: Thomson Learning.

Daly, F., Hand, D.J., Jones, M.G., Lunn, A.D. and McConway, K.J. (1995) *Elements of Statistics*, Wokingham: Addison Wesley.

Easterby-Smith, M., Thorpe, R. and Jackson, P.R. (2008) *Management Research* (3rd edn), London: Sage.

Lee, N. and Lings, I. (2008) *Doing Business Research: A Guide to Theory and Practice*, London: Sage.

Neuman, W.L. (2014) *Social Research Methods: Qualitative and Quantitative Approaches* (7th edn), Essex, England: Pearson Education Ltd.

Oppenheim, A.N. (2000) *Questionnaire Design, Interviewing and Attitude Measurement* (2nd edn), London: Pinter.

Rea, L.M. and Parker, R.A. (2014) *Designing and Conducting Survey Research: A Comprehensive Guide* (4th edn), John Wiley & Sons Inc.

Robson, C. and McCartan, K. (2016) *Real World Research*, John Wiley & Sons Ltd.

CHAPTER 20

COMPLETING AND PRESENTING THE RESEARCH

LEARNING OBJECTIVES

At the end of this chapter, the student should be able to:

● Conceptualize and present conclusions from research.

● Conceptualize and present recommendations for research projects.

● Complete the final written report of a research project.

● Present the research.

RESEARCH SKILLS

At the end of this chapter, the student should, using the exercises on Cengage Brain, be able to:

● Explain what a conclusion is in a research project, and what conclusions represent in terms of the research endeavour.

● Explain how good and useful recommendations are conceptualized and presented.

● Critique the conclusions and recommendations from a given research project.

The aim of this chapter is to explain the importance of the written report of the research project. To explain the concept of conclusions in research, to demonstrate how conclusions should be drawn, and to help you, the student, develop the skills needed to complete the write-up of a thesis. The means by which the research project is brought full circle is demonstrated in this chapter by explaining how the final conclusions of the research project respond to the research question or statement of the research project, respond to the aim of the research. The chapter explains how the final chapter of the thesis, or the final section of the research report, is designed to answer fully and completely the research question or the research statement.

INTRODUCTION

This final chapter explains and demonstrates what conclusions are, how they are drawn and what they are based on, and what is meant by the implications of the conclusions of the research project. The process of theorizing conclusions is explained and demonstrated. The chapter explains and demonstrates how **recommendations** are made in a research project.

> **recommendations** The courses of action that the researcher recommends based on the findings and subsequent conclusions drawn from those findings.

The chapter also considers the process of writing a thesis and presents tips for writing and the writing process. The means by which the written research project fits together, how it is structured and designed is explained and demonstrated. The importance and the limitations of the **first draft** of the thesis and the importance of the work of editing in the production of the final draft of the thesis/report of the research is explained. The importance of sequence, synthesis and integration in the **final draft** of the thesis are all considered.

> **first draft** The draft before the process of editing begins.
>
> **final draft** The edited and polished fully integrated and correct copy of the thesis that is finally submitted for examination.

Why should a careful researcher have to be a good writer, too? After the researcher has spent days, weeks or even months working on a project, preparation of the report may feel like an anticlimactic formality. All the 'real' work has been done; it just has to be put on paper. This attitude can be disastrous, however. Even if the project was well designed, the data carefully obtained and analyzed by sophisticated statistical and/or qualitative methods and important conclusions reached, unless the report of the research can effectively communicate this information, all of the earlier efforts will have been wasted. Frequently, the research report is the only part of the project that others ever see. The research report is a crucial means for communicating the whole project.

It is important in writing and presenting research that the study is written and presented as fully and as completely as possible. The writing and the presentation of research should be done in such a way as to facilitate clear and correct comprehension. The researcher writing up and presenting research is engaged in an exercise of communication with the reader. If the report is written for an academic audience, the communication should be structured to suit that audience. The final account of the research project should be communicated as fully, as comprehensively and as clearly as possible.

The model of the research project, presented in Chapter 1, Figure 1.1, shows how we have now come full circle in the research process. We are now at the stage of drawing conclusions from our research and making recommendations. We are finally completing the writing up and presentation of the research.

The research project detailed in the Value of Good Research box explains how two different accounts of one survey were published in *The Guardian* newspaper. The feature demonstrates how it is possible, regardless of how practised you are, to get it wrong in the writing and presentation of your research.

THE VALUE OF GOOD RESEARCH

An example of the potential complexities in reporting research

A reader of *The Guardian* newspaper wrote to the newspaper a few years ago, asking why a news story printed in the main paper and featured in the *Weekend* magazine, both published on the same day, reported seemingly conflicting findings. The focus of the study was teenage boys.

The survey was an online poll which used a panel of 1000 teenage boys living in England, Wales and Scotland as its base. Among the key findings were the findings that over 90 per cent of teenage boys are happy in their social lives; are happy in their home and family lives; are happy in their school or work lives; are ambitious about their future careers; and believe their career prospects are good. These findings were reported in the *Weekend* magazine.

The main section of the newspaper reported, on the same day, that less than 90 per cent of teenage boys were happy in their social lives; happy in their family lives; were happy at school or work; were ambitious; and believed they had good career prospects. Both sets of figures told the same story; the vast majority of teenage boys who took part in this survey said they were happy about their lives and prospects, but which findings were right?

The private research firm that carried out the research said that both sets of figures were correct. This was because the key findings presented in the *Weekend* magazine excluded people who gave the response 'neither agree nor disagree' to statements in the survey. The firm's research director said that the figures in the magazine gave a stronger picture by focusing solely on those respondents who had expressed an opinion.

Readers should have been told that the percentages reported in the magazine represented the responses of survey participants who expressed an opinion one way or the other.

While *The Guardian* did not 'get it wrong' exactly, neither did it precisely get it right either. It presented two different sets of results for the same survey and Siobhain Butterworth, the readers' editor of the newspaper, explained how this happened. Butterworth's concluding point (Butterworth, 2009) is useful for us in terms of this chapter. She states that the newspaper's weekender readers needed more information in order to be able to properly and fully understand the research as it was presented in the magazine section of the newspaper.

THE FINAL CHAPTER: DRAWING CONCLUSIONS AND WRITING RECOMMENDATIONS

In the final chapter of the thesis, or the final section of the research report, the researcher presents the conclusions and recommendations of the research project. Usually, the final chapter of the thesis or report is relatively short. There is an exception, however, to this general rule. If, for example, a grounded theory (GT) methodology has been used in the research project, the final chapter will be a substantial chapter; it will contain a full and detailed outline and explanation of the theory developed through the research. Remember, GT methodology is specifically designed to facilitate the development of new theory which is grounded in the data gathered for the research project. In general, the final chapter of the thesis/report of the research contains the overall conclusions drawn from the research, and the recommendations the researcher makes based on the conclusions drawn from the research.

All research undertaken within an academic setting must make a contribution to knowledge. Academic research, as explained in this textbook, emerges from a body of knowledge and, in turn, makes a contribution to that body of knowledge. In the final chapter, as well as presenting the findings of the research, the conclusions drawn from the research and the recommendations the researcher makes based on the research, if recommendations are appropriate, the researcher theorizes the conclusions drawn from the research.

The process of theorizing conclusions is the same as the process of **theorization** in the four stages of data analysis. The four stages, as explained in earlier chapters, are description, interpretation, conclusion and theorization. In the process of theorizing conclusions, the researcher draws on the work of other researchers and theorists and they knit their conclusions into the conclusions of these researchers and theorists. Through this process the researcher enriches the reporting of their conclusions. They connect their research to the research of other researchers in the field. It is in this way that the researcher makes their contribution to knowledge.

> **theorization** The researcher draws on the work of other researchers and theorists to enrich the reporting of their conclusions by connecting their research to the research of other theorists in the field. It is in this way that the researcher makes their contribution to knowledge.

Conclusions in research

A conclusion is essentially a judgement, or a final decision. At the end of the research process, the researcher comes to a final conclusion, or several final conclusions, about the research. This final decision or final judgement will relate to, or respond to, the research question or statement, to the overall aim of the research project. We have seen throughout this textbook how the four frameworks approach to the research project facilitates the researcher in building the research project on the conceptual framework, the research statement or question, the overall aim of the research. Now in this final phase of the research project, the researcher conceptualizes the overall conclusion of the research project. This must emerge logically and validly from the analysis of the data gathered, and from the findings of the research in such a way as to ensure that the overall conclusion responds to the research question or statement and accomplishes the aim of the research.

In presenting data analysis the researcher engages in the four stages of data analysis. First, they describe the data, then they interpret the data, then they come to some minor conclusion about the data, and finally they theorize the data. In every step of presenting the analyzed data and the findings of the research, the researcher presents minor conclusions drawn from the research. All of these minor conclusions add up into the overall conclusion that the researcher draws from the research.

The four frameworks

- Conceptual Framework
- Theoretical Framework
- Methodological Framework
- *Analytical Framework*

The overall conclusion that the researcher draws from the research is presented at the start of the final chapter, the chapter on conclusions and recommendations. This overall conclusion is a response to the research question or statement, a response to the overall aim of the research. It is the final accomplishment of the overall aim of the research project. It is the essential product of the research.

The overall conclusion from the research project is presented at the start of the final chapter, and it is thoroughly discussed and explained. This presentation, discussion and explanation of the overall conclusion is followed by the presentation and discussion of a number of main conclusions, all drawn from the overall conclusion.

The conclusions section in the final chapter of the thesis is the first part of the chapter. Following a brief introduction to the chapter, the conclusions are presented. The overall conclusion or overarching conclusion is presented and discussed first. Then the major conclusions are each detailed and discussed briefly. There then follows a general discussion of the conclusions, which are explored and examined. They are theorized. This means that the researcher briefly explains how the conclusions that they have drawn from their research fit with or contradict the conclusions that other researchers and theorists (as detailed in the literature review) have drawn about their own research. In this way, the researcher connects their research to the research of others and makes a contribution to knowledge.

Table 20.1 demonstrates how conclusions are drawn from findings and how recommendations are made based on conclusions.

Table 20.1 Drawing conclusions and making recommendations

Finding	Conclusion	Recommendation
One of the key findings of the research project was that all staff members were dissatisfied with the professional development training provided by the company.	The professional development programme provided by the company is failing to meet the needs of staff.	Either the professional training programme provided should receive a substantial overhaul or a new professional development training programme should be provided.
One of the key findings of the research was that junior managers felt isolated and unsupported.	The company is failing to maximize the resource that the junior managers represent.	A programme should be designed and put in place that will ensure that junior managers are properly supported.
All participants in the research agreed that the advertisement was attractive and engaging and they said that it would encourage them to purchase.	The advertisement is effective.	The new advertising campaign should be built around the advertisement.
The research found that students had reduced disposable incomes.	This has implications for the amount of money students will spend on meals out.	Monitor sales and react promptly to any reduction in sales with deals and special offers.
The data showed that while income from product line A increased month on month over the year, income from product line B decreased substantially in the final three months of the study.	Product line A is a better seller than product line B.	Increase volume of product line A. Decrease volume of product line B. Continue monitoring sales levels. If sales of product line B continue to decline, discontinue that product line.

The process demonstrated in the table is simplified. In reality, the conclusions drawn from findings can be very substantial and quite complex.

It is a good idea when writing the conclusions section of the final chapter to use your research diary to jot down the minor conclusions detailed in the data analysis chapter and the ideas and thoughts you have in relation to them. When you have done that, you should tease out the different aspects and elements of those conclusions. The more detail you can jot down in your research diary the better. Then, from that detail, you can create (conceptualize) the overall conclusion you wish to present in your thesis. You can use the detail from your research diary to illustrate in your writing the complexity of the conclusion, which should reflect the complexity of the research undertaken. The style of the research project should be consistent throughout. For example, when writing the conclusions of a qualitative study, the richness of the data gathered should be reflected in the concluding chapter, as it was in the data analysis chapter.

Once again, it is a good idea to examine the manner in which conclusions are drawn and presented in research projects similar to the research project you are carrying out. The journal articles that you have been using to model your research on will be useful in terms of modelling your approach to the presentation of your conclusions. It is important to pay attention to the style of the presentation in these models as well as their content. It is useful, too, to examine other theses in the library. There is a need, as always, to be critical of any published research project that you might consider using as a model for your own work. When you have identified the models you think are suitable, it is a good idea to show them to your thesis supervisor or your lecturer in research methodologies and to ask their opinions on them in relation to your intention to use them as models for your own work.

The process of theorizing conclusions is critical to the research endeavour. Simple examples of this process are presented in Table 20.2. As can be seen from the examples of theorization in the table, the researcher draws on the work of other researchers and theorists to enrich the reporting of their conclusions. At the same time they are connecting their work with the body of knowledge in their field and making their overall contribution to knowledge. The theorists that the researcher draws on should be detailed in the literature review of the research project. The researcher looks back at the literature review and sees how their research fits with the research detailed there. Then the researcher makes explicit connections between their research and the research of these other researchers. When the researcher has made the connections, the researcher then comes to a further conclusion(s).

Table 20.2 Drawing conclusions and examples of the theorization process

The main conclusion drawn from the research was that the professional development training programme provided by the company for the staff of the company did not meet the requirements of the staff. This conclusion echoes the conclusions of Edwards (2017), Edwards and Burke (2018) and Clark *et al*. (2018); all of these researchers found that the professional development training programmes of the companies they studied did not meet the needs of employees.
One of the conclusions drawn from the research was that the company is failing to maximize the resource that junior managers represent. This conclusion is similar to the conclusion drawn by Bryant and Yong (2018) in their research which found that junior managers tended to be excluded from management meetings and isolated from each other primarily because of their geographic locations in the organizations.
The key conclusion of the research was that students have less disposable income. This conclusion coincides with the conclusions of Hughes (2018), Al Maheri (2018) and Merkeert (2018), all of whom documented a retraction in levels of disposable income among third-level students.
The overall conclusion from the research was that the provision of incentives, in the form of special offers, did not impact on sales levels and there was, in fact, no change in the level of sales over the period of the study. This conclusion challenges the conclusions of Marks and Henry (2018), Habite and Mehabby (2018) and Orlean and Tuti (2017), all of whom found that the use of incentives, such as special offers, does impact positively on sales levels.
Note: All references in text are fictitious. They are presented here for the purposes of the exercise.

The examples in Table 20.3 show how the researcher continues to develop conclusions from the research until all of the possible conclusions that can be drawn from the research have been drawn. The researcher then edits the conclusions section to ensure that the most important conclusions are highlighted, and to make sure that the work fits within the word count allowed.

Table 20.3 Coming to further conclusions

The main conclusion drawn from the research was that the professional development training programme provided by the company for the staff of the company did not meet the requirements of the staff. This conclusion echoes the conclusion of Edwards (2017), Edwards and Burke (2018) and Clark *et al*. (2018). These researchers found in their studies that the professional development training programmes of the companies they studied did not meet the needs of the employees.
There is clearly a real need for companies to pay particular attention to the utility and fitness for purpose of the professional development programmes they provide for staff.
One of the conclusions drawn from the research was that the company is failing to maximize the resource that junior managers represent. This conclusion is similar to the conclusion drawn by Bryant and Yong (2018) who in their research found that junior managers tended to be excluded from management meetings, and isolated from each other through their geographic location in the organizations.
The evidence suggests that there is a serious problem in SMEs in the way in which they fail to properly and thoroughly engage junior managers and, through that failure, fail to properly and thoroughly maximize on the resource that junior managers represent.
The key conclusion of the research was that students have less disposable income. This conclusion coincides with the conclusions of Hughes (2018), Al Maheri (2018) and Merkeert (2017), all of whom have documented a retraction in levels of disposable income among third-level students.
It seems that there is a clear retraction in levels of disposable income among students and this will obviously have an impact across the board on small businesses providing services to students.
The overall conclusion from the research is that the provision of incentives, in the form of special offers, did not impact on sales levels. There was, in fact, no change in the level of sales over the period of the study. This conclusion challenges the conclusions of Marks and Henry (2018), Habite and Mehabby (2018) and Orlean and Tuti (2017), all of whom found that the use of incentives, such as special offers, does impact positively on sales levels.
It seems that although, in general, incentives are an effective means of improving sales, this is by no means the rule. If there are special circumstances, as in the current study where there was a documented retraction in the level of disposable income available to the market, then incentives designed to improve sales may have only a limited effect or perhaps no effect at all.
Note: All references in text are fictitious. They are presented here for the purposes of the exercise.

The entire research project is an exercise in logic. The conclusions that you come to in your research should be logical and reasonable. They should be based on the findings of the research project. The conclusions that you draw should be valid, sound and should stand up to scrutiny. They should be meaningful in terms of the overall aim and objectives of the research project.

Implications of conclusions

When the conclusions have been presented, the implications of the conclusions should be explored. The implications of the conclusions are the meanings that the conclusions have for different parties or constituents to the research project. For example, in the professional development example examined earlier, the conclusions drawn will have implications for the company, for the people giving the training and for the staff undergoing the training. The company will have the cost of developing a new training programme, and then the benefits of the new training programme. The people delivering the training will either have to improve the training being provided, or lose the job of providing the training; there will be cost implications either way. The staff will no longer have to undergo training that they do not value, instead they will benefit from a new training programme. The staff are likely to feel encouraged and affirmed as a result of the company responding to their needs, which is likely to lead to staff renewing their commitment to the company. The company will benefit from renewed commitment from staff. These are all possible implications of that conclusion.

It is important to tease out the implications of all of the conclusions drawn from the research for every group of people, organization and entity affected by the research and the conclusions drawn from it. Once again, it is a good idea to do this in as much detail as possible. Your research diary is the place to record these thoughts, ideas and insights initially. Then when you have all of that detail, you can begin to plan and structure what you intend to report on the implications of the findings. Plan which implications to present, and where and how, and in what order, they would best be presented.

RECOMMENDATIONS OF THE STUDY

The recommendations of the study are the ways forward from the research. Recommendations are courses of action that the researcher recommends based on the findings of the research and the conclusions drawn from those findings. The recommendations, following a brief introduction, can be presented as a bullet list. The following points should be kept in mind when conceptualizing the recommendations for the study:

- Recommendations should be succinct.
- They should be meaningful in relation to the aim and objectives of the research.
- They should respond to the research question or statement.
- Recommendations should be do-able or achievable. There is no point in making recommendations that cannot possibly be acted upon, perhaps because the necessary resources are not available, or because there would be too much opposition to them, or for other reasons.

Often a researcher will draw up a list of 20 or more recommendations in the process of listing all of the possible recommendations. It is a good idea to do this to begin with. Then, through a process of refining the recommendations, by collapsing some together, by eliminating some, by conceptualizing new recommendations, the researcher will produce a list of eight to ten meaningful recommendations for the research project.

The researcher may make separate recommendations for different constituents to the research. For example, using the example of the professional development training programme above, there might be recommendations for the company, for the training programme, for the trainers and for the staff of the company.

The research project detailed in the Theory in Research box is useful here. In the journal article, the aim of the research is clearly outlined. The aim of the research is to investigate the socialization experiences within the company of 30 newly hired engineers during the early stage of their employment with a large manufacturing company. The research was developed using a qualitative case study research design. The research questions are outlined, the sample is detailed, as is the sampling method used. There is a good explanation and discussion in the article of the data collection and data analysis carried out. It is interesting to note how the different aspects of methodology are theorized, i.e. connected to other theories and theorists. The findings of the research are clearly presented and discussed and the implications of the findings for human resource development and socialization practices are presented and discussed. A number of recommendations are made (in the list of bullet points at the end of the article). You will notice that the recommendations are useful and do-able and reasonable and they are well thought out, well written and well presented. They are simple and clear, yet substantial and meaningful in relation to the research carried out.

THEORY IN RESEARCH

We are told that current scholarship views organizational socialization as a learning process that is primarily the responsibility of the newcomer. Yet Korte states that recent learning research recognizes the importance of the social interactions in the learning process. See Korte (2009) 'How newcomers learn the social norms of an organization: a case study of the socialization of newly hired engineers', *Human Resource Development Quarterly, 20*(3): 285–306). The study, we are told, investigated how newly hired engineers at a large manufacturing company learned job-related tasks and the social norms of the organization. The author states that, from the perspective of social exchange theory, two major findings emerged from the data:

1. Relationship building was the primary driver of socialization.
2. The work group was the primary context for socialization.

The author states that these findings challenge the current views of organizational socialization by accentuating the relational processes that mediate learning during socialization. He writes that when asked what he wished he had learned in school to better prepare for the workplace, one practicing engineer lamented, 'I wish someone had taught me how to play the political game here.' He was referring to the unwritten rules governing behaviour – also known as the social norms of the organization.

Korte states that preliminary investigation of the experiences of engineers starting a new job indicated that the most troublesome experience was learning how to work within the informal social systems of the organization. He writes that in order to understand better the problems encountered by newcomers entering a workplace, his study investigated the experiences of 30 newly hired engineers during the early stage of their employment with a large manufacturing company.

The research methodology used was a qualitative case study research design. In justifying his use of this methodology, Korte writes that several authors describe a qualitative methodology as not only appropriate but also more likely to yield insights into complex social phenomena. He presents qualitative case study research as an appropriate design for acquiring in-depth understanding of the complex interactions and functions of people in the context of a specific situation.

We are told that the organization participating in this study is one of the world's largest manufacturers, employing more than 250 000 people around the world. According to the article the company, which is headquartered in the USA, has been a global engineering and sales leader for decades. Korte states that during the two years preceding the study the company hired nearly 200 new engineers, 30 of whom participated in the study. We are told that the participants in the study came from 26 work groups, and that while some of these work groups were well established, others were relatively new.

Three research questions guided the study. They were as follows:

1. How do new engineers learn the social norms of the organization?
2. What factors enable and constrain this learning process in the organization?
3. What factors determine how well new engineers learn and integrate into the workplace?

In terms of the sample used, Korte says that following the logic of theoretical or purposeful sampling, managers in the organization were asked to identify individuals to interview for the purpose of collecting rich, in-depth information addressing the research questions. He writes that the managers chose individuals according to length of employment, gender and experience. He explains that all of the participants had been with the company at least six months, and none had been employed with this company longer than 18 months. There were both men and women in the sample, and a mix of those who had previous job experience and those for whom this was the first job after graduating. We are told that the sample was composed of three groups:

- New graduates: 17 newly hired engineers starting their first job out of school.
- Experienced hires: 13 newly hired engineers with previous job experience.
- Managers: six managers of work groups with newly hired engineers.

Korte tells us that in his study, 'avoiding the purist extremes of qualitative and quantitative methodologies', he used a blended approach to analyze the data collected under a qualitative case study research design. Data for the study were generated from semi-structured interviews conducted and recorded by the researcher following the critical incidents technique. He asked questions in the interviews that prompted participants to recall a specific event or incident in which they learned something about 'the way things work here'. He probed their responses using subsequent questions designed to elicit detail on specifics: for example, what the incident was, what happened, who was involved, and what the participant learned from this. He explains that, in some cases, participants said there was no one specific incident. These participants recounted a series of small experiences that occurred over time which gave them an understanding of the norms of the organization. A professional transcriber converted the recorded interviews to text. The researcher checked the transcriptions for accuracy with the original recordings and analysis of the interview transcripts followed qualitative analysis procedures.

(Continued)

There were four steps in the qualitative data analysis process, outlined as follows:

1. The researcher carefully read the transcripts and attached predetermined codes to specific statements that described learning and norms.
2. The researcher retrieved all statements coded as 'learning and norms', carefully reread the retrieved statements and proceeded to open code the statements at a finer level of detail, staying close to the participants' language.
3. The researcher sorted the open codes into categories.
4. The researcher identified and described the categorical themes emerging from these data.

Korte explains that the emergent data indicated that relationship building was a critical process for newcomers. Furthermore, the data indicated that it was the quality of the relationships formed within the context of the work groups that enabled or constrained newcomer learning and integration into the workplace.

Korte tells us that the use of predetermined codes initially helped identify and categorize the experiences reported by newcomers into exchange and learning experiences related to the norms of the group. Then from these categories, common themes emerged that indicated how newcomers learned, what factors affected their learning, and how well they learned as they began their jobs. These themes are described by Korte in the findings section of the journal article.

He tells us that two major themes emerged from analysis of the data gathered from newcomers:

1. Relationship building was the primary driver of the socialization process – not individual capability for learning.
2. The work group was the primary context for socialization – not the organization.

He explains the data indicated that the quality of relationship building between the newcomers and members of their work groups mediated the quality of learning by newcomers. He writes that, overall, newcomers reported the necessity of building relationships with co-workers and their managers as a prerequisite for learning what to do and how to do it well.

Korte calculated frequency counts of learning incidents reported and attributed to different sources. He found that newcomers in the organization reported that co-workers were the primary source of learning the social norms of the work group (65 per cent of learning incidents reported). We are told that newcomers also reported learning from managers (15 per cent). Korte explains that the remaining learning interactions were reportedly self-directed, whereby newcomers relied on their personal knowledge and past experiences as a source of learning to understand and adapt to the social norms of the organization (18 per cent of learning incidents reported).

The implications of the study for human resource development and socialization practices are explored in the journal article and several recommendations are made.

THE VALUE OF GOOD RESEARCH

Focus on life history

Life history, as explained in Chapter 9, is the research methodology used to compile biographies of different people or biographies of different companies, organizations, entities. This methodology could be used, for example, to understand the changes that have occurred in the lives of a group of people, or the changes that have occurred in the life of a company.

One particular kind of life history research is oral history. Oral history is a vocalized account of some historical experience given by a witness or participant in that experience. The key data collection method used within a life history and an oral history research methodology is the life history interview.

The British Library has in its collection an oral history of Tesco, the supermarket chain. This oral history project, we are told, examines different functions across the business, distribution, information technology and personnel as well as retailing. The oral history comprises 39 in-depth interviews with Tesco employees from the checkout staff to the chairman. According to the website of the British Library, this is 'an unparalleled collection of first-hand witness accounts from those working within a major British retailer': www.bl.uk/reshelp/findhelprestype/sound/ohist/ohnls/nlstesco/tesco.html.

Other oral histories available in the British Library include an oral history of Barings Bank up to and including its collapse in 1995; oral histories of food and drink, documenting changes that have occurred in Britain's food industry over the course of the twentieth century; and an oral history project of the wine trade, comprising 42 life story interviews with workers in the wine trade.

Any business or business experience can usefully be studied using a life history or an oral history methodology. The contribution that such a project makes to knowledge rests on the quality of the research project, the insight the researcher brings to the project and the insights the researcher develops from the project.

You will find the following resources useful in relation to life history and oral history research methodologies:

National Life Stories: Tesco: An Oral History, British Library, www.bl.uk/reshelp/findhelprestype/sound/ohist/ohnls/nlstesco/tesco.html

Oral History Collection, Columbia University, New York, library.columbia.edu/locations/ccoh.html

Oral History Research, University of Winnipeg, Canada, www.oralhistorycentre.ca/business-oral-history

What is Oral History, historymatters.gmu.edu/mse/oral/what.html

WRITING THE RESEARCH PROJECT

The process of writing the research project is perhaps the most critical aspect of all aspects of the research process. It is through writing the research project that the researcher communicates the research, what it was about, how it was carried out, and what was accomplished through the research.

It is important to begin the process of writing the thesis as early as possible. Very rarely do researchers have enough time to conduct the research they wish to conduct (or at least this is usually how researchers feel). Because of this time constraint, it is important to get working on the research project as soon as possible. The research proposal is the first part of the research project. When the researcher has completed a good research proposal, the research is off to a good start. The research proposal, with a little adaptation, can become the first chapter in the thesis (see Table 20.4).

Table 20.4   Chapter 1: Introduction

Research statement or question	This is the conceptual framework for the research project.
Aim and objectives	The aim is the research statement or question restated as an aim. The objectives (usually not less than two, no more than six) can be presented in bullet point form (a bullet point is a short phrase).
Research Hypothesis/ Hypotheses	These are formal statements of the proposition(s) to be empirically tested through the research.
Population and sample	State the population of the research and the sample and sampling method, if a sample is used.
Methodology	State the methodology, explain it, the background to it and provide a brief explanation as to why you are using it in this research project, i.e. justify your choice of methodology, explain why it is the most appropriate methodology for this research project.
Data collection methods	Introduce the data collection methods and briefly outline them. Explain why this method is the most appropriate/why these methods are the most appropriate for this study.
Rationale for the research	Explain why you are undertaking this research and what it is that you hope to accomplish with the research.
Context for the research	Outline the context for the research. If you are undertaking the research as part of the requirements of a particular course of study, e.g. for a BSc in management, then state this. State where the study is being carried out. Any background detail you wish to provide for the study can be presented in this section.

The second chapter in the thesis is the literature review chapter and it contains the theoretical framework for the research project (see Table 20.5). The theoretical framework is built on the conceptual framework. The key concepts in the conceptual framework provide guidance and direction for the reading for the literature review and the structure of the literature review chapter.

Table 20.5   Chapter 2: Literature review

Introduction	A short introduction to the chapter. There may be two subsections or three, or four or five subsections. The subtitles of the subsections are drawn from, or informed by, the conceptual framework.
First subheading	Each of the subheadings is an indication of the contents of that subsection. Remember that one or two words do not make good subheadings, so develop a short (appropriate) phrase for each subheading.
Second subheading	Each of the subsections deals with a different but related aspect or element of the conceptual framework.
Third subheading	The subsections are presented in a logical, meaningful order.
Summary	A brief summary of the chapter.

The third chapter is the research methodology chapter and it contains all the information on how the research was carried out (see Table 20.6). This chapter contains the methodological framework for the research project, which is the third framework in the four frameworks approach. Every aspect of the methodological framework has to 'fit' with the research project: the methodology, the population and sample, the data-gathering methods, the kind of data gathered, the way in which the data are analyzed, the ethical issues considered.

Table 20.6 Chapter 3: Methodology

Introduction	Brief introduction to the chapter.
Research methodology	Theoretical background to the research methodology and a more detailed explanation of the methodology, following on from Chapter 1. A justification of the methodology (an explanation of why the methodology is appropriate for this research project).
Population and sample	Detailed description of population and sample, sampling method used.
Data-gathering methods	Detailed description and justification of data-gathering methods.
Issues of validity and reliability	Detailed discussion of the issues of validity and reliability and how these are dealt with in regard to the data-gathering methods used.
Triangulation	Has the research been triangulated and if so how?.
Pilot study	Detailed description of pilot study if pilot study has been carried out.
Data gathering	Detailed description of process of gathering data, any issues or problems encountered in data gathering and an explanation of how they were dealt with.
Data analysis	Detailed description of data analysis processes and procedures.
Ethical issues	Detailed discussion of ethical issues, routine ethical issues, informed consent and anonymity and confidentiality, as well as ethical issues specific to the research project. An honest, reflective account of how these issues were resolved.

The fourth chapter is the data analysis chapter and it contains the analytical framework for the research project (see Table 20.7). This is the fourth framework in the four frameworks approach to the research process. The chapter contains a synopsis of all of the analysis carried out on the data gathered for the research project. The structure of the chapter is based on the decisions the researcher makes about the story or narrative they wish to tell about the analyzed data. The narrative told should be the one that best explains the phenomenon under investigation. Although the researcher does not report every detail of the analyzed data, the researcher does use all of the analyzed data to present the best possible account, providing the best possible insight into that phenomenon.

Table 20.7 Chapter 4: Data analysis

Introduction	A brief introduction to the contents of the chapter.
First subheading	There may be two subsections or three, or four or five subsections. Each of the subheadings is an indication of the contents of that subsection. Each of the subsections deals with a different but related aspect or element of the analysis or analytical framework.
Second subheading	The subsections are presented in a logical order, in the order that best suits the narrative, or story, the researcher wishes to tell from the analyzed data.
Third subheading	The narrative told will be the narrative that best describes or explains the phenomenon under investigation.
Summary	A brief summary of the contents of the chapter.

The final chapter is the chapter on conclusions and recommendations (see Table 20.8). Table 20.9 contains a summary of the whole project.

The **list of references** or bibliography follows the final chapter. The appendices follow the list of references or bibliography.

> **list of references** A complete list of all of the works cited in your research project.

In terms of word count, the guidance usually given is that the word count for the completed thesis should come within a 10 per cent margin of the word count allowed. The title pages, the list of references and the appendices tend not to be included in the word count (see Table 20.10).

Table 20.8 Chapter 5: Conclusions and recommendations

Introduction	A brief introduction to the contents of the chapter.
Conclusions	The overall conclusion of the research is stated. This conclusion responds to the research question or statement. The overall conclusion is theorized and the implications of it are drawn out. Then the overall conclusion is broken down into major conclusions. Each of these is discussed and theorized and the implications of each are drawn out. Finally, minor conclusions are reported, explained and theorized.
Limitations of the research	A short paragraph considering the limitations of the research is appropriate. The research should not be undermined by this paragraph. The paragraph is simply a brief acknowledgement of the limitations of the research.
Recommendations	The recommendations of the research are laid out in bullet points. A list of (about) ten well-conceptualized, carefully considered, useful and meaningful in terms of the research undertaken, recommendations are presented.
Final short paragraph	There is often a final short paragraph in this chapter that summarizes the research and the accomplishments of the research. In this paragraph, the researcher can note or detail briefly what was accomplished by the research. They may also very briefly note what they themselves gained from the research.

Table 20.9 The thesis/report

Title page	This page contains the title of the research, the name of the researcher, and any other detail necessary, such as the name of the university and school. The university or college will have a convention governing this page.
Acknowledgements	It is usual to acknowledge the help and support you received throughout the research. In general, your research supervisor would be thanked, participants in the research would be thanked and any gatekeeper who facilitated the research would be thanked. In addition, it is customary to acknowledge the support of family and friends.
Abstract	This is a short one-paragraph summary of the thesis, for a 20 000-word thesis, the abstract would be 300 words long. It contains mention of all of the key concepts in the research project, the methodology and data-gathering methods used, the main conclusion and key recommendations.
Table of contents	This is a detailed table of contents of the thesis complete with page numbers. Again the university or college will have a convention governing this page.
Chapter One – Introduction	The first chapter in the thesis/report, it is structured around the conceptual framework, the first framework in the four frameworks approach to the research project.
Chapter Two – Literature review	The second chapter contains the theoretical framework.
Chapter Three – Research methodology	The third chapter contains the methodological framework.
Chapter Four – Data analysis	The fourth chapter contains the analytical framework.
Chapter Five – Conclusions and recommendations	The fifth and final chapter contains the conclusions and recommendations.
List of references	Constitutes a complete list of all references in the text. Again, the university or college will have a convention governing the presentation of the references in the list of references or bibliography.
Appendices	Included in appendices are copies of letters written requesting access to research sites, letters written inviting participation in the research. You place copies of questionnaires, interview schedules, focus group schedules, observation schedules, and so on in appendices. Also placed in appendices are copies of informed consent forms. Long lists and big tables, graphs and charts and other large images are also placed in appendices.

Table 20.10 Breakdown of typical word counts for theses and research projects

Total word count	20 000 words	15 000 words	12 000 words	10 000 words
Introduction	2000	1200	1000	1000
Literature review	5000	4000	3000	2500
Research methodology	4000	3000	3000	2500
Data analysis	6000	5000	3500	3000
Conclusions and recommendations	3000	1800	1500	1000

Completing the first draft of the thesis is a major milestone. It is at this point that you can see the scale of the research project and at first sight it is always impressive. Once the first draft of the thesis or report is complete, it is time to begin the process of rewriting and editing the thesis. It is at this stage, the polishing stage, that the final draft of the thesis comes into being. It is important to remember that the first draft is simply that, a first draft. A great deal of work goes into producing the final draft of the thesis. It is a good idea to submit the first draft for formal feedback from your thesis supervisor. The feedback you receive should then be incorporated into the final draft of the thesis. If you have received feedback from your thesis supervisor throughout the different stages of the research process, there should not be any major surprises in the feedback you get on the first complete draft of the thesis.

It is important in the editing and polishing stage to take as much time as is needed to produce the final draft of the thesis. The work involves rewriting, editing and re-editing. Hopefully, when you've finished this work you will have a complete, well-structured and well-integrated research project. You will have learned a great deal through the process of undertaking research about the substantive area that is the focus of your research and about research methods. You will be able to draw on the knowledge and skills you have developed through the research process all through your career. I wish you great success.

YOUR RESEARCH
Common research problems

One of the most common mistakes students make in writing research is that they do not take proper care with the language they use, or with spelling, grammar and syntax. Poorly written and poorly presented theses lose marks, and they lose a lot of marks, unnecessarily. The academic institution wherein English is the language used is merciless when it comes to written English, and to preserving an appropriate standard of written English, and this is the case whether or not English is the first language of the student. If you are studying within such an institution and English is not your first language, you will have needed to assure the academic institution of your ability to study in English, and write English to the appropriate standard, in order to secure a place on the course of study. If you feel that your written English is not as good as it should be, then you should have someone proofread your work before you submit it for examination. In proofreading your work, this person will highlight for you any spelling mistakes, grammatical errors and errors of syntax in your work. You can then correct these mistakes before you submit the work.

A simple test: there is a deliberate error in each of the sentences that follow. Can you spot them? If you cannot, you should get someone to proofread your work before you submit it for examination. (Answers at end of chapter.)

SPOT THE DELIBERATE ERROR

- There were too main reasons why the participants in the study did not enjoy the training programme.
- Respondents anger over the refusal of the company to provide the information requested was evident.
- Respondents indicated that they're anger was prompted by perceptions that the company was not listening to them.
- 'Your required to attend the training,' was the instruction in the document.
- The government have decided to rescind all tax incentives.

It is easier to maintain correct grammar and syntax in short sentences. Meaning and sense can be lost when writing long sentences. When writing, use all of the aids for good clear writing available to you: proper sentences and good spelling, good paragraphing, good headings and subheadings, and the use of bullet points when appropriate.

When you have finished writing a section, check back on it:

- Check for sentence structure, for syntax, grammatical errors and spelling errors.
- Check your paragraphing. Are the paragraphs too long or are they too short? Remember, a paragraph is a substantial amount of information. Generally half a page is long enough for a paragraph.
- Critique your subheadings. Are they meaningful? Do they adequately indicate the content of that subsection?
- Are any of your sentences too long? If any sentence goes on for three lines or more it is too long. Try to break the long sentences down into two or more short sentences.

Perhaps the most important element of writing is the need to write to a point. When you are reading a section of your research, ask yourself, what point am I making here? Is it an important point? Is it as clear as it could be? Remember, in writing you are attempting to communicate. You have to structure your communication in such a way as to help the reader understand what it is that you are saying.

All of the points that you make in your writing should contribute to your overall argument. You should never lose sight of your overall argument. What is your overall argument? How well are you making that overall argument? Try to argue persuasively in your writing.

Be careful to ensure that in your writing you are not evidencing biases, for example, in terms of gender, race, ethnicity, culture or religion, in the way in which you use language.

It is important to get feedback on your writing. Check with your thesis supervisor that you are on the right track. There is nothing so dispiriting as to complete a large amount of work only to find that, for one reason or another, it is not to the standard required.

Basic business research report

The following paragraphs explain the outline of a basic business research report. You will notice that essentially the outline follows the steps in the model of the research process outlined at the start of Chapter 1 of this textbook. The outline described in the following applies especially to applied business research projects. When pure or basic research reports are written, such as might be submitted and potentially published in an academic business journal, the outline changes slightly since some components become irrelevant. A common outline used in basic business research proceeds as follows:

1. Abstract
2. Introduction
3. Background
   a. Literature review
   b. Hypotheses
4. Research methods
5. Results
6. Discussion
   a. Implications
   b. Limitations
   c. Future research
7. Conclusions
8. List of references
9. Appendices

The material in the sections does not change very much between different business research problems, so here we only note exceptions. The basic research report will place a greater emphasis on how the current research is integrated into the previous literature dealing with the research topic. This section finishes with a specific set of theoretical hypotheses. The research methodology and results section may contain more statistical detail and jargon since the reader is expected to be knowledgeable in basic research methodology. A quick look at an academic business journal such as the *Journal of Business Research*, the *Journal of Marketing*, the *Journal of Finance* or the *Journal of Management* will give a reader a feel for this type of writing. Overall, however, both basic and applied business research reports involve technical writing and the principles of good technical writing apply.

Effective use of graphic aids

Used properly, **graphic aids** can clarify complex points or emphasize a message. Used improperly or sloppily, they can distract or even mislead a reader. Graphic aids work best when they are an integral part of the text. The graphics should always be interpreted in the text. This does not mean that the writer should exhaustively explain an obvious chart or table, but it does mean that the text should point out the key elements of any graphic aid and relate them to the discussion in progress.

> **graphic aids** Pictures or diagrams used to clarify complex points or emphasize a message.

The oral presentation

The conclusions and recommendations of most research reports are often presented orally as well as in writing. The purpose of an **oral presentation** is to highlight the most important findings of a research project and provide clients or line managers with an opportunity to ask questions. The oral presentation may be as simple as a short video conference with a manager at the client organization's location or as formal as a report to the company board of directors.

> **oral presentation** A spoken summary of the major findings, conclusions, and recommendations, given to clients or line managers to provide them with the opportunity to clarify any ambiguous issues by asking questions.

In either situation, the key to effective presentation is preparation. The researcher should select the three or four most important findings for emphasis and rely on the written report for a full summary. The researcher also needs to be ready to defend the results of the research. This is not the same as being defensive; instead, the researcher should be prepared to deal in a confident, competent manner with the questions that arise. Remember that even the most reliable and valid research project is worthless if the managers who must act on its results are not convinced of its importance.

As with written reports, a key to effective oral presentation is adapting to the audience. Delivering an hour-long formal speech when a ten-minute discussion is called for (or vice versa) will reflect poorly on both the presenter and the report.

Lecturing or reading to the audience is sure to impede communication at any level of formality. Presenters should refrain from reading prepared text word for word. By relying on brief notes, familiarity with the subject, and as much rehearsal as the occasion calls for, presenters will foster better communication. Presenters should avoid research jargon and use short, familiar words. Presenters should maintain eye contact with the audience and repeat the main points. Because the audience cannot go back and replay what the speaker has said, an oral presentation often is organized around a standard format: 'Tell them what you are going to tell them, tell them, and tell them what you just told them.'

Graphic and other visual aids can be as useful in an oral presentation as in a written one. While presenters can choose from a variety of media, most professional presentations are based on PowerPoint or comparable presentation software. For smaller audiences, the researcher may put the visual aids on posters or flip charts. Another possibility is to make copies of the charts for each participant, possibly as a supplement to one of the other forms of presentation.

Whatever medium is chosen, each visual aid should be designed to convey a simple, attention-getting message that supports a point on which the audience should focus its thinking. As they do in written presentations, presenters should interpret graphics for the audience. The best slides are easy to read and interpret. Large typeface, multiple colours, bullets that highlight, and other artistic devices can enhance the readability of charts.

Reports on the internet or intranet

Many clients want numerous employees to have access to research findings. One easy way to share data is to make executive summaries and reports available on a company intranet. In addition, a company can use information technology on the internet to design questionnaires, administer surveys, analyze data and share the results in a presentation-ready format. Real-time data capture allows for beginning-to-end reporting. A number of companies offer fully web-based research management systems – for example, WebSurveyor's online solution for capturing and reporting research findings.

The research follow-up

Research reports and oral presentations should communicate research findings so that managers can make business decisions. In many cases, the manager who receives the research report is unable to interpret the information and draw conclusions relevant to managerial decisions. For this reason, effective researchers do not treat the report as the end of the research process. They conduct a **research follow-up,** in which they recontact decision-makers and/or clients after the latter have had a chance to read over the report. The purpose is to determine whether the researchers need to provide additional information or clarify issues of concern to management.

research follow-up Recontacting decision makers and/or clients after they have had a chance to read over a research report in order to determine whether additional information or clarification is necessary.

CASE STUDY

In this paper (Bloom and Van Reenan, 2010, 'Why do management practices differ across firms and countries?', *Journal of Economic Perspectives*, *24*(1): 203–224), the authors present evidence to show that persistent differences in productivity at firm level and national level largely reflect variations in management practices. They say that, as British-born academics, they are used to reports that blame Britain's relatively low productivity on bad management. They say that this view is so common in the UK it has generated a strong export industry of television shows on bad management. They cite *The Office*, an example of bad management in the wholesale sector; *Fawlty Towers,* an example of bad management in private services; and *Yes Minister*, an example of bad management in the public sector.

The authors have undertaken a large survey research programme designed to measure management practices systematically across firms, industries and countries. In this paper, they explain how they measured management and explored some of the basic patterns in their data. Their explanation, which they developed from their research, as to why management practices vary so much across firms and nations, rests on 'a combination of imperfectly competitive markets, family ownership of firms, regulations restricting management practices and informational barriers'.

The ten conclusions they came to, based on their analysis of their data, are as follows:

1. Firms with 'better' management practices tend to have better performance on a wide range of dimensions: they are larger, more productive, grow faster and have higher survival rates.
2. Management practices vary tremendously across firms and countries. Most of the difference in the average management score of a country is due to the size of the 'long tail' of very badly managed firms. For example, relatively few US firms are very badly managed, while Brazil and India have many firms in that category.
3. Countries and firms specialize in different styles of management. For example, American firms score much higher than Swedish firms in incentives but are worse than Swedish firms in monitoring.
4. Strong product market competition appears to boost average management practices through a combination of eliminating the tail of badly managed firms and pushing incumbents to improve their practices.
5. Multinationals are generally well managed in every country. They also transplant their management styles abroad. For example, US multinationals located in the UK are better at incentives and worse at monitoring than Swedish multinationals in the UK.
6. Firms that export (but do not produce) overseas are better managed than domestic non-exporters, but are worse managed than multinationals.
7. Inherited family-owned firms who appoint a family member (especially the oldest son) as chief executive officer are very badly managed on average.
8. Government-owned firms are typically managed extremely badly. Firms with publicly quoted share prices or owned by private equity firms are typically well managed.
9. Firms that more intensively use human capital, as measured by more educated workers, tend to have much better management practices.
10. At the country level, a relatively light touch in labour market regulation is associated with better use of incentives by management.

It is interesting that in this paper we begin with a consideration of the conclusions, and then we move to reading about the research and the research methodology. The authors developed a new survey methodology. This is an interview-based evaluation tool that defines and scores from 1 (worst practice) to 5 (best practice) across 18 basic management practices. The survey instrument and the manner in which it was used in the study is explained in detail in the journal article.

(Continued)

The authors explain that their data are cross-sectional, across many firms and countries at roughly the same point in time. They present tables and graphs that highlight different trends and patterns in their data.

Questions: What do you think of the conclusions drawn by Bloom and Van Reenan in this study? Can you see how these conclusions have emerged from the data gathered? What do you think of the recommendations they make for further research in the field of economics? In preparing your answer, consider the work of Alasuutari (2010) as outlined in Chapter 18. There are very many ideas in terms of possible research projects in the synopsis above and in the original journal article which you should source and read.

END OF CHAPTER QUESTIONS

1 What are conclusions and how are they drawn in a research project?

2 What is the role of the overall conclusion in the research project?

3 What is meant by the term 'theorizing conclusions'?

4 Explain the following statement: there are different conclusions for different constituents.

5 What are recommendations and how are they developed?

6 What is meant by the term 'the limitations of the research', in the context of the final chapter of the thesis or report of the research?

7 Illustrate, using examples, the differences between findings, conclusions and recommendations in research.

8 Outline and briefly explain the model of the research process.

9 Outline and briefly explain the four frameworks approach to the research process.

10 Explain the value of the research diary.

11 What rules should be followed when preparing slides for presentations?

12 Why is it important to think of the research report from a communications perspective?

SPOT THE DELIBERATE ERROR ANSWERS

- There were **two** main reasons why the participants in the study did not enjoy the training programme.

- Respondents' anger over the refusal of the company to provide the information requested was evident.
- Respondents indicated that **their** anger was prompted by perceptions that the company was not listening to them.
- **'You're** required to attend the training,' was the instruction in the document.
- The government **has** decided to rescind all tax incentives.

REFERENCES

Alasuutari, P. (2010) 'The rise and relevance of qualitative research', *International Journal of Social Research Methodology*, 13(2): 139–155.

Bloom, N. and Van Reenan, J. (2010) 'Why do management practices differ across firms and countries?', *Journal of Economic Perspectives*, 24(1): 203–224.

Butterworth, S. (2009) 'Open Door, The readers' editor on . . . 1000 teenagers, one survey, and two sets of results', *The Guardian*, 19.10.2009, www.theguardian.com/commentisfree/2009/oct/19/teenage-boys-survey-statistics (Accessed 17.03.2018).

Korte, R.F. (2009) 'How newcomers learn the social norms of an organization: a case study of the socialization of newly hired engineers', *Human Resource Development Quarterly*, 20(3): 285–306.

National Life Stories: Tesco: An Oral History, British Library, www.bl.uk/reshelp/findhelprestype/sound/ohist/ohnls/nlstesco/tesco.html (Accessed 17.03.2018).

Oral History Collection, Columbia University, New York, library.columbia.edu/locations/ccoh.html. (Accessed 17.03.2018).

Oral History Research, University of Winnipeg, Canada, www.oralhistorycentre.ca/business-oral-history (Accessed 17.03.2018).

What is Oral History, historymatters.gmu.edu/mse/oral/what.html (Accessed 17.03.2018).

RECOMMENDED READING

Bell, J. and Waters, S. (2014) *Doing Your Research Project* (6th edn), Maidenhead: Open University Press.

Collis, J. and Hussey, R. (2013) *Business Research: A Practical Guide for Undergraduate and Postgraduate Students* (4th edn), Basingstoke and New York: Palgrave Macmillan.

Creswell, J. and Creswell, D.J. (2018) *Research Design: Qualitative, Quantitative and Mixed Methods Approaches* (5th edn), London, California, New Delhi, Singapore: Sage.

Denscombe, M. (2017) *The Good Research Guide: For Small-scale Social Research Projects* (5th edn), Maidenhead: Open University Press.

Easterby-Smith, M., Thorpe, R. and Jackson, P.R. (2008) *Management Research* (3rd edn), London: Sage.

Miles, M.B., Huberman, A.M. and Saldana, J. (2014) *Qualitative Data Analysis: A Methods Sourcebook* (3rd edn), California, London, New Delhi, Singapore: Sage.

Murray, R. (2017) *How to Write a Thesis* (4th edn), Maidenhead: Open University Press.

Neuman, W.L. (2014) *Social Research Methods: Qualitative and Quantitative Approaches* (7th edn), Essex, England: Pearson Education Ltd.

Robson, C. and McCartan, K. (2016) *Real World Research*, John Wiley & Sons Ltd.

White, B. and Rayner, S. (2014) *Dissertation Skills for Business and Management Students*, London: Cengage Learning EMEA.

GLOSSARY

abstract level In theory development, the level of knowledge expressing a concept that exists only as an idea, or a quality, apart from an object.

access Access to data and access to the field of the research project.

aim and objectives The aim is a precise statement of what the researcher intends to accomplish with the research. Objectives specify how the researcher intends to accomplish this aim.

aim of your research To keep things simple, the aim of your research is your research statement/question restated as an aim.

analysis of variance (ANOVA) Analysis involving the investigation of the effects of one treatment variable on an interval-scaled dependent variable – a hypothesis-testing technique to determine whether statistically significant differences in means occur between two or more groups.

analyzing The data are analyzed by means of description and interpretation.

analytical framework In the four frameworks approach to the research project, the analytical framework emerges from the conceptual framework, the theoretical framework and the methodological framework. The analytical framework is presented in the data analysis chapter in the thesis or in the data analysis section of the report of the research.

anecdotal evidence Evidence from anecdotes, evidence gathered in informal and/or casual conversation, and consequently deemed to have limited value.

anonymity Free from identification.

appendices Used to detail any document or artefact relevant to the research but not detailed in the body of the research project.

applied business research Research conducted to address a specific business decision for a specific firm or organization.

attitude An enduring disposition to consistently respond in a given manner to various aspects of the world, composed of affective, cognitive and behavioural components.

attribute A single characteristic or fundamental feature of an object, person, situation or issue.

back translation Taking a questionnaire that has previously been translated into another language and having a second, independent translator translate it back to the original language.

balanced rating scale A fixed-alternative rating scale with an equal number of positive and negative categories; a neutral point or point of indifference is at the centre of the scale.

basic business research Research conducted without a specific decision in mind that usually does not address the needs of a specific organization. It attempts to expand the limits of knowledge in general and is not aimed at solving a particular pragmatic problem.

behavioural differential A rating scale instrument similar to a semantic differential, developed to measure the behavioural intentions of subjects towards future actions.

bias Anything that contaminates or compromises the research or data.

bibliography The US term for a list of all of the published work cited in the research project. All published works cited in the research project must be listed in the bibliography. In the UK this list is called the *References*.

bivariate analysis Analysis conducted on two variables e.g. chi-square tests, one-way ANOVA, *t*-tests, correlation and simple regression.

business research The application of the scientific method in searching for the truth about business phenomena. These activities include defining business opportunities and problems, generating and evaluating ideas, monitoring performance and understanding the business process.

briefing session A training session to ensure that each interviewer is provided with common information.

case study methodology Useful in the in-depth study of bounded entities, such as an organization, or a single incident or event. A case study can focus on a single case or on a number of cases.

category scale A rating scale that consists of several response categories, often providing respondents with alternatives to indicate positions on a continuum.

census An investigation of all the individual elements that make up a population.

choice A measurement task that identifies preferences by requiring respondents to choose between two or more alternatives.

click-through rate (CTR) is the ratio of the number of users who view a web page and then click on a link on the web page to go through to another web page, to the total number of users who view the web page

closed questions Questions that elicit a defined limited range of responses, e.g. yes/no. Often used to establish factual information.

cluster sampling An economically efficient sampling technique in which the primary sampling unit is not the individual element in the population but a large cluster of elements; clusters are selected randomly.

coding key A guide to all of the codes used in coding data; used to input the data into a computer software program.

coefficient alpha (α) The most commonly applied estimate of a multiple-item scale's reliability. It represents the average of all possible split-half reliabilities for a construct.

comparative rating scale Any measure of attitudes that asks respondents to rate a concept in comparison with a benchmark explicitly used as a frame of reference.

composite measures Assign a value to an observation based on a mathematical derivation of multiple variables.

composite scale A way of representing a latent construct by summing or averaging respondents' reactions to multiple items each assumed to indicate the latent construct.

computer-assisted qualitative data analysis software (CAQDAS) Computer software designed to support qualitative data analysis.

concept (or construct) A generalized idea about a class of objects that has been given a name; an abstraction of reality that is the basic unit for theory development. Every discipline and theory is made up of concepts, e.g. key ideas, key-words, key phrases.

conceptual framework The conceptual framework of the research project is contained in the one sentence research statement or question. The conceptual framework contains all key concepts in the research project. The entire research project rests on the conceptual framework.

conclusion Essentially a judgement or a final decision drawn from evidence and argument.

confidentiality The non-disclosure of certain information.

constant-sum scale A measure of attitudes in which respondents are asked to divide a constant sum to indicate the relative importance of attributes; respondents often sort cards, but the task may also be a rating task.

construct A term used to refer to concepts measured with multiple variables.

construct validity Exists when a measure reliably measures and truthfully represents a unique concept; consists of several components including face validity, content validity, criterion validity, convergent validity and discriminant validity.

consumer panel A longitudinal survey of the same sample of individuals or households to record their attitudes, behaviour or purchasing habits over time.

content validity The degree to which a measure covers the breadth of the domain of interest.

contingency table A data matrix that displays the frequency of some combination of possible responses to multiple variables; cross-tabulation results.

continuous measures Measures that reflect the intensity of a concept by assigning values that can take on any value along some scale range.

convenience sampling The sampling procedure of obtaining those people who are most conveniently available.

convergent validity Concepts that should be related to one another are, in fact, related; highly reliable scales contain convergent validity.

conversation An informal qualitative data-gathering approach in which the researcher engages a respondent in a discussion of the relevant subject matter.

correlation coefficient A statistical measure of the covariation, or association, between two at-least-interval variables.

correspondence rules Indicate the way in which a certain value on a scale corresponds to some true value of a concept.

covariance The extent to which two variables are associated systematically with each other.

covert observation Carried out without the knowledge of those being observed.

criterion validity The ability of a measure to correlate with other standard measures of similar constructs or established criteria.

critical analysis A questioning analytical approach to any phenomenon.

critical perspective A reflective, thoughtful, evaluative perspective or view.

cross-tabulation The appropriate technique for addressing research questions involving relationships among multiple less-than-interval variables; results in a combined frequency table displaying one variable in rows and another in columns.

cross-validate To verify that the empirical findings from one culture also exist and behave similarly in another culture.

curbstoning A form of interviewer cheating in which an interviewer makes up the responses instead of conducting an actual interview.

data Information or evidence gathered for a research project.

data analysis The process of analyzing data gathered for a research project. The process of data analysis involves describing the data and interpreting the data. The process also involves drawing conclusions from the data and, in research undertaken in an academic institution (college or university), theorizing those data, i.e. connecting the data gathered with the theory laid out in the literature review.

data collection methods The means by which data are gathered for a research project; examples of data-gathering methods include observation, interviews, focus groups, questionnaires.

data management The correct, safe and secure management of data while data are being gathered, stored and analyzed.

data transformation Process of changing the data from their original form to a format suitable for performing a data analysis addressing research objectives.

deductive reasoning The logical process of deriving a conclusion about a specific instance based on a known general premise or something known to be true.

depth interview/in-depth interview A one-on-one interview between a professional researcher and a research respondent conducted about some relevant business or social topic.

descriptive analysis The elementary transformation of raw data in a way that describes the basic characteristics.

descriptive statistics Used to describe variables in the data such as gender, education, income, age, etc. Presented as percentages, ratios, ranges, averages and standard deviations.

dichotomous variable A variable with two values.

discourse analysis A way of analyzing the social world as it is produced and represented in language.

discrete measures Measures that take on only one of a finite number of values.

discriminant validity Represents the uniqueness or distinctiveness of a measure; a scale should not correlate too highly with a measure of a different construct.

disguised questions Indirect questions that assume the purpose of the study must be hidden from the respondent.

door-in-the-face compliance technique A two-step process for securing a high response rate. In step 1, an initial request, so large that nearly everyone refuses it, is made. Next, a second request is made for a smaller favour; respondents are expected to comply with this more reasonable request.

dummy tables Tables placed in research proposals that are exact representations of the actual tables that will show results in the final report with the exception that the results are hypothetical (fictitious).

empirical level Level of knowledge that is verifiable by experience or observation.

empirical testing Examining a reality using data.

epistemology Relates to knowledge, to what constitutes knowledge and to the processes through which knowledge is created.

ethics Moral principles governing the conduct of an individual, a group or an organization.

ethnography Represents ways of studying cultures through methods that involve becoming highly active within that culture.

face validity A scale's content logically appears to reflect what was intended to be measured.

field interviewing service A research supplier that specializes in gathering data.

field notes The researcher's descriptions of what actually happens in the field; these notes then become the text from which meaning is extracted.

fieldwork The means by which data gathering is undertaken in order to provide primary data for a research project.

fieldworker An individual who is responsible for gathering data in the field.

final draft The edited and polished fully integrated and correct copy (of the thesis) that is finally submitted for examination.

first draft The draft before the process of editing and getting feedback begins.

'fit' Every step in the research project, should 'fit' with every other step in the research project and 'fit' with the purpose and focus of the project and the philosophical framework within which the research project is situated.

focus blog A type of informal, 'continuous' focus group established as an internet blog for the purpose of collecting qualitative data from participant comments.

focus group An unstructured, free-flowing discussion with a small group of around six to 10 people. Focus groups are facilitated by a trained moderator who follows a flexible format encouraging dialogue among respondents.

foot-in-the-door compliance technique A technique for obtaining a high response rate, in which compliance with a large or difficult task is induced by first obtaining the respondent's compliance with a smaller request.

forced-choice rating scale A fixed-alternative rating scale that requires respondents to choose one of the fixed alternatives.

four frameworks approach An approach to carrying out research whereby the conceptual framework shapes, supports and directs the other three frameworks, the theoretical framework, the methodological framework and the analytical framework.

four stages of data analysis Description, interpretation, conclusions and theorization.

free-association techniques Record respondents' first (top-of-mind) cognitive reactions to some stimulus.

funded business research Refers to basic research usually performed by academic researchers that is financially supported by some public or private institution, as in government grants.

gatekeeper Any person or structure that governs or controls access to people, places, structures and/or to organizations.

generalizability The application of the findings of a research project beyond the specific context of the study.

graphic aids Pictures or diagrams used to clarify complex points or emphasize a message.

graphic rating scale A measure of attitudes that allows respondents to rate an object by choosing any point along a graphic continuum.

grounded theory A research methodology particularly focused on developing theory from data. Represents an inductive investigation in which the researcher poses questions about information provided by respondents or taken from historical records; the researcher asks the questions to him or herself and repeatedly questions the responses to derive deeper explanations.

group dynamic Energy that develops naturally within a group. It can be positive or negative and is often affected by strong personalities.

group interviews A researcher interviews the participants in a group.

hermeneutics Hermeneutics is defined as the theory of interpretation and the study of the processes of interpretation.

hermeneutic unit Refers to a text passage from a respondent's story that is linked with a key theme from within this story or provided by the researcher. Used in CAQDAS.

histogram A graphical way of showing a frequency distribution in which the height of a bar corresponds to the observed frequency of the category.

hypothesis A predicted or expected answer to a research question; a formal statement of an unproven proposition that is empirically testable.

hypothetical constructs Variables that are not directly observable but are measurable through indirect indicators, such as verbal expression or overt behaviour.

idea for a research project The broad area within which a researcher wishes to situate their research. Your idea for your research project, when refined through a process of key concept analysis, is properly expressed in your very well-conceptualized research statement or question.

image profile A graphic representation of semantic differential data for competing brands, products or stores to highlight comparisons.

importance–performance analysis Another name for quadrant analysis.

inclusion and exclusion criteria The criteria potential participants must meet in order to be included in the study. Exclusion criteria is the criteria on which potential participants will be excluded from participation in the study.

independent samples *t*-test A test for hypotheses which compares the mean scores for two groups comprising some interval- or ratio-scaled variable using a less-than interval classificatory variable.

independent variable In examining the relationship between two variables, the assumed cause is the independent variable. The independent variable is expected to influence the dependent variable in some way.

index measure An index assigns a value based on how much of the concept being measured is associated with an observation. Indexes often are formed by putting several variables together.

inductive reasoning The logical process of establishing a general proposition on the basis of observation of particular facts.

inferential statistics Inferential statistics infer, based on a study of a sample population, what the entire population might think or do.

informed consent Agreement given by a person to participate in some action, after being informed of the possible consequences.

in-house interviewer A fieldworker who is employed by the company conducting the research.

integrity The honesty and scholarship of the researcher in carrying out research.

internal consistency Represents a measure's homogeneity or the extent to which each indicator of a concept converges on some common meaning.

intersubjective certifiability Different individuals following the same procedure will produce the same results or come to the same conclusion.

interval scales Scales that have both nominal and ordinal properties, but that also capture information about differences in quantities of a concept from one observation to the next.

interval variables Data with a meaningful and measurable distance between values, e.g. an age.

intervening variable The means by which the independent variable affects the dependent variable.

interviews The social science researcher develops a series of questions or a series of points of interest to discuss with the interviewees.

interview schedule The list of questions the researcher develops to ask participants, the list of points or the key issues the researcher develops to discuss/explore with participants.

interviewer cheating The practice by fieldworkers of filling in fake answers or falsifying interviews.

interviewer verification An interviewer gives each of the interviewees a transcript of their interview. Each interviewee then verifies that the transcript is an accurate record of their interview.

intrusion Unwarranted, unnecessary or unwelcome engagement with a person or place.

judgemental (judgement or purposive) sampling A non-probability sampling technique in which an experienced individual selects the sample based on personal judgement about some appropriate characteristic of the sample member. The researcher selects participants for the study based on their capacity to inform the study, i.e. the participants selected for inclusion in the sample are key informants (they have particular expertise on the phenomenon being investigated).

justify The researcher is obliged to justify, or explain and defend, the choices they make, especially their methodological choices, in relation to their research.

key concept A key idea expressed in a word or phrase.

keyword searches A search of the literature, in library databases, carried out using the key concepts, the keywords and/or phrases, in the research project.

ladder of abstraction Organization of concepts in sequence from the most concrete and individual to the most general.

laddering A particular approach to probing, asking respondents to compare differences between brands at different levels that produces distinctions at the attribute level, the benefit level and the value or motivation level.

Likert scale A measure of attitudes designed to allow respondents to rate how strongly they agree or disagree with carefully constructed statements, ranging from very positive to very negative attitudes towards some object.

list of references A complete list of all of the works cited in your research project.

literature Research that has already been carried out and published.

literature review A review of literature; always undertaken in order to embed the researcher and research project in the body of knowledge. Literature is research already carried out and published, in books, in journal articles, in conference reports, in government reports and in the reports of non-governmental organizations (NGOs).

longitudinal research Research that takes place over a long period of time.

longitudinal study A study of respondents at different times, thus allowing analysis of response continuity and changes over time.

marginals Row and column totals in a contingency table, which are shown in its margins.

matrices Data displays that the researcher creates for the purposes of reduction and presentation of data.

measurement The process of describing some property of a phenomenon of interest, usually by assigning numbers in a reliable and valid way.

measures of central tendency The mean: the arithmetic average; the mode: the most commonly occurring value; the median: the middle value of a range of values.

measures of dispersion The interquartile range (IQR); the standard deviation; variance.

method Used to denote research methodology such as case study or survey, and data collection method(s) such as observation, interviews, focus groups and questionnaires.

methodological framework An outline and a justification of the methodology selected for the research project, e.g. justification of population, sample; an outline of all of the steps taken in order to carry out the research.

methodological pyramid A model showing how the fundamental philosophies fit with the different methodologies and the different data collection methods.

methodology The overall approach to the research project; the way in which the research is carried out, a means of supporting the philosophical assumptions that underpin the research project.

monadic rating scale Any measure of attitudes that asks respondents about a single concept in isolation.

multivariate analysis Analysis conducted on more than two variables, e.g. multiple regression analysis.

narrative analysis The analysis of data through the use of narratives (stories).

narrative research Narrative inquiry or narrative analysis is a research methodology that is used in the gathering and analysis of narratives (stories).

no contacts People who are not at home or who are otherwise inaccessible on the first and second contact.

nominal scales Represent the most elementary level of measurement in which values are assigned to an object for identification or classification purposes only.

nominal variables Each value is a distinct category and serves simply as a label. Categories cannot be ranked, e.g. gender, nationality, race.

non-participant observation Carried out when the researcher does not participate in the action or in the phenomenon being observed.

non-probability sampling A sampling technique in which units of the sample are selected on the basis of personal judgement or convenience; the probability of any particular member of the population being chosen is unknown.

non-respondents People who are not contacted or who refuse to cooperate in the research.

non-response error The statistical differences between a survey that includes only those who responded and a perfect survey that would also include those who failed to respond.

numerical scale An attitude rating scale similar to a semantic differential except that it uses numbers, instead of verbal descriptions, as response options to identify response positions.

objectives of the research The steps the researcher takes in order to accomplish the aim of the research.

observation A data collection method where the researcher engages in observing and recording the phenomenon under investigation or some part of it.

observation schedule An observation schedule, like an interview schedule, is a form or series of forms on which the results of an observation are recorded.

one-to-one interview The researcher interviews each participant, one at a time and in great depth and detail.

online focus group A qualitative research effort in which a group of individuals provides unstructured comments by entering their remarks into an electronic internet display board of some type.

online interviews Interviews conducted online. Can be synchronous (in real time) or asynchronous (outside of real time).

ontology Relates to the study of being, the nature of being and our ways of being in the world.

open questions Questions without defined response set. Used to explore understandings, feelings and beliefs. Usually require thought and reflection. Tend to generate relatively long responses.

operationalization The process of identifying scales that correspond to variance in a concept that will be involved in a research process.

operationalizing The process of identifying the actual measurement scales to assess the variables of interest.

opt in To give permission to receive selected email, such as questionnaires, from a company with an internet presence.

oral presentation A spoken summary of the major findings, conclusions and recommendations given to clients or line managers, to provide them with the opportunity to clarify any ambiguous issues by asking questions.

ordinal scales Ranking scales allowing things to be arranged based on how much of some concept they possess.

ordinal variables Values are ranked according to criteria, e.g. social class (upper, middle, working).

paired comparisons A measurement technique that involves presenting the respondent with two objects and asking the respondent to pick the preferred object; more than two objects may be presented, but comparisons are made in pairs.

paired-samples *t*-test An appropriate test for comparing the scores of two interval variables drawn from related populations.

participant–observation Carried out by the researcher when the researcher does participate in the action or in the phenomenon being observed; ethnographic research approach where the researcher becomes immersed within and participates in the culture that he or she is observing in order to draw data from his or her observations.

peer-reviewed sources Published accounts of research that have been subjected to critical review by the peers of the authors of the research.

phenomenology A philosophical approach to studying human experiences based on the idea that human experience itself is inherently subjective and determined by the context in which people live. A study of lived experience from the perspectives of those living the experience.

philosophical framework The worldview within which the research is situated.

photo-elicitation interview The researcher takes the interviewee through an exploration and analysis of a photograph or a series of photographs.

pilot study An aid to improving the rigour and the validity of the research. This is a test of the data-gathering instrument(s) designed for the research.

plagiarism The use and/or presentation of somebody else's work or ideas as your own. Plagiarism is a serious offence. It is generally avoidable through proper referencing.

population Every person who or every entity that could be included in the research.

population element An individual member of a population.

population (universe) Any complete group of entities that share some common set of characteristics.

potential harms A potential harm is a harm that might occur.

preliminary tabulation A tabulation of the results of a pretest to help determine whether the questionnaire will meet the objectives of the research.

primary sampling unit (PSU) A term used to designate a unit selected in the first stage of sampling.

privileged access Prior access to an individual or site that provides an advantage in securing access for the purpose of conducting research. Can present substantial ethical issues.

probability sampling A sampling technique in which every member of the population has a known, non-zero probability of selection.

projective technique An indirect means of questioning, enabling respondents to project beliefs and feelings onto a third party, an inanimate object or a task situation.

propositions Statements explaining the logical linkage among certain concepts by asserting a universal connection between concepts.

quadrant analysis An extension of cross-tabulation in which responses to two rating-scale questions are plotted in four quadrants of a two-dimensional table.

qualitative business research Research that addresses business objectives through techniques that allow the researcher to provide elaborate interpretations of phenomena without depending on numerical measurement; its focus is on discovering true inner meanings and new insights.

qualitative data Non-numerical data; data are textual, visual or oral; focus is on stories, visual portrayals, meaningful characterizations, interpretations and other expressive descriptions.

qualitative research Qualitative research is research that produces non-numeric data. Qualitative research focuses on words rather than numbers in the collection of data. Qualitative research as a research strategy is inductive and subjective, constructivist and/or interpretivist.

quantitative business research Business research that addresses research objectives through empirical assessments that involve numerical measurement and analysis.

quantitative data Data in the form of numbers, numerical data and/or data that can be coded in numeric format; representing phenomena by assigning numbers in an ordered and meaningful way.

quantitative research Focuses on the gathering of numeric data or data in numerical form, i.e. data in the form of numbers. Quantitative research is deductive. It is said to be objective and situated within a framework of positivism.

questionnaires Structured means of gathering data.

quota sampling A non-probability sampling procedure that ensures that various subgroups of a population will be represented on pertinent characteristics to the exact extent that the investigator desires.

random sampling error A statistical fluctuation that occurs because of chance variation in the elements selected for a sample; difference between the sample result and the result of a census conducted using identical procedures.

ranking A measurement task that requires respondents to rank order a small number of stores, brands or objects on the basis of overall preference or some characteristic of the stimulus.

rating A measurement task that requires respondents to estimate the magnitude of a characteristic or quality that a brand, store or object possesses.

rating scales The researcher asks participants to rate different aspects or elements of the phenomenon under investigation.

ratio scales Represent the highest form of measurement in that they have all the properties of interval scales with the additional attribute of representing absolute quantities; characterized by a meaningful absolute zero.

recommendations The courses of action that the researcher recommends based on the findings and subsequent conclusions drawn from those findings.

references Details of the source of literature, see list of references for example.

reflexivity Researcher's active thoughtful engagement with every aspect and development of their research, e.g. self-reflection, self-consciousness, self-awareness.

refusals People who are unwilling to participate in a research project.

reliability An indicator of a measure's internal consistency; dependability of the research, the degree to which the research can be repeated while obtaining consistent results.

representation The degree to which a sample selected from a population can be said to be representative of that population.

research ethics committee Convened by organizations to monitor and police the ethical standards of research projects in which the parent organization has some gatekeeping role.

research follow-up Recontacting decision makers and/or clients after they have had a chance to read over a research report in order to determine whether additional information or clarification is necessary.

research idea The broad area within which you want to situate your research.

research methodology Signals to the reader how the research was conducted and what philosophical assumptions underpin the research.

research methods Data collection methods.

research process The means or process by which research is carried out.

researchable A project is researchable if you have the time, money, data and the level of access to the data needed to carry out and complete the research.

respondent error A category of sample bias resulting from some respondent action or inaction such as non-response or response bias.

response bias A bias that occurs when respondents either consciously or unconsciously tend to answer questions with a certain slant that misrepresents the truth.

response rate A count of the number of valid responses received to a data-gathering exercise.

reverse coding A method of making sure all the items forming a composite scale are scored in the same direction. Negative items can be recoded into the equivalent responses for a non-reverse-coded item; changing the value of a response to a scale so it is the opposite of the original value, e.g. a scale from 1–5 is reversed so 1 = 5, 2 = 4, 3 = 3, 4 = 2 and 5 = 1. Done so negative items in a scale are scored in the same direction as positive items.

reverse directory A directory similar to a telephone directory except that listings are by city and street address or by phone number rather than alphabetical by last name.

rigorous For a research project to be rigorous, it must adhere to the scientific principles of research. The research must be systematic and valid.

sample A sample is a subset of a larger population. If probability sampling is used, the sample is said to be representative of the population.

sample bias A persistent tendency for the results of a sample to deviate in one direction from the true value of the population parameter.

sample survey A more formal term for a survey.

sampling frame A list of elements from which a sample may be drawn; also called working population.

sampling frame error An error that occurs when certain sample elements are not listed or are not accurately represented in a sampling frame.

sampling unit A single element or group of elements subject to selection in the sample.

saturation point Reached when the researcher gathering data for the project no longer hears any new thoughts, feelings, attitudes, emotions, intentions, etc. At this point continuing to engage participants would not be useful, necessary or ethically sound, as further participants and/or more data will not add to the knowledge being generated.

scales A device providing a range of values that correspond to different values in a concept being measured.

scanner-based consumer panel A type of consumer panel where participants record purchases using a barcode scanner.

scope The breadth and depth of a project.

scientific method A set of prescribed procedures for establishing and connecting theoretical statements about events, for analyzing empirical evidence, and for predicting events yet unknown; techniques or procedures used to analyze empirical evidence in an attempt to confirm or disprove prior conceptions.

search strategy The plan the researcher makes for their search of the literature for relevant literature for their literature review.

secondary sampling unit A term used to designate a unit selected in the second stage of sampling.

semantic differential A measure of attitudes that consists of a series of seven-point rating scales that use bipolar adjectives to anchor the beginning and end of each scale.

semi-structured observation Carried out when the researcher knows, broadly speaking, what aspects or elements of the research should or could be observed.

sensitivity A measurement instrument's ability to accurately measure variability in stimuli or responses.

sentence completion exercises A projective technique. The researcher starts a sentence and asks the respondent to complete it.

simple random sampling A sampling procedure that assures each element in the population of an equal chance of being included in the sample.

skips and filters Devices used in questionnaires to allow respondents to skip over questions that do not relate to them.

snowball sampling A sampling procedure in which initial respondents are selected by probability methods and additional respondents are obtained from information provided by the initial respondents.

social research Research conducted by social scientists on some aspect(s) of the social world.

sorting A measurement task that presents a respondent with several objects or product concepts and requires the respondent to arrange the objects into piles or classify the product concepts.

split-half method A method for assessing internal consistency by checking the results of one-half of a set of scaled items against the results from the other half; used to test equivalence reliability.

SPSS Statistical Package for the Social Sciences. A computer software package designed for the analysis of quantitative data.

Stapel scale A measure of attitudes that consists of a single adjective in the centre of an even number of numerical values.

statistical analysis Analysis of quantitative data through the use of statistics.

statistical base The number of respondents or observations (in a row or column) used as a basis for computing percentages.

statistical inference Uses the data gathered from a sample population to draw conclusions about the population.

stratified sampling A probability sampling procedure in which simple random subsamples that are more or less equal on some characteristic are drawn from within each stratum of the population.

structure The structure of a chapter, or any written work, is the way in which it is organized.

structured observation Carried out when the researcher knows precisely what aspects or elements of the research project should or could be observed.

structured question A question that imposes a limit on the number of allowable responses.

subjective The individual personal experiences and perspectives of participants. Results are researcher dependent, meaning different researchers may reach different conclusions based on the same interview.

summarizing statistics Examples of descriptive statistics. Descriptive statistics are statistics that are used to describe data.

summated scale A scale created by simply summing (adding together) the response to each item making up the composite measure.

survey Used to denote survey research methodology. A survey research methodology is particularly useful in facilitating the study of big populations and geographically scattered samples. A research technique or data-gathering method in which a sample is interviewed in some form or the behaviour of respondents is observed and described in some way.

systematic Systematic means there must be a system in place and the action is carried out in a systematic manner, using the system.

systematic error Error resulting from some imperfect aspect of the research design that causes respondent error or from a mistake in the execution of the research.

systematic (non-sampling) error Error resulting from non-sampling factors, primarily the nature of a study's design and the correctness of execution. These errors are not due to chance fluctuations.

systematic sampling A sampling procedure in which a starting point is selected by a random process and then every nth number on the list is selected.

tertiary sampling unit A term used to designate a unit selected in the third stage of sampling.

test of researchability Deems a research project feasible in relation to the time, money and data needed in order to carry out and complete the research.

test–retest method Used to estimate reliability. A questionnaire is used in a pilot test, then later, the same test is repeated and compared for consistency; administering the same scale or measure to the same respondents at two separate points in time to test for stability; process of assigning a numerical score or other character symbol to previously edited data.

thematic analysis The analysis of data through the use of themes.

thematic apperception test (TAT) A test that presents subjects with an ambiguous picture(s) in which consumers and products are the centre of attention; the investigator asks the subject to tell what is happening in the picture(s) now and what might happen next.

themes Identified by the frequency with which the same term (or a synonym) arises in the narrative description.

theoretical framework The theoretical framework for the research project is contained in the literature review. The literature review contains the theoretical framework for the research project. The key concepts in the conceptual framework guide and direct reading for the literature review and they provide the structure for the literature review.

theorization The researcher draws on the work of other researchers and theorists to enrich the reporting of their conclusions.

theorizing data Explaining and demonstrating how the research findings and conclusions of the research project support or contradict the current research as detailed in the literature review.

theory A formal, logical explanation of some events; in the context of a research project, theory is research that has already been carried out, completed and published.

thick description Developed by Clifford Geertz to explain the complex in-depth representation qualitative researchers attempt to accomplish when describing their research projects.

Thurstone scale An attitude scale in which judges assign scale values to attitudinal statements and subjects are asked to respond to these statements.

total quality management A business philosophy that emphasizes market-driven quality as a top organizational priority.

tracking study A type of longitudinal study that uses successive samples to compare trends and identify changes in variables such as consumer satisfaction, brand image or advertising awareness.

triangulation Studying the phenomenon under investigation from more than one perspective, e.g. researcher, theoretical, methodological and/or method triangulation.

unbalanced rating scale A fixed-alternative rating scale that has more response categories at one end than the other, resulting in an unequal number of positive and negative categories.

undisguised questions Straightforward questions that assume the respondent is willing to answer.

univariate analysis Analysis conducted on only one variable, e.g. frequencies.

unobtrusive observation Carried out unobtrusively, with or without the knowledge of the research participants.

unstructured observations Carried out when the researcher does not know what aspects of elements of the action or the phenomenon should or could be observed.

unstructured question A question that does not restrict the respondents' answers.

validity Relates to how logical, truthful, robust, sound, reasonable, meaningful and useful is the research; the accuracy of a measure or the extent to which a score truthfully represents a concept.

value Values make up different variables.

value labels Unique labels assigned to each possible numeric code for a response.

variable A characteristic with more than one value; anything that may assume different values.

verification Quality control procedures in fieldwork intended to ensure that data is properly and correctly gathered; that interviewers are following the sampling procedures and to determine whether interviewers are cheating.

vulnerable populations Populations that have some vulnerability in terms of their social position or their age or their state of well-being.

REFERENCES FOR FEATURES

The following features have been written specifically for *Business Research Methods*:

Chapter	Feature	References
1	The Value of Good Research: Research in the media	Elliott, L. (2017) 'We're being hurt by the fixation on economic growth at all costs', *The Guardian*, 20.11.2017, www.theguardian.com/commentisfree/2017/nov/30/fixation-economic-growth-gdp-pollution-gambling (Accessed 19.12.2017). OECD, 'How's Life 2017', 'New OECD data expose deep well-being divisions', www.oecd.org/newsroom/new-oecd-data-expose-deep-well-being-divisions.htm (Accessed 19.12.2017).
1	Real World Research: How theory influences research	Nanda, M., Pattnaik, C., and Lu, Q. (Steven) (2018) 'Innovation in social media strategy for movie success: A study of the Bollywood movie industry', *Management Decision*, 56(1), 233–251.
2	The Value of Good Research: Research in the media: 'UK's Top 10 fish and chip shops revealed'	Alexander, S. (2017) 'Britain's Best Fish and Chip Shops Revealed', *The Telegraph*, 25.01.2017, www.telegraph.co.uk/food-and-drink/news/britains-best-fish-chip-shops-revealed/ (Accessed 15.01.2018). Gander, K. (2017) 'UK's Ten Best Fish and Chip Shops Revealed', *The Independent*, 15.09.2017, www.independent.co.uk/life-style/food-and-drink/uk-best-fish-chip-shops-top-10-scotland-northern-ireland-england-north-east-west-london-a7947836.html (Accessed 15.01.2018). Seafish, 'The authority on seafood from catch to plate', www.seafish.org (Accessed 15.01.2018).
2	Real World Research: How theory influences research	Liang, J. and Xu, Y. (2018) 'Second-hand clothing consumption: A generational cohort analysis of the Chinese market', *International Journal of Consumer Studies*, *42*, 120–130.
2	Case Study	Na'amneh, M.M. and Al Husban, A.K. (2012) 'Identity in old clothes: the socio-cultural dynamics of second-hand clothing in Irbid, Jordan', *Social Identities: Journal for the Study of Race, Nation and Culture*, 18(5): 609–621.
3	The Value of Good Research: Research in the media	Ferguson, D. (2017) 'Start your own ethical business – it could make a world of difference', *The Guardian*, 07.10.2017, www.theguardian.com/money/2017/oct/07/start-ethical-business-financially-successful-socially (Accessed 26.01.2018). Huhman, H.R. (2018) 'Putting your employees first will be your best move in 2018', *Entrepreneur*, 25.01.2018, www.entrepreneur.com/article/307776 (Accessed 20.01.2018). Yeung, K. (2018) 'Chinese index ranking companies by social value commitment aims to help ethical investors', *South China Morning Post*, 19.01.2018, www.scmp.com/business/companies/article/2129721/chinese-index-ranking-companies-social-value-commitment-aims-help (Accessed 26.01.2018).
3	The Value of Good Research: Focus on case study research	Davies, I.A., Doherty, B. and Knox, S. (2010) 'The rise and stall of a fair trade pioneer: The Cafédirect story', *Journal of Business Ethics*, 92: 127–147. Yin, R.K. (2018) *Case Study Research and Applications: Design and Methods* (6th edn), London: Sage.
3	Real World Research: How theory influences research	Clegg, S., Kornberger, M. and Rhodes, C. (2007) 'Business ethics as practice', *British Journal of Management*, 18: 107–122. Donaldson, T. (2003) 'Editor's comments: taking ethics seriously? A mission now more possible', *Academy of Management Review*, 28: 363–366. Johnson, P. and Smith, K. (1999) 'Contextualizing business ethics: Anomie and social life', *Human Relations*, 52: 1351–1375. Parker, M. (ed.) (2003) 'Special issue on ethics politics and organization', *Organization*, 10(2): 187–203. Porter, M. and Kramer, M. (2002) 'The competitive advantage of corporate philanthropy', *Harvard Business Review*, 37–68.

Chapter	Feature	References
		Soule, E. (2002) 'Managerial moral strategies? In search of a few good principles', *Academy of Management Review*, 27: 114–124, journals.aom.org/doi/10.5465/amr.2002.5922420
		Tonge, A., Greer, L. and Lawton, A. (2003) 'The Enron story: you can fool some of the people some of the time', *Business Ethics, A European Review*, 12: 4–22.
		Veiga, J. (2004) 'Bringing ethics into the mainstream: an introduction to the special topic', *Academy of Management Executive*, 18(2): 37–39.
		Weaver, G.R., Treviño, L.K. and Cochran, P.L. (1999) 'Corporate ethics practices in the mid-1990s: an empirical study of the fortune 1000', *Journal of Business Ethics*, 18: 283–294.
		Werhane, P.H. (2000) 'Business ethics and the origins of contemporary capitalism: economics and ethics in the work of Adam Smith and Herbert Spence', *Journal of Business Ethics*, 24: 185–198.
		Wicks, A.C. and Freeman, R.E. (1998) 'Organization studies and the new pragmatism: positivism, anti-positivism and the search for ethics', *Organization Science*, 9: 123–141.
4	The Value of Good Research: Research in the media	Women and Hollywood, blog.womenandhollywood.com/. (Accessed 02.03.2018).
		Lauzen, M.M. (2018) 'It's a Man's (Celluloid) World: Portrayals of Female Characters in the 100 Top Films of 2017', womenintvfilm.sdsu.edu/wp-content/uploads/2018/02/2017_Its_a_Mans_Celluloid_World_Report_2.pdf. (Accessed 01.03.2018).
		Motion Picture Association of America (2017) 'Theatrical Market Statistics 2016', www.mpaa.org/wp-content/uploads/2017/03/MPAA-Theatrical-Market-Statistics-2016_Final.pdf. (Accessed 01.03.2018).
		Puente, M. (2018) 'Women in Film: Bad news all over with bright spots for women of color, annual study shows', *USA Today*, 28.02.2018, www.usatoday.com/story/life/2018/02/22/women-film-bad-news-overall-bright-spots-women-color-annual-study-shows/360242002/ (Accessed 01.03.2018).
4	Research in Practice: Carol's research project – a survey	Fowler, F.J. (2014) *Survey Research Methods*, Thousand Oaks, CA: Sage.
4	Research in Practice: Fiona's research project – a phenomenological study	Moustakas, C.E. (1994) *Phenomenological Research Methods*, Thousand Oaks, CA: Sage.
		Smith, J.A., Flowers, P. and Larkin, M. (2009) *Interpretative Phenomenological Analysis*, London: Sage.
		Rose, G. (2016) *Visual Methodologies: An Introduction to Researching with Visual Materials*, London and Thousand Oaks, CA: Sage.
4	The Value of Good Research: Focus on image-based research	Sun, Z, (2017) 'Exploiting femininity in a patriarchal postfeminist way: A visual content analysis of Macau's tourism ads', *International Journal of Communication*, 11, 2624–2646.
4	Real World Research: How theory influences research	Bullough, A., Moore, F. and Kalafatoglu, T. (2017) 'Research on women in international business and management: then, now, and next', *Cross Cultural & Strategic Management*, 24(2): 211–230.
4	Real World Research: How theory influences research	Kidwell, R.E., Eddleston, K.A. and Kellermann, F.W. (2018)'Learning bad habits across generations: How negative imprints affect human resource management in the family firm', *Human Resource Management Review*, 28: 5–17.
4	Case Study: The research diary	Nadin, S. and Cassell, C. (2006) 'The use of a research diary as a tool for reflexive practice: Some reflections from management research', *Qualitative Research in Accounting and Management,* 4(4): 208–217.
5	The Value of Good Research: Research in the media	Ahmed, N. (2014) 'Earth insight, "Nasa-funded study: industrial civilisation headed for 'irreversible' collapse?"', *The Guardian*, 14.03.2014, www.theguardian.com/environment/earth-insight/2014/mar/14/nasa-civilisation-irreversible-collapse-study-scientists *(Accessed June 10 2014).*
5	Real World Research: How theory influences research	Dubin, R. (1969) *Theory Building*, Free Press: New York.
5	The Value of Good Research: Focus on the scientific method	Pirsig, R.M. (1974) *Zen and the Art of Motorcycle Maintenance*, New York: Harper Collins.
5	Real World Research: Social network theory	www.facebook.com/pages/Social-network-theory/112159215470744. (Accessed 03.08.2011).
5	Real World Research: How theory influences research	Soboleva, A., Burton, S., Mallik. G. and Khan. A. (2017) '"Retweet for a Chance to…": An analysis of what triggers consumers to engage in seeded eWOM on Twitter', *Journal of Marketing Management*, 33(13–14): 1120–1148.

Chapter	Feature	References
5	Case Study	Li, C. (2015) 'Why No One Uses the Corporate Social Network', *Harvard Business Review*, hbr. org/2015/04/why-no-one-uses-the-corporate-social-network (Accessed 22.06.2018).
6	The Value of Good Research: Focus on content analysis	BBC World Service Trust, 'Using content analysis to measure the influence of media development interventions: elections training for journalists in Yemen', www.gov.uk/dfid-research-outputs/using-content-analysis-to-measure-the-influence-of-media-development-interventions-elections-training-for-journalists-in-yemen (Accessed 14.03.2018).
		Colorado State University, 'Introduction to content analysis', writing.colostate.edu/guides/page. cfm?pageid=1305&guideid=61 (Accessed 14.03.2018)
		Erlingsson, C., and Brysiewicz, P. (2017) 'A hands-on guide to doing content analysis', *African Journal of Emergency Medicine*, 7: 93–99.
		Neuendorf, K.A. (2017) *The Content Analysis Guidebook* (2nd edn), California and London: Sage.
		Research Methods Knowledge Base, 'Unobtrusive measures (indirect measures, content analysis, and secondary analysis of data)', www.socialresearchmethods.net/kb/unobtrus.php
		Schreier, M. (2012) *Qualitative Content Analysis in Practice*, California, London, New Delhi, Singapore: Sage.
		Yin Zhen, J., Coulson, K.R., Yu, J. and Zhou, J.X. (2017) 'Promoting business schools: A content analysis of business school's magazines', *Journal of Applied Business and Economics*, 19(3): 106–116.
6	Real World Research: How theory influences research	Kotler, P.R. (1967) *Marketing Management: Analysis, Planning and Control*, Englewood Cliffs, NJ: Prentice Hall.
		Mogaji, E., Czarnecka, B., and Danbury, A. (2018) 'Emotional appeals in business-to-business financial services advertisements', *International Journal of Bank Marketing*, 36(1): 208–227.
7	Case Study: FlyAway Airways	AQR Airline Quality Rating, airlinequalityrating.com/ (Accessed 17.03.2018).
		Queendom The Land of Tests, www.queendom.com/tests/index.htm (Accessed 17.03.2018).
8	The Value of Good Research: What's in the van?	Whaba, P. (2017) 'How Vans Skated Past a Big Retail Milestone', fortune.com/2017/03/31/vans-vfc/
8	Case Study: Malika's action research project	Brydon-Miller, M., Greenwood, D. and Maguire, P. (2003) 'Why action research?', *Action Research*, 1: 9–28.
		Katzenbach, J.R. and Smith, D.K. (2003) *The Wisdom of Teams: Creating the High-Performance Organization,* New York: McKinsey & Company.
		McCleskey, J.A. (2014) 'Situational, Transformational, and Transactional Leadership and Leadership Development', *Journal of Business Studies Quarterly*, 5(4): 117–130.
		McNiff, J. (2017) *Action Research*, London, California, New Delhi, Singapore: Sage.
		McNiff, J. and Whitehead, J. (2009) *Doing and Writing Action Research*, London: Sage.
		Morgeson, F.P., Scott DeRue, D. and Karam, E.P. (2010) 'Leadership in teams: A functional approach to understanding leadership structures and processes', *Journal of Management*, 36(1): 5–39.
		Vasilagos, T., Polychroniou, P. and Maroudas, L. (2017) 'Relationship between Supervisors Emotional Intelligence and Transformational Leadership in Hotel Organisations', in A. Kavoura, D. Sakas and P. Tomaras (eds) *Strategic Innovative Marketing. Springer Proceedings in Business and Economics*. Cham, Switzerland: Springer.
		Yuki, G. (2010) *Leadership in Organisations* (7th edn), New Jersey, USA: Prentice Hall.
9	Real World Research: How theory influences research	Holt, R. and Macpherson, A. (2010) 'Sensemaking, rhetoric and the socially competent entrepreneur', *International Small Business Journal*, 28(1): 20–42.
9	The Value of Good Research: Focus on narrative research/narrative inquiry/narrative analysis	Andrews, M., Squire, C. and Tamboukou, M. (eds) (2013) *Doing Narrative Research* (2nd edn), London, California, New Delhi, Singapore: Sage.
		Boje, D.M. (2001) *Narrative Methods for Organizational & Communication Research*, Sage Series in Management Research.
		Colorado State University Guide to Narrative Inquiry, writing.colostate.edu/guides/page. cfm?pageid=1346&guideid=63
		Fletcher, D. (2007) '"Toy Story": the narrative world of entrepreneurship and the creation of interpretive communities', *Journal of Business Venturing*, 22(5): 649–672.
		Kim, J-H. (2016) *Understanding Narrative Inquiry*, London, California, New Delhi, Singapore: Sage.
		Kohler Riessman, C. (2008) *Narrative Methods for the Human Sciences*, Sage.

Chapter	Feature	References
9	Case Study: Genji's case study research project: the methodological framework	Bryman, A. and Burgess, R.G. (1994) *Analysing Qualitative Data*, London: Routledge.
		Creswell, J. and Creswell, J.D. (2018) *Research Design: Qualitative, Quantitative and Mixed Methods Approaches*, Thousand Oaks, CA: Sage.
		Denscombe, M. (2017) *The Good Research Guide: For Small-scale Social Research Projects* (6th edn), Milton Keynes: Open University Press.
		Denzin, N. (1970) *The Research Act in Sociology*, Chicago: Aldine.
		Duffy, B. (2005) 'The Analysis of Documentary Evidence', in J. Bell *Doing Your Research Project*, Ch. 7, Maidenhead: Open University Press.
		Quinlan, C. (2011) *Business Research Methods*, Andover: Cengage Learning EMEA.
		Quinlan, C., Babin, B., Carr, J., Griffin, M. and Zikmund, W.G. (2015) *Business Research Methods*, Andover: Cengage Learning EMEA.
		Yin, R.K. (1989) *Case Study Research*, London: Sage.
		Yin, R.K. (2018) *Case Study Research and Applications: Design and Methods* (6th edn), Thousand Oaks, CA: Sage.
10	The Value of Good Research: Focus on discourse analysis	Braidford, P., Drummond, I. and Stone, I. (2017) 'The impact of personal attitudes on the growth ambitions of small business owners', *Journal of Small Business and Enterprise Development*, 4(4): 850–862.
		CADAAD (Critical Approaches to Discourse Analysis Across Disciplines), cadaad.net/ (Accessed 17.03.2018).
		Fairclough, N. (1995) *Critical Discourse Analysis*, London: Longman.
		Fairclough, N. (2013) *Critical Discourse Analysis: The Critical Study of Language*, Oxon and New York: Routledge.
		van Dijk, T.A. (1993) 'Principles of critical discourse analysis', *Discourse and Society*, 4(2): 243–289.
		Wang, J. (2006) 'Questions and the exercise of power', *Discourse and Society*, 7(4): 529–548.
10	Real World Research: How theory influences research	Dermody, J. and Scullion, R. (2004) 'Exploring the value of party political advertising for youth electoral engagement: An analysis of the 2001 British General Election advertising campaigns', *International Journal of Nonprofit and Voluntary Sector Marketing*, 9(4): 361–379.
10	Case Study: How to use a table of random numbers to randomly select a sample	Stat Trek, Teach Yourself Statistics, stattrek.com. (Accessed 17.03.2018).
11	The Value of Good Research: Focus on documentary research/documentary analysis	Bowen, G.A. (2009) 'Document analysis as a qualitative research method', *Qualitative Research Journal*, 9(2): 27–40.
		Denscombe, M. (2017) *The Good Research Guide for Small-scale Social Research Projects* (6th edn), Maidenhead: Open University Press.
		Kennelly, M., Corbett, H. and Toohey, K. (2017) 'Leveraging ambitions and barriers: Glasgow universities and the 2014 Commonwealth Games', *Marketing Intelligence & Planning*, 35(6): 822–838.
		McCulloch, G., (2004), *Documentary Research in Education, History and the Social Sciences*, Oxon and New York: Routledge.
		Scott, J. (1990) *A Matter of Record: Documentary Sources in Social Research*, Oxford: Blackwell.
		US Library of Congress, Guide to business history resources, www.loc.gov/rr/business/guide/guide1/businesshistory/intro.html (Accessed 17.03.2018).
		World History Sources, *Scholars Analyzing Documents*, George Mason University, chnm.gmu.edu/worldhistorysources/whmdocuments.html
		Yin, R.K. (2018) *Case Study Research and Applications: Design and Methods* (6th edn), Thousand Oaks, CA: Sage.
11	Template for a Research Proposal	Yallop, A.C. and Mowatt, S. (2016) 'Investigating market research ethics: An empirical study of codes of ethics in practice and their effect on ethical behaviour', *International Journal of Market Research*, 58(3): 381–400.

Chapter	Feature	References
11	Case Study: Tom's research project (using a documentary analysis research methodology)	Abrams, R. (2014) *The Successful Business Plan, Secrets and Strategies*, California: Planning Shop, Rhonda Inc.
		Barringer, B.R. (2014) *Preparing Effective Business Plans: An Entrepreneurial Approach*, Harlow: Pearson Education.
		Blackwell, E. (2017) *How to Prepare a Business Plan : Your Guide to Creating an Excellent Strategy, Forecasting your Finances and Producing a Persuasive Plan* (6th edn), London, New York and New Delhi: Kogan Page.
		Bohnsack, R. (2014) 'Documentary Method', in *The SAGE Handbook of Qualitative Data Analysis*, London, California, New Delhi, Singapore: Sage.
		DeThomas, A. and Derammelaere, S. (2015) *Writing a Convincing Business Plan* (Barron's Business Library), New York: Barron's Business Library.
		Jameson, D.A. (2009) 'Economic crises and financial disasters: The role of business communication', *Journal of Business Communication,* 46: 499–509.
		Johnson, R. (2003) *The Perfect Business Plan: All You Need To Get It Right First Time*, The Perfect Series, London: Century Business.
		McKeever, M.P. (2014) *How to Write a Business Plan*, Berkeley, CA: Nolo.
		Neuman, W.L. (2014) *Social Research Methods: Qualitative and Quantitative Approaches* (7th edn), England: Pearson Education Ltd.
		Prinson, L. (2013) *Anatomy of a Business Plan: The Step-by-Step Guide to Building a Business and Securing Your Company's Future* (8th edn), Tustin, CA: Out of Your Mind . . . and into the Marketplace Publishing Company.
		Prior, L. (ed.) (2011) *Using Documents and Records in Social Research*, SAGE Benchmarks in Social Research Methods.
		Quinlan, C. (2011) *Business Research Methods*, Andover: Cengage Learning EMEA.
		Quinlan, C., Babin, B., Carr, J., Griffin, M. and Zikmund, W.G. (2015) *Business Research Methods*, Andover: Cengage Learning EMEA.
		Raj, A. (2018) '3 New Year's resolutions for small business success in 2018', *CPA Practice Advisor, Ft Atkinson*, 28(1): 20.
		Richbell, S.M., Watts, H.D. and Wardle, P. (2006) 'Owner-managers and business planning in the small firm', *International Small Business Journal,* 24(5): 496–514.
		Vaughan, E. (2016) *The Financial Times Essential Guide to Writing a Business Plan: How to Win Backing to Start Up or Grow Your Own Business*, Harlow: Pearson.
12	Real World Research: Software for fieldwork? Ask Askia	Askia, www.askia.com. (Accessed 17.03.2018).
12	The Value of Good Research: Why is "why" important?	Calo Research Services, www.caloresearch.com/ (Accessed 17.03.2018).
12	Real World Research: Probing for deeper meaning at Olson Zaltman Associates	Olson Zaltman Associates, olsonzaltman.com/ (Accessed 17.03.2018).
13	The Value of Good Research	Lynd, R.S. and Lynd, H.M. (1959) *Middletown: A Study in Modern American Culture*, New York: Mariner Books.
13	Real World Research: How theory influences research	Oliver, J. and Eales, K. (2008) 'Re-evaluating the consequentialist perspective of using covert participant observation in management research', *Qualitative Market Research: An International Journal,* 11(3): 344–357.
13	Real World Research: ATTI shadows the fleet	Advanced Tracking Technologies, Inc. (ATTI) www.advantrack.com/contact-us/ (Accessed 17.03.2018).
13	The Value of Good Research: Focus on ethnography	Anderson, K. (2009) 'Ethnographic research: a key to strategy', *Harvard Business Review*, hbr.org/2009/03/ethnographic-research-a-key-to-strategy (Accessed 17.03.2018).
		Anderson, K., Faulkner, S., Kleinman, L. and Sherman, J. (2017) *Creating a Creators' Market: How Ethnography Gave Intel a New Perspective on Digital Content Creators, Ethnographic Praxis in Industry Conference Proceedings, Cases 3 – New Ventures and New Markets*, anthrosource.onlinelibrary.wiley.com/doi/epdf/10.1111/1559-8918.2017.01162 (Accessed 17.03.2018).
		Colorado State University, 'Writing guide: ethnography, observational research, and narrative inquiry', writing.colostate.edu/guides/guide.cfm?guideid=63

Chapter	Feature	References
		Ethnographic Research, Inc., www.ethnographic-research.com (Accessed 17.03.2018).
		Kozinets, R. (2015) *Netnography: Redefined* (2nd edn), London, California, New Delhi, Singapore: Sage.
		Lee, J. (2009) 'Open mic: professionalizing the rap career', *Ethnography*, 10(4): 475–495.
13	Case Study: Dabir's research idea	Russell, D.W. (2008) 'Nostalgic tourism', *Journal of Travel and Tourism Marketing*, 25(2): October, 103–116.
14	The Value of Good Research	Big Brother 2018, www.bigbrotherauditions.com/ (Accessed 17.03.2018).
		Wood, D. (2017) *What's Hot in Global Entertainment*, hub.editiondigital.com/whats-hot-in-global-entertainment (Accessed 17.03.2017).
14	Real World Research: How theory influences research	Guba, E. G. and Lincoln, Y. S. (1989) *Fourth Generation Evaluation*. Newbury Park, CA and London: Sage Publications.
		Guba, E.G. and Lincoln, Y.S. (1994) *Competing Paradigms in Qualitative Research*, www.uncg.edu/hdf/facultystaff/Tudge/Guba%20&%20Lincoln%201994.pdf.
		Outsios, G. and Kittler, M. (2017) 'The mindset of UK environmental entrepreneurs: A habitus perspective', *International Small Business Journal: Researching Entrepreneurship*, 6(3): 285–306.
14	The Value of Good Research: Focus on phenomenology	Abugre, J.B. (2017) 'A phenomenological study of time concept and management and productivity in a sub-Saharan African context', *International Journal of Cross Cultural Management*, 17(2): 197–214.
		Chan, G., Benner, P., Brykcynski, K.A. and Malone, R.E. (2010) *Interpretive Phenomenology in Health Care Research: Studying Social Practice, Lifeworlds, and Embodiment*, Sigma Theta Tau Intl, catalog.sit.edu/cgi-bin/koha/opac-detail.pl?biblionumber=86905.
		Edwards, A. and Skinner, J. (2016) *Qualitative Research in Sports Management*, Routledge.
		Ezzedeen, S.R. and Zikic, J. (2017) Finding balance amid boundarylessness: An interpretive study of entrepreneurial work-life balance and boundary management, *Journal of Family Issues*, 38(11): 1546–1576.
		Finlay, L. (2009) 'Debating phenomenological research methods', *Phenomenology & Practice*, 3(1): 6–25, ejournals.library.ualberta.ca/index.php/pandpr/article/viewFile/19818/15336.
		Griffith, J.N. and Jones Young, N.C. (2017) 'Hiring ex-offenders? The case of Ban the Box', *Equality, Diversity and Inclusion: An International Journal*, 36(6): 501–518.
		Groenewald, T. (2004) 'A phenomenological research design illustrated', *International Journal of Qualitative Methods*, 3(1): 1–26, www.ualberta.ca/~iiqm/backissues/3_1/pdf/groenewald.pdf
		Hemme, F., Morias, D., Bowers, M.T. and Todd, J.S. (2017) 'Extending sport-based entrepreneurship theory through phenomenological inquiry', *Sport Management Review*, 20(1): 92–104.
		Phillips, C.R., Haase, J.E., Broome, M.E., Carpenter, J.S. and Frankel, R.M. (2017) 'Connecting with healthcare providers at diagnosis: Adolescent/young adult cancer survivors' perspectives', *International Journal of Qualitative Studies on Health and Well-being*, 12(1), DOI: 10.1080/17482631.2017.1325699.
		Pisarik, C.T., Clay Rowell, P. and Thompson, L.K. (2017) 'A phenomenological study of career anxiety among college students', *The Career Development Quarterly*, 65(4): 339–352.
		Walters, J. (2017) *Phenomenological Research Guidelines*, Capilano University, www.capilanou.ca/psychology/student-resources/research-guidelines/Phenomenological-Research-Guidelines/.
		Zamani, N. and Mohammadi, M. (2017) 'Entrepreneurial learning as experienced by agricultural graduate entrepreneurs', *Higher Education*, 1–16, doi.org/10.1007/s10734-017-0209-y (Accessed 17.03.2018).
14	Case Study: The museum shop as a marketing tool for the Imperial War Museum	Kent, T. (2010) 'The role of the museum shop in extending the visitor experience', *International Journal of Nonprofit and Voluntary Sector Marketing*, 15(1): 67–77.
15	The Value of Good Research: Focus on survey methodology	American Statistical Association online guide, 'What is a survey?', www.whatisasurvey.info/ (Accessed 17.03.2018).
		Checkbox, www.checkbox.com. (Accessed 17.03.2018).
		Instant Survey, www.instantsurvey.com. (Accessed 17.03.2018).
		Methodspace, www.methodspace.com. (Accessed 17.03.2018).

Chapter	Feature	References
		Princeton University Survey Research Center (PSRC), www.princeton.edu/~psrc/ (Accessed 17.03.2018). Snap Surveys, www.snapsurveys.com. (Accessed 17.03.2018).
		Survey Monkey, www.surveymonkey.com. (Accessed 17.03.2018).
		Surveyspro, www.surveyspro.com. (Acccessed 17.03.2018).
		Trochim, W.M. (2006) *The Research Methods Knowledge Base* (2nd edn), www.socialresearchmethods.net/. (Accessed 12.05.2014).
15	The Value of Good Research: Access to the internet	BBC News, 'Internet access is "a fundamental right"', news.bbc.co.uk/2/hi/technology/8548190.stm (Accessed 17.03.2018).
		CNN (2009) 'Fast internet access becomes a legal right in Finland', 15 October, edition.cnn.com/2009/TECH/10/15/finland.internet.rights/index.html (Accessed 17.03.2018).
		Howell, C. and West, D.M. (2016) *The Internet as a Human Right*, www.brookings.edu/blog/techtank/2016/11/07/the-internet-as-a-human-right/ (Accessed 17.03.2018).
		The Brookings Institution, www.brookings.edu/about-us/ (Accessed 17.03.2018).
		UN Declaration of Human Rights, www.un.org/en/universal-declaration-human-rights/ (Accessed 17.03.2018).
15	Case Study: Strategy of celebrity endorsement	Samman, E., McAuliffe, E. and MacLachlan, M. (2009) 'The role of celebrity in endorsing poverty reduction through international aid', *International Journal of Nonprofit and Voluntary Sector Marketing,* 14(4): 137–148. Wiley-Blackwell.
15	The Value of Good Research: Overestimating patient satisfaction	Based on Mazor, K.M., Clauser, B.E., Field, T., Yood, R.A. and Gurwitz, J.H. (2002) 'A demonstration of the impact of response bias on the results of patient satisfaction surveys', *Health Services Research,* 37(5): 1403–1417.
16	Research in Practice: Is it positive emotionality, or is it LOVE?	Based on Myers, J. and Shurts, M. (2002) 'Measuring positive emotionality: A review of instruments assessing love', *Measurement and Evaluation in Counseling and Development,* 34: 238–254.
16	Real World Research: Students ask – are you responsible?	Based on Bush, M. (2008) 'Students rank social responsibility', *Advertising Age,* 79(August 4): 11.
16	Real World Research: Measuring website usability	Based on Tullis, T.S. and Stetson, J.N. (2004) 'A Comparison of Questionnaires for Assessing Website Usability', presented at the Usability Professionals Association (UPA) 2004 Conference, Minneapolis, MN, June 7–11, home.comcast.net/~tomtullis/publications/UPA2004TullisStetson.pdf. (Accessed 05.07.2014).
16	The Value of Good Research: How much is a healthy home worth?	Based on Spetic, W., Kozak, R. and Cohen, D. (2005) 'Willingness to pay and preferences for healthy home attributes in Canada', *Forest Products Journal,* 55(October): 19–24.
		Bower, J. (1999) *Healthy House Building for the New Millennium,* Bloomington, IN: Healthy House Institute.
16	Real World Research: Focus on attitude research	Ajzen, I. and Fishbein, M. (1980) *Understanding Attitudes and Predicting Social Behaviour,* Englewood Cliffs, NJ: Prentice Hall.
		Eagly, A.H. and Chaiken, S. (1993) *The Psychology of Attitudes,* Forth Worth, TX: Harcourt Brace and Company.
		QuestionPro, www.questionpro.com. (Accessed 17.03.2018).
		Surveyspro, www.esurveyspro.com. (Accessed 17.03.2018).
		Survey Resources Network, surveyresearch.weebly.com/survey-resources-network.html (Accessed 17.03.2018).
		What is an Employee Attitude Survey?, www.hr-survey.com/EmployeeAttitude.htm (Accessed 17.03.2018).
17	The Value of Good Research: Three cheers for the death of old economics	Goodman, D. (22.10.2017) *Nobel Laureates Stiglitz and Spence to Lead New Group to Tackle World's Economic Woes,* www.bloomberg.com/news/articles/2017-10-21/nobel-laureates-lead-new-group-to-tackle-world-s-economic-woes (Accessed 17.03.2018).
		Institute for New Economic Thinking (INET), ineteconomics.org (Accessed 17.03.2018).
		Kaletsky, A. (2009) 'Three cheers for the death of old economics: The orthodox mathematical model took no account of reality. The new George Soros Institute should bring back some sanity', *The Times,* 28 October.

Chapter	Feature	References
		Purkiss, A. (2010) 'Soros plans economics institute at Oxford University, *Times* says', 5 April, www.bloomberg.com/news/2010-04-05/soros-plans-oxford-university-economics-institute-on-markets-times-says (Accessed 06.07.2014).
		Soros, G. (2010) 'Anatomy of crisis – the living history of the last 30 years: Economic theory, politics and policy', presented at the INET Conference, King's College, April 8–11, 2010, ineteconomics.org/key-topics/economic-policy?page=26. (Accessed 06.07.2014).
		The Economist, (13.04.2013) 'The Institute for New Economic Thinking: A Slipping Taboo', www.economist.com/news/finance-and-economics/21576089-george-soross-attempt-shake-up-dismal-science-arrives-asia-slipping. (Accessed 17.03.2018).
17	Real World Research: How theory influences research	Resnik, D.B. (2009) 'International standards for research integrity: An idea whose time has come', *Accountability in Research,* 16(4): 218–228.
17	The Value of Good Research: Focus on semiotics	Chandler, D. (nd) 'Semiotics for beginners', visual-memory.co.uk/daniel/Documents/S4B/ (Accessed 17.03.2018).
		Koller, V. (2007) '"The world's local bank": glocalisation as a strategy in corporate branding discourse', *Social Semiotics,* 17(1): 111–131.
		Oswald, L. (2007) 'Semiotics and strategic brand management', University of Illinois, www.csun.edu/~bashforth/098_PDF/Semiotic_branding.pdf (Accessed 17.03.2018).
		Owyong, Y.S.M. (2009) 'Clothing semiotics and the social construction of power relations', *Social Semiotics,* 19(2): 191–211.
17	Case Study: Managing and analyzing data	Suboleski, S., Kincaid, C.S. and Dipietro, R.B. (2009) 'An exploratory study of multi-unit restaurant management training: A qualitative perspective', *Journal of Human Resources in Hospitality & Tourism,* 8(2): 199–214.
18	The Value of Good Research: Amplifon – redesigned and reinvigorated	Amplifon Charles Holland Award, www.amplifon.com/English/People/charles-holland-award/Pages/default.aspx (Accessed 09.07.2014).
		Amplifon Middle East, www.amplifon.com.eg/aboutus.asp (Accessed 09.07.2014).
		Amplifon Worldwide, www.amplifon.co.uk/information/worldwide/ (Accessed 09.07.2014).
18	The Value of Good Research: Focus on ground theory methodology	Corbin, J. and Strauss, A. (2014) *Basics of Qualitative Research: Techniques and Procedures for Developing Grounded Theory* (4th edn), Thousand Oaks, CA: Sage.
		De Massis, A. and Kotlar, J. (2014) 'The case study method in family business research: Guidelines for qualitative scholarship', *Journal of Family Business Strategy,* 5: 15–29.
		Glaser, B. and Strauss, A. (1967) *The Discovery of Grounded Theory: Strategies for Qualitative Research,* Chicago, IL: Aldine.
		Murphy, C., Klotz, A.C. and Kreiner, G.E. (2017) 'Blue skies and black boxes: The promise and practice of grounded theory in human resource management research', *Human Resource Management Review,* 27: 291–305.
18	The Value of Good Research	Kessous, A. and Roux, E. (2008) 'A semiotic analysis of nostalgia as a connection to the past', *Qualitative Market Research,* 11(2): 192–212.
18	Real World Research: How theory influences research	Alasuutari P. (1995) *Researching Culture: Qualitative Method and Cultural Studies,* London: Sage.
		Alasuutari, P. (2010) 'The rise and relevance of qualitative research', *International Journal of Social Research Methodology,* 13(2): 139–155.
		Cremer, R.D. and Ramasamy, B. (2009) 'Engaging China: strategies for the small internationalizing firm', *Journal of Business Strategy,* 30(6): 15–26.
		Denzin, N.K. and Lincoln, Y.S. (2000) *Handbook of Qualitative Research,* Thousand Oaks, CA: Sage.
		Payne, G., Williams, M. and Chamberlain, S. (2004) 'Methodological pluralism in British sociology', *Sociology,* 38(1): 153–163.
18	Case Study: A qualitative study using a diary method	Götze, E., Prange, C. and Uhrovska, I. (2009) 'Children's impact on innovation decision making: A diary study', *European Journal of Marketing,* 43(1/2): 264–295.
19	The Value Of Good Research	NASA (National Aeronautics and Space Administration), climate.nasa.gov/ (Accessed 17.03.2018).

Chapter	Feature	References
19	The Value of Good Research: Focus on experimental design	Harvard MIT Data Center, 'Guide to SPSS', www.hks.harvard.edu/fs/pnorris/Classes/A%20 SPSS%20Manuals/SPSS%20Statistcs%20Base%20User's%20Guide%2017.0.pdf (Accessed 17.03.2018).
		Hawthorne Experiments, Harvard Business School, www.library.hbs.edu/hc/hawthorne/09.html (Accessed 17.03.2018).
		Science Olympiad, 'Experimental design', scioly.org/wiki/index.php/Experimental_Design (Accessed 17.03.2018).
		Trochim, W.M. (2006) *The Research Methods Knowledge Base*, socialresearchmethods.net/ (Accessed 17.03.2018).
19	Real World Research: How theory influences research	Mullen, M.R., Budeva, D.G. and Doney, P.M. (2009) 'Research methods in the leading small business – entrepreneurship journals: A critical review with recommendations for future research', *Journal of Small Business Management,* 47(3): 287–307.
19	Case Study: A survey: Consumption of charity bracelets	Yurchisin, J., Yoo Jin, K. and Marcketti, S.B. (2009) 'Consumers of charity bracelets: Cause-supporters or fashion-followers?', *Journal of Fashion Marketing and Management,* 13(3): 448–457.
20	The Value Of Good Research: An example of the potential complexities in reporting research	Butterworth, S. (2009) 'Open Door, the readers' editor on … 1000 teenagers, one survey, and two sets of results', *The Guardian*, 19.10.2009, www.theguardian.com/commentisfree/2009/ oct/19/teenage-boys-survey-statistics (Accessed 17.03.2018).
20	Theory in Research	Korte, R.F. (2009) 'How newcomers learn the social norms of an organization: A case study of the socialization of newly hired engineers', *Human Resource Development Quarterly,* 20(3): 285–306.
20	The Value Of Good Research: Focus on life history	*National Life Stories: Tesco: An Oral History*, British Library, www.bl.uk/reshelp/findhelprestype/ sound/ohist/ohnls/nlstesco/tesco.html (Accessed 17.03.2018).
		Oral History Collection, Columbia University, New York, library.columbia.edu/locations/ccoh.html (Accessed 17.03.2018).
		Oral History Research, University of Winnipeg, Canada, www.oralhistorycentre.ca/business-oral-history (Accessed 17.03.2018).
		What is Oral History, historymatters.gmu.edu/mse/oral/what.html (Accessed 17.03.2018).
20	Case Study	Bloom, N. and Van Reenan, J. (2010) 'Why do management practices differ across firms and countries?', *Journal of Economic Perspectives*, 24(1): 203–224.

The following extracts and/or data have been used with full permission, or do not require permission:

Chapter	Feature	References
5	The Value of Good Research: Focus on the scientific method	Pirsig, R.M. (1974) *Zen and the Art of Motorcycle Maintenance: An Inquiry into Values (ZAMM)*, New York: Harper Collins Publishing
7	Figure 7.3: Susceptibility to interpersonal influence: an operational definition	Bearden, W.O., Netemeyer, R.G. and Mobley, M.F. (1999) *Handbook of Marketing Scales: Multi Item Measures for Marketing and Consumer Behavior Research* (2nd edn), Newbury Park, CA: Sage Publications.
		Hoffmann, A.O.I. and Broekhuizen, T.L.J. (2009) 'Susceptibility to and impact of interpersonal influence in an investment context', *Journal of the Academy of Marketing Science*, 37(4): 488–503.
15	Figure 15.4: Longitudinal research from a Harris poll	'Americans Feel More Isolated, Less Empowered, Poll Shows', *Wall Street Journal* (December 8, 2005), online.wsj.com
16	Figure 16.3: Semantic differential scales for measuring attitudes toward supermarkets	Yu, J.H., Albaum, G. and Swenson, M. (2003) 'Is a central tendency error inherent in the use of semantic differential scales in different cultures?', *International Journal of Market Research*, 45(2): 213–228.
16	Figure 16.4: Image profile of private versus public high schools	Andrewski, L., Carrasquillo, A., Kalhammer, T., Sansone, L. and Vornkahl, T. (2011) 'Perceptions of Private and Public High Schools in Peoria', Project for Bradley University Marketing Research Class.

Chapter	Feature	References
19	Table 19.9: Cross-tabulation tables from a survey of families regarding family responses to financial hardships	Bibliographic Citation:National Center for Family and Marriage Research, Judith A. Seltzer, and Suzanne M. Bianchi. Familial Responses to Financial Instability, Doubling Up When Times Are Tough: Obligations to Share a Home in Response to Economic Hardship, 2009 [United States] [Computer file]. ICPSR26543-v1. Ann Arbor, MI: Inter-university Consortium for Political and Social Research [distributor], 2010-05-20. doi:10.3886/ICPSR26543.v1.
19	Figure 19.7: Rise in internet access, UK households and individuals, 1998–2017	Reproduced with permission by the Office of National Statistics from Statistical Bulletin', Crown © Copyright 2009, Crown copyright material is reproduced under the terms of the Click-Use Licence; www.statistics.gov.u/statbase/Product.asp?vlnk=5672.
19	Figure 19.8: Annual percentage change in median full-time gross weekly earnings for all employees and those in continuous employment, UK, April 2005 to 2017	Reproduced with permission from *Economic & Labour Market Review*, 3(5), May 2009, Crown © Copyright 2009, Crown copyright material is reproduced under the terms of the Click-Use Licence.

INDEX